For Paul, Daniel, and Adam
My wonderful most immediate social world

Social Cognition

Making Sense of People

Ziva Kunda

A Bradford Book
The MIT Press
Cambridge, Massachusetts
London, England

This book was set in Melior and Helvetica by Asco Typesetters, Hong Kong.

Printed and bound in the United States of America.

Library of Congress Cataloging-in-Publication Data

Kunda, Ziva.
  Social cognition : making sense of people / Ziva Kunda.
    p.   cm.
  Includes bibliographical references and index.
  ISBN 0-262-11241-8 (hardcover : alk. paper).—ISBN 0-262-61143-0
(pbk. : alk. paper)
  1. Social perception. I. Title.
BF323.S63K86   1999
302′.12—dc21   98-56172
                                                                      CIP

Contents

Self-evaluation Maintenance Model · The Impact of Role Models on
the Self · **Self-regulation 507** · *Self-regulation Is Adaptive* ·
Self-regulation Is Effortful · **Summary 510**

Acknowledgments

The planning and completion of this book benefited greatly from the support and advice of several people. My colleague Mark Zanna generously offered to read each chapter as it came off the press. I am grateful to him not only for his many invaluable suggestions but also for his ongoing encouragement which helped sustain my own enthusiasm for the book throughout the lengthy writing process. I am also grateful to Mike Ross for his comments on select chapters, to two anonymous reviewers for their detailed and constructive criticisms, and to Christian Jordan for his assistance with references. Amy Brand at The MIT Press helped persuade me to undertake the project in the first place and helped bring it to fruition. Finally I thank the many undergraduate and graduate students at the University of Waterloo who provided reactions to an early draft of the manuscript. The social psychology graduate students at Waterloo deserve special thanks for providing me with a useful "writer's kit" containing the key words required for such a book.

While I was writing the book, my research was supported by the Social Sciences and Humanities Research Council of Canada and by the National Sciences and Engineering Research Council of Canada.

Last but not least, I thank Paul, Daniel, and Adam Thagard for their ongoing love, support, and inspiration. I dedicate this book to them.

1 Introduction

How do we make sense of other people and of ourselves? What do we know about the people that we encounter in our daily lives and about the situations in which we encounter them, and how do we make use of this knowledge when we attempt to understand, predict, or recall their behavior? Are our social judgments fully determined by our social knowledge, or are they also influenced by our feelings and desires?

These questions lie at the heart of a relatively new discipline, social cognition. Building on a long tradition of research and theory in social psychology, and invigorated by an infusion of new ideas and methods emerging from cognitive psychology, social-cognition researchers have shed new light on many classic social psychological questions, and have also endeavored into previously uncharted areas of investigation.

Background

For much of the first half of the twentieth century, experimental psychology was dominated by a behaviorist approach that dictated that psychologists should focus only on directly observable phenomena such as stimuli and responses. The goal of psychological research was to identify the laws that governed how behavior was influenced by events in the environment, in particular, events that amounted to rewards and punishments. The mental events that intervened between a stimulus noted in the environment and the response that it gave rise to were considered irrelevant; the mind was treated as a "black box" that psychologists could not and should not try to investigate (e.g., Skinner 1963). Cognitive events underlying perception, judgment, and decision making received little attention until the 1960s.

Social psychologists, however, never bought into this behaviorist view. Cognitions have always been central to social psychological theory and research (Markus and Zajonc 1985). Many of the central questions that social psychology has been concerned with from its earliest days—how we form impressions of others, how we explain their behavior, how our attitudes relate to our actions, how we resolve conflicts among our beliefs, how our reactions can be tainted by prejudice—revolved around complex mental processes. Research addressing all these questions focused on the investigation of cognitive elements such as beliefs and inferences.

Social psychologists were therefore especially well prepared to embrace the cognitive revolution that began to unfold in the late 1950s. At that point the insight that the mind could be understood and discussed as analogous to an information-processing computer led to an explosion of theory and research aimed at exploring the mental structures and processes used by human information processors. Armed with concepts such as knowledge structures, rules, and plans, cognitive psychologists launched the experimental investigation of many topics that had been considered taboo during the reign of behaviorism. Their newly developed theories and methods began to address questions about how people learn and represent concepts, how they store and access information from memory, and which rules they use to solve problems (for an analysis of the cognitive revolution, see Thagard 1992).

Social psychologists were quick to recognize the relevance of these new ideas to their own traditional concerns. Theories and methods developed to examine how concepts such as *bird* or *apple* are represented could be readily used to study the representation of social concepts such as *extravert* or *librarian*. Experimental tools used to determine when exposure to a word such as *bank* will automatically bring to mind related words such as *money* could be used to examine whether exposure to a member of a stereotyped group such African Americans would automatically bring to mind traits associated with the stereotype of that group. Insights from research uncovering the inferential rules that people use to make judgments about uncertain events such as coin tosses could be applied to exploring how people make judgments about uncertain social events such as the likely behavior of another individual. These insights led to an explosion of research on social cognition. By the early 1970s the field was in full swing.

In addition to its ongoing interest in cognitive elements such as beliefs and attributions, social psychology had historically maintained an interest in two other systems—motivation and affect. The notion that our motives can influence our beliefs lies at the core of one of the most influential social psychological theories, dissonance theory, which was based on the assumption that the motivation to reduce the unpleasant tension among conflicting beliefs could provoke attempts to modify one of the discordant beliefs (Festinger 1957). Another important line of social psychological research, the investigation of attitudes and their impact on behavior, has always regarded affect as central to the concept of attitudes (Eagly and Chaiken 1993). Despite the historical centrality of motivation and affect to social psychological theory, these two systems were somewhat neglected in the early days of social cognition, as researchers enthusiastically imported and extended ideas from cognitive psychology and focused on exploring the role of cognitive structures and processes in social judgment. Until the late 1980s most theory and research in social cognition focused on the relatively "cold" cognitions involved in representing social concepts and drawing inferences from them. More recently there has been renewed interest in the relatively "hot" cognitions underlying motivation and affect, leading social cognition researchers to examine how our goals, desires, and feelings can influence the way we remember and make sense of social events. This research has led to renewed theoretical efforts to integrate cognition, motivation, and affect. In this book I use the term *social cognition* broadly to refer to all these aspects of making sense of our social world—thoughts, goals, and feelings or, more technically, cognition, motivation, and affect.

Overview

The social cognition research reviewed in this book is rich and diverse, containing a multitude of insights about a broad variety of topics. Yet there are some unifying themes that are repeated throughout the book. Perhaps the most important one is that social events do not merely unfold before our eyes, complete with their inherent meaning and implications. Rather, we play an important role in making sense of social events and imbuing them with meaning. Our understanding of our social world is influenced by our concepts, beliefs, and theories as well as by our goals and feelings. Two different individuals may understand the identical social situation quite differently if they view it through different lenses. A remark regarded as witty banter by one person may be viewed as an offensive insult by another. A role model who gives rise to inspiration in one person may provoke discouragement in another. And a venture that seems like a sure bet to one person may be viewed as doomed to failure by another.

Such differences may arise because the same social situation may trigger very different associations in different people. The same woman may remind one person of her gentle mother but remind another of his hostile neighbor. The same African American doctor may evoke the negative stereotype of African Americans in one person but evoke the positive stereotype of doctors in another. The same challenging situation may lead one person to concentrate on achieving success but may lead another to focus on avoiding failure. And the same mention of vacations may give rise to a flood of happy memories in one person but to a host of depressing recollections in another. The different thoughts, goals, and feelings that the same situation triggers in different people can lead them to arrive at very different interpretations of that situation and may cause them to behave quite differently when they find themselves in it.

Even the same individual may understand the identical situation differently on different occasions if this individual encounters the situation with different thoughts, goals, and feelings in mind on each occasion. I may view the same shove as aggressive if I have just been thinking of violence but as playful if I have just been thinking of jocularity. I may consider the same argument persuasive when I wish to believe it but flawed when I wish to disbelieve it. And I may find the same person amusing when I am in a good mood but annoying when I am in a bad mood.

Much of these sense-making activities are carried out automatically. We may not realize that our understanding of another person's behavior can be influenced by the stereotypes and individuals that this person brings to mind, by our theories of social behavior, by the thoughts and feelings that happen to be on our mind at the moment, and by the goals we are pursuing on that particular occasion. The question of just how much control we can exert over such automatic processes is currently the topic of much debate. An especially lively ongoing debate concerns our ability to suppress unwanted negative stereotypes and prevent them from coloring our interpretations of members of stereotyped groups.

Another repeated theme that runs through the book is that our social knowledge and judgments can be faulty. Much of our repertoire of beliefs and theories about social behavior is reasonably accurate, and the rules we use to draw inferences about our social world often serve us well. However, we also carry mistaken beliefs and faulty rules that can often lead us astray. We may have inaccurate memories of our own past behavior and attitudes, believing, for example, that we had initially liked our roommate much more that we actually had. We may fail to recognize the causes of our own and other people's behavior, not realizing, for example, that an angry comment was caused by a provocation rather than by an angry disposition. We may be mistaken about the prevalence of various attitudes and behaviors among our peers, believing, for example, that many more of our friends favor heavy alcohol consumption than is actually the case. Our failure to grasp the relevance of appropriate statistical rules may lead us to view chance events as meaningful. For example, we may take randomly produced streaks of successful shots as evidence that a basketball player is "hot." We may be far too overconfident about the veracity of our predictions about our own or other people's future behavior, thinking, for example that we are much better able to foretell the outcome of our current romantic relationship than is the case. And we may undertake dangerous endeavors that we would have avoided if we had understood how risky they were.

Every one of the examples of idiosyncratic interpretations of events, mistaken beliefs, and erroneous thinking cited above is documented by research described in this book. An appreciation of the possibility that our understanding of events may be idiosyncratically constructed by us and may be swayed by often inappropriate associations, beliefs, and rules may not suffice to prevent us from falling prey to unwanted biases and errors. Nevertheless, it may leave us a little more humble about the veracity of our interpretations and memories, a little more open to dissenting opinions, and a little more cautious in our judgments and decisions.

Throughout the book I focus not only on *what* has been learned about each topic of interest but also on *how* it has been learned. To evaluate the validity of conclusions about human nature, it is essential to understand what these conclusions are based on. Laypeople and psychologists alike make many claims about the nature of social cognition. Any newspaper or magazine you pick up is likely to be rife with assertions and speculations about many of the topics discussed in this book. You may encounter media discussions of issues such as the accuracy of eyewitness memories, the impact of gender stereotypes on hiring, the extent to which decision makers are blinded by self-interest, or the differences between Japanese and American children. Whereas some of the claims you encounter may be backed by solid research, others may rest entirely on intuitions. As I document in this book, our intuitions can sometimes serve us well, but they can also be widely off the mark. Intuitions that are not based on research should therefore be treated with skepticism.

The conclusions presented in this book are therefore based on empirical research rather than on intuitions. Different experimental methods have different strengths and weaknesses. I attempt to provide enough detail of the methods used in the described studies to permit an appreciation of the generality and limitations of the conclusions that these studies point to.

Synopsis

The book is divided into three sections. The first focuses on *basic processes* in social cognition. It reviews research on concept representation, rules of inference, memory, "hot" cognition, and automatic processing. The second section focuses on three *basic topics* in social cognition: group stereotypes, knowledge of other individuals, and the self. The final chapter revisits many of the issues discussed in the book from a cross-cultural perspective.

Deciding what to cover in the basic processes chapters and what in the basic topics chapters was not easy. Most research uncovering basic processes relates to one of the three basic topics, and most research that sheds light on the basic topics also uncovers underlying processes. Nevertheless, I decided to divide the book in this manner because I believe that a thorough understanding of the basic processes is essential to understanding what has been learned about these basic topics. In the basic processes chapters I therefore present and discuss each study with a focus on how it speaks to the underlying process at hand, and I provide brief pointers to the implications for the basic topics. In the basic topics chapters, in contrast, I pull together the implications of diverse processes to provide a sense of what social cognition research has to say about how we think, feel and behave toward stereotyped groups and their members, other individuals, and the self. Finally the chapter on culture draws upon research relating to a variety of processes and topics. I turn next to a brief overview of the contents of the book.

Basic Processes

Chapter 2 focuses on concepts, the building blocks of thought. It notes that social concepts such as *lawyer, extravert, crying*, or *party* are essential to making sense of our social world. They allow us understand the social events that we encounter and to go beyond the information we observe directly, and they enable us to think about such events and to discuss them with others. The chapter examines how we represent social concepts—do we carry definitions of lawyers, lists of their typical attributes, or theories about what makes them tick? Finally it discusses models of how concepts may be interrelated. These models can account for how thinking about one concept can influence our thoughts about another concept.

Chapter 3 focuses on how people make judgments about uncertain events. It notes that people have some understanding of the statistical rules that govern such events and often use them appropriately. However, often, instead of using these statistical rules, people rely on very different heuristics, that is, rules of thumb. The chapter reviews the systematic biases and errors in judgments about other people and the self that can result from reliance on these heuristics. It also outlines factors that can influence whether people will apply statistical or alternative heuristics to the solution of a particular problem.

Chapter 4 begins with a discussion of how people go about testing hypotheses (Is Jane outgoing?) and assessing correlations (Do better scientists make better teachers?). It notes that the strategies they use to do so can lead to systematic biases; people are sometimes biased toward confirming their hypotheses, they often fail to detect correlations that exist in their world, and often "see" correlations that do not, in fact, exist. After discussing how people determine what is and was true of their world, the chapter turns to a discussion of how people contemplate what might have been true. It examines what kind of "if only ..." thoughts people are likely to entertain in different circumstances, and how these may influence feeling of regret and related judgments.

Chapter 5 focuses on memory. It notes that we do not recall events exactly the way they had happened. Rather, we reconstruct past events, and our recollections can be shaped by our state of mind at the time the events unfolded as well as by our current expectancies, theories, goals, and feelings. Memories of past events can therefore be inaccurate. We may recall our past attitudes as more consistent with our current ones than they really had been, and may recall the emotional tone of events as more consistent with our current emotions than was the case. We may also sometimes be mistaken about the source of our memories, and we are capable of mistaking imagined events for real and of recalling other people's ideas as our own.

Chapter 6 focuses on "hot" cognition, that is, cognition that is influenced by our desires and feelings. First, it examines the impact of different kinds of goals on judgment. It notes that the motivation to arrive at particular conclusions can bias people toward arriving at these desired conclusions, and the motivation to arrive at accurate conclusions can lead people to devote greater effort to their judgment. Next the chapter examines the impact of feelings on judgment. It notes that we evaluate our cars, our leaders, our lives, and many other objects more positively when we are happy than when we are sad, and discusses the different ways through which our moods may color our judgments.

Chapter 7 reviews evidence showing that many of our judgments and behaviors may be carried out automatically, that is, without awareness, intention, effort, or controllability. It notes that our judgments, feelings, and behaviors can be influenced by factors that we have never been aware of (because they were perceived subliminally), by factors that we were aware of at one time but can no longer recall, and by factors that we can still recall but whose influence we are unaware of. It next notes that automatic processes require very little effort, and so can proceed without disruption even when we cannot invest much effort in them because we are preoccupied with other tasks. The chapter describes how this insight has been used to determine whether different kinds of social judgment are carried out automatically.

Basic Topics

Chapter 8 addresses the topic of stereotypes. It first examines the circumstances under which stereotypes come to mind and influence judgments about members of stereotyped groups. It considers whether these processes take place automatically and whether they depend on one's level of prejudice. It next examines what it is like to be the target of stereotyping. It describes how members of negatively stereotyped groups may have trouble making sense of feedback they receive from others and discusses how their performance may be impaired when the relevance of the negative stereotypes is highlighted. Finally it examines how group stereotypes can be maintained even in the face of group members who disconfirm these stereotypes.

Chapter 9 examines people's knowledge about other individuals. It first notes that although people can be reasonably accurate about the proportion of individuals who show various attitudes and behaviors, they are also subject to systematic biases. Sometimes they exaggerate the extent to which others share their opinions. On other occasions they mistakenly assume that others' reactions differ from their own. The chapter next focuses on people's beliefs about the consistency of behavior. Although the extent to which any person's behavior reveals friendliness, honesty, or any other trait is influenced considerably by situational forces and is likely to vary notably from one situation to another, people mistakenly assume that such behavior is highly consistent, and they readily infer underlying traits from even a single behavior. The chapter also examines the reasons for these mistaken beliefs.

Chapter 10 focuses on the self. It describes how the contents and organization of knowledge about the self can influence the way people react to and make sense of information about themselves and about others. It next discusses people's desires to receive information that confirms their sense of self and information that enhances their self-views, and examines what happens when these two desires are in conflict (as when negative information would confirm one's sense of oneself as inadequate, but positive information would enhance one's self-views). The chapter then examines how self-knowledge comes into play when one considers other people's performance. Others may be measured against one's own accomplishments, and conversely, one's own achievements may assessed in relation to those of others. Finally the chapter discusses people's ability to regulate their thoughts, feelings, and behavior. Such self-regulation can be highly effortful, and the ability to exercise it can be adaptive.

Culture

Chapter 11 examines cultural differences in social cognition. It begins by contrasting Eastern cultures with Western ones. Whereas Western culture promotes a sense of self as an independent individual, many Eastern cultures promote a sense of self as interdependent with others and as intricately connected to a broader social web. These differences are associated with different kinds of self-knowledge, different ways of explaining others' behavior, and different goals. The chapter then examines cultural differences among Northern and Southern regions of the United States. Only the southern regions are home to a "culture of honor" in which men are extremely concerned with protecting their reputations and honor. These cultural differences are associated with greater acceptance of honor-preserving violence in the South than in the North. Southerners also construe and react to identical insults more negatively than do Northerners.

I Basic Processes

We rely on a variety of concepts to make sense of our social world. We have concepts for personality traits such as shy or responsible, concepts for categories of people such as students or African Americans, and concepts for social events such as parties of funerals. The chapter begins with a discussion of the different ways in which concepts help us make sense of our social worlds and guide our social judgments. Before it can figure in our judgments, a concept must come to mind. I discuss how the social context we find ourselves in as well as our own recent experiences, character, and goals can influence which concepts we activate and use on a given occasion. To understand how people use concepts, it is important to understand how they represent them. Do we carry definitions of students, lists of their most typical attributes, or theories of what they are like? I review the development of ideas on concept representation and describe the strengths and weaknesses of key theories on this issue. It is also important to understand how concepts are organized and interrelated. I describe how prevailing models of the way concepts are interrelated can explain why thinking about one concept can bring to mind related ones. For example, if you stereotype lawyers as aggressive, seeing a lawyer can bring aggression to your mind, and this in turn may lead you to view a friend's amusingly hostile comment as an insult rather than as a joke.

What Are Concepts?

Why are many women who believe in equal rights for men and women reluctant to call themselves feminists? Why are welfare offices across the United States being renamed as "job centers," "employment centers," or "family independence agencies?" (*NYT*, 7.5.1998). Such name changes and disputes over terminology are not unusual. Consider a Palestinian who has planted a bomb on an Israeli bus, killing several civilians. Whether this person should be called a terrorist or a freedom fighter has been the subject of heated debate. Or consider a six-year-old boy who kisses a classmate on the cheek. Should we view this behavior as sexual harassment, as did the Lexington, North Carolina, principal who suspended little Jonathan Prevette from school for a day on these grounds, or should we view this behavior as innocent play, as did the child's outraged parents? (*NYT*, 9.27.1996).

Each of these examples represents a search for the concept that best describes an object, a person, or a behavior. Concepts are the building blocks of cognition. A concept is a mental representation of a category, that is, a class of objects that we believe belong together (Smith 1990). I will return later to the question of what it is that makes us believe that a set of objects or individuals hang together as a meaningful category, but for now the important thing to note is that a concept is our representation of such a category in our minds. It embodies our knowledge about the category and its members. For example, our concept of lawyer may contain attributes that we think are associated with that class of people (intelligent, argumentative), theories about how these attributes relate to each other and to the category as a whole (must be intelligent to get into law school), and examples of particular lawyers we have come across (the characters on a TV show, the lawyer we turned to when we bought our house). Concepts do not necessarily represent what objects, people, or situations are really like; they represent what we believe them to be like. Some concepts, like those of an apple or a lecture, may be quite accurate. Others, like those of a librarian or a honeymoon may be less accurate. Concepts do not necessarily "cut nature at the joints," grouping objects, people, or events into objectively meaningful categories. Many concepts may reflect our own understanding of which groupings are most likely to be meaningful. People can be categorized by shoe size just as readily as by skin color. It is our theories of the world that lead us to view categorization by skin color as more meaningful.

Psychologists have used many different terms to refer to concepts. Some of these are general enough to refer to just about any concept. These include mental representations, knowledge structures, and schemas. Some contain specific assumptions about the nature of representation. These include prototypes and frames. Others refer to specific kinds of objects. These include scripts (for events) and stereotypes (of kinds of people). Among social psychologists, the single most popular term for mental representation has been schema. However, different researchers imbue this term with different meanings. Many use this term in its most general sense, as interchangeable with concept and mental representation. But others view the notion of schema as also containing particular assumptions about the nature of representation. Because the nature of representations has been a topic of some debate, I have chosen to use the simplest and most familiar of the general terms, concept, which makes no assumptions about the content or structure of representations.

Functions of Concepts

Without concepts, our world would make little sense. We would be unable to extract meaning from the huge amount of information that surrounds us, unable to generalize from one experience to another, and unable to communicate effectively with each other. Imagine, for example, how lost and confused you would be if you were to attend a wedding party without an appreciation of some key concepts such as marriage, bride, waiter, dance, photographer, or gift.

The many crucial functions of concepts include classification, inferring additional attributes, guiding attention and interpretation, communication, and reasoning.

Classification

As we encounter objects, people, or behaviors, we classify them as instances of particular concepts. Much of this is done automatically—we do not see an elongated yellow object with black stripes, we see a banana. Just as surely, we "see" police officers and beggars, shy behaviors and helpful acts, joyful expressions and angry outbursts (Trope 1986). Classification is important because it allows us to treat different objects as the same, and it enables us to use our knowledge about categories to make sense of individual members of these categories. When we apply our concept of doctor to a person wearing a stethoscope, we can better understand this person's behavior, and when we apply our concept of help to an offer to carry an old person's groceries, we can better understand the intention underlying that offer.

Inferring Additional Attributes

Once we have classified an instance as belonging to a concept, we can use this concept to go beyond the information given about that particular instance on that particular occasion (Bruner 1957). Having classified an animal as a dog, one may assume that it is capable of barking and biting. Having classified a person as a doctor, one may assume that this person is well-educated and well-off. And having classified a patient's illness as depression, a clinician may assume that this patient is in danger of committing suicide and is likely to respond well to cognitive therapy and to medication. It is this function of going beyond the information given that makes concepts often the subject of heated political debates: A person classified as a freedom fighter is also assumed to be noble and heroic, whereas a terrorist is assumed to be despicable and murderous.

Guiding Attention and Interpretation

Concepts provide a framework for making sense of incoming information. When you step into a classroom, the concepts of lecture, professor, and student allow you to understand what is going on. Without these, the interaction might seem quite strange. We often become aware of our heavy reliance on concepts only when we step into a very different culture and realize that we don't have a clue about what is going on.

Our concepts do not only help us identify the objects, events, and people that we encounter, they also color our reality. People applying different concepts to the same events may emerge with very different understandings of these events. This is especially true in the social world, where many behaviors and interpersonal situations can be ambiguous. The concepts we apply to them help us determine which of their multiple potential meanings is most appropriate for the present occasion because the very same behavior can be interpreted quite differently when viewed through the lenses of different concepts. When we observe a woman crying at a funeral, we will view her crying as an expression of sadness. Yet we will understand the identical behavior as an expression of joy when we observe it at a wedding (Trope 1986). Similarly, when we observe one person pushing another, we may interpret this behavior as a jovial shove if it is performed by a White person, but interpret the identical behavior as a violent push if it is performed by a Black person (Sagar and Schofield 1980).

This interpretive function of concepts lies at the heart of one of the central lessons of research in social cognition: When we observe our social world, we do not merely watch an objective reality unfold before our eyes. Rather, we take part in shaping our own reality; the concepts we impose on events determine the meaning we extract from them.

When incoming information can be readily interpreted with the aid of relevant concepts, we may not pay attention to seemingly irrelevant perceptual details, focusing instead on the broader meaning of behavior (von Hippel et al. 1993). We may notice, for example, that Alex pushed John but not notice what Alex was wearing at the time or where exactly he touched John.

These functions of permitting quick and easy identification of instances and guiding attention to relevant information are tremendously important. They simplify cognitive processing, reduce the effort needed to make sense of our world, and so free up precious cognitive resources that are needed to deal with other pressing judgment tasks (Macrae, Milne, and Bodenhausen 1994). They also enable us to understand behaviors and events that might otherwise seem meaningless. There is, however, a cost. Concepts may cause us to misinterpret information, and the seemingly irrelevant details that they lead us to ignore may actually be important. These costs are particularly disturbing when stereotypes are used to interpret people's behavior, leading to prejudice and discrimination (see chapter 8).

Communication

Concepts permit effective communication with others. Indeed, we take each other's understanding of concepts for granted when engaged in conversation. For example, if you ask me: "Why were you running?" the response "I saw a rattle snake" seems quite sufficient. Your rich conceptual knowledge permits you to readily infer what I thought the snake would do to me and what I was trying to accomplish by running. Concepts permit efficient communication because they allow the speaker to omit many details under the assumption that the listener already knows them. But for this reason concepts may also promote misunderstanding, which can happen if the speaker and listener have different concepts in mind or different representations of the same concepts.

Reasoning

Concepts are the constituents of thought. We can combine existing concepts to form new ideas and to describe new objects and situations. For example, we can readily make sense of novel combinations such as "Harvard-educated carpenter" by relying on what we know about people educated at Harvard and about carpenters, as well as on other related concepts. We may assume, for example, that such a person is intelligent, as befitting a Harvard graduate, and nonmaterialistic, as befitting someone who has chosen not to pursue a more lucrative occupation (Kunda, Miller, and Claire 1990).

Activating Concepts

The concepts that come to mind on a given occasion play a major role in determining how we understand the events and people that we encounter on that occasion. It is therefore of great interest to determine what leads us to activate and use the concepts that we do on each occasion. Why is it that the same person may apply different concepts to similar situations on different occasions? Why, for example, did I classify John's smile as friendly, but Ed's smile as condescending? And why might two people apply different concepts to make sense of the same situation? Why, for example, do some people understand "no" to mean "no," but others understand it to mean "try harder"? The activation of a concept on a given occasion is jointly determined by aspects of the stimulus, of the context in which it is observed, and of the observer.

Stimulus Features

Clearly, the features of the stimulus constrain which concepts may be applied to it. It is difficult to describe a very wrinkled person as young or a very exuberant behavior as withdrawn. This point has received little research attention, perhaps because it is so obvious and perhaps because social psychologists have been more interested in showing how aspects of perceivers and situations can influence concept activation, over and above what one might expect from the mere features of the stimulus (Higgins 1996). Such influences are particularly likely when the stimulus can be reasonably described in terms of more than one concept because it is ambiguous or because it belongs to multiple categories.

Salience

Context may make some aspects of a person more salient than others. A person who differs from everyone else present on a particular dimension may be especially likely to activate that dimension. The solo Black person in the room may be particularly likely to be classified as Black, and the solo woman may be particularly likely to be viewed through the lenses of the woman stereotype (e.g., Biernat and Vesico 1993; Taylor et al. 1978). Salience may also affect which concepts we use to describe ourselves. Children are particularly likely to describe themselves as having attributes that make them relatively distinctive from their classmates. For examples, in classes where boys are a minority, little boys asked to "tell us about yourself" are particularly likely to mention that they are boys (McGuire and Padawer-Singer 1976).

Priming

If you have just been reading an article about race relations, you may be particularly likely to think of a black person as an African American (rather than, say, as a woman, a doctor, or a friend). And if you have just been thinking about acts of hostility, you may be particularly likely to view a person who refuses to pay the rent until his apartment is painted as aggressive (rather than, say, as fair-minded or self-assured; Srull and Wyer 1979). In these examples, particular concepts—African American, aggression—have been primed, that is, made accessible, by a recent experience. The term *priming* refers to any experiences or procedures that bring a particular concept (or any other knowledgen structure) to mind (Higgins 1996).

Following the initial work of Tory Higgins and his colleagues, social psychologists have demonstrated repeatedly that a concept that has recently been primed is especially likely to be applied to the interpretation of novel information, even in unrelated contexts (e.g., Higgins, Rholes, and Jones 1976; Higgins and King 1981. For a review, see Higgins 1996). A variety of procedures have been used to prime concepts. These include asking participants to read synonyms of the concept, asking them to unscramble a series of sentences that are related to the concept (e.g., "leg break arm his" for aggression), or having them overhear a radio broadcast describing an incident related to the concept. The effects of such priming on judgment are then examined in a seemingly unrelated context.

There is now abundant evidence that priming traits such as *aggressive* or *reckless* and priming stereotypes such as *African American* or *elderly person* can influence the interpretation of a related ambiguous behavior encountered later. For example, participants asked to read a description of a person engaging in ambiguously aggressive behaviors rate this person as more aggressive if they have recently been primed with words or sentences related to the trait *aggressive* or with words related to the culturally prevalent stereotype of African Americans, which includes the trait *aggressive* (e.g., Devine 1989; Srull and Wyer 1979. For a review see Higgins 1996). Such priming effects are obtained even when the priming is unconscious. It is possible to flash words on a screen so fast that people will not realize that they have seen any word at all, and yet their judgments will be affected by their exposure to these words. For example, people rate a person who performed ambiguously aggressive behaviors as more aggressive after such rapid, subliminal presentation of words related to aggression or to the negative stereotype of African Americans, even though they are not aware of having seen these words (e.g., Bargh and Pietromonaco 1982; Devine 1989; see chapters 7 and 8).

It is also possible to prime people's attitudes or feelings toward a concept, and this too will make them more likely to use this concept in judgment. For example, under normal circumstances, people are equally likely to classify Mother Teresa as a humanitarian as they are to classify her as a Catholic nun. However, if they have just been asked to contemplate how much they like Catholic nuns, they become more likely to classify her as a nun than as a humanitarian (Smith, Fazio, and Cejka 1996). This is not due to mere priming of the concept; merely priming the concept (by asking people to determine whether it refers to an animate or inanimate object) does not lead to comparable results. We may be especially likely to use those concepts that evoke strong feelings in us. When we contemplate our liking for a category, our feelings toward it become more accessible, and we therefore become more likely to use the concept representing that category in judgment.

Chronic Accessibility

Each person has some concepts that tend to be accessible at all times and are applied wherever possible. For one person, intelligence may be chronically accessible. This person will tend to classify other people as smart or stupid and to classify behaviors as wise or foolish. For another person, gender may be chronically accessible. This person will be particularly likely to classify people and behaviors as masculine or feminine. Concepts tend to be chronically accessible if they are viewed as self-defining and important or if they figure prominently in many of one's descriptions of other people (Higgins, King, and Mavin 1982; Markus 1977). Chronically accessible concepts affect one's understanding of others: A person for whom masculinity is chronically accessible will be particularly likely to apply this concept to make sense of another's behavior, and a person for whom shyness is chronically accessible will be particularly likely to view as shy someone whose behaviors are ambiguous as to whether or not they reflect shyness (Bargh et al. 1986; Markus, Smith, and Moreland 1985). Because different concepts are chronically accessible to different people, two people entering identical social situations may extract very different meanings from these situations (for a detailed discussion, see chapter 10).

Goals

People may be able to activate or suppress particular concepts in the service of their goals. At times, you may wish to disparage another person, perhaps because this person has offended you in some way or perhaps because you are feeling especially vulnerable and so want to establish your superiority over another. If this person belongs to a negatively stereotype group, you may be especially likely to activate and use this group's stereotype to disparage him or her under such circumstances. There is some evidence that people may engage in such motivated activation and use of the negative ethnic stereotypes of African Americans or Jews if they have just experienced a personal failure or if they have just been criticized by a member of the group in question (Fein and Spencer 1997; Sinclair and Kunda 1998). People may also be able to suppress negative ethnic stereotypes if they wish to appear unprejudiced, or if they wish to avoid discrediting a member of that group whom they are motivated to view positively (Devine 1989; Kunda and Sinclair, in press; see chapter 8).

Structure of Concepts

The question of how concepts are represented in our minds has received a tremendous amount of research attention, yet many important issues remain unresolved. Psychologists' understanding of concepts has undergone major transformations over the last few decades (Medin 1989). The first involved a shift from the classical view of concepts as organized around necessary and sufficient defining features to a probabilistic view of concepts as organized more loosely around features that are typical but not defining. The second involved increased recognition that lists of unrelated features cannot adequately describe concepts; concepts also contain a wealth of causal information.

Classical View

Until quite recently most philosophers, linguists, and psychologists subscribed to what has been termed the classical view of concept representation (Smith and Medin 1981). The central assumption of the classical view is that concepts may be defined by a set of necessary and sufficient attributes. There should be, for example, a set of attributes that define the concept *student*. One may be considered a student only if one has all these attributes, and anyone who has all of them is a student. This view maps nicely onto our intuitions. Most of us tend to assume that we can define just about any concept in this manner. Indeed, scholars from many disciplines took the classical view for granted from the days of Aristotle until the middle of the twentieth century. However, following relatively recent analyses by philosophers and linguists and empirical investigations by psychologists that focused on how concepts are represented, the classical view lost favor.

Critique of the Classical View

Medin (1989) summarized the most serious problems with the classical view. These include:

1. *Difficulty in specifying defining features.* Although we assume that we can define concepts, in reality it is very difficult to come up with sets of necessary and sufficient attributes for most concepts. The philosopher Wittgenstein (1953) was the first to illustrate this problem in his now famous discussion of the concept of a game. What are the attributes that are necessary and sufficient to define a game? It turns out that there are no attributes that are common to all games. Some games involve competition and have winners and losers, but others, such as ring-around-the-rosie, do not. Some games, such as snakes and ladders, involve luck. Others, such as chess, involve skill. And still others, such as poker, involve both. Many games involve amusement but would still be considered a game even if no one were having fun. Some games are played alone, some in pairs, and some in large groups. In short, it is impossible to come up with a set of features that all games must have and that are sufficient for calling an activity a game as required by the classical view. And the problem is not restricted to games. Although it is possible to define many mathematical and geometric concepts such as an odd number or a triangle, even experts are unable to produce sets of necessary and sufficient defining attributes for most other concepts.

2. *Members vary in their typicality.* According to the classical view it should be possible to make clear-cut decisions about how any instance should be classified: If it has all the necessary and sufficient features of the concept, it is a member; otherwise, it is not. And all members are equally good examples of the concept; any triangle is as good a triangle as any other because all have the necessary defining features. But the pioneering work of cognitive psy-

chologist Eleanor Rosch suggests that in fact people view some members of a category as better examples than others (e.g., Rosch and Mervis 1975; Rosch, Simpson, and Miller 1976). For example, we think that a robin is a better example of a bird than is an ostrich or a chicken. Rosch and her colleagues and many subsequent researchers used a variety of experimental techniques to make this point (for a review, see Smith 1990). These include:

Typicality ratings. People are asked to rate the extent to which an instance (robin) is typical of a category (bird). People generally agree with each other on such ratings, and tend to rate some members as more typical than others. For example, apple and peach are considered typical fruits, raisin and fig less typical, and pumpkin and olive atypical.

Reaction times. People are asked to indicate as fast as they can whether an instance (robin) is a member of a category (bird) by pressing a button. When one examines the speed with which correct responses are made, it is apparent that people categorize typical members (e.g., robin or swallow) more rapidly than atypical members (e.g., owl or vulture).

Production of examples. People are asked to list all members of a category such as bird. They tend to list the more typical members first.

In short, it is clearly not the case that we consider all members of a category to be equally good examples of it, as would be predicted from the classical view. We regard some members as more typical and can classify these members more efficiently. These more typical members also come to mind more readily when we think about the category. Social psychologists Nancy Cantor and Walter Mischel were quick to note that the same is at least as true for social categories (Cantor and Mischel 1979). For example, among the people whom we consider extraverts, we view some as "better" extraverts than others. Subsequent researchers showed that many other social concepts are also made up of instances that vary in their typicality. When we think about the concept of love, for example, we view some behaviors and feelings such as *trust* and *caring* as more central to the meaning of love than other behaviors and feelings such as *miss other when apart* and *comfort other* (Fehr 1988).

3. *Unclear cases.* If the classical view were correct, we should have no trouble deciding whether any instance belongs to a category—all we need to do is check for the presence of the defining features. In reality, however, we often come across objects that we are not quite sure how to classify: Is a blackboard furniture? Is someone who holds a full-time job and takes correspondence courses a student? The difficulty we have with such examples suggests that we do not categorize by applying clear-cut definitions.

These and other problems have led psychologists to lose faith in the ability of the classical view to account for how people represent concepts, and to favor, instead, a probabilistic view of representation.

Probabilistic View

Wittgenstein, who launched the initial attack on the classical view, also laid down the foundations for the probabilistic view that psychologists turned to next (Wittgenstein 1953). According to the probabilistic view, a category can be described by a list of features that are typical of it, yet do not define it. For example, birds typically fly and nest in trees, but a chicken qualifies as a bird even though it does neither. Wittgenstein used the analogy of *family resemblance* to illustrate what category members have in common. Family members can share various features: blue eyes, curly hair, chubby cheeks, shy personality. Not every member has all these features; indeed it is possible that no single family member will have all of them. And some members have more of the family features than do others. In the same manner, category members are similar to each other in various ways but cannot be characterized by a set of necessary and defining features. Rather than having clear boundaries, categories are "fuzzy" and ill defined.

The probabilistic view holds that to determine whether an instance belongs to a category, we examine the similarity between the two. We classify the instance as belonging to the category if the similarity between the instance and the category is above a certain critical level. Because similarity plays such a central role in classification, it is also necessary to spell out just how we assess similarity. Theorists in this tradition typically view similarity as increasing with the number of features that the instance and the category have in common, and decreasing with the number of features that are unique to each (Smith 1990; Tversky 1977). To determine, for example, whether Jane is an extravert, we assess her similarity to other extraverts we know, or to some abstracted representation of extraverts. We do this by comparing Jane's features to the features we associate with extraverts. Our representation of extraverts may include the features friendly, talkative, has many friends, strikes up conversations with others, comfortable in social situations, often the life of the party. The more of these features that Jane has, the more similar she will be to our representation of extraverts, and so the more likely she will be to be classified as one. And the more Jane is characterized by features that are not part of our representation of extraverts, the less similar she will be to that representation and the less likely to be classified as an extravert.

Support for the Probabilistic View

The findings that are problematic for the classical view follow naturally from the probabilistic view. According to the probabilistic view, membership in a category can be a matter of degree rather than an all or none decision. Members who share more attributes with the category will be considered "better" or more typical members than those who share fewer attributes with the category. And one can be unsure about whether borderline instances belong to the category if their similarity to the category hovers around the critical value for inclusion.

The probabilistic view gained strong support from findings reported by Rosch and Mervis (1975). They showed that when people are asked to judge how typical members are of a category, there is a strong correlation between their typicality judgments and the number of features that instances share with the category—the category members that are viewed as most typical are those that share the most features with the category. Highly typical birds like robins share more features with the category *bird* than do less typical birds like penguins. Cantor and Mischel (1979) showed that the same was true for social categories such as extraverts: Individuals who are judged to be highly typical extraverts share more of their attributes with the category of extraverts than do less typical extraverts.

Within the probabilistic view, there are two different ways of conceptualizing categories:

The prototype view assumes that people possess summary representations of categories, termed prototypes. A prototype is an abstracted list of features that are typical of category members. The bird prototype, for example, may include the features flies, sings, lays eggs, is small, nests in trees, and eats insects (Smith 1990). To determine whether a creature is a bird, one compares it to this summary representation rather than to individual birds. In the same manner, people may be classified as students, extraverts, or gourmets based on their similarity to abstracted representations or stereotypes of such categories rather than on the basis of their similarity to individual category members.

The exemplar view assumes, in contrast, that categories are represented as sets of exemplars, that is, category members that one has encountered. On this view, concepts bring to mind not abstracted summary representations but, rather, groups of specific instances. For example, Smith and Zarate (1992) suggested that a White bigot may not hold a negative global stereotype of Black people. Rather, the bigot may have stored examples of several Black criminals, and these come to mind and determine judgments about newly encountered Black individuals. More generally, people may have no abstract representations of stereotypes, or of any other concept. Instead, they may create ad hoc "stereotypes" by retrieving particular sets of category members (and may retrieve different sets on different occasions). To determine whether an instance is a member of a category, one assesses the similarity between the instance and this set of retrieved category members, without consulting any abstract representation.

Prototypes or Exemplars? The debate about whether concepts are represented as abstract prototypes or as sets of more specific exemplars has not yet been settled. Much of the findings that gave rise to the probabilistic view are plausible under both views of representation. Consider, for example, the key finding that the category members viewed as most typical are those that share the most features with the category—robins share more feature with the category of birds than do penguins (Rosch and Mervis 1975). This finding holds regardless of whether similarity to the category is calculated by comparing the features of a robin to those of an abstracted representation of bird, as the prototype view suggests we should, or by comparing the robin to each of many other specific kinds of bird (swallow, vulture, chicken, etc.) and calculating the average of these similarity judgments, as the exemplar view suggests we should (Smith 1990).

Each view is also supported by some evidence that the alternative view has trouble accounting for. In support of the prototype view, there are studies showing that people's judgments about what a group is like can be independent of their memories about specific group members (e.g., Park and Hastie 1987). This suggests that as they observe group members, people develop an abstract representation of the group that they can then use to make judgments about the group without having to recall individual group members. Such findings are problematic for the exemplar view, because it assumes that there are no abstract representations of the group and that judgments about the group should depend on attributes of recalled group members. On the other hand, the exemplar view gains support from other findings that suggest that recalled exemplars often do influence judgments about groups and their members. For example, people who are reminded of some particularly corrupt politicians tend to view politicians in general as less trustworthy (Schwarz and Bless 1992). And judgments about a football player who happens to bring to mind a particular football star can be influenced by people's recollections of this star (Gilovich 1981).

Social psychologists have been persuaded by both camps. Most recent reviewers of the relevant research have come out in favor of a mixed model, holding that people store both abstract representations of categories and specific examples of them (e.g., Fiske and Taylor 1991; Hamilton and Sherman 1994; E. R. Smith 1996). On this view, our judgments about a newly encountered student may be guided by an abstract representation of what students in general are like as well as by our memories of one or more students we have known. Our judgments of different students will have much in common, but a student who reminds us of a recent dropout may be evaluated quite differently than a student who reminds us of a scholarship winner.

It is also important to note that both the prototype view and the exemplar view have one central assumption in common. Both regard categorization as based on similarity between the instance and the category. They differ only in their assumptions about whether this similarity judgment reflects a comparison of the instance to an abstract representation of the category or to a set of category members. This heavy reliance on similarity has been at the heart of a recent set of criticisms of the probabilistic approach which have led to some disillusionment with it.

Critique of the Probabilistic View

The probabilistic view has successfully accounted for an impressive range of phenomena and, as a result, has been enormously influential. Researchers in this tradition have been able to create precise measures of similarity between an instance and a category, and have shown that such measures predict the extent to which instances are viewed as typical of categories. These typicality judgments, in turn, can predict important aspects of categorization decisions, such as their speed and accuracy (Smith 1990). Such precision and predictive power can be invaluable. If we know the attributes of a category, we can use this theory to predict the classification of novel instances. If we identify, for example, the list of attributes and behaviors that customs officials associate with smugglers, we will be able to predict which individuals are most likely to be stopped for search and interrogation at the border. And if we know the list of attributes that professors value in graduate students, we will be able to predict which individuals are most likely to be admitted into graduate school.

Within social psychology the view of concepts as represented by lists of attributes that vary in their typicality or associative strength has had a tremendous impact on theory as well as on methodology. Most investigators interested in assessing people's stereotypes do so by obtaining lists of attributes that people associate with each stereotype (Stangor and Lange 1994). For example, the culturally prevalent stereotype of Blacks has been portrayed as a list of traits such as hostile, poor, and musical (Devine and Baker 1991). Similarly, people's impressions of other individuals are often represented as lists of attributes such as traits, behaviors, and attitudes. For example, impressions of fellow students have been portrayed as lists of items such as intelligent, dyed her hair pink, and is aware of her faults (e.g., Park 1986). People's representations of traits are also conceptualized and measured as lists of behaviors. For example, the trait gregarious has been portrayed as a list of behaviors such as introduced oneself to others, told jokes at a dinner party, and studied with a group (e.g., Buss and Craik 1983). In short, social concepts are typically measured as lists of unrelated attributes.

The broad acceptance of the probabilistic view has also led clinicians to revamp the key document used as a guideline for diagnosis, the *Diagnostic and Statistical Manual of Mental Disorders*. The 1968 version (DSM-II, American Psychiatric Association) still attempted to define disorders. For example, it defined depressive neurosis as "an excessive reaction of depression due to an internal conflict or to an identifiable event such as the loss of a love object or a cherished possession" (p. 40). By 1987 the lessons of the probabilistic view of concepts had clearly sunk in. The version published that year (DSM-IIIR) no longer attempted to provide definitions of disorders. Instead, it characterized mental disorders as lists of typical symptoms (and the same was true for the subsequent 1994 version, DSM IV). In these versions the same diagnosis of depressive neurosis requires that a person have a depressed mood for most of the day more days than not for at least two years and also have, while depressed, at least two of a list of six additional symptoms such as insomnia, appetite loss, fatigue, and low self-esteem everyday for at least two weeks. Remarkably, three different individuals can now be given the same diagnosis of depression even though there is no overlap in any of their symptoms other than depressed mood! Depressed individuals are now assumed to share a family resemblance rather than to possess the same defining features.

Despite its broad impact and appeal, the probabilistic view has been the focus of increasingly harsh criticisms. These question the central role allocated to similarity between instances and categories, and challenge the view of concepts as lists of unrelated attributes. Critics of the probabilistic view agree that similarity plays an important role in organizing categories—clearly, category members seem similar to each other. But they argue that similarity cannot alone account for categorization. Murphy and Medin (1985) pointed to some problems with relying on similarity as the sole determinant of category membership. These include:

1. *How do we decide what to base our similarity judgments on?* The influential theory of similarity developed by Tversky (1977) views similarity between objects as a function of the number of features common to both and the numbers of features unique to each, weighted by the salience or importance of each feature. But how do we know what to count as a feature? As Murphy and Medin (1985, p. 292) pointed out, any two objects share an infinite number of features. Plums and lawnmowers for example, "both weigh less than 10,000 kg (and less than 10,001 kg, ...), both did not exist 10,000,000 years ago (and 10,000,001 years ago, ...), both cannot hear well, both can be dropped, both take up space, and so on. Likewise, the list of differences could be infinite." One need not call on such absurd features to make the point that some features seem more meaningful to categorization than others. We are more likely to categorize people by their sexual preferences than by their food preferences, more likely to categorize by skin color than by shirt color, more likely to categorize by occupation than by hobby (e.g., Stangor et al. 1992). Clearly, some additional knowledge

about the nature of the world guides our choice of features and helps determine which will figure in our categorization judgments.

Even after we decide which features will figure in our judgments, we still have a problem: How do we know how to weight each feature? How do we determine their relative importance? This is crucial because similarity between two objects can vary with the weights we assign to features. A zebra will seem more similar to a barber pole than to a horse if the feature *striped* is considered important enough. It turns out that the salience and importance of features varies from context to context, and so the perceived similarity among objects also varies (Medin, Goldstone, and Gentner 1993; Tversky 1977). This leads to yet another problem: How can categories be based only on similarity if similarity varies from one occasion to another? The problem is even more acute when we attempt to classify people as belonging to social categories such as stereotypes, because each individual belongs to many such categories. A Black woman and a White woman may be seen as similar to each other and grouped together if they are the only women among fifty men of both races, highlighting the salience of gender for classification. But the same Black woman may be grouped together with a Black man rather than with other women if the two are the only Black people among fifty White people of both sexes (see Taylor et al. 1978).

It appears, then, that neutral atheoretical feature-based similarity judgments cannot fully account for categorization. At the very least, these judgments must be guided by additional information that helps determine which features are relevant and how important each of them is.

2. *Classification by similarity alone ignores relations among attributes.* Under the probabilistic view the features of objects and of categories are treated as lists of unrelated attributes, and categorization is based on the numbers of attributes that the instance and the category share as well as on the number of attributes unique to each. But this view ignores the fact that people also possess rich knowledge about the relations among attributes. Our concept of bird includes, in addition to the features "has wings" and "can

fly," the knowledge that birds can fly *because* they have wings. Just as surely, we know that lawyers are articulate *because* they need to be persuasive in the courtroom. We often rely on such causal knowledge in our classifications. For example, we may classify a person who jumped into a swimming pool fully dressed as drunk, even though our representation of "drunk" does not include that specific behavior. We do so because we know enough about the meaning of such behavior in its context and about the consequences of being drunk to infer that this behavior could indicate intoxication (Murphy and Medin 1985).

The realization that categorization requires knowledge that transcends similarity judgments prompted some theorist to propose a shift toward a view of concepts as theory based.

Concepts as Theory Based

Social psychologist have long assumed that the representations of concepts contain causal relations. The term *schema*, which has dominated social-cognition discourse about mental representations, has been defined as "'theories' about how the social world operates" (Markus and Zajonc 1985, p. 145; see also Taylor and Crocker 1981). However, for most social psychologists using the term, the view of schema as theory served as a background assumption rather than as the focus of empirical investigation. Social-cognition research focused, instead, on investigating how schemas are activated and on exploring their consequences for processing social information. Most findings generated by this research do not depend on particular assumptions about how concepts are represented. Moreover, as I pointed our earlier, social concepts have typically been measured and described as lists of unrelated traits rather than as theories.

More recently cognitive and developmental psychologists exploring the nature of concept representation have accumulated mounting support for the notion that concepts include causal knowledge. As a result several theorists have suggested that causal knowledge plays a central role in holding concepts together and in guiding categorization (Carey 1985; Keil 1989; Murphy and Medin 1985). The strongest statement of this view holds that the relation between a concept and an instance is analogous to the relation between a theory and data (Murphy and Medin 1985). Classification does not result simply from matching the attributes of the instance to those of the concept. Rather, it "requires that the example have the right 'explanatory relationship' to the theory organizing the concept" (Medin 1989, p. 1474). A weaker view of the role of theory in the representation of concepts holds that many concepts contain knowledge about causal relations (along with information about attribute typicality), and this knowledge can play a role in classification (Keil 1989).

Support for the Theory-Based View

Several different lines of research point to the role of theoretical knowledge in the representation and use of concepts. These are described next.

Category Membership Overrides Similarity Developmental psychologists Susan Gelman and Ellen Markman (1986) found that even for preschoolers, similarity-based judgments can be overridden by theory-based knowledge. In their studies they showed children sets of pictures in which perceptual similarity and category membership were in conflict. For example, a swallow was drawn to be very similar to a bat but quite different from a flamingo. Despite this, most children inferred that the swallow's feeding practices would resemble those of the flamingo (a fellow bird) rather than those of the perceptually similar bat. In other words, the children based their judgments on category membership rather than on perceptual similarity. Apparently, similarity judgments were overridden by knowledge about the kinds of attributes that members of the same category are likely to have in common.

The work of another developmental psychologist, Frank Keil (1989) points to the same conclusion. In his studies Keil tells children about a set of increasingly gruesome transformations performed on one animal so as to make it resemble another. In one of his scenarios, a raccoon was made to appear like a skunk by shaving and dying its fur and, with surgery, putting in its body "a sac of super smelly odor, just like a skunk has." Even though the transformed animal now looks and smells like a skunk, children believe it is still a raccoon. Once again, category membership overrides superficial similarity. When classifying or predicting the behavior of an animal, children rely on their underlying knowledge about the nature of animals.

Goal-Derived Categories A different kind of evidence for the importance of theories in organizing concepts comes from the existence of goal-derived categories (Barsalou 1983 1985). Consider, for example, a category that includes children, money, photo albums, and pets. You may find it difficult to see why these objects should be grouped together, until you are told that these are all "things to take out of one's home during fire." Once you know this, you can readily make decisions about whether new objects belong to the category (manuscripts do, refrigerators do not), and about how typical each object is of the category. This category hangs together despite the fact that its members share few family resemblances. One could argue that they do share some typical features —they are valuable, irreplaceable, and portable. But these features only hang together as a category because of their causal relation to its organizing principle. It is easy to think of similar examples of social categories that are held together by virtue of some underlying knowledge and theory rather than by atheoretical similarity. You may wish to generate members of the categories of "behaviors that would drive my mother crazy," "traits I would value in a spouse," or "prisoners who should receive parole." Clearly, background knowledge and theory can highlight the similarities between seemingly unrelated objects, behaviors, or people, and make them hang together as a coherent category.

Expertise People with deep understanding of a domain classify objects differently than do less knowledgeable people. For example, when asked to group physics problems together, novices grouped them according to superficial similarity whereas experts grouped them according to the underlying physical principles used to solve the problem (Chi, Feltovich, and Glaser 1981). Evidently the experts' theoretical knowledge led them to see superficially different problems as belonging together. Similarly, people who deal with the same objects in different professional roles tend to classify them somewhat differently. Scientists who study trees, landscapers who use trees in their projects, and maintenance workers who keep up trees in parks do not share identical taxonomies of trees. Landscapers, for example, are more likely than the other kinds of professionals to group trees according to whether they are weed trees or ornamentals. And maintenance workers are especially likely to pay attention to features such as wood strength (Medin, Lynch, and Coley 1997). The background knowledge conferred by different kinds of expertise along with the purpose that this expertise serves can influence categorization judgments.

Combined Concepts What is a pot fish? an ocean drive? a horse race? We can readily understand these combined concepts. Yet, as Murphy and Medin (1985) noted, we cannot figure out what the combination means simply by putting together the meanings of each individual concept, and there is no single rule that explains how we do make sense of such combinations. We know that a horse race is a race of horses, but an ocean drive is not a drive of oceans; we know that an expert repair is a repair done by experts, but an engine repair is not a repair done by engines. To understand such combined concepts, we appear to call upon causal knowledge embedded in each concept as well as on broader knowledge about the world.

Social psychological research has provided nice examples of reliance on causal reasoning when combining concepts. Asch and Zukier (1984) asked people to describe individuals characterized by two often conflicting traits: someone who is gloomy and cheerful; someone who is hostile and dependent; someone who is generous and vindictive. People often resolved these conflicts through causal reasoning. In some cases, one trait was viewed as a means for obtaining the other; a person may be strict and kind because one must be strict in order to protect a child. In other cases, one trait was viewed as the cause of the other; a person may be hostile and dependent because dependence breeds hostility. And in still other cases, explanatory events were inferred; a person who is intelligent and unambitious must have met with failure. As these examples illustrate, causal knowledge was used to resolve conflicts among traits, and must have also guided decisions about which mode of resolution was appropriate for each pair of traits. This suggests that trait concepts are embedded in a network of causal relations.

The same is true for stereotypes. Imagine someone who is Harvard educated and a carpenter, someone who is a lawyer and blind, someone who is gay and a construction worker. Kunda, Miller, and Claire (1990) found that people rely on causal knowledge to combine such pairs of surprising and seemingly incompatible stereotypes. Students' descriptions of such individuals often contained explicit causal reasoning: A blind lawyer must be hard working to have overcome the obstacles of law school; a gay construction worker must be trying to hide his true identity behind the image of a masculine profession. Moreover, descriptions of someone characterized by such combinations of stereotypes contained emergent attributes, that is, attributes that were not used to describe either of the original stereotypes. For example, a Harvard-educated carpenter was described as nonmaterialistic and a nonconformist, even though neither of these attributes was used to describe someone identified only as a Harvard-educated person or only as a carpenter. Such emergent attributes suggest that in forming impressions of someone who belongs to multiple stereotyped groups, people rely not only on the attributes contained in each of the stereotypes but also on broader world knowledge. These findings are inconsistent with the view of stereotypes as bundles of unrelated attributes.

Critique of the Theory-Based View

There appears to be considerable and compelling evidence that concepts contain causal knowledge which can influence judgments about how to classify instances, which attributes category members are likely to share with other members, and how concepts should be combined. Although this evidence suggests that theories do play a role in the organization of concepts, it is not clear just how big this role is. The evidence is not strong enough to support an extreme view, which holds that all concepts are organized entirely by theory such that every attribute has an explanatory relation to the concept as a whole as well as to other attributes. More likely, many concepts contain some causal information as well as other information that is unrelated to theory. For example, we know that lions have sharp claws and teeth, and this information is causally related to our knowledge that they are carnivores. But we also know that lions have manes, and we may have no idea as to why they should—we just noticed that they typically do. As Keil (1989, p. 278) put it, "Concepts may always be embedded in theories, but part of their structure may always be organized according to theory-independent principles."

The view of concepts as theory-based enriches our understanding of concepts and sheds light on phenomena that would be difficult to explain otherwise. But wholesale endorsement of this view would entail the loss of the precision and predictive power that made the probabilistic view so attractive. The notions of theory and causal relations are somewhat vague. To date, research has focused on demonstrating that theory must have played a role in the use of concepts, but there have been few attempts to measure theoretical knowledge and to predict its impact.

Interconcept Organization

So far, discussion focused on the internal structure of concepts. There has also been considerable work on how concepts may be related to each other. Many concepts are organized in hierarchies, with the most specific and narrow concepts at the bottom, and broader and more abstract ones at higher levels. In the biological world, for example, one hierarchy includes *animal* at a high, or superordinate level, *dog* at a lower level, and *Dalmatian* at a still lower, subordinate level. In the social world, one hierarchy includes *emotionally unstable person* at a high level, *phobic* at a lower level, and *claustrophobic* at a still lower level (Cantor and Mischel 1979). In such hierarchies, higher-level categories include all members of the categories below them: *Animal* includes all dogs, *dog* includes all Dalmatians. Therefore, the same creature may be classified at different levels of abstraction: We may refer to Rover as a Dalmatian, as a dog, or as an animal. It is important to know which level we are likely to use because categories at different levels of abstraction bring to mind different attributes: *Animal* may bring to mind *can breathe*, *dog* may bring to mind *can bark*, and *Dalmatian* may bring to mind *has spots*. It turns out that in many hierarchies, one of the possible levels of abstraction has a special status. Rosch and her colleagues have termed this special, privileged level the *basic level* (Rosch et al. 1976).

Basic-Level Categories

The basic level is the level at which we will most naturally name objects. When we see a picture of Rover, we will most likely refer to him as a dog (rather than as a Dalmatian or an animal). Basic-level concepts are also the ones learned first by children. What makes a particular level basic? Rosch originally thought that this is determined by nature—the basic level is the highest or most inclusive level at which objects have many common attributes that are distinct from the attributes of other categories at that level. For example, dogs have much in common with each other and are also quite different from birds and fish. At a lower level, Dalmatians also have much in common with each other, but they are not that different from poodles or bulldogs. And at a higher level, different kinds of animals do not have that many attributes in common. Basic levels are also the highest level at which one can readily create an image that would represent the category as a whole. One can readily imagine a generic dog or bird, but what would a generic animal look like? Categories identified in this manner as basic-level categories tend to be at an intermediate level of abstraction (Rosch 1978). This view of basic categories as "cutting nature at its joints" was challenged, however, by the realization that different levels of

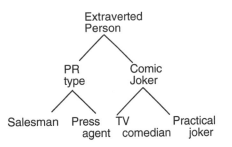

Figure 2.1   Hierarchy of social categories. Adapted from Cantor and Mischel (1979, fig. 2, p. 17). Copyright © (1979) by Academic Press. Adapted with permission.

abstraction may be basic for different people. For example, experts may consider lower levels in the hierarchy to be basic. You and I may think of Rover as a dog, but a dog trainer may think of him as a Dalmatian (Tanaka and Taylor 1991). Basic levels are also likely influenced by goals. When choosing a pet dog, we may be classifying potential candidates as poodles or terriers rather than as dogs.

Are there comparable basic-level categories for social concepts? This is an important question because, as discussed earlier, the categories applied to people and behaviors can affect our expectations about people and our interpretations of their behavior. We will form very different expectations about a person if we classify her at a high level of abstraction, as a woman, than if we classify her at a lower level of abstraction, say as a grandmother, feminist, or nun. Many hierarchies of social concepts do have privileged basic level categories, and as is true for natural categories, basic social concepts tend to be those at middle-level abstraction. Consider the hierarchy of social categories presented in figure 2.1. Cantor and Mischel (1979) showed that the intermediate-level categories in this hierarchy, *PR type* and *comic joker* have much in common with basic-level categories such as *dog* or *chair* identified by Rosch. They represent the highest level of abstraction at which concepts can be richly and vividly described, and they can be readily differentiated from other concepts at the same level of abstraction. As well, social stereotypes such as *comedian* and *politician* are often more rich and distinct than are broader trait concepts such as *extravert* (Andersen and Klatzky 1987). Perhaps, then, these rich and differentiated intermediate categories are also basic in that they are the ones that come to mind first when we observe people. There is some reason to believe that this is often the case. We tend to think of aged individuals in terms of intermediate-level stereotypes such as *grandmotherly type* or *elder statesman* rather than in terms of higher-level more inclusive stereotype such as *old people* (Brewer, Dull, and Lui 1981). And, when describing others' personalities, we often prefer intermediate-level traits such as *kind*, which represent the highest level of abstraction that can still describe behavior, over more specific subordinate traits such as *charitable*, or more abstract traits such as *good* which are so broad that they no longer imply concrete behaviors (John, Hampson, and Goldberg 1991).

Despite such findings we should not rush to assume that we can and have identified *the* basic levels of social concepts that people habitually use when thinking about others. This is because the level that we consider basic in hierarchies of social concepts seems far more likely to be flexible and to vary from one context to another, and more likely to depend on our goals than is the case for nonsocial concepts (Cantor and Kihlstrom 1987). Although this speculation has not been tested directly, it gains support from work showing that different kinds of social concepts may be activated spontaneously. Traits such as *generous* may be spontaneously used to describe some behaviors (Winter and Uleman 1984), and broad racial stereotypes such as *black* may be applied automatically to some individuals (Fazio et al. 1995). Rather than questioning which is more basic, it may be more useful to investigate the circumstances under which each is most likely to be used (Andersen and Klatzky 1987; Cantor and Mischel 1979; Hampson, John, and Goldberg 1986).

It is also the case that many social concepts do not fit neatly into mutually exclusive hierarchies. A Dalmatian is a dog, and is not a member of other categories at the same level of abstraction such as cat or horse. Further, all dogs are animals, but all animals are not dogs. Consider, in contrast, my neighbor. He is a man, an American, a professor, an Asian, an extravert, a gourmet, a sports fan, and the list could go on and on. Every person belongs to many such crosscutting categories that cannot be organized in a single hierarchy of increasingly inclusive categories. Without such a clear hierarchy, there can also be no basic-level categories akin to those described by Rosch. We run into the same problems for traits and behaviors. Consider the behavior *made rude comments to passing women*. We may classify this behavior as an instance of aggression. But we may also classify it as an instance of other traits such as unrefined and unfriendly. Many behaviors participate in multiple hierarchies as do many traits (Hampson et al. 1986; Kunda, Sinclair, and Griffin 1997). It is not that helpful to describe a given level, be it trait or social stereotype, as basic if we cannot also specify which of the many potential candidates at that level will be used—do we identify Jane as a comedian or as a math wiz? Do we view pushing as aggressive or as rude?

The search for basic-level social categories is further complicated by the fact that social hierarchies are messier than nonsocial ones. The subordinate-superordinate relations in nonsocial categories are usually clear-cut. It is obvious to us that a dog is a kind of animal but that an animal is not a kind of dog. In contrast, we may believe that to be unkind is a way of being inconsiderate and also believe that to be inconsiderate is a way of being unkind (Hampson et al. 1986). The same is true for stereotypes: We may see *doctor* as a kind of woman and also see a *woman* as a kind of doctor.

The messy relations among social concepts have led some to suggest that rather than thinking of social concepts as organized in structured hierarchies, we should think of them as arranged in *tangled webs* (Andersen and Klatzky 1987; Cantor and Kihlstrom 1987). Which concepts will be used on a given occasion then depends not so much on structural aspects of the concept such as its richness or distinctiveness but rather on situational and personal factors that serve to activate particular concepts.

Models of Representation

Cognitive psychologists have developed detailed models of knowledge representation that describe not only how concepts are represented and interrelated but also the processes through which knowledge may be activated and retrieved (e.g., Anderson 1983; Collins and Loftus 1975). Some social psychologists have also developed detailed models of how social knowledge is represented and used (e.g., Wyer and Srull 1986). But, for the most part, social psychologists have adopted some of the central assumptions of influential cognitive models without worrying too much about the specific details. Typically, social psychologists have focused not so much on mapping out the architecture of cognition but on spelling out the implications of aspects of this architecture for people's understanding of their social worlds. In particular, the assumptions of associative network models (Collins and Loftus 1975) have informed and inspired a great deal of research on social cognition. I therefore focus on spelling out these central assumptions rather than on the details, which may vary from one model to another (for more detailed reviews, see Carlston and Smith 1996; Fiske and Taylor 1991; Smith 1998).

Associative Network Models

These models view mental representations as networks of *nodes* that are connected to each other by way of *links*. Depending on the specific model, a node may represent a feature (attractive) a concept (woman) or a proposition (Dave helped the old lady cross the street). The links vary in strength—some associations are stronger than others. In many cognitive models the links are labeled. For example, the link connecting *dog* to *animal* can be labeled *is-a*, and the link connecting *dog* to *bark* can be labeled *can*. But most social psychological models simplify matters by using unlabeled links. Each node has a level of *activation* that varies from one occasion to another. The more activated a node, the more likely it is to be used, that is, to burst into awareness, to be recalled, and to be applied to incoming information. Activation *spreads* from one node to another by way of the connecting links. So, when one node such as *dog* is activated, others that are connected to it (e.g., *animal*, *bark*) are activated as well. After a node is activated, its level of activation gradually *decays*.

In their most general form, associative models make no assumptions about the internal structure of concepts or about their organization. Knowledge is represented as a web of concepts and features, and there are no gradients of typicality or hierarchies of concepts. However, such information can be incorporated into associative models by specifying the strength with which different instances are associated with a category (associations could be stronger for more typical instances), indicating which other concepts each concept is linked to (there could be direct links to superordinates and subordinates), and spelling out the nature of these links (they could specify that one concept is included in another, or that one describes another).

Figure 2.2 illustrates a segment of an associative network, portraying a set of associations among several behaviors, traits, and stereotypes (of course each of these would also have many other associations that are not represented in the figure). This network may be used to demonstrate how associative models can account for key social psychological findings about the activation and use of concepts. One important finding involves priming—a concept that has been recently activated can affect the interpretation of information encountered later (e.g., Srull and Wyer 1979). Consider the behavior *won't pay rent until house is painted* depicted in figure 2.2. If you have just been thinking about aggression, for whatever reason, the node *aggressive* will have relatively high activation. When you then hear that John won't pay his rent until his house is painted, this sends further activation to *aggressive*. Activation also spreads from the behavior to its other associates, *protests unfair treatment* and *wants nice house*. But these will not be as strongly activated as *aggressive* because only *aggressive* enjoys the benefit of the additional lingering activation due to its recent use. Therefore your impression of John will be dominated by *aggressive*.

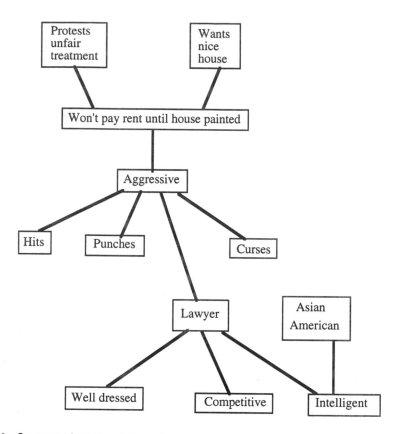

Figure 2.2 Segment of an associative network.

It is apparent from the figure that the meaning of an ambiguously hostile behavior can also be affected by the activation of stereotypes that are associated with aggression (Devine 1989). In this example, if you have been thinking about lawyers, activation will spread from *lawyer* to *aggressive*, and thereby affect your impression of the person who wouldn't pay his rent until his house was painted, just as it does when *aggressive* is activated directly.

The figure also illustrates one important weakness of associative network models: Activation may spread indefinitely throughout the network, often inappropriately. In this example, thinking about Asian Americans can also lead you to activate aggression. This is because activation spreads from Asian *American* to *intelligent*, and continues to spread from *intelligent* to *lawyer* and from *lawyer* to *aggressive*. But even though we may agree with the assumptions underlying these links, namely that lawyers and Asian Americans are stereotyped as intelligent, and that lawyers are also stereotyped as aggressive, it seems highly inappropriate for Asian Americans to activate aggression; if anything, they are stereotyped as unaggressive. It seems that there should be some constraints on how activation may spread. Some models avoid this problem by assuming that each concept is stored in a separate and independent bin so that activating Asian American will not lead to the activation of lawyer and, thereby, of aggression (Wyer and Srull 1986). A new class of models that have only recently been introduced to social psychology handles this problem by placing explicit constraints on the spread of activation.

Parallel-Constraint-Satisfaction Models

These models, which are often referred to as *connectionist models*, also view representations as networks of interconnected nodes, and assume that activation spreads along these connections. But they add an important assumption: Activated nodes not only can activate their neighbors, they also can *deactivate* them (Rumelhart and McClelland 1986). There are two basic kinds of links between nodes: If two nodes have a positive *excitatory link*, then activating one will increase the activation of the other. These links are akin to the ones in earlier, associative models. But two nodes may also have a negative *inhibitory link*. In this case activating one will decrease the activation of the other. Returning to figure 2.2, we may wish to add such a negative link between *Asian American* and *aggressive*, so that thinking about Asian Americans will make us less likely to entertain thoughts about aggression. It is important to incorporate such inhibitory links because there is increasing evidence that mental structures may be inhibited, that is, deactivated under some circumstances (Anderson and Spellman 1995; Macrae, Bodenhausen, and Milne 1995).

The positive and negative links act as *constraints* on the spread of activation. A positive constraint between two nodes means that the two should go together—they should both be activated or both deactivated. For example, if John is hostile, he should also be aggressive. If he is not hostile, he should not be aggressive either. A negative constraint means that the two nodes should not go together—if one is activated the other should be deactivated. For example, if John is hostile, he should not be friendly; if he is friendly, he should not be hostile. The challenge is to arrive at a final pattern of node activation that satisfies as many of these constraints as possible. It is often not possible to satisfy all of the constraints because they may conflict with each other. For example, a person who is manipulative should also be interpersonally skilled. But a person who is interpersonally skilled should also be loving, whereas a person who is manipulative should not. It will be impossible to satisfy all of these constraints simultaneously. Parallel-constraint-satisfaction models aim to satisfy as many of the constraints as possible while giving preference to the more important ones (Thagard and Kunda 1998).

There are two broad classes of parallel-constraint-satisfaction models that differ in the level of abstraction at which nodes are conceptualized. Models using *local* representations view nodes as representing identifiable concepts or propositions—traits, stereotypes, or behaviors, much like the nodes in the associative network illustrated in figure 2.2. Models using *distributed* representations view nodes as representing more basic, lower-level elements so that the meaning of higher-level concepts is distributed over many such nodes. So far, of the small number of models applied to social cognition, most have used local, intuitively meaningful representations (Kunda and Thagard 1996; Read and Miller 1993; Read and Marcus-Newhall 1993; Shultz and Lepper 1996; Spellman and Holyoak 1992). It has also been suggested that distributed models may be usefully applied to social psychological issues (Smith 1996).

Parallel-constraint-satisfaction models also differ in how they conceptualize links and constraints. The most simple models involve only positive and negative links and constraints (Kunda and Thagard 1996). Such simple models have been successfully applied to understanding how information from many, often conflicting sources (traits, behaviors, stereotypes) may be integrated into a coherent impression of a person. They may also readily account for phenomena such as priming that associative networks have been used to explain. Other models involve more elaborate, labeled links spelling out causal relations, and more elaborate sets of constraints (e.g., logical contradiction and simplicity; Read and Marcus-Newhall 1993; Thagard 1989). These have been applied to understand higher-level reasoning such as jury decision making.

Beyond these differences among parallel-constraint-satisfaction models, they all share the view that making sense of people involves an elaborate balancing act in which one attempts to satisfy many, often conflicting demands so as to arrive at coherent impressions of individuals, behaviors, or social situations.

Summary

A *concept* is a mental representation of a category, that is, a class of objects that we believe belong together. Concepts of social objects such as traits, stereotypes, and interpersonal situations allow us to classify behaviors, people, and events, to interpret our social world and make inferences about it that go beyond the information we have observed directly, and to communicate with one another.

The activation of a concept on a given occasion is jointly determined by aspects of the stimulus, the context in which it is observed, and the observer. The social context may increase the salience and use of some concepts. For example, the sole woman in a room full of men may be especially likely to be classified as a woman. Our own recent experiences can also influence which concepts are on our minds. If we have just been contemplating a particular concept in one context, it may remain activated and influence our judgments in another context. For each of us, some concepts are activated chronically, and these are likely to influence our judgments in a wide range of situations. Our goals, too, may influence which concepts we activate; we may be especially likely to activate and use those concepts that can help us draw desired conclusions.

Psychologists' understanding of the structure of concepts has undergone major transformations over the last few decades. The first involved a shift from the *classical view* of concepts as organized around necessary and sufficient defining features to a *probabilistic view* of concepts as organized more loosely around features that are typical but not defining. The second involved increased recognition that lists of unrelated features cannot adequately describe concepts; concepts also contain a wealth of *causal information*.

Prevailing *associative-network models* of knowledge representation view representations as networks of interconnected nodes (depicting features, concepts, or propositions). Activation spreads from each node to those that it is connected to. Therefore, thinking of one concept can increase the activation of associated concepts and, thereby, increase their use in judgment. More recent *parallel-constraint-satisfaction models* assume that nodes not only can activate their associates but also can deactivate them, depending on how they are connected. Each concept's final level of activation reflects a compromise among the various activating and deactivating messages it receives from its associates. Such models can explain how different, often conflicting kinds of information about a person can be integrated into a coherent impression.

You have just met a graduate of Bluevale High School, and she seemed pretty arrogant. Should you expect the next Bluevale graduate you meet to be arrogant as well? Your best friends had a wonderful time on their Florida vacation. Will you love Florida too? The personnel officer who interviewed Anthony thought he would make an outstanding manager. Will Anthony excel as a manager?

To answer each of these questions, you must consider probabilities: The probability that one graduate of a particular high school is arrogant given that another graduate of that school is, the probability that you will like a vacation spot given that your friends liked it, the probability that someone who seems outstanding on a job interview will excel on the job.

The question of how we reason about probabilities has received a great deal of attention. Much of this attention has focused on identifying our weaknesses—the ways in which we fail to understand and use the rules that govern probabilities, and the trouble that this gets us into. Studying cognitive errors and illusions is interesting in its own right. It is also important because it can shed light on how we reason, in general, much like studying visual illusions can shed light on the workings of our visual system. In this chapter I will begin with a brief history of people's reasoning about probability and then discuss more recent research demonstrating some of the problems that people have with statistical reasoning and the implications of these problems for reasoning about the social world. I will describe several important nonstatistical heuristics, or rules of thumb that people often rely on rather than using more appropriate statistical rules, and will describe some of the factors that determine when people are likely to follow appropriate statistical rules and when they are likely to use nonstatistical ones instead.

History of Probabilistic Reasoning

Probability theory is a relatively new intellectual accomplishment. People have been gambling since ancient times. In lieu of dice, ancient civilizations used polished animal knucklebones which, when thrown, could land in only four ways. Although such randomizing devices were prevalent, the rules governing them were not really understood until fairly recently. Philosopher Ian Hacking, in his book *The Emergence of Probability* (1975), argues that probability theory emerged only in the seventeenth century. Indeed, Hacking suggests that someone with only modest knowledge of probability mathematics could have won the whole of ancient Gaul in a week!

The fact that the understanding of probability developed so late in history is important because it indicates that people do not acquire such knowledge spontaneously, through everyday exposure to uncertain events that unfold in accordance with the rules of probability. Therefore we should not be surprised to find out that people still have many difficulties with probabilistic reasoning today. You might wonder, how is it possible to live in an uncertain world without developing a full understanding of the rules that govern uncertainty? The most likely answer is that we do develop a rudimentary understanding of these rules that allows us to get by and to handle many reasoning tasks adequately, but our understanding is limited enough that we can also fall victim to errors, especially when thinking about social events. You may find this state of affairs all the more compelling if you consider how similar these limitations on our ability to reason about uncertainty are to the limitations that characterize our reasoning about the physical world we live in. Our understanding of the rules that govern the physical world is good enough that we typically do not bump into walls when walking or into other cars when driving. Even young children can predict the trajectory of a thrown baseball well enough to enable them to run and catch it. Yet, even adults can make systematic errors in reasoning about the physical world. For example, pilots flying bombers during World War 1 often overshot their targets because they released their bombs directly over the target rather than releasing them, as they should have, before their airplanes reached the target. Their understanding of the physical world was not sophisticated enough for them to realize that a bomb dropped from a moving airplane will not fall down in a straight line. Many college students today show similar misconceptions about everyday physics (e.g., Kaiser, Proffitt, and McClosky 1986). It is not surprising that we also have misconceptions about everyday statistics.

Gradually statistical knowledge did evolve, and by the midtwentieth century probability theory was well established and widely applied to reasoning about uncertain events ranging from determining the likelihoods of possible outcomes of games of chance to calculating fair annuities from mortality curves. Despite the lack of relevant psychological research, it was generally assumed that people follow the dictates of probability theory in their everyday judgments. Indeed, much of modern economic theory is still predicated on the view of people as rationally using probabilities to calculate their likely economic gains and losses.

The psychological investigation of people's probabilistic reasoning began in earnest in the 1950s. Research by Nobel laureate Herbert Simon suggested that people do not always seek the best possible solutions to inferential problems in a perfectly rational manner. Simon characterized people as operating within *bounded rationality* in that rather than optimizing they *satisfice*, that is, seek solutions that are good enough for their purposes though less than perfect (Simon 1957). At about the same time, Paul Meehl compared the judgments reached by clinicians attempting to combine several source of information to those obtained through simple statistical combinations of the same information and found the clinicians lacking by comparison (Meehl 1954). And Ward Edwards and his colleagues showed that an important rule of probability, *Bayes's theorem*, could be used to evaluate the way people revise their beliefs when confronted with new evidence. From their research Edwards and his colleagues concluded that people are overly conservative Bayesians—they do revise their beliefs in the face of new evidence as they should, but their revisions are not nearly strong enough (e.g., Phillips and Edwards 1966).

These developments set the stage for the groundbreaking work launched in the 1970s by Daniel Kahneman and Amos Tversky (Kahneman and Tversky 1973). These authors suggested that, rather than using statistical rules imperfectly, people often rely on very different kinds of inferential *heuristics*, that is, rules of thumb for judgment. Although these heuristics often lead to effective reasoning, they also lead to systematic biases and errors. Following Kahneman and Tversky's seminal work, a great deal of research has focused on identifying people's inferential shortcomings and on exploring the circumstances under which people use inappropriate nonstatistical heuristics. In an important book Richard Nisbett and Lee Ross spelled out the implications of this research tradition to social judgment (Nisbett and Ross 1980). More recently there has been increasing recognition that in addition to the nonstatistical heuristics identified by Kahneman and Tversky, people also possess at least rudimentary understanding of statistical rules. This has led to attempts to discover what determines which heuristics—statistical or nonstatistical—will be used on each occasion (e.g., Gigerenzer 1991; Ginossar and Trope 1987; Nisbett et al. 1983). In the following sections I describe the major nonstatistical heuristics introduced by Kahneman and Tversky, and discuss the implications of each for how we understand our social world. I also describe more appropriate statistical heuristics that people sometimes use, and discuss factors that determine whether people use these heuristics or the less appropriate nonstatistical ones.

The Representativeness Heuristic

Is Susan likely to be a Democrat or a Republican? Does Jerry's recent string of rejections by women reflect a run of bad luck or a personality disorder? Many of the probabilistic questions we encounter are of such form: We are often called upon to judge the likelihood that an instance belongs to a category, or that an event originated from an underlying process. Kahneman and Tversky suggested that when answering such questions, we often rely on the *representativeness heuristic*: Our categorizations are based on the extent to which an instance represents the category, that is, is similar to it. If Susan seems very similar to our stereotype of Democrats, we will assume she is a Democrat. In the same vein, our causal judgments are based on the extent to which an event is representative of the process that generated it. If an uninterrupted run of rejections matches our expectations about the effects of an ongoing personality disorder, we will assume that Jerry suffers from one (Kahneman and Tversky 1972; Tversky and Kahneman 1974).

The representativeness heuristic most likely serves us well in many of our judgments because the similarity between an instance and a category is often a good indicator of category membership (see chapter 2). This is true when the features of the instance are highly diagnostic of the category, as is often the case for objects such as animals or fruits: Anything that looks like a duck, walks like a duck, and quacks like a duck is most likely a duck. But for many other categories, especially social ones, features are far less diagnostic of category membership. Someone who is White, wealthy, and tough on crime may resemble our stereotype of Republicans, yet we know that many Democrats also have these attributes. In such cases, when we base our probability judgments only on representativeness we may make serious errors because probability judgments should also be influenced by several other factors that do not affect similarity judgments. Kahneman and Tversky showed that we often ignore these other factors, as discussed next.

Ignoring Prior Probabilities of Outcomes (Base-Rates)

Consider the following question:

William is a short, shy man. He has a passion for poetry, and loves strolling through art museums. As a child, he was often bullied by his classmates. Do you suppose that William is (a) a farmer, (b) a classics scholar?

Upon reading this description, one is tempted to guess that William is a classics scholar. After all, he seems so much more similar to our image of classics scholars than to our image of farmers. Before jumping to that conclusion, however, consider a crucial piece of information: the *base-rates*, or the frequencies of these professions in the population. In our society there are many more farmers than classics scholars. Indeed, even if only a small proportion of North American farmers matches William's description, the number of such farmers may well exceed the total number of classics scholars in North America. Surely we should take these prior probabilities into account when estimating the likelihood that William belongs to each of these professions. It turns out, however, that we often ignore or underuse such prior probabilities or base-rates, relying instead on the representativeness heuristic.

To demonstrate that people rely on representativeness rather than on prior probabilities, Kahneman and Tversky (1973) conducted an experiment in which they intentionally manipulated people's beliefs about base-rates and then examined the impact of this manipulation on their judgments. Participants were informed that a panel of psychologists had interviewed and tested a group of 100 successful professionals—engineers and lawyers—and had written a thumbnail description of each. To manipulate the base-rates, different participants were given different information about the composition of the group: Half were informed that it consisted of 70 engineers and 30 lawyers, and the remaining half were informed that it consisted of 30 engineers and 70 lawyers. All participants then read a series of descriptions said to have been drawn at random from the 100 available ones. For each, participants were asked to indicate the probability that the person was an engineer. The descriptions varied in the extent to which they were representative of lawyers and engineers. One of the descriptions, created to resemble engineers, read as follows:

Jack is a 45-year-old man. He is married and has 4 children. He is generally conservative, careful, and ambitious. He shows no interest in political and social issues and spends most of his free time on his many hobbies which include home carpentry, sailing, and mathematical puzzles (p. 241).

How do we determine the probability that this person is an engineer? According to Bayes's theorem, two factors should influence such judgments: (1) The relative likelihoods of finding people who match this description among engineers and among lawyers. Believing that this kind of character is far more common among engineers than among lawyers is tantamount to assuming that this character description is more representative of engineers than of lawyers. Individuals who are highly representative of engineers should be judged as more likely to be engineers than individuals who are only moderately representative of engineers.[1] (2) The relative prior probabilities or base-rates of engineers and lawyers. People who believe that 70 percent of the population are engineers should judge the likelihood that every one of the individuals is an engineer higher than do people who believe that only 30 percent of the population are engineers.

However, in their responses, participants relied only on representativeness and ignored the base-rates—for each description, participants informed that 70 percent of the group were engineers and participants informed that only 30 percent of the group were engineers made essentially identical likelihood judgments. Likelihood judgments varied as a function of the extent to which the descriptions resembled lawyers and engineers but not as a function of the base-rates for lawyers and engineers. It was not that people were inherently unable to understand and use base-rates. When given no personality sketch, participants correctly judged the probability that an unknown individual was an engineer as identical to the base-rate they were given for engineers (i.e., .70 or 30 percent). But they ceased to use this information when given a

---

1. This is not meant as an endorsement of stereotypes. Lawyers and engineers may well be far more similar to each other in personality than common stereotypes suggest. However, if you subscribe to the stereotypes and view a character description as more representative of engineers than of lawyers, you should use this information if you wish your judgment to be logically coherent with your beliefs.

personality description, relying instead on the representativeness of the description.

These early findings triggered a great deal of research on whether and when people use base-rate information. It now appears that under some circumstances people do use base-rate information, though usually they do not weigh it as heavily as Bayes's theorem suggests they should (Kahneman and Tversky 1996).

People are more likely to use base-rates when these convey meaningful causal information. For example, the proportion of students who passed an exam has obvious meaning—if 75 percent of the students passed, the exam was easy, but if only 25 percent passed, the exam was difficult. People should readily recognize that any student is more likely to pass an easy exam than a difficult one. In other words, they should be able to use such meaningful base-rates in judgments about individuals. To examine this possibility, participants were given a brief blurb about a student, describing his abilities and study habits, and were asked to assess the probability that this student had passed an exam (Ajzen 1977). They were also given relevant base-rate information. For half the participants, this information was meaningful; they were told that the exam had been passed by 75 percent (or 25 percent) of the students who had taken it. These participants used the base-rates in their judgments—those given the 75 percent base-rate judged the student as considerably more likely to have passed the exam than did those given the 25 percent base-rate. The remaining participants were given the identical base-rate information but divorced of its implications for test difficulty; they were told that the professor who had selected the described students was especially interested in successful (or unsuccessful) students and had therefore selected a sample in which 75 percent (or 25 percent) of the students had passed. These arbitrary base-rate participants made much less use of the base-rates in their judgments than did those given meaningful base-rates. It appears, then, that meaningful base-rates are more likely to be used than seemingly arbitrary ones.

Other studies using problems similar to Kahneman and Tversky's original lawyer/engineer problem suggest that people are also more likely to use base-rates when chance factors are highlighted or when the base-rates are made more salient (e.g., Bar-Hillel and Fischhoff 1981; Gigerenzer, Hell, and Blank 1988; Ginossar and Trope 1987; Krosnick, Li, and Lehman 1990; Schwarz et al. 1991). Implying, implicitly or explicitly, that statistical reasoning is relevant seems to increase people's use of base-rate information. This point will be discussed in greater detail in the section on statistical heuristics.

These findings constitute important theoretical modifications of our understanding of people's use and failure to use base-rates. But they should not distract us from the bottom line. Though we do have some understanding of the importance of base-rates, and may be able to use them in our judgments under certain circumstances, our understanding is shaky enough that we are easily lured by the attractiveness of the representativeness heuristic and often ignore or underuse base-rates to our peril.

We may be all the more concerned about the peril when we consider some of the important decisions that are made by us and by others who have power over us, decisions in which base-rates should play a role but often do not. Many physicians fail to realize that when symptoms and medical tests are not perfect predictors of a disease, the prevalence of the disease should influence the estimates of the likelihood that a patient has it (Eddy 1982). Venture capitalists may fail to consider the (very high) failure rates of new businesses. Planners may fail to consider the typical completion times of similar projects. Newlyweds may fail to see the implications of divorce rates to the likelihood that their own marriage will survive. And aspiring basketball stars may fail to consider the odds of making it to the NBA. In all these cases, failure to use base-rates may lead people to vastly underestimate their risks, and to make mistaken judgments and decisions.

I am not saying that you should never undertake risky endeavors that carry low probabilities of success. There may often be good reasons to invest in high-risk enterprises, to shoot for scarce rewards, and to embark on ambitious but risky endeavors. What I am saying is that we often undertake such endeavors without full appreciation of risk and choose options that we would have avoided had we known just how dangerous they were. We often fail to see the danger because we fail to recognize the relevance of base-rates.

The insight that people often fail to use base-rates has been used to shed light on key social psychological topics such as attribution, stereotype use, and impression formation, as described next.

Consensus as Base-Rate   I have described how the understanding of people's probabilistic reasoning evolved from the insight that Bayes's theorem is relevant to many judgment tasks to the realization that people often fail to use it in their judgments. Within social psychology the understanding of how people make causal attributions about others' behaviors underwent a similar development, from the proposal of a normative model specifying which factors people should take into account when making attributions, to the realization that people do not always follow the dictates of this model.

Imagine that Eric became thoroughly depressed after talking with Diane. Should we see this as due to something about Eric (he is a depressive) or to something about Diane (she depresses people)? Harold Kelley's *covariation model of attribution* provided guidelines for how we should go about answering such questions (Kelley 1967). According to Kelley's model, we should take three factors into account: *Distinctiveness*, that is, does the effect occur only in the presence of one causal candidate? Does Eric get depressed only when he talks to Diane, or does he get depressed whenever he talks to anyone? *Consistency*, that is, does the effect occur repeatedly in the presence of this causal candidate? Does Eric get depressed whenever he talks to Diane, or was this a one-time occurrence? and *Consensus*, that is, does everyone respond in the same way to this causal candidate? Does everyone who talks to Diane get depressed, or is it only Eric?

Different combinations of these factors should lead us to make different causal attributions. If Eric gets depressed after talking to many different people (low distinctiveness), Eric always gets depressed when talking to Diane (high consistency), and most other people do not get depressed after talking to Diane (low consensus), we should conclude that Eric's depression on this occasion is due to something about him; he is probably someone who gets depressed readily. In contrast, if Eric gets depressed only when talking with Diane and not when talking with anyone else (high distinctiveness), Eric always gets depressed after talking with Diane (high consistency), and everyone else who talks to Diane gets depressed (high consensus) we should conclude that Eric's depression on this occasion is due to something about Diane; somehow she manages to depress people.

Originally it was assumed that people use all these types of information appropriately (see Nisbett and Ross 1980). However, studies that required participants to read vignettes in which the different types of information were systematically varied revealed that although people are quite sensitive to distinctiveness and consistency information, they are much less sensitive to consensus information. For example, when trying to understand why a man protected his house, people paid much less attention to consensus information (is it the case that almost every other man or hardly any other man protected his house?) than they paid to distinctiveness information (does this man protect almost every other house or almost no other house? McArthur 1972; 1976). Subsequent research led to the same conclusion—people underuse consensus information in their attributions (e.g., Major 1980).

Nisbett and Borgida (1975) recognized the parallel between the tendency to underuse consensus information in attribution and the tendency to underuse base-rate information in categorization. Consensus, after all, is a base-rate; it reflects the proportion of people performing a given behavior. Just like the proportion of lawyers in the population should influence estimates of the likelihood that Jack is a lawyer, the proportion of people who trip on Joan's feet should influence estimates of the likelihood that Ralph will (unless, of course, we have extremely strong reasons to predict that Ralph would or would not trip on Joan's feet. But we rarely have such clearly diagnostic information for social behavior). The likelihood that one will perform a behavior has clear implications for the attributions we can make about the causes of the behavior. If we expect Ralph to step on Joan's feet because we know that everyone else does, surely we shouldn't attribute this behavior to Ralph's unique personality or skill. Nisbett and Borgida reasoned that we fail to use consensus information in attribution because we fail to realize its implications for estimating the likelihood of an individual's behavior, a failure of statistical reasoning akin to the failure to use base-rates.

They set out to show that people indeed fail to realize that consensus information, that is, information about how most people behave in a given situation, should affect expectations about how any particular individual will behave in that situation (Nisbett and Borgida 1975). In one study, participants read about a classic social psychological experiment that examined how quickly students conversing over an intercom would move to help a fellow discussant who appeared to be having a seizure. This experiment was picked because of its surprising and counterintuitive results—most students failed to offer help quickly. Some of the participants in Nisbett and Borgida's study were told about these surprising results. These participants therefore had accurate if surprising consensus information at their disposal. Other participants were given no information about the results of the experiment. Both groups of participants were then given brief and not very informative descriptions of several students said to have participated in the original experiment and were asked to guess how each had behaved. The interesting finding was that participants given the surprising consensus information did not appear to use it. Their predictions were no different from those made by participants given no consensus information. Participants who knew that most students in the original study failed to help quickly tended to assume nevertheless that the ordinary, unremarkable individuals they had observed would offer quick help. In other words, they ignored the base-rate when making their predictions. Most likely, they relied on the representativeness heuristic instead. These ordinary individuals seemed more representative of decent, helpful people than of callous, unsympathetic ones and so were judged as likely to offer quick help.

It may seem surprising that people do not use base-rates to predict the likely behavior of individuals. Recall that people do use base-rates when these convey meaningful causal information. We do use information about the proportion of students who passed an exam to determine the likelihood that a particular individual passed it because this base-rate information conveys the difficulty of the exam (Ajzen 1977). But consensus information is meaningful too—it conveys the power of the situation. Situations in which everyone behaves in the same way clearly exert a very powerful impact on behavior. So why don't we recognize that other individuals will likely succumb to powerful situations, much like we recognize that other individuals will likely fail difficult exams? One of the central lessons of social psychological research is that we tend to underestimate the power of situations to influence behavior (Ross and Nisbett 1991). We do not realize that seemingly subtle situational differences can have dramatic impact on behavior, and we tend to assume that behaviors are driven predominantly by underlying personality dispositions (e.g., Jones and Davis 1965; Ross 1977; for details see chapter 9). In the absence of deep understanding of how situations may determine behavior, consensus information must seem more like an arbitrary base-rate than like the meaningful conveyer of causal information that it in fact is.

While acknowledging that consensus information may help predict strangers' behavior, many people do not accept the notion that they should take consensus information into account when predicting their own and their friends' reactions. You might be tempted to say "I don't care what other people did. I know myself well enough to be confident that I will behave differently. Other people's behavior is irrelevant to predicting my reactions (or those of my father or my roommate)." There is reason to believe, however, that such intuitions are often mistaken. Vallone et al. (1990) obtained students' predictions about how they and their roommate would behave over an extended period of time (an academic quarter or the entire year). The predictions concerned a diverse range of important behaviors in the domain of academics (e.g., would they drop any course, would they declare a major), social life (e.g., would they break up with their boyfriend or girlfriend, would they become close friends with their roommate), family relations (e.g., would they feel seriously homesick, would they return home for summer), and extracurricular activities (e.g., would they vote in the upcoming election, would they attend the "big game"). The authors were able to assess the accuracy of these predictions by comparing them to reports of actual behavior which they obtained from participants at the end of the specified period.

This design made it possible to examine whether the intimate and extensive knowledge that one has about oneself justifies predictions that defy population base-rates. The answer was a resounding no. Both for self-predictions and for predictions about one's roommate, accuracy dropped dramatically for predictions that went against the base-rates. In one study, when people's predictions went with the base-rates, that is, when people predicted that they themselves would do what most people did, they were accurate 78 percent of the time. In sharp contrast, when people's predictions went against the base-rate, that is, they predicted that they themselves would behave differently from what most other people ended up doing, they were accurate only 50 percent of the time. Results were even more dramatic when analysis focused only on items with strong base-rates, that is, items where at least 75 percent of the students behaved in the same manner. For these items, predictions that went with the base-rates were accurate 88 percent of the time, but predictions that went against the base-rates were accurate only 28 percent of the time. The authors point out that individuals would have been far more accurate if they simply predicted that they and their roommates would behave like most people in cases where base-rates were extreme, no matter what privileged knowledge they had about themselves or their roommates.

Participants in these studies cannot be faulted for not using the base-rates because they may well have been unaware of them. But a clear implication of these findings is that base-rates are undoubtedly relevant for predicting your own behavior. When you expect that you yourself will behave differently from most people, you should recognize that you run a substantial risk of being wrong.

Stereotypes as Base-Rates Commonly held stereotypes suggest that men are more assertive than women. Anne Locksley and her colleagues recognized that these and other stereotypes can be viewed as base-rates (Locksley et al. 1980; Locksley, Hepburn, and Ortiz 1982). Such stereotypes reflect the belief that men are more likely to be assertive than are women, or that the proportion of men who are assertive is greater than the proportion of women who are assertive. In other words, a stereotype, like a base-rate, defines the prior probability that any individual member of a group will have the attributes associated with that group's stereotype. It follows that stereotypes should "behave" like base-rates. Recall that people typically use base-rates to make judgments about an individual when they know nothing about this individual but ignore or underuse base-rates if they are given even a brief description of the individual, relying instead on the representativeness of that description. Locksley and her colleagues showed that people often use and ignore stereotypes in much the same way.

One study focused on the stereotype of men as more assertive than women. Participants read different kinds of information about several men and women, and were asked to indicate how assertive each of these individuals was. Some of the individuals were described only by a name. In this case participants used the stereotype: A person identified only as Paul was judged more assertive than a person identified only as Susan. Other individuals were identified by name as well as by a single behavior indicative of assertiveness. One such behavior was:

The other day Nancy was in a class in which she wanted to make several points about the readings being discussed. But another student was dominating the class discussion so thoroughly that she had to abruptly interrupt this student in order to break into the discussion and express her own views (Locksley et al. 1980, p. 827).

Half the participants read the above description as is. For the other half, the identical behavior was said to have been performed by a male student (e.g., Tom). Participants given male or female names along with this behavioral information no longer used the gender stereotype: Nancy who had abruptly interrupted another student was considered to be just as assertive as Tom who had done the same thing. It appears that when we are given such behavioral information, we rely entirely on the representativeness heuristic. Our judgments of the person's assertiveness are based only on the extent to which the person's behavior is indicative of assertiveness. We do not take into account the prior probability that the person is assertive, a probability that is dictated by the stereotypes that we subscribe to and use in the absence of any information about the person's behavior.

Although our failure to use stereotypes in this manner can be viewed as an inferential error, Locksley and her colleagues pointed to the bright side of this error: Many of the stereotypes people hold are inaccurate and demeaning. We may be happy to know that people are unlikely to apply such insidious stereotypes to individuals about whom they have some behavioral information. Our prejudices may be more likely to affect our judgments of strangers than they are to affect our judgments of more familiar individuals.

The initial work of Locksley and her colleagues led to an explosion of research on how stereotypes affect impressions of individuals. This research and its implications is discussed at length in chapter 8. For now, I will say only that Locksley's initial findings have been corroborated—people generally do not integrate behavioral information with the prior probabilities dictated by their stereotypes. But the optimistic implications have been toned down —stereotypes may nevertheless color judgments of individuals through other routes (e.g., stereotypes may color the meaning of the individual's behavior; for a review, see Kunda and Thagard 1996).

The Dilution Effect Although we do use stereotypes when evaluating individuals about whom we know nothing else, the effects of stereotypes can be reduced or eliminated when we are given some additional information about these individuals, even if we view this information as completely irrelevant to the judgment at hand. When given only an individual's first name, people judge Paul as more assertive than Susan (Locksley et al. 1980). But when people are also given information that has no bearing on assertiveness, for example, that the person's mother "earns $24,000 per year working for a bank in a city, and she commutes 30 minutes each way," this irrelevant information can undermine the effects of stereotypes on judgment. Paul whose mother works for a bank is viewed as no more assertive than Susan whose mother works for a bank (Hilton and Fein 1989). It appears that irrelevant or nondiagnostic information can dilute the impact of information that we consider diagnostic (in this case, gender).

Nisbett and his colleagues, who named this phenomenon *the dilution effect*, showed that nondiagnostic information can also dilute the impact of other kinds of diagnostic information (Nisbett, Zukier, and Lemley 1981). For example, people given information that they consider indicative of whether a social work client is likely to be a child abuser (e.g., "He is aroused by sadomasochistic sexual fantasies," "He has a drinking problem") viewed this person as quite likely to be a child abuser. But other people, who were given, in addition to this diagnostic information, some completely irrelevant information about the person (e.g., "He manages a hardware store," "He has an IQ of 110") viewed him as less likely to be a child-abuser. In other words, the nondiagnostic information diluted the impact of the diagnostic information on judgment.

Nisbett and his colleagues suggested that the dilution effect may be due to reliance on the representativeness heuristic. The nondiagnostic information about Paul or Susan reduces their similarity to the stereotypes of men and women because any feature of the person that is not part of the stereotype reduces the similarity between the two. In the same manner the nondiagnostic information about the social-work client reduces his similarity to the typical child abuser. It seems that we find it difficult to think of someone who has normal, ordinary attributes as depraved because our image of a depraved person is one of pure evil.

So far I have described how people often ignore or underuse base-rate information when making judgments such as guessing an individual's occupation, explaining an individual's behavior, or forming an impression of an individual. Instead, they base such judgments on the representativeness heuristic. I turn next to a discussion of other kinds of statistical information that people often ignore in favor of the representativeness heuristic.

Ignoring Sample Size

Consider the following problem (Tversky and Kahneman 1974, p. 1125):

A certain town is served by two hospitals. In the larger hospital, about 45 babies are born each day, and in the smaller hospital about 15 babies are born each day. As you know, about 50 percent of all babies are boys. However, the exact percentage varies from day to day. Sometimes it may be higher than 50 percent, sometimes lower.

For a period of 1 year, each hospital recorded the days on which more than 60 percent of the babies born were boys. Which hospital do you think recorded more such days?

a. *The larger hospital*
b. *The smaller hospital*
c. *About the same (that is, within 5 percent of each other)*

Most of Tversky and Kahneman's participants believed that the large and small hospitals would have about the same number of days in which more than 60 percent of babies born are boys. This, however, reflects a failure to appreciate the importance of sample size. In fact, small samples are far more likely to stray from the overall population mean than are large samples. Therefore the small hospital will stray from the overall population mean of 50 percent boys far more often than will the large hospital. People's mistaken belief that the frequency of days with 60 percent boys is the same for two hospitals is most likely based on the representativeness heuristic. The similarity of 60 percent to 50 percent is the same, regardless of hospital size. If you base your estimates only on this similarity or representativeness, you will judge the two hospitals to be equally likely to deviate from the population mean.

Subsequent research suggested that people are capable of appreciating the importance of sample size under some circumstances, much like they can sometimes use base-rates (Nisbett et al. 1983). However, as for base-rates, it is still the case that our understanding of the importance of sample size is shaky enough that we may easily be distracted from using it. An important implication for social judgment is that we may not realize that a brief interaction with someone is not nearly as informative about what this person is like as is a long-term acquaintance. Impressions gleaned from a brief interview with an individual are believed to be just as representative of underlying character as are impressions based on many encounters with the individual. We may therefore mistakenly give brief interviews the same weight that we give to information based on deeper acquaintance.

Imagine, for example, that a trusted colleague who has worked with John for several years recommends him to you as a competent and effective manager. You interview John for about an hour and are not impressed with his managerial skills. If you are tempted, as most of us are in such situations, to go with your own evaluation, perhaps you should pause to consider the sample sizes underlying your and your colleague's impressions. Yours is based on behavior over one hour, your colleague's on behavior over hundreds, perhaps thousands of hours. John's behavior during the brief interview, and the impression it gave rise to, is far more likely to be an atypical aberration than is his behavior over several years of acquaintance with your colleague. Unless you have reason to doubt your colleague's honesty or skill at evaluating managers, you should assume that your colleague's impression is more likely than yours to be accurate.

Misconceptions of Chance

When my two sons disagree about which TV program to watch, we typically settle the dispute by tossing a coin. At one point, after his third loss in a row, my older son complained that the coin liked his brother better. We may be amused by such logic in a seven-year-old. We may be less amused to learn that we too often behave as though randomizing devices such as coins and roulettes are endowed with humanlike cognitive abilities. People believe, for example, that when tossing a coin for heads (H) or tails (T) the sequence H–T–H–T–T–H is more likely than the sequence H–H–H–T–T–T (in fact the two sequences are equally likely). We make this error because the first sequence seems more random. In other words, it is more representative of the random process that is supposed to govern coin tosses (Tversky and Kahneman 1974). The mistake is to assume that this random process will manifest itself even in short runs of coin tosses.

You may observe this error in operation by spending some time by a roulette wheel at a casino. If you stay long enough, you are very likely to encounter a run of reds. Watch how more and more people place their bets on black as the run of reds grows longer. Why is the temptation to bet on black so strong after a run of reds? Most people mistakenly assume that black is now due. A run of reds followed by black seems more representative of the underlying random process than is a run of reds followed by yet another red. The roulette, however, does not have a memory any more than a coin has a tendency to like my youngest son. Black is no more likely after three reds than it is after any other three-trial sequence of reds and blacks; the probability of getting black on each trial remains 50 percent.

Our failure to understand the role of chance may lead us to consider individuals who have had a brief run of lucky breaks to be particularly skilled. Or we may consider those who have had a series of unfortunate accidents to be somehow responsible for their misfortune. In similar vein, we may consider a building where several employees were struck with cancer to be unsafe. What we don't understand is that in an uncertain world, occasional runs of successes, accidents, and illnesses are to be expected just from chance. This misunderstanding is beautifully illustrated in sports fans' belief in "the hot hand."

Belief in the Hot Hand   There is a widespread belief among basketball commentators and fans that players occasionally experience "the hot hand" and become, for a while, "streak shooters." The assumption is that after a couple of successful shots a player becomes confident and relaxed and, therefore, much more likely to succeed on the next attempted shot. Indeed, among 100 knowledgeable basketball fans queried by Thomas Gilovich, Robert Vallone, and Amos Tversky (1985), 91 percent believed that "a player has a better chance of making a shot after having just *made* his last two or three shots than he does after having just *missed* his last two or three shots," and 84 percent believed that "it is important to pass the ball to someone who has just made several (two, three, or four) shots in a row."

Gilovich and his colleagues suspected, however, that this belief in the hot hand arises from a misconception of chance. Consider a player whose shots are successful 50 percent of the time. Such a player can be expected to have occasional strings of four or more successful shots in a row just like a tossed coin can be expected to have occasional strings of four or more heads in a row. The crucial question is: Are such strings more frequent for a 50 percent player than they are for a tossed coin? Put more broadly, is any player really more likely to make a shot after having just made one, or two, or three than on other occasions? Are "shooting streaks" more common than what would be expected by chance alone? As you may have guessed by now, the answer to all these questions is no.

Gilovich and his colleagues were able to analyze the shooting records of the Philadelphia 76ers over an entire season. A series of analyses revealed that streaks were *not* more common than what would be expected by chance and that players were *not* more likely to make a shot after having just made one, two, or three shots than after having just missed one, two, or three shots. Whether or not a player will make any shot turned out to be independent of the player's performance on the previous few shots, just like whether or not a coin will land on heads on any toss is independent of where the coin landed on the previous few tosses. This is not to say that shooting success depends entirely on chance. It does not. A highly skilled shooter is more likely to make any shot than is a less skilled shooter. But the point is that for both players the likelihood of making the next shot is unaffected by how they performed on the last few shots (though it is affected by their overall ability).

Note that the mistaken belief in the hot hand can be costly. If players choose to pass the ball to a "hot" player (as they widely believe they should) rather than to another equally skilled but less heavily guarded player, their team's performance will suffer.

Some anecdotal evidence for the depth of our inability to appreciate the role of chance in producing random strings of events comes from the reactions of several prominent basketball coaches to these findings, as reported by Gilovich (1991, p. 17). Red Auerbach of the Boston Celtics declared: "Who is this guy? So he makes a study. I couldn't care less." Another well-known coach, Bobby Knight of the Indiana Hoosiers, was equally unimpressed: "... there are so many variables involved in shooting the basketball that a paper like this really doesn't mean anything." Not only did these coaches fail to recognize the operation of chance factors spontaneously, their unsubstantiated belief in the hot hand was strong enough to withstand evidence that challenged the existence of this phenomenon.

Failure to Understand Regression

When you take a test, your score is affected by your true overall knowledge of the topic as well as by some chance factors: perhaps you got lucky because an important question addressed the one topic that you happened to be particularly knowledgeable about, perhaps a headache prevented you from performing as well as you should have. If your score is extreme, one can make informed guesses about how your performance was influenced by chance, that is, about whether chance factors worked for you or against you. If you did extremely well, chances are that, in addition to being skilled, you also got lucky. And if you did extremely poorly, chances are that you had some bad luck. It is therefore probable that your true ability is less extreme than your extreme performance on this test, and your performance on similar tests is also likely to be less extreme. Put differently, whenever test scores are influenced at least in part by chance, people who perform extremely well on one occasion will, on average, probably perform somewhat less well on another occasion. And people who perform extremely poorly on one occasion will, on average, perform somewhat better on another occasion. People scoring at both extremes can be expected to *regress toward the mean*. This well-established statistical principle is highly counterintuitive.

Tversky and Kahneman (1974) describe how Israeli flight instructors came to believe that one should refrain from praising outstanding performance and should be sure to criticize poor performance, a belief that stands in stark contrast to established learning theory which assumes that praise is more effective than punishment. The flight instructors started off praising particularly smooth landings and criticizing particularly rough ones, and then noticed that outstanding performance declined after lavish praise, whereas terrible performance improved after harsh criticism. What the instructors failed to realize was that they were simply observing regression to the mean. Regardless of what the instructor says, outstanding performance can be expected to deteriorate on the next attempt, and terrible performance can be expected to improve.

Kahneman and Tversky (1973) also provided more formal demonstrations of our failure to appreciate regression to the mean. For example, even when people were told that a test of mental concentration was influenced by chance factors such as mood and fatigue and was only somewhat predictive of overall GPA, they still expected individuals with extreme scores on the mental concentration test to have equally extreme GPAs; their predictions were nonregressive. Kahneman and Tversky hypothesized that this was due to reliance on the representativeness heuristic, that is, the belief that the extremity of the outcome (GPA, in this case) should be representative of the extremity of the predictor (the mental concentration test).

One disturbing consequence of our failure to appreciate regression is that when we notice patterns that are due to regression to the mean, we will be tempted to invent causal theories to account for them, as were the flight instructors. We may form committees to determine how our corporation had failed outstanding job candidates who did not live up to their potential, we may generate psychological theories to explain why the children of brilliant people are not as brilliant as their parents or why the rookie of the year typically performs less well in the subsequent year (e.g., Fong, Krantz, and Nisbett 1986), and we may invest in instructional programs that seem to improve the performance of low achieving students. What we don't realize is that all these phenomena are to be expected simply from regression to the mean.

The Conjunction Fallacy

Consider the following problem (Tversky and Kahneman 1983, p. 297):

Linda is 31 years old, single, outspoken, and very bright. She majored in philosophy. As a student, she was deeply concerned with issues of discrimination and social justice, and also participated in anti-nuclear demonstrations. Which of the following alternatives is more probable?:

a. *Linda is a bank teller*
b. *Linda is a bank teller and active in the feminist movement*

If you chose the second alternative, you are not alone. Fully 85 percent of Tversky and Kahneman's participants made the same choice. It is, however, incorrect. Probability theory dictates that the probability of a conjunction, that is, a co-occurrence of two outcomes, cannot be greater than the probability of each outcome alone. Linda cannot be more likely to be both a bank teller and a feminist than she is to be only a bank teller. This may be easier to understand if you consider that all the feminist bank tellers who match this profile are, by necessity, included among all the bank tellers who match this profile. Tversky and Kahneman named people's failure to recognize this principle *the conjunction fallacy*.

Use of the representativeness heuristic may contribute to the conjunction fallacy. Linda is more similar to our image of a feminist bank teller than she is to our image of a bank teller. If we base our likelihood judgments only on this similarity, we will judge that she is more likely to be a feminist bank teller than a mere bank teller. We run into such problems because as the likely outcomes for Linda are enriched with details that are consistent with the kind of person that her description invokes, the probability of these conjoint outcomes decreases while their representativeness increases.

The conjunction fallacy may also affect our assessments of the plausibility of explanations. In one study students who were asked to determine why John chose to attend Dartmouth considered it quite unlikely that he did so because he liked the female/male ratio at Dartmouth. But when this unlikely reason was combined with a more likely one (he chose Dartmouth because he wanted to attend a prestigious college *and* because he liked the female/male ratio at Dartmouth), this combination of reasons was considered more probable than was the unlikely reason taken alone (Leddo, Abelson, and Gross 1984). This, of course, violates probability theory. Liking the female/male ratio may be an improbable reason for choosing a college. But liking that ratio *and* wanting prestige is even less probable. The combination of reasons is, however, more representative of our notion of what amounts to a good explanation of college choice, and that may be why we judge it as more probable.

In sum, I have outlined a wide range of judgment problems that people often solve by using the representativeness heuristic. When this strategy entails ignoring or underusing important statistical information such as base-rates or sample sizes and failing to appreciate important rules of probability theory such as those that govern conjunctions, it can lead to serious inferential errors.

Statistical Heuristics

Imagine your reactions to someone who says "I can't understand it; I have nine grandchildren and all of them are boys." You may find this statement perfectly reasonable, and agree that this is an oddity begging for an explanation. But now imagine that the person said, instead, "I can't understand it; I have three grandchildren and all of them are boys." You may find this statement rather odd, and proceed to explain to the misguided grandparent that chance alone could be responsible for this result; no further explanation seems called for. Nisbett and his colleagues suggested that in so doing, you are expressing valid statistical intuitions (Nisbett et al. 1983).

Tversky and Kahneman's early papers implied that fundamental statistical notions were simply "not part of people's repertoire of intuitions" (1974, p. 1125). This turned out to be a bit of an overstatement. Subsequent research suggests that people do possess a basic understanding of some statistical principles. Nisbett and his colleagues refer to these statistical rules of thumb as *statistical heuristics*. Unfortunately, people do not always use their statistical heuristics when they should. As a case in point, consider the contrast between the grandchildren thought experiment described above and Kahneman and Tversky's hospital problem described earlier. Although most of us recognize that the gender makeup in the smaller sample of grandchildren is far more likely to be atypical of the population than that of the larger sample, most of us fail to apply the very same rule to the hospital problem. In that case, we fail to realize that the smaller hospital is more likely to produce atypical samples than is the larger hospital. Thus, although our intuitions do include quite sophisticated statistical heuristics, we still lack well-developed intuitions about when to apply them.

The question then arises, what determines whether we will apply statistical or nonstatistical heuristics to problems we encounter? What is it that enables us to recognize the relevance of statistics to some probabilistic problems, but not to others? We do not yet have a complete answer to this question. However, some important factors that influence the choice of heuristics have been identified, as discussed next.

FACTORS THAT INFLUENCE THE CHOICE OF HEURISTICS
Which heuristic we choose to solve a particular problem will depend on our general understanding of the nature of events that the problem concerns and on our general knowledge of statistics. Be-

cause we typically possess many, often conflicting beliefs and have at our disposal a wide array of potentially relevant heuristics, contextual factors that make particular beliefs or rules accessible can influence our choice of heuristics.

A central aspect of our domain knowledge concerns our beliefs about what kinds of forces are likely to govern events in this domain. For example, when attempting to predict a student's performance on a standardized test, we may consider the extent to which this performance may depend on the student's academic ability, motivation, and anxiety, on the quality of the student's school and home instruction, and on unpredictable chance factors. Our beliefs about the likely impact of chance on this kind of event are of particular importance, because a crucial first step to statistical thinking in a domain is the recognition that chance plays a role in producing events in that domain. The recognition that events are influenced by chance depends on our general knowledge about the domain, on contextual cues that highlight the importance of chance factors or of alternative factors, and on our general knowledge of statistics (Nisbett et al. 1983). I next discuss each of these factors in turn.

Knowledge about the Domain

Chance factors play an important role in a wide variety of domains. Our performance on academic exams, our achievements at athletic competitions, and our interpersonal behavior on social occasions are all influenced by stable attributes such as underlying abilities and traits. But they are also influenced by chance factors such as whether or not we happen to have a headache, are about to go on vacation, or are in the midst of a nasty family dispute. Our ability to recognize the role of such chance factors depends on the nature of the domain itself as well as on our own expertise in the domain.

Clarity of the Sample Space in the Domain In some domains it is easy to break the flow of events into clear units, and easy to assign a score to each unit. In academics, an exam forms a natural unit, and the grades assigned to it are typically clear and unambiguous. The same is true for sports, where games may form natural units and game outcomes are clear-cut. In such objective domains it easy to keep track of repeated scores—grades on repeated exams, outcomes of repeated games. Such observation is an important first step for appreciating the role of chance in governing events and the relevance of statistics to reasoning about them. In contrast, in social interactions it is often not obvious how to unitize events or how to score them. What, for example, constitutes a unit of friendliness? Even if we form somewhat arbitrary units—a conversation, an hour—how do we score them for friendliness? Number of smiles per minute? Even such seemingly objective scores can be misleading—not all smiles are friendly. In such subjective domains that are relatively difficult to unitize and score the role of chance may be less transparent, and statistical reasoning less likely.

In support of this analysis, one study showed that people are more likely to give statistical answers to problems about objective domains such as sports and abilities than they are to problems about more subjective domains such as personal preferences and personality assessments (Jepson, Krantz, and Nisbett 1983). For example, the same participants were more likely to recognize that large samples were more reliable than smaller samples when the samples involved games of sport, an objective domain, than when they involved individuals' evaluations of courses, a subjective domain. Another study found similar results for people's use of base-rates: Participants did not use base-rates when given Kahneman and Tversky's original lawyer-engineer problem, but did use them when the same problem was reformulated as a card game in which each card provided a person's profession on one side and a personality sketch on the other side (Ginossar and Trope 1987). In card games the sampling space is clear and the role of chance obvious, and so statistical reasoning is more likely.

Experience with the Domain   As people become more familiar with a domain in which events are influenced by chance, they may gain greater appreciation of the role of chance in that domain, and so become more likely to apply statistical heuristics when thinking about it. Even in domains such as sports in which the role of chance is relatively easy to observe, people may gain full appreciation of the role of chance only after they have had many opportunities to observe its consequences. Experienced athletes may be more likely than novices to realize that an athlete's performance may vary from one occasion to another in an unpredictable manner.

If this intuition is correct, then experience with a domain should make people more likely to reason statistically about problems that relate to it. In one study designed to test this prediction, some participants were given a problem relating to sports: They were asked for the best explanation for a football coach's observation that the two or three boys who perform superbly at the try-out practice typically turn out to be only somewhat better than the rest. This outcome can be explained in terms of regression to the mean. Most of the participants who were experienced in sports favored an explanations that reflected this statistical principle ("The brilliant performances at try-out are not typical of those boys' general abilities. They probably just made some plays at the tryout that were much better than usual for them" (Nisbett et al. 1983, p. 354). In contrast, most participants who were inexperienced at sports favored nonstatistical causal explanations for the same outcome (e.g., the initially superb boys were trying to slack off so as not to make others jealous; or they were trying to coast through the season on their talent alone and were not putting in enough effort).

Other participants received an almost identically worded problem modified slightly so as to be about acting; they were asked why actors who performed superbly at an audition typically turn out to be less than superb. This time, it was experience in acting that made a difference: Most of the participants experienced in acting preferred the statistical explanation, whereas most inexperienced participants preferred the nonstatistical, causal explanations.

Although the finding that experience increases reliance on appropriate statistical heuristics is encouraging, it is also important to keep in mind that experience is unlikely to be very helpful in domains that do not lend themselves quite as readily to statistical reasoning. We are all very experienced at social interactions, yet the role of chance in these situations remains elusive, most probably because social events are so difficult to unitize and score.

Even in domains that are highly familiar to us, our familiarity may be restricted to samples of particular sizes. For example, we may be highly familiar with the distribution of genders in families of two, three, and four children, and so we may recognize that families of two are more likely to have all boys or all girls than are larger families, through chance alone. Nevertheless, this recognition of the role of chance and of the importance of sample size may not extend to much larger samples with which we have less direct experience. Recall that most people do not realize that a hospital with 15 births a day is likely to have more days in which the percentage of boys born deviates from the population mean of 50 percent than is a larger hospital with 45 births a day (Tversky and Kahneman 1974). Yet people showed much better understanding of this statistical principle when this hospital problem was slightly modified so that the small hospital had only 2 births a day (rather than 15), and participants were asked which hospital would have more days in which 100 percent of the babies born were boys (rather than 60 percent as in the original problem). A study in which participants were given either this modified version or the original one found that the percentage of participants who used the appropriate statistical heuristic and recognized that the small hospital was more likely than the large one to have deviant samples jumped from 31 percent for the original problem to 76 percent for the modified one (Pelham and Neter 1995). I believe the modified problem is so much easier and more transparent because people are much more familiar with the frequency with which samples of two children can be made up of all boys than they are familiar with the frequency with which samples of 15 children can have 60 percent boys. We may be more likely to recognize the role of chance in determining the makeup of samples of a given size if we have had many experiences with samples of that size.

Contextual Cues

Our choice of heuristics can also be influenced by aspects of the problem or the situation that highlight the salience of chance and, thereby, make us more likely to use statistical heuristics. Our reasoning can also be swayed by our assumptions about which rules others consider appropriate; we may be especially likely to use those heuristics that we assume others think we should use.

Salience of Chance Factors   Any information that reminds us of the operation of luck or chance can increase our use of statistical heuristics. In one study, participants were more likely to recognize that a large sample of one's peers' reactions to a college (based on many months at the college) may be superior to a very small sample of one's own reactions (based on a single day's visit) when they were also told that the small sample was selected randomly. This information likely served as a reminder that the small sample could be greatly influenced by chance (Nisbett et al. 1983)

Highlighting the role of random selection has also been shown to increase the use of base-rate information. Recall that in Kahneman and Tversky's (1973) lawyer/engineer problem, participants given diagnostic descriptions of individuals said to have been drawn randomly from a pool of 70 lawyers and 30 engineers (or 30 lawyers and 70 engineers) largely ignored the base-rates. A subsequent study attempted to highlight the salience of the fact that the descriptions had been selected randomly (Gigerenzer et al. 1988). This was accomplished by asking the participants themselves to draw the descriptions one at a time from an urn. Participants who underwent this procedure, which highlighted the relevance of chance factors, showed greater reliance on base-rates than did participants who had merely been informed that the descriptions had been selected randomly (though participants in the high salience condition still underutilized the base-rates). It appears that increasing the salience of chance factors can increase the perceived relevance of statistical heuristics.

Assumptions about Communicative Intent   In normal conversation we take certain rules of communication for granted, and we use these to make sense of what people tell us (Grice 1975). We assume, for example, that any information a speaker conveys is meant to be relevant and informative, and we therefore interpret it as such (for a review, see Schwarz 1994). However, in the context of psychology experiments, these rules are often violated. In research on judgment, experimenters often provide participants with information that they themselves consider redundant or worthless because they wish to see how participants view and use this information. If participants mistakenly assume that normal rules of conversation apply in the experimental context, they will infer that the experimenters consider any information they provide to be relevant and useful; "If the experimenters gave me a detailed description of someone's personality," a participant might reason, "surely they wanted me to use it in my judgments about that person." Some have suggested that the kinds of information and heuristics that participants use when solving problems designed to assess their use of base-rate information can be influenced by the assumptions they make about the experimenters' communicative intent (Krosnick, Li, and Lehman 1990; Schwarz 1994).

Krosnick and his colleagues (1990) noted that in most studies that had shown that people underuse base-rate information, participants were given the base-rates first and the descriptions of the target individuals last. If participants assume that the experimenter is trying to be relevant and informative, they may conclude that the experimenters provided the individuating descriptions on top of the base-rate information (which had clear implications for judgment in and of itself) because they considered these descriptions especially relevant and important. Moreover, if they assume, as people often do, that speakers present the information they consider most important last, participants may pay special attention to the information that comes at the end.

In a series of studies testing this hypothesis, participants were given variations of Kahneman and Tversky's lawyer/engineer problem in which the base-rate information was presented either first or last (Krosnick et al. 1990). Consistent with the view that people would consider the information provided last most important, participants were more likely to use the base-rate information when it was provided last rather than first. This was not simply because information provided at the end became more salient and memorable. Rather, this was due to assumptions participants made about the importance that the experimenters' attached to information provided last. When these assumptions about the experimenters' communicative intent were undercut by telling participants that the order of presentation had been determined randomly, information presented last no longer had any advantage.

These studies suggest that if people assume that others consider an individual's description especially important to determining that individual's occupation, they may be especially likely to use the representativeness heuristic which involves reliance on such information. On the other hand, if people assume that others consider base-rates especially important, they may be especially likely to use statistical heuristics that take base-rates into account. Our assumptions about the intentions of the person who posed a problem can highlight the salience and perceived relevance of particular houristics and thereby increase their use.

This line of work further highlights just how shaky our understanding of the importance of base-rate information is. We are capable of understanding the relevance of this information and of using it appropriately in our judgments. Yet we will fall back on less appropriate nonstatistical heuristics simply because we think others might consider these relevant. If our understanding of the relevance of base-rate information were robust, we would likely stick to our guns no matter what we thought others expected of us, preferring to appear intelligent rather than agreeable.

Predicting Single Events versus Long-Run Frequencies   In much of the research in the heuristics and biases tradition, participants were asked to predict the *probability of single events*—What is the probability that Linda is a bank teller and active in feminist movement? What is the probability that your answer to the problem you have just solved is correct? In a series of articles Gerd Gigerenzer and his colleagues have argued that people would be more likely to apply statistical heuristics to these problems if the problems were framed, instead, in terms of *long-run frequencies*—Of the 100 persons who fit Linda's description, how many are bank tellers and active in feminist movement? Of the 100 problems you have solved, how many did you get correct? (Gigerenzer 1991, 1996; Gigerenzer, Hoffrage, and Kleinbolting 1991).

Indeed, people are sometimes more likely to apply statistical heuristics to problems that ask about such frequencies than to formally identical problems that ask about the probability of a single event. Rephrasing problems in terms of frequencies has been shown to increase reliance on base-rate information, to decrease the conjunction fallacy, and to decrease people's tendency to be overconfident about their judgment (for a review, see Gigerenzer 1991). From the current perspective, framing a problem in terms of frequencies can increase use of statistical heuristics because such framing highlights the salience of chance factors and clarifies the sampling space by highlighting the fact that one is thinking about a sample rather than about an individual.

Gigerenzer (1991) makes the stronger argument that laypeople understand statistics to be only about the assessment of frequencies. They construe statistical rules as relevant only to frequentist problems; they don't apply these rules to assess the probabilities of single events because they view them as irrelevant to such judgments. Moreover, he argues, contrary to the conclusions of research in the heuristics and biases tradition, people do have a solid understanding of statistical principles, and apply these principles correctly to any relevant problem; cognitive illusions and biases disappear when people are asked problems that meet the assumptions of their frequentist statistical approach.

However, this view is inconsistent with the finding that people sometimes do apply statistical rules to assess the probabilities of single events, when other factors highlight the relevance of these rules. For example, as described above, people do rely on base-rate information to assess the probability that a single individual is an engineer when the role of chance has been made salient or when they assume the experimenter considers this information important (Gigerenzer et al. 1988; Ginossar and Trope 1987; Krosnick et al. 1990). Moreover it is not the case that people will always apply statistical heuristics to problems that are framed in terms of frequencies; they often fail to do so (Kahneman and Tversky 1996). It appears that framing a problem in terms of frequencies is but one of several ways of highlighting the salience and perceived relevance of statistical heuristics. People may apply statistical heuristics to problems that are not framed in terms of frequencies if other factors make these heuristic salient, and may fail to apply statistical heuristics when assessing frequencies if other factors make alternative heuristics more salient.

Gigerenzer (1991) takes the extra step of making the normative claim that probability theory applies only to judgments about the frequency of events over the long run, not to judgments about the probability of a particular event; along with statisticians who subscribe to the frequentist approach to probability, Gigerenzer holds that questions about the probabilities of single events are meaningless and cannot be addressed by probability theory. In other words, statistical information and rules cannot be applied to questions such as, What is the probability that Tom is a lawyer? What is the probability that this medication will relieve your symptoms? or What is the probability that it will rain tomorrow? Moreover, because such questions are inherently meaningless, they have no right or wrong answers.

I disagree with this view. As Kahneman and Tversky (1996) point out, a person claiming that the probability that it will rain tomorrow is 99 percent and the probability that it will *not* rain tomorrow is also 99 percent is clearly mistaken. By the same token, if your surgeon assures you that you have a 99 percent probability of surviving an operation, and you then find out that when making such assurances, this surgeon is correct only 75 percent of the time, you have every right to be angry and upset. Similarly, a physician who fails to take the population base-rates of disease into account when diagnosing individual patients will make more mistaken diagnoses that a physician who does apply base-rates to assess the probabilities of such single cases.

In conclusion, although people do possess statistical heuristics, they fail to apply them to a wide range of relevant problems. This can result in serious errors and biases. The question then arises, Can anything be done to increase people's use of statistical heuristics in everyday judgment? There is reason to believe that training in statistics may serve this purpose, as discussed next.

Statistical Education

Statistical education can sharpen people's understanding of statistical heuristics and increase their ability to apply these to some everyday situations. In one study students enrolled in a statistics course were contacted over the phone for a sports survey either early in the term, before they had learned any statistics, or later in the term (Fong, Krantz, and Nisbett 1986). One of the questions on the survey asked why the Rookie of the Year in baseball typically does not do as well the second year, the so-called sophomore slump. Students contacted toward the end of the statistics course were considerably more likely to give a statistical answer to this question. The statistics course helped them recognize that this phenomenon could be explained through regression to the mean. Other studies have shown that brief instruction in statistics, lengthy scientific training, and education in disciplines that highlight statistics (e.g., psychology) can all enhance the use of statistical heuristics in everyday problems (Fong, Krantz, and Nisbett 1986; Lehman and Nisbett 1990).

Training in statistics can improve your reasoning about problems that involve uncertainty. However, it cannot protect you against the biases and fallacies discussed in this chapter. Indeed, even experienced scientists often fail to use appropriate statistical heuristics (e.g., Kunda and Nisbett 1986; Tversky and Kahneman 1971). As Amos Tversky put it: "Whenever you find an error that statistically naive people make, you can find a more sophisticated version of the same problem that will trip the experts. If I say to my grad students, 'Do tall fathers always have tall sons?' they think of the textbook page on regression. But if I say something like 'Isn't it interesting that, in French history, the best monarchs usually had average prime ministers, and vice versa?' they say, 'Yes, that's fascinating! I wonder why.'" (McKean 1985, p. 31).

Problems that involve predicting other people's or our own behavior, attitudes, and preferences are particularly unlikely to trigger statistical reasoning. It is difficult to appreciate the role of chance in these domains, and they typically offer few cues that could remind us of chance. Moreover, whereas our culture often encourages us to reason statistically about domains such as sports and weather, and provides us with ample examples and reminders of the relevance of statistics (batting averages, probabilities of rain), our culture provides few such reminders of the relevance of chance and statistics to social behavior. As a result our reasoning about social behavior may be particularly vulnerable to error.

So far I have focused on the representativeness heuristic and on the statistical heuristics it often leads us to neglect. I turn next to a discussion of the second major nonstatistical heuristic introduced by Kahneman and Tversky, the availability heuristic.

The Availability Heuristic

How common is it for middle-aged men to suffer heart attacks? For college students to hold a job? For you to behave shyly? Tversky and Kahneman (1974) suggested that, when answering such questions, we often rely on *the availability heuristic*: We attempt to bring to mind examples of the events whose frequency we wish to determine, and we base our frequency judgments on the ease of imagining such examples, that is, on their availability. If we can readily bring to mind examples of middle-aged men who had heart attacks, of employed college students, or of our own shy behaviors, we will judge these occurrences to be quite common.

By and large, the availability heuristic can serve us well because it is usually easier to recall examples of common outcomes than examples of uncommon ones. As a case in point, we can more readily bring to mind examples of male politicians than of female politicians because males are more common in politics. But the availability heuristic will get us into trouble when the ease of imagining examples is influenced by factors that are not related to their frequency.

Such trouble was apparent in a simple study in which people were asked whether the letter R is more likely to appear as the first or as the third letter in words (Tversky and Kahneman 1973). In reality, words with R as a third letter are far more common than words that begin with R. But most people believed the opposite— they mistakenly assumed that words beginning with R were more common than words that have R as the third letter. Tversky and Kahneman suggested that this occurred because it is far easier to generate words that begin with R than words with R in the third place, and people rely on this ease of generation or availability of each kind of word when assessing its frequency. Unfortunately, in this case, ease of word generation is unrelated to actual word frequency, so the availability heuristic leads us to an incorrect answer.

Ignoring Biases in Available Samples

The availability of instances in our mind will fail to reflect the actual frequency of instances when, for whatever reason, the sample of instances that we come across is biased. In such cases, if we rely on availability to assess frequency without taking the bias into account, our frequency judgments will be off the mark. Your own interests and circumstances may bias your samples. One aging friend describes how, when his first child was born, he noticed people with babies everywhere, and now that he has developed arthritis, he notices people with canes everywhere. This friend could readily generate instances of people with babies or with canes, and so would likely overestimate their frequency. In contrast, someone lacking these particular interests may never notice babies or canes, and so might underestimate their frequency. In a similar vein, reporters and staff members who travel along with the campaign of a candidate for political office, and who observe the candidate being welcomed by cheering fans in one town after another, often overestimate the popularity of that candidate. This could be due to the availability heuristic—these reporters can readily conjure up images of enthusiastic supporters but have much fewer available examples of disgruntled opponents. They may fail to realize that their samples are biased—people who dislike the candidate stay home. In much the same way the availability heuristic could lead you to overestimate the success of a concert you have performed, a talk you have given, or a party you have thrown if these have been greeted with nothing but compliments. The greater availability of positive reactions may be misleading in such cases because people who disliked your efforts are probably holding their tongues.

Media coverage may also bias the availability of events, when the frequency with which events are reported does not correspond to their actual frequency. This tends to be the case for media coverage of different causes of death. In particular, the media are far more likely to cover violent, dramatic events such as homicides or tornadoes than less sensational causes as death such as disease. People's estimates of frequency follow suit. In one study, people evaluated death by homicide as more common than death from stomach cancer, when in fact death from stomach cancer was 17 times more common. It's just that one is not very likely to read about it in the evening newspaper (Slovic, Fischhoff, and Lichtenstein 1982). One disturbing implication is that public concern about dangers that seem probable because of their availability could lead to heavy investment in attempts to prevent these dangers. This could come at the expense of investment in dangers that are less psychologically available but more probable.

The media can also bias your perception of social groups. If, for example, the only African American people profiled in the media are criminals, individuals who have no other contact with African Americans may vastly overestimate the frequency of criminality in this group. Recognizing this, many American newspapers are consciously attempting to ensure that African Americans are portrayed not only in stories about crime and welfare but also in other stories involving more mainstream issues such as health, consumer behavior, or politics.

Social psychologists have shown that when the samples of data available to people are systematically biased, reliance on the availability heuristic can lead to predictable biases in attributions and judgments about social events, as discussed next.

Salience Before instances can come to mind, we must notice them. The salience or prominence of information can determine whether we notice it and how much attention we devote to it. If we pay more attention to highly salient information, it will become more available to us and so exert greater influence on our judgment (Taylor and Fiske 1975, 1978).

These ideas gain support from an ingenious series of experiments by Shelley Taylor and Susan Fiske (1975). In one study, observers watched a conversation between two people. Two observers were seated behind one of the discussants, an arrangement that guaranteed that these observers would focus their attention on the other discussant. Two other observers were seated in the opposite location, forcing them to focus on the opposite discussant. The remaining two observers were seated so that they could see both discussants equally well. All observers watched the identical conversation at the same time. Yet, when they were asked how much each discussant had influenced the conversation, their answers were affected by the salience of each discussant to them. They rated the more visually salient discussant as more influential. It appears that accidents of location that make a particular individual highly salient to you can lead you to see that individual as especially influential.

A particular individual may also grab your attention for other reasons. You may inadvertently pay more attention to the lone woman in the room or to the lone African American, and so view these individuals as playing a particularly important role in their social interactions (Taylor and Fiske 1978).

The availability heuristic can explain these effects of salience: Focusing our attention on a given individual will lead us to notice and recall more of this individual's contributions. When trying to assess how influential each of several individuals was in an interaction, this salient individual's contributions will be more available to us, and so we will view this individual as more influential.

People tend to attribute others' behavior to their personalities (she made a donation to charity because she is generous), but attribute their own behavior to the situation (I made a donation because of social pressure at work; Jones and Nisbett 1972). One reason for this difference among actors and observers may be that different information becomes salient when explaining one's own and another's behavior. When I observe your behavior, I focus on you. But when I myself am behaving, I cannot see myself; I focus instead on the situation. Because of these different focuses of attention, different information is available when I make causal judgments about your behavior and mine; for judgments about you, information about you is available, and so I attribute the behavior to you. But for judgments about me, information about the situation is available, and so I attribute my behavior to the situation (Nisbett and Ross 1980).

Egocentric Biases Choose a married couple you know, approach the husband and wife separately, and ask each what percentage of the housework he or she does at home. You may be surprised to discover that their estimates add up to more than 100 percent!

Michael Ross and Fiore Sicoly termed this tendency to assume that one has contributed more than one's fair share to joint endeavors an *egocentric bias*. Ross and Sicoly (1979) found egocentric biases in spouses' assessments of their contributions to housework, in students' assessments of their contributions to classroom discussions, and in basketball players' assessments of their team's contribution to important turning points in games. They suggested that the availability heuristic may play a role in producing the egocentric bias: We may overestimate our contributions to joint endeavors because our own contributions are more available to us. I am acutely aware of every time I take out the garbage, every time I wash the dishes. But I may be unaware of many of my husband's contributions, which often take place when I am not around. Ross and Sicoly found some evidence for this: People did generate more examples of their own than their partner's contributions, and the more they did this, the greater the egocentric bias they showed. And, in another study, asking people to focus on the contributions of their partner led them to assign greater responsibility to the partner. This last finding suggests that we may underestimate our partner's contributions not only because we are completely unaware of them; we may know about our partner's contributions but still not bring them to mind spontaneously. The next section describes more examples of the impact of such temporary accessibility (or inaccessibility) of examples on judgment.

Ignoring Biases in Accessible Cognitions

Even if the total pool of examples that we have at our disposal is unbiased, the availability heuristic could still lead us to bias if we temporarily bring to mind only a biased subset of the total pool. Several factors can lead us to do so, as discussed next.

One-Sided Questions   Most of us are shy on some occasions, outgoing on others. If asked, I could readily generate examples of my shyness (I am sometimes uncomfortable in social situations, I can be quiet at large dinner parties). I can just as readily generate examples of my extraversion (I have many friends, I sometimes introduce myself to strangers). If I am asked to describe only one of these aspects of my personality, behaviors related to that aspect will become more available, and this will affect my self-view. If I focus exclusively on my shyness, I will see myself as more shy; if I focus exclusively on my extraversion, I will see myself as more extraverted.

Russell Fazio and his colleagues demonstrated such an effect (Fazio, Effrein, and Falender 1981). In the first stage of their experiment, some participants were asked a series of one-sided questions designed to focus them on their extraversion (e.g., "What would you do if you wanted to liven things up at a party?"). Other participants were asked questions designed to focus them on their introversion (e.g., "What things do you dislike about loud parties?"). Following these interviews, participants led to focus on their extraversion rated themselves as more extraverted and behaved in a more extraverted manner than did participants led to focus on their introversion. It is clear that increasing the availability of a biased set of one's self-knowledge through one-sided questions can affect one's self-conceptions.

Ease or Difficulty of Recruiting Examples In one episode of the TV drama *Cracker*, a woman hoping to save her marriage seeks help from a therapist. He begins by asking her to think of all the things that she likes about her husband. Anyone familiar with the consequences of asking people one-sided questions will likely view this as a sound technique: Focusing the woman's attention on the positive aspects of her husband should make her regard him more positively, a crucial first step for rapprochement. Unfortunately, in this case the technique backfires. Realizing how difficult it is for her to conjure up anything positive about her husband, the woman storms out of the therapist's office and promptly files for divorce.

Do we base our judgments on such subjective experiences of ease or difficulty of recruiting examples? The availability heuristic was initially described precisely in this manner, as basing judgments on the ease of generating examples. But for a long time the evidence for the role of such subjective experience remained inconclusive. In studies demonstrating reliance on the availability heuristic, it is typically difficult to tell whether judgment is indeed affected by the subjective experience of ease or difficulty of recall, or whether judgment is affected, instead, by the contents of what has been recalled. Do we judge words beginning with R as more common than words with R as the third letter because it is easier for us to generate words that begin with R, or because, having attempted to generate both kinds of words, our list of generated words includes more words that begin with R?

Norbert Schwarz and his colleagues devised an ingenious way of teasing these two kinds of explanations apart (Schwarz et al. 1991). Imagine that you were asked to come up with a dozen examples of your past assertive behaviors. You will probably be able to recruit the first seven or eight examples with little effort. But beyond that point it gets more and more difficult to dredge up each additional example. Because you find it so difficult to bring to mind the requested examples of your assertiveness, you may conclude that you are not all that assertive. If this is the case, people asked for a dozen examples of their assertiveness should come to view themselves as less assertive than people asked for only half a dozen examples because it is so much more difficult to think of a dozen; this, despite the fact that those asked for twelve examples will have generated more examples than those asked for only six. If the people who had brought many examples to mind nevertheless viewed themselves as less assertive than the people who had brought only a few examples to mind, this would show that people base their judgments not only on the sheer number of recruited examples but also on the ease or difficulty of recruiting them.

Accordingly, in one experiment, Schwarz and his colleagues asked some participants to come up with twelve examples of situations in which they had behaved assertively, something they could do only with great difficulty. They asked other participants to come up with only six such examples, something they could do with ease. Two other groups of participants were asked to generate either twelve or six examples of situations in which they had behaved unassertively. Interestingly, even though participants asked for twelve examples of assertiveness had produced more such examples than did participants asked for only six, those asked for twelve rated themselves as *less* assertive than did those asked for only six (as shown in the left column of table 3.1). Participants generating unassertive behaviors showed a similar pattern—those asked for twelve examples of their lack of assertiveness rated themselves as *more* assertive than did those asked for only six such examples (as shown in the right column of table 3.1).

If you examine the top row of table 3.1, you will also see that results for participants asked for only six examples of their behavior followed the same pattern obtained in earlier studies using one-sided questions: Those led to focus on their assertive behaviors viewed themselves as more assertive than those led to focus on their unassertive behaviors. But this pattern was actually reversed for participants given the difficult task of generating twelve exam-

Table 3.1 Self-ratings of assertiveness by participants asked to recall six or twelve examples of their assertive or unassertive behavior

	TYPE OF BEHAVIOR	
NUMBER OF RECALLED EXAMPLES	ASSERTIVE	UNASSERTIVE
Six	6.3	5.2
Twelve	5.2	6.2

Source: From Schwarz et al. (1991, table 1, p. 197). Copyright © (1991) by the American Psychological Association. Reprinted with permission.
Note: Higher numbers indicate greater assertiveness.

ples of their behavior: Those asked for assertive behaviors rated themselves as *less* assertive than did those asked for unassertive behaviors (as shown in the bottom row of table 3.1). This suggests that people relied on the difficulty of generating the requested number of behaviors more than they relied on the recalled content.

In short, even if we are led to recall many examples of an outcome, we may judge that outcome to be relatively improbable if we experience the recall task as difficult.

Our attitudes may be affected in a similar manner by the ease or difficulty with which we can generate support for them. For example, people asked to come up with many arguments supporting a particular position (e.g., that public transportation is good) ended up viewing that position *less* favorably than people asked for only a few such arguments (Wanke, Bless, and Biller 1996). Apparently, when we have trouble generating arguments supporting a position, we lose faith in it.

One-sided questions and recall instructions focus our attention directly and explicitly on a biased subset of our knowledge, and so bias our judgments. Similar biases can be obtained in more subtle ways, as discussed next.

Explanation Take a moment to consider why it might be a good thing for firefighters to be risk-seekers. Most people can readily come up with a persuasive explanation—after all, firefighters must be willing to enter burning houses, and would be unable to perform their job effectively if they were reluctant to take on such risks. But suppose you were asked, instead, to consider why it might be a *bad* thing for firefighters to be risk-seekers. Most people can readily come up with a persuasive explanation for this as well—if firefighters take unnecessary risks, rushing into blazing buildings and out of high-up windows without taking appropriate precautions, they will endanger their own lives as well as the lives of the people they are meant to save. It turns out that not only can we readily generate explanations for such opposite theories, but, having generated support for these theories, we come to believe them.

In one set of studies demonstrating these consequences of explanation, people were asked to explain either why good firefighters tended to be less risky than poor ones, or why good firefighters tended to be more risky than poor ones (Anderson and Sechler 1986). Participants who had explained why being risky was good for firefighters came to believe that being risky was in fact better for firefighters than did participants who had explained the opposite causal relation. Moreover, these theory changes affected participants' evaluations of briefly sketched individuals described as applicants for positions as firefighters. Participants who had explained why being risky was good rated risk-seeking applicants more highly than they rated conservative ones, but participants who had explained why being risky was bad showed the opposite preference—they rated conservative applicants more highly than risk-seeking ones.

Similar findings have been obtained when people were asked to explain a variety of other causal relations. For example, people can readily explain why extraverts do better than introverts academically (e.g., extraverts rely on their social skills to get useful help from professors and friends). People can just as readily explain the opposite causal relation, namely that introverts do better than extraverts academically (e.g., introverts spend their time studying rather than partying). When people are asked to explain either of these causal relations, they come to view it as more plausible (Sanitioso, Kunda, and Fong 1990).

Why do people come to believe a causal relation they have explained when they also possess knowledge that supports the opposite causal relation? The most likely account is that the act of explanation makes the subset of one's knowledge that supports the explained relation highly available, and we rely on the availability of beliefs supporting a particular explanation when assessing its plausibility. What we don't realize is that the set of available beliefs is not a representative sample of our own knowledge on this topic because, in attempting to explain a one-sided causal relation, we have accessed a biased subset of our relevant knowledge.

I am often reminded of these findings when I come across socio-biological explanations of human behavior that account for current social behavior in terms of likely evolutionary pressures. Yes, it is easy to generate an account of how evolutionary forces would lead men to favor beautiful women, and women to favor smart men. But it is not that difficult to generate an account of how evolutionary pressures could have produced the opposite pattern, too.

Perseverance of Refuted Beliefs   Suppose that I told you yesterday that a test you have just taken revealed that you are unusually socially perceptive. Take a moment to let this information sink in. Now, let me tell you that I was just kidding, the test you had taken was phony, and I had made up the results. How socially perceptive do you now think you are?

Clearly, the information that you thought you were given about your perceptiveness has been thoroughly refuted; you have learned absolutely nothing about your perceptiveness, and so should regard yourself no differently than you had before. Research suggests, however, that my initial statement is likely to have a lingering impact on your self-views. Beliefs tend to persevere even when the initial evidence on which they were based has been discredited.

In one set of studies, participants were put in essentially the same situation you have just imagined for yourself (Ross, Lepper, and Hubbard 1975). First, they were given the task of distinguishing between real and fake suicide notes, and received false feedback about their performance: Some were told that they had done exceptionally well, some were told that they had done poorly, and some that their performance was average. Later, they were debriefed: They were told that the feedback they had been given was false, and that they had been randomly assigned to get positive, neutral, or negative feedback. Although the feedback had at this point been discredited, this feedback nevertheless continued to affect participants' self-views. Those who had received positive feedback still thought they had done better at the suicide-discrimination task and that they were generally better at this kind of sensitivity task than did those who had been told they were average. And those who had received negative feedback still thought they were relatively poorer at this and related sensitivity tasks.

The availability heuristic can account for the perseverance of refuted beliefs. The feedback that you are unusually sensitive may lead your to try to apply this information to what you know about yourself. You may recall how you had noticed that your neighbors' marriage was in trouble even before they had confided this to you, how you had guessed in advance that your friends were planning a surprise party for you, and how you have always known which gifts would most please your mother. All this information remains available even after the initial evidence that has led you to recruit it has been discredited, and so continues to affect your judgments of yourself. There is no direct evidence that the perseverance effect results from such increased availability of information. But, as discussed earlier, there is clear evidence that increasing the availability of self-related information can affect self-perceptions.

The recognition that refuted beliefs can nevertheless persevere provides insight into why slander can be so damaging. Once an accusation is voiced and a reputation tarnished, it may be extremely difficult to undo the harm to the accused person's reputation, even if the accusations are proved false.

Imagination Imagine that you are walking along a quiet street when suddenly a police car pulls up beside you, two police officers jump out, inform you that you are suspected of armed robbery, force you hard against their police car and search you, handcuff you, and drive you to the police station where you are arrested. Close your eyes for a moment, and try to imagine this scenario as vividly as you can. Now consider the following question: How likely is it that you might someday be arrested for armed robbery, regardless of whether you are innocent or guilty? Remarkably, the mere act of imagining such events may lead you to view them as more likely (for a review, see Koehler 1991).

In a series of studies demonstrating this consequence of imagination, people were asked to imagine themselves experiencing events such as being arrested for a crime, winning a free trip to Hawaii, or enjoying the benefits of cable TV (Gregory, Cialdini, and Carpenter 1982). Participants who had imagined these events later judged them to be more likely than did other participants who had not engaged in such imagination. Participants who had imagined themselves experiencing the benefits of cable TV were also more likely to subscribe to cable than were participants who had merely been informed about these benefits. Similar results were obtained in studies that asked participants to imagine themselves succeeding or failing at an anagram task and to explain the outcome they had imagined. Those imagining success expected to do better at the task than those imagining failure. Moreover, participants' actual performance was also influenced by the imagined outcome: Those imagining themselves succeeding at the task actually performed better than those imagining themselves failing at it (Sherman et al. 1981). Imagination has also been shown to increase the perceived likelihood of social events that do not involve the self, such as the election of a particular political candidate (Carrol 1978).

The availability heuristic can account for these findings. After one has imagined an event, images of it can be conjured up more readily, that is, they become more available. Our reliance on the availability of such images to assess the likelihood of events will lead us to view imagined events as more probable. At times, we may even come to mistake such imagined events for real, if the now available images seem as vivid and rich as our memories of events that actually happened (for a review, see Johnson, Hashtroudi, and Lindsay 1993; for a detailed discussion, see chapter 5).

Anchoring and Adjustment

Let's pick a random number, perhaps my brother's age, thirty-four. Now, do you suppose the number of African countries in the United Nations is greater or smaller than thirty-four? What do you suppose it is?

Obviously, my brother's age is completely irrelevant to your estimate and should have no impact on it. But it probably did. Tversky and Kahneman (1974) showed that such random and irrelevant starting points can have a dramatic impact on judgment. In one study, participants were asked to make the same estimates you were, using random starting points generated in their presence by spinning a wheel of fortune. Those given low numbers as starting points estimated the number of African countries in the United Nations to be only 25, whereas those given high numbers as starting points estimated their number to be almost twice as high, 45. The same thing happened even when participants were offered payoffs for accuracy. Initial starting points, even totally irrelevant ones, seem to serve as *anchors*. When we make our estimates by adjusting upward or downward from such an anchor, we often do not make a large enough adjustment. As a result our estimates can be biased toward the anchor. Tversky and Kahneman termed this phenomenon *anchoring*.

Anchors may bias judgments about a target by priming specific relevant knowledge (Strack and Mussweiler 1997). In the typical anchoring experiment, participants are first asked to make a comparative judgment (Is the number of African countries in the UN greater or smaller than 34?). To make this judgment, they construct a mental model of the target (African countries in the UN), using information that is maximally consistent with the anchor value. In other words, the model they construct of the target is biased toward the anchor. Having constructed this biased model of the target, they then rely on it to make their subsequent, absolute judgment about the target (How many African countries are there in the UN?). If it is true that an anchor biases judgments about a target because it prompts the construction of a biased model of that target, then the biasing impact of the anchor should be restricted to that particular target. Indeed, this turns out to be the case. For example, when participants were given an anchor in the context of a comparison judgment about one target (Is the height of the Brandenburg Gate in Berlin greater or smaller that 150 meters?) this anchor subsequently colored their judgments about the same target (the height of the Brandenburg Gate) but did not influence their judgments about a different target (the width of the Brandenburg Gate). To influence judgments about a target, anchors must activate knowledge that is deemed relevant to that target.

Anchoring effects have been found for a wide range of numeric judgments, including real-estate agents' appraisals of houses, survey respondents' assessments of the likelihood of nuclear war, and students' estimates of geographic distances (e.g., Northcraft and Neale 1987; Plous 1989; Tversky and Kahneman 1974). In these, and many other judgments, estimates are biased by the provision of irrelevant numbers that can serve as anchors.

Anchoring and Social Judgment

Although the early research on anchoring focused on the impact of numeric anchors on numeric judgments, social psychologists were quick to realize that anchoring could also occur when neither the anchor nor the judgment were obviously numeric. Consider the classic social psychological experiment in which some participants observe an experimenter asking an individual to write a pro-Castro essay, and other participants observe the experimenter asking for an anti-Castro essay. After reading the resulting pro- or anti-Castro essay, participants are asked to guess the individual's real attitude toward Castro. The typical finding of this and similar experiments is that participants reading a pro-Castro essay think the essay writer is more pro-Castro than do those reading an anti-Castro essay; this, despite the fact that the essay writer clearly had no choice in the matter and was only fulfilling the experimenter's request. In other words, people overattribute the individual's behavior to the individual's underlying attitudes and dispositions, and underattribute it to the constraints of the situation (Jones and Davis 1965; see chapter 9). This phenomenon has been termed *correspondence bias* or *the fundamental attribution error.*

George Quattrone proposed that anchoring may play a role in producing the fundamental attribution error: People use the essay as a starting point or anchor, and adjust their judgments upward or downward from there (Quattrone 1982). They may say to themselves something like, "This essay is really supportive of Castro, but I know that John was forced to write it, and is probably not nearly as supportive of Castro as appears from his essay, so I should guess he has a less extreme attitude." If people use the essay as a starting point or anchor in this manner but do not adjust their estimates sufficiently upward or downward, their estimates will be biased by the anchor.

Such anchoring may be pervasive in social judgment. We may anchor on our own traits and attitudes when trying to determine those of others, and we may anchor on others' opinions of us when trying to assess our own attributes. As a result we may view others as more similar to us than they are, and draw stronger conclusions than we should from flattery or criticism. We may anchor on a group's stereotype when evaluating a group member, or anchor on a member's behavior when assessing the stereotype. As a result we may view individuals as more similar to their social group than we should, and we may overgeneralize from a single individual to an entire group. We may anchor on examples of extreme performance when evaluating less extreme performance, or anchor on average performance when assessing extremes. As a result we may view individuals who remind us of a star more positively than we should, and view individuals who dramatically outperform their peers less positively than we should (all these examples are based on documented phenomena that will be discussed in later chapters).

Whenever we observe that people's judgments are biased by information that is provided or available to them, we need to consider the possibility that this is due to anchoring on the biasing information.

Can We Overcome Biases due to the Availability Heuristic and Anchoring?

Many of the biases produced by the representativeness heuristic are due to a failure to rely on more appropriate statistical heuristics. In many cases we possess all the information needed to make correct inferences, and even possess the correct statistical heuristics. Biases occur because we fail to apply these heuristics when we should. And, indeed, when we are reminded of the relevance of information such as base-rates and sample size, we often use it. Moreover, experience with uncertain domains and statistical education can increase reliance on statistical heuristics. Although even the most sophisticated statisticians can fall prey to bias, we may nevertheless remain optimistic that we can at least reduce the pervasiveness and magnitude of such biases.

A less optimistic picture emerges when we consider how we may overcome biases due to the availability heuristic and to anchoring. The availability heuristic entails using the information that comes to mind to assess frequencies or to make other judgments. Even if we become aware that the information that comes to mind may be biased, it is impossible to assess the magnitude of the bias. How, for example, can we determine the number of words with R as the third letter that we were unable to think of? Or how can we tell how many people hated our performance but failed to share this with us? If we have no objective information and do not rely on the availability of examples, how can we assess frequency?

The same problem occurs for attempts to get rid of biases due to anchoring. Here we are often aware that the anchor is either irrelevant or too extreme, and that is precisely why we adjust our judgments away from it. But how can we tell just how much to adjust? Now that we are aware that anchors can bias us, how do we get rid of their influence? If we try to correct for the effects of an anchor, how do we ensure that we do not undercorrect or overcorrect?

Unlike the representativeness heuristic, the availability heuristic and anchoring biases do not appear to be due to failure to know or use more appropriate heuristics. Rather, they may be viewed as a kind of *mental contamination* (by availability or by the anchor; Wilson and Brekke 1994). Even though we do not want our judgments to be contaminated in this manner, it is very difficult to eliminate the contamination.

Although we may be incapable of eliminating biases due to availability and anchoring, becoming aware of the potential for such bias should at the very least alert us to the possibility that our judgments may be in error, should cause us to be more cautious, and should lead us to seek more objective information where possible.

Careful Thinking and Use of Heuristics

Researchers in several areas of social cognition have developed *dual-process* models of cognition. Although these models differ in their details, they share the broad assumption that people alternate between different modes of thinking. Sometimes we engage in careful, detailed, and elaborate processing, devoting all of our attention to the problem at hand and aiming for the best possible solution. On other occasions we engage in more cursory, superficial processing, devoting little time and attention to the problem, aiming only for a quick and easy, albeit less than perfect, solution (for reviews, see Chaiken and Trope 1999; for a discussion of the impact of goals on modes of processing, see chapter 6).

When we encounter a persuasive message, for example, we may either carefully contemplate the strengths and weaknesses of its arguments or respond to more superficial cues such as the credentials of the speaker (for a review, see Eagly and Chaiken 1993). In a similar vein, when explaining a person's behavior, we may either carefully analyze the situation, trying to take into account the full range of forces operating on this person, or we may just jump automatically to conclusions about the person's underlying personality (for a review, see Gilbert 1989; see chapter 7). By the same token, when forming an impression of a person, we may engage in a thoughtful attempt to integrate everything we know about this person into a coherent impression, or we may merely try to "place" this person into obvious social categories (for reviews, see Brewer 1988; Fiske and Neuberg 1990). In short, we may tackle many judgment tasks either through careful, elaborate thinking or through "quick and dirty" processing.

Because the major nonstatistical heuristics discussed in this chapter—the representativeness heuristic and the availability heuristic—are often referred to as "quick and dirty" rules of thumb, some have equated their use with superficial, relatively mindless processing. On this view, people use these relatively simplistic heuristics when they engage in superficial, mindless processing, but rely on more complex and sophisticated principles when they engage in thoughtful, elaborate processing (e.g., Bodenhausen 1990). Contributing to the endorsement of this view, an important model of persuasion distinguished between "systematic processing," on the one hand, and "heuristic processing," on the other hand (Chaiken, Liberman, and Eagly 1989). This terminology may have inadvertently encouraged the assumption that heuristic processing, which is viewed as relatively superficial and mindless, entails heavy reliance on heuristics such as representativeness and availability.

It is not the case, however, that these nonstatistical heuristics are inherently more simple and effortless than statistical ones. When trying to explain, for example, why the rookie of the year usually does less well the subsequent year, the statistical answer "regression to the mean" can be produced with much less thought and effort than the nonstatistical causal accounts that people often struggle to generate ("well, the success goes to their heads ... and there's pressure to keep up the performance after the great first year ... and ..."; Nisbett et al. 1983, p. 361). It is also not the case that careful thinking is bound to decrease reliance on representativeness and availability. Research has shown that careful thinking can sometimes decrease the use of nonstatistical heuristics, sometimes increase their use, and sometimes have no effect on their use (for a review, see Kunda 1990).

Sometimes careful thinking reduces reliance on nonstatistical heuristics. For example, one study found that alert individuals were less likely than tired individuals to commit the conjunction fallacy, that is, to assume that a person is more likely to belong to a conjunction of categories (e.g., feminist and bank teller) than to belong to just one of these categories (Bodenhausen 1990). The conjunction fallacy is typically assumed to result from reliance on the representativeness heuristic, as discussed earlier. Apparently, the careful thinking that people engage in when alert (but not when tired) can decrease their reliance on the representativeness heuristic and increase their reliance on more appropriate statistical principles when making such judgments.

Other research, however, has yielded opposite results. On some occasions careful thinking can increase reliance on nonstatistical heuristics, thereby increasing bias and error. For example, in one study, participants induced to engage in careful processing (because they knew they would have to later explain their answers to the investigators) were more likely than participants engaging in more cursory processing to show dilution effects, that is, to moderate their predictions about a person when given irrelevant information about this person (Tetlock and Boettger 1989). Similarly, in another study, participants induced to engage in careful processing (because they were told that performance was diagnostic of intelligence) were more prone to respond erroneously to Kahneman and Tversky's hospital problem than were participants engaging in more cursory processing (Pelham and Neter 1995; see chapter 6 for a related discussion). Both the dilution effect and the misguided intuitions about the hospital problem are typically assumed to result from reliance on the representativeness heuristic, as discussed earlier. Therefore these studies suggest that careful thinking can increase reliance on the representativeness heuristic.

Why does careful thinking sometimes increase and sometimes decrease reliance on the representativeness heuristic? I believe that careful thinking makes people especially likely to choose the heuristic that they consider most appropriate to the problem at hand. Sometimes this will result in correct choice of the appropriate statistical heuristic over the representativeness heuristic. However, as noted throughout this chapter, statistical understanding is shaky enough that careful reflection can sometimes lead people to conclude that it is more appropriate to rely on representativeness than on statistical information such as prior probabilities or sample sizes.

In conclusion, there is no simple association between depth of processing and choice of heuristics. Both statistical and non-statistical heuristics may be used in the context of careful elaborate processing as well as in the context of more superficial, cursory processing. Careful thinking will lead us to favor those heuristics that we consider, upon careful reflection, to be superior. The heuristic we prefer upon reflection may be either statistical or non-statistical, depending on our understanding of the problem and its domain and on our general understanding of statistics.

Summary

When reasoning under uncertainty, people rely on a variety of *heuristics*, that is, rules of thumb. People do have at least some understanding of statistical rules, but they often use nonstatistical heuristics in their stead.

People use the *representativeness heuristics* to determine the probability that an instance belongs to a particular category or the probability that an event was produced by a particular cause. This heuristic entails basing such probability judgments on the similarity between the instance and category, or between the event and the causal process assumed to govern it. This heuristic can serve us well when the features of the instance or the event that are used in the similarity judgments are highly diagnostic of category membership or of causal processes. However, the heuristic can get us into trouble when these features are not highly diagnostic, and we rely on them exclusively, ignoring other important information such as prior probabilities and sample sizes, and failing to appreciate the relevance of important statistical principles. As a result we may make serious mistakes when trying to explain another person's actions, predict our own or someone else's likely behaviors and outcomes, determine someone's likely occupation, or form impressions of others.

Several factors determine whether we will apply the representativeness heuristic or a statistical heuristic to a given problem. These include our general knowledge about the role of chance in the domain in question, contextual cues that highlight the importance of statistical or nonstatistical information and heuristics, and our general knowledge of statistics.

People use the *availability heuristic* to assess the frequencies of events and make frequency-related judgments. This heuristic entails basing such judgments on the ease of bringing the events in question to mind, that is, on their availability. This heuristic can serve us well when the availability of events is strongly correlated with their actual frequencies, as is often the case. However, it can get us into trouble when the ease of imagining events is influenced by factors that are not related to their frequency. In such cases we may make mistaken judgments about issues such as the pervasiveness of various risks, the extent of our relative contributions to collaborative efforts, the impact of an individual on a group, or our own behavioral patterns.

When making judgments, people often use irrelevant values as *anchors*, and make insufficient adjustments from these anchors. As a result irrelevant numbers can bias judgments about topics such as the likelihood of nuclear war, the value of real estate, the attitudes of an individual, or the characteristics of a group. By and large, it is difficult to overcome biases due to availability and anchoring because we have no way of telling the extent to which our judgments have been contaminated by irrelevant factors.

This chapter discusses several judgment tasks that are central to the way we understand and experience our social worlds. Much of our social knowledge is accrued as we test particular hypotheses about the world: Is this person trustworthy? Will I enjoy this social event? Have I been fair minded? We also gain knowledge by assessing covariations among attributes and events: Are librarians especially shy? Do children become hyperactive after eating candy? In this chapter I review evidence suggesting that our ability to handle these inferential tasks is less than perfect. The strategies we rely on to test hypotheses and to assess covariations can produce systematic biases in our conclusions about our own and other peoples' attributes, can lead us to "see" covariations that do not in reality exist, and can prevent us from detecting covariations that do exist. I will also discuss some factors that can increase and decrease bias and inaccuracies when we test hypotheses and assess covariations and will explain why judgments about social events are especially vulnerable to error.

The way we understand and experience events is influenced not only by our beliefs about what actually happened but also by the thoughts we entertain about what might have happened. At times we may be tormented by thoughts of how things could have turned out so much better, "if only ..." At other times, we may feel extremely fortunate that things did not turn out much worse, as they might have. I will review some of the principles that govern the kinds of counterfactual thoughts we entertain in different circumstances, and show how these can color our evaluations of events and our emotional reactions to them.

Hypothesis Testing

Take a moment to bring to mind a single woman whom you know well. Now suppose that I tell you that my friend Frank is interested in meeting someone. He tends to like extraverted women; women who are friendly, outgoing, and comfortable around other people. Do you think he will like your friend? Is she extraverted?

How do you go about answering such a question? What information about your friend do you bring to mind when trying to determine whether she is extraverted? One strategy might be to consider all the relevant information you have about her: Bring to mind any evidence indicating that she may be extraverted—friendly behaviors, conversations with strangers, and so on, and also bring to mind any evidence indicating that she may not be extraverted—shy behaviors, avoiding social situations, and so on. With all this information in mind, you should be able to make a balanced assessment of her overall extraversion. It turns out, however, that we usually do not conduct such a balanced search for evidence. Rather, our searches tend to be one-sided. Most people would try to determine whether their friend is an extravert by seeking mostly evidence that she is in fact extraverted, and would not look nearly as hard for evidence that might suggest the opposite.

The Positive-Test Strategy

Klayman and Ha (1987) termed this one-sided approach to hypothesis testing the *positive-test strategy*. When you use this strategy, you test a hypothesis by seeking cases that match it. To determine whether your friend is extraverted, you search for examples of her extraversion. If you can find such evidence, you conclude that the hypothesis is true (she is, indeed, extraverted). If you cannot find such evidence, you conclude that the hypothesis is false. This broad strategy might serve you well in cases where the evidence is clear-cut. If, for example, your friend's behavior is uniformly extraverted or uniformly introverted, it will not matter that your search for evidence is one-sided; a more balanced search would yield identical results. But if the relevant evidence is mixed, the positive-test strategy could bias your evaluations. If, for example, your friend is extraverted on some occasions but shy on other occasions, seeking only examples of her extraversion will lead you to view her as more extraverted than she really is. In this case the positive-test strategy will bias you toward confirming your hypothesis.

People use the positive-test strategy to evaluate hypotheses both when searching through their memories for preexisting knowledge and when searching the external world for new evidence that could bear on their hypotheses. This strategy is particularly likely to lead to hypothesis confirmation when applied in the social domain because people's social behavior varies from one situation to another, and because our knowledge about others is often a mixed bag that contains information that could support either of two opposite hypotheses.

Hypothesis Confirmation in Evaluating Others

Biased Memory Search   We often find ourselves confronted with new questions about people we know well: Will my acquaintance make a good roommate? Will my child thrive in the neighborhood school? Will my brother succeed as a lawyer? Mark Snyder and Nancy Cantor (1979) set out to determine whether people test such hypotheses about familiar others by conducting one-sided searches through their relevant memories, searching for those memories that fit their hypotheses. To this end, they first provided participants with a set of mixed memories about a person, Jane. Participants read a lengthy description of a week in Jane's life, which portrayed her as behaving in an extraverted manner on some occasions and in an introverted manner on others. For example, she engaged in animated conversation in the doctor's office but refrained from socializing during her coffee break; she spoke to strangers while jogging but acted shyly at the supermarket. When participants returned to the lab two days later, they were asked to test one of two hypotheses about Jane: Half were asked to determine Jane's suitability for the job of real-estate agent; though this was not stated explicitly in

Table 4.1 Numbers of extraverted and introverted facts recalled about a person and judgments of her suitability to an extraverted job (real-estate agent) and to an introverted job (librarian) as a function of whether participants had been asked to test her suitability to the extraverted or the introverted job

	HYPOTHESIS	
	EXTRAVERTED	INTROVERTED
Recalled facts		
Extraverted	4.03	1.28
Introverted	1.00	2.56
Job suitability		
Real-estate agent	4.41	2.50
Librarian	3.29	5.00

Source: From Snyder and Cantor (1979, table 2, p. 338). Copyright © (1979) by Academic Press. Reprinted with permission.

the instructions, this job is typically stereotyped as requiring an extraverted personality. The remaining half were asked to determine Jane's suitability for the job of librarian, which is typically stereotyped as requiring an introverted personality.

Participants in both groups were asked to list the facts about Jane that they considered relevant to deciding her suitability for the job they were evaluating. As may be seen in the top two rows of table 4.1, participants clearly engaged in the positive-test strategy: Those testing Jane's suitability to the extraverted profession of real-estate agent recalled more extraverted than introverted facts about her. And the reverse was true for those testing her suitability for the introverted profession of librarian. It seems as though people were asking themselves, "What do I know about Jane that is consistent with her being suitable for this job?" and were not asking "What do I know that is inconsistent?"

Moreover, the biased recruitment of relevant facts about Jane resulted in hypothesis confirmation, as shown in the bottom two rows of table 4.1: Those testing Jane's suitability for the real-estate agent job thought she would make a better real-estate agent than librarian. But those testing her suitability for the librarian job arrived at the opposite conclusion—they thought she would make a better librarian than real-estate agent! When we have mixed evidence about a person, merely entertaining a one-sided hypothesis about this person can increase our confidence in this hypothesis.

Biased Evidence Seeking   We often find ourselves testing one-side hypotheses about newly encountered, unfamiliar others. These can be derived from prior expectations (Eliot's teachers say he is pretty smart; is he?), from stereotypes (lawyers tend to be aggressive; is this lawyer aggressive?), or from our goals (I want to hire a warm and caring person as a baby-sitter; is this person I am interviewing warm and caring?). Our reliance on the positive-test strategy when seeking the evidence we need to evaluate such hypotheses about others will often bias us toward hypothesis confirmation, because people's behavior on any personality dimension is rarely uniform. Such bias was demonstrated in a series of studies by Mark Snyder, William Swann, and their colleagues.

In one study, each participant was asked to evaluate the personality of a stranger waiting in another room (Snyder and Swann 1978). Half were told that their job was to find out whether this person's behavior and experiences matched those of the typical extravert. To this end they were given a brief profile of extraverts, which included attributes such as outgoing, confident, and enthusiastic. The remaining half were told to find out, instead, whether this person matched the profile of the typical introvert, which included attributes such as shy, quiet, and retiring. All participants were then given a list of 26 questions from which they were to choose 12 that they would pose to the other person so as to find out whether that person matched the profile. The list included two kinds of one-sided questions: The 11 extraverted questions asked for examples of extraverted behavior (e.g., "What would you do if you wanted to liven things up at a party?" "What kinds of situations do you seek out if you want to meet new people?"), and the 11 introverted questions asked for examples of introverted behavior (e.g., "In what situations do you wish you could be more outgoing?" "What factors make it hard for you to really open up to people?"). The remaining 5 questions were neutral (e.g., "What are your career goals?").

Participants favored those questions that matched the hypothesis they were asked to test: Those assessing whether the person was extraverted chose more extraverted than introverted questions. But those assessing whether the person was introverted showed the opposite preference—they chose more introverted than extraverted questions. In short, participants' choice of questions reflected reliance on the positive-test strategy.

What would happen if one actually posed such a biased set of questions to another person? Snyder and Swann reasoned that a list that includes mostly extraverted questions gives respondents many opportunities to reveal their extraverted side, but few opportunities to reveal their introverted side. As a result, the respondents might convey an image of themselves that is biased toward extraversion. In a similar manner, those asked mostly introverted questions would come across as overly introverted. This is precisely what happened in a follow-up study that used the same procedure as the original study with the addition that, after selecting the questions, participants actually got to pose these questions to another participant, the respondent. The investigators prepared an audio tape of each interview which included only the voice of the respondent (the questions were spliced out of the tape). A group of judges who knew nothing about the study listened to these tapes and rated the extraversion of each respondent (Snyder and Swann 1978).

As in the original study, participants favored those questions that matched the hypothesis they were asked to test. Moreover, these one-sided lists of questions constrained the impressions that respondents were able to convey: Those interviewed by someone testing whether they were extraverted actually came across as more extraverted than did those interviewed by someone testing whether they were introverted; this was true even though the extraversion ratings were made by judges who had no idea what questions respondents were being asked. It appears that the positive-test strategy used by interviewers to test their hypotheses yielded one-sided evidence that confirmed these hypotheses. More broadly, when I try to determine whether you are outgoing, shy, assertive, or anything else, my hypothesis-testing strategies may constrain your responses in ways that serve to confirm my hypothesis about you.

These conclusions were challenged by Trope and Bassok (1982, 1983) who pointed out that participants in Snyder and Swann's studies were not given an opportunity to ask truly diagnostic questions, that is, questions that could actually reveal whether or not someone was extraverted. They argued that when one is asked, for example, "What would you do to liven up a party?" one is essentially compelled to respond as an extravert; the only way one could reveal introversion would be to reject the assumption implied by the question (I don't usually liven up parties), something that is difficult to do in polite conversation. Therefore such a question cannot really distinguish between extraverts and introverts. They suggested that if given the opportunity to ask truly diagnostic questions, people may use a *diagnosing strategy*, that is, choose those questions that are most diagnostic of whether or not their hypothesis is true.

In one study testing these ideas, Trope and Bassok (1983) essentially replicated Snyder and Swann's original study, but using truly diagnostic questions (e.g., "Do you like loud parties?" "Do you shy away from social interactions?"). They also varied question diagnosticity so that some of the questions, like those just listed, were highly diagnostic of extraversion or introversion, and some were only somewhat diagnostic (e.g., "do you talk loudly?"). They found strong evidence for reliance on the diagnosing strategy: Participants favored highly diagnostic questions over less diagnostic ones, and diagnosticity was the most important determinant of their choice of questions. Participants even preferred highly diagnostic questions that did not match their hypotheses over less diagnostic ones that did. For example, those testing whether someone was extraverted favored the question "Do you shy away from social situations?", a highly diagnostic question that did not match their hypothesis, over the question "Do you talk loudly?", a less diagnostic question that did match their hypothesis.

But, in addition to relying on the diagnosing strategy, participants also relied on the positive-test strategy: They preferred to ask questions that matched their hypotheses. The same pattern of strong preference for diagnostic questions accompanied by a weaker preference for questions that matched participants' hypotheses was also found in other studies (e.g., Devine, Hirt, and Gehrke 1990; Skov and Sherman 1986; Trope and Bassok 1982). Reliance on the positive-test strategy also emerged in a study in which diagnosticity was not an issue because participants were given the choice between two equally diagnostic questions, one matching and one not matching their hypothesis. For example, those testing whether someone was extraverted preferred to ask an extraverted question over an equally diagnostic introverted one (Devine, Hirt, and Gherke 1990). People were also shown to use the positive-test strategy when allowed to construct their own questions: They asked interviewees whether they possessed attributes that matched the hypothesis rather than asking about attributes that matched its alternative. Interviewees tended to answer these one-sided questions positively (perhaps because they themselves relied on the positive-test strategy to generate answers), resulting in hypothesis confirmation (Zuckerman et al. 1995).

It appears, then, that we do not rely on the positive-test strategy to the point of ignoring important information about diagnosticity; we do try to ask the most informative questions we can. Nevertheless, we also rely on the positive-test strategy when seeking evidence needed to test our hypotheses, and this can bias our judgments. Even judgments about the self can be affected by reliance on the positive-test strategey, as discussed next.

Hypothesis Confirmation in Evaluating Oneself

Are you assertive? Friendly? Happy? Do you support a tax cut? A tuition raise? A welfare reform? Do you think you would enjoy a canoeing trip? A high school reunion? A philosophy lecture? In the course of our daily lives we are frequently called upon to answer such questions about ourselves. At times we may have a ready, prestored summary answer (being highly assertive may be a central part of your self-image). But often, we need to construct our answer on the spot, based on what we know about our related behaviors, thoughts, and feelings. In these cases, if we rely on the positive-test strategy, we may attempt to answer one-sided questions by selectively recruiting information that matches them. When I ask you if you are assertive, you may bring to mind evidence of your assertiveness, but when I ask you if you are unassertive, you may bring to mind evidence of your lack of assertiveness. Such one-sided recruitment of self-knowledge can influence one's self-views; due to reliance on the availability heuristic, people who have just brought to mind examples of their assertiveness may see themselves as overly assertive. Therefore people asked whether they are assertive will likely view themselves as more assertive than people asked whether they are unassertive.

To determine whether self-views can be influenced simply by asking people one-sided questions, my colleagues and I posed such questions to students (Kunda et al. 1993). In one study, half the participants were asked to list examples of their past thoughts, feelings, and behaviors that came to mind as they tried to answer the question, "Are you happy with your social life?" The remaining half of the participants were asked to do the same for the opposite question, "Are you unhappy with your social life?" Participants engaged in the positive-test strategy: Those asked whether they were happy recruited more happy thoughts and fewer unhappy thoughts than those asked whether they were unhappy. Moreover, this strategy resulted in hypothesis confirmation: Participants asked whether they were happy rated themselves as happier with their social lives than did participants asked whether they were unhappy. Indeed, only 4 percent of participants asked whether they were happy rated themselves as unhappy (i.e., gave negative ratings below the neutral midpoint of the scale). But the percentage of participants rating themselves as unhappy jumped to 19 percent for those asked instead if they were unhappy.

Follow-up studies revealed that one-sided questions about the self result in hypothesis confirmation only when the relevant knowledge base is mixed and so capable of supporting opposite hypotheses. The tendency to confirm hypotheses was eliminated when people's knowledge base was relatively uniform, as was the case when questions focused on relatively consistent domains of the self or when questions were addressed to individuals whose social behavior was relatively consistent. In such cases the direction of one-sided questions had no impact on self-views (Kunda et al. 1993). It appears, then, that when one-sided questions do bias self-views, this is due to one-sided searches through inconsistent memories and beliefs.

These findings have obvious implications for how one should conduct and interpret survey research. When you encounter a survey that relied on one-sided questions such as, "Do you support policy X?" you should recognize that the survey most likely provides an inflated estimate of public support for that policy. The opposite question, "Do you oppose policy X?" would likely yield considerably lower estimates of support for the very same policy.

You should also recognize that your assessment of your own attitudes, beliefs, and traits may be inadvertently biased by one-sided questions posed to you by others or by yourself. Before acting on your preferences, you may wish to ask yourself whether you have reason to believe that you might hold the opposite preference. Considering the opposite hypothesis in this manner may lead you to recruit a more balanced set of your relevant beliefs, one that is more representative of your true attitude (Lord, Lepper, and Preston 1984).

Choosing versus Rejecting

Imagine that you are serving on a jury whose task is to sort out a messy divorce case. You need to decide which of the two parents will receive sole custody of their child. One might think that asking yourself which parent should be awarded sole custody is equivalent to asking yourself which parent should be denied sole custody; after all, when you award sole custody to one parent you also, by necessity, deny it to the other parent. It turns out, however, that the direction of the question can influence your judgment. Eldar Shafir reasoned that this would occur when one parent seemed better than the other parent in some respects but worse in others. Consider, for example, the following pair of parents (Shafir 1993, p. 549):

Parent A: *Average income*
Average health
Average working hours
Reasonable rapport with the child
Relatively stable social life

Parent B: *Above-average income*
Very close relationship with the child
Extremely active social life
Lots of work-related travel
Minor health problems

There are several good reasons to prefer awarding custody to parent B rather than A: Parent B has a higher income and a better relationship with the child. But there are also good reasons to see Parent B as a worse candidate for custody than A: Parent B will be away often due to travel and has some health problems.

If we use the positive-test strategy when making this decision, then, when asked who should be awarded custody, we will focus on information that makes one parent superior to the other. Parent B is superior on several dimensions, and so we will award custody to that parent. But when asked who should be denied custody, we will focus on information that makes one parent inferior to the other. Parent B is inferior on several dimensions, and so will be denied custody. That is precisely what happened in Shafir's study: Most of the participants asked who should be awarded custody chose parent B, and most of the participants asked who should be denied custody also chose parent B!

This and similar studies conducted by Shafir suggest that when we are in the business of choosing winners—people who should receive an award, get admitted to graduate school, get elected for public office—we will favor complex people who have striking strengths and weaknesses over more bland and unremarkable ones, because we have more reasons for choosing the complex individuals. But when we are in the business of weeding out losers—people who should be eliminated from the short list for an award, be denied admission to graduate school, be cut from a list of political candidates—we will choose to reject the complex people over the more bland ones, because we have more reasons for rejecting the complex individuals. A selection committee that puts together a shortlist by looking for and including the best candidates may end up with a very different list than a committee that, instead, constructs its shortlist by looking for and rejecting the worst candidates.

Which of these strategies one uses may depend, in part, on the proportion of applicants expected to make the final list. If our task is to admit only a tiny proportion of applicants to our program (say we have 100 applicants competing for one or two spots), we may focus on reasons for excluding applicants and search for their weaknesses. But if our task is to admit a sizable proportion of applicants (say we have a 100 applicants competing for 50 spots), we may focus instead on reasons for including applicants, and search for their strengths (M. Ross and Ellard 1986). As a result our ratings of a given applicant's ability will be lower when we evaluate this applicant in the context of a tough competition for one of a scarce number of positions than when we evaluate the very same applicant in the context of an easier competition for one of many available positions.

Note also that we are likely to have more complex and elaborate views of familiar individuals whom we know well than of less familiar individuals. As a result we may have more reasons for choosing our acquaintances over strangers but also have more reasons for rejecting our acquaintances. Perhaps that explains why my son hails me, on some occasions, as the best mother in the world but also condemns me, on less happy occasions, as the worst mother in the world....

Analyzing Reasons for Predictions

Think of someone you have met only recently and whom you do not yet know well. Over the next few months, do you suppose you will go to at least one movie with this person? Will you go out of your way to avoid seeing this person? Before answering, take a moment to think of the reasons for why you may or may not perform these behaviors. One might imagine that contemplating the reasons for your predictions in this manner will increase the accuracy of your predictions. In fact the opposite is true.

When analyzing the reasons for such predictions, people may rely on the positive-test strategy, and so focus on reasons for why they will perform the behavior. Even if you don't particularly like the acquaintance you have brought to mind, you might think up some reasons for why you might go to the movies with this person. As a result you will consider it more likely that you will in fact do so. In a study designed to test these ideas, Wilson and LaFleur (1995) asked sorority members to make these and similar predictions about their likely behavior in the coming semester toward a newly met sorority member. Half the participants were also asked, before making each prediction, to list the reasons why they would or would not perform that behavior. At the end of the semester, Wilson and LaFleur obtained participants' reports of their actual behavior toward the designated person. These enabled them to examine the accuracy of participants' predictions.

Merely asking participants to analyze the reasons for their behavioral predictions made them view the behaviors as more likely. This suggests that, in relying on the positive-test strategy, they tended to recruit reasons for why they would perform the behaviors, and they based their predictions on this somewhat biased set of recruited reasons. However, analyzing reasons had no effect on actual behavior. Because analyzing reasons increased the expected likelihoods of performing the behaviors without changing the actual likelihoods, analyzing reasons resulted in reduced accuracy. Reason analysis will likely reduce accuracy in this manner when, in the absence of such analysis, people make reasonably accurate estimates, or when they already believe the behavior to be more likely than it actually is. In these situations, making even higher likelihood estimates will reduce accuracy. Of course, when people start off underestimating the likelihood of behavior, analyzing reasons can boost their accuracy by increasing their likelihood estimates.

We often expect that thinking hard about an issue will improve our reasoning. The counterintuitive conclusion of research on analyzing reasons is that careful reflection can sometimes do more harm than good. This will occur when careful reflection leads us to rely on heuristics such as the positive-test strategy that can increase bias (see Tetlock and Boettger 1989; see chapter 3 for a related discussion).

So far I have discussed how we test hypotheses that focus on a single attribute—Is Jane introverted? Will I go to the movies with her? I turn next to a discussion of how we go about testing more complex hypotheses that focus on the association or correlation between two variables.

Covariation Detection

Do computer hackers tend to lack interpersonal skills? Do better scientists make better teachers? Are children who are unruly at home also disruptive at school? Do you and your best friend tend to agree on your evaluations of movies? Each of these questions concerns a covariation between two variables. In the course of our daily lives, we often need to evaluate similar covariations. To understand our social world, we must determine covariations between group membership and behavior, covariations between behaviors in two kinds of situations, and covariations between the opinions of two individuals, to name but a few examples. Because so much of our social knowledge is based on beliefs about such covariations, it is of great importance to determine just how good we are at assessing

Table 4.2 Hypothetical data

	ABSENTMINDED	
	YES	NO
Professor		
Yes	600 (A)	400 (B)
No	300 (C)	200 (D)

covariations. It turns out that under some circumstances we assess covariations quite accurately. But often we run into considerable difficulty when assessing covariations and, as a result, end up with misconceptions about our social world.

Assessing Covariations from 2 x 2 Tables

Suppose that you were interested in determining whether there was a relationship, or covariation between being a professor and being absentminded. Are professors particularly likely to be absentminded? Imagine that I have already done much of the necessary information gathering for you: I walked around campus, identified people who were or were not professors, and also found out whether each of them was or was not absentminded. I summarized all this information in table 4.2. Take a minute to examine this (admittedly fictitious) information. Based on this information, are professors particularly likely to be absentminded?

How should one go about answering this question? To determine whether there is an association between being a professor and being absentminded, we need to find out whether the ratio of professors who are absentminded to professors who are not (in this case 600 to 400, i.e., 3 to 2) is greater than the same ratio for people who are not professors (in this case, 300 to 200, i.e., 3 to 2). Because the two ratios are identical in this example, in these hypothetical data there is no relationship between being a professor and being absentminded.

Most people, however, do not realize that all four cells in this table are relevant. Instead, people tend to focus on just one or two of these cells. Many focus only on the yes-yes cell, labeled A in the table (representing, in this example, people who are professors and are absentminded; Smelsund 1963; Jenkins and Ward 1965). Given the data in table 4.2, such a focus might mislead one to believe that professors are particularly likely to be absentminded because there are many people in the A cell. Another common strategy is to compare the A cell to the B cell (i.e., compare the number of professors who are absentminded to the number who are not). Once again, this strategy would lead one to see a covariation that does not in fact exist because there are more professors who are absentminded than professors who are not. Few people realize that all four cells are relevant (for a review, see Klayman and Ha 1987).

The tendency to focus on the yes-yes cell (A) may be viewed as an example of reliance on the positive-test strategy—when trying to determine whether professors are absentminded, we look for cases that match the hypothesis, namely absentminded professors. The tendency to compare cells A to B also reflects reliance on the positive-test strategy—we look for cases that match the hypothesized cause (being a professor) to determine whether the hypothesized effect (being absentminded) is present (cell A) or absent (cell B) (Klayman and Ha 1987).

I frequently encounter such examples of faulty covariation detection from people who argue that there is truth in astrology. They often support this claim by providing several examples of events that were predicted by their horoscope and then came true. This amounts to focusing only on the A cell and is not good enough. To properly assess this covariation, it is also necessary to know 'about events that were predicted by the horoscope and did not come true (the B cell). And even this is not enough. It is also important to know about events that were not predicted by the horoscope but happened anyway (the C cell) and, counterintuitive as it may seem, about events that were not predicted by the horoscope and never happened (the D cell) (Nisbett and Ross 1980).

Assessing covariations from contingency tables seems, on the surface, a lot simpler than assessing covariations from a series of events that unfold over time, as when one has numerous encounters over many months with professors and other people who may or may not be absentminded. When data are summarized in a 2 × 2 table, you are not hindered by faulty memory or by faulty coding of behavior as you would be when assessing covariations from many instances observed over time (Crocker 1981). The fact that we run into difficulty even in this relatively simple task does not bode well for our ability to detect covariations from more naturalistic observation. You might wish to argue, however, that people are simply inexperienced with reasoning from 2 × 2 tables and may do much better in more familiar reasoning tasks. But this is not the case. People have difficulty with more naturalistic covariation detection tasks as well, as discussed next. As a result we often "see" correlations that are not in fact present, and fail to detect actual correlations.

Illusory Correlations

There is a widespread belief among doctors and patients that arthritis pain is influenced by the weather. Yet scientific studies have found no consistent evidence for such an association. This led Redelmeier and Tversky (1996) to suspect that faulty covariation detection contributes to the belief that arthritis pain is related to weather: People may be "seeing" an *illusory correlation* that is not in fact there. To examine this possibility, they followed 18 arthritis patients for a period of 15 months. They obtained measures of pain and joint tenderness from the patients themselves as well as from their physicians twice a month. They also obtained local weather reports on barometric pressure, temperature, and humidity for the corresponding time period. Almost all of the patients believed that there was a strong relationship between the weather and their pain. Yet, when the researchers correlated each patient's reported level of pain at each point in time with the weather at that time, they found no significant correlations. The average correlation was close to zero.

The positive-test strategy may contribute to the perception of such illusory correlations: If our prior theories lead us to expect a correlation, we will pay special attention to cases that embody this correlation. Patients may focus on times when a change in the weather was accompanied by an increase in arthritis pain, and may pay less attention to times when their pain increased even though the weather remained stable, or their pain remained stable even though the weather changed. As a result, when patients attempt to asses the correlation between their pain and the weather, the confirmatory cases will be more available and easier to retrieve and so will unduly influence their estimates of the correlation.

The notion that prior theories and expectations may lead people to see illusory correlations that are not present in the data was tested more rigorously in a series of studies by Loren Chapman and Jean Chapman (1967, 1969). These authors set out to determine why clinical psychologists continue to use and believe in projective tests such as the Draw-a-Person test even though dozens of studies have shown that these tests are not valid indicators of personality characteristics. Chapman and Chapman suggested that this might occur because the clinicians' own experience with these tests leads them to see an illusory correlation between patients' responses to these tests and their symptoms. Their research demonstrated that the perception of such illusory correlations is driven by prior expectations, and can persist even in the face of data in which these correlations are nonexistent.

One set of studies focused on the enormously popular Rorschach test, in which people are shown cards portraying patterns of inkblots and asked what they see in each card. Chapman and Chapman examined how people assess the correlation among homosexuality and particular responses to the Rorschach. This is an especially interesting question because existing research on the Rorschach had pointed to two valid but counterintuitive correlations: Homosexuals were more likely than heterosexuals to see a monstrous creature on one of the cards and were more likely to see an ambiguous animal-human figure on another card. At the same time there were many intuitively appealing correlations that in fact did not exist. Contrary to common intuitions, homosexuals were no more likely than heterosexuals to see anal content, feminine clothing, or humans of uncertain gender.

Chapman and Chapman first established that clinicians experienced with the Rorschach did in fact believe in the highly intuitive but invalid correlations. They also showed that naive students held the same beliefs, suggesting that clinicians' views were likely based on broad cultural assumptions rather than on their unique clinical experience. Chapman and Chapman then set out to determine whether people will in fact "see" these intuitively appealing correlations in data sets in which these correlations do not exist. To this end, they showed participants a series of Rorschach cards. Each was accompanied by a sheet that contained one person's response to that card as well as a couple of sentences describing that person's characteristics. Some of the responses to the cards reflected the valid but counterintuitive signs of homosexuality (e.g., "a giant with shrunken arms"), some reflected the invalid but intuitively appealing signs (e.g., "a woman's laced corset"), and some were neutral (e.g., "a map of Spain"). Some of the personal descriptions associated with these responses suggested that the person was homosexual, and some made no mention of sexual orientation. The data set was constructed such that there was no correlation between any of the response types and any of the personal descriptions—people described as homosexuals were not more or less likely than other people to give any kind of response.

Participants saw these cards briefly, one at a time, and then estimated what kind of response was associated with each personal description. Participants reported seeing correlations between homosexuality and the intuitively appealing responses, even though, in fact, there were no such correlations in the data set they had observed. In follow-up studies the investigators actually created negative correlations between the intuitive responses and homosexuality—homosexuals were less likely than heterosexuals to provide the responses that people mistakenly associate with homosexuality. Even this did not reduce the magnitude of illusory correlations. It appears that participants' prior belief that homosexuality was associated with a particular type of response led them to see such an association in the data they had observed despite the fact that in reality there was no such association in these data. Moreover, they saw positive associations even when the actual associations were negative.

These data should make you suspicious of any claims about correlations that are based on personal experience rather than on scientific investigations. Just as clinicians and students "see" nonexistent correlations between test responses and diagnoses, managers may "see" nonexistent correlations between employees' race or gender and performance, husbands may "see" nonexistent correlations between their wives' moodiness and biological cycles, parents and teachers may "see" nonexistent correlations between children's sugar consumption and unruly behavior, and students may "see" nonexistent correlations between their peers' college majors and personalities. Much of what we "learn" from experience may reflect our prior theories about reality rather than the actual nature of reality. Some of the resulting illusory correlations may be of little consequence. But some may serve as the basis for unjust social policies and inappropriate personal decisions.

Stereotype Formation through Illusory Correlation

There are few superstars in the media, and relatively few African Americans. And African American superstars such as Bill Cosby or Oprah Winfrey are very rare indeed. David Hamilton and his colleagues suggested that we may pay special attention to such rare and distinctive individuals. As a result African American superstars will be more memorable than White superstars and more available when we attempt to assess the correlation among race and stardom. We may therefore come to believe that African Americans are particularly likely to be media superstars even if in fact the proportion of media superstars among African Americans we have observed is no different from the proportion of media superstars among Whites we have observed. In other words, we will "see" an illusory correlation.

Put more broadly, we are likely to overestimate the frequency of rare behaviors among members of relatively small groups. When both the group and the behavior are rare, their co-occurrence (i.e., a group member who performed the behavior) will be even rarer. Such distinctive individuals will be especially noticeable and memorable, and so will give rise to an illusory correlation between group membership and the behavior.

To test these ideas, Hamilton and Gifford (1976) introduced their participants to two groups, one large and one small, identified only as Group A and Group B. Participants read information about 39 individuals, one at a time. They were informed about each individual's group membership and about a behavior performed by that individual (e.g., "Bruce, a member of Group B, did volunteer work for a political candidate;" "Joe, a member of Group A, made the other person very uncomfortable by his sarcastic remark"). The stimuli were created such that Group A was twice as big as Group B, and positive behaviors were more than twice as common than negative ones. But there was no relationship between group membership and the positivity of behaviors—the ratio of positive to negative behaviors was identical for both groups. Despite this lack of actual correlation, the researchers predicted that participants would see an illusory correlation. Members of the smaller Group B performing the less frequent, negative behavior were quite rare and distinctive and were therefore expected to be especially memorable and so to exert undue influence on participants' impressions of that group.

That is exactly what happened: Participants saw an illusory correlation between group membership and the positivity of behavior, and they overestimated the frequency with which members of the smaller Group B performed the rarer negative behaviors (in contrast, they were quite accurate about Group A). The end result was that they viewed Group B more negatively than Group A. In other words, they had developed a relatively negative stereotype of Group B from data that lent no support to such stereotyping.

Subsequent research using the same paradigm suggested that such illusory correlations are indeed due to the fact that rare and distinctive individuals capture our attention and become particularly memorable (for a review, see Hamilton and J. Sherman 1994). The best evidence for this comes from a study showing that participants spent more time examining sentences describing distinctive cases, that is, describing a member of the small group performing an infrequent behavior, than they spent on any other kind of sentence. This suggests that they were paying special attention to the distinctive cases. Moreover, the differential attention paid to distinctive and common individuals influenced estimates of the frequency of the different kinds of behavior among each group and, thereby, the liking for each group (Stroessner, Hamilton, and Mackie 1992; different results were obtained for participants who had been put in positive and negative moods, but those are less relevant to the present concerns). The increased attention to distinctive co-occurrences also appears to affect their memorability: In another study, participants remembered a greater proportion of the distinctive behaviors than of any other kind of behavior (Hamilton, Dugan, and Trolier 1985). The fact that we pay more attention to members of small groups who perform rare behaviors and are particularly likely to remember them can explain why we come to view small groups as especially likely to perform rare behaviors.

Consider the implications for the stereotyping of minority groups. Negative behaviors tend to be relatively infrequent. Members of minority groups performing such infrequent behaviors will be particularly distinctive, noticeable, and memorable. As a result their group may be viewed as particularly likely to perform such negative behaviors, even if it is not. The work by Hamilton and his colleagues suggests that even in the absence of prior expectations, minority groups may be negatively stereotyped because of the special attention paid to minority members performing relatively rare negative behaviors. Of course, negative prior expectations will exacerbate the problem. If, for example, we expect a particular minority group to be especially likely to produce criminals, we will pay special attention to criminal members of that group not only because they are distinctive but also because they confirm our hypotheses. As a result we may "see" support for our negative stereotypes where none exists.

I have focused on negative stereotypes because these are particularly disturbing. Note, though, that the same processes can give rise to unwarranted positive stereotype as well. Rare positive behaviors can be just as distinctive as rare negative ones, and so exert undue influence on judgment (Hamilton and Gifford 1976).

Failure to Detect Actual Correlations

Prior expectations and theories can lead people to see illusory correlations that do not in fact exist (Crocker 1981; Nisbett and Ross 1980). But, in the absence of prior theories, people may sometimes fail to see unexpected correlations that do in fact exist. This was the case when Chapman and Chapman (1969) created data sets that contained real correlations between homosexuality and the counterintuitive but valid signs of homosexuality. Participants failed to detect these unexpected correlations. A similar failure to detect actual correlations was obtained in a study by Jennings, Amabile, and L. Ross (1982). These authors created several data sets representing different objective correlations among pairs of variables. Each data set contained ten pairs of observations (e.g., ten drawings of men of varying heights holding walking sticks of varying heights; ten pairs of numbers). After studying each set of observations, participants estimated the strength of the relationship between the two variables (e.g., between the heights of the men and the lengths of their sticks). Because the choice of variables was rather arbitrary, participants were unlikely to have any preconceptions about the correlations among them. Therefore this study tests people's ability to detect unexpected correlations in simple data sets.

Participants were able to detect extremely strong correlations (.80 or above), and rated their magnitude as high. But they rated even quite strong correlations (.70) as at best moderate, and often failed to detect more modest correlations (.20 to .40), rating their magnitude as close to zero. As Jennings and his colleagues pointed out, many important real-world correlations in our social world are of this modest magnitude or lower. For example, the correlation between personality traits and behavior rarely exceeds this magnitude (Mischel 1968). People's inability to detect such modest correlations even from simple and sanitized data sets implies that we will likely also fail to detect many real-world correlations when these are not predicted by our theories.

Accuracy in Covariation Detection

Despite the demonstrated difficulties that we have in assessing covariations, we are also capable of remarkable accuracy when assessing some everyday correlations. When discussing people's statistical reasoning, I noted that people are likely to reason statistically in familiar domains in which events are easy to code (Nisbett et al. 1983; see chapter 3). The same factors also facilitate covariation detection. Our estimates of correlations are most likely to be accurate when we are familiar with data that are highly codable, as suggested by a series of studies that Richard Nisbett and I conducted (Kunda and Nisbett 1986).

The studies compared people's assessments of correlations in several domains that varied in familiarity and codability to the actual correlations in those domains. The first set of studies examined perceptions of the degree of agreement among people on evaluations that varied in familiarity. Evaluations tend to be easy to code. When Jane tells me she likes Tom, the unit is clear (one person's evaluation), and the evaluation is relatively easy to score and to compare to my own evaluation of Tom. The expectation was that in such codable domains, people would be more accurate in their assessments of the covariation among evaluators the more familiar they were with the domain of evaluation.

People were remarkably accurate in their estimates of covariations in familiar domains. One such domain concerned the agreement among people in their assessments of others' personalities.

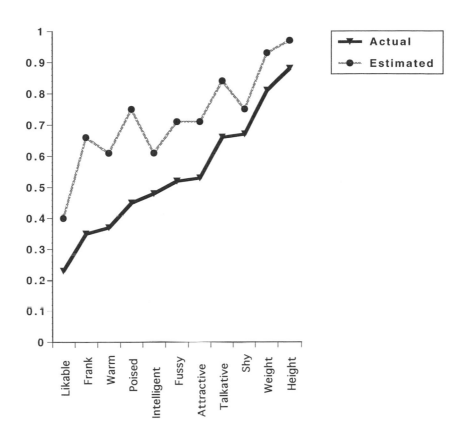

Figure 4.1 Actual and estimated agreement (*r*) among any two individuals about the attributes of other individuals. From Kunda and Nisbett (1986, fig. 2, p. 205). Copyright © (1986) by Academic Press. Reprinted with permission.

People spend a great deal of time discussing other people, and so are highly familiar with the extent to which they agree with others when evaluating different aspects of personality. We determined the actual level of agreement by asking sorority members to rate each other on a series of personal attributes such as likable, intelligent, and shy and calculating the average correlation among any two individuals on each attribute. Other participants estimated the magnitude of these correlations.

Figure 4.1 portrays the actual agreement among individuals (the solid line) and participants' estimates of the degree of agreement (the broken line). You may see that participants were quite accurate in their estimates of covariations in this highly codable and familiar domain. They knew, for example, that people are far more likely to agree with one another when evaluating their acquaintances' talkativeness than when evaluating their likability.

Undergraduates were less accurate in their estimates of agreement among psychologists in their evaluations of grant proposals submitted to funding agencies and of manuscripts submitted to professional journals, a domain with which they have no familiarity (and professional psychologists, who also have little familiarity with such agreement, did not fare much better). Taken together, these studies suggest that people may be quite inaccurate in their assessments of unfamiliar correlations but can also be quite accurate in their assessments of highly familiar correlations.

Familiarity, however, can only be an asset if the data are also codable, as discussed in chapter 3. Some familiar behaviors are very difficult to code. Behaviors that reflect abilities such as academic and athletic skills are both familiar and codable; they are easy to unitize (a unit may be a test or a game) and are also easy to score. In contrast, social behavior, although highly familiar, is far less codable. It is often unclear what constitutes a unit of behavior, and the behavior itself is often difficult to interpret. If codability facilitates accuracy, people should be more accurate in estimates of correlations in the domain of abilities than in the domain of personality traits.

In a study designed to examine this possibility, participants estimated the degree of consistency in people's behavior from one situation to another for two abilities, spelling and basketball, and for two traits, honesty and friendliness (Kunda and Nisbett 1986). In other words, they estimated the correlations between people's behavior in one situation and their behavior in another situation. Participants were quite accurate about correlations in the familiar and highly codable domain of ability. But they were quite inaccurate about the correlations in the equally familiar but less codable domain of personality; they vastly overestimated the consistency of social behavior from one situation to another. These data suggest that we think people are far more consistent than is the case. As a result we will often be surprised to find that people who seemed friendly, honest, or incompetent when we encountered them in one situation seem quite different when we encounter them in another situation. The implications of our inability to detect correlations in the social domain accurately will be discussed in greater detail in the chapter on our understanding of others (chapter 10).

Explanation-Based Judgment

Much of the research on hypothesis testing and covariation detection has assumed, implicitly or explicitly, that we make judgments by recruiting independent pieces of data—instances of extraverted and introverted behaviors, cases in which group membership and negative behaviors co-occurred. We then somehow add up or average the implications of the recruited instances by assessing their relative frequency or the ease with which they were recruited, to come up with our final judgment. Many of our judgments may indeed have this form. But many judgments require more complex causal reasoning. These may include the judgments made by jurors trying to determine a defendant's guilt or innocence, the judgments of medical scientists evaluating a new theory of disease, the judgments of foreign policy experts evaluating the likelihood of a stable peace in the Middle East, and your own evaluations of the likely outcome of your current romantic relationship. These and many other judgments may require elaborate causal analysis that draws on extensive world knowledge to relate different pieces of evidence to each other and to likely outcomes. As I noted when discussing concepts (chapter 2), many of our concepts are imbued with such causal knowledge (Murphy and Medin 1985).

Story Models in jury Decision Making

Consider the famous California trial in which celebrity O. J. Simpson was accused of murdering his ex-wife. Do you suppose that O. J. was guilty? If you followed the trial and formed an opinion about it, chances are you did more than adding up the number of incriminating pieces of evidence and comparing them to the number of exonerating pieces of evidence. More likely, you tried to choose among two accounts, or stories, that could explain and give meaning to all the relevant evidence. One story, put forth by the prosecution, held that O. J. was guilty as charged. This story included the information that he had a motive, a history of wife abuse, and an opportunity to commit the crime, and that a glove stained with the victim's blood was found in his yard. The alternative story, put forth by the defense, held that O. J., who is African American, was framed by racist police officers. This story included the information that a police officer had a history of racist behavior, that the police department was corrupt and incompetent, and that the bloodied glove did not fit O. J. Each piece of evidence brought up at the trial had a different meaning under the two stories. For example, the incriminating glove was either dropped by O. J. in his yard as he returned from the scene of the crime or planted there by a corrupt police officer. People following the trial were clearly trying to decide which of these stories could better account for the presented evidence, and their understanding and organization of the evidence was undoubtedly influenced by the story they came to prefer. In a series of elegant studies, Nancy Pennington and Reid Hastie demonstrated that such *story models* do indeed play a key role in jury decision making (Pennington and Hastie 1986, 1988, 1992).

In the first stage of their research, Pennington and Hastie showed that when people view a filmed trial from the perspective of a juror, they spontaneously construct stories about the events described at the trial (Pennington and Hastie 1986). Participants asked to talk about their thinking as they reached a verdict did not list a series of unrelated pieces of evidence. Rather, they described stories detailing what they thought had happened. A typical story contained a logical sequence of events (e.g., The defendant's girlfriend asked the victim for a ride. The defendant became angry and pulled a knife on the victim). Participants often inferred psychological states that were never directly mentioned in the trial but that helped make sense of events (e.g., the defendant was jealous). On the other hand, they often failed to mention evidence that was presented at the trial but that was not related to their stories. Participants reaching different verdicts constructed stories that differed dramatically in their chains of causal events (what led to what and why).

These initial findings suggested that jurors do arrive at their verdicts by constructing stories that make sense of the data. However, it also seemed possible that participants first arrived at their verdicts through some other cognitive process, and then constructed their stories later so as to justify their verdicts. This alternative account was ruled out by the next series of studies. Pennington and Hastie (1992) reasoned that if they could influence people's verdicts by manipulating the ease or difficulty with which one could construct the defense and prosecution stories *from the same evidence*, this would show that the verdicts were indeed based on the constructed stories.

All participants read the identical evidence about a murder trial. But this evidence was presented in different orders that affected the ease or difficulty of constructing the prosecution and the defense stories. A story was easy to construct when evidence pertaining to it was presented in a "story order" which preserved the causal and temporal sequence of events, starting, for example, with testimony about events that preceded the killing, followed by testimony about the fight that led to the killing, and ending with testimony about the arrest and autopsy. A story was difficult to construct when evidence was presented in a jumbled order that did not preserve the original sequence of events, going, for example, from testimony about the fight to testimony about the nature of the wound to testimony about events on the day before the fight.

All participants read the same evidence but in different orders: In one condition, the prosecution evidence was presented in story order and so was easy to construct, but the defense evidence was presented in a jumbled order and so was difficult to construct. In another condition, the defense evidence was presented in story order, but the prosecution evidence was presented in a jumbled order. This order manipulation had a dramatic impact on verdict decisions: When the prosecution story was easy to construct but the defense story difficult to construct, fully 78 percent of participants chose the guilty verdict. But when the prosecution story was difficult to construct and the defense story easy to construct, fewer than half as many participants, 31 percent, chose the guilty verdict. Two other conditions in which both stories were equally easy to construct or equally difficult to construct yielded intermediate levels of guilty verdicts. It is quite disturbing to realize that altering the order of evidence presentation without altering its content can more than double the likelihood that the defendant will be found guilty.

Clearly, we do not merely add up the independent implications of each piece of evidence to arrive at a verdict. Rather, we arrive at our verdict by constructing a story; factors that affect the relative ease of constructing alternative stories will also affect our verdicts.

Coherence of Explanations

The work on story models suggests that, when faced with alternative accounts of reality, we will choose the story that hangs together best, that is, the story that provides the most coherent explanation of all the relevant evidence. But how do we decide which explanation is most coherent? Philosopher of science Paul Thagard developed a theory of *explanatory coherence* that spells out the principles that determine the coherence of explanations (Thagard 1989).

Imagine that you are trying to explain why your girlfriend, Lisa, yelled at you at dinner. You are entertaining a couple of hypotheses: Perhaps she doesn't like you anymore, or perhaps she has had a rough day at work. Both of these hypotheses can explain Lisa's behavior toward you equally well. But you may still end up preferring one over the other based on how each relates to other information that you have about Lisa. Imagine that Lisa also seems tired and that you overheard her snapping at her mother on the phone. Both of these behaviors can be well explained by the fact that Lisa had a rough day at work, but not by the fact that she no longer likes you. This makes the rough-day hypothesis more plausible—it explains more of the evidence. More generally, we prefer those hypotheses that have greater *explanatory breadth*. As well, if you chose to believe that Lisa yelled at you because she doesn't like you, you would still have to find additional explanations for her tired appearance and for her rudeness to her mother. The rough-day explanation is simpler in that it provides a single explanation that can account for all of Lisa's behaviors. More generally, we prefer those hypotheses that have greater *simplicity*, that is, require fewer additional hypotheses or assumptions to account for the full range of evidence.

Now imagine that you know that Lisa has been working extra hard over the last few weeks because several of her coworkers have been laid off. This provides an explanation for why Lisa might have had a rough day at work and makes this hypothesis all the more plausible. More generally, we prefer those hypotheses that can be *explained* by other information. As the rough-day hypothesis becomes more plausible, the she-doesn't-like-me hypothesis seems less likely. More generally, our evaluation of competing hypotheses is *comparative*; increasing the plausibility of one hypothesis reduces the plausibility of its alternative.

In sum, our faith in a hypothesis increases with its explanatory breadth, its simplicity, and the extent to which it, in turn, can be explained by other information. As our faith in one hypothesis increases, our faith in competing hypotheses decreases.

Thagard (1989) constructed a computer program that embodies these and several additional principles of explanatory coherence and applies them jointly to evaluate the coherence of competing explanations. This program was able to successfully simulate a diverse array of judgments, ranging from scientists' preferences for competing scientific theories to jurors' preference for the defense and prosecution stories. The finding that the program "favors" the same explanations favored by scientists and jurors suggests that the theory provides a plausible model of human judgment.

Steven Read and Amy Marcus-Newhall (1993) took this work a step further by showing that people follow these principles of coherence when trying to explain social behavior. Read and Marcus-Newhall constructed scenarios that included many facts about an individual—behaviors, thoughts, desires, social circumstances—and asked participants to evaluate several explanations for these facts. In different studies the competing explanations differed in the number of facts they could explain, the number of additional assumptions they required, and in whether or not they themselves could be explained. Participants preferred those explanations that were broader, simpler, and that could be explained. In addition, their evaluations of competing explanations were comparative: Increasing the coherence of one explanation reduced the plausibility of alternative explanations. Moreover, the computer program developed by Thagard to simulate judgments of explanatory coherence favored the same explanations that the experimental participants had favored. This successful simulation of empirical results lends support to the notion that the principles of coherence used by the program are also used by us.

The question of how people explain social behavior has always been of central concern to social psychology. Much of the work on attribution has focused on how people choose between two competing explanations of behavior—was the behavior due to the actor's underlying personality or due to the situation? (for a review, see Jones 1990; see also chapter 9). The work on explanatory coherence provides guidelines for determining which of these competing explanations people will find most plausible under different circumstances (Read and Miller 1993; Thagard 1989). This work also permits addressing some important questions that have received little attention from attribution theorists: How do we choose among competing dispositional explanations (Did Jonathan smile because he is friendly or because he is manipulative?) or among competing situational explanations (Is Ellie misbehaving because she is under the influence of bad friends or because her parents have been neglecting her?).

The implications of the work on explanatory coherence to Pennington and Hastie's (1986) story model of juror decision making are obvious. The principles of coherence can help determine which story will seem most plausible to jurors. Others have suggested that, just as we construct elaborate stories to explain a defendant's actions, we may also construct stories or person models of individuals we encounter in other circumstances (Park, DeKay, and Kraus 1994). You may construct elaborate stories to explain why a friend's marriage broke up, why an acquaintance has failed to hold a steady job, or why your fifth-grade teacher never liked you. Different people may construct very different models of the same individual or event, especially if they hold different theories about the nature of the social world. The principles of explanatory coherence may be used to determine which person models people are likely to favor.

So far, I have discussed how people determine the nature of their past and present realities. I turn next to consideration of alternatives to these actual realities, namely counterfactual ones.

Counterfactual Thinking

In the Jewish tradition there is a special prayer, *Hagomel*, used by survivors of serious accidents, grave illnesses, wars, and any other life-threatening events to thank God for sparing their lives. Why do people who have just experienced such a misfortune, and who are often still suffering injury and loss, nevertheless feel thankful and fortunate? We may feel lucky after narrowly escaping disaster because it is so easy to imagine a more disastrous ending for the same incident. We cannot escape the thought that if events had unfolded only slightly differently, we would have surely died. When things do turn out disastrously, on the other hand, we may be haunted and tormented by thoughts about how easily disaster could have been avoided. Many events lead us to generate such *counterfactual outcomes,* that is, outcomes that run contrary to what had actually happened, outcomes that might have, could have, perhaps should have happened but did not. The counterfactuals that we generate in response to an event can influence our understanding of that event and our emotional reactions to it.

Event Normality

Some counterfactuals are easier to imagine than others (Kahneman and Tversky 1982). Imagine, for example, that after spending thirty unlucky minutes at a slot machine, you finally quit, several dollars in the hole. Another person steps up to the machine you have just vacated and, on the first try, hits the jackpot, winning ten thousand dollars. Chances are that you will feel more frustrated and disappointed than any of the other nonwinners present because it is so much easier for you to imagine that you had hit the jackpot; if only you had inserted just one more coin. . . .

Daniel Kahneman and Dale Miller (1986) termed events that can easily be imagined otherwise *abnormal*. They proposed that each event evokes a *norm* that reflects prior expectancies about it as well as the counterfactual thoughts that it gives rise to—how the event was expected to unfold and how it seems, after the fact, that it might have unfolded. The more an event deviates from its evoked norm, the more abnormal it will seem. Events can differ in their normality even if they do not differ in their prior likelihoods, if they give rise to different counterfactuals. In the slot-machine example, your prior odds of hitting the jackpot were no different from anyone else's; yet failure to hit the jackpot seems more abnormal for you because the counterfactual can be generated more readily for you than for anyone else.

The more abnormal an event seems, the stronger one's emotional reaction to it. That is why you are more disappointed than other people who have also failed to win the jackpot, even though you have all experienced similar outcomes. Moreover, we are often aware that some events might be particularly regrettable; *anticipatory regret* can lead us to avoid actions that might lead to such events. For example, most people (90 percent) agree to exchange a pen for an identical pen plus a small amount of money. After all, a pen plus money is better than just a pen. Yet, when given the same exchange offer, but this time with lottery tickets instead of pens, much fewer (less than 50 percent) are willing to make the exchange (Bar-Hillel and Neter 1996). Most likely, we are reluctant to exchange lottery tickets because we know we will want to kick ourselves if our forgone ticket turns out to be the winning one. Knowing that we might have won, if only we had kept our ticket, makes not winning appear highly abnormal and so most regrettable.

But what governs these judgments of normality? Why are some counterfactuals easier to imagine than others? We do not yet have a complete answer to this question, but some determinants of counterfactual thought have been uncovered, as discussed next.

Closeness of the Counterfactual to the Actual Event   Consider the following scenario (Kahneman and Tversky 1982):

Mr. Crane and Mr. Tees were scheduled to leave the airport on different flights, at the same time. They traveled from town in the same limousine, were caught in a traffic jam, and arrived at the airport 30 minutes after the scheduled departure time of their flights.
Mr. Crane is told that his flight left on time.
Mr. Tees is told that his flight was delayed, and just left five minutes ago.
Who is more upset? Mr. Crane or Mr. Tees?

Most people reading this scenario (96 percent) have a strong intuition that Mr. Tees, who had missed his flight by only five minutes, would be more upset. But why should he be? After all, his objective situation is no different from that of Mr. Crane; both are stranded at the airport. The answer lies in the availability of counterfactuals: It is easier for Mr. Tees than for Mr. Crane to imagine that he could have made his flight. The counterfactual, making the flight, seems closer to what had actually happened for Mr. Tees than for Mr. Crane. As a result Mr. Tees's fate seems more abnormal and so more regrettable.

What determines closeness? Miller, Turnbull, and McFarland (1990) speculated that we construct *mental models* of events that include causal information about how different factors could influence possible outcomes. Our model of driving to the airport might include the information that we could be delayed by red traffic lights or by road construction and could make up time through faster driving. A counterfactual seems close to an actual event if we need to make only a small number of modifications to our model of the actual event so as to arrive at the counterfactual. It is relatively easier for Mr. Tees to imagine how he could have arrived five minutes earlier (if only the driver had gone a little faster!), or how his plane could have left five minutes later, because closing a five-minute gap requires fewer hypothetical modifications to actual events than does closing a twenty-five-minute gap. Much of the research on counterfactual reasoning has focused on determining why some aspects of events are more *mutable*, that is, more easy to undo mentally, than others.

Although such causal reasoning may play an important role in determining closeness, counterfactuals may also appear closer to actual events through sheer proximity, even when they are not causally closer. For example, if the number on your lottery ticket differs by only one digit from the winning number, you will probably be more disappointed than someone with a radically different number, even though judgments of the closeness of the counterfactual to the actual numbers are not based on causal factors (Turnbull 1981). Recall that when discussing concepts, I concluded that the closeness of category members to each other can be based on a combination of causal relations and perceptual similarities (see chapter 2); the same appears to be true for the closeness of actual events to their alternative counterfactuals (see Roese and Olson 1995).

The missed-airplane scenario suggests that the availability of a close counterfactual can increase the regret and disappointment that one feels after experiencing a bad outcome. It can also affect observers' reactions to victims, and judgments about victim compensation. In one study participants read about someone who had died from exposure after surviving a plane crash in a remote area and were asked how much compensation should be given to the victim's family. Some participants read that the victim had died within 75 miles of safety, others that he had died within a 1/4 mile of safety. It is easy to imagine how the "close" victim, who had almost made it to safety, might have actually made it. Therefore his death seems more abnormal than that of the "distant" victim and so arouses more sympathy. Indeed, participants reading that the victim had been close to safety awarded more compensation to his family than did participants reading that he had been further from safety (Miller and McFarland 1986).

In these studies, people who have experienced or observed identical negative outcomes feel worse if they can generate positive counterfactuals more readily. More surprisingly, even people who are objectively better off than others can feel worse if they can imagine a still more positive outcome more readily. Consider the bronze and silver medalists at an Olympic competition; who do you suppose is happier? In such competitions there is a qualitative difference between the gold medalist and everyone else; only the gold medalist has won the competition, attained glory, and can expect lucrative commercial endorsements. The silver medalist in such a competition has come closer to winning gold than has the bronze medalist, and so is more likely to be tormented by thoughts of what might have happened. In contrast, the bronze medalist has come dangerously close to winning nothing at all, and may therefore be especially pleased at having avoided this misfortune. If the silver medalist is upset because "I could have won gold" whereas the bronze medalist is gratified because "At least I won a medal," the silver medalist may feel less happy than the bronze medalist, despite being objectively better off.

Medvec, Madey, and Gilovich (1995) tested these ideas in a series of studies. From TV coverage of the 1992 Summer Olympic games, they created two master videotapes. One portrayed the immediate reactions of all televised bronze and silver medalists at the time they had learned how they had done (e.g., as a swimmer touched the wall of the pool and learned that he had come in second, as an athlete completed her last long jump and realized she had won a bronze medal). The second videotape showed athletes as they stood on the medal stand during the award ceremony. Twenty students watched these videotapes without sound, and rated the athletes' apparent happiness. For both tapes, winners of bronze medals were rated as happier than winners of silver medals. Were silver medalists less happy because they were more likely than bronze medalist to be tormented by the notion that they had almost won gold? Most probably, yes. Analysis of the responses of Olympic medalists in televised interviews as well as the self-ratings of athletes in a prominent amateur competition revealed that silver medalists were more likely than bronze medalists to voice the thought that they had almost done better.

Similar reactions can be observed in students receiving test results. As many professors and students know, it can be very upsetting to find out that you have missed making an A by just one point. When this happens, you might be considerably less happy than another student who has gotten the same grade as you, but with a score that is several points lower than yours and so not as infuriatingly close to an A (Medvec and Savitsky 1997). Apparently, people who are objectively better off can feel worse than others who had not done as well because they are tormented by the even better result that they had come so close to achieving.

Exception versus Routine A friend once canceled a long-anticipated trip to Israel after a highly publicized terrorist attack there. Yet he was on his way to New York City, even though he believed that the streets of New York were considerably more dangerous than the streets of Tel-Aviv! He explained that traveling to New York was a normal, routine activity for him; the entailed risks seemed par for the course. In contrast, he was sure that his wife would never forgive him if got killed by terrorists in Israel. Traveling to Israel was a highly exceptional event for him and, as such, one that could be readily avoided. Therefore, if anything went wrong there, he knew he would be held more blameworthy. Research suggests that his intuitions about his wife's likely reactions were probably correct. People are more upset by negative outcomes when these result from exceptional behavior than they are when the identical outcomes result from routine behavior.

To illustrate this, Kahneman and Tversky (1982) created a scenario describing the events leading to a fatal car accident in which Mr. Jones was killed on his way home from work. In one version, Mr. Jones left work at the regular time but took an unusual route home to enjoy the view along the shore. In another version, he left work unusually early to do some chores but took his regular route home. Participants were asked how they thought Mr. Jones' family would complete "If only ..." sentences. Participants were more likely to undo the exceptional event ("If only he had left at his regular time," "If only he had taken his normal route") than they were to undo the routine events; attempts to undo routine events ("If only he had left earlier that day") were quite rare. Another scenario study showed that people also felt that someone involved in a car accident while taking an unusual route home would be more upset than someone involved in a similar accident while taking the normal route home (Kahneman and Miller 1986). The tendency to undo exceptional rather than routine events is particularly strong when the events lead to exceptional outcomes (Gavanski and Wells 1989).

The tendency to view misfortunes that follow exceptional events as particularly regrettable influences the compensation awarded to victims of such misfortunes. In one study, people read the identical description of a man injured in a robbery. In one condition, the robbery took place in a store that he went to regularly and, in another condition, it took place in a store that he did not usually go to. Participants recommended much more compensation (over $100,000 more) when the person was injured at an unusual location than when he was injured at a normal location, even though the remaining circumstances that led to the injury were identical (Miller and McFarland 1986). It seems that people find exceptional events easier to undo and therefore view them as more regrettable.

People also find the actions of exceptional individuals easier to undo than those of more "normal" individuals. Consider the gender gap that has characterized the voting patterns of Americans in the past few presidential elections: Women have been more likely than men to favor the Democratic candidate, whereas men have been more likely than women to favor the Republican candidate. Miller, Taylor, and Buck (1991) noticed that media discussions of this gender gap tended to focus on trying to explain and undo women's preference. Pundits often wondered why the Democratic candidate was so appealing to women and the Republican one so unappealing to them, or noted that if only women felt more like men, the Democrat would not have as strong a lead over the Republican. There was a remarkable lack of attempts to explain and undo the other half of the gender gap, namely men. Reporters were not wondering why the Democrat was unappealing to men, or bemoaning the fact that men were not more like women.

Miller and his colleagues proposed that this disparity occurred because men are viewed as more typical voters than are women. Because women are more atypical in this context, their actions are more mutable. A series of studies supported these ideas. In categories where men were considered more typical than women— voters, college professors—people were more likely to explain gender gaps in terms of the relatively atypical women than in terms of the more typical men, and tended to mentally undo the gap by changing the actions of women. For example, they were more likely to explain the gender gap in voting preference by using women-centered explanations (e.g., Women believe that the Democrat is more concerned with women's issues) than by using men-centered explanations (e.g., Men believe the Republican will spend more money on defense). But people do not always explain gender gaps in terms of women. When faced with a gender gap in a category for which women are more typical than men—elementary school teachers—people were more likely to explain this gap in terms of the more atypical men than in terms of the relatively typical women, and tended to mentally undo the gap by changing the behavior of men rather than that of women. It appears that like exceptional events, exceptional individuals are more mutable than normal, typical ones. In both cases we attempt to undo outcomes by mentally replacing exceptional occurrences with more normal ones.

Controllability The scenario described earlier, in which Mr. Jones was killed in a car accident, also included the information that the accident was caused by the other driver, a teen-aged boy who was under the influence of drugs. Although the drugged teen-ager was clearly responsible for the accident, few of the respondents asked to imagine how Mr. Jones' relatives would complete "If only ..." statements did so by removing the boy from the scene of the accident. Instead, they focused mostly on imagining how Mr. Jones could have behaved differently (Kahneman and Tversky 1982). A similar pattern of counterfactuals was observed among bereaved people who had actually lost a loved one in accidents caused by a drunken driver. The majority of bereaved individuals reported engaging in thoughts that mentally undid the outcome. Yet not one of them attempted to undo the outcome by removing the drunken driver from the scene; instead they focused on what they or their loved one could have done differently (Davis et al. 1995).

These findings suggest that people attempt to undo actions that are under the control of the individual they are focusing on. When focusing on the victim of a crime, we tend to presuppose the actions of the perpetrator, which become part of the immutable background, and we attempt to undo the victim's actions (Kahneman and Miller 1986). That may be why victims are often blamed for their misfortunes (Lerner and Miller 1978). It is interesting that people generate quite different counterfactuals when they are asked to focus on the perpetrator. When participants who had read the Mr. Jones scenario were asked to complete "If only ..." statements on behalf of the relatives of the drugged boy, most did so by removing the boy, rather than Mr. Jones, from the scene of the accident (Kahneman and Tversky 1982). A disturbing implication of these findings is that the more one identifies and emphasizes with a victim, the more likely one is to contemplate how the victim might have behaved otherwise and therefore to blame the victim (Kahneman and Miller 1986).

Further evidence that actions are more mutable when they are controllable comes from lab studies that found that, when attempting to undo the outcome of a game, people chose to undo those aspects of the game over which they had more control (Markman et al. 1995). Controllable actions may be particularly mutable because it is easy to imagine that the person might have chosen to behave otherwise.

Action versus Inaction   Consider the following scenario (Kahneman and Miller 1986):

Mr. Paul owns shares in company A. During the past year he considered switching to stock in company B, but decided against it. He now finds that he would have been better off by $1,200 if he had switched to the stock of company B. Mr. George owned shares in company B. During the past year he switched to stock in company A. He now finds that he would have been better off by $1,200 if he had kept his stock in company B.
Who is more upset? Mr. Paul or Mr. George?

Almost everyone reading this scenario (92 percent) believes that Mr. George, who suffered loss through his own action, would feel more regret than Mr. Paul, who suffered the same loss through inaction. Mr. George seems far more likely to be tormented by thoughts such as, "I could have avoided this loss" and "If only I had behaved otherwise...." Kahneman and Miller suggested that action is more regrettable than inaction because it is easier to undo action by mentally erasing it than it is to undo inaction by mentally adding the action not taken (Gleicher et al. 1990; Landman 1987). It seems that inaction is taken to be the norm, or default. Action is more abnormal and so more readily undone and more regrettable.

Because we have such strong intuitions that we are more likely to want to kick ourselves in self-recrimination when our actions lead to misfortune than when inaction leads to the same misfortune, we may sometimes avoid taking risky action so as to avoid subsequent regret. An elegant demonstration that such *anticipatory regret* can guide behavioral choices was described by Miller and Taylor (1995). They created a simulated game of Black Jack. In this game, you and the dealer are each dealt a series of cards, and their face values are added up. You win if you come closer than the dealer to 21 but lose, or bust, if you go over 21. You are first dealt two cards and need to decide whether you wish to request more. When your first two cards add up to 18 or more, you should clearly stay with what you have and not request more cards to avoid busting. And when your first two cards add up to 10 or less, you should clearly request another card. But the decision is far more difficult when your first two cards add up to 16; 16 is low enough that the dealer will probably come closer to 21, but high enough that you will probably bust if you get another card. In this situation anticipatory regret comes into play. Miller and Taylor reasoned that people may be particularly reluctant to ask for another card in this case (even when they are objectively more likely to win if they do) because they know that if they ask for another card and bust, they will want to kick themselves; such a loss, through one's own action, is expected to be more painful than losing through failure to act.

But what if things were framed such that obtaining another card was the normal default, and people had to actively request that they be given no more cards when they wanted no more? Miller and Taylor reasoned that in this situation, losing through action would still seem more regrettable than through inaction, but this time the regrettable action would be blocking the additional card, that is, staying with one's initial ones. To test these ideas, they devised a computer simulation of Black Jack in which requesting another card was framed either as an action or as an inaction. In the action version, participants were asked on each trial whether or not they wanted to hit, that is, receive another card. To obtain one, they had to respond "yes." In the inaction version, participants were asked instead whether or not they wanted to stand, that is, receive no more cards. To obtain another card, they had to respond "no." The prediction was that people would expect busting through their own action to cause more regret than busting through inaction. Therefore, when their first two cards added up to 16, they would be less likely to request another card when such a request was framed as an action than when the same request was framed as inaction. That is exactly what happened.

These and similar studies have suggested that people regret and anticipate regretting actions more than inactions. However, Gilovich and Medvec (1994, 1995) observed that the very opposite pattern is obtained when people look back on their lives. When we are asked to describe our biggest regrets in life we are most likely to relate things we have failed to do: "I wish I had worked harder in college," "I wish I had spent more time with my children," "I wish I had pursued the woman I loved." Indeed, adults asked to report their biggest regrets in life reported almost twice as many failures to act (63 percent) than actions (37 percent). The most commonly regretted inactions were missed educational opportunities, failure to "seize the moment," and failure to spend enough time with friends and family. Many people regretted not pursuing interests such as golf or stamp collections; none regretted wasting time on such interests, reinforcing the point that, when looking back on our lives, it is our failures to act that we regret, not our actions.

How can this tendency to regret our lifelong failures to act be reconciled with the experimental results suggesting that we regret our actions more than our inactions? Gilovich and Medvec proposed that the pattern of regret we experience depends on the passage of time: In the short term our actions seem most regrettable, but in the long run our failures to act cause us the most grief. Several studies lend support to this analysis (Gilovich and Medvec 1994). In one, people were asked to recall their single most regrettable action and inaction from the past week and from their entire lives. Then, for each time period, they indicated which they regretted more, the action or the inaction. When considering their lifelong regrets, most people (84 percent) found their inaction more regrettable than their action. But when considering their more short-term regrets, pertaining to the past week, much fewer people (47 percent) regretted their inaction more than their action. In short, actions were regretted most in the short term, inactions in the long run.

People seem to be aware of this temporal pattern of regret. In another study, participants read about two unhappy students who were considering transferring to another school. Ultimately, one decided to transfer and the other decided to stay where he was, and the decision turned out badly for both; both remained unhappy. Most participants (76 percent) believed that the person who had transferred, and therefore had experienced misfortune through his own action, would feel greater regret over the short term. However, most (63 percent) believed that the person who had failed to act and had stayed where he was would experience greater regret over the long run. In short, even when considering the same pair of action and inaction, the action is expected to provoke greater regret in the short term, but the inaction is expected to cause more pain after some time has elapsed.

Why do we experience this temporal shift in the pattern of our regrets over actions and inactions? Gilovich and Medvec (1995) proposed several reasons. We may find failures to act particularly disturbing as they recede into the past because often, in retrospect, we are unable to understand why we had failed to act. Obstacles that loomed large at the time no longer seem so insurmountable when we look back at our lives. In one study demonstrating that obstacles may recede over time, current Cornell students felt that adding a challenging course to their workload would have a considerable negative impact on their lives; it would lower their grades, reduce the amount of sloop they got, diminish the quality of their social lives. Yet Cornell alumni assessing how adding such a course would have affected them in a typical semester thought the impact would have been relatively trivial (Gilovich, Kerr, and Medvec 1993). In retrospect, we think we could have handled with ease tasks that at the time seemed all but impossible. As time passes, regret over inaction becomes intensified because the failure to act becomes inexplicable; today we cannot understand what stopped us back then from approaching that attractive person, what prevented us from getting a better education.

Another reason why inactions become more regrettable than actions as time passes is that it is easier to determine and deal with the consequences of our actions (Gilovich and Medvec 1995). We know where the road we have chosen has led us. And, when our actions have brought about bad consequences, we have often dealt with these through corrective action (e.g., quitting an unpleasant job) or corrective thought (maybe things are not all that bad). But the road untaken remains shrouded in mystery. We will never know how wonderful the missed romance might have been, or how satisfying the missed career opportunity. Therefore, we may continue to be haunted by missed opportunities whose promise is bounded only by our imagination.

Ease of Replicating Events Mentally   So far I have discussed ways in which events become less normal if it is easy to mentally undo them. Events may also become more normal if it is easier to *mentally replicate* them, that is, to imagine other ways in which the same event might have happened (Miller, Turnbull, and McFarland 1989). To illustrate this point, imagine that you have a child who loves chocolate chip cookies. You buy packages that contain chocolate chip as well as oatmeal cookies, and your child typically takes only the chocolate chip ones, leaving the oatmeal ones to go stale. To avoid this, you instruct your child to go to the cookie jar, close his eyes, and take whichever cookie he grabs. A moment later, your child reports happily that he has followed your instructions, and just happened to get a chocolate chip cookie. How suspicious are you that the kid had peeked into the jar before selecting the cookie?

Your level of suspicion will most likely be influenced by your knowledge of your child. It may also be influenced by your knowledge of the contents of the cookie jar; you might be more suspicious if only a small percentage of the cookies were chocolate chip than if most were. Miller and his colleagues proposed that your suspicion may also be influenced by another factor. Consider two slightly different versions of the scenario. In one, the cookie jar contains 1 chocolate chip cookie and 19 oatmeal ones. In the other version, it contains 10 chocolate chip cookies and 190 oatmeal ones. How suspicious would you be in each case? In both, the percentage of chocolate chip cookies is identical, 5 percent, and people know this. Yet participants reading that there was only 1 chocolate chip cookie in a jar of 20 were more suspicious than those reading that there were 10 chocolate chip cookies in a jar of 200!

This finding suggests that the extent to which we are suspicious that the chocolate chip cookie was not selected through chance is influenced not only by the prior probability of selecting a chocolate chip cookie but also by its normality. When there are 10 different chocolate chip cookies, there are 10 possible ways of selecting one.

But when there is only one such cookie, there is only a single way of selecting a chocolate chip one, and therefore its selection is more abnormal.

The ease of replicating events mentally can also affect judgments of fairness and of foul play in situations that do not involve random draws. In another study by Miller and his colleagues, participants read about a supervisor who had been accused in the past of discriminating against women (Miller et al. 1989). The supervisor gives all candidates for promotion an exam, grades it, and reports that the highest mark was obtained by a man. Participants read one of two identical versions of this scenario that differed only in the absolute number of men and women who had taken the exam. In one version, the exam was taken by 1 man and 9 women. In the other, it was taken by 10 men and 90 women. Participants were more suspicious that the supervisor had graded the exams unfairly when the highest mark went to the only man in a group of 10 than when it went to one of the 10 men in a group of 100. Once again, it appears that suspicion is governed not only by the prior probability of selecting a man, which was identical in both case, but also by normality. When there were 10 men, there were 10 different ways in which a man could have achieved the highest mark. But when there was only one man, there was only a single route through which a man could be selected; therefore the selection of a man was more abnormal and gave rise to greater suspicion.

Functions of Counterfactual Thoughts

I have described many examples of counterfactual thoughts that give rise to regret and self-recrimination. We are often haunted and tormented by thoughts about how things might have turned out better; how fatal accidents might have been avoided, how failed opportunities could have been seized upon. Why do people engage in thoughts that make them miserable? We do not have a complete answer to this question. But part of the answer may lie in the possibility that, miserable as such thoughts make us, they also serve a useful function. Through thinking about how misfortune might have been avoided, we may identify the causes and circumstances that led to the misfortune and be better prepared to deal with such circumstances in the future (Wells and Gavansky 1989). The distressing thought that "If only I had left home earlier I would have made my flight" highlights what we need to do to avoid similar misfortunes in the future and thereby helps ensure that we will not find ourselves in the same predicament again. Counterfactual thoughts are particularly likely to be triggered when we are feeling badly; they may provoke us into action that will ameliorate the negative affect as well as action that will prevent the recurrence of the misfortune that had given rise to that affect (for reviews, see Gleicher et al. 1995; Roese 1997; Roese and Olson 1995, 1997).

There is some evidence that entertaining thoughts about how bad outcomes could have been avoided can serve to prevent such outcomes in the future (Roese 1994). In one study, students were asked to recall a recent exam on which they had done poorly. Some students were then asked to generate counterfactuals describing how they could have done better, and some were not. Generating these counterfactuals made students see themselves as more likely to engage in behaviors that could improve their academic performance, such as studying their notes frequently and attending all lectures. Imagining how we could have avoided our past failures can motivate us to do what it takes to avoid similar failures in the future. Counterfactuals that make us unhappy in the short term can nevertheless prove useful in the long run.

Other counterfactuals may help us feel better in bad situations, when we imagine how things could have been even worse (e.g., Roese 1994). This too can be a useful function.

Unfortunately, not all counterfactuals serve such useful purpose (see Sherman and McConnell 1995). What use is there in contemplating how one should have spent more time with one's children while they were young, when they have long since grown up? Or in imagining how one might have chosen a better career, when one has already retired? (Though others who are willing to listen might benefit from such misgivings). There is even less use in musing over how we might have won the lottery if our number had differed by just one digit; such musings do not highlight any causal factors, nor do they help us increase our odds of winning in the future. Yet they force themselves upon us with undeniable strength.

Summary

When testing hypotheses, people rely on the *positive-test strategy* which entails seeking cases that match the hypothesis. People use this strategy both when searching their memories for preexisting knowledge and when searching the external world for evidence that bears on the hypothesis. When the evidence base being searched is mixed, containing information that confirms the hypothesis as well as disconfirming information, use of the one-sided positive-test strategy can bias people toward confirming their hypotheses. Because information about the social world is typically mixed and inconsistent, we may often be biased toward confirming any hypothesis we entertain about our own or other people's attributes.

We also rely on the positive test-strategy when assessing covariations among variables. We may pay special attention to those cases that match our hypotheses about what correlates with what, and so overestimate the magnitude of the hypothesized covariation. When we have a strong prior theory that one variable is correlated with another, we may "see" illusory correlations that do not actually exist in the data, because we are especially likely to notice and remember cases that embody the theorized correlation. Other factors, such as distinctiveness, that increase the salience and memorability of particular co-occurrences of events can also give rise to illusory correlations. Because members of minority groups who perform unusual behaviors are especially distinctive, people may form illusory correlations between group membership and the unusual behavior. On other occasions we may fail to detect real but unexpected correlations. Despite these shortcomings people can detect many everyday correlations with impressive accuracy. We are especially likely to be accurate about correlations in domains such as sports that are both highly familiar and easy to code. Unfortunately, social behavior, though familiar, is typically difficult to code. We may therefore be especially prone to "seeing" illusory correlations and failing to see actual ones in the social domain.

When we test more complex hypotheses about individuals, such as a defendant's likely guilt, we construct elaborate "stories" about the events in question and select the one that seems most coherent. In general, we follow reasonable principles when evaluating the coherence of accounts, preferring those that explain more evidence, those that require fewer additional assumptions, and those that can be explained by other information. Nevertheless, irrelevant factors, such as the order with which we encounter information, which influence the ease with which we can construct a particular account can also influence our judgments.

Many events lead us to generate *counterfactual* outcomes that can influence our understanding of the event and our emotional reactions to it. Events that can be easily imagined otherwise seem *abnormal*, and the more abnormal they seem, the stronger our emotional reactions to them. An event seems more abnormal if our model of it is very *close* to a model of an alternative, counterfactual event; if only a few things had been different, the outcome would have been quite different. When the close counterfactual is more positive than what actually happened we may feel especially upset about having failed to achieve it, and when the close counterfactual is more negative than what actually happened, we may feel especially gratified about having narrowly missed it. We are also especially likely to generate counterfactuals and to experience regret when confronted with *exceptional* rather than ordinary behavior or individuals, and when we believe that the individuals we are focusing on were able to exercise *control* over the events. When we contemplate events that resulted from *action or inaction*, our emotional reactions depend on the passage of time. Actions provoke greater regret in the short term, but inaction provokes greater regret over the long run. The counterfactual thoughts that we generate in response to events influence our emotional reactions to these events, and also color our judgments about issues such as blame, appropriate compensation to victims of misfortune, and the likelihood that foul play had contributed to the event.

The movie *The Assault* (1986) describes the struggles of a man plagued by traumatic memories. The opening scenes of the movie portray the traumatic incident as it unfolds: During one awful night at the end of World War II Anton, a little Dutch boy in the Nazi-occupied Netherlands, witnesses the events that lead to the execution of his parents and brother by the Nazis. The remainder of the movie shows Anton, now a grown man and a successful physician, striving to make sense of these events. Gradually he remembers different scenes from that dreadful night: The fateful actions of his neighbors, the argument between his brother and his parents, the words of the woman with whom he had spent the rest of the night in a dark prison cell. These recalled scenes are portrayed as replays of the events shown early on; Anton recalls the events *exactly as they had originally taken place*. In this chapter I will show that, Hollywood to the contrary not withstanding, memory is nothing like a replay of a well-preserved movie. We do *not* recall events exactly as they had happened. Rather, we *reconstruct* our memories of events as well as of the circumstances in which we came by these memories. Our recollections are shaped by the way we had processed events as they were occurring as well as by our current understanding of events, our current goals and moods, and many other factors. Rather than replaying old movies in our mind's eye, we use the past and the present to construct new ones.

State of Mind When Encoding Events

Our state of mind at the time we observe events, as we encode them and store them in memory, may affect how we later recall these events. We may be particularly likely to recall those events that we had paid special attention to as they occurred, for whatever reason. The way we recall events later will be influenced by the way we had initially interpreted them.

Expectancies and Interpretation

We often approach people and events with prior expectancies. These may arise from concepts such as stereotypes; you may expect Laura to be warm and supportive because you know she is a social worker. Expectancies may arise from other sources as well; you may harbor these expectations about Laura because I have told you that she is warm and supportive, or because she has behaved warmly toward you in the past. Whatever their source, the expectancies that you bring to your encounter with Laura may influence your subsequent recollections of this encounter.

Your expectancies may determine the very meaning you ascribe to Laura's behaviors as you observe them, especially if these are ambiguous and can be understood in more than one way. You may understand the same smile as reflecting warmth when you expect Laura to be warm, but as reflecting arrogant self-satisfaction when you expect her to be cold (Kelley 1950). Numerous studies have shown that expectancies can guide the interpretation of behavior. For example, the same act of crying may be viewed as an expression of sadness when observed at a funeral, but as an expression of joy when observed at a wedding (Trope 1986), and the same responses to a test may be viewed as a strong performance when the child taking the test is believed to come from a high socioeconomic background, but as a mediocre performance when she is believed to come from a low socioeconomic background (Darley and Gross 1983); I discussed this point when describing the functions of concepts (see chapter 1), and will discuss it again when describing the consequences of stereotypes (see chapter 8) and our knowledge about others (see chapter 9).

For now, the important point is that our initial understanding of events will determine the way we later remember them. Once we know enough about Laura's behavior to infer that she is warm, we will be able to retrieve this trait, warmth, independently, without having to retrieve the behaviors on which it had been based (Sherman and Klein 1994). Moreover, with the passage of time, we may come to forget the specific behavioral details we had observed, and recall only their gist, that is, the meaning we had imposed on them (e.g., Schul 1983). Rather than remembering that Laura walked toward us with a big smile on her face and hugged us, we may recall only that she behaved warmly. Once this happens, it will be impossible for us to retrieve any details that could, in retrospect, lend different meaning to an observed behavior.

Expectancies and Attention

Even when events have clear meaning and are not open to multiple construals, our expectancies can still influence our memory by directing the amount of attention we devote to different aspects of reality as we observe it and by determining how new information is linked to existing knowledge.

Expectancy-Congruent Information   You may be particularly likely to notice information that is congruent with your expectancies; if you expect Laura to be warm, you may pay special attention to her warm behaviors. As a result you will be especially likely to recall these in the future. You may be most vulnerable to such effects when stressed or aroused (Jamieson and Zanna 1989). Reliance on the positive-test strategy can cause people to pay special attention to events that match their hypotheses and expectations and, thereby, can increase the memorability of these events. The increased memorability of congruent events can lead people to overestimate the extent to which the information they have observed supports their hypotheses (Klayman and Ha 1987; see chapter 4). In a similar vein, people may come to believe in illusory correlations because they pay special attention to cases that embody those correlations that they expect to see. For example, if you believe that Asian Americans are especially good at math, you may be especially likely to pay attention to any Asian American math whiz you encounter. Thanks to the increased attention they receive, such individuals, who embody the correlation you expect to find, will later be particularly memorable, leading you to overestimate their frequency (Garcia-Marques and Hamilton 1996; Chapman and Chapman 1967, 1969; see chapter 4).

Numerous studies have shown more directly that expectancies can increase the memorability of information that matches them (for reviews, see Higgins and Bargh 1987; Olson, Roese, and Zanna 1996; Stangor and McMillan 1992). For example, in one study, participants watched a videotape of a woman interacting with her husband (Cohen 1981). Before viewing the video, half the participants were told that the woman was a librarian, and half that she was a waitress. The video portrayed many of the woman's attributes and behaviors. Of these, some were consistent with the stereotype of librarians but inconsistent with the stereotype of waitresses (e.g., wears glasses, listens to classical music). Other attributes were consistent for waitresses but inconsistent for librarians (e.g., affectionate with husband, drinks beer). Later, participants' memories about the woman were assessed. Participants were more likely to recall the information that was consistent with their stereotype of the woman than they were to recall the inconsistent information. In other words, the woman recalled by participants was more similar to the stereotype they had brought to their encounter with her than was the actual woman they had seen.

Events that are congruent with our expectations may be particularly memorable not only because we pay greater attention to them but also because they are more strongly related to our existing beliefs (Hastie 1980). Our prior knowledge provides a meaningful structure that enables us to link diverse pieces of new information to each other as well as to existing beliefs, and this rich pattern of associations can increase the memorability of newly encountered information. We are considerably more likely to recall items that are part of a conceptually meaningful unit than we are to recall lists of unrelated items. Imagine, for example, that you are told that John is creative, temperamental, unconventional, sensitive, and individualistic. Your ability to later recall these traits will likely be substantially improved if you are also told that John is an artist. All these traits are stereotypic of artists, and the stereotype lends coherence to them. Indeed, in a study that tested this possibility, participants who had been given an appropriate stereotyped category along with such lists of stereotypic traits describing an individual later recalled more than twice as many of the individual's traits than did participants who had seen the same traits without the benefit of the stereotype (Macrae, Milne, and Bodenhausen 1994). Importantly, providing the stereotype label did not increase the memorability of traits unrelated to the stereotype, suggesting that the stereotypic traits had become more memorable because of their meaningful association with the stereotype. More generally, our expectancies can provide conceptual coherence to congruent events and, thereby, can increase their memorability.

Expectancy-Incongruent Information You may also be particularly likely to notice and recall information that violates your expectations; if you expect Laura to be warm, you may find her acts of cold indifference particularly noticeable. The surprise that you experience when you encounter such unexpected events may cause you to pay special attention to them and, thereby, may increase their memorability. Recall that illusory correlations may be created through this route, too. People are particularly likely to pay attention to members of minority groups performing a rare behavior because the co-occurrence of a member of a scarce group performing an uncommon behavior is so unusual; as a result, they subsequently overestimate the frequency of such distinctive individuals, and form a mistaken belief that minority members are especially likely to perform that uncommon behavior (Hamilton, Dugan, and Troiller 1985; Stroessner, Hamilton, and Mackie 1992; see chapter 4).

Numerous studies have shown that people are especially likely to recall information that violates their expectancies. For example, in one series of studies, participants were first led to expect that a person had a particular trait (e.g., intelligent; Hastie and Kumar 1979). They then read a list behaviors performed by this person. Of these, some were consistent with the person's trait description (e.g., "won the chess tournament"), some were inconsistent (e.g., "made

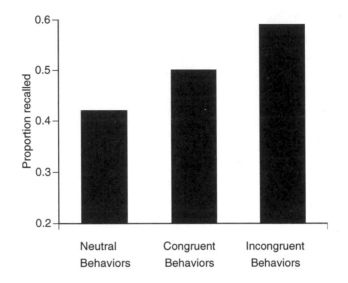

Figure 5.1 Proportion of neutral, expectancy-congruent, and expectancy-incongruent behaviors recalled by participants shown six congruent, six incongruent, and four neutral behaviors. From Hastie and Kumar (1979, table 2, p. 29). Copyright © (1979) by the American Psychological Association. Adapted with permission.

the same mistake three times"), and some were irrelevant to that trait (e.g., "took the elevator to the third floor"). Later, they were asked to recall the person's behavior. As shown in figure 5.1, participants were most likely to recall those behaviors that violated their expectancies about the person. These were recalled even better than behaviors that were congruent with expectancies. Both incongruent and congruent behaviors were recalled better than were the behaviors that were irrelevant to participants' expectancies.

Events that violate our expectancies may be especially well remembered not only because they capture our attention but also because we may work hard to reconcile these incongruent events with our expectancies (Hastie 1984; Hastie and Kumar 1979); we may, for example, try to understand why the usually warm Laura behaved so coldly today, and may think about how this behavior relates to other things we know about Laura, such as her strained relationship with her parents. All this cognitive work will render Laura's cold behavior particularly memorable, because it will now be related to a wealth of other information about her. Indeed, when we are operating under information overload, and do not have sufficient cognitive resources to engage in such attempts of reconciling incongruent information with our expectancies, the recall advantage of incongruent information disappears (e.g., Srull, Lichtenstein, and Rothbart 1985; for reviews, see Olson, Roese, and Zanna 1996; Stangor and McMillan 1992). Another reason why unexpected events may be especially well remembered is that the same cognitive structures that lend coherence to behaviors that are consistent with expectations may also serve to group and impose meaning on inconsistent behaviors, and so increase their memorability.

A great deal of research has focused on trying to determine which pieces of information will be recalled better, those that are congruent with our expectancies or those that are incongruent. This was the topic of some controversy because some studies suggested that congruent information would be more memorable whereas others suggested, instead, that incongruent information would be more memorable. After reviewing this extensive literature, Stangor and McMillan (1992) resolved the controversy by concluding that incongruent information will be relatively better recalled when people are motivated to form an accurate impression that takes all relevant information into account. When so motivated, people will work hard to reconcile incongruent information with their expectancies, and so recall it especially well. In contrast, when people are less concerned about accuracy and are not particularly motivated to invest effort in reconciling incongruent information with their expectancies or when they are incapable of such effort because they are already preoccupied with other cognitive tasks, they may pay less attention to incongruent information, and will be especially likely to recall information that fits with their expectations. This view gains support from other research that has shown more directly that goals may influence the initial processing of information and its subsequent recall, to be discussed in the next section. But perhaps the most important lesson from this line of research is that both congruent and incongruent events are recalled better than neutral events that are unrelated to one's expectancies. The expectancies we have about other people influence the way we process their attributes and behaviors and, thereby, help determine what we later recall about these people. Our memories can be systematically biased because they reflect not only the reality we have observed but also the manner and extent to which we have processed that reality. These may be influenced not only by our beliefs and expectancies but also by our goals and desires, as discussed next.

Goals

Imagine that Alan has responded to an ad which you have placed in search of a roommate, and you are having dinner together to decide whether the two of you wish to share an apartment. It is very important to you to determine what kind of a person Alan is, and so you try hard to form an accurate impression of him. You may pay special attention to any comments that seem to reveal various aspects of his personality, and may organize your impression along the dimensions you consider important in a roommate— friendliness, honesty, considerateness. Now imagine instead that you are having dinner with Alan because you were both stranded at the airport at the same time. You do not expect to ever see him again, and you do not particularly care what kind of a person he is; you are just trying to pass time pleasantly. Even if you have essentially the same conversation that you would if you were trying to decide whether or not to room with Alan, chances are that when trying to recall the airport conversation, you will remember less of it, and your memories will be less well organized. Put more broadly, the goal of forming an impression of another can lead you to pay more attention to information about that person and invest greater effort in making sense of that information. This will allow you to organize the information in a meaningful way and to find ways of relating one piece of information to another. As a result of this increased attention and organization, you will recall the information better.

Several studies have shown that people instructed to form an impression of another person recall even more about this person and organize this information more meaningfully than do people who are instructed to recall as much as they can about this person (e.g., Hamilton, Katz, and Leirer 1980; Srull 1981; Wyer and Gordon 1982). But does expecting to interact with someone in the future lead you to form such impression-formation goals yourself, even when not instructed to? The answer appears to be yes. In one study, participants read information about five different people (Devine, Sedikides, and Furhman 1989). They were given special instructions about one of these people. Some participants were told that this person would be their partner in an upcoming problem-solving task. Other participants were simply told to form an impression about this person, and still others were asked to try to memorize the information about this person. Later, participants were asked to recall as much of the information about each of the five people as they could. The investigators assessed the amount of information recalled about each target as well as its organization. They reasoned that if participants had organized information about a particular individual, drawing associations among the individual's various attributes, they should be especially likely to recall this individual's attributes contiguously. Therefore, they assessed organization by calculating the probability that after recalling one item about a particular individual, the next item recalled would also be about the same individual.

Participants expecting to interact with the target person showed enhanced memory and increased organization for information about this person, much like participants instructed explicitly to form an impression of the target, as shown in table 5.1. Both groups recalled information about the target better than did participants instructed to memorize this information, and only the expected-interaction and impression-formation groups showed better recall for the target than for the other four individuals they had read about. Participants expecting an interaction showed even better organization of information about the target than did participants instructed to form an impression. Perhaps the need to form an impression of another person and the resulting increase in efforts to make sense of this person are greater when the impression-

Table 5.1 Mean numbers of attributes recalled and mean conditional probabilities for the target individual and for the remaining individuals, on average, made by participants given different instructions about the target

	INSTRUCTION SET		
	ANTICIPATED INTERACTION	FORM IMPRESSION	MEMORIZE INFORMATION
Number of recalled attributes			
Target	4.38	4.00	3.00
Average other	1.80	2.33	2.23
Conditional probability[a]			
Target	.844	.578	.281
Average other	.328	.438	.297

Source: From Devine et al. (1989, table 2, p. 686). Copyright © (1989) by the American Psychological Association. Reprinted with permission.
a. Probability of recalling one item about an individual given that another item about that individual has just been recalled.

formation goal arises from one's own interpersonal concerns than when it arises from an experimenter's instructions. Whatever the source of our goals, this and similar studies suggest that the goals we bring with us to an interaction with another person will influence the way we attend to and process information about this person and, thereby, influence our memories of this interaction. The way we process an event and its resulting memorability are also affected by the personal significance that the event carries for us, as discussed next.

Event Significance

It was about eight o'clock in the evening of January 18, 1991. The crisis in the Persian Gulf had been going on for a while, and the

U.S.-led counterattack against Iraq had begun the day before. I was in the upstairs bathroom of our New Jersey home bathing my young son, vaguely aware of the sounds of the TV drifting up from downstairs, when my husband appeared at the door, his face ashen, his voice trembling with emotion, to tell me that Iraq had launched a missile attack on Israel. My thoughts flew immediately to my family near Tel-Aviv. I had visions of my parents huddled together in their safe room, wearing their gas masks. I rushed to the phone.

It is now more than seven years since these events took place, yet I recall them with great vividness, as though they had happened just yesterday. Such vivid recollections of the circumstances surrounding highly emotional events have been termed *flashbulb memories*, a term meant to imply a moment of great clarity amid our more hazy recollections of the past (Brown and Kulik 1977). Flashbulb memories typically concern the circumstances surrounding one's first encounter with an event—how one found out about it, who else was present, what one was wearing at the time, and so on—rather than details of the event itself. Many Americans have such flashbulb memories of the moment they had first heard of the 1989 California earthquake, of the 1986 explosion of the space shuttle *Challenger*, and of the assassination of President John F. Kennedy.

Initially it was thought that flashbulb memories are highly accurate, that they contain information that has been somehow "frozen" in memory through a special mechanism (Brown and Kulik 1977; for a review, see Schacter 1996). Certainly, people experiencing such memories typically have great faith in their accuracy (Neisser and Harsch 1992). Memories of the circumstances surrounding dramatic and shocking events of great personal significance may indeed correspond closely to one's initial description of these circumstances, and they may be more accurate than memories of more mundane events that took place at about the same time (Christianson 1989; Conway et al. 1994). The importance of the personal significance of events to cementing memories of the circumstances surrounding these events was illustrated in one study that compared how well Americans and British people remembered how they had found out about the surprising resignation of then British prime minister Margaret Thatcher. A year after this event, British people, for whom it was likely of greater personal significance, remembered more accurately how they had heard about Thatcher's resignation than did Americans, for whom this event must have been less personally significant (Conway et al. 1994). Note, though, that British citizens most likely had considerably more media exposure to this event than did Americans, and so their improved memory may have been due to their increased exposure to the event rather than to its personal significance to them.

Personally significant memories may be better recalled because of their emotional significance (Brown and Kulik 1977). There is little direct evidence that emotional intensity increases the memorability of dramatic events, but there is some intriguing evidence that the stress hormones released as people view videos depicting highly emotional scenes such as a bloody car accident can contribute to the memorability of these scenes (Cahill et al. 1994; for a review, see Schacter 1996). Flashbulb events may become particularly memorable for other reasons as well, because such dramatic, shocking events differ from more mundane events not only in their emotional significance but also in other ways that could contribute to their greater memorability. People may work harder to make sense of the shocking events and the circumstances that surround them, and may recall them better for that reason. People may spend a great deal of time discussing the shocking events with others, and comparing notes about how they first found out about them. They may also go over these circumstances in their minds frequently as they recall them. These public and private rehearsals could increase the memorability of the events and the circumstances surrounding them. At this point, it remains unclear to what extent these and similar "normal" memory mechanisms contribute to the memorability of flashbulb events. It is quite possible that intense emotions and more normal memory mechanisms contribute jointly to the memorability of dramatic events (Brewer 1992).

Although flashbulb memories may be more accurate than memories for more mundane events, it is important to note that the accuracy of flashbulb memories is far from perfect. Ulric Neisser and Nicole Harsch, who were interested in this topic, jumped into action immediately upon hearing of the *Challenger* explosion. Within less than 24 hours of the disaster, they asked over 100 Emory students to write an account of how they had first found out about it (Neisser and Harsch 1992). Two and a half years later, the researchers were able to track down 44 of the original participants, and asked them once again to write down a description of how they had first found out about the *Challenger* disaster.

None of the participants had perfectly accurate memories, and many of their recollections were quite off the mark. For example, one student reported on the morning after the disaster that she had heard about it in her religion class, from other students. Two and a half years later, she recalled hearing about it in her dorm room, from the TV. Yet she was extremely confident that her memories were accurate. Most participants were correct about some aspects of the original situation, and incorrect about some. Most were also highly confident of their accuracy, and this confidence was not correlated with their actual accuracy; the most confident people were not necessarily the most accurate, and some of them were highly inaccurate. These findings suggest that no matter how vivid our memories, or how convinced we are of their accuracy, we must recognize that they may be at least somewhat inaccurate.

In summary, as we observe an event unfold, our expectancies about this event, the goals we hope to accomplish in it, and its personal significance to us may all influence the way we process this event; they may influence which aspects of the event we pay attention to, how much attention we pay to each, and also our physiological reactions to the event. These factors, in turn, will help determine how we later remember the event. All these factors concern the ways in which our state of mind at the time the event takes place can influence our recollections of it. Our expectancies, goals, and feelings at the time we are recalling an event may also affect our memories of it, as discussed next.

State of Mind When Retrieving Events

Expectancies and Retrieval

Even when we encode events in a relatively unbiased manner, our recollections of these events may still be biased by our expectancies at the time of retrieval. I have already discussed research showing that people asked to entertain one-sided hypotheses about other people or about themselves rely on the positive-test strategy and are therefore particularly likely to recall information that matches their hypotheses; when trying to determine whether someone is extraverted, we may be especially likely to recall this person's extraverted behaviors and so may exaggerate their relative frequency (Kunda et al. 1993; Snyder and Cantor 1979; see chapter 4). Expectancies can provoke similar biases of recollection, perhaps because expectancies give rise to one-sided hypotheses. If I expect, for whatever reason, that you are extraverted, I may spontaneously set out to determine whether my expectation is correct. This will lead me to selectively retrieve those memories of you that match my expectation.

To demonstrate that memory for earlier events is biased by current expectancies, it is important to rule out the possibility that the bias was caused by expectancies held at the time of encoding, which, as discussed earlier, can also influence memory. Several studies have accomplished this by providing participants with particular expectancies about a person only *after* they had already encountered and encoded information about this person. When discussing the impact of expectancies on encoding, I described a study in which participants observed a videotape of a woman said to be a librarian or a waitress and subsequently recalled her behavior as consistent with the stereotype of her profession (Cohen 1981). That study also contained two additional conditions in which participants were informed about the woman's profession only after they had seen the video. For these participants, stereotype-based expectancies could not have influenced encoding because these expectancies were not present at the time of encoding. Yet these expectancies influenced memory; participants were more likely to recall information consistent with their stereotype of the woman's profession than they were to recall inconsistent information. Thus, expectancies acquired after an event has been observed can also influence one's recollections of that event.

Expectancies that derive from a person's own behavior can bias memories about this person in a similar manner. In one study, after hearing about a series of positive and negative behaviors performed by a person, participants viewed a self-description written by this person in which she came across either as arrogant and contemptuous or as modest and respectful (Pyszczynski, LaPrelle, and Greenberg 1987). This self-description created an expectancy about the person's character which then influenced which of her previously observed behaviors participants recalled: When asked to write down all that they could remember about the person, participants were more likely to recall behaviors that matched their expectations about her character than behaviors that conflicted with their expectations. Expectancies can lead not only to selective retrieval of a biased subset of observed behaviors but also to memory distortion, transforming one's recollections of particular behaviors. Other studies have shown that people may recall information that violates current expectancies as more consistent with these expectancies than it really had been (Hirt, Erickson, and McDonald 1993).

In addition to influencing which memories we retrieve, current expectancies can also determine how we interpret retrieved memories (for a review, see Ross 1989). Through the lenses of a woman's current belief that her husband is cheating on her, the flowers he had recently given her are retroactively transformed from a gesture of love to an act of deceit. When we are unable to recruit clear memories about a person, current expectancies may also lead us to "fill in the gaps" in ways that are consistent with our understanding of this person. If we now know that Betty is a lesbian but have trouble recalling exactly what she was like in high school, we may guess that she did not date men (Bellezza and Bower 1981).

Subtly conveyed expectancies may also influence how we reconstruct observed events. Elizabeth Loftus and John Palmer showed participants films depicting traffic accidents and then interrogated them about the speed of the vehicles involved in the collision (Loftus and Palmer 1974). Subtle differences in the wording of the question about speed led to substantial differences in participants' estimates. For example, those asked how fast the cars were going when they *smashed* each other estimated the speed at about 41 mph. But those asked how fast the cars were going when they *contacted* each other estimated the speed at only 32 mph. It appears that the expectancies conveyed by the questions affected participants' memories of the event. Eyewitness testimony may thus be influenced by subtle messages conveyed wittingly or unwittingly at the time of interrogation.

These different sources of bias can all contribute to the same phenomenon: We may recall people's past behaviors as more consistent with our current expectancies about them than they really had been. Our memories reflect not only what we have observed but also what we expect to have observed. So far I have discussed expectancies that arise from the behavior or group membership of an observed individual. I turn next to expectancies that arise from our general theories of personality. As we will see, these too can bias memory.

Theories about Stability and Change

Think of someone whom you have known for at least a year. How much did you like this person when you had only just met him or her? How did you go about answering this question? Often, we have vivid memories of our first encounters with others, and can retrieve these readily. You may recall falling in love with someone at first sight, or recall determining to avoid any further contact with someone after your first meeting. But in many cases we are unable to retrieve such clear memories of our past reactions. Michael Ross suggested that in such circumstances we may attempt to reconstruct our past attitudes, beliefs, or behaviors based on our present ones (Ross 1989). You might start off by asking yourself, "How much do I like this person now?" and then ask, "Is there any reason to believe that I felt differently about this person a year ago?'' To answer this latter question, you may invoke *implicit theories* of your likely stability.

We tend to believe that we are stable on many dimensions; I am the same person today that I was yesterday and a year ago, and hold the same preferences for certain kinds of people, sports, politicians, foods, and many other things. Invoking a theory of stability can lead you to conclude that because you like (or dislike) a particular person today, you must have always felt the same way. We also believe, however, that some aspects of ourselves are likely to have changed over time. Often this is because we have experienced events that are associated in our culture with change and growth, events such as puberty, graduation, marriage, parenthood, trauma, therapy, or retirement. To illustrate such culturally held beliefs about change, Ross cites a best-selling greeting card that reads, "When we first started dating you never belched or farted or picked your nose.... Marriage has changed all that. Happy anniversary." Invoking a theory of change may lead you to conclude that your initial attitude toward a person was quite different from your current one; even though you like someone a great deal today, you may believe that your general outlook on life has become much more positive since your marriage, and so conclude that you probably did not like that person nearly as much at the time of your first meeting, when you were not yet married.

When our theories of stability and change are accurate, using them as an aid for reconstructing our past selves can increase the accuracy of these reconstructions. Sometimes, however, our theories are wrong. Our preferences may have changed over time without our realizing it. Or, we may have failed to change even though we have experienced events that were expected to change us. When we use such mistaken theories to reconstruct our past state of mind, our reconstructions will be systematically biased. Reliance on theories that exaggerate stability can lead us to believe that our past preferences were more similar to our current ones than is the case. And reliance on theories that exaggerate change can lead us to believe that our past preferences were more different from our current ones than is the case. There is evidence for both types of bias, as discussed next.

Exaggerating the Consistency between the Past and the Present There are several studies in which people were induced to change their attitudes in the context of an experiment, and were then asked to recall their earlier attitudes. Not realizing that they have undergone an attitude change, participants typically recall their past attitudes as more similar to their newly minted ones than they really were (for a review, see Ross 1989). For example, it is possible to change people's attitudes toward important and controversial issues such as the merits of busing school children so as to eliminate racial segregation, without them realizing that their attitudes have been manipulated. If, after such an experience, you are asked to recall your earlier attitude, you may say to yourself, "Right now I believe that busing is an excellent idea, and I have no reason to believe that I felt differently a week ago." As a result you will conclude, mistakenly, that you had held the same attitude the previous week (Goethals and Reckman 1973).

Recollections about our past behaviors may also be biased by our current attitudes (Ross, McFarland, and Fletcher 1981). In one study, participants first listened to an expert deliver one of two messages about dental hygiene that had been shown to effectively change attitudes toward toothbrushing. Some heard the expert explain that frequent toothbrushing was good, others that it was bad (one should floss instead). Later, in a seemingly unrelated experiment, participants were asked how often they had engaged in many different behaviors over the past two weeks, including toothbrushing. Participants who had learned that toothbrushing was harmful reported less frequent toothbrushing than did participants who had heard that toothbrushing was good. If we don't realize that our attitudes toward toothbrushing have changed, we may believe that we have always behaved in accordance with our current attitudes.

This phenomenon does not require that our attitudes be changed through subtle, tricky experimental manipulations. We may also be oblivious to gradual attitude change that takes place naturally as we age and mature, and so we may exaggerate the extent to which our past attitudes and behaviors were similar to our current ones. For example, when people interviewed for a political survey were asked to recall how they had responded to the same survey nine years earlier, they recalled their past attitudes as more similar to their current ones than was the case (G. Markus 1986). They must have failed to realize that their attitudes had shifted over time.

Our recollections about our romantic partners may be biased in a similar way. In one study, university students rated the personalities of their dating partners on attributes such as honesty, kindness, and intelligence (McFarland and Ross 1987). Two months later they were asked to rate their partners on these same attributes again, and also to recall their earlier ratings. To encourage them to be as accurate as possible in their recollections, they were informed that the investigators would compare their recalled ratings to their actual ones. Nevertheless, the students' recalled impressions were systematically biased by their current ones. Some of the students had come to view their partners more negatively than they had two months earlier; these students recalled their earlier impressions as more negative than they had in fact been. Others had come to view their partners more positively; these students recalled their earlier impressions as more positive than they had been. Not realizing that our attitudes have changed over time, we exaggerate the extent to which our past attitudes resemble our current ones.

This phenomenon may help explain the *interview illusion*, that is, people's mistaken belief in their ability to predict, based on a brief conversation with someone, how they will evaluate this person in the future (Kunda and Nisbett 1986; see chapter 9). The interview illusion persists even though we undoubtedly have many experiences of gradually changing our opinions of people as we get to know them better. We may think that our reactions to a person after a brief interview predict how we will feel once we know the person well because we simply do not realize that we no longer feel the way we had at the time of the interview; we believe we have always felt the way we do now. After many such experiences of mistakenly recalling our initial reactions to a person as similar to our current ones, we may come to believe that the reactions we experience when we first meet a person are highly predictive of how we will feel toward this person once we get to know him or her well.

The tendency to exaggerate the extent to which our past selves were similar to our current ones may also help explain why professors routinely complain that their students are so much less impressive than their own generation of students was, and why, since ancient times, every generation of parents has insisted that when they were young, children were so much better behaved than the current crop of children (Ross 1989). Older people may exaggerate the extent to which their younger selves resembled their current ones. Their unrealistically embellished recollections of their past selves seem far superior to today's youth. In the words of Vaillant (1977), "It is all too common for caterpillars to become butterflies and then to maintain that in their youth they had been little butterflies. Maturation makes liars of us all" (p. 197).

Whereas theories that exaggerate the stability of behavior over time may lead us to recall our past selves as more similar to our current ones than they really had been, theories that exaggerate the extent to which behavior changes over time may lead us to recall our past selves as less similar to our current ones than they really had been, as discussed next.

Exaggerating the Difference between the Past and the Present
Amy has always believed that once she gets married, she will be much more self-assured and secure. She has now been married for several years and is often troubled by self-doubts and insecurity. Yet her theory about the bolstering role of marriage persists. Why? Although Amy feels pretty insecure today, she recalls herself as being far more insecure back when she was single. When our theories lead us to expect that we have changed even though no actual change has occurred, we may recall our past selves as far more different from our present ones than they really were. This may be one reason why people are often satisfied with useless self-

improvement programs. Even if we recognize that following the treatment, we are not doing all that well, we may exaggerate how badly off we were prior to the treatment, and so believe that the treatment was effective (Ross 1989).

This is exactly what happened to students enrolled in a study-skills program created by Conway and Ross which, like many similar programs, turned out to be quite useless (Conway and Ross 1984). University students interested in participating in a study-skills program were invited to an initial meeting during which they evaluated their study skills. They were then randomly assigned either to participate in the study-skills program or to a waiting-list control group. The three-week program was modeled closely on one offered regularly at a local university. It covered topics such as task definition, effective note taking, and reading. After the completion of the program, participants who had attended it and waiting-list participants were all asked to indicate how much their study skills had improved, to predict the grades they would get at the end of that term, and to recall their initial evaluations of their study skills. Program participants thought their skills had improved more than did control participants, and also expected higher grades. But these high expectations were not borne out. In fact, the program had no impact on academic grades; the grades of program participants were no better than those of controls. Memory distortions may have contributed to participants' unrealistic belief in the program's effectiveness: Program participants recalled their initial self-evaluations as worse than they actually had been. Control participants showed no such bias. We may maintain our faith in useless self-improvement programs by retrospectively disparaging our performance prior to enrolling in these programs.

In sum, our theories about stability and change may color our recollections of our past selves. When we expect stability, we may exaggerate the similarity between our past and present selves, and when we expect change, we may exaggerate the difference. Such theories may affect the reconstruction of our earlier attitudes, behaviors, traits, and general well-being. When we plan to base important judgments and decisions on such reconstructions of our past selves, we should recognize the potential for bias. When a candidate for political office asks you to consider whether you are better off now than you were four years ago, when a therapist asks you whether your level of functioning has improved, and when you ask yourself whether your new romantic relationship has made you happier, you should realize that your recollections of your earlier well-being may be colored not only by your current state but also by your theories of stability and change.

Our memories of the beliefs and expectations that we held at an earlier time may also be influenced by events that have taken place since that time, as discussed next.

The Hindsight Bias

Consider the most recent election in your country. Now imagine that I had asked you, six months before it had taken place, to guess how it would turn out. What do you suppose you would have predicted? Do you think you are capable of completely ignoring your current knowledge when trying to remember your earlier state of mind? Now that you know the results of the election, can you accurately reconstruct the knowledge and beliefs that you had held before you knew these results? It turns out that it is very difficult to accurately reconstruct the way we had understood events before we had known about their eventual outcomes. Once we know that something has happened, we believe that it was bound to have happened. Moreover, now that we know the outcome, we have a strong conviction that "I knew it all along."

A series of studies by Baruch Fischhoff demonstrated that our attempts to reconstruct our past state of knowledge are often characterized by a *hindsight bias*; we tend to exaggerate the extent to which we could have predicted currently known outcomes. Fischhoff (1975) gave participants a detailed description of a historical or a clinical event that could have ended in several different ways. Different groups of participants were led to believe that the event resulted in different outcomes, and all were asked to estimate the prior likelihood of each outcome. For example, one scenario

Table 5.2 Mean probabilities assigned to each outcome by participants informed that different outcomes had occurred

| | OUTCOME EVALUATED | | | |
OUTCOME PROVIDED	BRITISH VICTORY	GURKA VICTORY	STALEMATE	PEACE SETTLEMENT
None	33.8	21.3	32.3	12.3
British victory	**57.2**	14.3	15.3	13.4
Gurka victory	30.3	**38.4**	20.4	10.5
Stalemate	25.7	17.0	**48.0**	9.9
Peace settlement	33.0	15.8	24.3	**27.0**

Source: From Fischhoff (1975, table 1, p. 291). Copyright © (1975) by the American Psychological Association. Reprinted with permission.
Note: Numbers in bold typeface are probabilities assigned to outcomes said to have occurred.

described a war between British forces stationed on the Northern frontier of Bengal and the Gurkas of Nepal. Some participants were informed that the war had ended in British victory, some that it had ended in Gurka victory, some that it had ended in a stalemate without peace, and some that it had ended in a stalemate with peace. A control group was not told what the final outcome had been. Knowing that a particular outcome had occurred led participants to believe that this outcome had been more likely. For example, as shown in table 5.2, participants told that the Gurkas had won viewed Gurka victory as more likely than did controls, and as more likely than any other outcome. In contrast, participants told that the British had won viewed that outcome as the most likely. In general, participants judged the outcome they were informed about as more likely than did controls. Participants also viewed all the evidence pointing to the outcome they were told occurred as more relevant to the event's outcome than did other participants.

This hindsight bias was not due to participants' failure to realize that they were expected to reconstruct their earlier state of knowledge, before learning of the outcome. A similar pattern was obtained in follow-up studies in which participants were explicitly asked to answer "as they would have had they not known the outcome," or to guess the answers of other participants who did not know the outcome (Fischhoff 1975). In short, finding out that an outcome has occurred leads us to view this outcome as more likely, and we are unaware of this impact of outcome knowledge on our judgments. We believe that we "knew it all along," and that the signs pointing to the outcome were there in advance, for anyone to see. We don't realize that the relevance of these signs is only obvious now that we have the benefit of retroactive knowledge.

These studies showed that knowledge of outcomes can bias our estimates of what we would have predicted without outcome knowledge. Outcome knowledge can also bias our recollections of what we had actually known before the fact (Fischhoff and Beyth 1975). In 1972 President Nixon made a historic, unprecedented trip to China. On the eve of the trip, students were asked to estimate the probabilities of various outcomes such as: "President Nixon will meet Mao at least once" and "President Nixon will announce that his trip was successful." More than two weeks after the visit, participants were asked to recall the probabilities that they had given earlier. The experimenters emphasized that they were seeking accurate recall and that they would examine participants' recollections for accuracy. Nevertheless, participants' recalled probabilities were systematically biased by their current knowledge of what had actually happened. They recalled giving higher probabilities than they had in fact given to events known to have happened and recalled giving lower probabilities than they had in fact given to events known not to have happened. In short, they remembered their predictions as more accurate than they really had been; knowing how the visit had unfolded, they believed that they "knew it all along."

Hindsight bias has been demonstrated for a wide range of events, including historical events, scientific experiments, sports games, elections, medical, legal, and psychiatric cases, and accidents (for a review, see Hawkins and Hastie 1990). There are several reasons why we retroactively exaggerate the extent to which we could have and did anticipate the ultimate outcome of such events. Preceding events take on new meaning and importance as they are made to cohere with the known outcome. Now that we know that our friends have filed for divorce, any ambiguous behavior we have seen is reinterpreted as indicative of tension, any disagreement gains significance, and any signs of affection seem irrelevant. It now seems obvious that their marriage was doomed from the start. Such reinterpretation of relevant evidence is the most commonly found reason for hindsight bias (for a review, see Hawkins and Hastie 1990). Moreover, having adjusted our interpretations in light of current knowledge, it is difficult to imagine how things could have happened differently. When making likelihood judgments, we often rely on the availability heuristic: The more difficult it is for us to imagine an outcome, the more unlikely it seems (Kahneman and Tversky 1973; see chapter 3). Therefore, the difficulty we experience imagining how things might have turned out differently makes us all the more convinced that the outcomes that did occur were bound to have occurred.

Our inability to reconstruct our earlier state of knowledge correctly may lead us to be overly harsh toward others and ourselves following decisions that turned out badly. Now that the bad outcome has occurred, it seems to us that it was inevitable and that anyone should have been able to anticipate it in advance; we cannot understand how anyone could have made so stupid a decision. We don't realize that the negative outcome did not seem nearly as obvious at the time the decision was made. Because we all have perfect hindsight vision, we mistakenly believe we should have had perfect foresight vision as well.

Our memories of the past may be influenced not only by our current knowledge and theories but also by the goals and desires that now motivate us, as discussed next.

Goals

Take a moment to think of behaviors you have performed in the past that, you feel, reflect how kind or unkind you are. If, like most people, you wish to see yourself as a kind person, your search for relevant memories may have been biased by this desire. We may be especially likely to recall those of our past behaviors that match our desired self-image. Much like expectancies, goals may bias our recollections by leading us to pose one-sided questions (Kunda 1990). If I wish to see myself as kind, I may ask myself whether I am, indeed, kind. The positive-test strategy may then lead me to selectively retrieve those memories that match my desired self-view (Klayman and Ha 1987; see chapter 4).

In a series of studies, my colleagues and I have shown that motivation may bias autobiographical memories in this manner (Sanitioso, Kunda, and Fong 1990). We first informed participants that a given trait—extraversion or introversion—was associated with academic and professional success, and asked them to explain why this might be so. Explaining such a relation increases one's belief in its truth (Anderson and Sechler 1986; see chapter 3). We reasoned that believing that a trait is associated with success would motivate people to see themselves as having that trait. This motivation would lead them to selectively recruit those memories associated with that trait. This was indeed the case. When asked to list memories of their past behaviors that reflected their standing on the extraversion-introversion dimension, participants for whom introversion was made desirable were more likely to list introverted memories first, and they listed more such memories than did participants for whom extraversion was made desirable. In another study, participants motivated to see themselves as extraverted or introverted were asked to recall specific incidents of their past extraverted behavior (e.g., a time when you initiated a conversation with a stranger) and of their past introverted behavior (e.g., a time when you stayed away from a social situation). Those motivated to see themselves as introverted were faster to generate incidents of their introverted behavior and slower to generate incidents of their extraverted behavior than were those motivated to see themselves as extraverted. These findings all suggest that memories associated with the desired trait had become especially accessible. Our memory of how we have behaved in the past can be colored by how we wish we had behaved.

As discussed earlier, expectancies can lead us to remember past events as more consistent with current expectancies than they really had been. The extent to which such memory distortions occur may depend on our motivation to confirm or disconfirm these expectancies. McDonald and Hirt (1997) showed that expectancies about a person lead to the distortion of memories about this person when one harbors no specific motivation and when one is motivated to confirm the expectancies, but not when one is motivated to disconfirm the expectancies. When recalling a smart but disliked person's past performance, our expectancy that he had been successful may be overridden by our desire to see him as a failure; we may therefore recall his performance as less stellar than it really had been. Thus, motivation may not only influence which incidents we bring to mind but also influence how we reconstruct and distort our memories of particular incidents.

Our current state of mind includes not only our beliefs, expectancies, and goals but also our moods and feelings. These too can influence our recollections of past events, as discussed next.

Mood

Mood-Congruent Memory   Try to recall an event from any time in your past that has something to do with a piano. How pleasant was the event that you recalled? Your answer may depend on your mood at this moment. People are particularly likely to recall memories that are congruent with their current mood: In a good mood one might recall a pleasant evening of making music with friends, but in a bad mood one might recall instead the embarrassment of showing up to a piano lesson unprepared. A considerable amount of research has demonstrated such *mood-congruent memory* (for reviews, see Blaney 1986; Isen 1987; Singer and Salovey 1988).

To investigate the effects of mood on memory in controlled experiments, investigators first induce positive or negative moods in participants and then assess their memory. In one such series of studies, Eric Eich and his colleagues induced positive or negative moods by having participants listen to happy music while concentrating on ideas or images that would make them feel pleasant or listen to sad music while concentrating on ideas or images that would make them feel unpleasant (Eich, Macaulay, and Ryan 1994). Once the appropriate mood was obtained, participants heard a series of emotionally neutral words such as *candle* and *kitchen* and, for each word, were asked to remember a specific event from any time in their past that was brought to mind by that word. They described each event in detail and rated how positive or negative it had seemed when first experienced. The emotional tone of the recalled events was influenced by participants' emotional state at the time of recall: Those experiencing a positive mood recalled more positive events and fewer negative events than did those experiencing a negative mood. These and similar studies suggest that we may tend to preferentially recall those events whose emotional tone is congruent with our mood at the time of recollection.

In this particular set of studies, it could be argued that it was not the mood per se that affected the emotional tone of participants' memories. Participants were aware that they were taking part in an investigation of mood, and their mood was monitored throughout the study; this may have led them to theorize that the researchers were seeking mood-congruent memories. As well, they were encouraged to think of ideas and images consistent with the mood they were meant to experience. These ideas and images may have primed thematically related material, and so may have increased the likelihood that it would be recalled. Therefore, the effects could have been due to demand characteristics or to cognitive priming rather than to the direct impact of mood on memory. There is reason to believe, however, that mood can indeed influence memory. This is because mood-congruent memory was also obtained in other studies that used more subtle procedures of mood induction and are therefore less vulnerable to these alternative accounts (for a review, see Blaney 1986). In one study, for example, a positive or a negative mood was induced through exposure to a pleasant or an unpleasant odor (Ehrlichman and Halpern 1988). In another set of studies, moods were induced by asking participants to arrange their facial muscles into configurations that amounted to a smile or a frown (Laird et al. 1982). In these studies it is unlikely that participants were aware that the researchers were interested in the impact of their mood, and the mood-induction procedures were unlikely to directly prime related cognitive structures. Yet both of these mood manipulations provoked mood-congruent memory. These and similar studies have led most reviewers of the relevant literature to conclude that mood can facilitate the recollection of mood-congruent material (Blaney 1986; Fiske and Taylor 1991).

Studies that have examined the impact of naturally occurring moods on memory have also found evidence of mood-congruent recall. When compared to people who are not depressed, depressed individuals show better recall for negative material encountered in the lab and poorer recall for positive material. In other words, they show mood-congruent memory (for a review, see Blaney 1986). People who are depressed also tend to recall their personal past as more bleak than do people who are not depressed (for a review, see Lewinsohn and Rosenbaum 1987). Of course, it is possible that people who endure episodes of depression have, in fact, experienced more negative events throughout their life, and that may be why they recall their life more negatively. But one study suggests that the psychological state of depression can itself contribute to the negativity of the memories of depressed individuals (Lewinsohn and Rosenbaum 1987). Participants who were depressed at the time of the study recalled their parents as having been more emotionally rejecting than did participants who had never been depressed. In contrast, participants who had experienced depression in the past but were not depressed at the time of the study did not recall their parents as particularly rejecting; their recollections did not differ from those of participants who had never experienced depression. This suggests that the bleak recollections of depressed individuals are due to their depression rather than to other, more permanent factors that remain in effect even when they are no longer depressed.

Although mood can facilitate the recollection of mood-congruent memories, such effects are not inevitable. Sometimes, when we are in a bad mood, we may attempt to cheer ourselves up by thinking of something happy. Such attempts at mood regulation may lead us to preferentially recall mood-incongruent rather than mood-congruent material. A handful of studies has obtained such mood-incongruent recall (e.g., Parrott and Sabini 1990). This may also be why it is often the case that positive moods provoke greater mood-congruent recall than do negative moods (Blaney 1986). We typically have no desire to eliminate positive moods, and so do not attempt to regulate them. In contrast, we may actively attempt to get rid of negative moods, and these attempts may override the tendency to favor mood-congruent recollections.

Mood-Dependent Memory Mood may also influence memory in another way. Events that are encoded in a certain mood may be best recalled when we are again in that same mood. This phenomenon, termed *mood-dependent memory*, focuses on the fit between mood at retrieval and mood at encoding. When such a fit exists, memory for material observed on the earlier occasion will be improved, regardless of the affective tone of that material; when you are happy, you will have improved recall of both positive and negative material that you had encountered on previous happy occasions. This is quite different from mood-congruent memory, in which current mood facilitates memory for mood-congruent material, regardless of one's mood at the time that material was first acquired (Blaney 1986).

The phenomenon of mood-dependent memory has had a tortuous history (Eich 1995). After some promising clinical and experimental demonstrations, there seemed to be strong reason to believe in the reality of this phenomenon (Bower 1981). However, the phenomenon proved so difficult to replicate that the earlier demonstrations began to seem more like unreliable chance events (Bower and Mayer 1989). Reluctant to give up on the effect, Eich and his colleagues identified a series of conditions that seemed important to obtaining mood-dependent memory, and were able to demonstrate that the effect is indeed obtained under these conditions (Eich 1995). Based on a review of relevant research, Eich proposed that we would be especially likely to show mood-dependent memory when the recalled events are internal (thoughts, feelings, imaginations) rather than external, when we are not explicitly reminded of these events at the time of recollection, and when our moods at encoding and at retrieval are sufficiently intense.

A series of experiments that met these conditions obtained the expected mood-dependent memory (Eich, Macaulay, and Ryan 1994). The first stage of these experiments was described in the section on mood congruence: Participants were first put in a positive or a negative mood; when their mood was sufficiently intense, they generated a series of autobiographical memories in response to neutral prompts. Two days later, participants underwent mood induction again. Half were put in the same mood induced in their first session, and half were put in the opposite mood. They were then asked to try to recall the gist of as many as possible of the events they had generated in the earlier session. Their recollections showed mood dependence: Participants who were in the same moods when generating and when recalling events showed greater memory for the generated events than did those who were in different moods on the two occasions. This was true regardless of the emotional tone of the recalled events. For example, compared to participants who were happy when generating events but sad when recalling them, participants who were happy on both occasions showed better memory not only for the positive events they had generated but also for the negative ones.

In sum, it appears that when we are happy we may be particularly likely to recall happy events (mood-congruent memory), and may be particularly likely to recall events experienced on previous happy occasions (mood-dependent memory). Other moods, such as sadness or anxiety, can be expected to exert similar influences on memory. In real life the two mood-related phenomena often go hand in hand. In happy moods we may be particularly likely to

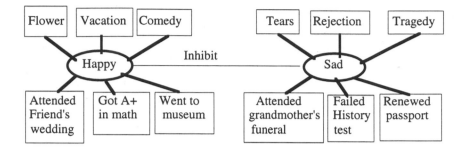

Figure 5.2 Schematic portrayal of a network in which emotions such as *happy* and *sad* are associated with events typically associated with that emotion (e.g., *attended funeral*) as well as events that had been experienced while in that emotion (e.g., *renewed passport*). Semantic associates of the emotions are portrayed in the top row. The two emotions are connected with an inhibitory link. The remaining links portrayed are all excitatory.

experience happy events. On future happy occasions these events may be especially memorable both because their affective tone matches the current one and because they were first experienced in a similar mood.

What causes these effects of mood on memory? Most theorists believe knowledge is stored as a network of interconnected nodes, and assume that activation can spread from one node to another along these connections (e.g., Anderson 1983; Collins and Loftus 1975; see chapter 2). Bower (1981) proposed that emotions may also be represented as nodes in such a network; a representation of a happy event is linked to a *happy* node, and a representation of a sad event to a *sad* node. Events experienced when one is happy or sad are also linked to these emotion nodes. When you are happy, activation spreads from the *happy* node to its associates. This increased activation increases the likelihood that you will retrieve these associates. Figure 5.2 depicts these ideas. Note that in the figure, in addition to their associations with events, the *happy* and *sad* nodes each also have many semantic associations. For example, *happy* is associated with *flower* and *vacation*, *sad* is associated with *tears* and *rejection*. These semantic associations are also expected to become activated by mood (see chapters 6 and 7).

This network theory of affect has dominated discussion of the influence of mood on memory (Blaney 1986; Singer and Salovey 1988). Some have questioned its appropriateness, especially when the reality of mood-dependent memory was in doubt (Bower and Mayer 1989). Nevertheless, in the absence of a plausible alternative, the network theory of affect remains the leading theory in this field. Some have suggested that the theory could account for much of the existing research if it were expanded to incorporate the notion that motivation can sometimes lead us to search for happy memories so as to eliminate sadness (Blaney 1986; Singer and Salovey 1988). Based on current parallel-processing theories of representation, it is also reasonable to assume that emotions not only activate congruent material but also inhibit incongruent material and incongruent emotions (e.g., Kunda and Thagard 1996; Rumelhart and McClelland 1986; see chapter 2).

Whatever the reason for these effects, it may be useful to bear in mind that our recollections can be colored by our moods. Our overall experiences with a loved one may not have been quite as positive as the ones that come to mind following a wonderful romantic evening, nor may they have been quite as negative as the ones that come to mind following a nasty fight. We should be hesitant to base important decisions on the rush of memories that come to mind in the wake of highly emotional incidents. We may have more balanced recollections once the intensity of emotion has subsided.

In summary, our memories of past events are reconstructed. They are influenced by the expectancies, beliefs, goals, and feelings that were on our mind when we first experienced the events as well as by those that are on our mind at the time of recollection. These factors may all bias our memories in systematic ways. Our beliefs about the sources of our memories are also reconstructed, and, therefore, subject to bias. As a result we may be mistaken about whether we had actually experienced or merely imagined an event and about how we came by our current knowledge of it, as discussed next.

Source Memory

Distinguishing Reality from Imagination

Take a moment to recall a particular visit you have made to the library. Now consider this recollection: How do you know that this visit actually took place, that you did not just imagine it? You may find this question baffling at first. The reality of recalled events often seems so obvious and compelling that it does not occur to us to question it or to wonder where this sense of reality comes from. Yet, like many other aspects of memory, our belief in the reality of recalled events is constructed. To distinguish recalled reality from imagination, we rely on perceptual aspects of the memory along with broader theories of plausibility and background knowledge (for a review, see Johnson, Hashtroudi, and Lindsay 1993). Memories of actual events have more temporal and spatial attributes than do memories of imagined events (you may recall the exact time of your visit to the library and remember which floor you visited), more sensory attributes (you may recall the color of the shirt you wore that day), more detailed and specific information (you may recall which books you checked out, which other people were present, what the librarian said), and more emotional information (you may recall your boredom and frustration as you stood in the long checkout line). You may also have supporting memories (you may still have the book you checked out that day), and your memories may be corroborated by those of others (your friend reports remembering going to the library with you that day). We rely on all these cues to distinguish real from imagined events. We may also rely on our reasoning powers: If the memory includes logically impossible events (books jumping off the shelf to greet you), you may conclude that this event must have been imagined. On the other hand, if the recalled events seem coherent and logically interrelated, you may view the memory as more accurate (Ross, Buehler, and Karr, 1998).

Because we rely on such cues to construct the reality of recalled events, we may sometimes confuse reality and imagination when the cues mislead us. As imagined events become more rich and detailed, we become more likely to mistake them for real. These ideas gain support from an extensive program of research on reality monitoring conducted by Marcia Johnson and her colleagues. In one study, for example, participants saw pictures of common objects on some trials (Johnson et al. 1979). On other trials, they were asked to imagine one of these pictures without actually seeing it. The investigators varied the number of times each picture was seen and imagined. Later, in a surprise test, participants were asked to estimate how many times they had actually seen each of the pictures, ignoring the times they had imagined it. Despite the instructions to ignore instances of imagining pictures, these instances did influence participants' recollections of actually seeing the pictures: The more often participants had imagined a picture, the more often they thought they had seen it. Clearly, participants were mistaking some of the imagined occurrences for actual ones. Moreover, participants who were particularly good at visual imaging were particularly likely to confuse imagined occurrences with actual ones. Most likely, these good imagers showed greater confusion between imagination and reality because their imagined pictures were more similar to their actual perceptions in richness and detail.

This kind of confusion between memories for reality and imagination lies at the heart of common everyday failures at reality monitoring. If you ever engage in imagined conversations with your loved ones, in which, for example, you rehearse recounting an amusing incident, you may later find it difficult to tell whether you have already told them about this incident or have only imagined doing so. As a result you may on occasion be embarrassed to find that you are repeating yourself. On other occasions, you may discover that your loved ones know nothing about an incident that you thought you had told them about. Imagined conversations with strangers are far less likely to be mistakenly recalled as real because of the constraints of plausibility (you know full well that you have never met the president of the United States).

The research on reality monitoring has disturbing implications for how stereotypes may be maintained even when they receive no objective confirmation. We may imagine group members engaging in stereotypic behaviors, and then mistakenly recall these imagined events as real. Consider the thoughts a White man might entertain as he is walking through a Black neighborhood on a dark night. He may conjure up images of the terrible things that residents could do to a White person who happens into their neighborhood, and may imagine that each approaching individual is planning to mug him. Later, he may come to confuse these images for reality. So, paradoxically, even though he had walked through the Black neighborhood without incident, an event that, if anything, should weaken his stereotype of Black people as criminal, his stereotype may actually be strengthened by this event.

Morgan Slusher and Craig Anderson showed that stereotypes can indeed lead us to imagine stereotypic behavior which we later mistake for actual behavior (Slusher and Anderson 1987). Participants read a series of sentences describing members of different occupational groups engaging in different activities. Some of the sentences contained explicit mentions of stereotypic traits. For example, the sentence "Arthur, a wealthy lawyer, is taking a swim in his backyard pool" confirms the stereotype of lawyers as wealthy. Other sentences, seen by only some of the participants, described a setting in which a stereotypic trait could be imagined, but these sentences did not actually mention that trait. For example, when reading the sentence "John, a lawyer, is standing in front of his home" one might imagine the home as a mansion in an affluent neighborhood. The study found that such imagined construals of wealth were later mistaken for actual mentions of wealth. For example, reading about a lawyer standing in front of his home led participants to believe they had seen lawyers described as wealthy more often. Importantly, this occurred only if the trait that could be imagined was stereotypic. Reading about a clergyman standing in front of his home did not affect memories of how often clergymen had been described as wealthy; most likely, this sentence did not conjure up an image of a clergyman in a wealthy setting that could then be mistaken for an actual mention of a wealthy clergyman.

It is clear from these and similar studies that when we experience a series of similar actual and imagined events that are of little personal relevance and that are unrelated to the broader fabric of our lives, we are capable of confusing real events with imagined ones. But what exactly are the implications for memory of everyday events? In real life, can we come to believe falsely that we have experienced complex and elaborate events that never actually happened outside our imagination? Research on the power of suggestion suggests that such confusions may occur, as discussed next.

Suggestion and False Memories The renowned developmental psychologist Jean Piaget described a vivid recollection of how he had almost been kidnapped at the age of two (Piaget 1962). He could clearly recall how his nanny had bravely stopped the kidnapper, and could still envision the resulting scratches on her face. Yet he also knew that when he was about fifteen, the nanny confessed that she had made up the entire story. The event had never taken place, and despite its vividness, his memory for it must have been false. It is not difficult to come up with such anecdotal evidence of false memories. Moreover, the proliferation of cases in which people recall being kidnapped by aliens, or recall events that took place in the first months of their life or in previous lives also contributes to the suspicion that people may hold some memories that are false (for a review, see Schacter 1996). Elizabeth Loftus and her colleagues have attempted to determine whether it would actually be possible to implant false memories in the minds of ordinary people (Loftus, Feldman, and Dashiell 1995).

In one study, the investigators enlisted trusted family members to try to convince five individuals that, at the age of five, they had been lost for an extended time (Loftus and Coan in press). Four of these individuals later reported remembering these fabricated events. For example, 14-year-old Chris was "reminded" by his older brother of the time he had been lost at a mall until he was rescued by an elderly man. Chris later reported that he could remember what the man had looked like, what he had worn, and what his mother had said when they were finally reunited. Because of its very small sample size—five—this study is only suggestive of the possibility that people may be induced to remember events that never happened. Moreover, in this case, it is possible that the individuals were putting together fragments of events that actually happened and confusing them with this particular, confabulated event. It is quite conceivable that Chris really had been lost for a while at some point in his childhood. However, other researchers were able to demonstrate similar constructions of false memories for events that were considerably less likely to have actually taken place.

In one study, the parents of college students provided information about events that had taken place when their children were young (Hyman, Husband, and Billings 1995). The students were later queried about their memories for some of these actual events and also for memories about fabricated events such as an overnight hospitalization at the age of five which, according to their parents, had never actually occurred. When first queried, none of the participants could recall the fabricated events. However, when queried about these fabricated events again one to seven days later, 20 percent of the participants reported some memories of these events. At this point, their memories of the thoughts and feelings they had experienced when first queried about these events must have been mistaken for memories of actual events. In short, although most participants in this study did not generate false memories, a substantial minority did. Subsequent research showed that people are more likely to create false memories if they are also asked to imagine the fabricated events and if they are good imagers (for a review, see Schacter 1996). This is consistent with results obtained in the laboratory studies of reality monitoring described above, namely that one is particularly likely to confuse imagined events with reality when the imagined events resemble real ones in richness and detail (Johnson, Hashtroudi, and Lindsay 1993).

The question of whether people may hold false memories and whether it is possible to implant false memories in others has been central to what is arguably the most hotly debated and controversial dispute about psychological issues in the public arena, namely the dispute about whether people may come to hold false memories of childhood abuse. Over the last decade or so there has been a virtual epidemic of cases in which adults, typically women, come to remember, usually in the course of psychotherapy, that during their childhood they had been sexually abused by a parent or a close relative. The alleged abusers typically vehemently deny these accusations. Do these thousands of cases all involve memories of real events? Or is it possible that at least some of these recovered memories of abuse are false?

Debate on this issue is fueled by intense emotions. Survivors of childhood abuse have picketed scientific gatherings in which memory researcher Elizabeth Loftus has participated (Schacter 1995). They feel that her argument that some recovered memories of abuse could be false invalidates the reality of their own very painful memories, and they are deeply disturbed by the possibility that the denials voiced by perpetrators of abuse will carry greater weight than the accusations voiced by their victims. Emotions also run high among parents who feel they have been falsely accused of abusing their children. Such accusations can tear families apart, and can irreparably destroy reputations. In 1992, in response to the proliferation of cases of recovered memories of abuse, a group of accused parents along with a number of professionals founded the False Memory Syndrome Foundation whose aim is to collect and disseminate scientific information related to false memories and to help parents who feel they have been falsely accused of abusing their children. Many prominent psychologists serve on the foundation's advisory board (Freyd 1998).

Most psychologists who have suggested that recovered memories of sexual abuse may sometimes be false have also been careful to emphasize that childhood abuse is a real and widespread problem of great concern. There seems to be little reason to doubt the memories of people who have always recalled their abuse. Many recovered memories of events that had been forgotten for a while may be accurate as well. I doubt that any serious scholar would wish to trivialize the magnitude or the seriousness of such abuse, or its devastating consequences. And yet, many are deeply disturbed by the possibility that some recovered memories may be false. What is the evidence for this?

Several conclusions may be drawn from the relevant literature (Schacter 1996; see also Bowers and Farvolden 1996; Brandon et al. 1998). Although there are some striking case studies, there is no direct evidence from controlled experiments that false memories of sexual abuse can be implanted in the course of psychotherapy or in any other manner. Nor is there ever likely to be such evidence, for obvious ethical reasons. Yet, there are many reasons to believe that some therapists may have provoked the creation of false memories by their clients. Several lines of evidence lend support to this conclusion. Recall that it has been shown that memories for less traumatic events can be implanted. This suggests that people may come to hold false memories of abuse as well. Memories that have been recovered during psychotherapy are especially suspect, because many therapists rely on techniques that seem particularly likely to foster false memories. One such technique that is common among therapists who suspect abuse is guided imagery, in which the therapist instructs the client to try to imagine the suspected abuse in vivid detail. Research on reality monitoring discussed earlier has shown that such vivid imaginations are particularly likely to be confused with reality at a later date. Indeed, this technique has led people to recover outlandish memories of past lives and alien abductions whose reality few would take seriously. In addition, many people who had at one point thought that they had recovered memories of abuse have subsequently retracted their accusations, and have come to believe instead that their therapists had driven them to false memories. When a person first professes to recall abuse and then retracts the recollection, it is not obvious which of these two states of belief reflects objective reality. But the proliferation of retractors does at the very least raise the possibility that the initially recovered and subsequently retracted memories of abuse may have been false.

If one believes that some recovered memories are true but others are false, one is left with the obvious question: How do we tell the true memories from the false ones? Sadly, we do not yet have a good answer. There is no litmus test for the reality of memories. There are many useful truth criteria that we can and do rely on, such as the richness and detail of the memory, its plausibility, and the extent to which it is congruent with the recollections of other people. But, unfortunately, these criteria offer no guarantee of success at determining the reality of our own or anyone else's memories (Ross 1997). When confronted with a woman insisting that she has recovered memories of abuse at the hands of her father, and a father who vehemently denies this accusation, it may be impossible for us to determine what had really transpired in this tormented family.

The legal systems in North America have undergone a shift in beliefs about the reality of recovered memories. When this phenomenon first surfaced in the 1980s, recovered memories of abuse were often considered sufficient evidence for convicting the alleged abuser. One Canadian man, for example, was sentenced in 1994 to six years in prison based on his daughter's memories, recovered in therapy, of incidents in which he had sexually abused and physically assaulted her throughout her childhood, starting when she 18 months old (*Globe and Mail*, 11.6.1997). With the increasing awareness of the possibility that such recovered memories may be false, the courts have become reluctant to convict anyone on the basis of recovered memories that are not corroborated by additional evidence. In Canada, the president of the Criminal Lawyers Association has asked the justice minister to review all cases of men already convicted on the basis of recovered memories (so far, she has refused. *Globe and Mail,* 5.9.1998).

The courts have also begun accepting the view that mental health professionals who induce recovered memories in their patients may be guilty of professional misconduct. For example, in 1997 a jury awarded $5.8 million to a Houston woman who had accused her therapist of implanting memories of murder, satanism, and cannibalism (*NYT*, 11.6.1997). In several cases, lawsuits filed against therapists have been settled out of court. The largest settlement to date, $10.6 million, was awarded in 1997 to a woman who claimed that while undergoing psychiatric treatment at a Chicago hospital, she was induced by her doctors to recover false memories of being part of a satanic cult, being sexually abused by several men, and abusing her own two sons. In another case, involving demonstrably false recovered memories, a church in Missouri settled on a payment of $1 million dollars to a woman who claimed that under the guidance of a church counselor, she had recovered memories that her father had raped her, got her pregnant, and then performed a coat-hanger abortion on her. In this case it was possible to thoroughly refute the "recovered" memories—the woman was still a virgin and her father had had a vasectomy (details of these and similar cases were reported in *NYT*, 11.6.1997). These developments in legal circles reflect a growing consensus among academic psychologists and psychiatrists that recovered memories, especially those recovered in therapy, can be false (e.g., Brandon et al. 1998).

So far I have focused on how we monitor the reality of our memories, and have discussed how this reality monitoring is sometimes faulty. I turn next to a discussion of how we monitor memories about information derived from external sources. Like reality monitoring, external-source monitoring can be less than perfect; we may sometimes forget the circumstances under which information was first acquired, as we occasionally do for our flashbulb memories.

Monitoring External Sources

During his 1980 presidential campaign, the CBS program *60 Minutes* showed Ronald Reagan recounting a moving story about an act of heroism performed by a U.S. pilot in World War II. Although Reagan described the incident as real, his account of it was remarkably similar to a scene from a Dana Andrews movie released in the 1940s (Johnson et al. 1993). It appears that Reagan remembered the incident accurately but was mistaken about its source. Such confusion about the source of one's memories is more common among elderly than young people, but young people are not immune from it (for a review, see Johnson et al. 1993). In everyday life, you may think that you had heard from your father an item of news that had actually come from your mother, you may think that a tabloid headline you had scanned at your grocery store was actually encountered in a more respectable newspaper, and you may think that you had come up with a brilliant idea that you had actually heard from someone else. Like reality monitoring, external-source monitoring is more likely to break down as the similarity among different sources increases.

Of the nine judges sitting on the U.S. supreme court in 1997, two—Justice Ruth Bader Ginsburg and Justice Sandra Day O'Conner—were women. Justice Ginsburg noted amusedly that twice that year, distinguished lawyers arguing before the Court began their responses to her questions with, "Well, Justice O'Conner ..." (*NYT Magazine*, 10.5.1997). It is a safe assumption that the two justices are confused with each other by virtue of their shared gender. There is also reason to believe that when recalling Court proceedings, people may sometimes confuse one of these judges' statements with those of the other. An ingenious experimental technique first introduced by Shelley Taylor and her colleagues showed that we are particularly likely to misattribute one person's statements to another if the two belong to the same social group (Taylor et al. 1978).

Participants listened to a discussion among a group of three White and three Black men. As each spoke, his picture was projected on a screen. The pairings of voice with picture were varied, so that the same voices were paired with different pictures in different conditions. Later, participants were given a page with pictures of all the discussants and a list of the various suggestions made in the course of the discussion and were asked to recall which discussant had made each suggestion. Errors in which a statement was mistakenly attributed to another person of the same race as the original speaker were considerably more common than errors in which a statement was mistakenly attributed to someone of a different race. It is clear that we can be mistaken about who said what, and are particularly likely to mistakenly attribute one person's statements to another when we perceive the two as similar.

What makes us see two individuals as similar and leads us to confuse one for another? Recall that our general theories of the world· play an important role in determining which objects we group together (Murphy and Medin 1985; see chapter 2). One would therefore expect source confusion to be triggered not only by objective similarity among the sources but also by the extent to which we find their similarity meaningful and informative. This is precisely what was found in a series of studies by Charles Stangor and his colleagues which used the same method used by Taylor and her colleagues (Stangor et al. 1992). As in the earlier study, participants were more likely to confuse two individuals of the same race with one another than they were to confuse a Black person with a White person. But participants were not any more likely to confuse two individuals wearing the same colored shirt with one another than they were to confuse someone wearing a black shirt with someone wearing a white shirt. Clearly, in our society it is more meaningful to categorize people by the color of their skin than by the color of their shirt. When we categorize people as members of the same group, we are more likely to mistake one for another when trying to recall what each had said.

A dimension that normally seems irrelevant for categorization can be made meaningful and so give rise to source confusion. In another study, Stangor and his colleagues (1992) showed that normally people are not more likely to confuse one individual's statements with another's just because both are dressed in the same style. However, if people are asked to choose the person who would make the best media representative, style of clothes becomes a meaningful dimension. Under these circumstances people are more likely to confuse similarly dressed people with one another than they are for differently dressed people.

Individuals differ in the extent to which they find different dimensions meaningful and so differ in the kinds of sources they are likely to confuse with one another. People who view race as more meaningful for categorization may be more likely to fall prey to within-race confusions. In another study, Stangor and his colleagues (1992) showed that highly prejudiced people were considerably more likely to make within-race confusions than they were to make between-race confusions. But the same was not true for people who were extremely low in prejudice; they were no more likely to confuse one Black person with another than they were to confuse a Black with a White person. Highly prejudiced people may be particularly likely to represent a person who is Black as a Black person rather than as, say, Tyrone or Rashid. They may be particularly likely to make within-race confusions because it is easier to mistake one Black person for another than it is to mistake Tyrone for Rashid.

Forgetting who said what is one kind of failure of external-source monitoring. Another kind of problem arises when we forget important information that we initially had about the source and that may have influenced our initial reactions to it. We may forget, for example, that we had initially doubted the source's credibility, as discussed next.

The Sleeper Effect Imagine that you hear a representative of a tobacco company proclaim that there is considerable evidence that cigarette smoking is neither harmful nor addictive. Given your assumptions about the likely vested interests of the speaker, you may have little faith in the credibility of this statement; your attitudes toward smoking will remain unchanged. A few weeks later, though, when discussing smoking with your friends, you may recall this statement without remembering exactly where you had heard it. If you no longer remember that the speaker lacked credibility, you may, at this point, be influenced by the contents of the speech and come to view smoking more positively than you might have if you had never heard that speech. Social psychologists have termed this phenomenon, in which the attitude change provoked by a discredited communication is greater after a delay than it is immediately, the *sleeper effect*. Most theorists have viewed this effect as due to a dissociation between the message and the information that discredited it, that is, as due to a failure at source monitoring (e.g., Hovland, Janis, and Kelley 1953; for a review, see Eagly and Chaiken 1993).

The sleeper effect has had a somewhat tortuous history (Eagly and Chaiken 1993). After some initial demonstrations of the sleeper effect in the 1950s, it gained widespread acceptance. However, after pointing to the weakness of the empirical evidence for the sleeper effect, and after failing to obtain it themselves in a series of seven studies, Gillig and Greenwald (1974) suggested that it is "time to lay the sleeper effect to rest" (p. 132). This conclusion was challenged by Gruder and his colleagues who argued that the sleeper effect should only be obtained under certain theoretically important conditions which were not met by Gillig and Greenwald's studies (Gruder et al. 1978). A sleeper effect requires that the communication be effective so that it can be influential once it is dissociated from the information that discredits it; the information discrediting the source must also be persuasive; and the attitudes must be measured at an optimal time delay: Enough time must have elapsed since the message was first heard to permit dissociation between the message and the information that discredited it, but the delay should not be long enough for the message itself to be forgotten. Gruder and his colleagues were able to show that the sleeper effect is obtained under these conditions, but not when they are violated.

In one condition that met the requirements for the sleeper effect, participants read a 1,000-word magazine article arguing against a four-day work week (Gruder et al. 1978). A note from the editor at the end of the article contained the discrediting information; it stated that since the article had gone to press, a more recent comprehensive study had demonstrated that the conclusion of the article was false. The article provoked little attitude change immediately after it had been read; at that point the discrediting information had successfully undermined the article's impact. However, five to six weeks later, participants who had read the article showed greater agreement with its conclusions than participants who had not. This was a true sleeper effect: The delayed persuasive impact of the article was greater than its immediate impact.

In an experiment reported ten years later, Pratkanis and his colleagues also obtained a sleeper effect under these same conditions (Pratkanis et al. 1988). In another condition, these authors failed to obtain a sleeper effect when the information discrediting the article was read before rather than after reading the article itself; in part, this occurred because, under these circumstances, the article was not discredited as much initially, leaving less room for the sleeper effect to emerge. Pratkanis and his colleagues argued that these results, along with similar results from sixteen additional experiments that used different methods, could be better accounted for by a different theory of the sleeper effect, which holds that, rather than being dissociated from the source, the discrediting information is simply forgotten more rapidly. Others, however, have challenged this conclusion, and pointed out that the sixteen other experiments did not meet the basic requirement that enough time must elapse because they all provided discredited messages and examined whether these provoked sleeper effects within the same brief session (Eagly and Chaiken 1993).

Thus, the exact mechanism underlying the sleeper effect remains unclear. But regardless of whether the sleeper effect is due to the fact that the discrediting information is dissociated from the message or to the fact that it is forgotten more rapidly than the message, it is clear that the sleeper effect results from a failure of source monitoring. We remember the initial message without remembering, at the same time, that it had been discredited so effectively that we did not initially believe it. Through such failures of source monitoring, information that we initially deem worthless can subsequently contaminate our judgments.

In conclusion, although many of our memories may depict reality quite accurately, some may not. We may sometimes be mistaken about the details of earlier events, may misrecall our prior expectations for past events, may have biased recollections of our own past behaviors and attitudes as well as those of others, and may misrecall the sources of our memories. Unfortunately, our memories in and of themselves hold no foolproof cues to their accuracy. We should therefore be careful not take it as a foregone conclusion that our own and other people's memories are faultless, no matter how real they seem. When important decisions rest on the accuracy of memories, it is important to try to gather corroborating evidence for the recalled events.

Summary

Our state of mind at the time events unfold may influence the way we encode these events and, therefore, the way we later remember them. The expectancies we have about other people can influence the way we process their attributes and behaviors and, thereby, help determine what we later recall about these people. Events that are congruent with our expectancies and events that are incongruent with them are recalled better than neutral events that are unrelated to our expectancies. The goals we bring with us to an interaction with another person also influence the way we attend to and process information about this person and, thereby, influence our memories of this interaction. If we are motivated to form an impression of a person, we subsequently recall our interactions with this person better. We may also have especially good memories for events that have great personal significance to us.

Our state of mind at the time we retrieve events may also influence the way we remember them. We may recall people's past behaviors as more consistent with our current expectancies about them than they really had been. Our memories for our own past reactions may also be influenced by our theories about the likely stability of such reactions. This can result in biased memories when our theories are mistaken. Reliance on theories that exaggerate stability can lead us to believe that our past preferences were more similar to our current ones than is the case. And reliance on theories that exaggerate change can lead us to believe that our past preferences were more different from our current ones than is the case. Our memories of our past expectations for events may be influenced by our current knowledge about how these events actually unfolded. This can produce a *hindsight bias*: Once we know that something has happened, we believe that it was bound to have happened and that we knew so all along. Our current goals may also influence our memories; we may be especially likely to recall those events that lend support to our desired conclusions. Our current moods may also influence which events we recall. For example, when we are happy, we may be particularly likely to recall happy events (*mood-congruent memory*) and may be particularly likely to recall events experienced on previous happy occasions (*mood-dependent memory*).

Our beliefs about the sources of our memories are also subject to bias. We rely on cues such as the vividness, detail, and plausibility of a memory to decide whether it concerns a real or an imagined event. When these cues are misleading, we may mistake imagined events for real. We may also sometimes forget how we came by our current knowledge. As a result we may misattribute one person's statements to another. Such confusions are more likely the more similar the two individuals are to each other. We may also come to espouse arguments that we had initially disbelieved, if we later remember the arguments without remembering that we once had good reasons for disbelieving them.

Much of the discussion in the preceding chapters concerned the way we represent, reason about, and retrieve social knowledge. These relatively intellectual, information-driven processes are sometimes referred to as "cold" cognition, mostly in order to distinguish them from the more motivational, affect-laden processes of "hot" cognition. Hot cognition refers to those mental processes that are driven by our desires and feelings—those cases where our goals and moods color our judgment. Until the late 1980s many doubted that hot cognition even existed, preferring to explain seemingly hot phenomena in terms of colder mechanisms of information processing. More recent evidence has pretty much put these doubts to rest, and there is an emerging consensus that motivation and affect can and do affect judgment (e.g., Dunning, in press; Gollwitzer and Moskowitz 1996; Forgas 1995; Kruglanski 1996; Kunda 1990).

In this chapter I will describe the evidence for hot cognition and show that our judgments can be influenced by a variety of goals and moods. I will also discuss the mechanisms for these effects. I will argue that motivation and affect influence judgment by influencing the cognitive processes we engage in to arrive at a judgment. Both motivation and affect may influence which concepts, beliefs, and rules we apply to a judgment; we may be especially likely to apply those that are congruent with our goals and moods. Motivation and affect may also influence our mode of processing information, determining whether we rely on quick and easy inferential shortcuts or rely on elaborate, systematic reasoning.

Motivation

DIRECTIONAL GOALS

For much of her adult life, my mother was a heavy smoker. As a young woman she smoked heavily throughout her three pregnancies (back then it was not commonly known that this might not be a good idea). Years later, after reading an article about the effects of smoking during pregnancy on one's babies, she exclaimed, "This article is full of nonsense. It says that if you smoke during pregnancy you will have small babies. Look at my 'small' babies!" (Both of my brothers are about 6′4″). I too had read the article and couldn't help pointing out that it also said that smoking during pregnancy could cause lung problems in your babies. I reminded her that both of my huge brothers had suffered from spastic bronchitis throughout their childhood, and suggested that perhaps there was some truth to the article. "Oh, come on," she said dismissively, "that's only a sample of two."

In my research career I have spent a considerable amount of effort trying to demonstrate that this kind of motivated reasoning is not restricted to my mother; on occasion, we all come to believe what we want to believe because we want to believe it (Kunda 1987, 1990). *Directional goals*, that is, the goal of arriving at a particular conclusion, can bias our judgment. You may consider this idea to be self-evident. Indeed, you may have observed such biases in your own mother and friends (though, most probably, not in yourself ...). We all know that lovers may be blind to any fault in their loved ones, and mothers to imperfections in their children. We are not surprised to discover that each party to an argument is genuinely convinced that only the other is at fault. And we may distrust the judgments of "hired guns" who have a vested interest in reaching a particular conclusion. Yet, although the notion that our desires can color our judgment is well entrenched in our culture, this issue has been a topic of considerable controversy within social psychology.

Motivational versus Cognitive Accounts of Bias

Imagine the following study: Undergraduates at an elite university are given a brief test of intelligence. They are then given false feedback on their performance: Half are told that they have excelled, and half that they have done quite poorly. All are then asked to evaluate the validity of the test, that is, to indicate how good a measure of intelligence it is. Not surprisingly, those informed that they had excelled think the test is excellent, whereas those informed that they had done poorly think it is pretty lousy. Could these different evaluations of the test be due to the different motivations of the two groups? They certainly could. Those told they had excelled at the test are most probably motivated to believe in its validity. If the test is valid, their excellent performance on it proves that they are really smart, a highly desirable conclusion. In contrast, those told they had done poorly on the test are most probably motivated to believe that it is not valid. If it is invalid, their poor performance on it need not imply that they are unintelligent. The overarching motivation to maintain and enhance one's self-regard creates a desire to believe in a test that one has excelled at and to disbelieve in a test that one has failed, and these desires could lead the two groups to evaluate the test quite differently.

But could these different evaluations of the test by those who had excelled and those who had done poorly at it also be due to other, nonmotivational factors? Just as certainly, they could. Students enrolled at an elite university typically have a long history of strong academic performance. Each has excelled at countless exams, and given their superb academic records, all have strong reason to expect that they will perform well on an intelligence test. You and I, who have no vested interest in this matter, would expect the same of them. When such students are informed that they have indeed excelled at the test, this merely confirms their expectations. The test has provided a plausible result, and so it seems valid. But when such students are informed that they have done poorly at the test, this constitutes a major violation of a well-entrenched expectation. Surely, they must think, it is unlikely that this brief test provides a better measure of their intelligence than do their many years of academic excellence. Therefore it seems reasonable for them to conclude that the test must be invalid. In this manner, we have accounted for the different evaluations of the test by the two groups in purely cognitive terms, without invoking motivation at all. The two groups evaluate the test differently not because they are motivated to validate their success and to invalidate their failure but because success seems plausible and failure implausible, given their expectations.

In the mid 1970s and early 1980s, several theorists reviewed the literature purporting to demonstrate motivated reasoning, and all arrived at the same conclusion: The results of all relevant experiments could be explained in purely cognitive terms, without invoking motivation (Miller and M. Ross 1975; Nisbett and L. Ross 1980; Tetlock and Levi 1982). One line of research, for example, had shown that people take responsibility for their successes and attribute them to themselves, but deny responsibility for their failures, attributing them instead to external factors such as bad luck or task difficulty. Although such results had been explained as due to the motivation to see oneself in the best possible light, the reviewers pointed out that they could also have been due to alternative, cognitive factors—the expectation that one would succeed, or the knowledge that one had invested a great deal of effort in the task. Some reviewers argued that it would never be possible to obtain indisputable evidence for the impact of motivation on judgment because it would always be possible to reinterpret any finding as due to purely cognitive mechanisms (Tetlock and Levi 1982).

If you can interpret the same finding as due to motivation or as due to cognitive mechanisms, which explanation should you prefer? Some argued that you should prefer the cognitive explanations because they allowed for a more parsimonious theory, that is, a simpler theory that required fewer constructs (Dawes 1976; Miller and M. Ross 1975; Nisbett and L. Ross 1980). At the time, there was a great deal of independent evidence for the cognitive mechanisms invoked to explain these controversial findings. For example, it was already well established that expectancies could color judgment (for a review, see Olson, Roese, and Zanna 1996). In contrast, there was no independent evidence for the impact of motivation on judgment; all the relevant evidence came from studies that could also be reinterpreted in purely cognitive terms. Why, then, invoke yet another construct, motivation, for which there is no independent evidence, when we can explain all relevant research perfectly well without it?

At the time, this argument seemed persuasive. However, it no longer does. By 1990 researchers had succeeded in obtaining independent evidence for the impact of motivation on judgment and had begun exploring the mechanisms underlying such processes, as I describe next (Kunda 1990).

Outcome Dependency

Much of the research about allegedly self-serving judgment that had been questioned by critics was open to reinterpretation in purely cognitive terms because it concerned the self. It is inevitable that our detailed self-knowledge will give rise to expectations about our likely performance; when both expectations of success and the motivation to be successful predispose us to arrive at the same conclusion, it is difficult to tell whether we drew this conclusion because of our expectation or because of our motivation. However, if we examine motivated judgments about a stranger, about whom we have no prior knowledge or expectations, this problem should not arise. How could you be motivated to hold particular beliefs about a stranger? One way of creating such motivation is through making you dependent on this person for some important goal. If you are about to go on a blind date with someone, you may be strongly motivated to believe that this person is likable. And if you know that the success of your team depends on the competence of your new teammate, you may be strongly motivated to believe that this person is competent. Several studies have shown that such *outcome dependency* does indeed bias judgment.

In one study participants were recruited to take part in a dating study (Berscheid et al. 1976). Before meeting their dating partner, they watched a videotaped discussion among three people, one of whom was said to be their future partner. There were three groups of participants, each expecting to date a different one of the three discussants, and an additional control group that was not expecting to date any of them. One would expect that participants would be motivated to see their future dating partner in the best possible light. And, indeed, they did. Participants rated their expected date as more likable than the other two discussants, and as having a more positive personality. Other outcome dependency studies have yielded conceptually similar results. People given some information about a stranger rate this person more positively when they are dependent on this person because they expect the person to be their partner in an intimate sexual discussion, because they expect that rewards for their own efforts will depend on this person's performance, or because they expect this person to be their partner rather than their opponent on a team competition (Darley and Berscheid 1967; Klein and Kunda 1992; Neuberg and Fiske 1987).

It is difficult to construct nonmotivational accounts for these studies. In all of them, participants had no prior expectations about the target person. Moreover, the motivation to see this person positively was manipulated in a manner that provided no additional information about the target person and so could not give rise to any expectations about this person. The fact that participants nevertheless came to view the person whom they wanted to like and respect as especially likable and competent in these studies therefore provides strong evidence for the role of motivation in judgment. Two additional lines of work were able to implicate motivation even in judgments about the self, as I discuss next.

The Crucial Role of Arousal

Dissonance theory provided one important arena for the debate between proponents of motivational influences and proponents of cognitive mechanisms. In the typical dissonance study, participants are induced to support a position that runs contrary to their attitudes. For example, students may be asked to write an essay in favor of police brutality, higher tuition, or Cuba's Fidel Castro, all anathema to the typical participant in these studies. If they are also induced to believe that they had written the essay of their own free will, their attitudes shift toward the position they had expressed—they become more supportive of police brutality, higher tuition, or Fidel Castro. Originally such findings were interpreted as due to motivation, although theorizing about the precise nature of the underlying motives underwent change as the theory evolved (Festinger 1957; for a review, see Cooper and Fazio 1984).

The originator of dissonance theory, Leon Festinger, believed that attitude change in such experiments resulted from an attempt to reduce the unpleasant tension, or dissonance, between two conflicting beliefs: I oppose X, and I have just written an essay in favor of X. This dissonance would be reduced if I came to believe that I actually support X (Festinger 1957). Subsequent theorists suggested that dissonance arousal required a threat to the self. On this view, the conflicting beliefs are: I have done something bad or foolish, and I am a decent, intelligent person (Aronson 1968; Greenwald and Ronis 1978). Dissonance would be reduced if I came to believe that what I had done was not so foolish, and I could believe that if I assumed that I actually support the attitude I had expressed. Note that both the original and the modified view hold that people are motivated to adopt the attitude they had been led to express, and it is this motivation that provokes attitude change.

This view was challenged by Daryl Bem, who proposed an alternative, nonmotivational account of such findings (Bem 1972). Bem argued that people often have no direct way of determining what their attitudes are. Instead, they determine their attitudes by observing their own behavior and inferring that their attitudes must be consistent with it. If I have volunteered to write an essay in favor of Castro, I must be pro-Castro. This self-perception theory accounts for the attitude change that results from counterattitudinal behavior in purely cognitive terms, without invoking motivation. The deadlock between the motivational and self-perception accounts of dissonance findings was resolved by an ingenious set of studies by Mark Zanna, Joel Cooper, and their colleagues that demonstrated that self-perception cannot fully account for such attitude change (Zanna and Cooper 1974; for a review, see Cooper and Fazio 1984).

Bem's self-perception account of dissonance findings assumes that attitude change results from a cool-minded inference; detached observers would be expected to make the same inference. In contrast, the motivational account assumes that one is upset and disturbed by one's behavior, and it is this distress that provokes attitude change; one is motivated to reduce the distress. Emotions such as distress are typically accompanied by physiological *arousal* —we feel the blood rush to our face, our heartbeat quickens, our palms get sweaty. This arousal tends to be nonspecific, so one's interpretation of it depends on one's understanding of the situation. The same arousal can be taken to reflect euphoria, fear, or distress, depending on whether one is surrounded by clowns, tigers, or crying babies; one uses the cues available in the situation to make sense of one's arousal (Schachter and Singer 1962). Arousal plays a key role in shaping our beliefs about our emotional states. The more aroused we are, the more likely we are to assume we are experiencing strong emotion, and if we have reason to believe that this emotion is negative, the more likely we are to do something about it. More recent research by neuroscientists has confirmed that people rely on their arousal to infer that they are concerned about threats. Brain-damaged patients who do not experience such arousal do not avoid dangerous situations even when they are aware of the danger (for a review, see Damasio 1994; see chapter 7).

Zanna and Cooper (1974) recognized the implications of these ideas about how we infer our emotions to dissonance theory. They reasoned that the inference that one is upset in a dissonance experiment requires two components: Arousal, and information that would lead one to attribute this arousal to distress over one's actions. If it is the motivation to reduce such distress that drives attitude change in dissonance experiments then both these components should be essential for attitude change—eliminate arousal, and people won't assume that they are upset, or, provide an alternative reason for the arousal, and people won't attribute it to their distress over their actions. Indeed, in a series of experiments, Zanna, Cooper, and their colleagues were able to show that the presence of arousal along with the belief that it was caused by one's counterattitudinal behavior play a crucial role in provoking attitude change. First, they predicted that if people induced to perform a counterattitudinal behavior could be tricked into misattributing their resulting discomfort and the unpleasant arousal that accompanies it to a different source, they would not think they are upset about their behavior, and so would not change their attitudes.

To demonstrate this, they conducted a typical dissonance experiment in which participants were asked to perform a counterattitudinal behavior, but they added a new twist: Participants were also asked to ingest a pill (Zanna and Cooper 1974). In fact the pill was a placebo, a sugar pill that had no side effects. Control participants were told, truthfully, that the pill would have no effect on them. These participants showed the kind of attitude change obtained in typical dissonance studies—they became more supportive of the attitude they had been induced to express. Another group of participants was informed that the pill would make them feel aroused and tense. These participants were expected to feel the same discomfort and arousal experienced by the control participants, and for the same reason—they were disturbed by their behavior. But, unlike control participants, these participants were given an alternative explanation for their arousal—the pill. If they misattributed their arousal to the pill, they would be unlikely to realize that they were disturbed by their behavior and, therefore, would have little motivation to change their attitude. This is exactly what happened—participants who believed the pill would cause arousal showed no attitude change. Yet another group of participants were informed that the pill would make them feel relaxed. These participants showed even greater attitude change than did controls. Expecting relaxation, they must have concluded from their surprising arousal and discomfort that they were extremely disturbed by their behavior and, therefore, that their motivation to change their attitudes must have been especially strong.

This study showed that attitude change in dissonance experiments requires the correct attribution of arousal to one's counterattitudinal behavior. Follow-up studies further implicated the crucial role of arousal, by showing that attitude change in such experiments was virtually eliminated when unsuspecting participants were given a tranquilizer that reduced their arousal and was exaggerated when they were given amphetamines that increased their arousal (Cooper, Zanna, and Taves 1978). Note that if participants were merely inferring their attitudes from their behavior as suggested by Bem's self-perception theory, their actual level of arousal and their belief about its likely source should have had no impact on their attitudes. The finding that attitude change in such experiments occurs only in the presence of arousal that is attributed to concern about one's behavior suggests, then, that the attitude change results from an attempt to deal with the source of this concern. In short, it is driven by motivation.

Other researchers were quick to use the logic of these experiments to demonstrate that self-serving attributions about one's own success and failure also required arousal, suggesting that motivation plays a role in these too (for a review, see Pyszczynski and Greenberg 1987). The dissonance paradigm also gave rise to another line of work that provided strong evidence for the important role of motivation in provoking attitude change by showing that such attitude change is driven by the need to affirm one's sense of oneself as a fine person, as I discuss next (Steele 1988).

Self-affirmation

Imagine you have just found yourself, to your horror, publicly endorsing a political party whose policies you actually find quite offensive (countless dissonance studies suggest that it would be remarkably easy to get you to do this). Naturally, such an act can provoke intense self-recrimination: What kind of a person am I? How could I have been so stupid? What happened to my moral fiber? But before you have had a chance to dwell on these challenges to your self-image, a friend calls to tell you about a new show at a local art gallery. You are reminded that you are an art-lover, a fine, cultured person of great value. Would this be enough for you to dismiss any doubts about your self-worth that your behavior had given rise to? Research by Claude Steele and his colleagues suggests that it might be (for a review, see Steele 1988).

Steele and his colleagues reasoned that the counterattitudinal behaviors that people are led to perform in dissonance studies provoke attitude change because they pose a threat to one's self-image. These behaviors challenge one's sense of oneself as an intelligent and decent person and so create a need to reaffirm one's self-worth. One may obtain such *self-affirmation* by changing one's attitudes— if the position I have endorsed is not that bad then I am not so bad a person. But that is not the only route to self-affirmation. Any thoughts and actions that bring to mind valued aspects of one's self-concept can also serve to reestablish one's sense of oneself as a worthy person, even if these are completely unrelated to the counterattitudinal behavior. For a scientist, self-worth could be reaffirmed through reading a scientific journal, for a religious person through prayer, and for an art-lover through a visit to an art gallery. If, following a counterattitudinal behavior, one is reminded of these valued aspects of oneself, this will reaffirm one's global self-worth and, therefore, reduce the need to change one's attitude in the service of such self-affirmation.

In a series of studies Steele and his colleagues demonstrated that the attitude change provoked by counterattitudinal behavior could indeed be undercut by an opportunity to affirm other valued aspects of one's self. One study demonstrating this included two kinds of participants: students who cared about politics and economics, and students who did not (Steele and Liu 1983). These students, who were also known to be strongly opposed to tuition hikes, were induced to write an essay supporting substantial increases in tuition. This traditional forced-compliance manipulation was expected to provoke attitude change in participants who believed that they had chosen to write this counterattitudinal essay freely. Such attitude change was indeed obtained in control conditions for both types of participants. But the study also included another set of conditions in which participants were asked to complete a questionnaire about politics and economics before they were asked about their attitudes. For participants who valued politics and economics, this questionnaire served as a reminder of a valued aspect of themselves and, as such, provided an opportunity for self-affirmation. If the need for self-affirmation drives attitude change then these participants, who have already achieved self-affirmation through this alternative route, should no longer need to change their attitudes. In contrast, participants who did not value politics and economics should be unable to derive any self-affirmation from the questionnaire and so should still need to reaffirm themselves through attitude change. This is exactly what happened. Answering a questionnaire about politics and economics eliminated the attitude change for participants who valued these domains but not for participants who did not.

This and similar studies suggest that the motivation to reaffirm oneself can drive attitude change following counterattitudinal behavior. When this motivation is satisfied through other routes, attitudes do not change. Note that Bem's self-perception theory cannot account for such findings. If one simply inferred one's attitudes from one's behavior, such inferences should not be affected by answering unrelated questionnaires that happen to affirm one's self-worth on a different dimension.

The same logic has been used to demonstrate the motivational underpinnings of other kinds of judgment as well. In one study, for example, participants rated a woman as less competent when she appeared Jewish than when she appeared Italian (Fein and Spencer 1997; see chapter 8). But this tendency to derogate the Jewish woman was eliminated when participants were given an opportunity to affirm valued aspects of the self. This suggests that such prejudice is driven, at least in part, by the need to affirm one's own self-worth; derogating a Jew, an African American, or a gay person may serve to highlight one's own superiority. When the need for self-affirmation is satisfied through other means, one is less compelled to derogate members of negatively stereotyped groups.

In sum, two independent lines of work point to the important role that motivation plays in provoking attitude change in forced compliance experiments. The first implicated motivation by showing that attitude change is obtained only when people also experience arousal and attribute it to their behavior. The second implicated motivation by showing that attitude change is eliminated when people are given other means of satisfying their need to reaffirm their self-worth. Both kinds of logic have been widely accepted as evidence for the impact of motivation, and both have been used to show that motivation drives other types of judgment as well. When these lines of work are viewed alongside the outcome-dependency studies which obtained evidence for motivated reasoning that could not be readily reinterpreted in purely cognitive terms, the case for motivated reasoning seems quite compelling. Many researchers have now accepted this conclusion and have begun addressing the question of just how motivation might affect judgment, as I discuss next.

Mechanisms for Motivated Reasoning

In his 1987 book *And the Band Played On* Randy Shilts tracked the reactions of various communities to increasingly disturbing findings about a then-unknown deadly disease that had begun to show up in gay men, a disease now known as AIDS. The gay community, the scientific community, the U.S. government, and the blood banks, all initially refused to believe the signs pointing to a devastating conclusion, namely that the disease was infectious and could be transmitted sexually. It was clear to all that if this were true, the disease could claim a horrendous number of lives within and beyond the gay community. In addition, the gay community would have to forgo much of its characteristic lifestyle, the blood banks would have to acknowledge that their blood was unsafe and to dramatically modify their procedures at great cost, and the government would have to deal with the vast financial and social implications. The motivation to believe that this horrific scenario could not be true was tremendous. And, indeed, all these communities attempted at first to justify rejecting the dreaded infectious-disease theory, with some success. Scientists expended great effort following every lead that pointed to alternative explanations, focusing, for example, on environmental factors such as drugs that are unique to the gay community. Within the gay community, a popular alternative theory postulated a right-wing conspiracy to undermine the gay lifestyle. The disease raged while, as Shilts put it, the band played on. Yet these motivated efforts at denial eventually gave way to reality. As the evidence mounted, most people came to believe that AIDS was indeed caused by a virus and could be transmitted sexually as well as through blood transfusions. The blood banks altered their procedures, and gay organizations began preaching safe sex.

This brief history illustrates my own account of how motivation affects judgment (Kunda 1990; for similar ideas, see Kruglanski 1980; Pyszczynski and Greenberg 1987). Motivation can color our judgments, but we are not at liberty to conclude whatever we want to conclude simply because we want to. Even when we are motivated to arrive at a particular conclusion, we are also motivated to be rational and to construct a justification for our desired conclusion that would persuade a dispassionate observer. We will draw our desired conclusion only if we can come up with enough evidence to support it. But despite our best efforts to be objective and rational, motivation may nevertheless color our judgment because the process of justification construction can itself be biased by our goals. To construct justifications for desired conclusions, we search through our memory for beliefs and rules that support these conclusions directly and use existing knowledge to construct new general beliefs and theories from which our desired conclusions can be derived. As discussed in chapter 4, when we attempt to determine whether a hypothesis is correct, our search for relevant memories and beliefs may be one-sided and may be biased toward finding support for it (Klayman and Ha 1987). This may be all the more true when we are also motivated to believe the hypothesis.

When you are trying to determine your likely academic performance, you are most probably motivated to see yourself as highly successful. When you search your memory for relevant information, you may be particularly likely to recall your past successes (that A+ in history) and may be less likely to recall your past failures. You may also construct broader theories about how your personal background makes you particularly likely to succeed. If you are the first in your family to attend college, you may reason that this gives you an especially strong drive to succeed. With these beliefs in mind, you may feel justified in concluding that you will indeed be successful. What you don't realize is that you also have knowledge that could be used to support the opposite conclusion. You have experienced some failures (remember that botched physics exam?). And as for your theory about the benefits of your background, it is just as easy to justify an opposite theory. If you had come from a long line of college graduates, you might have reasoned instead that your family culture and ethics made you especially well-prepared for academic success. So we think we are being rational, carefully weighing evidence and applying inferential rules to its evaluation. We don't realize that both the evidence that we have recruited and the rules we have used to evaluate it are biased by motivation. If our goals had been different, we might have recruited different evidence and used different rules. Note, however, that although motivation can bias our judgments, it does not blind us to reality. Because we feel compelled to be rational, we will only draw our desired conclusions if we can justify them. Our understanding of reality imposes constraints on our ability to draw desired conclusions.

There is now evidence for such *motivated memory search and belief construction*, as well as for the *constraints* imposed by reality on motivated reasoning. In discussing the impact of goals on memory, I described studies showing that people with different motives bring different memories to mind (see chapter 5). For example, people motivated to see themselves as extraverted or introverted were especially likely to recall those of their past behaviors that were consistent with their desired self-view. This enabled them to see themselves as higher on the desired trait (Sanitioso, Kunda, and Fong 1990). A follow-up study showed that people's ability to construct such desired self-images is constrained by their prior self-knowledge.

Two types of participants were selected for the study: extremely extraverted students and extremely introverted ones (Sanitioso

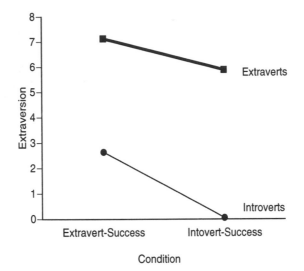

Figure 6.1   Self-ratings of extraverts and introverts who were motivated to see themselves as extraverted (extravert-success) or as introverted (introvert-success). From Sanitioso et al. (1990, fig. 2, p. 238). Copyright © (1990) by the American Psychological Association. Reprinted with permission.

et al. 1990). As in the earlier studies, participants were led to believe that either extraversion or introversion was conducive to academic and professional success. Most probably, participants therefore wanted to see themselves as extraverted or as introverted. Then, in a seemingly unrelated study, participants were asked to rate their own introversion/extraversion. These self-ratings are portrayed in figure 6.1. You may see that both extraverts and introverts rated themselves as more extraverted when they were motivated to see themselves as extraverted than when they were motivated to see themselves as introverted; their self-views were affected by motivation. But you may also see that these shifts in self-conceptions were clearly constrained by participants' prior knowledge about themselves. Extraverts in both conditions rated themselves as more extraverted than did introverts. Indeed, extraverts who wanted to see themselves as introverted still saw themselves as more extraverted than did introverts who wanted to see themselves as extraverted! Even when motivated, we will only draw those conclusions that seem feasible, given our understanding of reality.

Our ability to selectively access those beliefs that best support our goals may also enable us to construct causal theories that support desired beliefs. For example, we may come to believe that our own attributes and background are especially conducive to desired outcomes. It has been shown that people view their own attributes as more conducive than other attributes to another person's success at school or at achieving a happy marriage (Kunda 1987). For example, participants whose own mothers had been employed outside the home when they were young and participants whose mothers had stayed home when they were young developed quite different theories about the roots of marital success. Each group believed that their own kind of mother was more likely than the other kind to predispose her children toward having a happy marriage. In short, people with opposite attributes constructed opposite theories about how these attributes might relate to success. Another set of studies suggested that the construction of such self-serving theories is driven at least in part by the motivation to see oneself in the best possible light. Motivation was implicated by showing that the tendency to construct such self-serving theories was especially strong after participants had experienced failure, when their need to boost their self-regard was enhanced (Dunning, Leuenberger, and Sherman 1995).

Our own attributes may also influence our definitions of ability. If I am more mathematically than verbally inclined, I may believe that math skills are most central to intelligence. But if, instead, my verbal skills are stronger than my mathematical ones, I may believe that verbal skills are most central to intelligence. One study making this point included two kinds of participants, people-oriented ones and goal-oriented ones (Dunning, Perie, and Story 1991). When these participants were asked which attributes best captured their image of a leader, people-oriented participants rated interpersonal skill as more central to leadership than did goal-oriented participants, whereas goal-oriented participants rated attributes such as ambition and persistence as more central than did people-oriented participants.

Our ability to define traits idiosyncratically may contribute to our belief that we are better than others. There is considerable evidence that most people see themselves as above average on a wide variety of dimensions. Most of us think we are better than our average peer in our academic skills, our driving ability, our leadership ability, our marriage prospects, and our health, to name but a few examples (see Dunning, Meyerowitz, and Holzberg 1989). Naturally, we can't all be better than average. We may believe that we are in part because we base our definitions of excellence on our unique strengths. Someone who is highly creative but not very good with numbers may believe he is extraordinarily intelligent if he assumes that creativity is the most central feature of intelligence. If self-serving trait definitions contribute to the "I'm above average" effect, people should be less likely to view themselves as above average when their ability to define a trait idiosyncratically is constrained. A series of studies by David Dunning and his colleagues suggests that this is indeed the case. People rated themselves as more extraordinary on ambiguous traits such as *sensitive* or *idealistic* which could be understood in many different ways than they did on more clearly defined traits such as *well read* and *punctual*. Moreover, even for ambiguous traits, people's tendency to see themselves as above average was reduced when they were required to base their trait ratings on a small number of criteria supplied by the investigators (Dunning et al. 1989). It appears that we only view ourselves as above average on a given trait if we can justify this, based on our own self-knowledge and our understanding of the trait. We may not realize, though, that our self-knowledge can influence our understanding of the trait; we define traits so as to portray ourselves in the best possible light.

Motivation may also influence which inferential rules people are likely to select and use. Recall that my mother complained about small sample size when evidence from the sample of her two sons suggested that smoking during pregnancy may be harmful, but she was.perfectly happy to use evidence from that very same sample of two to make the point that smoking was harmless. Such motivated use of rules about the sufficiency of small samples has also been demonstrated in more rigorous research. In one study, participants were given either desirable information, namely that their own group was more prosocial than a different group, or undesirable information, namely that their own group was less prosocial than a different group (Doosje, Spears, and Koomen 1995). This information was based either on a small sample or on a large sample. When the sample was large, and therefore difficult to dismiss, people accepted its conclusions even when these were undesirable; they were forced to conclude that the out-group was superior to the in-group. This shows, once again, that people's ability to draw desired conclusions is constrained by their understanding of reality and feasibility. In contrast, when the sample was small, people generalized from it only when it pointed to a desired conclusion, namely that their in-group was superior. When it pointed to an undesirable conclusion, they failed to generalize from it, and did not conclude that their own group was inferior. In other words, they dismissed a small sample as too small when it pointed to an undesirable conclusion but not when it pointed to a desirable one.

Motivation may lead to selective use of other inferential rules as well. Imagine that you were shown data about the leadership skills of all the executives and office workers in a particular corporation. A simple count shows that there are many more men than women who are good leaders. On the face of it, these data suggest that men are more likely than women to be good leaders. Yet more careful examination of the data reveals that this correlation between gender and leadership skills is spurious—within each of the two professional groups, executives and office workers, women are just as likely as men to be good leaders. Gender appears to be correlated with leadership skills only because executives are far more likely than office workers to be good leaders, and men are far more likely than women to be executives. The correlation is due to the unequal distribution of genders among the two professions rather than to the superiority of men over women within each profession.

Schaller (1992) predicted that men shown such data would accept the spurious correlation at face value. Women, in contrast, would be motivated to debunk any notion of female inferiority, and this motivation would lead them to retrieve the inferential rules needed to see through the spurious correlation between gender and leadership skills. Indeed, women shown such data were considerably more likely than men to notice that the correlation between gender and leadership was spurious and was due to the unequal distribution of men and women in the two professional categories. It is not the case that women are simply more adept than men at this kind of reasoning. Follow-up studies in which participants were shown comparable data about artificially created in-groups and out-groups provided a conceptual replication of these results among both women and men. It appears that we are more likely to notice that a correlation is spurious when we are motivated to disbelieve it.

Research on inferential rules has shown that we have at our disposal a wide array of heuristics, and a variety of factors influence which of these will be used on a particular occasion; we may use the representativeness heuristic to solve a particular problem on one occasion but use a statistical heuristic to solve the same problem on another occasion (Ginossar and Trope 1987; Nisbett et al. 1983; see chapter 3). The studies just described suggest that motivation may be one of the factors that influences our choice of heuristics. We may be particularly likely to call on those heuristics that allow us to arrive at our desired conclusion.

Motivation may affect not only which memories, beliefs, and rules we access but also the *amount* of effort we invest in searching for relevant beliefs and rules in the first place (Ditto and Lopez 1992; Kruglanski 1980). When we come across evidence that supports our desired conclusions, we may accept it at face value. But when we come across comparable evidence that challenges our desired conclusions, we may evaluate it more critically and work hard to refute it. In a telling study by Charles Lord, Lee Ross, and Mark Lepper, opponents and proponents of capital punishment read about two studies on the deterrent effects of capital punishment, one suggesting that capital punishment was an effective deterrent, and one that it was a worthless deterrent (Lord, Ross, and Lepper 1979). The two studies involved different methodologies, and the materials were counterbalanced such that each method was associated with the pro-capital-punishment conclusion for half of the participants and with the anti-capital-punishment conclusion for the other half. Both opponents and proponents of capital punishment thought that the study that disconfirmed their own beliefs was more poorly conducted than the one that confirmed their beliefs. In other words, the same methodology was viewed as acceptable when it resulted in support for their beliefs but as unacceptable when it challenged their beliefs. The end result was that after viewing the same mixed bag of evidence, each group became even more convinced of its original position.

It is unclear whether participants in this study were biased because they were motivated to believe the study that confirmed their own position or because they considered it more plausible, given their prior beliefs. Evidence for the importance of motivation for such biases was provided in a later study in which participants were exposed to arguments for or against their own position on capital punishment. This study too found that the same argument was judged to be stronger when it supported participants' own position than when it challenged it. Moreover such bias was especially pronounced for participants who had indicated high emotional involvement in the issue, which suggests that motivation had contributed to the bias (Edwards and Smith 1996). This study also obtained more rigorous evidence that people invest greater effort in evaluating undesirable evidence than in evaluating desirable evidence, and that their effort is directed at refuting the undesirable evidence. When asked to list the thoughts that came to mind when considering the conclusion they were asked to evaluate, participants generated more thoughts overall and more refutations when the argument challenged their own position than when it supported their position. It appears that the amount of time and effort we expend in evaluating evidence depends at least in part on how much we wish to believe it. When the evidence is undesirable, we will work especially hard at undermining it.

In summary, our judgments may be biased by our motives because we selectively access those beliefs and rules that support our desired conclusions and try especially hard to refute undesirable conclusions. However, we will only draw our desired conclusions when we succeed at justifying them. Our ability to justify desired conclusions is constrained by our understanding of reality.

Revisiting the Motivation versus Cognition Debate

Recall that in the absence of independent evidence for motivated reasoning, the major argument for preferring cognitive mechanisms over motivational ones was parsimony; the cognitive account was simpler in that it required fewer constructs. However, now that there is independent evidence for the role of motivation, it is possible to turn this parsimony argument on its head. It now seems that a single construct, motivation, may account for many different phenomena, ranging from self-serving attributions about oneself, through motivated beliefs about others, to biased evaluation of scientific evidence. Many of these phenomena cannot be accounted for in strictly cognitive terms. For many others it is possible to construct cognitive accounts, but these require many speculative assumptions. For example, to explain why people with different family backgrounds would construct different theories about what predicts academic success, you could propose that they have been inadvertently exposed to different information about the precursors of such success. But there is no evidence for such differential exposure, whereas there is evidence that people are motivated to believe that they will succeed. Under the current state of knowledge, the motivational account, which requires fewer auxiliary assumptions, seems more parsimonious.

Having said this, let me add that with the new insights into the mechanisms underlying motivated reasoning, the distinction between motivational and cognitive processes has begun to blur (see Sorrentino and Higgins 1986). I am sure that it has not escaped your notice that the mechanisms that have been proposed to account for motivated reasoning are cognitive: memory search, rule use, belief construction. Motivation appears to have its effects by harnessing the cognitive system to its service. In its underlying mechanisms, the process of confirming our desired conclusions, typically billed as "hot cognition" seems indistinguishable from the process of confirming our expectations, which is typically billed as "cold cognition." The parallel between goals and expectancies becomes even stronger if one recognizes that our seemingly cold expectancies may themselves be imbued with motivation. The prospect of having to abandon a well-established belief may be every bit as unpleasant as some of the undesirable conclusions investigated under the rubric of "hot cognition." It was this insight that led Festinger, the founder of the quintessentially motivational dissonance theory, to speculate that you would experience strong dissonance if you found yourself standing in the rain without getting wet (Festinger 1957).

Normative Considerations

The philosopher David Hume stated that "Reason is and ought to be the slave of passion." Do you agree? Do you think it is a good thing that our judgments can be colored by our motives and desires? In an influential article, Shelley Taylor and Jonathon Brown argued that motivated reasoning and the optimistic illusions that it gives rise to can be highly adaptive (Taylor and Brown 1988). These authors reviewed a series of positive illusions that most of us entertain: Our self-perceptions are overly flattering, we exaggerate the extent to which we can control events in our lives, our expectations about the future are unrealistically rosy. There is one group of people who do not display any of these illusions—depressed people. Perhaps, then, these unrealistically positive beliefs contribute to our general happiness and well-being; without them, the threats and difficulties of daily life would doom us to misery and depression. Moreover, our glowing views of ourselves and our prospects and our exaggerated sense of control may do more than make us feel good. They may also increase our motivation and effort, and lead us to persist at difficult tasks even in the face of initial failure. As a result these positive expectations may become self-fulfilling; if you believe in yourself, you will often do what it takes to make these beliefs come true (for a review, see Armor and Taylor 1998).

Positive illusions about others may be adaptive as well. In one study of intimate relationships, partners in 180 married and dating couples each rated themselves and their partner on a series of positive and negative attributes, and also rated their satisfaction with their relationship (Murray, Holmes, and Griffin 1996; for a related discussion, see chapter 10). Overall, intimates tended to idealize their partners; they saw their partners even more positively than the partners saw themselves. Such idealization appeared to promote satisfaction—individuals were happier in their relationship the more they idealized their partner. Individuals were also happier the more their partner idealized them. In such a study, it is difficult to know which measure best reflects reality; it is possible that people's self-views reflect reality, and their partners' more glowing views of them reflect a positive illusion. It is also possible, though, that people are overly modest in their self-ratings, and it is their partners who see them more realistically. Nevertheless, these data do show that the more positively you view your partner in an intimate relationship, the more satisfied you are likely to be with this relationship. When you view your partner in the best possible light, you may feel happier and more secure in your relationship, and both you and your partner may have the generosity and good will needed to overcome inevitable daily conflict. Ultimately, positive illusions about intimate partners may be self-fulfilling.

Despite these advantages of positive illusions, it is important to note that motivated illusions can sometimes get you into serious trouble. This is especially true when motivated reasoning leads you to play down the significance of real threats and prevents you from carrying out behaviors that could protect you from danger. Motivated reasoning that leads you to ignore early symptoms of severe illness such as skin cancer or to distrust evidence pointing to the dangers of smoking could literally cost you your life. Unrealistically rosy views of yourself and others can also be costly. If you pursue goals that are beyond your reach, you may have to deal with failure. And if you pursue romantic relationships with unsuitable individuals, you may have to deal with abuse or divorce. It should be noted, however, that there have been few attempts to document the consequences of positive illusions empirically; most researchers have focused on identifying these illusions rather than on exploring their consequences (Armor and Taylor 1998).

Positive illusions may be especially beneficial when they concern global judgments that do not serve as the basis for immediate action. There may be little harm in holding an exaggerated view of your likability and kindness, or in believing that your marriage is more loving and stable than most people's. But motivated reasoning can be costly and dangerous when it is used to guide important behaviors and decisions, especially in situations where more objective reasoning could give rise to more appropriate behavior. People may have some inkling of these considerations. They seem most likely to engage in positive illusions in situations where their unrealistically positive expectations are unlikely to be put to the test of reality because they concern global rather than specific outcomes, because they pertain to ambiguous or subjective outcomes, because they pertain to outcomes in the distant future, or for any other reason that makes immediate, clear-cut disconfirmation unlikely (for a review, see Armor and Taylor 1998).

So far I have focused on directional goals that motivate people to draw a particular conclusion. I turn text to a different kind of goal, the goal of arriving at the most accurate conclusion possible, whatever it may be.

ACCURACY GOALS

Allison, a personnel officer at a large corporation, is reviewing the folders of two engineers who have applied for a job at her company. She knows that after she makes her choice, she will have to give her boss a full account of her decision, and explain the reasons for her preference. The same two engineers have also applied for a job at Gail's company. Gail's position gives her complete control over hiring decisions, and she will not have to explain her reasoning to anyone. Which of the two do you suppose will spend more time going over the folders and musing over the decision? Which will make the better decision? The first of these questions is a lot easier to answer than the second. Chances are that Allison, who needs to justify her decision to her boss, will think longer and harder about it than Gail, who is accountable to no one. But whether this more extensive and elaborate thinking will actually result in a better decision depends on a variety of factors. Hard thinking can improve judgment under some circumstances but can make it worse under others (as noted in chapter 3).

We may assume that Allison is more strongly motivated than Gail to make an accurate and correct decision. Accuracy goals differ importantly from the directional goals discussed in the previous section. When you have a *directional goal*, you are motivated to arrive at a particular conclusion. In contrast, when you have an *accuracy goal*, you are motivated to arrive at the most accurate conclusion possible, whatever it may be (Kruglanski 1980; Kunda 1990; Pyszczynski and Greenberg 1987). Accuracy goals may arise for different reasons. You may be motivated to be accurate because, like Allison, you know you are accountable to others. You may also be motivated to be accurate because you know a lot rides on your decision. Chances are that you will have strong accuracy goals when you expect that a wrong decision could cost you a great deal of money, ruin your reputation, undermine a project you care deeply about, or cause you to treat others unfairly.

There is considerable evidence that such accuracy goals lead people to invest greater effort in the judgment task and to search harder for the best possible reasoning strategies. People alternate between different modes of thinking. Sometimes we engage in careful, systematic, elaborate processing aimed at arriving at the best judgment possible. On other occasions we engage in more cursory, superficial, "quick and dirty," heuristic processing aimed at arriving at a good enough, if imperfect judgment (for reviews, see Chaiken and Trope 1999; see chapter 3). Accuracy goals lead people to favor the elaborate over the cursory processing. Put differently, rather than "freezing" their judgment process as soon as they arrive at a semblance of an answer, people motivated to be accurate will continue thinking and reasoning until they are satisfied that they have arrived at the best possible conclusion (Kruglanski 1980). These enhanced efforts will result in greater accuracy when, upon reflection, people turn to strategies that are indeed better. Sometimes, however, reflection may lead people to retrieve poorer strategies that they mistakenly view as better. In such cases accuracy goals will decrease accuracy (for a review, see Kunda 1990; see chapter 3).

The clearest evidence that accuracy goals can increase the complexity of thought comes from a study by Philip Tetlock and Jae Kim, who motivated some participants to be accurate by leading them to expect that after making their judgments, they would have to explain their thinking to the researchers (Tetlock and Kim 1987). Other participants were told, instead, that their judgments would remain confidential and that even the experimenter would not know how they had responded. Participants were then shown the responses made by three people to 16 questions about their personality. After reading these responses, they wrote a description of each respondent's personality, and then predicted how each would respond to 16 other personality questions. Participants motivated to be accurate wrote more cognitively complex descriptions of the respondents: They relied on a greater number of attributes to describe each person, were more likely to note contradictions within a person's character, and were also more likely to develop an integrated view of the person by drawing elaborate connections among distinct attributes. This increased complexity of thought paid off—participants motivated to be accurate did in fact make more accurate predictions about how the respondents would answer the second set of questions, and this was due, in part, to the increased complexity of their impressions.

Many studies have shown that accuracy goals can improve judgment, presumably because they lead people to rely on better inferential strategies. For example, in a series of studies, Arie Kruglanski and his colleagues showed that people who were motivated to be accurate because they expected to be evaluated, because they expected to have to justify their judgments to others, because they expected their judgments to be made public, or because they expected their judgments to have a real impact on other people's lives were less likely to show a variety of cognitive biases: They were less likely to show a primacy effect in impression formation, that is, to be overly influenced by information observed early on; their evaluations of essays were less influenced by the ethnicity of the essay writer; and they were less likely to anchor on irrelevant numbers when making probability judgments. Participants with strong accuracy goals probably showed less bias because they engaged in more careful and elaborate thinking. Indeed, when participants' ability to engage in lengthy thought was curtailed by a requirement to respond quickly, all of these biases were exaggerated (Freund, Kruglanski, and Shpitzajzen 1985; Kruglanski and Freund 1983).

As I noted earlier, accuracy goals do not guarantee increased accuracy. In several studies, monetary incentives or admonitions to be accurate failed to eliminate bias. Accuracy goals created in this manner did not decrease reliance on the availability heuristic, did not increase reliance on difficult statistical rules, and did not eliminate the hindsight bias (e.g., Fischhoff 1977; Kahneman and Tversky 1973). When we do not possess a superior reasoning strategy or when we fail to recognize its relevance and superiority, no amount of thought will improve judgment. Worse, when careful thought leads us to bring forth more faulty rules, accuracy goals will increase errors and biases. For example, it has been shown that asking people to reflect carefully upon the reasons for their preferences can lead them to focus on the wrong criteria and, thereby, reduce the quality of their judgment (Wilson and Schooler 1991). Several studies have shown that accuracy goals, and the complex reasoning that they give rise to, can have similarly unfortunate effects.

In one study, participants motivated to be accurate (because they expected to justify their judgments) were more likely than others to show the dilution effect, that is, to make less extreme judgments about another person when given irrelevant information about this person (Tetlock and Boettger 1989). In another study, participants motivated to be accurate (because they were told that performance reflected intelligence) were more likely than others to give erroneous responses to difficult problems such as Kahneman and Tversky's hospital problem (see chapter 3), and this increased error rate was due to an increased reliance on faulty heuristics. Interestingly, the same accuracy goals led to improved performance on easier versions of the same problems for which the relevance of the correct rules was more transparent (Pelham and Neter 1995). In short, it is not always the case that more elaborate and complex thought will lead to improved judgment. There are situations in which the harder we think, the more likely we are to resort to faulty reasoning strategies. In such situations accuracy goals can, ironically, increase error and enhance bias.

In sum, both directional goals and accuracy goals affect judgment by influencing our choice of beliefs and rules. However, directional goals lead us to favor those beliefs and rules that can support our desired conclusions, whereas accuracy goals lead us to favor those beliefs and rules that seem most appropriate to the task. I turn next to a discussion of some circumstances that could give rise to accuracy and directional goals.

Deliberative and Implemental Mindsets

When you are contemplating buying a house, you may work hard to ensure a correct decision. You may note the advantages and disadvantages of each house you see, and consider their implications in a careful and objective manner. Your aim is to buy the best house possible, and you don't want to be confronted with any nasty surprises once the deal is done. But once you have decided on a particular house, you turn your attention to doing what it takes to make the deal go through: Getting the owner to accept your offer, securing a mortgage, lining up contractors for your planned renovations. This is not a time for doubts and indecision; it is a time for action.

Research by Peter Gollwitzer and his colleagues suggests that people who are in the process of making a decision develop a *deliberative mindset* which leads them to consider relevant information in a careful and balanced manner. Put differently, deliberative mindsets give rise to accuracy goals. In contrast, people who have just made a decision develop an *implemental mindset* which leads them to focus on the thoughts and actions necessary to achieve the outcome that they have decided to pursue. The determination to achieve chosen outcomes may give rise to directional goals that foster a belief in one's ability to bring these desired outcomes about. Once elicited, these mindsets may carry over into unrelated tasks. When you are carefully deliberating buying a house, you may deliberate your own strengths and weaknesses just as carefully, but once you have decided to buy a house and are focused on getting the best deal possible, you may also see yourself in the best possible light (Gollwitzer and Kinney 1989; Taylor and Gollwitzer 1995; for a review, see Gollwitzer and Moskowitz 1996).

In a series of studies, Gollwitzer and his colleagues elicited deliberative and implemental mindsets by asking participants to focus on their own life tasks. Participants were put in a deliberative mindset through a set of instructions guiding them to think about an unresolved personal problem and to contemplate the positive and negative consequences of taking an action that would change the way things were. Other participants were put in an implemental mindset through a set of instructions guiding them to think about a project they had already decided to undertake, to list the steps necessary for bringing that project to completion, and to describe how they would execute these steps. Control participants were given no mindset manipulation. In one study, after their mindsets were manipulated in this manner, participants turned next to the seemingly unrelated task of estimating the amount of control they had over the onset of a red light that they were attempting to turn on by pressing or by not pressing a button. In fact, they had no control at all over the light—it turned on frequently regardless of what they did (Gollwitzer and Kinney 1989).

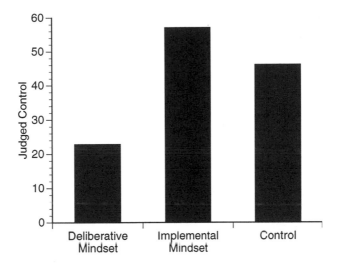

Figure 6.2 The amount of control that participants in a deliberative mindset, participants in an implemental mindset and control participants thought they had over the onset of a light. Gollwitzer and Kinney (1989, fig. 2, p. 539). Copyright © (1989) by the American Psychological Association. Reprinted with permission.

Results suggested that a deliberative mindset can reduce the tendency to exaggerate the extent to which one can control uncontrollable events. As shown in figure 6.2, participants in a deliberative mindset thought they had exercised substantially less control over the light than did participants in an implemental mindset or control participants. Participants in an implemental mindset thought they had somewhat more control than did control participants, but this difference was not statistically significant. This study suggests, then, that a deliberative mindset that arises when we contemplate an unresolved issue in our life can lead us to suspend our normal illusions about our ability to control other, unrelated events in our life.

Another series of studies that manipulated mindsets in the same manner found that mindsets can also influence self-perceptions and beliefs about one's vulnerability to risk (Taylor and Gollwitzer 1995). An implemental mindset increased participants' tendency to believe that they were better than their peers on a variety of desirable skills and attributes, whereas a deliberative mindset reduced this tendency. Implemental mindsets also reduced participants' sense of vulnerability to risks such as divorce and disease. It appears, then, that the accuracy goals elicited by deliberative mindsets can decrease the positive illusions we normally entertain about ourselves, whereas the directional goals fostered by implemental mindsets can exacerbate these illusions.

CLOSURE GOALS

President Truman once quipped in exasperation that he wished he could find a one-handed economic advisor, one who wouldn't qualify every recommendation with "but on the other hand,...." A person who must decide on a course of action may have little patience for equivocation. Arie Kruglanski and his colleagues proposed that sometimes achieving *closure*, that is, arriving at a clear conclusion, becomes a goal in its own right (Kruglanski 1980; Kruglanski and Webster 1996). We may be motivated to obtain quick closure if we are operating under time pressure, if we find the decision-making task so tedious that we are eager to get it over with, or if we know we can turn to a more enjoyable activity as soon as we have completed the one we are working on. Some people have an ongoing need for closure and find any lack of closure disturbing. When we are motivated to achieve closure, we may "freeze" our thinking process early on, as soon as we have arrived at what seems like a good enough solution. We may also fall back on those rules and beliefs that are most readily available and easy to use. Often, such "quick and dirty" thinking will increase error and bias. Indeed, Kruglanski and his colleagues have shown that a variety of biases can be exacerbated by time pressure (Freund et al. 1985; Kruglanski and Freund 1983).

At other times, we are motivated to *avoid closure* and, to this end, attempt to prolong the judgment process and to postpone arriving at a clear conclusion for as long as possible. Accuracy goals may provoke a motivation to avoid closure. If we are afraid of making a mistake, and know that once we have committed ourselves to a particular conclusion we will be open to criticism and punishment, we may wish to put off the moment of truth. We may also wish to extend the judgment process because we find it inherently enjoyable, or at least more enjoyable than the task we know we must turn to next. When we are motivated to avoid closure, as when we are motivated to be accurate, we expend greater effort on the judgment. Therefore, the consequences of closure avoidance can be expected to be the same as the consequences of accuracy goals—greater accuracy and fewer biases when increased efforts yield reliance on better reasoning strategies, but not otherwise.

A series of studies by Donna Webster showed that closure goals can influence judgments about another person (Webster 1993). In one study, participants watched a video of a woman reading a speech expressing a negative view of student exchange programs. Half were informed that she had chosen to read this speech, and half that she had had no choice in the matter. In such circumstances, people typically assume that the speaker's own opinions are consistent with her expressed views even when they know that she had not chosen freely to express these views. In other words, they exaggerate the extent to which her attitude corresponds to her behavior (see Jones 1990; see chapter 9). People are especially likely to display this bias when they have too few cognitive resources to carefully consider the implications of the situational constraints, that is, the fact that the person was required to read this essay (Gilbert, Pelham, and Krull 1988; see chapter 7). Perhaps, then, the goal of achieving quick closure, which leads people to invest less effort in the judgment, will increase the correspondence bias, and the goal of avoiding closure, which leads people to invest extra efforts in the judgment, will reduce the bias. Webster set out to investigate this possibility. Some participants were motivated to achieve quick closer, because they expected that, as soon as they were done, they would be able to turn to the far more attractive task of watching a collection of comedy clips. Others were motivated to avoid quick closure, because they expected that they would have to turn next to a lecture on statistics, a prospect they found extremely unattractive. Control participants

Table 6.1 Ratings made by participants with different closure goals of the true attitude of a target who had delivered a speech, with or without free choice, in which she opposed student exchange programs

| | GOAL OF PARTICIPANTS | | |
CONSTRAINT	QUICK CLOSURE (NEXT TASK MORE ATTRACTIVE)	NEUTRAL (NEXT TASK EQUALLY ATTRACTIVE)	AVOID CLOSURE (NEXT TASK LESS ATTRACTIVE)
No choice	2.31	3.76	7.08
Free choice	1.69	2.27	2.13

Source: From Webster (1993, table 2, p. 265). Copyright © (1993) by the American Psychological Association. Reprinted with permission.
Note: Lower ratings indicate less support for exchange programs, that is, greater correspondence to the attitude expressed in the speech.

expected to turn next to a task that was essentially the same as the first one.

Participants motivated to achieve quick closure did spend less time on the task than did controls, and participants motivated to avoid closure spent more time on it. These different levels of effort had the predicted impact on participants' judgments, as shown in the top row of table 6.1. Participants motivated to achieve quick closure showed an exaggerated correspondence bias. Even when they knew that the woman had been given no choice about the contents of her speech, they were more likely than controls to assume that the woman, like her speech, opposed exchange programs. These participants must have simply based their judgments of the speaker on the contents of her speech, without stopping to reflect on the constraints she was under. In contrast, participants motivated to avoid closure showed a decrease in the correspondence bias when they knew the women had acted without choice. These participants must have spent enough time and effort on evaluating the woman to realize that her speech was not a good indicator of her opinions because of the constraints of her situation. This interpretation is strengthened by the finding that when participants thought that the woman had chosen freely to read her speech, their goals had little impact on their ratings of her attitude, as shown in the bottom row of table 6.1. In this situation, the inference that the woman must subscribe to the attitudes she is expressing is so simple and straightforward that it is unlikely to change with an increase or a decrease in effort.

A follow-up study that examined closure goals arising from ongoing differences among people obtained the same pattern (Webster 1993). Participants completed a measure of their need for closure which asked for their agreement with statements reflecting a preference for closure (e.g., "I'd rather know bad news than stay in a state of uncertainty" and "when I am confused about an important issue, I feel very upset") as well as with statements reflecting a preference for avoiding closure (e.g., "I tend to put off making important decisions until the last possible moment" and "I like to have friends who are unpredictable"). Participants scoring in the top and bottom quartiles of this measure were classified as high in need for closure and as high in need to avoid closure, whereas those scoring in the middle 50 percent were classified as neutral controls. As in the earlier study, correspondence bias was especially strong among participants with a chronically high need for closure and was eliminated among participants with a strong need to avoid closure. Neutral controls showed an intermediate level of correspondence bias. It appears, then, that closure goals can influence the amount of time and effort we devote to our judgment tasks and thereby influence the quality of judgment. When elaborate thought results in more appropriate reasoning, as seems to be the case in situations that can give rise to the correspondence bias, the more elaborate scrutiny triggered by the need to avoid closure can eliminate bias.

In conclusion, directional goals, accuracy goals, and closure goals all influence judgment by influencing the cognitive processing of relevant information. Goals may influence which beliefs and rules we access and apply to the judgment at hand, and may also influence the amount of time and effort we devote to the judgment. As a result people with different goals may arrive at very different judgments, and the same individuals may find themselves drawing different conclusions from the same information as their goals shift.

The impact of goals and desires on judgment constitutes one aspect of "hot" cognition. Our cognitions may also be "hot" in another regard; they may be colored by our moods, or feelings. I turn next to a discussion of the impact of affective states on judgment.

Affect

Mood-Congruent Judgment

Take a moment to think of a situation that would make you really happy. Try to imagine this situation as vividly as you can and to feel the same way you would feel if you were actually in it. Now, consider the following questions: All things considered, how satisfied or dissatisfied are you with your life right now? How happy or unhappy was your childhood? How much do you like grocery shopping? Your romantic partner? Your country's leader? How likely are you to develop high blood pressure? A great deal of research suggests that your answers to all these questions may have been influenced by the brief mood manipulation at the start of this paragraph (for reviews, see Forgas 1995; Isen 1987; Schwarz and Clore 1996). We tend to give more positive answers to such questions when we are in a good mood, and more negative answers when we are in a bad mood. In other words, our judgments tend to be congruent with our moods.

In a classic study by Alice Isen and her colleagues, happiness was induced by means of an unexpected gift (Isen et al. 1978). A confederate approached people at a shopping mall and gave them a small gift to "introduce them to the company's products." Women received a note pad and men a nail clipper, each worth 29 cents. Control participants were not approached by the confederate. An experimenter standing about 50 yards away, who did not know whether or not the person had received a gift, then asked the person to participate in a brief consumer survey. When asked to rate the performance of their cars and TV sets, participants who had received the gift rated these more highly than participants who had received no gift. This study suggests that even seemingly trivial gifts can suffice to put us in a good mood and, thereby, make us see our belongings in a more positive light.

Many subsequent studies have obtained similar evidence for mood-congruent judgment using a variety of mood manipulations and diverse judgment tasks. I will describe only a handful of these to provide a sense of the different mood-induction techniques that have been used and of the range of judgments that have been shown to be influenced by the resulting moods. In one study, people were approached on the street just after they had seen a happy movie, such as *Beverly Hills Cop* or *Back to the Future*, or a sad movie, such as *Birdy*, or *Killing Fields* (Forgas 1994). To rule out the possibility that any differences between the judgments of viewers of the two kinds of movies resulted from inherent differences among the kinds of people who chose to attend each kind of movie (happy people may be especially likely to go see happy movies), control participants were approached as they were entering the same happy and sad movies. The movies did have the expected effects on mood: People who had seen a happy movie were happier than controls who had not yet seen any movie, and people who had seen a sad movie were less happy than controls. Participants' judgments about conflicts they had experienced in their own intimate relationships were congruent with these moods: Compared to controls, participants who had seen a happy movie were less likely to blame themselves for such conflicts, and participants who had seen the sad movie were more likely to blame themselves. Thus, our moods can influence how we understand and explain important events in our lives.

In another study, people suffering from the common cold or flu were put in different moods through tape-recorded instructions to imagine a situation that would make them feel happy, sad, or neutral (Salovey and Birnbaum 1989). Participants' ratings of their mood revealed that this procedure had successfully induced the intended moods in the three groups. Moreover, participants' ratings of their own symptoms were congruent with these moods: Relative to participants in a neutral mood, sad participants reported more aches and pains and greater discomfort whereas happy participants reported fewer such symptoms. If you are feeling sick, you would be well advised to watch a comedy; it may not only raise your spirits but also alleviate your symptoms. But stay away from tragedies; these can make you feel sicker.

In yet another study, mood was manipulated through music (Esses and Zanna 1995). Participants were asked to describe any imagery that came to mind as they listened to happy music, such as Handel's *Arrival of the Queen of Sheba*, sad music, such as Tchaikovski's *Pathetique*, or emotionally neutral music, such as Chopin's *Nocturne #17*. Participants' ratings of their mood revealed that this procedure had successfully induced the intended moods in the three conditions. These moods influenced participants' descriptions of ethnic groups that are negatively stereotyped in Canada, where the study was conducted (Arabs, Pakistanis, Native Indians). Participants in a negative mood described these groups in more unfavorable terms than did those in neutral or positive moods. However, unfortunately, positive moods did not make participants see these groups any more positively. Bad moods, then, may increase our prejudice toward negatively stereotyped groups and lead us to see them in even more negative terms.

Similar mood manipulations have been shown to influence a host of other judgments, including assessments of one's own competence, one's general satisfaction with life, estimates of the likelihood that one will fall prey to various misfortunes and diseases, evaluations of the quality of political leaders, estimates of the number of annual fatalities from different causes, evaluations of the strength of persuasive messages, and many other judgments (for a review, see Forgas 1995). A striking aspect of all the mood manipulations used in such research is that they seem so minor, and so common in our daily life—a little gift, an emotion-laden fantasy, a piece of classical music, a movie. Yet so many of our judgments about people, objects, and events in our lives can be influenced by the moods that these manipulations induce. Why do our judgments tend to be congruent with our moods? I turn next to the major theories that have been proposed to account for mood-congruent judgment.

Mood as a Source of Priming As you may recall, our mood can lead us to retrieve mood-congruent memories; when happy, we are especially likely to retrieve happy memories, and when sad, sad memories (Blaney 1986; see chapter 5). Gordon Bower proposed that mood-congruent judgments result from mood-congruent memory (Bower 1981; 1991). In Bower's *network model*, when a node representing an affective state such as *happy* is activated, activation spreads to nodes representing other people, objects, or events that are also associated with that affective state (see figure 5.2). Many objects have positive as well as negative associations; I may be happy with the quality of image on my TV set but unhappy with the quality of sound. I may be proud of some aspects of my behavior in last night's fight but ashamed of some of things I said. When happy, we may be especially likely to retrieve the more happy aspects of such complex objects and events, and when sad, the unhappy ones. When evaluating such objects, we tend to rely on the availability heuristic, basing our judgments on the subset of relevant information that comes readily to mind (Kahneman and Tversky 1973; see chapter 3). Because the subset of retrieved memories tends to be congruent with our mood, our judgments are as well.

Through such processes, mood may change the very meaning of a variety of attributes. Imagine, for example, that you believe a certain group of people to be proud. Being proud has positive as well as negative connotations; you may value and respect people who delight in their own achievements, but disdain people who appear haughty and superior. When you are sad, you may be especially likely to bring to mind the negative aspects of being proud. As a result, you will put a negative spin on this trait, and view the group that possesses it negatively (Esses and Zanna 1995).

The notion of mood-driven priming provides a plausible account for many mood-congruent judgments. The evidence for mood-congruent memory is strong (see chapter 5; for a review, see Blaney 1986). There is also evidence that affect-laden concepts can increase the accessibility of other concepts that connote the same affect, even if they have little else in common; *divorce* may increase the accessibility of *toothache, sunshine* may increase the accessibility of *chocolate* (Bargh et al. 1992; Fazio et al. 1986; see chapter 7 for a more detailed discussion of this research). Thus there are strong reasons to believe that mood often influences judgment because it primes mood-congruent material relevant to the judgment. However, not all mood-congruent judgments can be accounted for in this manner, as discussed next.

Mood as Information   Imagine that you are asked how much you like your neighbor, Scott. You may stop to reflect on everything you know about Scott, consider his many positive and negative behaviors and traits, and integrate these into an overall judgment. But you may also use an alternative route. Because you were asked for you feelings, you may try to assess these directly; just how do you feel about Scott? This strategy can often give you a good answer; your liking for Scott should indeed reflect your feelings about him. However, this strategy may also leave you open to error because it is not always easy to tell where your feelings come from. Imagine that as you are considering your liking for Scott, the radio is playing cheerful music that raises your spirits. Not realizing that your positive feelings come from the music, you may mistakenly attribute them to Scott and conclude that you like him a great deal. More generally, we may use our moods as a *direct source of information* about our judgments. When we are unaware of the actual source of a mood, we may mistakenly attribute it the object of judgment. As a result, our judgments will be congruent with our moods.

Norbert Schwarz, Gerald Clore, and their colleagues argued that the notion that moods can serve as a source of information leads to some important predictions about mood-congruent judgment that cannot be readily accounted for through mood-congruent recall

(Schwarz and Clore 1983; 1996; Schwarz 1990). One such prediction is that *the impact of mood should depend on its perceived informational value.* If you realize that your good feelings come from the cheerful music you happen to be listening to, you will discount them as a valuable source of information about Scott. Therefore they should not influence your evaluation of him. Note that if moods affect judgment only through mood-congruent recall, the informational value of the mood should not determine its impact; even if you realize that your good mood is irrelevant to your evaluation of Scott, activation spreading from this mood should still make you especially likely to activate and retrieve Scott's positive qualities and, thereby, should color your evaluation of him.

A clever study by Schwarz and Clore (1983) tested these ideas by examining the impact of mood induced by weather. Noting that people are generally happier on sunny than on miserable days, these investigators reasoned that if people's assessments of their general happiness and satisfaction with life are influenced by mood, then people should report greater life satisfaction on sunny than on rainy days. To determine if this were so, students at the University of Illinois at Urbana-Champaign were contacted over the phone on either sunny or rainy weekdays. The interviewer explained that she was calling from Chicago to conduct a survey of students' life satisfaction, and asked several questions about global happiness (e.g., "How happy do you feel about your life as a whole?") and, at the end, also asked about the respondent's happiness at that moment. Students contacted on sunny days were indeed happier at that moment than those contacted on rainy days. Moreover, their judgments of their overall life satisfaction were congruent with these moods: On sunny days students reported greater overall happiness with their lives than on rainy days, as may be seen in the top row of table 6.2.

In another crucial set of conditions, other students, who were also called either on sunny or on rainy days, were asked casually at the start of the interview "By the way, how's the weather down there?" These students, too, were in a better mood if contacted on a

Table 6.2 Ratings of their overall happiness with life made by students questioned on sunny or on rainy days with or without a reminder of the weather

	SUNNY DAY	RAINY DAY
No reminder	7.43	5.00
Weather reminder	7.29	7.00

Source: From Schwarz and Clore (1983, table 3). Copyright © (1983) by the American Psychological Association. Reprinted with permission.
Note: Higher numbers indicate greater happiness.

sunny day than on a rainy day. But these students had just been reminded of the reason for their mood—the weather. Such a reminder should undermine the informational value of mood—if one's lousy mood is due to the lousy weather, it cannot serve as a basis for assessing one's overall happiness. Indeed, for students reminded of the weather, weather, and the mood it gave rise to, had no impact on overall happiness; students contacted on rainy days reported being just as happy with their lives as did those contacted on sunny days, as seen in the bottom row of table 6.2. This study and several conceptually similar ones suggest that we may use our mood as a rough indicator of our overall life satisfaction, unless we are reminded that our mood may be due to a transient factor such as the weather that has no bearing on our satisfaction with life. Given such a reminder, we attribute our mood to this transient factor, discount its relevance to other judgments, and no longer make mood-congruent judgments.

Note that such findings cannot be due to mood-congruent memory; asking people about the weather should not have any impact on the extent to which their mood increases the activation of mood-congruent material. Therefore, these findings suggest that the impact of mood on judgment is due, at least on some occasions, to its informational value. Another prediction derived from the view of mood as information that cannot be readily explained through mood-congruent recall is that *the impact of mood on judgment should not depend on the extent to which the material used to induce the mood is relevant to the judgment task.* If you are sad because you have just read about a child dying of cancer, and then use this bad mood as an indicator of your feelings about other issues, this sadness should have the same impact on judgments that are closely related to the story you have read (e.g., risks of cancer and other diseases) as it has on unrelated judgments (e.g., your life satisfaction, the quality of your TV).

In contrast, the network model at the base of the mood-congruent-memory account of judgment assumes that mood is but one of several sources of activation. Semantic associations should also increase the activation of memories and beliefs. Therefore mood effects should be stronger when the mood is induced by thoughts that are relevant to the judgment because, in such cases, both the contents of the mood induction and the mood itself increase the accessibility of relevant material. If you have read about a sick child, material related to other illnesses gets activation both through its semantic association with sickness and through its association to negative affect. Such material should be more strongly activated than negative material relating to your TV set which receives activation only from its association with negative affect. Therefore, if mood-congruent judgment results only from the priming of mood-related material, the impact of mood on judgment should be greater the stronger the semantic associations between the mood-inducing material and the object of judgment. But this is not the case.

In one study, three groups of participants were put in a bad mood by reading a sad story about a student who died unexpectedly either by leukemia, homicide, or fire. A fourth, control group read a story unrelated to death (Johnson and Tversky 1983). Participants then rated the extent to which they were worried and concerned about each of 18 causes of death, including the three used in the mood-induction procedures and others that varied in their similarity to these three causes (e.g., lung cancer, traffic accidents, tornadoes). They also estimated the annual number of U.S. fatalities due to each of these causes. All three stories had successfully induced bad moods, and these negative moods provoked mood-congruent judgment: Participants who had read a sad story reported greater concern about the presented causes of death and estimated the annual fatalities from each as much higher than did control participants who had not read a sad story. More important to the present discussion, these enhanced perceptions of concern and risk generalized to the full range of risks and were completely unrelated to the similarity between the evaluated risks and the topic of the story read by participants. For example, the increase in estimates of the frequency of leukemia was just as high for participants who had read about death by fire as it was for participants who had read about death by leukemia. It is difficult to account for such content-free generalized effects of mood on judgment in terms of mood-congruent memory. However, these and similar findings are consistent with the view that mood is used to inform judgment (Schwarz 1990).

In sum, mood can affect judgment both by priming mood-related material and by serving as a source of information that bears on the judgment. When will each of these effects of mood come into play? I turn next to a theory that has attempted to grapple with this question.

The Affect Infusion Model   Joseph Forgas developed the *Affect Infusion Model* to predict when affect will have any influence on judgment and, when it does, through what mechanism (Forgas 1995). The model assumes that the influence of affect depends on the kind of reasoning strategy one engages in. Affect is assumed to have little impact on judgments that can be made through *direct retrieval* of a prestored conclusion; if I know I love chocolate ice cream, I will tell you I love it, regardless of my mood. Affect is also assumed to have little influence on judgments that are guided by the motivation to satisfy strong *directional goals* because these may override affective influences. Judgments that are infused with affect, that is, mood-congruent judgments, arise from two other kinds of reasoning strategies. In identifying these, Forgas builds on a distinction made in several other areas of social cognition between *heuristic processes,* that is, processes that involve reliance on quick and easy heuristics, inferential shortcuts, and minimal effort, and more labor intensive *substantive processes,* that is, processes that involve extensive searches through memory and more elaborate, analytic, and systematic reasoning (see chapter 3). You may recall a similar distinction in the discussion of the impact of goals on judgment: The goal of achieving quick closure gives rise to quick and easy reasoning, that is, to heuristic processes, whereas accuracy goals give rise to elaborate reasoning, that is to substantive processes.

Forgas proposes that the mechanism through which affect influences judgment will depend on which of these two strategies one engages in. When people engage in heuristic processing, they will use mood to inform their judgment. Rather than engaging in an elaborate analysis of all that they know about the target of judgment, they will use the much easier strategy of asking themselves, "How do I feel about it?" In contrast, when people engage in substantive judgment, they will conduct an elaborate search through memory for relevant information. What they retrieve will inevitably be colored by their mood, due to priming. Therefore, judgments that arise from substantive processing will be influenced by mood because they rely on mood-congruent memories.

This analysis of when the two kinds of mechanisms for mood-congruent judgment will come into play remains controversial, however (Schwarz and Clore 1996). It is not obvious why all the judgments that have been shown to rely on mood as information should be assumed to be based on heuristic strategies. Some of these judgment tasks, such as evaluating one's overall life satisfaction or one's concern about different risks to one's life, seem quite complex. To obtain unequivocal evidence for the predictions of the affect infusion model, it would be necessary to lead people to apply different reasoning strategies to the same judgment task (perhaps by manipulating accuracy goals) and show that mood affects judgment through a different mechanism under each strategy. To my knowledge, no such data exist.

I also question the assumption that mood-congruent judgment must result either from mood-congruent memory or from reliance on mood as information, never from both. Complex judgments that rely on extensive memory search need not exclude the informational value of mood; one's feelings could be one of the many factors taken into account (e.g., "He's smart, he's handsome, and I feel great about him"). If this were true, both the informational value of a mood and the mood-congruent memories that it primes could jointly influence the same judgment. In sum, there is reason to believe that both kinds of mechanisms can give rise to mood-congruent judgment. The jury is still out on when each will come into play.

Mood as a Determinant of Cognitive Strategies

In addition to influencing the *contents* of judgment, affect may also influence the *cognitive strategies* we apply to the judgment (for a review, see Taylor 1991). When we are in a bad mood, we may be especially likely to use elaborate, systematic processing strategies, for at least two reasons. First, a bad mood may inform us that we have a problem that we should be dealing with. We then mobilize our cognitive resources to solve the problem, and this intensified processing may generalize to other judgment tasks as well (Schwarz 1990; Schwarz and Clore 1996). Second, bad moods are inherently unpleasant. In an attempt to rid ourselves of such unpleasant states, we may throw ourselves into any distracting task that comes our way (Isen 1987). When we are in a good mood, on the other hand, we may be especially likely to use more heuristic, simplified processing strategies, for similar reasons. A good mood may inform us that all is fine with the world; there is little need for careful evaluation of our circumstances. This "What me worry?" state of mind may carry over into other judgment tasks (Schwarz 1990; Schwarz and Clore 1996). Second, because good moods are pleasant, we may wish to extend them, and so may avoid any task that might disrupt our good mood; hard thinking may be viewed as one such task, and so avoided when possible (Isen 1987). Happy moods may also bring to mind a host of well-integrated happy thoughts; dwelling on these may leave less cognitive capacity for other judgment tasks, and so provoke cursory, heuristic processing (Isen 1987).

Although there is still some debate about exactly *why* moods influence the choice of cognitive strategies, several lines of research support the conclusion that happy moods are often conducive to heuristic processing and sad moods to more systematic processing, as discussed next.

Mood and Persuasion   Current theories of persuasion assume that when people hear a persuasive message, they may either process it *systematically*, carefully analyzing its arguments to determine whether they should be persuaded, or process in *heuristically*, relying on quick and easy cues such as the likability or credentials of the person presenting the message rather than on careful analysis of its contents (see chapter 3). A great deal of research has shown that when people are capable of processing a message in a systematic manner, they are more persuaded by strong arguments than by weak ones (for reviews, see Eagly and Chaiken 1993; Petty and Cacioppo 1986). For example, when students are asked to support a decision to institute comprehensive exams for seniors at their university, they are more persuaded by strong arguments (e.g., such exams would enhance academic excellence and would improve the university's national ranking) than they are by weak arguments (e.g., parents had written in support of such an exam and the exam would cut costs by eliminating the need for other tests; Petty, Harkins, and Williams 1980). However, people find strong arguments more persuasive than weak ones only if they process the message systematically. If, for whatever reason, they allocate fewer cognitive resources to the message and process it in a "quick and dirty" heuristic manner, they no longer find strong arguments more persuasive than weak ones; they simply do not base their reactions on the quality of the arguments, relying instead on cues such as the attractiveness, likability, or expertise of the person delivering the message.

This robust pattern of findings provided an excellent testing ground for the hypothesis that people should be more likely to engage in systematic processing when sad than when happy. If this were true, they should be more sensitive to the strength of arguments in persuasive messages when sad than when happy. Several studies have shown that this is often the case (e.g., Bless, Mackie and Schwarz 1992; Mackie and Worth 1991; for reviews, see Eagly and Chaiken 1993; Schwarz and Clore 1996). The typical finding in studies that have examined the effect of mood on the impact of counterattitudinal messages is that sad participants show considerable attitude change in response to strong arguments but none in response to weak arguments. In contrast, happy participants show equal, moderate attitude change in response to the two kinds of arguments; they are not sensitive to argument strength. It appears that we are more likely to pay careful attention to the contents of persuasive messages when sad than when happy; sadness gives rise to systematic processing, happiness to heuristic processing.

Under some circumstances, however, happy moods can increase rather than decrease systematic processing of persuasive messages. Duane Wegener and his colleagues reasoned that happiness decreased systematic processing of persuasive messages in previous research because, in that research, the messages were always counterattitudinal and so unpleasant to contemplate (Wegener, Petty, and Smith 1995). Happy people, intent on preserving their happiness, may scrutinize all potential activities especially carefully to ensure that they avoid any activity that could undermine their good mood. They avoid careful consideration of counterattitudinal messages because of the likely unpleasantness of this activity. It follows that if the initial scrutiny suggests that the activity may be pleasant and mood enhancing, happy people will be especially likely to engage in it. Indeed, Wegener and his colleagues found that happiness increased sensitivity to the strength of arguments in a message about how to improve foster care and increase its benefits, a positive message that was neither counterattitudinal nor mood threatening.

A follow-up study showed that happy people were also especially sensitive to information about the likely consequences of a message to mood ("the primary quality of the article you are about

to read is that it makes people feel HAPPY/SAD"). Happy participants were more persuaded by strong than by weak arguments
when they expected the message to be uplifting but not when they
expected it to be depressing. Happiness, then, can increase systematic processing that is expected to be pleasant and mood
enhancing but can decrease systematic processing that is expected
to be unpleasant. A different pattern emerges for sad people.
Wegener and his colleagues reasoned that when one is sad, just
about any activity will be more pleasant than dwelling on one's
sadness (Wegener et al. 1995). There is therefore little need to
scrutinize activities so as to determine how good they will make
one feel. Sad people will therefore throw themselves wholeheartedly into any activity that comes their way, with the hope that
it will at the very least distract them from their sadness. Indeed, sad
people appeared to process the message systematically regardless
of whether they expected it to be uplifting or depressing. They were
more persuaded by strong than by weak arguments in both cases.

In sum, the literature on mood and persuasion has found consistent evidence that when we are sad, we are especially likely to
engage in systematic processing. When we are happy, we tend to
avoid systematic processing that seems likely to dampen our good
mood, but we are especially likely to engage in systematic processing that promises to be uplifting.

Mood and Stereotyping   Mood may also influence the extent to
which we rely on stereotypes when evaluating individuals. Some
theorists have suggested that stereotypes may provide a quick and
easy manner of evaluating people; when evaluating a particular
woman, it is sometimes easier to fall back on our expectations for
women in general than it is to contemplate and integrate everything
we know about this particular woman, especially if her behavior is
difficult to interpret (for reviews, see Brewer 1988; Bodenhausen
1993; Fiske and Neuberg 1990). Therefore, conditions that give rise
to quick and easy heuristic processing may also give rise to stereo-
type-congruent judgments. Another reason for this prediction is
that we often attempt to inhibit stereotypes so as to avoid being
prejudiced. Such inhibition requires resources and effort, and is

often successful if we work hard enough at it (Devine 1989; for a review, see Kunda and Sinclair, 1999). But our ability to inhibit stereotypes may break down if we allocate too few cognitive resources to the judgment task and try to breeze through it using low-effort mental shortcuts. When this happens, we may show greater reliance on stereotypes in our judgment.

If happiness makes us more likely to engage in quick and easy heuristic processing, it should therefore make us more likely to rely on stereotypes in our judgment. There is some evidence that this is the case (for reviews, see Bodenhausen 1993; Schwarz and Clore 1996). In a series of studies, Galen Bodenhausen and his colleagues investigated the effects of happiness on the use of stereotypes (Bodenhausen, Kramer, and Susser 1994). In one study, half of the participants were put in a happy mood through instructions to recall an event that had made them particularly happy. Control participants recalled mundane, emotionally neutral events. Then, in a seemingly unrelated study on legal thinking, they read a summary of a disciplinary hearing involving a student's alleged misbehavior, and were asked to assess the student's guilt. The identity of the student was varied so that he either was or was not a member of a group stereotyped as likely to engage in that offense. For example, one scenario involved a case in which a student had assaulted his roommate. For half of the participants, the student's name was Hispanic, a group stereotyped on that campus as likely to commit assault, and for the other half his name was ethnically nondescript.

Among participants in a neutral mood, the student's category membership had no effect on their assessment of his guilt; they did not use the stereotype when making this judgment. In contrast, happy participants did rely on the stereotype; they viewed the student as more guilty if he belonged to a group stereotyped as likely to commit the alleged offense. A follow-up study revealed that this tendency of happy students to base their judgments of an individual on his group's stereotype resulted from their reliance on low-effort heuristic processing (Bodenhausen et al. 1994). When happy participants were led to engage in more effortful processing (because they were told that they would be held accountable for their judgments just as though they were serving on a real disciplinary panel), the stereotypes no longer influenced their guilt assessments.

In these studies it is unclear whether happiness increases our reliance on stereotypes because it reduces our reliance on other pertinent information or because it leads us to forgo our attempts at suppressing negative stereotypes. In either case, it is clear that happiness can lead us to engage in less effortful processing and thereby can increase our use of stereotypes when evaluating others. On the positive side, we are not doomed to be prejudiced whenever happy; we are capable of investing greater effort when we are motivated to be accurate, and when we do, we cease to make stereotypic judgments. Note also that the judgment task here, determining guilt for an unpleasant offense, is of the sort that could be expected to dampen our mood. That may be why happy people handled it through heuristic processing. The research on the effects of mood on persuasion described earlier suggests that a different pattern may emerge when one is asked to contemplate more positive outcomes—who should win desirable awards, for example (Wegener et al. 1995). In such cases, if the judgment is expected to be pleasant and mood-enhancing, people in a happy mood may invest more, not less effort in it, and may be equally or less likely than people in a neutral mood to rely on stereotypes. It remains to be determined whether this is the case.

Sadness can also influence stereotype use. If sadness makes us more likely to engage in effortful, systematic processing, it should decrease our reliance on stereotypes. Some studies have suggested, consistent with this expectation, that sad people do engage in more effortful processing and therefore rely less on group stereotypes when evaluating individuals (for a review, see Schwarz and Clore 1996). This seems to be true only for negative stereotypes; in one set of studies, sadness reduced reliance on negative stereotypes but did not affect the use of positive stereotypes (Lambert et al. 1997). The elaborate thought induced by sadness may lead people to recognize the inappropriateness of using negative stereotypes and to therefore curtail their use. Positive stereotypes, in contrast, are not deemed inappropriate, and so their use is not curtailed even upon the careful reflection induced by sadness.

In sum, several lines of research suggest that mood can influence the mode of processing. For the most part, sadness gives rise to more elaborate, systematic processing. Happiness often gives rise to more cursory, heuristic processing, but this tendency can be overcome if happy people expect elaborate reasoning to be pleasurable or if they have other reasons to engage in elaborate reasoning, such as a desire to be accurate.

In conclusion, the term "hot cognition" has proved to be remarkably apt. It captures the fact that our judgments and decisions can be "heated up" by our desires and emotions as well as the fact that the "heat" operates on and through cognitions. Motives and moods may influence which cognitive strategies we use and which cognitive structures we bring to mind. These, in turn, may color our judgment.

Summary

Directional goals, that is, the motivation to draw a particular conclusion, can color judgment. They do so by biasing the selection of beliefs and rules one accesses in the process of reasoning: We are particularly likely to access those beliefs and rules that support our desired conclusions. Directional goals also influence the amount of effort we invest in judgment; when we encounter undesirable evidence, we work especially hard at refuting it. Nevertheless, although motivation can bias our judgments, it does not blind us to reality. We will only draw our desired conclusions if we can justify them, and our ability to do so is constrained by reality and plausibility.

Reasoning driven by directional goals may result in *positive illusions*. These may be beneficial in that they may lead to an increase in our motivation, effort, and persistence at difficult tasks, and they may ultimately become self-fulfilling. However, positive illusions may also get us into serious trouble when they lead us to play down the gravity of real threats and prevent us from taking necessary precautions.

Accuracy goals, that is, the motivation to arrive at the best possible solution, whatever it may be, lead people to invest greater effort in the judgment task, to engage in more complex and elaborate reasoning, and to search harder for the best possible reasoning strategies. This can improve judgment when the reasoning strategies that one favors upon reflection are indeed superior. However, accuracy goals can also reduce the quality of judgment when they lead people to retrieve poorer strategies that they mistakenly view as better.

The kinds of goals we entertain can be influenced by our mindset. While in the process of making a decision, we may be in a *deliberative mindset* which entails careful consideration of all options and gives rise to accuracy goals. However, once our decision is made, we may shift to an *implemental mindset* which entails a focus on achieving the chosen option and gives rise to directional goals.

Our judgments may also be influenced by our moods. We view our possessions, our leaders, our well-being, and many other issues more positively when happy than when sad. Mood often influences judgment because it brings to mind mood-congruent material relevant to the judgment. Mood can also affect judgment by serving as a source of information; to determine how much we like an object, we may ask ourselves how we feel when we think about that object. Sometimes, though, our current feelings may be influenced by other factors as well, such as music or the weather. If we are unaware of the actual source of a mood, we may mistakenly attribute it to the object of judgment. However, when we believe that our mood is not indicative of our feelings toward an object, as we do when we attribute the mood to a different source, the mood no longer influences our judgment of that object. Moods may also influence our choice of cognitive strategies: When we are sad, we tend to favor systematic processing. In contrast, when we are happy we often favor heuristic processing, though we may turn to systematic processing instead if we expect to enjoy it.

7 Automatic Processes: Judgment and Behavior without Awareness, Intention, Control, or Effort

Much of the social psychological research carried out up to the mid 1970s assumed, explicitly or implicitly, that people were aware of the cognitive processes underlying their judgments and behavior and were capable of monitoring and controlling these processes. That has changed. Once cognitive psychologists began questioning these assumptions, social psychologists were quick to follow. By the late 1980s it had become clear that a wide variety of mental processes could be carried out with little awareness or intention (for reviews, see Uleman and Bargh 1989; Wegner and Bargh 1998). In this chapter I will review evidence showing that we may have automatic reactions to various objects, people, and situations and that these can color our judgments and influence our behavior even if we have no idea that this is happening.

Many of the ideas discussed in this chapter are highly provocative. I will therefore devote considerable attention to discussing the methods on which they are based, and I will attempt to answer questions such as: How can we tell that people are unaware that their judgments had been influenced by a particular factor? How can we show that stimuli perceived only unconsciously can nevertheless color judgment? How can we determine that people jump to conclusions about others automatically and effortlessly, with little thought or analysis? How can we examine people's ability to exercise control over their own thoughts?

Automatic versus Controlled Processes

Why did you interrupt your friend so curtly? Why did you decide to hire Anne over Philip? Why does Gary make you feel so uncomfortable? We often answer such questions about the reasons for our behaviors, thoughts, and feelings with great confidence. We believe, quite correctly, that we have privileged access to a great deal of relevant information—we know what was going on in our minds at the time, know our likes and dislikes, know how we usually think and behave. Yet our behavior, thoughts, and feelings may also be influenced by factors that we are unaware of. You may not realize that you interrupted your friend because you had just been reading about forceful, assertive people, you may be unaware that your desire to hire a woman led you to interpret Anne's background more favorably, and you may fail to recognize that Gary makes you uncomfortable because he resembles a hated high school teacher.

Freud and his disciples popularized the notion that much of our mental life takes place outside of awareness. In Freudian theory, material is often pushed out of consciousness because it is too threatening to contemplate. In contrast, the modern view of unconscious processes does not require such active repression. Rather, it is now assumed that the structures of our cognitive and affective systems are such that we simply do not have introspective access to many processes, and we are often unable to control and monitor their execution (for a review, see Kihlstrom 1987).

Empirical investigation of such unconscious, automatic processes began in the 1970s. At that point theorists drew a distinction between automatic and controlled processes (e.g., Shiffrin and Schneider 1977). *Automatic processes* were those processes that *occurred outside awareness*, were carried out *without intention*, were *uncontrollable* in that one could not stop them once they had begun, and were highly *efficient* in that they required few cognitive resources and could occur in parallel with other processes. Many aspects of perception are automatic in this manner. For example, the mental calculations that we rely on to determine an object's size and distance are completely automatic—they require no effort or intention and are not open to conscious scrutiny or control. *Controlled processes*, on the other hand, were characterized by the opposite set of features—they were carried out with intention and awareness, could be controlled and monitored, and required considerable effort, so much so that they could be disrupted when cognitive resources were limited.

Originally it was thought that automatic and controlled processes were completely distinct and mutually exclusive. Each process was assumed to be either fully automatic, that is, characterized by all four features of automaticity, or fully controlled, that is, characterized by all four features of controllability. However, it later became evident that few if any higher-order cognitive processes satisfy these stringent criteria (Bargh 1989, 1994, 1996; Zbrodoff and Logan 1986). Rather, many processes are automatic in some regards but controllable in others. For example, if you are an experienced driver, you may drive for miles without any awareness of the mechanics of driving, and your driving may be so effortless that you can listen to music and carry on a conversation at the same time. In these ways your driving is automatic. Yet your driving lacks other features of automaticity. It cannot be considered unintended; you had made a conscious decision to go on this car ride. Nor is your driving uncontrollable; you may choose to stop or monitor it at any time. Many processes of social judgment have a similar mix of automatic and controlled features. For example, when White Americans encounter an Asian American person, the Asian American stereotype may come to their mind spontaneously, without any intention on their part. Yet this will only occur if they have sufficient cognitive resources (Gilbert and Hixon 1991). In other words, stereotype activation may be unintended (a feature of automatic processes) but also effortful (a feature of controlled processes).

The notion that many of our judgments, feelings, and behaviors are carried out automatically and are influenced by factors that we are unaware of and are unable to control seemed highly provocative at first, and researchers focused on demonstrating that this was indeed the case. By now, these ideas have gained broad acceptance, and there is considerable agreement about what constitutes good evidence that a process is automatic. Current research efforts focus on applying these methods toward exploring which of our reactions are likely to be automatic: Do we activate and apply stereotypes automatically? Do we infer people's character from their behavior automatically? What kinds of objects and events provoke automatic affective reactions?

Most social psychological research aiming to demonstrate automatic processing has focused on two of the criteria for automaticity, lack of awareness and efficiency (though lack of awareness is often assumed to also imply lack of intention and control—if I am not aware that a factor influenced my judgment, I most probably did not intend for this to happen, and if I am unaware that a process is taking place I cannot control its execution). How can one show that people are unaware of what determined their judgments, feelings, and behavior? How can one show that a process is carried out with great efficiency? The following discussion of automatic processes is organized around the major methods that have been used to answer these questions.

Lack of Awareness

Failure of Introspection

In a highly influential article, Richard Nisbett and Timothy Wilson argued that we often have little introspective access to higher-order cognitive processes; we can be completely unaware of the role that various factors had played in influencing our judgments and preferences (Nisbett and Wilson 1977). We may not realize that our political attitudes had shifted as a result of a friend's comments, that our brilliant solution to a problem was actually triggered by a subtle cue from a teacher, or that we chose a particular brand of toothpaste because of its location on the supermarket shelf. In such cases, we often provide confident reports about how we had arrived at our judgment, but our reports cannot be trusted because they are not based on direct introspection. Instead, they are based on our causal theories about which factors are likely to influence different kinds of judgment.

To demonstrate such failures of introspection, Nisbett and Wilson described a series of studies that all had the same form: An experiment demonstrates that a particular factor, say a comment by the experimenter, influenced judgments; people who had heard this comment made different judgments than people who had not. Yet, when participants are interviewed, they deny that this factor had exerted any impact on their judgment, and typically insist that their judgment was due to different factors. Such denials of the influence of a factor in the face of evidence that it had in fact been influential are taken as evidence for failure of introspection.

Nisbett and Wilson noted that participants in many classic social psychological experiments seemed unaware of the influence of factors that had in fact played a critical role in their judgment. Leading dissonance researchers confirmed that this was often the case in dissonance studies; typically participants denied that the dissonance-provoking manipulations had influenced their attitudes. For example, one classic study had found that people liked a group more if they had been required to undergo a more painful initiation rite in order to participate in it (Aronson and Mills 1959). Dissonance theory assumed that people increase their liking for the group so as to justify their willingness to undertake the painful initiation, an act that would seem foolish otherwise. Yet participants in that study denied any such process, as Aronson reported: "When I explained the theory to the subjects, they typically said it was very plausible and that many subjects had probably reasoned just the way I said, but not they themselves" (Nisbett and Wilson 1977, p. 238). Another classic set of studies had shown that people are less likely to help a person in distress the greater the number of other witnesses and bystanders around (Latane and Darley 1970). Yet participants in these studies routinely insisted that their behavior had not been influenced by the presence of other people.

Nisbett and Wilson conducted a series of studies to demonstrate the breadth of this phenomenon. In all, they created situations in which they believed people would be wrong about the effects of key factors on their judgment. They reasoned that if people's accounts of what had influenced their judgment are based on their prior causal theories rather than on direct introspective access, then people would provide inaccurate accounts when their judgments had been influenced by factors that seemed highly counter-intuitive. In one study conducted at a mall, passersby were asked which of four pairs of stockings was of the best quality, and, after making their choice, were asked to explain the reasons for it. In fact, the four pairs of stockings were identical. Yet participants showed a strong tendency to prefer the rightmost one. None of the participants mentioned spontaneously that the positions of the stockings had influenced their evaluations, and virtually all strongly denied this when queried directly about it.

In another of Nisbett and Wilson's studies, participants watched one of two videotapes of an interview with a professor who had a heavy European accent. The professor appeared warm and pleasant on one of the tapes, cold and unpleasant on the other. Those who had seen the warm professor found his accent, mannerisms, and appearance attractive, whereas those who had seen the cold professor found these same qualities irritating. Clearly, the warmth and pleasantness of the professor had influenced participants' evaluations of his personal qualities. But participants strongly denied this. Instead, those who had seen the cold professor claimed that the causal direction was opposite; they thought their liking for the professor was decreased because of his annoying accent, mannerism, and appearance.

These and similar studies suggest that our judgments are often automatic in that we are not aware of the cognitive processes that underlie them. More recently, Bargh and his colleagues used a similar strategy to show that complex social behaviors may also be automatic at times (Bargh, Chen, and Burrows 1996). In one study, these authors first primed the concepts of rudeness and politeness, and then, in a seemingly unrelated context, examined whether such priming could lead people to behave in a rude or polite manner. Participants were told that they would take part in two separate studies on language. Their first task was to unscramble a series of scrambled sentences. Each included five scrambled words such as "he it hides finds instantly" from which participants were to construct a correct four-word sentence as fast as they could. This task was used to prime the desired concepts. Participants received

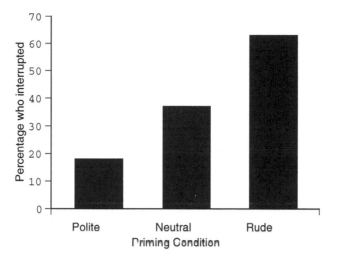

Figure 7.1 Percentage of participants who interrupted the experimenter within the ten-minute period, by trait-priming condition. From Bargh et al. (1996, fig. 1, p. 235). Copyright © (1996) by the American Psychological Association. Reprinted with permission.

one of three versions of this task. In one, intended to prime the trait *rude*, half the sentences included words related to rudeness such as bold, rude, and intrude. In a second version, intended to prime the trait *polite*, these sentences included, instead, words related to politeness such as, polite, courteous, and considerate. A third, control version included only words unrelated to rudeness or politeness. The experimenter did not know which of these versions the participant had completed.

Participants were left alone to complete this task, and were told to come out and get the experimenter when they were done. When they did so, they found the experimenter engaged in a lengthy conversation with another participant who seemed to be having trouble understanding the instructions (actually, a confederate). The experimenter never acknowledged or made eye contact with the participant, and continued to answer an endless stream of questions from the befuddled confederate. This conversation went on for 10 minutes, or until the participant attempted to interrupt it with something like "excuse me" or "sorry." As may be seen in figure 7.1, the priming manipulation had a dramatic influence on whether or not participants interrupted the experimenter. Compared to participants primed with neutral words, those primed with rude words were substantially more likely to interrupt the conversation, and those primed with polite words were substantially less likely to interrupt. Yet, when queried, none reported any suspicion that the priming manipulation had influenced this behavior. It appears that we may be completely unaware of the ways in which subtle aspects of the situation can govern our social behavior.

This paradigm, in which one concludes that people are unaware of the causes of their judgment and behavior because they deny the role of causes known to have influenced their reactions, provides strong evidence that people cannot be trusted to correctly report on how various factors had influenced their responses. This conclusion, and its implications for psychological methods, have been broadly accepted. It is now common wisdom that we should not assume that our experimental manipulations had achieved (or failed to achieve) the desired effects just because participants said so.

But does this paradigm also prove that people can be completely unaware of the determinants of their reactions? This conclusion has been more controversial. Critics have pointed to reasons why this paradigm may not provide conclusive evidence of unconscious processing (e.g., Ericsson and Simon 1980; Smith and Miller 1978). It is possible that participants were in fact aware of the actual causal factors at the time of their judgment or behavior but that they subsequently forgot about them. It is also possible that people remain aware that these factors had influenced their judgment, but choose not to report this because they do not wish to appear foolish or for a variety of other reasons. Although these and related alternative accounts often seem far fetched when applied to particular experiments, it is difficult to rule them out completely for this paradigm. Therefore, this paradigm is considered to provide relatively weak evidence of unconscious processing. It is not unusual for articles describing studies that rely on this method to also include studies that rely on more stringent methods so as to rule out explanations that rely on conscious, strategic processes (e.g., Bargh et al. 1996). I next describe more stringent methods for demonstrating unconscious influences on judgment.

Implicit Memory

Injuries to certain areas of the brain may cause amnesia. An amnesic patient will have normal perceptual, linguistic, and intellectual functioning but will be unable to consciously remember recent experiences. If you teach such a patient a new skill, novel information, or a new list of words, the patient will, on subsequent occasions, have little conscious memory of what had been taught. Indeed the patient may even be unable to remember that the teaching episode had ever taken place. Yet neuroscientists have discovered a remarkable phenomenon: Although amnesic patients have little conscious memory of past experiences, their subsequent judgments and behavior can nevertheless be influenced by traces of these experiences. A patient's performance on a practiced motor skill will improve even though the patient cannot remember practicing. A patient will be able to recount newly learned facts despite being unable to remember learning them. And a patient who cannot tell that a particular word was included on a list seen a little earlier will nevertheless come up with that word when given its first three letters (for reviews, see Schacter 1987; 1996).

The performance of brain-damaged people can provide novel insights into the workings of normal brains. When considered together, the memory failures and successes of amnesic patients imply that there may be more than one kind of memory. It might be useful to draw a distinction between *explicit memory*, that is, conscious recollections of earlier experiences, and *implicit memory*, that is, unconscious influences of past experience on current judgments, feelings, or behaviors. The amnesic patients had clear deficits of explicit memory, but their implicit memory was relatively unimpaired. Could the same dissociation be found in normal people? Is it possible for our reactions to be influenced by experiences that we cannot even remember? A large number of studies suggest that the answer is yes (for a review, see Schacter 1987).

If you study a list of words that includes *octopus* and are later asked to complete the word fragment O __ T __ __ U S, you will come up with the correct completion much more readily than someone who had not had the benefit of seeing *octopus* earlier on a word list. This is a standard, not particularly surprising priming effect. What is surprising, though, is that you will have this advantage even if you no longer consciously remember seeing the word octopus. In one study demonstrating such a dissociation between explicit and implicit memory, people studied a word list and were then given two different memory tests either one hour or one week later (Tulving, Schacter, and Stark 1982). One test, tapping explicit, conscious memory, examined whether or not participants could recognize that a word had appeared on the list. Participants were given the list of 24 previously seen words intermixed with 24 new words, and they were asked to indicate whether each had appeared on the study list. Not surprisingly, participants' ability to accurately recognize the words they had seen was much poorer after a week than after an hour. But a different pattern emerged for the second test, which assessed priming by examining whether participants would correctly complete word fragments with words from the original list. The words that had appeared on the list were indeed primed, and, these priming effects were just as strong after a week as they were after an hour. This was true despite the fact that conscious recognition of the primed words had declined substantially over the week-long delay. Moreover, priming for words that participants could not remember seeing was just as strong as for words that they did remember. Put differently, implicit memory persisted even when explicit memory declined. Many other studies produced conceptually similar results (e.g., Jacoby and Dallas 1981). It appears that past experiences can influence our judgment even when we can no longer recall these experiences.

One unfortunate result of such implicit influences of a prior experience that cannot be explicitly recalled may be unintended plagiarism (Brown and Murphy 1989). An idea that you had come across when attending a lecture, reading an article, or chatting with a friend, may pop into your mind at a later date. If, at that point, you no longer remember where you had first come across this idea, you may mistake it for your own. This may be one reason why disputes over the authorship of ideas are not uncommon among scientists and artists. Freud, for example, described how, when he was developing a new theory, a former colleague claimed to have given Freud the idea for that theory several years earlier. At the time Freud denied that there was any truth to that claim, but later, to his embarrassment, he did remember the earlier incident. In another famous example, George Harrison of the Beatles was accused in a lawsuit of having copied the tune for his song "My Sweet Lord" from an earlier song by the Chiffons, "He's so Fine." Harrison admitted having heard the earlier song before composing his own, but denied that he had copied it intentionally. The court acknowledged that the copying may have been unintentional, but nevertheless found Harrison legally responsible for infringing on copyrighted material (for descriptions of both these incidents, see Brown and Murphy 1989). Controlled experiments have also shown that people may mistake ideas generated by others for their own (Brown and Murphy 1989).

One may even plagiarize one's own ideas unknowingly (Brown and Murphy 1989). One eminent social psychologist was fond of recounting self-disparagingly how, every now and again, he would come up with what seemed like a brilliant new idea. Excited, he would sit at his desk working out the ramifications and implications of this new insight and designing experiments that would prove it true. On a good day, he would realize by noon that he was redesigning the experiments from his dissertation, conducted several decades earlier. On a bad day, he would not come to this realization until dinner time.... Such unintended plagiarism from others or from oneself may be viewed as an example of a failure of source memory; one recalls previously encountered information without recalling its source (Johnson et al. 1993; see chapter 5).

Discussions of implicit memory have often avoided using the term "unconscious" influences so as to avoid controversy. Critics have noted that it is difficult to prove that the effects revealed in implicit measures are completely unconscious, or that explicit measures that appear to show no conscious recollection reveal the full range of conscious experience (e.g., Jacoby, Lindsay, and Toth 1992). For example, when people complete a word fragment with a previously seen word, it is difficult to prove that they have no awareness that they have seen the word before. Even when they fail to identify the word as belonging to the earlier list, they may still be conscious, at some level, of having seen it before. These concerns may be alleviated when conscious processes are pitted against unconscious ones, as discussed next.

Pitting Conscious Processes against Unconscious Ones

When you tell a friend a joke, this joke becomes more accessible in your memory. As a result of this increased accessibility, you should be inclined to tell the same joke again. What prevents you from being a repetitive bore is your conscious recollection of having already told this particular joke to this particular friend. In this example, the unconscious influence of the past experience and the conscious recollection of that experience are pushing you in opposite directions. If you were only subject to the unconscious priming of the joke, you would repeat it. But if you also remembered telling it, you would avoid such repetition. Larry Jacoby and his colleagues recognized that a paradigm that places conscious and unconscious processes in such opposition can yield strong evidence for unconscious processing (Jacoby et al. 1989).

In many studies of implicit memory, conscious and unconscious memories can be expected to influence participants in the same direction. For example, both the conscious recollection of having seen a word before and the unconscious experience of being primed by that word will lead you to correctly complete a fragment of that word. In such cases, it is possible that priming effects that seem unconscious are actually due to conscious effects that the experimenter simply failed to detect. But this is not a concern when the two processes work in opposition. It is clear that you will repeat a joke only if conscious memory fails you. Any repetition can therefore be seen as evidence for unconscious influences. Using this logic, Jacoby and his colleagues were able to obtain strong evidence for unconscious influences on judgment, as described next.

Becoming Famous over Night Is Sebastian Weisdorf famous? At the moment, you would probably say no. You may be quite confident that you have never seen this name before. But what if I asked you this question again tomorrow? At that point, you will have seen this name briefly, right here, as an example of a nonfamous person. If you remember exactly where and why you had come across Sebastian Weisdorf, you will say with confidence that he is not famous. But what if you no longer remember that this is where you saw that name? The name may still appear vaguely familiar; after all, you will have seen it before. If you base your judgment of fame on such a sense of familiarity, you will mistakenly call the name famous. In this manner Sebastian Weisdorf may become famous over night.

Note that in this example conscious and unconscious memories should influence you in opposite directions. Reading the name gives rise to unconscious priming that should lead you to call it famous. But the conscious memory that it was given as an example of a nonfamous person should lead you to call it nonfamous. Therefore, if you mistakenly call it famous, you are doing so because of unconscious priming influences. To demonstrate such unconscious influences, Jacoby and his colleagues examined whether people would come to mistake previously seen nonfamous names for famous (Jacoby et al. 1989). The first phase of their experiment was introduced as a study on the accuracy of pronunciation. Participants were shown a series of 40 nonfamous names on a computer screen one at a time, and were asked to read them out aloud. The second phase, in which participants made fame judgments, took place either immediately or 24 hours later. Participants were reminded that all the names seen in the first phase were nonfamous, and were told that they would be given a list that included those nonfamous names as well as new nonfamous and famous names. They were told that the famous names would not be of extremely famous people and that they would not have to describe what the person had done to become famous. They were then given a list that included the 40 old nonfamous names, 20 new nonfamous names, and 60 moderately famous names (e.g., Minnie Pearl, Christopher Wren), and were asked to indicate whether or not each name was famous.

When participants were tested immediately, mistakes in which a nonfamous name was called famous were less common for the previously seen nonfamous names than they were for the new nonfamous names. This suggests that immediately after having seen the names in the experiment, participants could still consciously remember seeing them there and so were able to avoid mistaking them for famous. A different pattern emerged after the 24-hour delay. It was expected that by this point participants would have trouble remembering which names they had seen in the previous phase but that the previously seen names would still be primed. Indeed, after the 24 hour delay, mistakes in which a nonfamous name was called famous were *more* common for the previously seen nonfamous names than they were for the new ones. This enhanced error rate for previously seen nonfamous names must have been due to unconscious priming; if participants had still been able to consciously remember seeing the names on the earlier list, they would not have called them famous. Studies such as this, in which unconscious processes are pitted against conscious ones, provide the strongest evidence for unconscious influences on judgment.

Mistaken fame judgments may be viewed as another example of failure of source monitoring (Johnson et al. 1993; see chapter 5). People correctly recognize a name as familiar but misidentify the source of familiarity. They misattribute the name's familiarity to its fame rather than to its presence on the previously seen list. This phenomenon also provides another example of people's reliance on their subjective experiences to make judgments (Schwarz and Clore 1996). Much like we rely on our moods to judge our attitudes toward people (see chapter 6), rely on the ease with which we can retrieve instances to judge their frequency (see chapter 3), and rely on the extent to which we are aroused to judge the extent to which we are upset (see chapter 6), we rely on the extent to which a name seems familiar to judge its fame. The problem with relying on sub-jective experiences in this manner, as we have seen before, is that it is easy for us to be mistaken about the source of the experience. When this happens, we may make faulty judgments. One reason why we can be so wrong about the sources of our experiences is that we are often unaware of the factors that give rise to these experiences.

In sum, there is considerable evidence that we can be unaware of the influence exerted by various experiences on our judgments, thoughts, and feelings, and these influences may persist even when we are unable to recall the original experiences. The studies dis-cussed so far all deal with situations in which people were initially aware of an experience but were unaware of the impact of this experience on their later reactions. Can we also be influenced by experiences that we have never been aware of? Can information perceived subconsciously also exert an impact on our thoughts, feelings, and behavior? There is a growing consensus that this can indeed happen, as discussed next (Greenwald 1992; Kihlstrom 1987; Merikle 1992).

Subliminal Perception

It is possible to flash words or images in front of you so fast that you will have no awareness that anything has been flashed, and no ability to report on what you have seen. If, despite your lack of any conscious experience of the flashed stimuli, these stimuli never-theless influence your subsequent reactions, it could be argued that you had perceived these stimuli subliminally or subconsciously. Many researchers have relied on this logic to demonstrate sublimi-nal perception. There is now a large body of studies that have suc-cessfully obtained evidence for priming by stimuli that people cannot report seeing: Briefly flashed stimuli can affect performance on tasks that tap unconscious priming such as word fragment completion even though explicit measures such as word recogni-tion suggest that the participants are unaware of having ever seen these words (for reviews, see Kihlstrom 1987; Merikle 1992).

Because such studies are based on a dissociation between measures of implicit and explicit memory for the subliminally presented stimuli, they are open to the same criticism voiced against studies using this dissociation method to demonstrate implicit memory. The assumption that the stimuli were perceived unconsciously relies on the finding that explicit measures show no evidence of conscious awareness. But how can we be sure that these measures tapped the full range of conscious experience? It is difficult to rule out the possibility that participants were conscious of the stimuli but the explicit measures were simply not sensitive enough to tap this. As was the case for implicit memory, it is possible to rule out this concern by pitting conscious processes against unconscious ones (Debner and Jacoby 1994; Merikle, Joordens, and Stolz 1995).

In one study relying on this method, a prime word (e.g., spice) was presented briefly on each trial (Debner and Jacoby 1994). Following its presentation, participants were given a word stem (e.g., spi___) and were asked to complete it with any word they wished *except* the one they had just seen. If participants know they have just seen the word *spice*, they should avoid using it to complete the word stem. Indeed, when the prime word was presented for long enough to permit conscious awareness (for 500 milliseconds), participants were less likely to use the word if they had been primed by it than if they had not. This shows that conscious perception led to successful exclusion of the primed words. In contrast, when the prime word was presented too briefly to permit conscious awareness (for 50 milliseconds), participants were *more* likely to use the word in their stem completions if they had been primed by it than if they had not. These participants must have been unable to exclude the primed word because they were unaware that they had just seen it. Yet, it influenced their responses, suggesting that is was perceived outside of awareness.

Studies using this method of pitting conscious processes against unconscious ones provide strong evidence that we are capable of unconscious perception; we can be influenced by stimuli that we have never been aware of. Moreover, results from these studies lend credibility to the reality of subconscious perception obtained in studies using less stringent methods. For example, now that it is established that stimuli presented for a brief 50 milliseconds can only be perceived subliminally, it is reasonable to assume that other studies in which stimuli were presented for equally brief times also involved subliminal perception, even though those studies did not use the method of pitting unconscious processes against conscious ones. Most social cognition studies exploring the influence of subliminal perception have not used the method of opposing processes, relying instead on the less stringent method of demonstrating implicit influences in the absence of explicit recognition. Nevertheless, the assumption that they have indeed demonstrated unconscious influences seems reasonable in view of the evidence for such influences obtained from studies using the more stringent designs.

Social psychologists were interested in whether more complex social judgments could also be influenced by stimuli presented subliminally. Many studies had shown that when a personality trait is primed in a person, it may influence the way this person evaluates others on that trait. For example, when hostility was primed in participants through a task that required them to unscramble sentences implying hostility (e.g., "he kicked her bit"), these participants later viewed a person they encountered in a seemingly unrelated setting as more hostile (Srull and Wyer 1979). John Bargh and Paula Pietromonaco set out to determine whether the same would also be true if the traits were primed subliminally, outside of awareness. Would these traits still influence social judgments? In their study, participants first completed a "vigilance task" that required them to press a button every time they saw a flash on the screen in front of them so as to indicate the location of the flash (Bargh and Pietromonaco 1982). In fact, each flash represented a word that was presented very briefly (for 100 milliseconds) and was followed by a string of Xs that effectively masked it. It is extremely difficult to consciously detect words presented under such conditions. Of the 100 words presented in this manner, a certain proportion were words related to hostility (e.g., hostile, curse, punch). The percentage of hostile words in the different conditions was 0,

20, or 80 percent, representing no priming with hostility, weak priming, or strong priming.

To establish that participants were not aware of the priming words, a different group of participants was exposed to the same procedure used in the strong priming condition. Unlike the experimental participants, these participants were informed that a word would flash on each trial, and were asked to guess the words. They guessed fewer that 1 percent of the hostile words correctly, suggesting that they were unable to consciously detect these words. Could such undetectable words nevertheless influence judgment? The other participants (who had not been asked to guess the words) next proceeded to another task in which they read a description of a man named Donald engaging in somewhat hostile behaviors. It was unclear from the description whether he had behaved this way because he was truly hostile or because of situational pressures (e.g., "he was refusing to pay the rent until the landlord repaints the apartment"). Although participants were unaware of seeing the hostile words, these words influenced their evaluations of Donald. The more hostile words they had seen, the more negatively they rated him. This was the first study to demonstrate that our judgments of others can be influenced by information observed outside of awareness.

Many other studies have since demonstrated that information presented subliminally can influence our judgments, feelings and behavior. Much of this research has focused on the automatic activation of stereotypes, and is discussed in greater detail in chapter 8. A brief example will suffice for now. The culturally prevalent stereotype of African Americans includes the attribute *hostile* (Devine 1989). It has been shown that this stereotype can be activated by subliminal presentation of stereotype-related material, and will then influence subsequent judgments and behavior. White Americans exposed subliminally to words related to other aspects of that stereotype rated the ambiguously hostile Donald described above more negatively (Devine 1989). Similarly, non–African American students exposed subliminally to photographs of African Americans behaved in a more hostile manner toward an experimenter

(Bargh et al. 1996). These and similar studies suggest that stereo-type-related information can influence our judgments and behavior even if we have never been aware of seeing this information. A separate line of work has investigated the influence of material perceived unconsciously on our feelings, as discussed next.

Mere Exposure   You may have heard that familiarity breeds contempt. But a great deal of evidence suggests otherwise: The more familiar we are with people, faces, colors, geometrical shapes, odors, foods, and many other things, the more we like them (for a review, see Bornstein 1989). Robert Zajonc termed this phenomenon the *mere exposure* effect to indicate that the mere repeated exposure to an object suffices to increase one's liking for it (Zajonc 1968). It now appears that mere exposure to an object is especially likely to increase liking for that object when people are unaware of this exposure (Bornstein 1989; Bornstein and D'Agostino 1992).

A now classic study by Kunst-Wilson and Zajonc (1980) established that people will come to prefer previously seen objects even if they have never been aware of seeing them. In the first phase of this study, participants were exposed five times to each of 10 different irregular octagons. These exposures were so brief (1 millisecond) so as to make conscious detection all but impossible. Then, in the second phase, each of the old octagons was paired with a different new one that participants had not previously seen. For each such pair, they were asked to guess which octagon they had seen previously. Their responses revealed that they were unable to recognize the previously seen octagons; their accuracy was no better than what would be expected by chance alone (48 percent). And yet, despite their inability to recognize the objects they had been exposed to, their liking for these objects was influenced by this exposure: For most pairs (60 percent) they liked the old octagons better than the new ones.

Many subsequent studies have replicated this mere exposure effect. Robert Bornstein conducted a meta-analysis of over 200 experiments that examined the effects of mere exposure on liking (Bornstein 1989). In a meta-analysis, the results of many experiments that examine the same phenomenon can be integrated to provide an overall estimate of the strength of this phenomenon, and factors that influence results can be identified. The meta-analysis of the mere-exposure studies revealed that the effect of prior exposure on liking was substantially larger in studies that used subliminal exposure than it was in studies that used conscious exposure. Inspired by this conclusion, Bornstein and D'Agostino conducted a series of experiments designed to test it directly (Bornstein and D'Agostino 1992). And, indeed, they were able to show that repeated exposure to the same stimuli (photographs of women or geometrical shapes) enhanced liking for these stimuli more when the stimuli were presented subliminally (i.e., for only 5 milliseconds) than when they were presented with conscious awareness (i.e., for 500 milliseconds).

These findings suggest that the mechanism underlying the mere exposure effect may be similar to those that lead names to "become famous over night" (Jacoby et al. 1989). It seems likely that the repeated exposure to a stimulus creates a sense of vague familiarity, sometimes termed perceptual fluency. This warm glow of familiarity is then mistaken for liking. When people realize that the stimulus appears familiar because they have just seen it, they do not use this sense of familiarity as a basis for their liking judgments.

Individual Differences in Automatic Reactions

Henry Kissinger, at one time one of the most powerful men in America, noted that "power is the ultimate aphrodisiac." Does power automatically bring sex to mind? Will a man be especially likely to see a woman in a sexualized manner when he has power over her? Research by Bargh and his colleagues suggests that there may indeed be an automatic link between power and sex, but not for all men. Men who are likely to be sexually aggressive toward women may be especially likely to have this automatic link.

In their first study on the power-sex link, Bargh and his colleagues examined whether subliminal exposure to words related to power would lead men to automatically activate sex-related material, and whether subliminal exposure to words related to sex would lead them to automatically activate power-related material (Bargh et al. 1995). To this end, they constructed a list that included words related to power (e.g., executive, boss, mighty, tough), words related to sex (e.g., bed, date, hard, wet), and neutral words (e.g., chalk, house). On each trial, a target word taken from this list was presented on a computer screen and participants were asked to pronounce it as fast as they could. Unbeknownst to the participants, the presentation of each target word was preceded by a subliminal presentation of another word taken from that list, the prime (participants experienced the primes as mere flashes on the screen). On different trials, each of the power and sex words was primed by a power word, by a sex word, or by a neutral word. In this procedure, if the target word is activated by the prime word, participants should be able to pronounce it faster. For example, if power activates sexuality, then the sex-related word *date* should be pronounced faster when primed with a power word such as *boss* than when primed with a neutral word such as *chalk*.

Bargh and his colleagues were also interested in whether they could identify men for whom such automatic priming was especially likely. Therefore, after the priming session, participants completed, among other things, a questionnaire that measured the extent to which they found sexual aggression attractive. This questionnaire included items assessing the attractiveness of rape and of forcing a woman to do something she does not want to do, along with items about other sexual practices. The men who scored in the top and bottom 25 percent of the attractiveness of sexual aggression measure (i.e., those who found sexual aggression most and least attractive) were included in the analyses.

As expected, power cues activated sex-related material for men who found sexual aggression attractive, but not for men who did not. Put differently, responses to sex-related words were speeded up by subliminal power primes only for those men who found sexual aggression attractive, as shown in figure 7.2. This power-sex link was unidirectional. Priming did not work in the opposite direction: Sex-related words did not activate power for either group of men. These findings have important implications for how power may

Attractiveness of Sexual Aggression

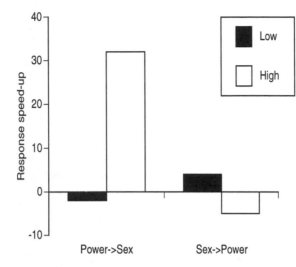

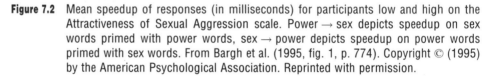

Figure 7.2 Mean speedup of responses (in milliseconds) for participants low and high on the Attractiveness of Sexual Aggression scale. Power → sex depicts speedup on sex words primed with power words, sex → power depicts speedup on power words primed with sex words. From Bargh et al. (1995, fig. 1, p. 774). Copyright © (1995) by the American Psychological Association. Reprinted with permission.

affect the way some men see women. If power cues can activate sexual thoughts in some men automatically, without them realizing that this was happening, then power cues could also lead such men to view any woman present in a more sexualized manner. If the man does not realize that his sexual thoughts are triggered by power, he may mistakenly assume that they are provoked by the woman.

Bargh and his colleagues examined this possibility in a follow-up study (Bargh et al. 1995). This time, they primed power in some participants by asking them to complete a list of word fragments that included six power-related words (e.g. BO__S). Other participants were primed with neutral words instead. Participants were then asked to rate the attractiveness of a female confederate masquerading as another participant. After a distracter task, participants completed the same questionnaire assessing the attractiveness of sexual aggression used in the earlier study. Once again, only participants scoring in the top and bottom 25 percent of this measure were included in the analyses.

Men who found sexual aggression attractive rated the female confederate as substantially more attractive if they had been primed with power than if they had not. No such priming effect was found for men who found sexual aggression relatively unattractive; they rated the woman as equally attractive regardless of the contents of the priming. It appears that those men for whom sexual thoughts are triggered automatically by power cues will also view women as more attractive in the presence of such power cues. In these studies the power cues were lists of words constructed by the investigators. But it is easy to imagine that cues deriving from real power differentials will have similar effects. If a man who automatically links power to sex finds himself in a position that gives him power and authority over a woman, his power over the woman may lead him to find her particularly attractive. Because power can activate sexual thoughts without the person realizing that this is happening, the man may not realize that he finds the woman attractive *because* she is his subordinate. He may find the same woman considerably less attractive if he were to meet her on an equal footing in a different setting.

These findings also make the broader point that different individuals may have different automatic reactions to the same situations, depending on their overall cognitive and affective structure. Other studies have also found individual differences in automatic reactions to the same stimuli. For example, photographs of African Americans lead to automatic activation of negative affect in some White Americans. But other, less prejudiced White Americans and African Americans show no such automatic negative reaction, and some show an automatic positive reaction instead (Fazio et al. 1995; see chapter 9). Our idiosyncratic pattern of automatic associations to different situational cues may lie at the very core of our personality (Mischel and Shoda 1995; see chapter 10).

In summary, there is considerable evidence that our judgments, feelings, and behaviors can be influenced by factors that we have never been aware of, by factors that we were aware of at one time but can no longer recall, and by factors that we can still recall but whose influence we are unaware of. A great deal of social cognition may be automatic in this regard; many of our judgments may be influenced by our past experiences in a manner that is not open to introspection (Greenwald and Banaji 1995). For example, our evaluations of others may be influenced by our liking for them, by our goals, by our moods, and by our stereotypes of their groups, as well as by many aspects of the situation and a variety of recent experiences. To the extent that we are unaware of these influences and are unable to report them, they should be considered implicit. Moreover, we should recognize that people's judgments may be influenced by a prior experience, attitude, or belief even when they deny this vehemently ("My dislike for him has nothing to do with his race!" "I would marvel at her brilliance even if she were not my child!" "I evaluate my students' papers entirely on their merit; I never allow my expectations or feelings to influence my grading."). Such claims may be made with great sincerity. Nevertheless, they may be wrong because people are simply unaware of many subtle influences on their judgments.

Efficiency

Another hallmark of automatic processes is that they are highly efficient, that is, their execution requires very little time and effort. They can be carried out even under severe time pressure, and even when cognitive resources are scarce. In contrast, controllable processes require sufficient time and resources. Therefore, researchers who wish to identify and study automatic processes often attempt to preempt controlled processing by restricting the amount of time available to participants or by overloading them with other tasks that sap their cognitive resources. Any process that can be carried out even under such restricted conditions is assumed to be automatic in that it is highly efficient (for reviews, see Bargh 1994, 1996).

Scarce Time

If you have just seen the word *bird*, specific kinds of birds such as *robin* will be highly activated in your mind. If you are then asked to determine as fast as you can whether *robin* is a word, you will be able to do this faster than if you had not just been primed with *bird*. There is a great deal of evidence for such semantic priming (for a review, see Ratcliff and McKoon 1988; see chapter 2). An important study by James Neely showed that people can override such priming effects *if they have enough time* (Neely 1977). When people are told that the prime *bird* will be followed by a target word representing a body part, they do not activate *robin* when primed with *bird* if the time between the onset of the prime and the onset of the target word exceeds 500 milliseconds. This suggests that, under these conditions, participants attempt to avoid activating words that are semantically related to the prime, and that these attempts are successful. However, if the time between the onset of the prime and the onset of the target word is less 500 milliseconds, participants do activate semantic associates of the prime even though they are trying not to.

People's inability to exercise control over processes that happen so rapidly suggests that these processes are automatic in several regards. In addition to being highly efficient (in that they require so little time), processes that occur within this very limited time frame are also assumed to be uncontrollable and to take place without intention (because they occur even despite an intention to do otherwise). These conclusions have been generally accepted, and most researchers assume that any priming that occurs within less than 500 milliseconds is predominantly automatic (see Blair and Banaji 1996). This assumption has guided research on the automatic activation of affect, as discussed next.

Automatic Activation of Affect　　Just about any object has an affective association—you either like it or dislike it. You may like sunshine, candy, and vacations and may dislike war, weeds, and vomit. Does this affect get triggered automatically when you encounter a liked or disliked object, without any intention on your part? Will you experience an automatic *yeah!* reaction upon hearing the word *vacation*, and an automatic *yuck!* reaction upon hearing the word *vomit*? If affect is activated automatically by such words, the activated affect should carry over to other judgment tasks. Russell Fazio and his colleagues reasoned that it should be possible to detect automatically triggered affect by examining its consequences for subsequent judgments (Fazio et al. 1986).

To understand the logic of their experiments, imagine that you are asked to indicate as fast as you can whether the word *attractive* is good or bad. For you to make this decision, your representation of either *good* or *bad* must reach a level of activation that is above a critical level. You will respond as soon as this happens. Now, if you have just been thinking about something that you really like such as sunshine, and *sunshine* has led you to activate positive affect, then *good* will have already received some activation; not that much more is needed to arrive at the critical threshold, and so you will be able to respond faster. In short, exposure to *sunshine* should speed up your decision that *attractive* is good. At the same time, it should slow down your decision that *repulsive* is bad. This is because the activation of *bad* will be inhibited and decreased by the positive affect triggered by *sunshine*, and therefore more activation and time will be required for *bad* to reach the critical level of activation. In the same manner, exposure to *vomit* should speed up your decision that *repulsive* is bad and slow down your decision that *attractive* is good.

Fazio and his colleagues reasoned that affect would be most likely to be triggered automatically by objects that people felt strongly about (Fazio et al. 1986). Therefore, the first step in each of their experiments was designed to identify, for each participant, a set of such affect-laden objects as well as a set of objects that provoked only weak affective reactions. To this end, participants were asked to indicate as fast as they could whether each of a list 70 objects was good or bad, by pressing an appropriate key. Based on the speed of their reactions, a list of strong primes was constructed for each participant. This list included the four words to which the participant had responded *good* most quickly (common examples were gift, music, party, and cake) as well as the four words to which the participant had responded *bad* most quickly (common examples were death, hell, guns, and crime). In addition a list of weak primes was constructed for each participant. This list included the four good and the four bad words that the participant had responded to most slowly (common good examples were crosswords and Republicans, common bad examples were mazes and radiation). With this list in hand, the experimenters were able to prime each participant with objects that were strongly or weakly associated with positive or with negative affect for that participant.

On each trial of the second phase of the experiment, participants were shown a target word that was either positive (e.g., appealing, delightful) or negative (e.g., repulsive, awful), and were asked to indicate as fast as they could whether it was good or bad. Each target word was preceded by a positive or negative prime selected from the participant's idiosyncratic list or by a letter string (e.g., BBB) included to serve as a baseline against which primed responses could be evaluated. The prime was presented very briefly (for 200 milliseconds), and the target word was presented after a very brief interval (100 milliseconds). After participants indicated whether the target word was good or bad, they were asked to recite the prime. This was done to ensure that they had read it. Note that the interval between the onsets of the prime and the target was only 300 milliseconds, well below the 500 millisecond cutoff for automatic processes. Moreover, because participants were not asked to attend to the affective connotations of the prime or to use these in their judgment, it is unlikely that they had consciously intended to do so. Therefore, any priming by the affect-laden words can be considered automatic.

Responses to the target words were indeed influenced by the primes. When participants were primed with strongly positive words such as *gift*, they were faster to indicate that words such as *appealing* were good and slower to indicate that words such as *repulsive* were bad (as compared to their baseline responses). Similarly, when they were primed with strongly negative words such as *death*, they were faster to indicated that words such as *repulsive* were bad, and slower to indicate that words such as *appealing* were good. In short, their automatic affective reactions to the strong primes speeded up their reactions to words with congruent affect and slowed down their reactions to words with incongruent affect.

Further evidence that the influence of affective reactions triggered by the strong primes was automatic was provided by a follow-up study that varied the interval between the onsets of the prime and the target (Fazio et al. 1986). The priming effects described above were replicated when this interval was very brief (300 milliseconds) but not when it was long enough to permit controlled processing (1000 milliseconds). There may be several reasons for the elimination of the affective priming at the longer interval. It is possible that the primed affect simply dissipated rapidly. It is also possible that participants were actively attempting to suppress it because it seemed irrelevant to their task, but were able to do so only when given sufficient time. In either case, this finding strengthens the interpretation that the obtained priming influences were automatic because, as discussed above, any process that occurs only in a very restricted time frame is especially likely to be automatic.

The weak primes did not lead to similar priming effects in these two studies, which suggests that not all objects will provoke an automatic activation of affect. Nevertheless, such automatic activation is quite widespread. The third study by Fazio and his colleagues did obtain affective priming even for weak primes (Fazio et al. 1986). Moreover, a series of studies by Bargh and his colleagues indicated that the range of objects that can trigger automatic affective reactions is quite broad (Bargh et al. 1992). Such automatic reactions are not restricted to extremely affect-laden words such as gift and death. Using procedures identical to those used by Fazio and his colleagues, Bargh and his colleagues showed that less extreme and quite mundane words such as magazine, clothes, litter, and hangover can also give rise to automatic affective priming.

In the studies described above, participants were engaged in an evaluation task (is *appealing* good?) which may have led them to focus on the affective connotations of the prime words as well. Could this be the main reason why the affect associated with the primes was activated? Apparently, not. Another set of studies demonstrated that affect is activated automatically by mildly positive and negative words even in the absence of any evaluative intent (Bargh et al. 1996). In these studies, participants were only asked to pronounce positive and negative words that had been preceded by positive or negative primes. Once again, the intervals between the onsets of the prime and the target were brief enough to ensure that any obtained priming would be automatic (300 milliseconds). Participants were faster to pronounce the target words when these words were primed by a word with congruent affect than when they were primed by a word with incongruent affect. This was true even when both the prime and the target were only mildly pleasant or unpleasant, and were completely unrelated semantically. For example, priming with *dentist* speeded up responses to *exam*, and priming with *pie* speeded up responses to *priest*. It appears that we have automatic affective reactions to many, perhaps most, of the objects we come across in the course of our daily lives, and these reactions can influence the way we think about other objects. Our automatic affective reactions to a given object may be stronger, though, if our attitude toward that object is more accessible to us (Fazio 1993).

Because the influence of the affect triggered by liked and disliked objects appears to be automatic, affective priming can be used as a subtle and uncontrollable indicator of people's feelings toward various objects, issues, or individuals. Our inability to control this process suggests that affective priming is unlikely to be contaminated by any desire to hide our feelings so as to present ourselves in the best possible light. For example, bigoted White Americans may be reluctant to tell you that they dislike African Americans, but their reaction times will reveal their true feelings (Fazio et al 1995; see chapter 8).

So far I noted that a cognitive process can be shown to be efficient by demonstrating that it can take place very rapidly and can occur even within highly restrictive time frames. A cognitive process may also be shown to be efficient by demonstrating that it can be carried out even with very limited cognitive resources, as discussed next.

Scarce Resources

We have a limited amount of cognitive and attentional resources. If we are engaged in a cognitively demanding task, we may have too few resources left over for many other tasks. If, when driving, you encounter a tricky stretch of highway, you may have to focus your attention on the road. As a result you may be unable to continue an ongoing conversation—you simply have too few resources for it. Similarly, when you are having an animated conversation with a friend at a party, you may be unable to also listen in on other people's conversations; you will not notice or remember what they say. But you may still be able to carry on some simultaneous activities—you may continue sipping your drink throughout your conversation. And, even though you are not really listening to other conversations, you will jump to attention if someone happens to mention your name. Those activities that you are able to continue without disruption even while you are engaged in a cognitively demanding task may be considered relatively automatic in that they are highly *efficient*; that is, they require very few cognitive resources.

Controlled processes require substantial cognitive resources and are therefore disrupted when resources are restricted. In contrast, automatic processes are so efficient that they can continue without disruption even with minimal cognitive resources. These ideas led to an important insight: It should be possible to determine whether a process is controlled or automatic by examining whether or not it is disrupted by an increase in cognitive load. If the process can continue without disruption even when one is loaded with other demanding tasks, it can be considered automatic. But if the process is disrupted by cognitive load, it can be assumed to be controlled. This insight has led to many experiments that have examined the impact of high cognitive load (created, for example, by asking participants to keep a long series of numbers in memory) on a variety of tasks (for reviews, see Bargh 1994, 1996, Wegner and Bargh 1998). One such influential line of work concerns the kinds of attributions that people make about another person's behavior, as discussed next.

Automatic and Controlled Processes in Attribution   Imagine that you have just observed the following sequence of events: Larry teases and makes fun of Justin. Justin gets mad and punches Larry. What do you make of Justin's behavior? What do you make of Justin? Daniel Gilbert and his colleagues have suggested that the person-perception process you are likely to go through in such a situation involves three components: *Categorization* of the behavior (punching is an aggressive behavior), *characterization* of the actor (Justin is an aggressive person), and *correction* of the characterization, taking situational factors into account (Justin was provoked by Larry, so maybe he is not all that aggressive). Gilbert and his colleagues assumed that the processes of categorization and characterization are relatively automatic, whereas correction is a more cognitively demanding, controlled process (Gilbert, Pelham, and Krull 1988). Attribution takes place in two stages: People first categorize the behavior and characterize the actor in a relatively automatic manner. This leads them to view the person as having the disposition implied by his or her behavior (Justin is aggressive). They then correct this attribution by making allowances for the constraints of the situation (he was provoked), but only if they have sufficient cognitive resources.

If it is true that dispositional inferences are carried out automatically whereas correcting for situational constraints requires deliberate effort, then only the process of correction should be disrupted by cognitive load. When preoccupied, you should still arrive at the effortless conclusion that Justin is aggressive. But you should be unable to make allowances for the provocation he had suffered; you will not have the resources necessary for the elaborate and effortful thought that such correction requires. One implication of this analysis is that when people are under a heavy cognitive load they should be more likely to engage in the *fundamental attribution error* (also known as the *correspondence bias*). Recall that this error involves overestimating the role of dispositions in producing behavior and underestimating the impact of the situation (for a review, see Jones 1990; see chapter 9). If people are capable of taking situational constraints into account only when they have sufficient resources, their tendency to underestimate the impact of the situation should be exaggerated when their resources are depleted. Gilbert and his colleagues explored these predictions in a series of studies (for a review, see Gilbert 1989).

Recall the classic study of correspondence bias, in which participants evaluated another student's attitude toward Cuba's Castro after reading a pro- or anti-Castro essay written by that student (Jones and Harris 1967; for relaaded discussions, see chapters 3, 6, and 9). The intriguing finding was that participants viewed the essay writer's true attitude as more supportive of Castro when the essay was pro-Castro than when it was anti-Castro even when they knew that the student had been required to write the essay in question. In other words, their attributions about the person corresponded to the attitude he had expressed and did not make sufficient allowances for the situational constraints he had been under, namely the fact that he had been required to express that particular attitude.

Gilbert and his colleagues replicated this classic study, with the addition that half of their participants were put under high cognitive load (Gilbert et al. 1988). Participants listened to a student read either a pro- or an antiabortion speech that he had been required to write. Half the participants merely listened to this speech. The other half listened with the expectation that they themselves would have to write and read a speech later in the session. It was assumed that this expectation would lead them to plan and mentally rehearse their own speech while listening to the target person read his; these cognitively demanding activities would deplete the cognitive resources available to them for thinking about the target person. If people's ability to correct their attributions for situational constraints depends on the availability of sufficient cognitive resources, those participants operating with the additional task of mentally rehearsing their own future speech should have greater

Table 7.1 Participants' perceptions of the target's attitude toward abortion as a function of whether they had only one cognitive task (listening to the target's speech) or an additional task (mentally rehearsing their own future speech)

TARGET ESSAY	ONE TASK (LOW LOAD)	TWO TASKS (HIGH LOAD)
Proabortion	8.7	10.6
Antiabortion	5.4	4.2
Difference	*3.3*	*6.4*

Source: From Gilbert et al. (1988, table 4, p. 737). Copyright © (1988) by the American Psychological Association. Reprinted with permission.
Note: Higher numbers indicate more proabortion attitudes.

difficulty taking the target person's situational constraints into account; their perceptions of his true attitude should correspond even more closely to the contents of his speech.

As may be seen in table 7.1, this was indeed the case. Participants operating under relatively low load did show the correspondence bias: They saw the target person as more proabortion if he had read a proabortion speech than if he had read an antiabortion one. But this bias was substantially larger for participants operating under high load; they made fewer allowances for the fact that the target had been required to write a particular kind of speech, and based their assessments of his true attitude more strongly on the contents of his speech.

In a series of related studies, Gilbert and his colleagues conceptually replicated these findings using a variety of cognitive load manipulations. These included requiring participants to keep in mind a long string of numbers or words, requiring them to monitor and respond to letters flashing on a screen, and asking them to try to make someone else laugh (for a review, see Gilbert 1989). As in the study described above, the general finding is that high cognitive load does not interfere with people's ability to infer that the actor's personality corresponds to his or her behavior, but high load does disrupt their ability to correct this inference for the likely impact of the situation.

These findings suggest that as we see another person deliver an insult, a joke, or a helping hand, we automatically assume that the person's underlying personality corresponds to the behavior we have observed. What we "see," even when we are preoccupied with other cognitive tasks, is an aggressive, amusing, or helpful person (see also Trope and Alfieri 1997; Winter, Uleman, and Cunniff 1985; for a detailed discussion, see chapter 9). Whereas these personality characterizations are drawn in a relatively automatic manner, making allowances for situational constraints requires more controlled, effortful processing, and can be disrupted when we are preoccupied. It appears, then, that one reason we fall prey to the fundamental attribution error is that we are often too preoccupied to make sufficient allowances for the impact of the situation on another person's behavior. Such preoccupation is not the only reason for the fundamental attribution error, though. To be able to correct for the impact of the situation, we must first be able to recognize and appreciate this impact. One of the central lessons from social psychological research is that people often fail to understand and appreciate the power of the situation (for a review, see Ross and Nisbett 1991). When we do not understand the ways in which people's behaviors are influenced by the situations they are in, we will make the fundamental attribution error no matter how abundant our cognitive resources (see chapter 9).

Cognitive load manipulations have been used to examine the automaticity of a variety of other aspects of social cognition. For example, it has been shown that the activation of stereotypes is not fully automatic; it can be disrupted when resources are scarce (Gilbert and Hixon 1991; see chapter 8). It has also been shown that people compare themselves to others in a relatively automatic way (Oh no! She did better than me!), but take into account differences in their own and the other's circumstances only if they have sufficient resources (Well, she has had more instruction; Gilbert, Giesler, and Morris 1995). And it has been shown that depressed individuals process negative information about the self more automatically than do nondepressed individuals; individuals who are not depressed have trouble processing negative information about themselves when under heavy cognitive load, but depressed individuals can still process such negative information rapidly even when cognitively overloaded (Bargh and Tota 1988). In these and similar studies, a process is assumed to be relatively automatic if it is not disrupted by cognitive load, and is assumed to be controlled if it is. This logic has also been used to explore the processes through which we attempt to control and suppress unwanted thoughts, as discussed next.

Ironic Processes in Thought Control   As you are reading the following section, please try *not* to think about your mother. We are often quite good at controlling our attention, thoughts, and feelings. We can successfully concentrate on important tasks while ignoring irrelevant distractors, we can avoid entertaining amusing thoughts in circumstances that call for seriousness, we can relax and go to sleep when we want to. But you have undoubtedly noticed that you cannot always control your thoughts and feelings. Indeed, we are often haunted by the very thoughts we are trying to suppress. When dieting, you may find yourself thinking of nothing but food. When trying to put a bad experience out of mind, you may be constantly reminded of that experience. When you are determined to avoid thinking of someone in terms of a negative ethnic stereotype, you may find that this very stereotype springs to mind when you encounter that individual. And I suspect that you have probably just been thinking about your mother even if you have been trying, as requested, not to.

Daniel Wegner noted that our attempts at mental control often result not only in failure but, worse, in an intensification of the very thoughts we are trying to suppress. In other words, when we try to control our thoughts, we often experience an *ironic reversal*; the more we try to suppress a thought, the more it plagues us (Wegner 1994). Why is it that our attempts at mental control result in success on some occasions but in dramatic failure on others? Wegner reasoned that the key to the answer lies in the availability of mental capacity. Mental control is successful when we have sufficient cognitive resources. But when our resources are depleted because we are distracted, tired, preoccupied, or for any other reason, our attempts at control may not only fail but also backfire and result in ironic reversals.

Mental capacity is essential to mental control because successful mental control requires two processes: We need to suppress the unwanted thought, but we also need to remember what it is that we are trying to suppress. There are two processes needed to accomplish these goals:

1. *An intentional search for distracters.* When we are trying to avoid thinking about food, we must search for something else to think about—sports, politics, work, a friend, anything but food. This search process is controlled and effortful, and can be disrupted when cognitive resources are depleted.

2. *An automatic search for the target.* To avoid thinking about food, we need to be on the lookout for any food-related thought so that we can suppress it. This monitoring is carried out outside of conscious awareness and requires little effort.

When we have sufficient cognitive resources, the two processes work hand in hand to produce successful mental control. The intentional search for distracters occupies our mind with alternatives to the thoughts we wish to suppress. Meanwhile the automatic search for signs of the unwanted thoughts continues surreptitiously, and when any traces of such thoughts are detected, a renewed search for distracters is launched. But when our cognitive resources are scarce, mental control breaks down. With reduced capacity, we are unable to conduct an effective search for distracters. Yet the automatic search for the contents we are trying to suppress continues with little disruption. In other words, we continue to search for the thoughts we wish to avoid, but we are unable to defend ourselves against these thoughts when we find them. The end result is an ironic reversal—we become hypersensitive to the very thoughts we wish to suppress.

To illustrate the flavor of research on the hyperaccessibility of suppressed thoughts, I would like you to try not to think about the word *house*. Next, you will see a list of words. As you read each, your task is to come up with an association to it, and say it out loud. You must do this very quickly; you have only three seconds for each word. And remember, you should still be trying not think about *house*. Now, come up with an association to each of the following words: *hill, home, bus, child, roof, drive, little, brick.*

If, despite, yourself, you found yourself saying *house* in response to some of these words, you are not alone in this. In a study that used this task, participants were asked either to concentrate on a target word (e.g., *house*) or to try not to think about it (Wegner and Erber 1992). They were then asked to provide associations to a series of prompts, some of which were related to the target word (e.g., *home, roof*), and some of which were unrelated to it (e.g., *hill, bus*). They responded to half the prompts, as you did, under high time pressure (within 3 seconds), and responded to the other half under low time pressure (within 10 seconds). Under high time pressure, mental capacity is severely restricted. These are the circumstances that should produce ironic reversals; people trying to suppress the word *house* should be especially likely to come up with that very word in response to a related cue, when operating with scarce cognitive resources. As may be seen in figure 7.3, this is precisely what happened.

Under low time pressure, participants' attempts at suppressing the target word were successful: Those trying to suppress a word came up with it as an association to a related cue less often than did those concentrating on the same word. But mental control broke down and backfired under high time pressure: Participants trying to suppress a word came up with it *more* often than those concentrating on it. In other words, when mental capacity was restricted by severe time pressure, the thoughts people were trying to suppress had, instead, become hyperaccessible.

Wegner and his colleagues obtained similar ironic reversals in a series of studies examining different kinds of attempts at mental control under different kinds of restrictions on mental capacity (for a review, see Wegner 1994). The findings are quite consistent: Under normal cognitive load, people demonstrate effective mental

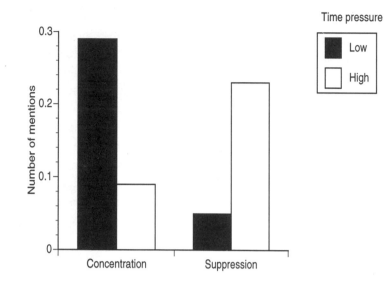

Figure 7.3 Average number of times the target word (the word that participants were attempting to suppress or were concentrating on) was mentioned in response to target-related cues, under high and low time pressure. From Wegner and Erber (1992, fig. 1, p. 906). Copyright © (1992) by the American Psychological Association. Reprinted with permission.

control. For example, when they try to, people can make themselves feel happy or sad, stop themselves from coming up with sexist associations, or fall asleep rapidly. But all these attempts at mental control lead to ironic reversals when people's cognitive resources are made scarce by instructing them to keep a series of numbers in mind, putting them under severe time pressure, or bombarding them with noisy and disturbing music. Under such circumstances people trying to be sad become happy instead, people trying to avoid being sexist become especially prone to sexist reactions, and people trying to fall asleep quickly stay awake for longer instead (Wegner 1994).

The finding that ironic reversals are especially likely when people attempt to control their thoughts while their cognitive resources are scarce lends support to Wegner's view that attempts at mental control trigger a controlled process that is disrupted when resources are scarce, along with an automatic search for the unwanted thoughts that continues unabated even when resources are restricted and results in hyperaccessibility of the very thoughts one is trying to avoid.

In conclusion, the recognition that is possible to identify highly efficient, automatic processes by demonstrating that they continue without disruption even when cognitive resources are scarce has enabled researchers to examine the automaticity of a variety of processes. This has shed new light on old problems such as the fundamental attribution error and stereotyping and has opened up newer areas of investigation such as mental control. This research has revealed that many of our cognitive processes can be launched and carried out automatically. I turn next to a discussion of how a mental process may come to be automatic.

Forming Automatic Reactions

As should be clear by now, a wide range of our thoughts, feelings, and behaviors can be triggered automatically by particular config- urations of cues, without any intention or awareness on our part. We may automatically infer people's character from their behavior, automatically experience affective reactions to a variety of objects, automatically behave in line with traits cued by recent experiences, and automatically engage in a variety of other mental processes as well. We may also differ from each other in our automatic reac- tions; for example, some people will automatically think of sex when cued with power, others will not.

What produces these automatic reactions? And why do we differ in our automatic reactions to various cues? In his *auto-motive model* developed to account for automatic thought, feeling, and action, Bargh suggested that automatic reactions are learned from experience (Bargh 1997). If we have the same reaction to an object every time we encounter it, we will build a strong association between the object and our reaction to it; once this happens, the reaction will be triggered automatically when we encounter the object. For example, if every time we see one person hit another we come to view the act and the person as aggressive, eventually we will think "aggressive" automatically whenever we observe such an act. Similarly, if every time we encounter vomit we experience disgust, eventually the mere thought of vomit may provoke disgust. Some automatic associations, such as disgust at the sight of vomit, may be universal. But because many aspects of our experience are unique, we will each also develop our own unique set of automatic reactions to different configurations of cues.

Some support for this model comes from animal research conducted by neuroscientist Joseph LeDoux and his colleagues (for a review, see LeDoux 1996). In exploring the neural pathways that develop as an animal learns to fear a sound (because it is accompanied by shock), LeDoux and his colleagues made an intriguing discovery: As would be expected, the animal develops connections between the brain region representing the sensory features of these sounds (the sensory thalamus) and the region in which higher-level processing of such sensory information is conducted (the sensory cortex), which in turn is connected to the brain region associated with emotional reactions (the amygdala). LeDoux termed this pathway *the high road*; it represents a process through which, after the stimulus is perceived, the animal identifies it and analyzes its meaning and then responds with the appropriate emotion. But in addition to this high road, the animal also establishes a *low road*, that is, a direct connection between the sensory thalamus, where the sensory features of the sound are represented, and the amygdala, which is responsible for emotional reactions, completely bypassing the sensory cortex in which stimuli are analyzed for meaning. This direct pathway allows for a quick emotional reaction before one fully knows what one is reacting to. As such, it provides compelling evidence for Zajonc's provocative claim that "preferences need no inferences" (Zajonc 1980). Moreover, this direct pathway points to the mechanisms through which automatic affective reactions can be acquired and produced.

Neuroscientist Antonio Damasio and his colleagues have suggested that such acquired automatic affective reactions play a crucial role in human decision making (for a review, see A. Damasio 1994). Their ideas were triggered by examination of the behavior of brain-damaged individuals whose damage was concentrated in the prefrontal cortex, an area that controls emotional reactions. Such patients show a puzzling profile. Their cognitive abilities seem intact: They appear intelligent and knowledgeable, their performance on many tests of intellectual abilities is comparable to that of normal individuals, they can understand and appreciate the consequences of various kinds of behavior, and they can distinguish between appropriate and inappropriate social behaviors. And yet, their everyday decision making is disastrous. They make extremely costly interpersonal and professional errors, have trouble holding on to jobs they had succeeded at before their injury, may squander their money on misguided business ventures, and tend to experience great discord in their personal relationships. Why is it that these individuals, who seem fully cognizant of the severe costs of inappropriate behaviors, nevertheless recklessly engage in these behaviors?

Damasio and his colleagues reasoned that this may be due to the patients' damaged ability to experience emotions. Emotions, they suggested, play a crucial role in alerting us to the fact that we have reason for concern; they serve as a red light, a signal that we are experiencing a problem (or, when positive, a signal that all is well). You may recall that social psychologists have documented the crucial role of arousal in signaling to us that we are concerned about something we have done or observed; we engage in motivated reasoning aimed at reducing a threat only when we experience arousal that we attribute to this threat (e.g., Zanna and Cooper 1974; see chapter 6). Social psychologists have also noted that we may rely on such emotional reactions when trying to determine our attitudes and beliefs (Schwarz and Clore 1996; see chapter 6). Damasio and his colleagues have expanded these ideas and applied them to a broader range of behaviors and decisions; they assume that we will feel compelled to make the right choice only when our emotions inform us that we care. Moreover, with experience, appropriate emotions will come to be triggered automatically, and will guide our decisions even if we cannot fully articulate why we are drawn to a particular option.

An ingenious study lends support to these ideas (Bechera et al. 1997). Normal individuals and patients with prefrontal damage were given a gambling task: Participants were given $2,000 in facsimile money, and were told to try to maximize their winnings and minimize their losses in a card game. On each of the 100 trials of the game, they were to pick a card from one of four decks. Most cards in each deck carried a monetary reward (which was revealed when the card was turned over), but some, unpredictable, cards in each deck carried a penalty instead. The participants were not informed about this, but there were two kinds of decks: Decks A and B carried high rewards ($100) but also high penalties; playing mostly from these decks would lead to overall loss in the long run. In contrast, decks C and D carried lower rewards ($50) but also lower penalties; playing mostly from these decks would lead to overall gain. Participants were connected to a device that recorded their skin-conductance response before the selection of each card; this provided a measure of their physiological arousal. In addition, after their twentieth trial and after every subsequent 10 trials they were asked to report how they conceptualized the game and what strategies they were using.

The results were quite striking. After encountering a few losses (usually by card 10), normal individuals began to show an elevated skin-conductance response as they were reaching for the "bad" decks. In other words, they were experiencing anticipatory arousal as though they were expecting punishment. They began reversing their preference, favoring the good decks over the bad ones. Yet, even by card 20, these normal individuals were reporting that they did not have a clue about what was going on. Put differently, these individuals were making advantageous choices, guided by automatic affective reactions, before they became aware of the fact that some decks were better than others. Once they became aware of the differences among the decks (usually somewhere between trials 50 and 80), they showed an overwhelming preference for the good ones.

A very different pattern emerged for the brain-damaged patients. These patients never experienced anticipatory arousal; their skin-conductance responses did not show any elevation as they approached the bad decks. Moreover, even after they recognized which decks would prove more advantageous, these patients continued to make disadvantageous choices, preferring the "bad" decks that they knew would yield greater short-term gains but larger overall losses. These patients appeared to lack the emotional "red light" indicating danger; they therefore ignored the danger even when they were aware of it. It appears that automatic emotional reactions can be learned rapidly and can guide our decisions even in the absence of conscious knowledge. But without such emotional reactions, we may behave foolishly even when we know better.

So far there has been little research on the acquisition of automatic reactions that involve complex judgments and behavior. Nevertheless, although we may not yet know exactly how such automatic reactions are established, there is, as we have seen, mounting evidence for the existence of such automatic reactions—many different kinds of thoughts and behaviors have been shown to be triggered automatically in response to situational cues. Each of us has a unique configuration of automatic reactions that we experience as we encounter various kinds of individuals and social situations. We may be aware of some of these, knowing for example, that vomit inevitability produces disgust, but may be completely unaware of others, not realizing, for example, that familiarity breeds liking. Moreover, many of our more complex social judgments involve an elaborate interplay between relatively automatic, unintended reactions and more controlled effortful thought. It is often difficult to tell whether and to what extent our attempts at careful reasoning have been contaminated by unintended and unwanted automatic associations. For example, a male manager may have trouble determining the extent to which his liking for his female secretary is influenced by her behavior, her looks, his power over her, his mood at work, or his stereotypes of women and of secretaries. Although, due to their very nature, we will often be unaware of our automatic reactions, we should be aware of the possibility that we, and others, may experience such reactions.

Moreover, people's failure to recognize that their judgments have been influenced by a particular factor cannot be taken as incontrovertible evidence that they were not in fact swayed by it.

Summary

Much of our mental life goes on automatically. Unlike controlled processes, automatic processes *occur outside awareness*, are carried out *without intention*, are *uncontrollable* (i.e., one cannot stop them), or are highly *efficient* (i.e., require few cognitive resources).

Our judgments, feelings, and behaviors can be influenced by factors that we have never been aware of and have only been exposed to subliminally, by factors that we were aware of at one time but can no longer recall, and by factors that we can still recall but whose influence we are unaware of. Consequently, our evaluations of others may be inadvertently influenced by our liking for them, by our goals, by our moods, by our stereotypes of their groups, by many aspects of the situation, and by a multitude of recent experiences, without our recognizing these influences. Therefore, people's reports on the reasons for their judgments and actions cannot always be trusted; people may simply be unaware of the extent to which they have been swayed by a variety of factors.

We also have automatic affective reactions to many, perhaps most, of the objects we come across in the course of our daily lives; some provoke positive affect and some negative affect. Our automatic emotional reactions can be learned rapidly, can guide our decisions and judgments, and can influence our thoughts about other objects even if we are not consciously aware of these reactions. People may differ in their automatic reactions to the same objects.

Some of our cognitive processes are so efficient that we can perform them even within highly restrictive time frames and even when we are preoccupied with other tasks. A process is assumed to be automatic in this sense if it is not disrupted when the time available for it is very brief or when one's cognitive resources are strained. Research driven by this insight has shed new light on old problems such as the fundamental attribution error and stereotyping, and has opened up newer areas of investigation such as mental control. For example, it now appears that when we observe a person behave, we jump automatically to conclusions about the person's underlying traits, but can correct these judgments to account for situational constraints only if we have sufficient cognitive resources; this is one reason for the fundamental attribution error. It also appears that successful suppression of undesired thoughts requires the conjoint operation of an intentional, controlled search for distracters and an automatic search for the unwanted thoughts (so as to suppress them when detected). When cognitive resources are scarce, the controlled search for distracters is disrupted, but the automatic search for the unwanted thoughts continues unabated, resulting in hyperaccessibility of the unwanted thoughts.

II Basic Topics

During the summer of 1998, Serbs engaged in "ethnic cleansing" of Albanians in the Yugoslav region of Kosovo, Hutus massacred Tutsis in Rwanda, three White Americans dragged an African American to his death in the United States, Protestants and Catholics clashed violently in Northern Ireland, and widespread abuse of female military recruits by their male counterparts came to light in Canada. The list of atrocities and indignities inflicted by people on other people who differed from them in nationality, ethnicity, gender, or religion during that summer alone could go on and on. Social psychological research and theory on stereotypes was initially driven by a desire to gain insight into the causes of such intergroup hatred and violence, issues that loomed especially large in the wake of World War II. As the social climate in the United States evolved and, following the civil liberties movement, explicit expression of negative racial and gender stereotypes became less and less socially acceptable, research on stereotypes began focusing on more subtle, sometimes unintended manifestations of stereotypes. In particular, research has examined how group stereotypes may color people's judgments about group members and affect their behavior toward them. Though relatively subtle, these processes may nevertheless be insidious, resulting in differential treatment and discrimination in schools, in the workplace, in the courtroom, and in a variety of interpersonal settings. Even in the absence of overt discrimination, the mere fact that the negative stereotypes are "in the air" may result in a social climate that can hinder the performance of negatively stereotyped individuals. Much of this chapter is devoted to a discussion of such relatively subtle influences of stereotypes on thoughts, feelings, and behavior.

Many theories of stereotypes start with an attempt to understand where stereotypes come from in the first place. The answers that

have been proffered fall into three broad categories: First, stereotypes are assumed to be a product of the prevailing culture; children learn them from their parents, their friends, and the media.
Second, stereotypes are assumed to result from deep personal
needs, most notably the need to belong to one's own group, the
need to feel superior to others, and the need to justify existing
social order. Finally, stereotypes are assumed to result from ordinary cognitive processes of categorization and covariation assessment (for a review, see Hamilton and Sherman 1994; for discussions
of these cognitive processes, see chapters 2 and 3). Although the
question of the origins of stereotypes has received a fair amount of
attention, the vast majority of research on stereotypes has taken the
contents and the existence of stereotypes as given, and has focused
on trying to understand when, how, and to what effect stereotypes
come into play. That is also the focus of this chapter.

After a brief discussion of the nature of stereotypes, I turn to an
examination of stereotypes from the point of view of the perceiver,
and discuss the circumstances under which people do (or do not)
activate stereotypes and use them to form impressions of members
of stereotyped groups. I next shift to the point of view of the person
at the receiving end of stereotyping, and discuss some psychological consequences of belonging to a negatively stereotyped group.
Finally, I review research that has attempted to change people's
stereotypes, and discuss why it is often so difficult to bring about
stereotype change.

What Are Stereotypes?

African Americans, lawyers, housewives, homosexuals, teen-agers
—each of these labels brings to mind a host of associations. You
probably have strong expectations about the traits, behaviors, and
circumstances likely for each of these groups, and you probably
experience a particular emotional reaction to each. In other words,
you have a stereotype for each of these groups. The term *stereotype*
has a long history. It was introduced to social psychology in 1922
by Walter Lippman, who described stereotypes loosely as "pictures

in our heads." In his 1954 book *The Nature of Prejudice*, Gordon Allport narrowed the definition of stereotypes to "an exaggerated belief associated with a category." The notion of beliefs associated with categories still dominates thinking about stereotypes, though current definitions do not include assumptions about the extent to which these beliefs are accurate or exaggerated. From the perspective of social cognition, stereotypes are typically viewed as cognitive structures that contain our knowledge, beliefs, and expectations about a social group (e.g., Hamilton and Sherman 1994). There is also growing recognition that group labels bring to mind feelings as well as thoughts (e.g., Esses, Haddock, and Zanna 1993; Fazio et al. 1995).

The view of stereotypes as mental representations of social categories highlights the similarity between stereotypes and other social as well as nonsocial concepts. Since the realization that stereotypes could be viewed as concepts, many of the ideas and debates emerging from research and theory about other concepts have been applied to stereotypes. Indeed my discussion and conclusions about the structure, function, and organization of concepts in chapter 2 are fully applicable to stereotypes, and I will therefore not provide a detailed discussion of those issues in this chapter.

Briefly, most theorists view stereotypes as containing a mix of abstract knowledge about a group (lawyers are aggressive and articulate) along with exemplars of group members (my neighbor the lawyer, the lawyer on my favorite TV show; for a review, see Hamilton and Sherman 1994). Stereotypes are typically measured and reported as prototypes, that is, lists of unrelated attributes that vary in typicality (e.g., African Americans are stereotyped as poor, uneducated, and criminal), though there is increasing recognition that stereotypes are also imbued with theoretical, causal knowledge (e.g., the discrimination and declining economic opportunities experienced by African Americans have restricted their educational opportunities and produced poverty and criminality; Wittenbrink, Gist, and Hilton 1997). Like other categories, stereotypes can be organized hierarchically, so that higher-level categories (African Americans) can contain subordinate categories, termed *subtypes*

(African American businessmen, African American athletes, African American ghetto dwellers; Devine and Baker 1991).

Stereotypes also contain knowledge about variability (for a review, see Hamilton and Sherman 1994). This is important because when we see a group as more invariable, we are more willing to generalize from a small number of group members to other group members and to the group as a whole, and we are also more willing to apply the stereotype of the group to individual members (Park and Hastie 1987; Park, Judd, and Ryan 1991; Park and Rothbart 1982; Quattrone and Jones 1980). If you believe, for example, that feminists are all pretty much the same, you may assume that "if you've seen one, you've seen them all." In contrast, if you assume that women can be very different from each other, you will not assume that your experiences with a particular woman can tell you much about what other women are like, nor will you assume that your general knowledge about women permits accurate prediction of the characteristics of a woman you have just met.

Group stereotypes can guide our expectations about group members and can color our interpretations of their behavior and traits (for a review, see Kunda and Thagard 1996). Like any other concept, stereotypes can tie together and give meaning and structure to attributes that you might have trouble making sense of otherwise. You may find it easier to make sense of someone described as intelligent, shy, hard working, and short if you also know that this person is an Asian American, a group often stereotyped as possessing all these attributes. And because the stereotype makes it easier for you to form an impression of such a person, the effort saved in the impression-formation task can be applied toward other tasks (Macrae, Milne, and Bodenhausen 1994).

Although much can and has been learned about stereotypes from research and theory about nonsocial concepts, there are some issues that are relatively unique to stereotypes. When you come across an apple, you will typically categorize it as an apple and expect it to have the features that you associate with apples. But, whereas encounters with apples will lead us to activate our concept of apples automatically, it is not obvious that encounters with

African Americans will lead us to activate our stereotype of African Americans automatically, nor is it obvious that our thinking about any African American that we encounter will be guided by our African American stereotype. This is because any African American person can be understood through the lenses of so many other concepts as well. Bill Cosby, for example, is not only an African American. He is also a man, an actor, a millionaire, a bereaved father, and the list of applicable social categories can go on and on. We might use any one of these categories to make sense of Bill Cosby, but we may also choose to focus on his behavior instead, noting that he can be funny and exudes warmth. For these reasons a great deal of theory and research has focused on trying to determine when stereotypes are activated in the minds of perceivers and when they are applied to make sense of individual members of stereotyped groups. I turn next to detailed discussion of these two questions.

The Perceiver's Perspective

STEREOTYPE ACTIVATION

When you come across an African American, do you find yourself spontaneously entertaining thoughts of crime and violence? Do you feel fear or anger? Do you view other people as especially aggressive? Does your own behavior become more hostile? If so, can you control and eliminate any of these responses? Are you even aware of them? Do you suppose your own ethnicity has any bearing on your spontaneous reactions to African Americans? If you are African American, do you suppose your spontaneous reactions to another African American differ from those of White or Asian Americans? If you are not African American, do you suppose your reactions to a member of this group depend on the extent to which you are prejudiced toward it? These and similar questions have engendered a considerable amount of research over the last decade.

By the mid-1980s it had become clear that many of our thoughts and feelings can be activated automatically, without any awareness or intention on our part, and can then color our judgments (for a review, see Kihlstrom 1987; see chapter 7). It didn't take long for social psychologists to begin asking whether our stereotypes, too, might be activated and used automatically. If so, this could shed new light on the dynamics of prejudice and discrimination: Could our judgments of others be influenced by racial stereotypes without our realizing that this was happening? Is it possible that even people who do not subscribe to negative stereotypes at a conscious level nevertheless use them unconsciously? Can we do anything to curtail unwanted stereotype activation?

Perhaps because the social implications of these possibilities are so important and disturbing, these questions, once raised, have captured the imagination of many researchers and have given rise to a lively and productive debate about the automaticity and inevitability of stereotype activation. Numerous studies have focused on whether exposure to members of a stereotyped group or to anything that reminds us of that group gives rise automatically to stereotype-related thoughts, feelings, and behaviors, whether we differ from one another in the extent to which we spontaneously activate culturally prevalent stereotypes of different groups, and whether we can control the activation and use of stereotypes when we want to. By now, there are clear answers to some of these questions, as discussed next.

Stereotypes Can Be Activated Automatically

Regardless of your own personal beliefs, you are probably aware of the very negative stereotype of African Americans that is prevalent in the United States. When Patricia Devine asked White University of Wisconsin students to articulate this cultural stereotype, there was considerable agreement on its contents. One of the most frequently mentioned traits, named by the majority of respondents, was *aggressive* (Devine 1989). Do White Americans activate this stereotype automatically when they encounter African Americans or anything that reminds them of this group? When they hear *Black*, do they automatically think *aggressive*? To explore this question, Devine exposed White participants subliminally to words that are related to the stereotype of African Americans but that are not directly related to aggression. She reasoned that if these words served to activate the stereotype of African Americans, they should also activate traits that are strongly associated with this stereotype such as *aggressive.* If *aggressive* were to become activated by stereotype-related cues even though it had never been mentioned explicitly, this would suggest that the cues provoked an automatic activation of the full-blown stereotype of African Americans.

Devine modeled her procedure on an earlier study that had demonstrated that subliminal exposure to words related to hostility could lead people to view a person who had behaved in an ambiguously hostile manner more negatively (Bargh and Pietromonaco 1982; see chapter 7). But, rather than priming participants with words related directly to hostility, Devine primed them with words that were related to the African American stereotype but were unrelated to hostility (one such set was: Negroes, lazy, Blacks, blues, rhythm, Africa, stereotype, ghetto, welfare, basketball, unemployed, plantation). Participants were exposed subliminally to a list of 100 words, of which either 80 or 20 percent were related to the African American stereotype (the rest of the list was made up of neutral words such as *then, would,* and *about*). Each word was presented very briefly (for 80 milliseconds) and followed by a masking string of letters. Under such conditions people cannot detect the words; they experience them instead as mere flashes of light. Indeed, a separate group of participants who were informed that each flash represented a word and were asked to guess these words guessed fewer than 2 percent of the words correctly. And another group of participants was unable to reliably pick out the words they had seen from a list that included those words along with an equal number of similar words that they had not seen. In short, participants were unaware of the words they had been exposed to and did not realize that they had been primed with the African American stereotype. Nevertheless, their judgments were influenced by the priming.

Experimental participants, who were not informed that they had been exposed to any words, next proceeded to their second task, in which they were asked to form an impression of a person who had performed a series of ambiguously hostile behaviors (they read the same description of Donald used to demonstrate the impact of subliminal priming with hostile words; Bargh and Pietromonaco 1982. Because Donald's ethnicity was not specified, he was probably assumed to be White). The striking finding was that participants who had received a heavy dose of priming with the African American stereotype (i.e., for whom 80 percent of the primed words were stereotype related) rated Donald as more hostile than did participants who had received only a mild dose of priming (i.e., for whom only 20 percent of the primed words were stereotype related). In other words, heavy priming with stereotype-related words appeared to activate the construct of hostility, even though none of these words related directly to hostility, and even though participants were not aware that they had been exposed to any words at all. This suggests that White Americans may activated the African American stereotype automatically, outside of their awareness, and this can color their judgments without their realizing that any of this is going on. This finding is particularly disturbing because if one is completely unaware of such processes, one is unlikely to be able to exercise any control over them.

Can we conclude from this study that mere exposure to an African American person, or to a neutral reminder of this group (e.g., the words *African American* or *Black* or a photograph of an African American person) will suffice to automatically bring to mind the full-blown cultural stereotype of African Americans with all its negative components? One may wish to argue that this study did not really provide a completely fair test of these ideas. After all, the words used to prime the stereotype were hardly neutral; they were mostly negative (lazy, welfare, ghetto, etc.). It is certainly interesting that some negative components of a stereotype can bring to mind other, unmentioned components of the negative stereotype such as aggression; this suggests that when activated, the negative stereotype comes to mind as a whole, with all its negative components. But perhaps this occurs only when the negative stereotype is primed directly as it was in this study; perhaps exposure to African

Americans in a neutral setting or exposure to neutral stereotype-related words will not lead to automatic activation of the negative stereotype. Unfortunately, subsequent research has ruled out this possibility.

Even a brief exposure to African American faces can suffice for other Americans to activate the negative stereotype of this group. One study demonstrated that subliminal presentation of photographs of African Americans can cause other Americans to activate the construct of hostility and can lead them to behave in a more hostile manner (Bargh, Chen, and Burrows 1996). Non–African American participants were engaged in an extremely tedious and boring task: On each trial, a picture depicting a large number of circles was presented briefly on a computer screen, and the participant had to decide whether the number of circles was odd or even. Unbeknownst to the participants, each such picture was preceded by a subliminal presentation of a photograph of a young man. For half the participants, these photographs depicted African Americans, and for half they depicted Caucasians. Each such photograph was presented very briefly (for no longer than 26 milliseconds) and was followed by a masking picture so that participants were unaware that they had seen any faces.

The tedious odd-even task went on and on until, on the 130th trial, an error message indicating a data-saving failure appeared on the computer, and the participant was informed that it would be necessary to do the entire task over again. A hidden video camera captured participants' reactions to this unwelcome news, and these were coded for hostility by observers who were unaware of the participant's experimental condition. The experimenter, who was also unaware of the participant's condition, also rated the hostility of the participant's reaction. Both these sets of hostility ratings told the same story: Participants who had been primed subliminally with African American faces responded in a more hostile manner than did participants who had been primed with Caucasian faces.

It appears that the mere exposure to an African American face can suffice for other Americans to activate the construct of hostility, which, in turn, can lead them to behave in a more hostile manner.

And all this can take place automatically, without their realizing that they have even seen an African American face or that this perception has had any impact on them. Other studies have also found that the negative African American stereotype can be activated automatically in the minds of other Americans by neutral reminders of that group. Brief exposure to photographs of African Americans can lead White Americans to automatically activate negative affect (Fazio et al. 1995). Subliminal exposure to the word *Black* can prime negative aspects of the African American stereotype such as poor, lazy, and violent in the minds on non–African Americans (Wittenbrink, Judd, and Park 1997). And subliminal exposure to neutral words related to the stereotype of Black people in Britain (e.g., Blacks, West Indians) can lead White British nationals to view an ambiguously described target person as more aggressive and unreliable (Lepore and Brown 1997). In short, neutral reminders of Black people can automatically trigger in other people negative thoughts, feelings, and behaviors, without any awareness on their part that they have even been reminded of this group.

Much of the research on the automatic activation of stereotypes has focused on the African American stereotype, undoubtedly because the most pressing problems of race relations in the United States revolve around African Americans. But the effect is not restricted to this particular stereotype; other stereotypes can be triggered automatically as well. For example, there is evidence for the automatic activation of the stereotypes of old and young people and of gender stereotypes (Blair and Banaji 1996; Purdue and Gurtman 1990).

All the studies discussed so far demonstrated stereotype activation under conditions that preclude controlled processing, namely subliminal presentation of cues or very brief intervals between the onsets of the prime and target stimuli (see chapter 7). I focused on these studies to demonstrate that stereotypes can be activated automatically. Note, though, that stereotypes can also be activated and used under conditions that do permit controlled processing, namely full awareness of stereotype-related material and plenty of time. There is a fair amount of evidence for the activation of racial stereotypes under such conditions (e.g., Dovidio, Evans, and Tyler 1986; Gilbert and Hixon 1991; Macrae, Bodenhausen, and Milne 1995). There is also a great deal of evidence that group stereotypes triggered under conditions that permit controlled processing can be used in judgments about group members (for a review, see Kunda and Thagard 1996; see the section on stereotype application in this chapter).

A particularly disturbing consequence of the automatic activation of stereotypes is that it may give rise to a vicious and escalating cycle of increasingly negative responses. If an African American person automatically activates thoughts of aggression in me, I may behave more aggressively toward this person, and this, in turn, could lead this ill treated person to respond in kind. As a result I may find that African American people do indeed behave more aggressively toward me than do White people, reinforcing my negative stereotype of African Americans. Sadly, I will not realize that the hostile reactions I get from African Americans may be entirely due to my own negative behavior toward them, which is fueled by automatic stereotype activation of which I am unaware. More generally, an activated stereotype may affect our behavior toward stereotyped individuals, and this may affect their reactions to us. A negative group stereotype may lead one to treat members of that group poorly which, in turn, may lead them to behave poorly, thereby confirming the stereotype.

In one telling demonstration of such a cycle, White participants each interviewed a White and a Black job applicant (Word, Zanna, and Cooper 1974). In fact, these "applicants" were confederates trained to respond in a standard manner. Nevertheless, participants treated the White and the Black applicants quite differently: They maintained a greater physical distance between themselves and the Black applicant, made more speech errors while interviewing him, and ended the interview more rapidly. A follow-up study revealed that the kind of treatment the Black applicant received—brusque, inarticulate, and distant—can undermine anyone's performance. This time, White Princeton students were interviewed for a job by trained White confederates (Word et al. 1974). Half were treated much like the White applicants had been treated by participants in the earlier study, whereas the other half were treated as the Black applicants had been (for these, the interviewer was more physically distant, made more speech errors, and kept the interview shorter). Two judges, who knew nothing about the study's purpose, viewed a videotape of each interview (showing only the applicant), and rated the applicant's competence. The interviewer's behavior had a remarkable impact on the applicants' performance: Those given the "Black treatment" were judged less adequate for the job than were those given the "White treatment." Together, these studies suggest that African Americans interacting with White people may sometimes come across as relatively incompetent simply because they are treated in a manner that undermines their ability to perform competently.

A more recent study suggests that even stereotypes that are activated outside of consciousness may influence our behavior toward others and, thereby, their reactions to us (Chen and Bargh 1997). White participants were first exposed subliminally to photographs of either African American or White men. Then, each of these participants was paired with a partner, who had not been exposed to any photographs, and the two played a word-guessing game. The investigators created two separate audiotapes of each game (one containing only the words of the primed participant, one those of the partner). Two judges who were unaware of the study's hypotheses listened to these audiotapes and rated each player's level of hostility. In keeping with earlier research on automatic stereotype activation, participants primed subliminally with African American faces showed greater hostility than did those primed with White faces. It other words, they had automatically activated the Black stereotype, and this affected their behavior. More remarkably, the behavior of the partners of these primed participants was also influenced by the priming: Those interacting with a participant who had been primed with African American faces showed greater hostility than did those interacting with a participant who had been primed with White faces. These partners, who had not themselves been primed with any faces, must have become hostile in reaction to their primed partners' hostility toward them.

It is interesting that in both of these studies behaviors consistent with the negative stereotypes of African Americans as incompetent and as hostile were elicited not from African Americans but from White Americans subjected to the same kind of treatment one may assume African Americans often receive. This helps pinpoint the impact of people's stereotype-driven behavior toward others on others' reactions to them. These behavioral confirmations of the African American stereotype had nothing to do with the race of the individuals who performed them; they were due entirely to the manner in which these individuals were treated by others who had the African American stereotype on their minds or who had been trained to imitate the behavior of White Americans interacting with African Americans. These studies suggest that people who automatically activate the negative African American stereotype upon encountering an African American individual may, through their own behavior, cause this individual to behave in a manner that confirms their negative stereotype. Moreover, this entire cycle may be initiated without any intention or awareness on the part of the perceivers, who may not realize that they are entertaining the stereotype or that they are behaving in keeping with it.

Is this unfortunate cycle bound to come into play whenever African Americans interact with other Americans? Or do non-Black individuals differ from one another in their automatic reactions to African Americans? I turn next to this question.

Individual Differences in Automatic Stereotype Activation

Most of us are familiar with the culturally prevalent negative stereotype of African Americans, and as discussed above, this stereotype can be activated automatically, without any awareness or intention. Does the broad familiarity with this negative stereotype guarantee that it will spring to mind automatically upon exposure to anything that reminds one of African Americans? Is it possible that even people who do not subscribe to this stereotype, indeed, who find it unacceptable and offensive, will nevertheless activate and use it automatically in their judgments? In a highly influential article Devine (1989) argued for this position, although, as we will see, subsequent research suggests otherwise.

Devine argued that because the culturally prevalent negative stereotype of African Americans is so well entrenched, other Americans will all automatically activate this stereotype when they come across anything that reminds them of this group, regardless of their own personal beliefs. Non-Black Americans do, however, differ in their personal beliefs about African Americans. Some subscribe to the common negative stereotype and consider it true. But others are convinced that this stereotype is quite inappropriate and mistaken. Such people, who are familiar with the cultural stereotype of African Americans but who do not themselves subscribe to it, will still experience an automatic activation of the negative stereotype when exposed to relevant cues. But they will be able to override and suppress the activation of this stereotype if they are aware that it has been activated and if they have sufficient time and resources to suppress it. Put differently, Devine argued that the activation of the negative stereotype is automatic and inevitable, regardless of one's personal beliefs. In contrast, the suppression and inhibition of this activation requires controlled processing. Therefore, people who do not subscribe to this stereotype and who wish to inhibit it will only be able to do so if the circumstances permit controlled processing.

Devine predicted that both people who were high in prejudice toward African Americans and people who were low in such prejudice would automatically activate the negative stereotype of African Americans when cued with stereotype-related material, but only people low in prejudice would suppress this stereotype when circumstances permitted such suppression. To explore such predictions, it is necessary to first identify people who are high and low in prejudice. This is easier said than done; given the prevalent cultural norms against any expression of prejudice, even people who believe the worst about African Americans may be reluctant to disclose these beliefs, knowing as they do that such beliefs are likely to be frowned upon by many.

Investigators aware of this problem have developed a more subtle measure of racial attitudes. This measure, the Modern Racism Scale, was designed to allow people to express negativity toward racial groups by responding to statements that do not necessarily imply prejudice (McConahay 1986). Some examples of such statements are: "It is easy to understand the anger of Black people in America," "Over the past few years,. the government and news media have shown more respect to Blacks than they deserve," and "Over the past few years, Blacks have gotten more economically than they deserve." It was assumed that prejudiced people who would be reluctant to endorse more blatantly racist statements such as "Black people are generally not as smart as Whites" would nevertheless be willing to endorse these more subtle statements because, in each case, the prejudiced response could also be explained as due to a race-neutral ideology (if you found yourself cringing at some of these statements and wondering why they were considered subtle, this may be because norms have continued to evolve since the scale was first developed. I will soon return to this point; see Fazio et al. 1995).

Devine used this Modern Racism Scale to identify White participants who were high and low in prejudice (Devine 1989). When they were asked to list the thoughts that came to mind when considering Black Americans, a task carried out with full awareness and plenty of time, participants low in prejudice did in indeed come across as less prejudiced; they listed fewer negative and more positive thoughts than did those high in prejudice. But a different pattern emerged under conditions that permitted only automatic processes. Automatic activation was assessed in Devine's central experiment, which I have already described. The crucial finding for the current discussion was that participants primed subliminally with words related to the African American stereotype activated this stereotype *regardless of their level of prejudice*; both high and low prejudice participants viewed the ambiguously described Donald as more hostile after such subliminal priming. This led Devine to conclude that when circumstances preclude controlled processing, White Americans all activate the negative stereotype of African Americans automatically when cued with stereotype-related material, regardless of their own personal beliefs about this group. Even those who are unprejudiced and who do not endorse the culturally prevalent negative stereotype of African Americans will activate this stereotype automatically when they are unable to engage in the controlled processes needed to override this activation. No matter how prejudice free we are at a conscious level, our judgments could still be tinged with prejudice.

Devine's provocative conclusion that there are no individual differences in the automatic activation of stereotypes did not go unchallenged. Russell Fazio and his colleagues noted that this conclusion rests on the finding that individuals identified through the Modern Racism Scale as high or low in prejudice did not differ from each other in the extent to which they experienced automatic stereotype activation (Fazio et al. 1995). But perhaps, they argued, the Modern Racism Scale is simply not a good enough measure of prejudice; perhaps Devine found no differences among people high and low in prejudice because she did not successfully identify such people in the first place. To determine whether there are, indeed, meaningful individual differences in automatic reactions to African Americans, Fazio and his colleagues devised a measure of automatic affective reactions to photographs of African American faces and examined whether this measure was related to other measures of prejudice.

Earlier work had shown that automatic affective reactions to a word representing one object can speed up or slow down evaluations of other positive and negative words (Fazio et al. 1986; see chapter 7). For example, if you are primed with *war* you may be faster to say that *awful* is a bad word and slower to say that *pleasant* is a good word. This is because *war* gives rise automatically to negative affect that facilitates the evaluation of affectively congruent words and inhibits the evaluation of incongruent ones. Fazio and his colleagues reasoned that if people experience an automatic negative reaction to African Americans, then exposure to photographs of African Americans should have a comparable effect—it should speed up the evaluation of negative words and slow down the evaluation of positive ones (of course, if the automatic reaction to such photographs is positive, the opposite pattern would be expected).

In order to relate their findings to Devine's, Fazio and his colleagues used the Modern Racism Scale to preselect participants who were high or low in prejudice (they scored among the top or bottom 10 percent of respondents). Most of the selected participants were White, but some were African American. Participants were told that the study involved word meaning as an automatic skill. In the first phase of the study, they were shown 12 positive words (e.g., attractive, wonderful) and 12 negative words (e.g., annoying, disgusting), and were asked to indicate as fast as they could whether each was good or bad by pressing an appropriate button. Their reaction times to this task provided a nonprimed baseline against which their primed responses could be evaluated. After several intermediate phases that involved memory for faces, the crucial priming phase took place. Participants were told that this activity examined whether they could do the evaluation task and the face memory task simultaneously. They were asked once again to indicate whether each of the 24 positive and negative words was good or bad. But this time, each word was preceded by a brief presentation of a photograph of a Black or a White person. The interval between the onset of the priming photograph and the onset of the target word was brief enough (450 milliseconds) to preclude controlled processing. Each adjective was evaluated four times, twice after priming with a Black face and twice after priming with a White face. And each face was used to prime two positive and two negative adjectives.

To determine the impact of the primes on the speed of evaluating the adjectives, a facilitation score was calculated for each participant's reaction times to each adjective. This score represented the difference between the participant's baseline speed of responding to an adjective and the speed of responding to that adjective after priming by each face. In other words, the facilitation score reflected the extent to which each face had speeded up or slowed down the participant's response to the adjective. For each participant, the investigators calculated average facilitation scores representing the extent to which Black faces facilitated positive words and negative words, and the extent to which White faces facilitated positive words and negative words.

Results for White participants indicated that their automatic reactions to Black faces were more negative than their reactions to White faces, as shown on the left panel of figure 8.1. On positive adjectives, these participants showed less facilitation when primed by a Black than by a White face. In contrast, on negative adjectives, they showed more facilitation when primed by a Black than by a White face. In short, relative to White faces, Black faces slowed down reactions to positive words and speeded up reactions to negative words. An opposite pattern emerged for African American participants, as shown on the right panel of figure 8.1. Relative to White faces, for these participants Black faces speeded up reactions to positive adjectives and slowed down reactions to negative adjectives. These findings showed that White and African American people experience different automatic reactions to African Americans; the automatic reactions of White people were relatively negative, whereas those of Black people were relatively positive. This was the first indication that there can be meaningful individual differences in automatic stereotype activation.

The investigators also calculated, for each participant, a single score representing the extent to which their responses to positive and negative adjectives depended on whether these adjectives had been primed by Black or White faces. This score was constructed so that more negative numbers reflect greater negativity toward African Americans. This measure, too, revealed that White participants responded negatively to Black faces whereas African American participants responded positively to the same faces. But, importantly, there were substantial individual differences among the reactions of White participants: Some were very negative whereas others were quite positive. Could these differences be meaningfully related to other measures of prejudice? To examine this, in the final stages of the experiment, participants were given an opportunity to reveal their prejudice in several other ways. One of these involved

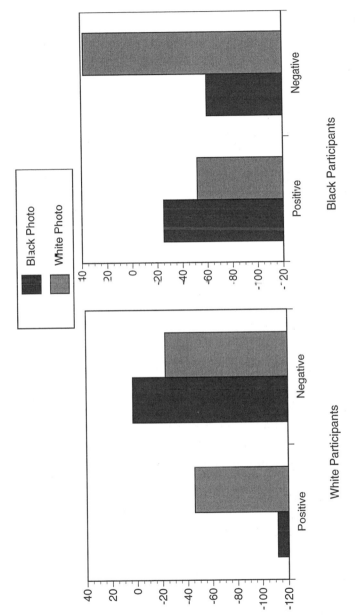

Figure 8.1 Mean extent (in milliseconds) to which the responses of White and Black participants to positive and negative adjectives were facilitated by exposure to photos of Black and White faces. Higher scores indicate greater facilitation. Adapted from Fazio et al. (1995, fig. 1, p. 1018). Copyright © (1995) by the American Psychological Association. Adapted with permission.

a 10–minute interaction with an African American experimenter who explained the study to them (actually, the explanation was bogus, and focused on the attractiveness of faces). The experimenter rated the friendliness and interest shown by each participant during this interaction. It turned out that participants' automatic reactions to the Black and White faces were meaningfully related to their behavior toward the African American experimenter: There was a significant positive correlation between the two measures, indicating that participants who showed more negative automatic reactions to the Black faces also behaved more negatively toward the Black person.

In another measure tapping their attitudes toward African Americans, participants were asked some questions about the events that followed the infamous 1992 Rodney King trial. In that trial four White Los Angeles police officers were acquitted in the beating of an African American, Rodney King. The brutal beating had been videotaped by a bystander and televised nationwide, and had caused an uproar. When the not guilty verdict was announced, African Americans reacted with outrage, and there was an explosion of looting and rioting in Los Angeles. Participants were asked to consider this trial and, among other things, to indicate the degree to which they would attribute responsibility for the riots to Whites and to Blacks. This measure, too, was positively correlated with their automatic reactions to Black and White faces. Those who had shown more negative automatic reactions to Black faces also assigned relatively more responsibility for the riots to Blacks than to Whites.

In summary, participants' automatic affective reactions to Black faces were meaningfully related to their own racial identity, to their behavior toward an African American experimenter, and to the extent to which they assigned responsibility to Blacks versus Whites for the riots that followed the Rodney King verdict. All this suggests that the measure of automatic affective reactions is a valid measure of people's attitudes toward African Americans. Yet these automatic affective reactions were not related to participants' responses to the Modern Racism Scale. Those shown by this scale to be low in prejudice were no less likely to respond to Black faces with automatic negative affect than were those shown to be high in prejudice. These results mirror those obtained by Devine (1989), and also serve to invalidate some of Devine's conclusions. It appears that Devine obtained no differences in the automatic reactions of individuals high and low in prejudice because her measure of prejudice was not good at distinguishing among such individuals. Had she used a better measure, she might have found, as did Fazio and his colleagues, that people with different attitudes toward African Americans experience different automatic reactions toward this group.

Fazio and his colleagues conducted several additional studies to understand why the Modern Racism Scale was not working. Briefly, they concluded that although this scale may have appeared subtle at one point, it no longer seemed that way to participants; participants recognized that it was tapping prejudice, and those who were interested in suppressing their prejudice tailored their responses accordingly. The measure also, and inappropriately, tapped conservatism; participants who were conservative obtained high scores on this measure even if their attitudes toward African Americans were positive (Fazio et al. 1995). As a result, at this point in time, the Modern Racism Scale does not reliably distinguish between racist and nonracist individuals.

Another challenge for Devine's conclusion that there are no individual differences in the automatic activation of stereotypes has focused on the nature of the priming words used in her study. Recall that many of these words were very negative (e.g., lazy, ghetto, welfare). Two sets of studies have found that there are meaningful individual differences in the thoughts and judgments that are triggered automatically in response to stereotype-related cues when these cues are neutral. One set of studies conducted in Britain identified individuals who were high and low in prejudice through a measure modeled after the Modern Racism Scale but modified to reflect current British realities (e.g., "It should be made easier to acquire British citizenship," "The number of Black members of parliament is too low, and political parties should take active steps to increase it"; Lepore and Brown 1997). When White British nationals were primed subliminally with neutral words related to the stereotype of Black people in Britain (e.g., Blacks, West Indians), only highly prejudiced individuals experienced automatic activation of the negative cultural stereotype; only they rated the target as more aggressive and unreliable when primed with the Black words. No such effect was obtained for individuals low in prejudice.

Interestingly, when the primes related to the negative contents of the stereotype (e.g., rude, dirty, drugs), as was the case in Devine's study, individuals high and low in prejudice no longer differed from each other; both groups showed automatic activation of the negative stereotype. This suggests that when primed with the information that is directly related to the negative stereotype, all people will automatically activate this stereotype, regardless of their prejudice. But only prejudiced people will also activate the negative stereotype of Blacks when primed with neutral reminders of this group.

In a similar vein, another study found that several measures of prejudice, including the Modern Racism Scale, predicted the extent to which the negative stereotype of African Americans and the positive stereotype of Whites were activated in response to subliminal priming with neutral category labels (*Black* or *White*; Wittenbrink, Judd, and Park 1997). Put differently, highly prejudiced people were more likely than people low in prejudice to activate the negative stereotype of African Americans automatically when cued with neutral reminders of that group. It is not clear why the Modern Racism Scale and its British variant predicted automatic stereotype activation in these studies despite the inability of this scale to predict automatic affective reactions in the studies by Fazio and his colleagues. But the general conclusion from both sets of studies is the same—highly prejudiced individuals are more likely than those low in prejudice to automatically activate negative thoughts and feelings in response to neutral cues that remind them of Black people.

In summary, we do differ in our automatic reactions to African Americans. People who are highly prejudiced toward this group automatically activate the negative traits associated with the stereotype of African Americans along with negative affect when they are exposed to anything that reminds them of this group; the word *Blacks* or a Black face can suffice to trigger the full-blown negative stereotype in prejudiced individuals. People who are less prejudiced toward African Americans are just as familiar with the negative cultural stereotype of this group, and they may activate it automatically when it is cued directly by negative stereotypic material. When cued with *ghetto* and *welfare*, even nonprejudiced individuals may automatically think *aggression*. But this does not mean that nonprejudiced individuals will activate the same negative thoughts and feelings automatically whenever they are reminded of African Americans. They do not activate the stereotype automatically when they come across neutral information that reminds them of African Americans without explicitly eliciting the negative stereotype; they do not think *aggressive* whenever they see an African American or whenever they hear *Blacks*.

Implicit measures of stereotype activation and use offer the exciting prospect of developing ways of gaining insight into people's hidden racial attitudes (Fazio et al. 1995). Many individuals who privately hold negative attitudes toward minority groups may choose to keep these attitudes private. Not wishing to be denounced as racists, such prejudiced people will respond to explicit measures of prejudice in a nonprejudiced manner; indeed, their answers to explicit questions may be indistinguishable from those of nonprejudiced individuals. But subtle, unobtrusive measures of prejudice that rely on automatic and uncontrollable reactions may nevertheless reveal their true attitudes. More work needs to be done on how these unobtrusive measures relate to prejudiced behavior in other settings. But existing research suggests that it might be possible to use people's automatic reactions to reminders of a stereotyped group to predict their behavior toward members of this group.

Stereotype Activation Can Require Effort

Although stereotypes can be activated without awareness and intention, their activation may nevertheless depend on the availability of sufficient cognitive resources. Cues that lead us to activate a racial stereotype when our resources are plentiful may fail to provoke comparable stereotype activation when we are preoccupied with a demanding task. In other words, cognitive busyness can disrupt the spontaneous activation of stereotypes. In a pair of studies that made this point, White participants were asked to complete a series of word fragments (Gilbert and Hixon 1991). These were presented by means of a videotape of an Asian or White assistant who held up a series of cards, one at a time, each displaying one word fragment. As they saw each fragment, participants were given 15 seconds to generate as many completions as they could for it. Five of the fragments could be completed with words associated with the stereotype of Asian American students. For example, S __ Y could be completed as shy, POLI __ E as polite, RI __ E as rice. Note that each of these fragments could also be completed with words that have nothing to do with the Asian American stereotype. For example, S __ Y could also be completed as sky or as say. The logic underlying this measure is that if the stereotype is activated, the stereotypic words will become more accessible, and so will be more likely to be used to complete the fragments. Therefore, the number of stereotypic completions generated by each participant served as a measure of the extent of stereotype activation.

Under normal circumstances, exposure to an Asian person did lead to the activation of the Asian American stereotype; participants exposed to the Asian assistant generated more stereotypic completions than did participants exposed to the White assistant, as shown in the left column of table 8.1. Can cognitive busyness disrupt such spontaneous stereotype activation? To examine this question, half of the participants were made cognitively busy while they performed the word-fragment completion task. These participants were asked to rehearse an eight-digit number while they watched the videotape and completed the word fragments dis-

Table 8.1 Number of stereotypic completions made by busy and not busy participants exposed to an Asian or a White assistant

	BUSYNESS	
ASSISTANT'S RACE	NOT BUSY	BUSY
Asian	3.82	3.12
White	3.00	3.24
Difference	*0.82*	*0.12*

Source: From Gilbert and Hixon (1991, table 1, p. 511). Copyright © (1991) by the American Poyohologioal Accooiation. Roprintod with pormission.

played in it. This cognitively demanding mental rehearsal task completely undermined the activation of the Asian American stereotype; among cognitively busy participants, those exposed to the Asian assistant did not generate any more stereotypic completions than did those exposed to the White assistant, as shown in the right column of table 8.1. In short, participants who were not cognitively busy activated the Asian American stereotype when they saw an Asian person, but busy participants did not.

These results suggest that the spontaneous activation of stereotypes is not inevitable; it will occur only if we have sufficient cognitive resources. You might wish to argue that the Asian American stereotype is simply not powerful enough to be activated when resources are limited. Despite these findings, it may still be possible that more powerful and entrenched stereotypes will be activated even when resources are scarce. The African American stereotype has been shown to be powerful enough to be activated automatically even by subliminal cues. Perhaps, then, exposure to African Americans will lead to automatic stereotype activation even in preoccupied individuals. A recent study suggests otherwise (Spencer et al. 1998). In this study, participants were exposed subliminally to drawings of Black or White faces before the presentation of each word fragment that they were to complete. They performed the word-fragment completion task either with or without performing an additional resource-consuming mental rehearsal task. The word fragments included six that could be completed with words related to the African American stereotype (e.g., hostile, dangerous, welfare). Despite the fact that this study focused on the potentially more powerful African American stereotype, the results were conceptually the same as those obtained by Gilbert and Hixon for the Asian American stereotype: Subliminal exposure to Black faces led to activation of the African American stereotype among nonbusy participants but not among busy ones. Once again, cognitive busyness served to undermine stereotype activation.

This study provides a clear illustration that the activation of stereotypes can be automatic in some regards but controlled in other regards (Bargh 1996). The stereotype activation was automatic in that it occurred without awareness or intention; it was cued by subliminally presented faces that participants did not even realize they had seen. At the same time this automatic, unconscious activation resembled controlled processes in that it was effortful; it took place only when cognitive resources were ample and was disrupted by cognitive busyness.

Spencer and his colleagues showed further that when the situation presented additional cues associated with stereotype activation, stereotypes were activated even by cognitively busy participants. They argued that a recent experience of failure may become associated with stereotype activation because, after failing, we often try to make ourselves feel better by using negative stereotypes to derogate others, a derogation that can make us look superior by comparison (Fein and Spencer, 1997; see the section on stereotype application). As suggested by Bargh's auto-motive theory, after many such repeated experiences we may develop a strong association between personal failure and negative stereotypes (Bargh 1997; see chapter 7). Therefore, a recent failure experience along with a reminder of a stereotyped group may give rise to an automatic activation of the negative stereotype of this group. The association between the stereotype and these cues may be so powerful that the stereotype will be activated even when one is cognitively busy. This was indeed the case.

In this study, participants first completed a bogus intelligence test and were told that they had either succeeded or failed at it (Spencer et al. 1998). Then, in a seemingly unrelated study, all participants were made cognitively busy and completed a word-fragment completion task while being primed subliminally with Black or White faces. Participants who had just succeeded behaved just like cognitively busy participants in the earlier studies; they did not activate the African American stereotype when primed with Black faces. But participants who had just failed did activate that stereotype when primed with Black faces, even though they were cognitively busy. This set of studies shows that the spontaneous activation of stereotypes usually requires effort and, therefore, is disrupted when our cognitive resources are depleted. But when the situational cues are powerful enough, stereotypes will be activated even when resources are scarce. The combination of a recent failure experience along with a reminder of a stereotyped group appears to have such power; under such circumstances even cognitively busy individuals experience automatic stereotype activation.

The finding that stereotype activation usually requires plentiful cognitive resources adds an optimistic note to a disturbing picture. True, we may often activate negative stereotypes without even realizing that we are doing so, and this could lead to many unfortunate consequences. But such activation is not inevitable. It may be that when we encounter members of negatively stereotyped groups in settings that require us to focus our attention on demanding tasks, we will be too preoccupied with these tasks to activate the negative stereotypes. Preoccupation with cognitively demanding tasks may be common in the workplace, where we may have to focus on solving work-related problems, as well as in social situations that present us with interpersonal problems. The spontaneous activation of negative stereotypes may be preempted in many such circumstances. The finding that stereotype activation requires effort also points to the possibility that we may be able to exercise some control over stereotype activation by directing our attention elsewhere. I turn next to examining this possibility.

Stereotype Activation Can Be Inhibited

When we want to suppress a stereotype, perhaps because we wish to avoid thinking about someone in stereotypic terms, can we do this? Can we inhibit the activation of stereotypes? Only a handful of studies have addressed this question, but these do indicate that stereotypes may sometimes be inhibited (for a review, see Kunda and Sinclair, 1999). One may assume that a stereotype has been inhibited, or pushed out of mind, if its activation drops to a level that is lower than the normal baseline. One study suggested that when we come across a person who belongs to more than one stereotyped group, say a Chinese woman, we may activate one of these competing stereotypes and inhibit the other (Macrae, Bodenhausen, and Milne 1995). Participants who observed a Chinese woman eating noodles from a bowl with a pair of chopsticks, a behavior intended to cue the Chinese stereotype, did indeed activate the Chinese stereotype. More interesting, they inhibited the other stereotype applicable to that person, that of women. In contrast, participants who observed the same Chinese woman engage in a behavior intended to cue the stereotype of women, putting on makeup, activated the stereotype of women and inhibited the Chinese stereotype. Macrae and his colleagues suggested that people suppress the less dominant of the two applicable stereotypes in order to avoid distraction and interference. It is unclear from these studies whether or not the obtained inhibition was intended, but these studies did provide the first evidence that the activation of an applicable stereotype may sometimes be inhibited.

Another series of studies showed that we can sometimes inhibit the activation of stereotypes if we are motivated to do so (Sinclair 1998; Sinclair and Kunda 1998). Exposure to an African American man may lead other Americans to automatically activate the negative African American stereotype. However, if this man proceeds to praise their abilities, they may wish to suppress this negative stereotype so as to avoid casting any doubts on his credibility; after all, the praise is only meaningful if it comes from a competent person who is skilled at evaluating others. To examine whether such motives will provoke stereotype inhibition, non-Black participants received positive or negative feedback on their performance from a Black or a White man. Other participants observed someone else receive the same feedback. Then, allegedly as part of an unrelated study, participants performed a word-fragment completion task which included several fragments that could be completed with words relating to the stereotype of Black people in Canada, where the study was conducted.

In the absence of a strong motivation to inhibit the Black stereotype, exposure to the Black man led to spontaneous activation of the Black stereotype. Participants who had received negative feedback from the Black man were, if anything, motivated to activate the Black stereotype so as to discredit their harsh evaluator. And participants who had observed someone else receive negative or positive feedback from the Black man had little personal stake in preserving or undercutting his competence; the credibility of the Black man had few implications for their own competence. And, indeed, all these groups of participants, who had been exposed to the Black man and who had little motivation to inhibit the Black stereotype, did activate that stereotype; they made more stereotypic completions than did participants exposed to a White man delivering comparable feedback.

Can such spontaneous activation of the Black stereotype be inhibited when one wants to suppress it? Apparently, yes. Participants who had received positive feedback from the Black man, and who were therefore motivated to suppress the Black stereotype so as to avoid casting doubt on his credibility, were able to do so. These participants made even fewer stereotypic completions than did baseline participants who had received comparable feedback from a White man. In other words, participants motivated to inhibit the Black stereotype so as to boost their own self-worth did indeed inhibit it. It appears that exposure to the Black man led to the spontaneous activation of the Black stereotype when participants had little reason to inhibit the stereotype. However, participants who were motivated to inhibit the stereotype were able to do so. Motivation, then, can override the spontaneous activation of stereotypes.

Moreover, motivation may lead people to pick and choose among the many stereotypes applicable to an individual, activating those that support their desired impression of this individual and inhibiting those that conflict with it, as suggested by a follow-up study (Kunda and Sinclair, in press; Sinclair 1998). Participants who had been praised by a Black doctor, and who were therefore motivated to think highly of him, inhibited the stereotype of Black people and activated the stereotype of doctors (as compared to participants who had received comparable feedback from a White doctor or no feedback at all). In marked contrast, participants who had been criticized by the Black doctor, and were therefore motivated to discredit him, showed the very opposite pattern—they activated the stereotype of Black people and inhibited the stereotype of doctors. Due to such selective activation and inhibition of stereotypes, we may therefore expect that a Black doctor will be viewed by non-Black people predominantly as a doctor if they wish to think highly of him, but predominantly as a Black person if they wish to disparage him.

It appears that when we want to, we can inhibit a stereotype that would otherwise be activated. In these studies, people were motivated to inhibit the activation of a stereotype because it had the potential of undercutting their desired impression of a stereotyped individual. These findings are encouraging to anyone concerned about the spontaneous activation of stereotypes because they imply that other goals, too, may be able to undercut such activation. Most important, the goal of avoiding prejudice may suffice to inhibit stereotype activation and therefore may also eliminate the subtle and unintended consequences that activated stereotypes can have on our perceptions of others and on our behavior toward them. However, this is only likely to happen if we realize that an undesired stereotype has been cued. If the stereotype is activated outside of our awareness, we may be able to do little to curtail its activation. Even when we do succeed at suppressing unwanted stereotypes over the short term, this suppression may sometimes backfire over the longer run, as discussed next.

Suppressed Stereotypes May Rebound

During Tom's lunch with Emma, the topic of affirmative action comes up. Tom feels he should watch his words carefully. From his experience with Emma, he believes her to be extremely sensitive to any hints of sexism. On several past occasions, remarks that he thought were quite innocent she took to be sexist. As he is talking to Emma, then, Tom works hard to ensure that he will not express any negative thoughts or feelings about women or any opinions that might be viewed as sexist. After lunch Tom returns to work, grading students' essays. The name on the first essay he picks up is Debbie Walker. What associations do you suppose the name Debbie will bring to Tom's mind? Having worked so hard at suppressing the negative stereotype of women over lunch, how likely is this stereotype to pop up in his mind now that lunch is over? Recall that when we try to control our thoughts, we often experience ironic reversals; trying to suppress a thought may, instead, make us especially likely to entertain that very thought (Wegner 1994; see chapter 7). Stereotypes are no exception to this rule (for a review, see Monteith, Sherman, and Devine 1998).

A series of studies by Neil Macrae and his colleagues investigated the consequences of suppressing a stereotype to its subsequent accessibility and use (Macrae et al. 1994). These studies focused on the stereotype of skinheads, a group viewed quite negatively in Britain where these studies were conducted. In the first phase of each study, students were shown a photograph of a male skinhead and were asked to write a brief description of a typical day in his life. Half the participants were instructed to suppress the stereotype. They were told that impressions of others are biased by stereotypic preconceptions, but that they should try to avoid thinking about the target person in this manner. The remaining, control participants were given no such instructions.

Table 8.2 Ratings of the stereotypicality of a passage describing a skinhead individual written by participants instructed to suppress the stereotype of skinheads and by controls given no such instruction, and latencies of identifying stereotype-related and stereotype-irrelevant words

	INSTRUCTION		
DEPENDENT MEASURE	SUPPRESS STEREOTYPE	CONTROL	BASELINE
Passage stereotypicality	4.83	6.83	—
Latencies[a] to identify:			
Stereotype-related words	571	690	778
Stereotype-irrelevant words	773	782	790

Source: From Macrae et al. (1994, table 2, p. 813). Copyright © (1994) by the American Psychological Association. Reprinted with permission.
Note: Baseline participants were not exposed to any skinhead and wrote no passage.
a. Latencies are presented in milliseconds.

Participants asked to suppress the stereotype clearly complied with this request. Their descriptions of the target were judged by raters who were unaware of participants' experimental conditions as less consistent with the stereotype of skinheads than were the descriptions written by control participants who were not trying to suppress the stereotype, as shown in the top row of table 8.2. How did this stereotype suppression influence the activation and use of the stereotype on a later occasion?

Subsequent tasks revealed that the initial suppression of the stereotype led to an increase in its activation and use in other settings encountered shortly thereafter. One study examined the activation of the stereotype by asking participants to indicate whether each of a series of letter strings was a word or a nonword. The list included 14 words related to the negative stereotype of skinheads and 14 other negative words that were irrelevant to that stereotype. The logic underlying this task is that if a word is already activated in participants' minds, they should be faster to correctly identify it as a word. Therefore the speed of response to the stereotypic words served as a measure of stereotype activation. As shown in table 8.2, participants who had initially suppressed the stereotype were faster to respond to stereotypic words than were control participants (the two groups did not differ in the speed of their responses to the stereotype-irrelevant words). In other words, following an experience of stereotype suppression, the suppressed stereotype had become especially accessible.

Another study showed that the increased accessibility of the stereotype may also carry over into behavior (Macrae et al. 1994). After writing their initial description of the skinhead target, participants were taken to another room where they were to meet this person. However, when they arrived there, they were confronted with a row of eight empty seats. The skinhead had apparently left the room briefly, leaving behind a jacket and bag which were placed on the first seat. The participant was asked to sit down and wait for the other person's return. The question of interest was how much distance would the participants choose to keep between themselves and the skinhead target, that is, how many seats away from that person's belongings would they choose to sit. Participants who had previously been asked to suppress the skinhead stereotype chose to sit further away from the belongings of the skinhead they were about to meet than did control participants who had not suppressed the stereotype. Presumably, the previously suppressed negative stereotype had rebounded, and made participants wish to maintain a larger social distance from the stereotyped individual.

These and similar studies show that when others instruct us to suppress a stereotype, we can effectively do so for the task at hand. But as we move to other tasks and are no longer actively trying to suppress the stereotype, it may spring to mind with greater intensity than it might have otherwise. The same may be true when we ourselves are the source of the directive to suppress stereotypes (Macrae, Bodenhausen, and Milne, 1998; for a review, see Monteith et al. 1998). Our concentrated efforts to avoid prejudice in one setting may inadvertently make us more likely to entertain prejudiced thoughts and actions once we have moved to another setting and have let down our guards.

So far I have focused mostly on the extent to which we activate stereotypes in different circumstances and on the factors that influence the activation and inhibition of stereotypes. I turn next to examine the manner and circumstances in which group stereotypes can color judgments about individual group members.

STEREOTYPE APPLICATION

Stereotypes Color the Meaning of Information about a Person

Differing Interpretations   Imagine that as a White student is walking around campus she come across a young Hispanic man crouched over a bicycle, fidgeting with the lock. What will she think he is doing? Would she interpret the same behavior differently if the young man happened to be White rather than Hispanic? Several studies suggest that it is quite possible that she would. If one's stereotypes hold that Hispanic men are more likely than White men to be criminal, one may assume that a Hispanic man fidgeting with a bicycle lock is trying to steal the bike whereas a White man doing the same thing is trying to unlock his own bike. In other words, one's stereotypes may lead one to interpret the identical behavior quite differently.

In one study demonstrating this phenomenon, White students watched a videotape of a discussion between two men (Duncan 1976). As they were watching, they were beeped periodically, and whenever this happened, they were to categorize the behavior they had just observed into one of several categories (e.g., dramatizes, gives information, asks for opinion, playing around, violent behavior, aggressive behavior). Gradually the discussion they were watching got more and more heated. The men were saying things such as "You must be crazy!" and "You're just too damned conservative. With an attitude like that you'll never get ahead!" Finally one of the men shoved the other, and at this point a beep indicated that participants were to categorize this behavior. Different participants watched different versions of the videotape. In one version the man delivering the shove was White, in another he was Black. This made a big difference to how the shove was interpreted: When delivered by a White man, it was viewed most often as "playing around," or as "dramatizes," but when delivered by a Black man, the identical shove was typically viewed as a violent or aggressive behavior.

It appears that when behaviors are somewhat ambiguous, the identical behavior will be understood quite differently when performed by individuals who belong to differently stereotyped groups. This conclusion is supported by several additional studies that have shown that stereotypes associated with race, social class, or profession can lend different meanings to the same ambiguous behaviors (e.g., Darley and Gross 1983; Dunning and Sherman 1997; Kunda and Sherman-Williams 1993; Sagar and Schofield 1980). Sadly, this conclusion is also supported by the daily indignities suffered by members of ethnic minorities in the United States. Many African Americans recount, for example, that they cannot walk through a department store examining merchandise without being tailed by a suspicious clerk. These actions, which are interpreted as normal consumer behavior when performed by White shoppers, are often viewed as evidence of criminal intent when performed by African American shoppers.

Undoubtedly such stereotypic interpretations of behavior may often reflect explicit prejudice and intentional discrimination. But this need not always be the case. As already discussed, exposure to an African American individual may spontaneously bring to mind traits such as *aggressive* or *criminal* which then influence the interpretation of ambiguous behaviors (e.g., Devine 1989). A disturbing aspect of this process is that perceivers, from their own perspective, may not realize that they are being prejudiced. They may not even know that their stereotypes have colored their impression. All they may know is that they have "seen" a violent or criminal act.

Even when stereotypes do not influence the way a behavior is categorized, they may still color its meaning by influencing the way it is explained. For example, the success of a White man may be attributed to his outstanding ability, whereas the same success by a woman or by a Black man may be attributed to their hard work or good luck (e.g., Deaux and Emswiller 1974; Jackson, Sullivan, and Hodge 1993; Yarkin, Town, and Wallston 1982). The way one explains others' behavior may depend on whether or not they belong to one's own social group: The behavior of a member of one's own group may be explained in more positive terms than the behavior of a member of an out-group. The same negative act may be attributed less to the actor's underlying personality and more to situational forces when the actor belongs to one's own group than to an out-group (Pettigrew 1979; Taylor and Jaggi 1974). Such a differential pattern of attributions, sometimes called "the ultimate attribution error," may result from people's holding more positive stereotypes of their own group than of rival groups.

Stereotypes may also influence the way we understand a trait used to describe a person. When we hear a lawyer described as aggressive, we may understand this to mean that the lawyer is argumentative and sarcastic. In contrast, when we hear a construction worker described as aggressive, we may understand this to mean that the construction worker is likely to yell insults and to get into barroom brawls (Kunda, Sinclair, and Griffin 1997). The identical trait gains different meanings when applied to differently stereotyped individuals.

A stereotype applied to an individual may also influence the interpretation of other stereotypes that apply to the same individual. One stereotype may lead to the activation of a particular subtype of another. When we hear that a carpenter is also a Harvard graduate, we may assume the carpenter to be a special kind of carpenter, a master carpenter. And when we hear that a nurse is a man, we may assume that he is a special kind of nurse, a psychiatric nurse (Hastie, Shroeder, and Weber 1990; Kunda, Miller, and Claire 1990).

In sum, our stereotypes can lead us to interpret identical behaviors, traits, and group memberships quite differently when these pertain to differently stereotyped individuals (for a review, see Kunda and Thagard 1996). As discussed earlier, such stereotype-driven construals may often take place automatically, without any intention or awareness on our part (e.g., Devine 1989). As a result we may often believe that our reactions to a stereotyped individual are free of prejudice because they are based on the individual's behavior and attributes rather than on the stereotype. What we may not realize is that the very meaning of these behaviors and attributes has been colored by the stereotype. If the person had belonged to a different group, we might have imbued the same attributes with very different meanings.

Shifting Standards It is obvious to most of us that a piece of writing viewed as superb for a first grader could be viewed as pitiful for a sixth grader. Clearly, very different standards of excellence apply to children in different grades. It may be less obvious that racial and gender stereotypes may give rise to different standards in a similar manner. If female college students are viewed as better at English than are male college students, their performance may be evaluated against different standards. The same 80 percent score on an English test may be viewed as excellent for a man but as only OK for a woman because the woman is measured against a higher standard.

It also follows that the same description of a student's performance may have different meanings depending on the student's gender. When we say that John did well on his English essay, we may mean that he got a B (which we consider good for a man), whereas when we say that Joan did well, we may mean that she got an A- (which we consider good for a woman). Therefore, even if we use the same *subjective* term, *good*, to describe identical performances by a man and a woman, it remains possible that our evaluation of these performances was nevertheless colored by gender stereotypes. If asked to report our evaluation on an *objective* measure such as a letter grade, it would become clear that our evaluations were indeed colored by our gender stereotypes.

In one study that demonstrated the impact of such shifting standards on subjective evaluations, participants were asked to read and evaluate a magazine article attributed to either Joan T. McKay or John T. McKay (Biernat and Manis 1994). Half of the participants evaluated the article on objective scales (e.g., a letter grades scale ranging from A+ to E), and the remaining half evaluated the article on subjective scales (e.g., a scale ranging from *excellent* to *terrible*). Some participants read an article on a masculine topic (e.g., fishing), some read an article on a feminine topic (e.g., eye makeup), and some read an article on a gender-neutral topic (e.g., health). The expectation was that women would be stereotyped as worse than men at writing a masculine article, as better than men at writing a feminine article, and as equal to men at writing a neutral article, and that these stereotypes would color participants' evaluations of the articles.

Examination of the objective ratings revealed that this was indeed the case: The same masculine article was assigned a lower letter grade when written by Joan than by John, the same feminine article was assigned a higher grade when written by Joan than by John, and the neutral article was assigned the same grade when written by Joan and by John. Although their stereotypes had clearly led participants to assume that an article was better written when attributed to an author whose gender was stereotyped as more competent at the article's topic, subjective measures revealed no evidence of such stereotype-driven evaluations. On these measures, all articles were rated as equally good regardless of the gender of their authors. When making subjective evaluations, participants must have implicitly measured men and women against different standards. For example, both Joan's and John's essays on eye makeup may have been rated as *good* even though Joan's was viewed as objectively better; her A- was viewed as good for a woman, whereas John's B was viewed as good for a man (who couldn't be expected to be an expert on this topic).

This and similar studies suggest that when we use a subjective measure to describe someone's performance, we may have a different level of performance in mind when we describe differently stereotyped individuals. We may believe a *good* performance by an African American athlete to be better than a *good* performance by a White one, because African Americans are measured against a higher standard of athletic excellence. We may also believe a *good* verbal performance by an African American student to be less competent than a *good* verbal performance by a White student because, in this domain, African Americans are measured against a lower standard of excellence (Biernat and Manis 1994). For this reason researchers interested in examining the impact of stereotypes on judgment would be well advised to choose their measures carefully. If they use only subjective measures, they may fail to detect large stereotype-driven differences in perception that might have been detected with more objective measures.

Using Stereotypes in the Presence of Individuating Information

We tend to assume that Andrew is more assertive than Ann, that attorney Miller is more outgoing than librarian Miller, that English major Smith attends more movies than computer-science major Smith. It has been shown repeatedly that if all we know about a person is that he or she belongs to a particular group, the stereotype associated with this group will color our impressions of the person (e.g., Locksley et al. 1980; for a review, see Kunda and Thagard 1996). But what if we also have some additional information about the person—a behavior, a trait, family circumstances? There has been considerable debate about whether and when stereotypes will affect impressions of an individual who is also known to be characterized by such *individuating information.*

Initially Anne Locksley and her colleagues argued that because stereotypes amount to base-rates (i.e., they provide the prior probabilities that members of different groups will show various behaviors and traits), they should also "behave" like base-rates (Locksley et al. 1980, 1982). Recall that people typically use base-rates to make judgments about an individual when they know nothing else about this individual, but they tend to ignore base-rates if they are given individuating information about the person, and base their judgments instead only on this individuating information (Kahneman and Tversky 1973; see chapter 3). Locksley and her colleagues proposed that stereotypes are used and ignored in the same manner. For example, they showed that when given only a name, participants believed that Nancy was less assertive than Tom. But when also told about an assertive behavior performed by this person, they believed Nancy who had behaved assertively in class to be every bit as assertive as Tom who had behaved assertively (Locksley et al. 1980; see chapter 3 for a more detailed discussion).

Initially such findings gave rise to an optimistic and encouraging conclusion: Admittedly, we may apply inappropriate stereotypes to total strangers, but as soon as we get to know anything about a person, we will no longer use the stereotype; even a single behavior may suffice to undercut the insidious impact of offensive stereotypes. Unfortunately, however, even though the basic finding obtained by Locksley and her colleagues has been replicated many times, other findings have substantially restricted the circumstances under which it holds true. As a result the initial optimism that these findings seemed to promise has been dampened considerably (for a review, see Kunda and Thagard 1996). It is true that usually people do not seem to integrate the implications of stereotypes (or any other base-rate) with those of individuating information as statistical rules suggest they should. People are extremely unlikely to go through an attempt at integration such as "she behaved in a very assertive manner, but she is after all a woman, so I will say she is only somewhat assertive." Instead, when they have individuating information about a stereotyped person, people seem to base their impressions of this person only on this information, ignoring the stereotype. This may be especially true when the stereotype is relatively weak and the individuating information relatively strong (Krueger and Rothbart 1988). But even when people fail to integrate the stereotypes with the individuating information, the stereotypes may nevertheless influence their impressions through other routes; they may influence the way the individuating information is construed in the first place, and they may continue to influence expectations about the individual's future behavior. These alternative routes are discussed next.

Ambiguous versus Unambiguous Information   John, a construction worker, hit someone who annoyed him. Try to imagine in as much detail as you can exactly how this event unfolded. Now, try to imagine a different scenario. Jane, a housewife, hit someone who annoyed her. How do you suppose this event unfolded? When these imagination tasks were given to two different groups of undergraduates, it was clear that the two groups had envisioned very different scenarios (Kunda and Sherman-Williams 1993). The construction worker was typically envisioned as punching a co-worker, a highly aggressive act, whereas the housewife was typically envisioned as spanking a naughty child, a much less aggressive act. In other words, the stereotypes had influenced the construal of the construction worker's and the housewife's behavior.

Such stereotype-driven construals may provide a route through which stereotypes can affect our impressions of a stereotyped individual even when we base these impressions only on the individual's behavior: The stereotypes can determine the very meaning that we attach to this behavior. Even though we judge the construction worker and the housewife only on their behavior, we have a very different behavior in mind for each, due to the impact of our stereotypes. Of course, this can only happen if the behavior is ambiguous enough to allow us to imbue it with different meanings; stereotypes should have little or no impact on impressions when the behavior is unambiguous because a behavior that is not open to much further interpretation is likely to be understood in the same manner regardless of who performed it.

In a study that examined these ideas, participants read that either a construction worker or a housewife had engaged in one of three behaviors (Kunda and Sherman-Williams 1993). For one-third of the participants, this behavior was the general and ambiguous "hit someone who annoyed him [or her]." As noted above, this behavior is likely to be construed differently when performed by a construction worker than when performed by a housewife. For the remaining participants, the behavior was one of two specific con-

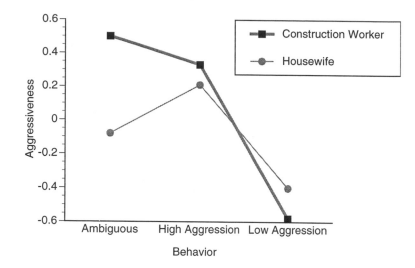

Figure 8.2 Ratings of the aggression of a housewife and a construction worker who had performed a behavior described in ambiguous terms (hit someone who annoyed him or her), as a disambiguated, highly aggressive construal of that behavior (decked a neighbor who had taunted him or her), or mildly aggressive construal (spanked a child who had trudged mud on the carpet). Ratings are reported in standardized scores. Higher numbers reflect greater aggression. From Kunda and Sherman-Williams (1993, p. 93). Copyright © (1993) by Sage Publications, Inc. Reprinted with permission.

struals of this general, ambiguous behavior. One of these was a typical, highly aggressive, example of the way in which a construction worker had been envisioned hitting someone (decked a neighbor who had taunted him or her). The other specific behavior was a typical, mildly aggressive, example of the way in which a housewife had been envisioned hitting someone (spanked his or her son for trudging mud on the carpet). Neither of these more specific behaviors left room for much further construal. Participants were asked to evaluate the extent to which the construction worker or the housewife was aggressive.

When participants were given the specific unambiguous descriptions of the behavior, their aggressiveness ratings were based only on the behavior. As you can see in figure 8.2, both the construction worker and the housewife were viewed as considerably more aggressive when they had decked a neighbor than when they had spanked a child. And in both cases, the housewife and the construction worker were viewed as equally aggressive. In other words, when a housewife or a construction worker was known to have performed an unambiguous aggression-related behavior, the different stereotypes associated with housewives and construction workers had no impact whatsoever on participants' impressions of these individuals' aggression; participants judged the individuals only on their behavior. This was not the case, however, when the behavior was the ambiguous "hit someone who annoyed him [or her]." In this case, the construction worker was viewed as substantially more aggressive than the housewife. In other words, the stereotypes clearly influenced the impressions of individuals who had performed an ambiguously aggressive behavior. It seems likely that in this case, too, participants were judging the targets only on their behavior. But they envisioned very different behaviors for the construction worker and for the housewife, and they therefore judged them differently.

In sum, when we have any relevant individuating information about a stereotyped person, we judge this person's personality only by the individuating information, not by the stereotype. But the stereotype may nevertheless color our judgments of the person because it can determine how we understand and interpret the individuating information. Stereotypes can still exert a powerful impact on impressions of individuals in the presence of individuating information if this information is ambiguous and open to multiple construals. Unfortunately, the impact of stereotypes on impressions of others' personalities is likely to be pervasive because many social behaviors lend themselves to multiple construals.

Trait Judgments versus Behavioral Predictions As discussed above, even though we may believe that John the construction worker is more aggressive than John the accountant, we will consider them equally unaggressive if we also know that each had performed a clearly unaggressive behavior such as walking away from an insult, furious yet silent. But which of the two will we consider more likely to get into bar fights after work? To make rude comments at passing women?

Even though we now consider the construction worker and the accountant to be equally unaggressive, we may still want to say that these crude behaviors are more likely for the unaggressive construction worker than for the unaggressive accountant. This is because although the unaggressive behavior has effectively undercut the impact of stereotypes on the trait *aggressive,* other aspects of the stereotype remain intact. In particular, we still view the construction worker as a member of the working class and the accountant as a member of the upper-middle class. These aspects of the two professional stereotypes may exert their own independent influence on our judgments of the likelihood of certain aggressive behaviors: We may believe that working-class people are more likely than upper-middle-class people to get into fights in bars and to make rude comments at women. Therefore, the working-class construction worker who had walked away from an insult will still seem more likely to perform these working-class aggressive behaviors than will the upper-middle-class accountant who had walked away from an insult, despite our belief that both are equally unaggressive.

This analysis suggests that stereotypes may influence predictions about a person's trait-related *behavior* even when their impact on the *trait* itself has been undermined by individuating information, because behavioral predictions can also be influenced by other aspects of the stereotypes that have not been undercut by the person's behavior. In one study that examined these ideas, participants read about John who, following an incident in which an acquaintance taunted him about his marriage and made fun of his wife, walked away without saying a word even though he was very angry (Kunda, Sinclair, and Griffin 1997). John was said to be either a construction worker or an accountant. As expected, John' unaggressive behavior completely undermined the impact of his professional stereotype on participants' impressions of his aggressiveness; they considered John the construction worker to be just as unaggressive as John the accountant. Nevertheless, participants still thought that John the construction worker would be more likely than John the accountant to engage in a range of stereotypically working-class aggressive behaviors such as get into bar fights, make rude comments at women, and punch someone back who punched him. Their expectations about the likelihoods that the two would perform each behavior diverged more the more the behavior was associated with social class; the behaviors that were most strongly associated with working-class status were especially likely to be seen as more probable for the construction worker than for the accountant.

Once again, it appears that our stereotypes do not influence our judgments of another person's traits in the presence of clearly diagnostic individuating information about that person. Nevertheless, our stereotypes may still influence our expectations about the stereotyped individual's likely behavior. This is because these expectations can also be influenced by other aspects of the stereotype that have remained unchallenged. Our expectations about how a person will behave in different situations undoubtedly play an important role in guiding our interactions with this person. Therefore, our stereotypes may shape our reactions to stereotyped individuals even when these individuals are familiar to us.

In sum, when Locksley and her colleagues first found that the impact of stereotypes on impressions can be undercut by individuating information, this finding gave rise to the optimistic conclusion that as soon as we get to know a stereotyped individual, we will put our stereotypes to rest; stereotypes will have no impact on our impressions of people with whom we are familiar (Locksley et al. 1980). Unfortunately, subsequent research suggests that this initial conclusion was overly optimistic. It now appears that the finding that relevant individuating information undercuts the effects of stereotypes on impressions does not hold when the individuating information is ambiguous and open to multiple construals, and it does not hold when the impressions involve predictions about future behaviors rather than trait ratings. Under these circumstances, stereotypes influence impressions even in the presence of individuating information. Because much of social behavior is ambiguous and many of our interactions with others are guided by how we expect them to behave, the impact of stereotypes on impressions is likely to be very pervasive indeed, even in the presence of individuating information.

Mental Capacity and Stereotype Application There is another reason why stereotypes often influence our judgments. *Not* using stereotypes seems to require effort. When we are tired, distracted, or pressed for time, we may be unable to invest the effort necessary to purge our judgments from the impact of stereotypes. Therefore, when our mental capacity is restricted for these or other reasons, we may be especially likely to base our impressions of stereotyped individuals on stereotypes that we might not have used had our cognitive resources been more plentiful.

You must know some people who are "morning people"—they are at the peak of their abilities early in the day, and are typically worn out by nightfall. And you must also know others who are "night people"—they wake up groggy and tired, and don't reach their cognitive peak until late in the day. In an ingenious study, Galen Bodenhausen relied on this difference among people to demonstrate the impact of reduced mental capacity on stereotype use (Bodenhausen 1990). He reasoned that if people are more likely to apply stereotypes to others when their mental capacity is strained, they should be especially likely to use their stereotypes when they are caught during their "off-peak" hours. In his study, participants read about cases involving the alleged misconduct of college students and were asked to evaluate each student's guilt. The alleged offenses were chosen because each was viewed as especially likely for a particular stereotyped group. One case involved a student accused of cheating on an exam (an offense stereotypic for campus athletes), another involved a student accused of physically attacking his roommate (an offense stereotypic for Hispanics), and another involved a student accused of selling drugs (an offense stereotypic for African Americans). For each case, half of the participants were led to believe that the alleged offender belonged to the group stereotyped as likely to commit that offense (he was described as an athlete or identified by a stereotypic name), and the other half were given no such stereotypic expectations. Both groups read the identical case descriptions, which provided suggestive but inconclusive evidence of guilt.

Would participants' stereotypes be especially likely to influence their guilt judgments when these judgments were made at an off-peak time? To address this question, participants took part in the study in the morning (9:00 a.m.), in the afternoon (3:00 a.m.), or in the evening (8:00 p.m.). Participants were classified as either morning people or evening people, based on their responses to a questionnaire that assessed this trait. If participants were relying on their stereotypes when making their guilt judgments, they could be expected to view the alleged offender as more guilty when he belonged to the group stereotyped as likely to commit the offense in question than when he did not. For example, a campus athlete accused of cheating would be found more guilty than a nonathlete who faced the same accusation. As expected, participants showed such stereotypic influence when they were caught off-peak but not when alert: Morning people relied on their stereotypes only in the afternoon and evening, and evening people only in the morning. Although we may feel tired at different times of day, we may all be especially likely to let our stereotypes color our judgments when we are tired.

Other circumstances known to reduce mental capacity have also been shown to increase stereotype application. These include time pressure, moods such as happiness and anger, and cognitive busyness (e.g., Bodenhausen, Kramer, and Süsser 1994; Kruglanski and Freund 1983; for a review, see Kunda and Thagard 1996). One study, for example, created cognitive busyness in half of the participants by asking them to perform a visual search task as they watched a video of either an Asian or a White person describing a series of mundane events from her life (Gilbert and Hixon 1991). Participants applied the stereotype of Asian Americans to their impressions when cognitively busy, but not otherwise: Only cognitively busy participants viewed the Asian target as more likely than the White target to have stereotypically Asian American traits such as timid and intelligent; nonbusy participants made the same personality ratings, regardless of the target's race.

Why do we become more likely to apply our stereotypes to stereotyped individuals when our mental capacity is taxed? There are two plausible explanations for this phenomenon (see Gilbert and Hixon 1991). The most commonly offered explanation is that stereotypes are easier to use than individuating information (e.g., Bodenhausen 1990; for a review, see Hamilton and Sherman 1994). Proponents of this view argue that stereotypes serve as quick and easy *heuristics* whose use requires little effort, whereas the processing of individuating information is far more effortful and, therefore, is disrupted by cognitive load (see also Fiske and Neuberg 1990; see chapters 3 and 6 for discussions of quick and easy versus effortful thinking).

Although this view has gained broad acceptance, I would like to point out that the evidence for it is inconclusive. The available data speak to only half of this argument: They show that stereotype use increases when cognitive capacity is reduced, but they do not show that use of individuating information is decreased at the same time. To demonstrate that use of individuating information is disrupted by cognitive load, it is necessary to provide participants with different kinds of individuating information (e.g., strong and weak evidence of guilt) and to show that people become less sensitive to this information when their mental capacity is strained. Unfortunately, none of the studies examining the impact of mental capacity on stereotype use has done so; all have relied on a single description of the target person, which was presented to different participants as associated with differently stereotyped individuals (Kunda and Thagard 1996). Therefore, there is no evidence that people are less likely to use individuating information when their resources are strained. Alternatively, it may be that cognitive load increases reliance on individuating information much like it increases reliance on stereotypes. When preoccupied, we may rely more heavily on each straightforward piece of relevant information rather than attempting a more complex and thoughtful integration of all relevant evidence.

Another reason for doubting the view that stereotypes are processed less effortfully than behaviors or other kinds of individuating information is that people have been shown to infer traits automatically from behavior (e.g., Gilbert et al. 1988, see chapter 7; Winter, Uleman, and Cunniff 1985, see chapter 10). This contradicts the notion that the processing of such individuating information is always effortful, and suggests that individuating information may be processed just as effortlessly as stereotypes. It remains possible, though, that making sense of more complex and multifaceted individuating information such as a detailed evidence pertaining to a crime will indeed require considerable cognitive effort.

The second plausible interpretation for the finding that we tend to rely more on our stereotypes when our mental capacity is strained is that *inhibiting* stereotypes may be effortful. As discussed earlier, stereotypes can color our judgments automatically. If we become aware that this is happening, we may wish to avoid basing our judgments on stereotypes, but this may require effortful, controlled processing (Devine 1989). The evidence for this interpretation is inconclusive as well. It is clear that people who are low in prejudice do not wish to appear prejudiced in their judgments and behavior, that they attempt to inhibit stereotype-based responses that imply prejudice, and that they feel guilt and compunction when they discover that prejudice has crept inadvertently into their reactions (Devine et al. 1991; Monteith 1993; Monteith, Devine, and Zuwerink 1993). However, there is no evidence that inhibiting stereotypes requires greater effort than using them.

In sum, when our mental capacity is reduced, our use of stereotypes increases. It is unclear whether this occurs because the absence of sufficient resources undercuts our ability to fully process alternative, individuating information or because it undercuts our ability to suppress stereotypes. But it is clear that, whatever the reason, when we are tired, preoccupied, or under time pressure, our impressions of stereotyped individuals may be especially likely to be colored by our stereotypes.

Motivated Application and Inhibition of Stereotypes   Imagine that you have just received a blow to your self-esteem; you may have failed an important test, or been denied a coveted promotion. Your need to restore your sense of self-worth when this happens may become especially strong. One way of gaining a sense of competence and self-worth is through comparison to less competent others. You may therefore go out of your way to try to disparage anyone you come across so as to make yourself seem superior by comparison. If, when you are so strongly motivated to boost your self-worth, you encounter someone who happens to belong to a negatively stereotyped group, you may seize upon this negative stereotype and use it to disparage the ill-fated individual. A series of studies by Steven Fein and Steven Spencer suggest that we may indeed become especially likely to apply negative stereotypes to stereotyped individuals when we are motivated to reaffirm our self-worth (Fein and Spencer 1997).

In one study, participants first took an intelligence test and were given either positive or negative feedback about their performance at it. Then, in a seemingly unrelated study, they were asked to evaluate a woman described as a candidate for a job as personnel manager, based on her job application forms and videotaped excerpts from her job interview. The woman was portrayed as either Jewish or non-Jewish. This was accomplished by giving her a Jewish or non-Jewish name and background, and by making minor modifications to the photograph attached to her application (e.g., she wore a Star of David or a cross). At the time the study was run at the University of Michigan, there was a well-known negative stereotype of the "Jewish American Princess" on campus. It was expected that participants would be especially likely to use this stereotype to derogate the Jewish woman when their need to boost their own self-worth had just been enhanced through the an experience of failure. This is exactly what happened, as may be seen in figure 8.3.

Participants who had received positive feedback rated the woman equally highly regardless of whether or not she was Jewish. These participants had just received a boost to their self-esteem, and had little need to boost it further, and therefore little need to use the negative Jewish stereotype to derogate the Jewish woman.

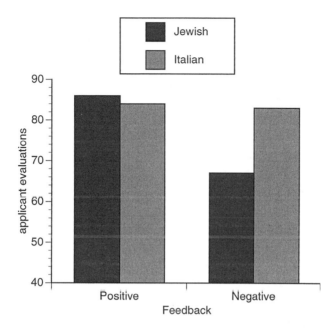

Figure 8.3 Evaluations of a Jewish and a non-Jewish job applicant by participants who had just been given positive or negative feedback on an intelligence test. Higher numbers reflect more positive evaluations. From Fein and Spencer (1997, fig. 3, p. 38). Copyright © (1997) by the American Psychological Association. Reprinted with permission.

Lacking a strong motivation to apply the stereotype, they refrained from applying it. In contrast, participants who had received negative feedback did rate the Jewish woman less highly than the non-Jewish one. These participants had just received a blow to their self-esteem, and were probably attempting to reaffirm their self-worth by using the negative stereotype to derogate another person. Indeed, the opportunity to derogate the Jewish woman gave these participants the desired boost to self-esteem, a boost not experienced by participants in any of the other conditions. In short, participants applied the negative stereotype to the stereotyped individual only when they were motivated to restore their threatened self-worth. We may be especially likely to apply negative stereotypes when we are down in the dumps because we have learned that derogating another person can make us feel better about ourselves.

Other motives may also lead us to apply negative stereotypes to stereotyped individuals. After receiving a bad evaluation from a stereotyped individual, we may call upon the negative stereotype so as to discredit the harsh evaluator and, thereby, dismiss the validity of the evaluation. If we believe the evaluator is incompetent, we don't have to take the negative evaluation we have received from this person to heart. In a series of studies, Lisa Sinclair and I found that White men disparaged Black and female evaluators if these had evaluated them poorly but not if these had evaluated them highly (Sinclair, 1998; Kunda and Sinclair, in press). A Black person or a woman who had given participants a negative evaluation were rated as less competent than a White man who had provided the identical negative evaluation. In contrast, a Black person and a woman who had given participants a positive evaluation were rated just as highly as a White man who had given the identical evaluation. In short, only participants who had received a negative evaluation from a stereotyped individual used their stereotype to disparage that individual. Apparently, they did this because they were motivated to protect themselves from the self-deflating evaluation they had just received. Indeed, other participants who had observed the same stereotyped targets delivering the same negative feedback to someone else rather than to themselves, and whose own self-worth was therefore not at stake, did not disparage the stereotyped individuals.

We obtained similar results when we asked male and female undergraduates to evaluate the quality of the professors who had instructed them the previous term (Kunda and Sinclair, in press). As you may have noticed, students' evaluations of their professors depend on the grades they receive from them—the higher the grades, the better the professor (Greenwald and Gillmore 1997). We found that this was especially true when the professor was female because female professors were particularly likely to be disparaged after providing low grades. Students rated female professors who had given them high grades just as highly as they rated male professors who had given them similarly high grades. However, students rated female professors who had given them poor grades as less competent then they rated male professors who had given them equally poor grades. Interestingly, this was true regardless of the students' own gender. Female students were just as likely as male students to use the negative stereotype of women to disparage the female professor who had graded them harshly.

These two sets of studies show that self-protective motives can lead us to apply negative stereotypes that we might not have used otherwise. They also suggest that even when we are motivated to disparage another person, we will do so only if we feel we have a good justification for this (Kunda 1990). In both sets of studies, mainstream targets suffered relatively little disparagement at the hands of participants motivated to reaffirm or protect their self-worth, probably because these participants were unable to come up with a good reason for disparaging the mainstream individuals no matter how much they wanted to. A negative stereotype can give us the needed justification for disparaging a member of the stereo-typed group, and will therefore be seized upon and applied when we are so motivated.

Serial versus Parallel Processing of Stereotypes and Individuating Information It has happened to me on more than one occasion at a restaurant that after deciding to ask my waiter for the check at the end of the meal, I realized, much to my embarrassment, that I could not pick out the person who had taken my order, served my meal, and stopped by several times to ask if everything was OK, from among all the other uniformed waiters. How could I have failed to notice what my waiter looked like? Two influential models of impression formation suggest that this failure of recollection is probably not due entirely to my advancing age. Rather, when we encounter a stereotyped individual in whom we have little personal interest, we may simply pay no attention to nuances of this person's appearance and behavior unless these are particularly striking or unusual. Instead, our impression of this person may be based predominantly on the stereotype (Brewer 1988; Fiske and Neuberg 1990). Intuitively, such *category-based* impressions seem especially likely when our dealings with a stereotyped individual are confined to interactions dictated by his or her stereotyped role, as is often the case when we interact with waiters, sales persons, or customs officials.

However, if we want to get to know a person, for whatever reason, or if the person's behavior and attributes clash with our stereotypes, we may pay more attention to these individuating characteristics and, as a result, rely on them more heavily when forming an impression of the person. There is some evidence that people may pay more attention to individuating information about a stereotyped person when this information clashes with their expectations as well as when they are motivated to see this person in an accurate manner or in the best possible light (e.g., Neuberg and Fiske 1987; for a review, see Fiske and Neuberg 1990).

These and related findings have given rise to two similar models of impression formation, Susan Fiske and Steven Neuberg's (1990) *continuum model* and Marilynn Brewer's (1988) *dual process* model. There are several important differences in the contents and emphases of these two models, but they share some basic assumptions that have gained wide acceptance. Both distinguish between *stereotype-based* processes, which result in impressions dominated by stereotypes, and *attribute-based* processes, which result in impressions dominated by individuating information. Neuberg and Fiske allow, in addition, for a range of intermediate processes that result in impressions that are based on a mix of stereotypes and individuating information. And Brewer allows, in addition, for an alternative, *personalized*, mode of impression formation in which stereotypes serve as but one of many features of the person, and impressions reflect an integration of all features, be they stereotypes, behaviors, or traits.

Both of these models are *serial* in that they assume that people first, perhaps automatically, identify and categorize the person as a member of a stereotyped group. At this early stage, then, impressions are based entirely on the stereotype. People often stop at this point. They may move to more attribute-based or personalized impressions if they are motivated to gain deeper understanding of the person, or if they cannot readily reconcile the person's attributes or behavior with any particular stereotype. In this sense, both models assume that stereotypes play a special, dominant role in impressions.

Paul Thagard and I proposed an alternative, *parallel-processing* model of impression formation (Kunda and Thagard 1996). This model recognizes that sometimes, as in the waiter example, one may notice only the stereotyped category to which another person belongs and pay little attention to the person's individuating features. In these cases, stereotypes will indeed dominate impressions, as suggested by the serial models. However, if one also notices the person's behavior, clothes, personal circumstances, or any other individuating information, stereotypes will have no special status. Rather, the stereotypes and the individuating information will jointly and simultaneously influence impressions. In the processes, the various kinds of information about the person will constrain and influence each other's meaning (see chapter 2 for a more detailed description of parallel-constraint-satisfaction models).

Imagine, for example, that you notice a professionally dressed woman shoving a man. The continuum model assumes that you will go through the following stages of impression formation (Fiske and Neuberg 1990). First, you will categorize this person using the dominant stereotype, in this case probably that of women. If you have no particular interest in her, you will stop at that. If you are interested in her, for whatever reason, you will then attempt to confirm that her behavior and attire are consistent with your stereotype of women. If you decide that shoving someone does not fit with your stereotype, you may try to make a different stereotype fit, perhaps that of professionals. If this one, too, fails to fit, you may finally resort to an attribute-based process, in which you attempt to integrate the full range of the person's attributes, with minimal influence from your stereotypes.

The parallel-processing model assumes, instead, that as you notice the woman delivering the shove, her gender, her behavior, and any other attributes that you notice will each bring to mind a host of associations that will color each other's meaning and jointly determine your impression. The stereotype of women as gentle and unaggressive along with the stereotype of professionals as refined may lead you to see the behavior as playful rather than violent or as an act of self-defense. At the same time, the forward nature of this behavior may lead you to see her as a special kind of woman, perhaps a feminist. Notice that both the continuum model and the dual-process model allow for the possibility of such simultaneous integration of information at some point. However, they differ from the parallel-processing model in that they assume that you first need to go through a range of other processes before arriving, if at all, at this point of simultaneous integration.

After reviewing the relevant research, Thagard and I concluded that there was simply no need to assume these additional processes (Kunda and Thagard 1996). We argued that the parallel-processing model could explain every phenomenon accounted for by the serial models, and then some. For example, a phenomenon that is better accounted for by the parallel-processing model is the finding, described above, that stereotypes can influence our expectations about a person's trait-related behavior even when their impact on our impressions of the trait itself have been undermined by the person's behavior (Kunda et al. 1997). Recall that a construction worker and an accountant who had behaved in an unaggressive manner were viewed as equally unaggressive, yet the construction worker was considered more likely than the accountant to punch someone. The serial models would be hard pressed to explain why stereotypes should exert different influences on these two kinds of judgment; in these models, the impact of stereotypes depends on the kind of process one engages in, and should be the same for all kinds of judgment. In contrast, the parallel-processing model can readily explain these differences; they arise from the fact that some aspects of the stereotype that have not been undermined by the individuating information (in this example, social class) are more strongly associated with the behavior than with the trait in question (see the more detailed discussion earlier).

In sum, there are many areas of agreement between the serial and the parallel models. All would predict that stereotypes dominate impressions under circumstances where individuating information is simply not noticed. All would predict that stereotypes would dominate impressions if one becomes aware of them before one notices the individuating information, as when you first find out a person's gender, race, and profession, and then gradually learn about the person's behaviors and background. Stereotypes should dominate impressions in this case because they provide a framework for interpreting the individuating information. The models diverge, however, in their predictions about what happens when stereotypes and individuating information are noticed at the same time, as when you come across a woman, an African American, or a police officer in the act of performing a distinct behavior. The serial models assume that you will first process these individuals through the lenses of the salient stereotypes, and that you will integrate the implications of the stereotype with those of the behavior only if you are especially interested in the person or if you cannot reconcile the behavior with the stereotype. In contrast, the parallel model assumes that the stereotype and the behavior will influence your impressions simultaneously.

The Target's Perspective

So far I have focused on how stereotypes figure in the mind of the perceiver, examining when and how our impressions of others are influenced by our stereotypes. I turn next to a discussion of what it feels like to be the target of stereotyping. How might the knowledge that others may be viewing you through the lenses of a negative stereotype influence your understanding of their behavior toward you? How might knowing that people like you are expected to perform poorly affect your performance?

Attributional Ambiguity

When Jan Wong, a respected author and reporter for Canada's leading newspaper, *The Globe and Mail*, returned to Canada from covering the 1996 Olympics in Atlanta, a blond immigration officer glanced at her Canadian Passport, questioned her briefly, and then referred her to a special waiting room for further security checks. In a furious article describing the incident, Wong, who is of Chinese descent, expressed the conviction that her treatment was due to the color of her skin and accused the immigration officers of racism (Wong, 8.10.1996). Following the publication of her article, the *Globe and Mail* was flooded with two kinds of responses from readers. Some readers, also members of ethnic minorities, wrote to describe similar incidents of racist treatment by immigration officers. But other, White readers, wrote to report that they, too, had been subjected to the same kind of treatment, for which they offered a very different explanation: "The immigration officers were simply doing their job—ensuring that Canada remains one of the safest, and best, countries in the world" (Leger, 8.17.1996).

Being stopped by immigration officers is never pleasant. But if you belong to a group that is often at the receiving end of discrimination, this adds an extra dimension of unpleasantness to the experience. Even if you recognize that the officers who stopped you may have simply been doing their job, conducting a random search or responding to irregularities in your passport, you cannot help wondering whether, perhaps, you have been singled out because of the color of your skin.

Such attributional ambiguity can be even more devastating when more is at stake. In his book, *The Rage of a Privileged Class*, Ellis Cose describes the anger and confusion of Black managers who feel they have been passed over for promotion. They cannot but wonder whether they have failed to achieve more because they are not capable of more or because they were being discriminated against. "'You usually end up suspecting that race is a factor,' but the truth is difficult to know" (Cose 1993, p. 75). Of course, many White managers also fail to achieve desired promotions, but in their case the message is usually easier to interpret. In the current social climate, making a promotion can also be fraught with ambiguity for Black managers; they may wonder whether they were promoted because of their outstanding ability, or thanks to affirmative action policies. If you are Black, or female, or a member of any other group

that has been the victim of discrimination, both positive and negative feedback from mainstream individuals and organizations can
be difficult to interpret. You may never know whether such feedback reflects an assessment of your ability or a reaction to your race
or gender. Regardless of your actual performance, you may remain
insecure about your ability and about how it is perceived, because
you can trust neither negative nor positive feedback.

A clever study by Jennifer Crocker and her colleagues documented the difficulty that Black students experience when they try
to make sense of feedback received from their White peers, and also
explored the consequences to their self-esteem (Crocker et al.
1991). Black and White students were invited to participate in a
study on the development of friendship. Upon arrival, each was
told that their partner for the session had already arrived and was
sitting in an adjacent room. The partner was always described as
White and of the same gender as the participant. The room to
which participants were taken was equipped with a one-way mirror covered with a blind. Half of the participants were told that the
blind would remain down so that their partner in the adjacent room
would be unable to see them. The other half were told that the
blind would be raised so that their partner could see them. Thanks
to this manipulation, participants expected that their partner was
either unaware or aware of their race. Participants then completed
a measure of self-esteem and a form asking about their likes and
dislikes, strengths and weaknesses, and personal qualities. They
were told that this form would be shown to their partner who
would use it to determine whether the two could be friends. After
the participant completed this form, the experimenter left to show
it to the partner, and returned a little later with the partner's reaction. In fact the partner did not exist, and participants received a
bogus response which was either very positive or very negative.
Participants were then given a questionnaire designed to tap their
reactions to this positive or negative feedback.

Would Black participants react differently to feedback from a
White peer when they assumed that this peer knew their race (and
so might be responding to it) than when they assumed that this peer

was unaware of their race? The answer was yes. Black participants who assumed their partner had seen them thought that prejudice had played a greater role in their partner's reactions to them than did Black participants who assumed their partner had not seen them. This was true not only when their partner's reaction to them was negative but also when it was positive. If you attribute another person's reactions to you to prejudice, you need not take them at face value.

Participants' responses to a second self-esteem measure suggested that they were indeed dismissing the feedback. Black students who assumed their partner did not realize they were Black, and who therefore had little reason to dismiss the partner's reaction as due to prejudice, did indeed take this reaction to heart. Their self-esteem decreased after they received negative feedback and increased after they received positive feedback. The same was not true for Black participants who assumed their partner had seen them and so knew that they were Black. These participants seemed to dismiss the relevance of the negative feedback as due to prejudice; it provoked no reduction in their self-esteem. But they were also unable to take credit for the positive feedback, which did not lead to an appropriate increase in their self-esteem; if anything, positive feedback seemed to decrease their self-esteem. These effects of enabling or preventing their partner from seeing them were clearly due to Black participants' assumptions about their partner's prejudice. For White participants, whether or not they assumed their partner could see them made little difference to their reactions.

Members of stigmatized groups, then, can buffer themselves from the personal implications of negative feedback by attributing it to prejudice. This may be one reason why, despite their stigmatization, the self-esteem of members of many negatively stereotyped groups such as African Americans, Chicanos, or facially disfigured individuals is as high or higher than that of nonstigmatized individuals (for a review, see Crocker and Major 1989). Whenever a stigmatized individual is criticized, ostracized, or experiences any other negative interpersonal outcome, he or she can attribute this outcome to prejudice rather than to a personal inadequacy. Such attributions can protect self-esteem, but they do carry a cost. They may prevent the individual from learning important lessons from appropriate negative feedback that might have led to self-improvement as well as to a realistic appraisal of one's abilities. By dismissing all feedback as due to prejudice, members of negatively stereotyped groups also bar themselves from enjoying the implications of positive feedback because it, too, is not taken at face value. They cannot tell whether the appreciation and liking expressed by others are genuine or, instead, reflect an attempt to be "nice" to a poor, stigmatized person. Therefore, after receiving any feedback, be it positive or negative, stigmatized individuals may remain uncertain about their actual ability and about how it is really perceived by others.

Stereotype Threat

Anyone who volunteers an answer in a math class carries the risk of getting it wrong and appearing incompetent. But some people, those who belong to groups stereotyped as incompetent at math, carry an extra vulnerability. A girl who gives a wrong answer risks confirming the stereotype that girls just can't do math, and a Black child who gives a wrong answer risks confirming the racial inferiority of African Americans. Such individuals are operating under a cloud of suspicion of intellectual inferiority; they fear that any mishap on their part may confirm this suspicion. Failure, then, becomes doubly threatening; it may reveal not only that they themselves are incompetent, but that their entire race or gender is inferior. Sadly, the resulting fear and anxiety can interfere with performance, leading the negatively stereotyped individual to confirm the stereotype. Claude Steele has used the term *stereotype threat* to refer to this fear that one will be reduced to the negative stereotype of one's group. Along with his colleagues, Steele has documented that situations that give rise to stereotype threat can undermine the performance of African Americans and of women (for a review, see Steele 1997).

In the United States, there is a well-documented and persistent gap between the academic achievements of White and Black students at all levels of schooling. Even among those who make it to college, the national dropout rate (measured as the percentage of students who fail to obtain a degree within six years) is considerably higher for Black students (70 percent) than it is for White students (42 percent). Black students who do graduate do so with a grade average that is two-thirds of a letter grade lower than that received by graduating White students. In part, this achievement gap may be due to background factors that leave Black students less well prepared for school than White students. But poor preparation cannot fully account for this achievement gap because it remains true even among very well prepared students. If you examine the academic achievements—GPA, dropout rates, time to graduation, and so on—of students who have received different scores on the Scholastic Aptitude Test (SAT), you will find that at every level of performance on the SAT, Black students have poorer achievements than do White students *with the same SAT score* (for these and related statistics, see Steele 1997; Steele and Aronson 1995). In other words, compared to White students, Black students with the same level of preparation underachieve at college.

Steele and his colleagues believe that this underachievement may be due in part to the fact that stereotype threat depresses the performance of Black students on academic tests. They reasoned that if this were so, the gap between the achievements of Black and White students should be narrowed or even eliminated in situations that carry only minimal levels of stereotype threat. In one study, Black and White Stanford undergraduates were given a test of verbal ability described as very difficult (Steele and Aronson 1995). Half of the participants responded under conditions designed to enhance stereotype threat. They were informed that the test was diagnostic of intellectual ability and that they would be given feedback that "may be helpful to you by familiarizing you with some of your strengths and weaknesses." This focus on assessing intellectual ability was intended to highlight the relevance of the stereotype of Blacks as intellectually inferior. The

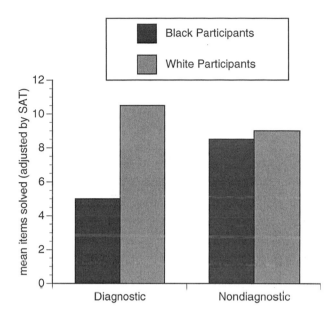

Figure 8.4 Test performance of Black and White students under high stereotype threat (diagnostic test) or low stereotype threat (nondiagnostic test). From Steele and Aronson (1995, fig. 2, p. 802). Copyright © (1995) by the American Psychological Association. Reprinted with permission.

other half responded under conditions designed to minimize stereotype threat. They were led to believe that the test was not diagnostic of ability and that the feedback they would receive would merely familiarize them with "the kinds of problems that appear on tests they may encounter in the future." It was assumed that if the task was not portrayed as an ability test, Black students would not view themselves as operating under the suspicion of incompetence. All participants took an identical test.

The results of this rather subtle manipulation were quite striking, as may be seen in figure 8.4. When participants were informed that the test was diagnostic of academic ability, Black students performed considerably worse than their equally prepared White peers, thereby replicating the well-documented gap between the test performances of Black and White students. But, remarkably, this gap was completely eliminated when stereotype threat was reduced by leading participants to believe that the test did not bear on their academic abilities. When so informed, Black students performed just as well as White students.

These results suggested that when the test was portrayed as diagnostic of ability, Black participants were reminded of the negative stereotype of Blacks that put them under suspicion of inferiority, and the anxiety provoked by this stereotype threat undermined their performance. However, Steele and Aronson recognized that diagnostic tests could also undermine the performance of Black students for other reasons that have little to do with stereotype threat. Perhaps, for example, Black students had simply learned to fear academic situations. The notion that their performance on the diagnostic test was undermined by stereotype threat would be strengthened if it could also be shown that the prospect of taking such a diagnostic test makes Black students especially likely to activate the Black stereotype. Steele and Aronson conducted a follow-up study to this end.

Black and White students were led to expect that they would be taking a test of word recognition followed by a difficult test of abstract reasoning (Steele and Aronson 1995). As in the earlier study, they were informed either that the test would be indicative of their ability in these domains (information intended to elicit stereotype threat) or that the test was not intended to evaluate their ability (information intended to minimize stereotype threat). They were then given the word recognition test which, in reality, was a measure of stereotype activation. It contained a list of word fragments that participants were asked to complete. The list included several fragments that could be completed with words relating to the Black stereotype, such as __ __ CE (race) or LA __ __ (lazy). Control participants were given this measure without any mention of verbal ability.

As expected, when under stereotype threat, Black students were especially likely to activate the Black stereotype. As may be seen in figure 8.5, Black students informed that the test was diagnostic of ability made more stereotypic completions than did Black students informed that the test was nondiagnostic or than Black control

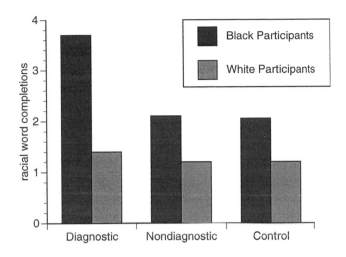

Figure 8.5 Number of racial completions made by Black and White participants under high stereotype threat (diagnostic test) and under low stereotype threat (nondiagnostic test and control). From Steele and Aronson (1995, fig. 3, p. 805). Copyright © (1995) by the American Psychological Association. Reprinted with permission.

students. Indeed, Black students under stereotype threat showed greater activation of the Black stereotype than did Black or White students in any other condition (for White students, the supposed diagnosticity of the test had no impact on stereotype activation, which was low in all conditions). In short, the one condition shown in the earlier study to depress the performance of Black students relative to their White peers was also the one condition in which Black students showed increased activation of the Black stereotype. This strengthens the interpretation that it was this stereotype activation, and the anxiety it gave rise to, that undermined the performance of Black students who were expecting to put their ability on the line.

Stereotype threat is not unique to African Americans. It may depress the performance of members of any group stereotyped as incompetent when they find themselves in situations that appear to test their ability in the domain of their alleged incompetence. For example, women's performance at math could be undermined by stereotype threat (Spencer, Steele, and Quinn 1999). Although girls do as well as boys at math in the early school years, they start to fall behind in high school, and this gender gap increases as they mature into adulthood. In difficult college math courses, women tend to do less well than men with comparable SAT scores (for relevant statistics, see Steele 1997).

Does stereotype threat contribute to women's underachievement at math? To address this question, male and female University of Michigan students who were good at math were given a challenging math test (Spencer et al. 1999). Before they took the test, half of the students were given information intended to elicit stereotype threat in women: They were told that the test generally showed gender differences (the stereotype of women as relatively incompetent at math is strong enough that there was no need to actually spell out the direction to the alleged gender differences). The other half were given information intended to undercut stereotype threat for women: They were told that the test showed no gender differences, implying that the stereotype of women as incompetent was not relevant to their performance on this particular test. All participants then took the identical test.

The results were quite dramatic. When participants were informed that the test produced gender differences, women performed substantially worse than men, thereby reproducing the well-documented gender gap. However, the gender gap was completely eliminated for participants informed that the test was gender neutral. When so informed, women performed just as well as men. Follow-up research suggested that the disruptive impact of stereotype threat on women's performance was due to the anxiety produced by this threat.

The results of these two sets of studies are extremely disturbing, but they also offer a window of hope. It is distressing that the clouds of suspicion hanging over African Americans in all domains of academic achievement and over women in the domain of math can so undermine their performance. The consequence of this depressed performance can have life-long ramifications, affecting, for example, college attendance, graduation rates, career choices, and income levels. It is especially distressing to realize that even when negatively stereotyped individuals attend the same classes as mainstream individuals, receive the same instruction, and take the same tests, they inhabit quite different worlds. Even if their instructors and fellow students never mention or react to their ethnicity or gender, the mere fact that they are attempting tasks on which they are stereotyped as inferior can suffice to create debilitating stereotype threat for stereotyped individuals.

The window of hope comes from the finding that stereotype threat can be undercut. Women and African Americans can perform just as well as White men when situational cues lead them to construe their tasks as irrelevant to the threatening stereotypes. The challenge, then, is to create school environments that minimize stereotype threat and enable stereotyped individuals to rise to their full potential. How might this be done? Based on their research, Steele and his colleagues reasoned that it is important to create a supportive environment for stereotyped individuals without signaling to them that they need this support because of their group membership. A remediation program aimed at overcoming the poor preparation of African Americans sends a clear signal that African Americans are at risk of failure. As such, remedial programs can do more harm than good. Indeed, in one study, strong African American students participating in a remedial program did worse than African American students with comparable ability who participated in no program at all (Steele 1997).

What then should a good intervention consist of? Steele and his colleagues at the University of Michigan created an intervention designed to improve the performance of African American students, guided by their insights about the importance of overcoming stereotype threat (Steele 1997). For one thing, the program was not restricted to African Americans. The makeup of its participants reflected the ethnic proportions on campus, though African Americans were overrepresented, constituting 20 percent of the sample. Another important element was that the program was portrayed as honorific rather than as remedial. When recruited, students were told that they had survived a very competitive selection process, and that the program was intended to help them maximize their strong potential. The program itself continued to communicate that the students had a strong intellectual potential by offering voluntary "challenge" workshops. In addition, students participated in weekly discussions on issues related to adjustment to college which were intended to convey that difficulties were common and not restricted to any particular ethnic group.

Early results, in the form of first year grade point averages (GPAs), were very promising. Control participants, who did not take part in any program, showed the usual pattern of Black underachievement. Among controls, Black students at any level of SAT performance obtained lower GPAs than did White students with comparable SAT scores. In dramatic contrast, there was practically no underachievement for Black students enrolled in the intervention. This was especially true for Black students with above average SATs; their GPAs were as high as those of White participants with the same SATs and substantially higher than those of Black students with comparable SATs who had not participated in the program.

An applied intervention like this one is bound to have so many different elements and unique circumstances that it is difficult to tell what exactly is responsible for its success. Nevertheless, its success is highly encouraging. It suggests that African Americans are not doomed to inevitable underachievement. Even without changing the broader social climate and without bringing about a modification of the widespread negative stereotype of African Americans, it may be possible to create schooling environments that undercut the extent to which African Americans see the stereotype as relevant to their own daily performance, enabling them to operate without the constant double burden of stereotype threat and its resultant anxiety, and allowing them to maximize their potential for achievement.

Stereotype Maintenance and Change

As should be clear by now, negative stereotypes can have devastating effects. There have been ample demonstrations throughout history of open and intended, often murderous discrimination arising from negative group stereotypes. The social psychological research documented in this chapter has focused on more subtle influences on judgment whose consequences can nevertheless be quite pernicious. Stereotypes can influence the way members of stigmatized groups are perceived, understood, and treated by others. Even people who have no prejudicial intent can inadvertently view stereotyped individuals through the lenses of negative stereotypes, without even realizing that they are doing so. For their part, stereotyped individuals often assume that they are operating under a cloud of stereotype-based suspicion of inferiority, and this can cause them to experience enough anxiety to undermine their performance.

As you contemplate the vast social costs of mistaken negative stereotypes, you may be wondering if anything can be done to correct such misperceptions. Is it possible to change people's stereotypes? This question has also intrigued many social psychologists. Their research efforts have given rise to another question, namely, Why is it so difficult to bring about stereotype change? These issues are discussed next.

The Contact Hypothesis

Early intuitions suggested that if we come to meet members of groups that are unfairly stereotyped in negative terms, we will soon recognize and correct our errors. If non-Blacks encounter enough intelligent, hard-working, and mild mannered African Americans, surely they will realize that it is inappropriate to view this group as unintelligent, lazy, and aggressive. These ideas gave rise to the *contact hypothesis*, which held that social contact between members of majority and minority groups will reduce prejudice. From the start, it was recognized that not any contact will do. Walking through an urban inner city or visiting Chinatown seems highly unlikely to change anyone's views of the ethnic minorities that reside there. Having an African American janitor seems unlikely to do the trick either. Rather, Gordon Allport suggested in 1954, to reduce prejudice through contact, the contact must be among people of equal status in pursuit of common goals. If, for example, a prejudiced White person has to cooperate at work with an African American teammate, this would eventually lead to liking and respect for this teammate which would then generalize into a more positive view of African Americans.

Although the contact hypothesis seemed intuitively appealing, it proved very difficult to change stereotypes through contact. In their classic Robber's Cave experiments, Muzafer Sherif and his colleagues created a sense of rivalry and hostility among two groups of boys, and then attempted to change their negative views of each other and eliminate their mutual dislike (Sherif et al. 1961). Sherif and his colleagues recruited well-adjusted middle-class White boys for a summer camp. Initially the boys did not know each other, and were unaware that they were participating in an experiment. After living together in the same cabin for a few days, the boys were separated into two groups. The investigators asked each boy who his best friend was, and made sure that the two would end up in different groups. The two groups were kept completely apart for a while, as each engaged in various activities designed to create group spirit. Once each group had acquired strong group spirit, the investigators initiated a series of activities intended to produce friction among them—a sports tournament, a competitive treasure hunt, and so on. Pretty soon, the boys were referring to members of the other groups as "stinkers," "sneaks," and "cheats." They began showing their mutual animosity by making threatening posters, planning raids, and burning the other group's banner after a game.

Having successfully created two hostile groups, the investigators began addressing the true purpose of the study—getting rid of the hostility. They began by creating opportunities for pleasant social contact such as watching movies together and eating in the same dining room. This proved to be a total failure. The social events only provided an opportunity for the rival groups to berate and attack each other. They shoved each other in the line for food, threw paper and food at each other, and made rude comments. The investigators then turned to a more elaborate tactic. They created a series of urgent situations that forced the boys to work together.

These included a breakdown in the water supply that required the boys to search the water line for the trouble spot, a failure of their truck to start that required the boys to all pull it together with a rope, and an opportunity to rent a movie that the two groups could only afford if they pooled their resources. Although the two groups were able to work together harmoniously on these tasks, their joint efforts did not lead to an immediate reduction in hostility. Initially, as soon as the task was completed, the boys returned to bickering and name calling. But gradually the friction and hostility between the groups was reduced, until, by the time the camp ended, they were seeking opportunities to mingle, entertain, and treat each other.

Recall that the rival groups in this study were made up of essentially similar boys with no prior history of hostility. Even for such groups, intergroup hostility was not reduced through sheer contact on an equal footing in a pleasant situation. And even cooperative contact did not lead to an immediate reduction in hostility. The outlook for groups with a long history of dislike and well-entrenched negative stereotypes of each other seemed even less promising. Indeed, extensive research on the contact hypothesis gives little reason for optimism. For contact to reduce prejudice, the members of the two groups must have equal status, an opportunity to get to know each other, exposure to evidence that disconfirms the stereotypes, shared goals, and active cooperation. And even then, contact is not always effective at reducing prejudice. Negative stereotypes often resist change even in the face of intense manipulations involving cooperation with members of the stereotyped group over long periods of time (for a review, see Stephan 1985).

Why do our group stereotypes so often remain unchanged even in the face of contact with group members whose behavior and attributes are nothing like our stereotypic expectations? One reason is that we may simply not realize that such individuals disconfirm our stereotypes because our interpretation of their behavior can be biased by our stereotypes; we may view their neutral and innocent behaviors as consistent with our negative stereotypes. But even when we recognize that individuals clearly disconfirm the stereotype of their group, we may still fail to generalize from them to the group as a whole because we consider them atypical of their group, as discussed next.

Subtyping Counterstereotypic Individuals

When you encounter a wealthy African American, an aggressive housewife, a respectful teenager, or a member of any other social group who disconfirms your stereotype of that group, you may hang onto your stereotype by "fencing off" this individual (Allport 1954; Rothbart and John 1985; Weber and Crocker 1983). Yes, a White American might say to himself, my African American neighbor Marcus is wealthy and successful, but you can't really learn anything from him about what African Americans in general are like because he is so atypical of African Americans; he belongs to an unusual subgroup of African Americans, African American executives. Much like one views ostriches as an unusual kind of bird that teaches little about the size and flying capabilities of birds in general, one may view African American executives as an unusual kind of African American that teaches little about the behavior and attributes of African Americans in general. By allocating counterstereotypic individuals like Marcus to a subtype that is considered atypical and unrepresentative of the group as a whole, one may be able to maintain one's global stereotype of the group even though one knows that some group members do not fit the bill.

Through this mechanism, one may be able maintain a negative stereotype of African Americans and a strong dislike for this group even though one's favorite entertainer is Bill Cosby, one's favorite singer is Michael Jackson, and one's favorite athlete is Michael Jordan (all of whom, one knows quite well, are African Americans). These liked and respected individuals can be dismissed as irrelevant to the stereotype of the group as a whole if they are viewed as belonging to atypical subtypes such as African American entertainers, African American singers, or African American athletes. In the same vein, the notion of subtyping explains how one can be a prejudiced bigot despite proclaiming that "Some of my best friends are Jews [or Blacks, or members of any other stigmatized group]." The "best friends" are simply fenced off as atypical of their still disliked group.

A landmark article by Renee Weber and Jennifer Crocker suggested that we may be less likely to change our stereotypes when we are confronted with individuals who disconfirm them if we can readily subtype these counterstereotypic individuals (Weber and Crocker 1983). In one study, these investigators attempted to change participants' stereotype of lawyers as well-dressed, industrious, and intelligent. In one set of conditions, participants read descriptions of 30 lawyers, each described by three sentences that implied different attributes. Participants in all conditions saw the same set of 90 sentences, which included 30 that implied attributes inconsistent with the stereotype of lawyers (e.g., "Larry has difficulty analyzing problems and developing logical solutions" implies unintelligent), 15 sentences that implied attributes consistent with the stereotype (e.g., "Ken often skips lunch and works overtime to finish projects" implies industrious), and 45 sentences that implied attributes irrelevant to the stereotype of lawyers (e.g., religious). In different conditions this identical set of sentences was distributed differently among the 30 lawyers. Most important, in the *dispersed* condition, the 30 counterstereotypic sentences were dispersed across all lawyers, so each had one disconfirming attribute. In contrast, in the *concentrated* condition, the 30 counterstereotypic attributes were all concentrated in 10 lawyers, such that this third of the lawyers each had 3 disconfirming attributes, whereas the remaining two-thirds had no disconfirming attributes.

Concentrating the disconfirming attributes within a small subgroup should make it easier to designate this group to an atypical subtype and, thereby, to dismiss its relevance to the overall stereotype. Indeed, participants in the concentrated condition appeared to show less stereotype change than did participants in the dispersed condition, who could not readily subtype the disconfirming individuals. Put differently, participants generalized less from the same examples of unlawyerly behavior when these examples were concentrated in a small subgroup of the observed lawyers than when they were dispersed across the entire sample. Other researchers have since replicated this finding (e.g., Johnston and Hewstone 1992). When we can, we subtype counterstereotypic individuals, and this enables us to maintain our global stereotypes.

It is easier to subtype and dismiss counterstereotypic individuals if they all share another common attribute that provides a good reason for viewing them as atypical. If, for example, the poorly dressed lawyers we encounter are all Black, it is easy to explain why they should differ from lawyers in general—perhaps they are pro bono lawyers, perhaps they come from impoverished backgrounds. With this explanation in mind, it seems reasonable to subtype them as atypical of lawyers as a whole, and it is then unnecessary to generalize from them to other lawyers. Indeed, several studies have shown that people are less likely to generalize from group members who disconfirm the stereotype on one dimension to the group as a whole when all of these counterstereotypic individuals also violate the stereotype on another dimension (Rothbart and Lewis 1988; Weber and Crocker 1983; Wilder, Simon, and Faith 1996). Put differently, individuals who disconfirm the stereotype of their group on one dimension are most likely to lead us to modify our stereotype if they are typical of their group's stereotype in all other ways. As assertive woman is most likely to provoke people into changing their stereotype of women as unassertive if she seems feminine in all other ways—wears makeup and feminine clothes, is warm and caring, and so on. An assertive woman who, in addition, dresses and behaves in a manner that violates the stereotype of women may provoke less stereotype change because she can so readily be subtyped as atypical and dismissed as irrelevant.

The subtyping of counterstereotypic individuals often results from an active attempt to maintain our stereotypes. We may be motivated to preserve our stereotypes because these help us to justify our social order, our own discriminatory behavior, or our sense of superiority to others (Allport 1954; Fein and Spencer 1997). But we may attempt to dismiss the relevance of counterstereotypic individuals to our stereotypes even in the absence of such motives. An individual who violates a well-entrenched stereotype may seem so surprising and improbable that we may attempt to explain this individual away, much like we do when we come across information that challenges any other expectancy that we harbor (Hastie 1984; Snyder 1984; Wong and Weiner 1981). For these reasons, when we encounter a member of a stereotyped group who violates our stereotype, we may ask ourselves, in effect, "Do I have any good reason for believing that this person is atypical of the group as a whole?" If the answer is positive, we may feel justified in not generalizing from the individual to the group. Recall that when we ask ourselves such one-sided questions, we tend to engage in an equally one-sided search for answers, which often biases us toward confirming our hypotheses (Klayman and Ha 1987; see chapter 3). Therefore, we will often find good reason for dismissing counter-stereotypic individuals as irrelevant.

As discussed above, if the counterstereotypic individuals possess another atypical attribute, this provides a good reason for subtyping and dismissing them as unrepresentative of their group. More recent research has shown that the additional attribute characterizing a stereotype-disconfirming individual can facilitate subtyping even if it is not atypical of the stereotype to begin with. We may be able to use even neutral information about a counterstereotypic person as grounds for viewing this person as atypical of his or her group (Kunda and Oleson 1995). For example, if we come across an outspoken, assertive woman who violates our stereotype of women as compliant and unassertive, we may feel compelled to revise our stereotype if we have no additional information about her. But we may be able to use any additional information about her as grounds for subtyping and dismissing her as atypical of women in general.

If we know, for example, that this assertive woman had (or did not have) brothers, that her parents were supportive (or unsupportive), that she was attractive (or unattractive), or if we have any other knowledge about her background, we may attempt to use this knowledge to explain why women with this particular attribute are, unlike most women, assertive. We are so good at generating explanations relating just about any attribute to just about any outcome that we should have little trouble coming up with a good explanation (e.g., Andersen and Sechler 1986; see chapter 3). We may theorize, for example, that women with brothers are likely to be assertive because they had the benefit of growing up with assertive role models. Or we may theorize that women without brothers are likely to be assertive because they had the benefit of growing up without being oppressed at home by domineering males. In either case, having successfully assigned the woman to an atypical subtype, we need not generalize from her to other women.

In one study designed to test these ideas, participants read an interview with a lawyer in which he came across as quite introverted, which challenged their stereotype of lawyers as outgoing (Kunda and Oleson 1995). Participants given no additional information about this lawyer did generalize from him to lawyers in general; they rated lawyers, on average, as more introverted than did control participants who had read no interview. A different pattern emerged for two additional groups that were given additional information about this introverted lawyer. One group was told that he worked for a small law firm, the other that he worked for a large law firm. Pretests had shown that lawyers who worked for small or large firms were not expected to differ in their introversion from other lawyers. In other words, participants in these two groups were given one of two opposite attributes that were both neutral in their implications for lawyers' introversion.

Although both these attributes were initially neutral, it is not difficult to construct an explanation for why either might make lawyers especially likely to be introverted. One may reason, for example, that either kind of lawyer may be able to get by despite being introverted—small-firm lawyers because they don't need to deal with many people and large-firm lawyers because in large firms some lawyers may be able to specialize in tasks that require few interpersonal skills. Either attribute, then, may be used as grounds for viewing the introverted lawyer as belonging to an atypical subtype. Indeed, unlike participants given no additional information about the introverted lawyer, those who were also told that he worked for a small or a large firm did not feel compelled to generalize from him; their stereotype of lawyers remained unchanged. In sum, participants generalized from a counterstereotypic individual when given no additional information about him. But providing them with an additional neutral attribute sufficed to undercut this generalization. In the process, the neutral attributes also lost their neutrality; they came to be viewed as associated with introversion. Together, these findings suggest that the neutral attributes undermined generalization from the counterstereotypic individual because they served as grounds for subtyping this individual as atypical.

Even if we have no further information that can be used as grounds for subtyping a counterstereotypic person, we may still be able to dismiss this person as an irrelevant exception if the person's deviation from our stereotype is extreme enough (Kunda and Oleson 1997). Consider Colin Powell, the African American general who orchestrated the successful execution of the Persian Gulf War, or Margaret Thatcher who ruled Britain with an iron fist. These individuals may violate our stereotypes of their groups so extremely that we may feel justified in viewing them as exceptions that don't prove the rule. We may believe that the sheer extremity of their deviance from our stereotypes provides us with a good enough reason for dismissing them as atypical and irrelevant.

In a series of studies that examined these ideas, participants read about a person who violated their stereotype either extremely or only moderately (Kunda and Oleson 1997). In one study, participants' stereotype of public relations (PR) agents as extraverted was challenged by a PR agent who was either extremely or only moderately introverted. In another study, participants' stereotypes of feminists as assertive were challenged by a feminist who was either extremely or only moderately unassertive. Stereotype change was assessed by comparing ratings of the stereotyped group made by these participants to those made by control participants who had not been exposed to any group member. In both cases, the person who deviated from the stereotype only moderately provoked greater stereotype change than did the person who deviated extremely.

Indeed, the extremely unassertive feminist provoked no stereotype change at all, whereas the moderately unassertive one did lead participants to view feminists as less assertive. If we want to change people's stereotypes of African Americans, we are more likely to succeed by introducing them to moderately successful African American individuals than by introducing them to extremely successful ones such as Colin Powell or Bill Cosby. These famous individuals deviate so extremely from their group's stereotype that people may view the sheer extremity of this deviation as a good enough reason for dismissing their relevance to the stereotype.

It is ironic that the more individuals deviate from the stereotype of their group, the less likely they are to bring about stereotype change. One disturbing implication is that the more inaccurate our stereotype of a group, the less likely it is to change spontaneously following encounters with group members. This is because the more inaccurate our stereotype, the more discrepant it will be from the typical group member. Put differently, the typical group member will deviate more extremely from more inaccurate stereotypes, and so will be dismissed more readily as an exception. This may be one reason why it is so difficult to change racial stereotypes through contact with individuals who disconfirm them (Stephan 1985). These stereotypes may be so inaccurate that average group members are perceived as extremely deviant from their group and, therefore, dismissed as extreme exceptions to the rule. It also follows that the individuals whose stereotypes one would like most to change, namely those holding extremely inaccurate negative stereotypes, will be the least likely to reduce the negativity of their stereotypes following exposure to group members who disconfirm them. For such extreme perceivers, the average group member will seem like an extreme and irrelevant deviant. Indeed, in these studies, extreme individuals became, if anything, even more extreme in their stereotypes following exposure to individuals who disconfirmed them.

On the positive side, the finding that people who moderately disconfirm perceivers' stereotypes of their group can provoke stereotype change is encouraging. In everyday life we may be more likely to encounter such moderate violations of our stereotypes than we are to encounter extreme violations. There are far more moderately assertive women than there are Margaret Thatchers. This may be why stereotypes can and do evolve over time.

Despite the difficulty of changing stereotypes through short-term interventions, examination of historical records and of the findings of longitudinal research suggest that over more extended time periods, dramatic changes in stereotypes can occur. Consider a group widely viewed as dirty, drunken, incompetent, brawling, slum-dwellers. You may be surprised to hear that this was the stereotype of the Irish in the United States in the mid-eighteen hundreds, when job ads specifying "No Irish need apply" were common (Sowell 1981). The stereotype of Irish Americans has clearly undergone dramatic change.

Other stereotypes have changed substantially as well. In a series of studies termed "The Princeton trilogy," different generations of Princeton students were asked to rate several ethnic groups on the same set of adjectives in 1933, 1951, and 1969 (Katz and Braly 1933; Gilbert 1951; Karlins, Coffman, and Walters 1969). Many of the stereotypes appeared to have changed considerably over this period. For example, there was a substantial decline in the extent to which Jews were seen as shrewd and mercenary, and an increase in the extent to which they were seen as ambitious and intelligent. And there was a dramatic decline in the extent to which Blacks were seen as superstitious and lazy, and an increase in the extent to which they were seen as musical. Admittedly, these changes may reflect not only actual changes in stereotypes but also changes in norms toward sanctioning open expression of prejudice (in itself, an encouraging development). Yet, when considered along with historical reports of stereotype change over the long run and experimental demonstrations that stereotype can be changed, these findings point to an optimistic outlook. Groups that are currently stereotyped inappropriately in negative terms may look forward with hope to a future in which they are subject to less prejudice and discrimination. As they gain greater insight into how people use their stereotypes and how they may come to change them, social psychologists may help bring this future about.

Summary

When we encounter a member of a stereotyped group or any information that we associate with this group, we may activate the group's stereotype automatically, with little awareness and intention. Once activated, the stereotype may color our judgments and behavior. Moreover, as we behave in keeping with the stereotype, we may cause the stereotyped individual to respond in kind, thereby fulfilling the stereotype. Stereotype activation may also be controlled in that it can require ample cognitive resources. Therefore, information that might lead us to activate stereotypes spontaneously when we have sufficient cognitive resources may fail to provoke stereotype activation when we are preoccupied with other tasks.

People may differ in their automatic reactions to a particular group. Whereas prejudiced White individuals may experience automatic negative reactions to any information that reminds them of African Americans, nonprejudiced White individuals and African Americans have no such automatic negative reactions, and may have automatic positive reactions instead.

Sometimes we may be able to inhibit the activation of stereotypes if we are motivated to do so. For example, when we are motivated to think highly of an individual, we may inhibit any applicable negative stereotype that, if activated, might interfere with our desired impression. Although we may successfully inhibit stereotypes over the short term, such inhibition may backfire in the long run; the previously inhibited stereotype may become hyperaccessible once we are no longer concentrating on inhibiting it.

We sometimes use group stereotypes to make sense of the behavior of group members. We may understand the identical behavior quite differently when it is performed by members of different social groups. Such stereotype-driven construals may take place automatically, without any intention or awareness on our part. We may often believe that our reactions to a stereotyped individual are free of prejudice because they are based on the individual's behavior and attributes rather than on the stereotype; we may not realize that the very meaning of these behaviors and attributes has been colored by the stereotype.

We apply a group stereotype to a member of that group when all we know about this individual is the group membership. However, when we have additional individuating information about a stereotyped person such as a behavior or a trait, we tend to base our impressions of this person only on this information, ignoring the stereotype. Nevertheless, the stereotype may still color our impressions of the individual by influencing our construal of the individuating information and our expectations about the individual's future behavior. When our cognitive resources are strained because we are tired, preoccupied, under time pressure, or for any other reason, our impressions of stereotyped individuals may be especially likely to be colored by our stereotypes. We may also be especially likely to use applicable negative stereotypes when evaluating an individual if we are motivated, for whatever reason, to disparage that individual.

Members of negatively stereotyped groups may find it difficult to determine whether others' evaluations of them reflect an assessment of their own performance or a reaction to their group membership. This *attributional ambiguity* may leave them insecure about their own abilities. They may also be hampered by *stereotype threat*; their fear that they may confirm others' negative expectations about them and their group may be debilitating enough to undermine their performance. Subtle manipulations that eliminate stereotype threat in test situations also eliminate the performance gaps that otherwise obtain between Black and White students and between female and male students.

It is very difficult to change well-entrenched stereotypes. Often, these persist even in the face of extensive interactions with members of the stereotyped group who violate the stereotype. One reason we do not modify our stereotypes in the face of individuals who disconfirm them is that we may allocate such individuals to atypical subtypes of the group. We may be able to maintain our overall dislike for a group even though "some of my best friends" belong to it, if the "best friends" are fenced off as atypical of the disliked group. We may be especially likely to subtype individuals who violate the stereotype of their group if we have or can readily construct a justification for viewing them as atypical.

Much of our social behavior is governed by our beliefs about other people's likely reactions. What will they think? What will they do? Our ability to answer such questions accurately may determine the quality of our decisions and the effectiveness of our interpersonal strategies. Just how good are we then at estimating our peers' likely attitudes, beliefs, and habits? How good are we at predicting people's future behavior when we know how they have behaved in the past? This chapter addresses these questions.

In the first section of this chapter, I examine our ability to assess the popularity of various attitudes, norms, and behaviors. I point to some systematic biases that color our attempts to determine how many people share our reactions, so that we sometimes exaggerate and sometimes underestimate the extent to which others react like we do. I also note that we are nevertheless capable of estimating the distributions of various reactions in the population with reasonable accuracy.

In the next section, I examine our ability to assess people's character and to predict their future behavior from our observations of their past behavior. I first review evidence showing that there is surprisingly little consistency in people's friendliness, honesty, or any other personality trait from one situation to other, different situations. I then show that we often fail to realize this, and tend to assume that behavior is far more consistent and predictable than it really is. As a result, when we observe people's behavior, we jump to conclusions about their underlying personality far too readily and have much more confidence than we should in our ability to predict their behavior in other settings.

Knowledge about the Prevalence and Distribution of Attributes in the Population

Do you suppose you know what percentage of college students favor equal rights for women? What percentage feel depressed frequently? Do you know how common it is for college students to get drunk? How most students feel about the drinking norms on their campus? Can you predict how your peers will react if you approach them with a small request? We often use our beliefs about others' thoughts, feelings, and behavior to guide our own behavior. Consider the social knowledge that you must use if you plan to throw a party for your friends. What music are your friends likely to enjoy? How much are they likely to eat? How many alcoholic and non-alcoholic drinks are they likely to consume? When can you expect them to arrive? How late will they stay? Your beliefs about their values and opinions may also guide your conduct at the party. What will they think of you if you drink too much? What if you drink too little? Which jokes will they laugh at and which will they find offensive? How will they react if you kiss your romantic partner in public?

Just how good are we at answering such questions? Dozens of studies have examined the accuracy of people's knowledge about other people's attributes. In discussing this research, I will first describe some systematic biases that we show when estimating others' attributes, and then I will discuss our overall accuracy, given these biases.

False Consensus

Imagine that you are enrolled in an introductory psychology class that requires you to participate in several experiments. To fulfill this requirement, you sign up for a study on communication techniques. When you arrive at the designated place, the experimenter explains that the study concerns people's reactions to messages presented on sandwich boards. You are asked to put on a sandwich board that carries the sign "Repent" and walk around campus for 30 minutes, keeping track of people's reactions. The experimenter explains that if you are not willing to do this, you will still get your experimental credit although you will miss a chance to have an interesting experience and to do the experimenters a big favor.

Would you choose to wear the sign or to withdraw from the experiment? What percent of your peers do you estimate would choose to wear the sign?

When Lee Ross and his colleagues put Stanford students in exactly this situation, about half agreed to wear the sign and half refused (Ross, Greene, and House 1977). More interesting, participants' estimates of others' likely reactions depended on their own choices: Those who agreed to wear the sign estimated that 63 percent of their peers would also agree to wear it, whereas those who refused to wear the sign estimated that only 23 percent of their peers would agree to wear it. Ross and his colleagues termed this phenomenon the *false consensus effect*. False consensus exists when people's own choices, attitudes, or beliefs bias their estimates of those of other people, leading them to view their own reactions as relatively common while viewing alternative reactions as relatively uncommon. False consensus is revealed when people making a particular choice consider this choice more common than do people making the opposite choice.

False consensus has been shown to color people's estimates of the prevalence of just about any choice, attitude, or behavior that has been examined, in domains as diverse as everyday habits and preferences, personality traits, and political opinions. For example, fans of white bread think more people would choose white bread over brown bread than do fans of brown bread, optimists believe optimism is more common than do pessimists, Americans who prefer the Republican presidential candidate believe that support for the Republican is more widespread than do those who prefer the Democratic candidate, and those who support cuts in public spending believe that more people support such cuts than do those who oppose them (for reviews, see Krueger 1998; Marks and Miller 1987; Mullen et al. 1985).

It is important to understand that false consensus is a *relative* effect. You don't have to believe that your own group is in the majority to show false consensus. If, for example, you belong to the minority of filmgoers who prefer European dramas to American comedies, you may recognize that you are in the minority, and estimate that only 20 percent of filmgoers share your preference for European dramas. Yet your estimate of the proportion of people who prefer European dramas could still be higher than the estimates made by people who prefer American comedies, who might think that only 10 percent of the population prefer European dramas. Moreover, false consensus can exist even if you do not overestimate the proportion of people who share your responses (relative to the actual proportion). To continue with the movie example, the set of judgments described above would reflect false consensus even if the actual proportion of people who preferred European dramas was 30 percent. In this case, even fans of European dramas (who estimate that 20 percent of the population share their preference) are underestimating the actual proportion of people who prefer European dramas. But they think preference for European dramas is more common than do people who prefer American comedies (who estimate that only 10 percent of the population prefer European dramas). This set of judgments would be considered an example of false consensus because false consensus is defined as a difference between the estimates of people with different opinions, or as a positive correlation between one's own opinions and one's estimate of other people's.

Why do we show the false consensus effect? A host of factors combine to bias our estimates of the prevalence of our own beliefs and preferences (see Gilovich 1991; Marks and Miller 1987). One reason for the correlation between our own reactions and our estimates of those of other people is that when we know nothing about other people's responses, we may quite reasonably base our estimates on the one individual whose responses we are familiar with, namely our own self (Dawes 1989). However, the false consensus effect is unlikely to be due only to inference from our own responses. We may show the false consensus effect even when we are familiar with the responses of many other individuals as well, because the samples available to us may be biased; we may simply be more familiar with people like us. Jocks hang out with other jocks,

Republicans socialize with other Republicans, and churchgoers meet like-minded individuals at church. Recall that we often rely on the availability heuristic when making our estimates of the prevalence of different kinds of responses, basing our estimates on the ease with which we can conjure up examples of each kind of response (Kahneman and Tversky 1973; see chapter 3). The fact that individuals who react like we do come more readily to mind could therefore lead us to overestimate the prevalence of our own reactions. Support for the notion that the availability heuristic plays a role in producing the false consensus effect comes from the finding that people's estimates of the prevalence of smoking are correlated with the number of people they know who smoke—the more smokers you know personally, the more common you believe smoking to be (Sherman et al. 1983).

Motivation may also contribute to false consensus. I may feel better about my own reactions and opinions if I believe that many others share them. This motivation may be especially strong if I have just experienced failure—my failure may seem less humiliating if many others have experienced similar failure. Indeed, following a failure experience, people are especially likely to show the false consensus effect (Sherman, Presson, and Chassin 1984).

The extent to which we show false consensus may also depend on our theories about the causes that underlie our choices. If we believe that our own reactions are governed by external forces, we will be especially likely to expect others to react like we do because we assume that they are subject to the same forces that govern us. But if we believe that our reactions are due to our own idiosyncratic quirks, we will be less likely to expect others to react like we do. Indeed, it has been shown that when people are asked to estimate others' choices, they show greater false consensus for choices that they think depend mostly on the characteristics of the two choice options (e.g., choosing between purchasing stock in Exxon or in IBM) than for choices that they think depend mostly on their own personal characteristics and idiosyncrasies (e.g., choosing between watching gymnastics or track and field). When we assume that our own choices are dictated by powerful aspects of the situation, we expect that others will succumb to the same forces and make the same choices we do (Gilovich, Jennings, and Jennings 1983).

Another reason for false consensus is that we often interpret the questions we are asked in idiosyncratic ways. If we do not realize that the same questions are open to multiple construals, and that others' construals may differ from our own, we may exaggerate the extent to which others will react like us. For example, when you are asked whether you prefer American comedies to European dramas, you may have in mind a choice between witty classics of American comedy such as Woody Allen's *Annie Hall* and incomprehensible surrealistic European fare. Not only will you vote for *Annie Hall*, you will expect most people to do the same. What you may not realize is that other people may construe the same question quite differently. Another person may construe American comedies to mean vacuous summer fare such as *Ernest goes to Camp*, and construe European dramas to mean engaging classics such as *The Bicycle Thief*. With these construals in mind, you too might have come out on the side of the Europeans. False consensus, then, may arise because different people construe the same choices differently, and people fail to recognize this fact and to make allowances for it when estimating others' likely reactions. Consistent with this view, Gilovich (1990) obtained greater false consensus when participants were given a choice between two broadly defined categories that were open to multiple construals (e.g., between an American and a European snack) than when they were given a choice between specific examples of these broad categories that left little room for further construal (e.g., between apple pie and chocolate mousse). However, the evidence for the role of construal in producing false consensus remains tentative because in two subsequent studies false consensus was as large for participants given specific construals to choose from as it had been for participants given more general choice categories (Gilovich 1990).

In summary, many factors act in concert to produce false consensus. Our inferential heuristics, our causal theories, our motives, and our unique construals all contribute to our tendency to expect others to react like we do. This tendency is further exacerbated by our failure to appreciate the impact that these factors exert on our estimates of others' likely reactions. The end result is that we often exaggerate the extent to which others share our opinions, and we believe our opinions to be far more common than do people holding different opinions. There are also circumstances, however, when we show the opposite tendency, and exaggerate our uniqueness, as discussed next.

Pluralistic Ignorance

Imagine that you are sitting in class, baffled and confused, unable to make any sense of the lecture. The professor pauses to ask if there are any questions. Mortified at the thought that you might come across as a fool, you say nothing. As you look around the classroom, none of the other students seems to be in any difficulty. They all look confident and composed. Not a single hand is raised. You are now convinced that you are the only one who hasn't been following the lecture. What is curious about this conclusion is that your own behavior is identical to that of everyone else. It is just that you interpret it differently: You believe that you are remaining silent because you are embarrassed to show how little you understand, yet you assume that everyone else is silent because they understand the lecture and need no further clarification. If everyone reasons like you do, it is quite possible to have a situation in which nobody is understanding the lecture, but everyone believes they are the only one experiencing any difficulty. Such failure on the part of most people to realize that others' share their own private reactions has been termed *pluralistic ignorance.*

The term pluralistic ignorance was coined by Floyd Allport (1933) to describe a situation in which almost everyone privately rejects a group norm, yet believes that most other group members accept it. In one early example of pluralistic ignorance, members of a strict Methodist church assumed that most other members endorsed the church's prohibitions against card playing, smoking, and alcohol. Yet, in fact, most members privately rejected these prohibitions and practiced the banned behaviors in the privacy of their own homes (Schanck 1932). Pluralistic ignorance was fostered in this case because members' public behavior did not reflect their private attitudes; publicly they voiced stronger support than they actually felt for the dictates of the church. Although each member realized that he or she expressed public support for these norms out of fear of disapproval and rejection, each assumed that others expressed support for these norms because they truly embraced them.

As these examples illustrate, the stage for pluralistic ignorance is set when people's public behavior does not reflect their private attitudes. Such a mismatch between public and private reactions will breed pluralistic ignorance if people assume that their own private reactions differ from those of others despite the fact that their public behavior is identical. They may assume, for example, that their own behavior is driven by fear of rejection or embarrassment while assuming that other people's identical behavior reflects their genuine attitudes and beliefs. Even when people realize that their own behavior belies their true feelings, they may take others' identical behavior at face value.

Why would we attribute our own and others' identical behaviors to different causes? We may do so because we simply do not realize that others are just as prone to fear and embarrassment as we are; we are keenly aware of our own fears and insecurities but have little evidence of the fears and insecurities of others. This is especially true in cases where we all try to hide our own fears and keep them private, and successfully come across as far more calm and composed than we really are. Moreover, even if we recognize others' fears, we may fail to realize what powerful motivators these fears are. For example, we may assume mistakenly that other students' need to understand the professor will override their fear of revealing their lack of understanding (Miller and McFarland 1987; Miller and Prentice 1994; Prentice and Miller 1996).

Pluralistic ignorance may be one reason why bystanders become less likely to intervene in an emergency when they are in the presence of others. It has been shown that when coming across a person in distress or when confronted with a potentially dangerous occurrence such as smoke filtering into their room, people are less likely to lend a helping hand or to take risk-preventing action if others are present than if they are alone (Latane and Darley 1970). As such emergencies occur, people may appear outwardly calm and collected despite their inner confusion and fear. Others take these calm appearances at face value, and assume that no one is particularly concerned about what is taking place. In this manner, emergency situations give rise to pluralistic ignorance about the true reactions of others and their construals of the situation. A group of people experiencing inner turmoil may each assume that everyone else sees little reason for concern. Each may then fail to act on their own true feelings because they accept the majority's construal as reality, or because they are afraid of coming across as foolishly fearful and panicky and becoming the target of scorn and derision.

There are many documented cases of pluralistic ignorance about a diverse range of beliefs, opinions, and values (for reviews, see Miller and McFarland 1991; Miller and Prentice 1994; Prentice and Miller 1996). Pluralistic ignorance can occur among transient groups of strangers thrown together in an emergency, among closely knit groups of individuals who know each other well, among members of large organizations such as universities, and in society at large. In different studies it has been shown, for example, that prison guards thought other guards were more strongly in favor of harsh disciplinary practices than they themselves were, that students at a notoriously liberal college (Vassar, circa 1972) assumed that most other students at the college were more liberal than they themselves were, and that, as the civil rights movement in America gained force, White Americans assumed that other Whites supported segregation more strongly than they themselves did (for a review, see Miller and McFarland 1991).

A particularly disturbing aspect of pluralistic ignorance is that it can breed widespread conformity to norms that no one actually believes in. This may not be of much concern when the norms are prosocial and represent the moral high ground. But pluralistic ignorance can also lead people to conform to antisocial, dangerous norms. For example, one study of juvenile delinquents found that each was privately uncomfortable with his own antisocial behavior but was reluctant to express these feelings to the others (Matza 1964). Not wanting to appear "chicken" to their seemingly tough peers, the boys engaged in mischief that none was actually comfortable with.

A series of studies by Deborah Prentice and Dale Miller demonstrated similar pluralistic ignorance among Princeton students about the extent to which their fellow students were comfortable with the drinking norms that prevailed on their campus (Prentice and Miller 1993). Alcohol has long been central to social life at Princeton. The eating clubs, which are at the center of social life on campus, have alcohol on tap around the clock and rely on drinking games when selecting and initiating new members. When compared to other major events in the United States, the level of alcohol consumption at Princeton alumni reunions is second only to that at the Indianapolis 500 (Prentice and Miller 1993). The norms at Princeton, as at many other North American campuses, are quite clear: Alcohol consumption is essential to social life, and one must be comfortable with it if one wants to participate fully in social events on campus.

At the same time, students cannot but notice the problems caused by excessive alcohol consumption. The deaths of students from alcohol-related poisoning or accidents receive considerable attention in the national media. In 1997, for example, there were highly publicized cases of students dying after drinking heavily at campus or fraternity parties at MIT, at the University of Virginia, at Louisiana State University, and on several other campuses as well (*Chronicle of Higher Education*, 1.4.1998). Following just about every weekend, students' newspapers on many campuses report cases of students arriving at emergency rooms with alcohol poisoning or alcohol-related injuries. Many students have also undoubtedly witnessed or experienced firsthand cases in which heavy drinking led to inappropriate behavior, memory losses, illness or injury, and declining academic performance. All this led Prentice and Miller to suspect that alcohol norms at Princeton would provide a perfect setting for pluralistic ignorance: Students would privately have doubts and misgivings about the strong pro-alcohol norms on campus but would not realize that others shared these misgivings. This was indeed the case. When students were asked how comfortable they were with the drinking habits at Princeton and how comfortable the average Princeton undergraduate was with these habits, their responses revealed pluralistic ignorance: Students believed that they themselves were far less comfortable than the average Princeton student with the alcohol drinking habits of Princeton undergraduates (Prentice and Miller 1993).

Clearly, then, there was a gap between students' own feelings about alcohol use and their beliefs about how their peers felt. What is likely to happen to such a gap over time, as students gain greater familiarity with their peers and their institution, and greater experience with alcohol? One disturbing possibility is that the students might come to accept the norm they assume everyone else subscribes to; their private beliefs may shift toward the perceived norms. Alternatively, as they remain keenly aware of the harmful effects of excessive drinking, students may persist in their belief that they are less comfortable than others with the drinking norms; the gap between their private feelings and their beliefs about others' feelings may persist, and they may come to experience increasing alienation from the group. To examine these possibilities, Prentice and Miller surveyed second-year Princeton undergraduates twice: Once in September, when they had just returned from summer vacation and had little recent exposure to the norms and behavior of their fellow students, and then again in December, after they had spent several months on campus. On both occasions, students were asked about their own and the average Princeton undergraduate's level of comfort with the alcohol drinking habits of students on campus.

At the beginning of the term, in September, both men and women revealed pluralistic ignorance about their peers' feelings, as may be seen in table 9.1. Both groups thought that they themselves were less comfortable than the average Princeton undergraduate with the drinking habits on campus. However, men and women responded

Table 9.1 Students' ratings of their own and the average student's comfort with alcohol drinking on campus

	SEPTEMBER		DECEMBER	
	SELF	AVERAGE STUDENT	SELF	AVERAGE STUDENT
Women	6.08	7.16	5.94	7.74
Men	5.84	7.48	7.08	7.58

Source: From Prentice and Miller (1993, table 3, p. 248). Copyright © (1993) by the American Psychological Association. Reprinted with permission.
Note: Higher numbers indicate greater comfort.

differently to the gap between their own feelings and their beliefs about the feelings of other students. By December, men had brought their own attitudes in line with the perceived norm; their own level of comfort with alcohol habits increased, and there was no longer a gap between their own feelings and their beliefs about the feelings of their peers. In short, the mistaken assumptions that male students entertained about their fellow students in September had become a reality by December. In contrast, female students did not come to internalize the norm. For women, there remained a gap even in December between their own feelings and their beliefs about the feelings of their fellow students.

It is difficult to nail down the exact reason why Princeton men and women reacted differently to the gap between their private feelings and the norm they perceived. It is possible that men in general are more vulnerable to conformity pressures, that they are especially vulnerable to such pressures in the domain of alcohol use which may be more central to male than to female culture, or that identifying with Princeton, an institution that had long been dominated by men, was more important to Princeton men than to Princeton women (Prentice and Miller 1993). Although they differed, both the reactions of men and of women carried potentially harmful consequences. Men came to embrace potentially dangerous norms despite their initial discomfort with these norms. And women, who continued to believe that their own feelings deviated from the norm, may have come to experience increasing alienation. Indeed, a follow-up study revealed that the belief that one deviates from one's group may breed alienation and promote disidentification with the group. Princeton students who perceived a gap between their own feelings about alcohol-related issues and the feelings of the average student on these issues were less likely than students who perceived no such gap to identify with Princeton; they expected to attend fewer Princeton reunions after they graduated (Prentice and Miller 1993).

Imagine that you are a student on a campus where alcohol dominates social life. Personally you feel quite uncomfortable with the pro-alcohol norms on campus, but you have been reluctant to reveal these feelings because you believe that most other students are far more comfortable with these norms than you are. Moreover, you often feel compelled to drink more alcohol than you would like to so as to avoid derision and social isolation. How do you suppose you would be affected by a lecture on pluralistic ignorance that included a presentation of data revealing that most students are privately uncomfortable with these norms but do not realize that others share their discomfort? Would you feel liberated by this knowledge? Would you now feel free to drink as little as you are comfortable with?

In a study designed to address this question, entering Princeton students were assigned to participate, during their first week on campus, in one of two sessions about alcohol use (Schroeder and Prentice 1995, reported in Prentice and Miller 1996). One included a discussion that focused on pluralistic ignorance. Participants were shown data about the discrepancy between students' own comfort with drinking alcohol and their beliefs about others' comfort with alcohol, and discussed the likely consequences of the misperceptions of others' attitudes. Participants in the other, control, condition also discussed alcohol use, but their discussion focused on how individuals can make responsible decisions about drinking alcohol; they learned nothing about pluralistic ignorance on this issue. Four to six months after these discussions, all participants were asked to report on their alcohol consumption in the past week and in the typical week.

Remarkably, dispelling pluralistic ignorance had a substantial impact on alcohol consumption: Students who had participated in the discussion of pluralistic ignorance about attitudes toward alcohol reported drinking substantially fewer drinks per week than did those who had participated in the control discussion. Follow-up analyses suggested that this occurred at least in part because students who had learned about pluralistic ignorance felt less social pressure to drink excessively.

In summary, there are many situations in which our public behavior misrepresents our private sentiments. In such situations, we may remain ignorant of the fact that others share our sentiments. Believing that others embrace norms that we personally reject, we may become all the more reluctant to reveal our private opinions, for fear of public embarrassment and social ostracism. If everyone behaves as we do, and none of us realizes that everyone else's behavior is driven by the same fears and insecurities that are driving us, pluralistic ignorance will persist. This may lead to the perpetuation of norms and behaviors that are in reality quite unpopular. However, this cycle depends on our remaining ignorant of others' true opinions. Once we become aware of each other's true sentiments, we will no longer feel pressure to conform to norms that none of us really embraces. This analyses suggests that polls of public opinion which have become central to modern democracies may play an important role in reducing pluralistic ignorance and preventing widespread adherence to norms and behaviors that are in fact unpopular.

False Consensus versus Pluralistic Ignorance

On the face of it, pluralistic ignorance, which refers to our tendency to underestimate the extent to which others share our views, appears to conflict with false consensus, which refers to our tendency to see more support for our views than do people holding opposite views. It is important to note, however, that this conflict is only apparent. It is quite possible to have pluralistic ignorance and false consensus at the same time. This is because false consensus is a relative effect which occurs when people holding a given attitude think that this attitude is more prevalent than do people holding the opposite attitude, whereas pluralistic ignorance is an absolute effect which occurs when people think their own attitude is less prevalent than it really is. For example, students who are uncomfortable with alcohol use may believe that such discomfort is more widespread than do students who are comfortable with alcohol; this would be a false consensus effect. At the same time, students who are uncomfortable with alcohol may underestimate the actual prevalence of discomfort with alcohol; this would be an example of pluralistic ignorance. Indeed, the studies of pluralistic ignorance about students' comfort with alcohol also revealed false consensus (Prentice and Miller 1993).

It is also the case, however, that factors that facilitate pluralistic ignorance may sometimes undermine false consensus. Pluralistic ignorance occurs when, even though our own behavior is identical to that of others, we attribute it to different causes. Such divergent attributions are especially likely when we attribute our own behavior to embarrassment and assume that we are far more driven by such embarrassment than other people are (Miller and McFarland 1991). Recall that false consensus is least likely to occur when we attribute our behavior to relatively idiosyncratic causes (Gilovich et al. 1983). Therefore, situations in which one attributes one's own reactions to relatively idiosyncratic insecurities should be especially likely to breed false uniqueness and especially unlikely to yield false consensus.

Research on false consensus and on pluralistic ignorance has focused on uncovering errors and biases in our beliefs about others' sentiments and behaviors, and there is compelling evidence that such errors and biases are widespread. Does it follow that we are completely ignorant about others' reactions? Is there any truth to our beliefs about other people's attitudes, behaviors, and values? The studies on false consensus and pluralistic ignorance were designed to detect bias and error; they do not provide a means of assessing how well-calibrated we are, if at all, when assessing people's reactions in a wide range of domains. Other studies have addressed this question, as discussed next.

Knowledge of Social Distributions

It seems that if we are to function effectively in our social worlds, we must have at least some knowledge of the distributions of important opinions, values, and behaviors. If we wish to follow accepted norms of behavior and want to avoid offending others, we must have some sense of the values and beliefs of the typical person. Such knowledge is also necessary for inferences about the meaning of an individual's reaction. If you are aware, for example, of the typical attitudes toward health care in the United States and in Canada, you will recognize that an American who voices support for socialized medicine holds radical opinions whereas a Canadian who voices the same support holds mainstream views; even though their attitudes are identical, you may therefore infer that the American is a revolutionary and the Canadian a conformist.

When planning our social interactions, we also need to have a sense of how behaviors and attitudes are distributed across the spectrum of possible reactions. When you propose a new initiative, you need to know not only how the average person will respond to it but also how many people will embrace it enthusiastically and how many will oppose it vehemently. And when you encounter someone whose behavior or attitudes deviate from the norm, you will be able to understand this person better if you also know whether he or she is part of a sizable minority or is but an aberrant exception.

To assess the accuracy of people's knowledge about social distributions, Richard Nisbett and I asked University of Michigan undergraduates for their beliefs about the distributions of a wide range of attitudes and behaviors among their peers (Nisbett and

Kunda 1985). Participants were asked to imagine that 100 of their fellow students were asked to report their liking for items such as McDonald's hamburgers, Saudi Arabians, the movie *Star Wars*, and the Moral Majority; their opinions on current issues such as drug use by students, the availability of abortion on demand, and the conduct of then-president Ronald Reagan; and the frequency with which they performed behaviors such as attending religious services, attending concerts, playing tennis, drinking alcoholic beverages, and feeling blue. Participants were given a scale such as the following:

Dislike very much	Dislike somewhat	Neither like nor dislike	Like somewhat	Like very much

Participants were asked, for each item, to distribute the 100 students among the possible response options on the appropriate scale, that is, to indicate how many of the 100 would choose each option. From these estimated distributions, we were able to calculate each participant's beliefs about the average response and the variability of responses, and we were able to assess each participant's beliefs about the shape of each distribution. Participants also indicated their own responses to each of the items. From these, we were able to assess the actual distributions of opinions and behaviors.

How accurate were participants' estimates? We found that, despite some systematic biases, the students were remarkably well calibrated about the average reactions of their fellow students as well as about the distributions of these reactions, as shown in figure 9.1. When each participant's estimates of the mean response to each item were correlated, across items, with the actual means, the average correlations were moderately to highly positive, ranging from .42 to .73 for different items. Participants recognized correctly, for example, that their fellow students liked Saudi Arabians better than they liked the Moral Majority and that they got drunk more frequently than they played tennis. Their absolute accuracy was impressive as well. On average, students' estimates of the

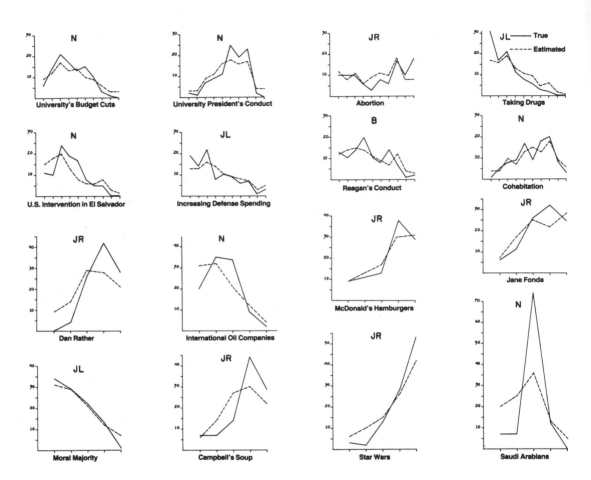

Figure 9.1 Actual and estimated distributions of attitudes. Letters at the top of each distribution denote its shape: N = normal, JL = J left, JR = J right, B = bimodal. From Nisbett and Kunda (1985, fig. 2, p. 305). Copyright © (1985) by the American Psychological Association. Reprinted with permission.

mean of each distribution were only about one scale point away from the actual mean for 10-point scales and about half a scale point off for 5-point scales.

Participants' estimates about dispersion were also fairly accurate. As for the means, there were moderate positive correlations between estimated and actual measures of dispersion (i.e., standard deviations). Participants recognized correctly, for example, that students varied more in the frequency with which they attended religious services than in the frequency with which they attended movies. As may be seen in figure 9.1, participants also tended to be accurate about the shapes of the different distributions, correctly producing distributions shaped like the actual ones, be they normal bell-curved distributions (e.g., university budget cuts), distributions skewed strongly to the right (e.g., McDonald's hamburgers), or distributions skewed strongly to the left (e.g., taking drugs).

This impressive accuracy was found despite the presence of some systematic biases. For example, there was a clear false consensus effect, revealed by a positive correlation between participants' own opinions and their estimates of the average opinion. This suggests that participants used their own positions on each issue as one source of information about others' positions. There was also a tendency to somewhat overestimate dispersion, most likely because people with extreme reactions may be more salient and available in mind than people with more moderate reactions. Taken together, these results suggest that our own attitudes and behaviors as well as those of other highly salient others may somewhat bias our estimates of social distributions, but will not blind us to social reality. The biases were systematic and reliable, but they were relatively modest in magnitude, and occurred within a context of substantial overall accuracy.

Most likely, the impressive accuracy resulted from students' familiarity with the behaviors and opinions of their peers. Indeed, other research has shown that we tend to be more accurate about highly familiar groups to which we belong than we are about less familiar out-groups. In one study, engineering and business majors at the University of Colorado were each asked to estimate the distributions of eight traits and attitudes among engineering majors and among business majors, and each also indicated their own positions on these items (Judd, Ryan, and Park 1991). The items were all stereotypic either of engineering majors (e.g., analytical and reserved) or of business majors (e.g., extraverted and impulsive).

When students' estimates of the means and standard deviations for these items were compared to the actual means and standard deviations, it appeared that the students were more accurate about their in-group than about the out-group; both business majors and engineering majors were more accurate about the distributions of traits and attitudes within their own major than within the other major. Overall accuracy, even for out-groups, was substantial for estimates of means and more moderate for estimates of standard deviations. Despite the accuracy, there existed systematic biases— participants tended to exaggerate the extent to which the two groups conformed to their group stereotypes, and were especially likely to do so for the out-group. For example, business majors showed much greater overestimation of the extent to which engineering majors conformed to the engineering stereotype than did engineering majors. Participants' greater familiarity with members of their in-group may have led them to base their estimates on these familiar members rather than on the group's stereotype. This may also be why they were more accurate about in-groups than about out-groups.

In summary, we can be remarkably accurate about the distributions of important social variables such as attitudes, traits, and behaviors within large social groups. We will be especially accurate if we are familiar with the social group in question. This is true despite the fact that our estimates of the distributions of other people's responses can be biased by our own responses, by the responses of other salient individuals, by our stereotypes of the social group they belong to, and, in all likelihood, by many other factors as well. This is not to say that we will always be accurate; as discussed earlier, we are certainly capable of substantial errors, and may be completely off the mark in many of our estimates. But it does appear that for many of the issues that we are likely to come across when interacting with others, we do have at least a rough idea of where others stand on these issues; for the most part, we typically have the kind of knowledge needed to guide our social conduct.

So far I have focused on knowledge about the prevalence and distribution of attributes in the population. I turn next to a discussion of knowledge about the very nature of attributes. As discussed earlier, such knowledge can influence our willingness to assume that others share our reactions; we will be less likely to assume such consensus when we believe that our reactions are driven by our own enduring, idiosyncratic dispositions than when we believe that our reactions are governed by external forces powerful enough to sway anyone. Knowledge about the nature of attributes, especially personality traits, is also important for many other inferences we draw about people, as discussed next.

Knowledge about the Consistency of Traits

My dad is really dependable. Watch out for Albert, he's not very honest. I wish Sarah weren't so shy. When describing what other people are like, we rely heavily on personality traits (at least in Western cultures; for cultural differences, see chapter 11). The central role that traits play in our impressions of others is supported not only by everyday experience but also by numerous studies (for a review, see Ross and Nisbett 1991). For example, when Bernadette Park asked students enrolled in a small seminar to provide detailed (and confidential) descriptions of each other, she found that traits clearly dominated their impressions (Park 1986). Traits such as humorous, intelligent, and easy going accounted for fully 65 percent of the information included in the students' descriptions. The next most frequently used category, behaviors such as "dyed her hair pink" and "would enjoy playing strategic games such as chess" accounted for only 23 percent of the information, and reliance on any other kind of information was negligible. Evidently we assume that personality is best captured and conveyed through traits. Our fondness for traits is also reflected in the English language. If you go through an English dictionary, as Allport and Odbert did in 1936, you will find more than 4,000 different words denoting personality traits.

We also use traits to make sense of other people's behavior. We spontaneously understand behaviors in terms of their underlying traits. When we hear that Christine didn't leave a tip at the restaurant, we understand that she is stingy, and when we hear that Roy carried an old woman' groceries home for her, we understand that he is helpful (Winter and Uleman 1984). When trying to understand why others behaved as they did, we turn, once again, to traits. We assume that Josh attacked other kids on the playground because he is aggressive, and that Lynn cheated on her taxes because she is dishonest (Miller 1984).

When we use a trait to describe someone, we are implying a stable underlying disposition, consistent across time and situations. When we say that Christine, who failed to leave a tip, is stingy, we are conveying expectations about her likely future behavior: We expect that she won't leave a tip on her next visit to a restaurant either. More generally, we expect her to show *temporal stability*, that is, to demonstrate consistent behavior from one situation to the same situation at different times. We expect her stinginess to manifest itself in other ways as well; we may expect her to buy cheap Christmas gifts and to give little to charity. More generally, we expect her to show *cross-situational consistency*, that is, to demonstrate consistent behavior from one situation to different situations that are presumed to tap the same trait. Such consistency across time and situations is central to the meaning of traits. If trait-related behavior is not consistent in these ways, the trait becomes meaningless; it does not permit any inferences from current behavior to behavior in future situations.

Because traits are so central to ordinary people's theories of personality (as well as to the theories of many personality psychologists), it is of great importance to find out just how consistent our trait-related behaviors really are, and it is of great interest to determine the accuracy of our beliefs about the consistency of traits. These topics have received a considerable amount of research attention, and have been at the focus of heated debates. To presage my conclusions, decades of research on these issues suggest that we tend to see far more consistency than there really is in people's trait-related behavior.

The Actual Consistency of Traits

Cross-situational Consistency Is Low If Rachel was friendly at dinner yesterday, will she also be friendly at dinner today? Will she be friendly in the dentist's waiting room? On a job interview? At a party? Just how consistent is Rachel's, or anyone else's, friendliness across time and situations? How might one go about answering this question? We could ask Rachel to tell us how consistent she is, or ask her mother and best friend to tell us about her consistency, but this wouldn't really be good enough. Their answers might reflect their beliefs and theories about Rachel's consistency (which may or may not be correct) rather than her actual consistency. To determine the actual consistency of behavior, we must go out and examine actual behavior, in real-life situations. If we wish to assess the consistency of friendliness, we need to measure the friendliness of many people in a variety of situations. Such measurement will enable us to determine the extent to which friendliness in one situation is correlated with friendliness in another situation—are the people who are more friendly than average at dinner parties also more friendly than average in doctors' waiting rooms?

Needless to say, such a study is extremely difficult to conduct. Just consider the logistics: One must find a community of people who all participate in a variety of events, and one must then follow these people from one event to another and rate the extent to which the behavior of each individual at each event is friendly (or reveals any other trait of interest). Not surprisingly, few have endeavored to undertake this ambitious enterprise. Yet the handful of studies that have risen to the challenge over the last seven decades or so have yielded remarkably similar conclusions: People often behave quite consistently when they encounter the same situation at different times, but there is very little consistency in their trait-related behavior from one situation to other, different situations. More technically, the temporal stability of trait-related behaviors is high, but their cross-situational consistency is minimal (for a review see Ross and Nisbett 1991).

The earliest study on this topic was published by Hartshorne and May in 1928; it examined the consistency of behaviors related to honesty. These investigators created a variety of situations in which thousands of elementary school children had the opportunity to cheat, lie, and steal in diverse settings ranging from the classroom to party games to athletic contests. In all of these situations children were led to believe, mistakenly, that the detection of any dishonest behavior would be impossible. For example, in one situation, children, believing themselves to be unattended, had the opportunity to steal some money that had been left on a classroom table. In another situation, they had the opportunity to cheat (by peeking) at a game in which they were supposed to be blindfolded. And in yet another situation, they had the opportunity to falsify and improve upon their scores on a test.

Hartshorne and May, who had expected to document a broad honesty disposition, were quite surprised by their own findings. Admittedly, the temporal stability of behavior was quite high: The average correlation between the children's honesty in a given situation on two separate occasions was an impressive .70. What this means is that a child who steals money from an unattended desk today will probably do the same tomorrow, and a child who falsifies scores on a particular test today will probably, if given the chance, do the same tomorrow. Yet, although behavior within a given situation was quite consistent over time, there was little consistency in behavior from one situation to another: The average correlation between the children's honesty in one situation and their honesty in a different situation was only a modest .23. What this means is that if you know that a child stole money from an unattended table, this tells you little about whether or not this child will also falsify test scores. Moreover, as the difference between any two situations increased, behavior from one to the other became less consistent. Clearly, honest behavior was governed not only by underlying honesty but also, perhaps predominantly, by key features of the situations in which the opportunities to be dishonest arose.

In 1929 Theodore Newcomb reported a study with even greater scope. He examined the consistency across time and situations of nine different traits broadly related to extraversion such as talkativeness, curiosity, and gregariousness. The study was conducted at a summer camp for "problem" adolescent boys. At the end of each day, camp counselors completed a lengthy questionnaire about each boy, rating the boy's performance that day on a series of behaviors related to each of the traits of interest. For example, the questions tapping behavior related to talkativeness were: "Did he tell of his own past, or of exploits he had accomplished?" "Did he give loud and spontaneous expressions of delight and disapproval?" "Did his conversation with counselors confine itself to asking and answering necessary questions?" "How did he spend the quiet hour?" and "How much of the time did he talk at the table?"

Newcomb's analyses focused mostly on the cross-situational consistency of behaviors. He, too, found this consistency to be remarkably low. The average correlation between any two behaviors presumed to tap the same trait was only .14. In other words, knowing how talkative a boy was at lunch does not permit you to predict with confidence how voluble he will be during the quiet hour or when interacting with counselors. Note also that the estimates of the correlations between behavior in any two situations are exaggerated in both Newcomb's study and Hartshorne and May's study. This is because in both studies behaviors were aggregated over several identical situations before the correlations were calculated. As will be discussed shortly, such aggregation boosts correlations. This makes the remarkably low cross-situational consistencies obtained in these studies all the more remarkable. Low as these correlations are, the correlations between any two single situations can be expected to be even lower.

Newcomb's study had another important feature. He also asked the camp counselors to provide, at the end of the camp, ratings of the frequency with which each boy had demonstrated each of the behaviors assessed in the daily records. Comparison of the consistency among these recalled patterns of behavior to the actual consistency obtained from the daily records revealed a striking finding: The counselors' overall impressions, at the end of the camp, yielded a considerably higher degree of consistency among conceptually related behaviors (.49) than was obtained from their own daily records of these same behaviors (.14). This was one of the first indications that we tend to "see" more consistency than there really is among trait-related behaviors.

In case you are wondering, the low cross-situational consistency of trait-related behaviors is not restricted to children; a more recent study revealed that college students are just as inconsistent (Mischel and Peake 1982). Students at Carleton College were observed repeatedly in a variety of situations that tapped friendliness and conscientiousness. For example, behaviors related to conscientiousness included class attendance, study-session attendance, assignment neatness, assignment punctuality, appointment punctuality, room neatness, and personal-appearance neatness.

By now, the findings should come as no surprise. The students showed modest temporal stability but little cross-situational consistency in their behavior. On average, the correlation between behavior in any two identical situations at different times was .29, whereas the correlation between any two different situations presumed to tap the same trait was only .08 (unlike in the earlier studies, these correlations are between pairs of single behaviors rather than between pairs of aggregates and so are not inflated). This means that if you noticed, for example, that the assignment that David handed in yesterday was messier than most students', this information allows you to predict with modest confidence that the assignment he will hand in next week will also be on the messy side. But the messiness of his assignment tells you practically nothing about how messy his room or his clothes are likely to be.

Trait theories of personality rest on the assumption that behavior is consistent across many diverse situations. In his 1968 book *Personality and Assessment*, Walter Mischel suggested that it was time to question that assumption. Reviewing the evidence from studies like the ones described above, he noted that the correlation between any two different behaviors presumed to tap the same trait was usually below .20. He concluded that rather than conceptualizing behavior as determined by broad underlying traits, one should recognize that behavior depends on the specifics of the situation in which it takes place. And he urged personality psychologists to launch a search for new ways of conceptualizing how personal and situational factors combine to govern behavior. Mischel's critique, and a similar one published that same year by Donald Peterson (1968) challenged the very foundations of trait theories of personality. In the heated, often acrimonious debate that ensued, personality theorists proposed different ways of salvaging the trait construct.

The Power of Aggregation One of the most influential solutions came from Seymour Epstein, who acknowledged that the consistency of trait-related behavior from one situation to another is indeed low, but challenged Mischel's conclusion that the notion of traits as broad constructs should therefore be abandoned (Epstein 1979, 1983). Epstein's argument was based on a well-known statistical fact: Even though the correlation between any two behaviors is low, the correlation between two *aggregates* of behavior can still be quite substantial. To illustrate why, consider the following example. You might not be able to predict a baseball player's performance in tomorrow's game with any certainty from his performance in yesterday's game. Yet you should be able to predict his overall performance next season with considerable confidence from his overall performance last season. This is because performance at any single game is quite unpredictable; it depends not only on the player's ability but also on many chance factors—the weather, the amount of sleep he got the previous night, his mood, and so on. But over many games, these chance factors cancel each other out, and one is left with a pretty good estimate of the player's true ability. By pooling and averaging the player's performances over many games, you obtain a reliable estimate of the player's ability that should be strongly correlated with other equally reliable measures of ability.

By the same token, Epstein argued, you might not be able to predict someone's talkativeness at dinner from her talkativeness in the doctor's waiting room or on a job interview. But if you measured her talkativeness in all these and several other situations, and averaged these measures to obtain a score of her overall talkativeness, you would be able to predict from this how talkative she will be, on average, in a range of other situations. Put differently, if Jane is more talkative than John at dinner, this tells you very little about whether or not she will be more talkative than him at the doctor's. But if, on average, Jane is more talkative than John in the dozen or so situations in which you have encountered them last month, there is a very good chance that, on average, she will also be more talkative than him in the dozen or so situations in which you expect to encounter them next month.

No one can argue with Epstein's analysis; it rests on solid statistical ground. But one can argue about its implications, and indeed the argument persisted. Epstein felt that by aggregating across situations he had solved the problem of trait consistency and had demonstrated the importance and viability of traits as broad personality constructs. But Mischel felt that such aggregation was akin to throwing away the baby with the water. It completely overlooked the fact that different situations could draw out different behaviors from different people, and made it impossible to assess each individual's unique pattern of behavior as it varied from one situation to another (Mischel and Peake 1982). To me, it seems that both arguments have merit. Whether one finds aggregation useful and traits meaningful depends on one's goals.

Often, we are interested in behavior over the long run. You may want to know how a friend or lover will treat you over the duration of your relationship, and may not be particularly concerned with momentary variations. A bank may be satisfied with a measure of honesty that predicts employees' behavior over the long haul. Using such a measure to weed out dishonest individuals could produce large savings over time, even if the measure cannot predict behavior in any single situation with any certainty. Measures of traits that are aggregated over many situations can be extremely useful for such purposes, and allow for considerable predictability over the long haul. Indeed, research using aggregated measures of personality has revealed that an individual's traits tend to remain quite stable across the life span (for a review, see Caspi and Bem 1990). In that sense, traits as broad dispositions are alive and well.

On other occasions, we are interested in predicting behavior in one situation from behavior in another. This we cannot do with any certainty; the correlation between any two situations is too low. If you expect that the person who treated you politely when you encountered her at work will treat you with equal politeness at a party, you may be in for a rude surprise. Moreover, even if we have an aggregated measure of a person's behavior in one situation, reflecting his average performance in this situation on many different occasions, it will still not do a good job of predicting aggregates of his behavior in another situation. In the Carleton students study described earlier, the average correlation between any two aggregates of behavior in a given situation was only .13 (Mischel and Peake 1982). The average messiness of David's many class assignments still tells you little about how likely his room or his clothes are to be messy, on average.

Practically, this means that even when we know a person well, we cannot do a good job of predicting this person's behavior in novel situations. The friend who seems so easygoing and confident at school may turn out to be fussy and apprehensive on a hiking trip. And the graduate student who seems so insecure and self-effacing when interacting with professors may prove to be poised and self-assured once she becomes a professor herself. Of course, when our information about a person is based on only a very brief acquaintance, we will do even worse when attempting to predict long-term behavior in novel situations. Job interviews, for example, correlate very poorly with actual performance on the job, with the typical correlation falling below .10 (Hunter and Hunter 1984). Therefore, the person who seemed respectful and humble on a job interview may well turn out to be contemptuous and arrogant on the job, and the person who seemed nervous and agitated during the interview may turn out to be calm and composed in the context of everyday work.

Accuracy from Thin Slices of Behavior   There is one line of work which, on the face of it, seems to challenge these conclusions. Many studies have shown that people observing only a very thin slice of another's behavior, often as little as a 30-second videotape with the sound turned off, can predict this person's long-term performance with remarkable accuracy (for a review, see Ambady and Rosenthal 1992). In one study, 13 graduate student teaching fellows were videotaped while teaching undergraduate courses (Ambady and Rosenthal 1993). The investigators created a master tape which included three 10-second clips of each teacher. This tape was shown, with the audio turned down completely, to nine undergraduates who were asked to rate the nonverbal behavior of each teacher on 15 dimensions broadly related to the quality of teachers' performance (e.g., accepting, active, enthusiastic, competent, optimistic).

How well can such personality ratings, based on 30 seconds of nonverbal behavior, predict the teachers' actual performance? The surprising answer was, remarkably well. To assess the teachers' actual performance, the investigators obtained the ratings of overall quality given to each teacher at the end of the term by the actual students in his or her videotaped class. The average personality ratings given to the teachers by observers of the brief video clips were highly correlated with the average quality ratings given to these teachers by their students. The more active, confident, dominant, enthusiastic, likable, optimistic, warm, and supportive the teacher appeared to be to observers of the brief video, the higher that teacher was rated by his or her students. On average, the correlation between teachers' overall ratings by their students and the ratings given to them on any personality dimension by viewers of the videotape was an impressive .76. Students' evaluations of their instructors depend a great deal on the instructors' charisma, and charisma can be assessed quite accurately from thin slices of performance.

Similar findings have been obtained in a variety of other domains as well. For example, thin slices of behavior have been shown to permit surprisingly accurate estimates of the quality of clinical therapists and the outcomes of their patients, of teachers' liking for different students, and of whether a speaker was telling the truth or lying (for a review, see Ambady and Rosenthal 1992). It appears that when we observe another person, even briefly, we are able to pick up, consciously or unconsciously, nonverbal cues that may reveal enduring truths about this person.

Does this mean that contrary to the conclusions of the previous section, you will be able to predict another person's long-term performance quite accurately from your observation of that person in a single, brief situation? No. It is important to note that in all studies demonstrating accuracy of prediction from thin slices of behavior, ratings of the thin slices were aggregated across many judges. Aggregation across judges boosts correlation much like aggregation across situations does. Each judge's rating reflects not only the target's actual personality but also the judge's idiosyncratic biases and errors. When impressions are averaged across many judges, these idiosyncrasies can cancel each other out, resulting in a more reliable estimate of the target's personality. Therefore, the accuracy of any individual judge will be far lower than the accuracy of the average judgment of a group of judges.

When one knows the reliability of an aggregate of items and the number of items it comprises, it is possible to calculate the reliability of a single item, or, in this case, a single judge (for the algorithm, see Nunnally 1978, p. 243). Ambady and Rosenthal (1991), who conducted a meta-analysis of 38 separate findings on this topic, found that the average correlation between ratings of thin slices of individuals' behavior and some other measure of these individuals' performance was a pretty impressive .39. The median number of judges rating the thin slices of behavior in these studies was 37. From this I calculated that the correlation expected for any single judge was only about .02. A single person cannot assess thin slices of behavior with much accuracy.

Where does all this leave us? If you walk by an open classroom door and catch a glimpse of an unfamiliar professor in action, your impressions of the professor will tell you very little about the professor's quality. But if several of your friends follow your lead, and you all pool your impressions together, you will have a pretty good idea of how this professor is likely to be evaluated by students attending the class. Note, though, that the predictive power of your pooled impressions remains restricted to the classroom. Given the well-documented low consistency of behavior from one situation to another, there is little reason to believe that you will be able to predict the professor's behavior in other settings with any accuracy. Even when you rely on aggregated impressions of the professor's classroom behavior, you will still know little about how the professor will treat you if approached during office hours, and will know even less about how the professor will behave toward colleagues, friends, and family members.

The bottom line is that although we can predict average, across the board levels of behavior from similarly aggregated measures of behavior with some accuracy, we cannot predict a person's behavior in one situation from that person's behavior in another situation with any confidence. And a single observation of a person in a single situation is unlikely to be very informative about this person's character. Do we know this? Do we realize how little predictability is afforded by a single behavior? Do we know how little we can generalize from one situation to another? Apparently, we do not, at discussed next.

Beliefs about the Consistency of Traits

It is easy to come up with anecdotes illustrating our profound failure to appreciate the extent to which behavior can vary from one situation to another. It is almost a cliché for newspaper articles about serial killers to be accompanied by interviews with astonished neighbors insisting that "he seemed like such a nice guy." The newspaper excerpt depicted in figure 9.2 is a striking case in point. It describes a friend's reactions to the news that Helmut

Waterloo man cited in war crimes
Developer was a member of 'killing unit,' government says

Longtime Friend can't believe charges
Accused man is a 'good, upstanding citizen," says associate of 30 years
By Brian Caldwell

Rudy Tavonius doesn't believe the things they're saying about his long time boss and friend--not for a miunute.

During 30 years in busines together, he's sure there would have been some sign that Helmut Oberlander was capable of taking part in the executions of civilians by the Nazis.

But Tavonius, 57, said he never noticed anything to indicate Oberlander, who has lived and worked in the Kitchener-Waterloo area since coming to Canada 40 years ago,

was anything other than the "upstanding citizen" he appeared to be.

"I was surpirsed the government would move against him," Tavonius said Friday. "I've known him a long time and he's just not the criminal kind. He was a good private and corporate citizen--and I've had a good look at him.

"He's never been charged with a crime--no drunk driving, nothing. He's been a good, upstanding citizen. If they're saying he committed criminal acts during the war, I just do not believe it."

Figure 9.2 From the front page of *The Saturday Record*, 4. 29. 1995. Copyright © (1006) by the Kitchener-Waterloo Record. Reprinted with permission.

Oberlander, a land developer in the Canadian city of Waterloo, had been accused by the federal government of being a member of a Nazi "mobile killing unit" responsible for executing thousands of Jews during the Second World War. The friend of this accused Nazi cannot imagine that the upstanding Canadian citizen he has known for years could possibly have committed any of the atrocities he is accused of. His staunch faith in his friend's innocence makes one wonder about his underlying theory of the nature and consistency of personality. Just what kind of behavior should we expect from a man who, as a youth in Nazi Germany, committed government-sanctioned atrocities in the company of supportive peers, once he has emigrated to the staid and civilized postwar Canada? Should we really expect former Nazis living in small Canadian cities to commit crimes such as drunken driving? To be mean to their neighbors? To torture animals? Or should we recognize that extremely different situations can bring our dramatically different behaviors in the same individual?

We need not rely on such extreme examples to reveal our tendency to overestimate the consistency of behavior from one situation to another. The widespread reliance on job interviews as a means of screening job applicants reflects the equally widespread failure to recognize that job candidates' behavior on an interview can be very different from their behavior on the job. Most of us seem to have strong faith in our ability to tell what a person is like from even a brief conversation, and this faith remains unshaken even though our initial impressions of others are often refuted by their subsequent behavior. In the following sections I will first document the evidence that we have exaggerated faith in the consistency of traits, and then attempt to understand the roots of this exaggerated faith.

Several lines of research speak to our tendency to overestimate the predictability afforded by single behaviors and to exaggerate the cross-situational consistency of traits. There is evidence that we overestimate the power of traits to determine behavior and underestimate the power of situations, that we consider single behaviors and brief encounters to afford far greater predictability than is the case, and that we spontaneously jump to conclusions about traits from trait-related behavior. I next discuss each of these points in turn.

The Fundamental Attribution Error   Before earning a PhD degree, candidates must face the often dreaded orals, a public event in which they field questions about their dissertation research from a panel of established professors. For psychologist Lee Ross this was a humbling experience that left him wondering if he would ever be as brilliant and insightful as his astute examiners. Fortunately he was treated to a corrective experience several months later. This time round, as a faculty member at Stanford, he had the privilege of sitting at the other side of the table, posing rather than attempting to answer questions. He emerged from this experience feeling confident in his own expertise; the candidate, on the other hand, confessed to feeling much like Ross had at his own orals. It was obvious to Ross that he had not achieved a dramatic gain in expertise in the few months that had passed since his own orals. More likely, his seemingly superior performance this time round was due to the tremendous advantage conferred by the role of examiner:

Examiners get to ask the questions and so can focus only on their own areas of expertise; they need not reveal any areas of ignorance. Candidates, on the other hand, have little power to determine the domain of discourse, and may be queried about esoteric topics that few besides the examiner are familiar with.

Ross was struck by the failure of participants in such events to appreciate the advantages and disadvantages of these two asymmetric roles and by their willingness to jump to unwarranted conclusions about the relative abilities of individuals occupying these different roles. More broadly, he noted that people often make what he termed the *fundamental attribution error*; namely they underestimate the extent to which behavior is shaped by the constraints of the situation and overestimate the extent to which it is shaped by people's underlying dispositions (Ross 1977; for reviews, see Gilbert and Malone 1995, Jones 1990). The now classic Quiz Game experiment was designed to demonstrate this phenomenon (Ross, Amabile, and Steinmetz 1977). Stanford students arriving in pairs were randomly assigned the role of "questioner" or "contestant" in a quiz game. The questioner's job was to compose 10 "challenging but not impossible" general knowledge questions and pose them to the contestant. The contestant's job was to answer these questions.

Drawing on their own esoteric knowledge, questioners posed difficult questions that few could answer, such as "What is the longest glacier in the world?" "What do the initials W. H. in W. H. Auden's name stand for?" Not surprisingly, contestants were able to answer, on average, only 4 of the 10 questions posed to them. In this setting, then, the questioner appeared considerably more knowledgeable than the contestant. Of course this apparent superiority was due entirely to the advantages conferred by the role of questioner. It is a safe bet that if the tables had been turned, the contestant would have been just as capable of generating questions that would have stumped the questioner. Did participants realize this? As may be seen in table 9.2, questioners may have recognized that they were not really more knowledgeable than contestants. But contestants clearly did not. They rated themselves as considerably less knowledgeable than they rated their questioners. In a follow-

Table 9.2 Ratings of the general knowledge of questioners and contestants made by participants and observers of a quiz game

ROLE OF RATER	RATING OF QUESTIONER	RATING OF CONTESTANT
Questioner	53.5	50.6
Contestant	66.8	41.3
Observer	82.9	48.9

Source: From Ross et al. (1977), excerpts from table 1 and the results of experiment 2. Copyright © (1997) by the American Psychological Association. Reprinted with permission.
Note: Higher numbers indicated greater knowledge.

up study, observers watching a reenactment of the quiz game also failed to appreciate the advantages conferred by the role of questioner, as shown in table 9.2. They, too, rated the questioner as far more knowledgeable than they rated the contestant. When we don't understand the power of a role, or any other constraining aspect of the situation, we will assume that people's behavior in that situation is far more informative about their underlying dispositions than is the case.

Many other studies have also demonstrated that we are often too quick to jump to conclusions about others' abilities, traits, and attitudes based on small samples of their behavior; we fail to appreciate the extent to which situational forces had contributed to that behavior. Rather than attributing behaviors to the situations that provoked them, we tend to attribute behaviors to the enduring traits or abilities of the person who had performed them. Put differently, we tend to infer that people's underlying dispositions correspond to their behavior. This tendency, also termed the *correspondence bias*, has been documented in numerous studies (for reviews, see Gilbert and Malone 1995; Jones 1990). We may assume, for example, that a person who had been required to write a pro-Castro essay supports Castro. We may assume that a student engaged in an embarrassing discussion of her intimate life is an anxious person. And we may assume that workers randomly assigned to supervise their peers are better leaders than are the workers they have been assigned to supervise.

In many of these cases, we don't take the situational pressures into account because we do not appreciate them. Often, we simply don't realize how powerful the situation is and do not understand that most people who find themselves in it would behave similarly. We do not fully comprehend the advantages conferred by the role of manager or examiner, we do not recognize the pressure one feels to comply with seemingly mild requests, and we underestimate the force of peer pressure. In all such cases, people's behavior will lead us to make unwarranted inferences about their underlying traits.

Even when we do recognize situational constraints, we will not always take them into account. Most of us know that discussing embarrassing topics can make a person nervous, that a punitive boss can make employees act meekly, and that the need to gain favor with an interviewer will make job candidates behave in an especially agreeable manner. But this knowledge does not always guide our impressions of people observed in such situations. Often, we first automatically jump to conclusions about the person's underlying trait (she is acting nervously, she must be a nervous person). We may then correct this conclusion, taking situational constraints into account (maybe talking about her intimate life is making her act nervous; she may not be that nervous a person). However, such corrections can require effort; we may be unable to perform effortful situational corrections if our mental capacity is strained (Gilbert 1989; for a detailed discussion, see chapter 7). Therefore, when we are preoccupied, tired, intoxicated, or in a hurry, and so unable to devote careful thought to making sense of others, we may fail to correct our impressions for situational constraints even if we understand these constraints. Instead, we will assume that people's behavior is driven by corresponding dispositions.

Further, even when we appreciate the impact of the situation, want to correct our inferences for it, and have the cognitive resources necessary for doing so, we may still fail to make sufficient corrections. If we use the trait inferred from a person's behavior as a starting point, or anchor and then attempt to adjust our inferences so as to take the situational pressures into account, we may fail to make sufficient adjustments; our inferences will remain biased toward the initially inferred trait (Quattrone 1982; see chapter 3). Our ultimate conclusions about a person may remain contaminated by our initial inferences about this person's character even if we consider these inferences unwarranted and attempt to rid ourselves of this contamination (Wilson and Brekke 1994).

In sum, we make the fundamental attribution error, overattributing behavior to dispositions and underattributing it to situations, because we often do not appreciate the power of situations. We may make this error even when we do understand situational constraints if we lack the mental resources needed to take them into account. Our failure to recognize the power of roles and situations to shape behavior and our willingness to draw broad conclusions about people's character from their behavior in a single situation may reflect a deeper failure to appreciate the extent to which a person's behavior can vary from one situation to another. Our tendency to make the fundamental attribution error implies that we do not realize just how low the cross-situational consistency of behavior really is. I turn next to research that has examined beliefs about the cross-situational consistency of behavior more directly.

Beliefs about Cross-situational Consistency of Behavior   How may one measure people's beliefs about the consistency of behavior? It would be nice if we could simply ask them to estimate the correlation between people's behaviors in any two situations: What is the correlation between students' honesty in one situation and their honesty in another situation? Unfortunately, most people are not familiar with statistical terms such as correlation. Richard Nisbett and I therefore devised an indirect way of assessing beliefs about correlation (Kunda and Nisbett 1986). We used questions with the following format:

Suppose that you observed Jane and Jill in a particular situation and found that Jane was more honest than Jill. What do you sup-

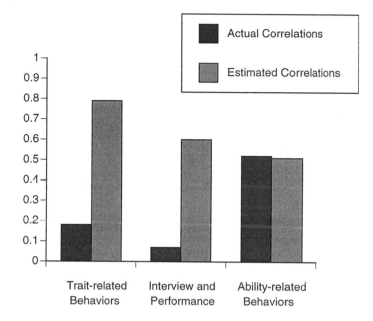

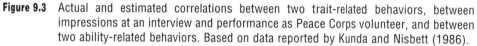

Figure 9.3 Actual and estimated correlations between two trait-related behaviors, between impressions at an interview and performance as Peace Corps volunteer, and between two ability-related behaviors. Based on data reported by Kunda and Nisbett (1986).

pose is the probability that in the next situation in which you observe them you would also find Jane to be more honest than Jill?

Participants answered these questions on a scale from 50 to 100 percent, in which an estimate of 50 percent was tantamount to saying there was no way of predicting which of the two would be more likely to be honest in the next situation and higher estimates reflected greater predictability. Such percentage estimates could be easily converted into correlation coefficients, and these estimated correlations could then be compared to the actual correlations obtained in studies that had assessed the cross-situational consistency of such behaviors (e.g., Hartshorne and May's 1928 study on honesty and Newcomb's 1929 study on extraversion).

It was clear that participants dramatically overestimated the consistency of traits, as can be seen in the leftmost bars in figure 9.3. The actual correlation between behaviors in any two situations tapping traits such as honesty or friendliness is at best .15, yet participants believed it to be close to .80! In terms of the percentage estimates requested in the question quoted above, participants should have estimated that the probability that Jane would be more honest than Jill again in the next situation was about 55 percent. Instead, they estimated it at about 80 percent. Participants were just as likely to overestimate the consistency of behavior from one situation to another when the question spelled out the nature of the situation, making it very clear that participants were being asked to predict behavior in a very different kind of situation. These data suggest that we assume that trait-related behavior is far more consistent than it really is.

People were similarly mistaken when asked to estimate how well behavior on the job could be predicted from brief interviews. In one study using similar question formats, participants were told that a psychiatrist had interviewed applicants to the Peace Corps, and were asked to estimate how well these interviews could predict the applicants' performance as community organizers working for the Peace Corps in third-world countries (Kunda and Nisbett 1986). Their estimates were compared to actual correlations obtained from an earlier study on Peace Corps volunteers (Stein 1966). As may be seen in the middle set of bars in figure 9.3, participants thought a brief interview with a psychiatrist could predict performance in a new role in a foreign country with considerable accuracy; they estimated the correlation between the interview and performance at about .60. In fact, the correlation was an almost negligible .07. We may substantially overestimate the extent to which job performance can be predicted from interviews.

It may have occurred to you that participants may have simply been unable to understand the questions they were asked; their percentage estimates may not have reflected their actual beliefs. However, there are reasons to believe otherwise. In cases where people could be expected to be accurate, participants' estimates showed remarkable accuracy. The rightmost set of bars in figure 9.3 portrays actual and estimated correlations for the consistency of ability-related behaviors such as performance at basketball games and on spelling tests (Kunda and Nisbett 1986). Participants were expected to be more accurate about abilities than about traits because the correlations for abilities are easier to detect; it is easy to break the flow of ability-related behavior into meaningful units (a game, a test) and easy to determine the score achieved in each unit (number of points, grade). It is more difficult to detect correlations in the domain of personality traits because trait-related behavior is much less codable. There are no comparable, ready-made units of friendliness, and it is far more difficult to determine the precise degree of friendliness expressed by a given behavior (for a related discussion, see chapter 4). Indeed, as can be seen in figure 9.3, participants were far more accurate about the consistency of abilities than they were about the consistency of traits. For traits, we simply do not realize how little consistency there is from behavior in one situation to behavior in another situation.

Spontaneous Trait Inference The librarian carried the old woman's groceries across the street. The receptionist stepped in front of the old man in line. The plumber slipped an extra $50 into his wife's purse. Although you were not asked to make any inferences about any of these characters, chances are that you inferred that the librarian is helpful, the receptionist rude, and the plumber generous. Perhaps because we do not realize the extent to which behavior is shaped by situations, we tend to spontaneously infer such traits from behavior. These trait inferences can be automatic in that they are carried out with little effort or intention. I have already described research indicating that trait inferences can require so little effort that people draw them readily even when preoccupied with other tasks (Gilbert 1989; Trope and Alfieri 1997; see chapter 7). Other research has shown that people tend to make trait inferences spontaneously when they encounter trait-related behaviors, even when they have no explicit intention of doing so (for a review, see Uleman, Newman, and Moskowitz 1996).

If it is true that when we encounter a man carrying an old woman's groceries across the street we spontaneously assume that he is helpful, then this inferred trait, *helpful*, should become part of our stored memory of this event. Information that is stored along with a particular memory can later help bring this memory to mind; if two pieces of information are encoded in memory together, then when we later come across one we will be reminded of the other (Tulving and Thompson 1973). Therefore, if *helpful* was inferred from the grocery-carrying behavior and stored alongside it, then if I ask you later to recall the behavior described in this paragraph, you may be better able to do so if I also give you as a clue the word *helpful*. Put differently, if the clue *helpful* serves to remind you of this behavior, we can assume that you inferred *helpful* from the grocery-carrying behavior as soon as you heard about it, and stored this inferred trait alongside the behavior. Laraine Winter and James Uleman (1984) used this logic to demonstrate that traits can be inferred spontaneously from related behaviors.

Participants were given a series of sentences similar to the ones that opened this section, each describing a behavior that implied a different personality trait, and were asked to study them for a later memory test. After a brief distracter task they were asked to recall as many of these sentences as they could. The recall sheets on which they wrote their responses contained different kinds of cues. For each sentence, some participants were cued by the trait implied by the behavior. For example, the trait cue for the sentence "The librarian carries the old woman's groceries across the street" was *helpful*. Other participants were cued, instead, by a word that was semantically related to the actor, in this case, *books* for librarian. Still other participants were given no cue at all. The design was carefully counterbalanced so that each participant received a mixture of trait cues, semantic cues, and no cues for different sentences, and each sentence was cued by a trait for one group of participants, by a semantic associate for another group, and by nothing for yet another group.

Not surprisingly, the semantic cues improved recall. For example, people cued with *books* were better able to remember the librarian and her behavior than were people given no cue, and people cued with *pipes* were better able to remember the plumber and his behavior. More interesting, the trait cues were every bit as effective. For example, *helpful* helped people remember the sentence about the person carrying groceries for an old woman, and *generous* helped people remember the sentence about the person slipping money into his wife's purse. Several subsequent studies obtained the same basic results: Trait cues improved memory for sentences that implied those traits and were as good or better at improving memory as were other semantic associates of the words in the sentences. This occurred despite the fact that the semantic cues were typically more strongly associated with the words in the sentence than were the trait cues (for a review, see Uleman et al. 1996). The effectiveness of traits as memory cues for related behaviors suggests that these traits had been stored alongside the behaviors. Because the traits had never been mentioned explicitly in the sentences, these findings suggest that the traits had been inferred spontaneously from the behaviors. When we hear "carried groceries for an old woman" the word *helpful* spontaneously comes to mind.

It is reasonable to assume that trait inferences were made spontaneously in these studies because these inferences were made even though participants had no explicit intention of forming impressions. Indeed, trait cues improved memory for sentences describing trait-related behaviors even when participants were led to believe that these sentences were mere distracters included only so as to draw their attention away from their central task (Winter, Uleman, and Cunniff 1985). And participants, when queried, seemed unaware of having made any trait inferences and doubted that trait cues could have improved their memory. We may infer traits spontaneously from behavior even if we have no intention of doing so and even if we do not realize we are making such inferences.

In this kind of study, it is possible that participants had not inferred the traits when they first encountered the behaviors. Rather, it may be that they made the connection between the trait and the behavior only later, at the time of retrieval, when they saw the trait cue. Such an interpretation would undermine the conclusion that traits are inferred spontaneously from behaviors as one encounters them. However, other studies using different methods have found more clear-cut evidence that traits are inferred spontaneously at the time a related behavior is observed. These studies were based on the assumption that if traits are inferred spontaneously from behavior they should become more accessible following exposure to a relevant behavior. There is evidence for such increased trait accessibility. For example, after reading about a trait-implying behavior such as "stepped on his partner's foot while dancing," people are faster to recognize the trait (clumsy, in this case) as a word, and are more likely to come up with the trait when asked to complete a word fragment (e.g., clumsy for CL __ __ __ __; for a review, see Uleman et al. 1996). Trait-related behaviors bring to mind the traits that they imply.

The conclusion that people infer traits spontaneously from behaviors gained further support from a different series of studies (Carlston and Skowronski 1994; Carlston, Skowronski, and Sparks 1995). These studies were based on the assumption that if you infer a trait from a person's behavior spontaneously when you first encounter it, this will make it easier for you to learn to associate that person with that trait on a later occasion, because you will have already formed that association. In one study, participants viewed photos of different faces, each accompanied by a statement, allegedly made by the photographed individual, which implied a particular trait (Carlston and Skowronski 1994). For example, the statement "I hate animals. Today I was walking to the pool hall and I saw this puppy. So I kicked it out of my way" implied, as you have most likely inferred yourself, the trait *cruel*. Before viewing these photos, participants were given different instructions. Some were instructed explicitly to think of a trait that described each person's personality. Others were instructed, more vaguely, to form an impression of each person's personality. Still others were instructed merely to familiarize themselves with the materials. Any trait inferences by these latter participants could be considered spontaneous because they were never instructed to infer traits.

To determine whether participants had inferred traits from the photographed individuals' behaviors, they were asked, after a brief interval, to perform a learning task: They were shown a series of photos of faces, each paired with a trait word, and were instructed to remember the word paired with each photo. Twelve of these trials presented participants with new information to learn. On these control trials, both the faces and the traits were new and unfamiliar. In contrast, on 12 other trials, each face was paired with the trait implied by the statement that had accompanied that same face in the earlier task. If participants had already inferred this trait when they first encountered the statement, this learning task would have required them to merely "relearn" an association they had already formed, a relatively easy learning task. To determine how well they had learned the face-trait associations, participants were later shown each photo and asked to recall the trait word that had been paired with it.

As one might expect, participants who had originally been instructed to infer traits from the behavioral statements were able to recall many more traits from the relearning trials than from the control trials, as shown by the leftmost pair of bars in figure 9.4. These participants knew to associate each individual presented in the relearning trials with the appropriate trait because they had previously inferred that trait from the individual's behavior. More interesting, the same was also true for participants instructed only to form a general impression of the persons or to merely familiarize themselves with the materials, as shown in the middle and rightmost pairs of bars in figure 9.4. Moreover, the improved recall on the relearning trials obtained for these participants, who were not instructed to infer traits, was just as large as that obtained for participants told explicitly to infer traits. Most likely, the explicit instruction to infer traits carried no added benefit because participants in the other conditions had also inferred the traits. Since they had not been instructed to do so, they must have made these trait inferences spontaneously. When someone tells us that he has kicked a puppy, we don't need to be instructed to infer that he is cruel; that inference springs to mind spontaneously.

The ease and readiness with which we draw trait inferences from behavior suggest that when we come across a person hitting another, what we may "see" is an aggressive person, when we come

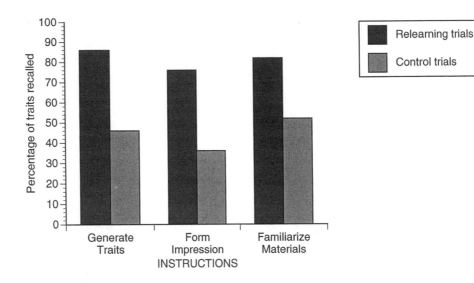

Figure 9.4 Percentage of traits recalled on relearning trials and on control trials by participants instructed to generate a trait describing the personality of the person performing each behavior, by participants instructed to form an impression of the person's personality, and by participants instructed merely to familiarize themselves with the materials. From Carlston and Skowronski (1994, fig. 1, p. 845). Copyright © (1994) by the American Psychological Association. Reprinted with permission.

across a person comforting a child, what we may "see" is a nurturant person, and when we come across a person blushing and stammering, what we may "see" is an anxious person. Even if we have no intention of forming impressions of people or of making sense of their actions, we will spontaneously go beyond their observed behavior and draw inferences about their underlying character.

Before this conclusion is endorsed wholeheartedly, however, one should note an important limitation of research on spontaneous trait inference. In all this research, participants read verbal descriptions of behavior rather than observing actual individuals in action. The trait implications of behavior may be more obvious and inescapable when one encounters such verbal descriptions than they are when one observes actual behavior. There is evidence that actual behavior does give rise to trait inferences and that such inferences can even be automatic in that they require little effort

(Gilbert 1989). It would be nice to supplement this research with evidence that trait inferences from actual behavior can also be automatic in that they are carried out with little intention and awareness, much like trait inferences from verbal descriptions.

In sum, we do not realize the extent to which people's behavior can be shaped by the situations of their life, and we fail to appreciate how inconsistent trait-related behavior can be as one moves from one situation to another and comes under the influence of different situational forces. When we observe or hear about another person's behavior, we often fail to appreciate the extent to which this behavior may have been shaped by circumstances. Instead, we tend to assume that the behavior was driven by the person's enduring underlying dispositions. Moreover, our tendency to view behavior in dispositional terms may be so ingrained that we often jump to conclusions about traits from behavior automatically, with little intention, awareness, or effort. (Note that these inferential tendencies may be restricted to Western culture; see chapter 11 for a discussion of cultural differences.)

How Could We Be So Wrong? In the course of our daily lives we encounter huge amounts of information about our own and other people's behavior in various settings. We see our friends at school, at work, and at play. We see them interacting with a variety of people. We are with them in good times and bad. We should have plenty of evidence for the low cross-situational consistency of behavior. Why, then, can't we read this evidence? Why don't we realize how much people's behavior can vary from one situation to another?

Many factors contribute to our failure to appreciate the low cross-situational consistency of behavior. First, familiarity with events does not guarantee accurate covariation detection (see chapter 4). As noted earlier, covariation detection may be especially problematic for trait-related behavior because of the great difficulty of coding such behavior (Kunda and Nisbett 1986). If we cannot readily break the flow of behavior into units and assign scores to such units, we will not be able to track changes in scores from one setting to another. In the absence of accurate covariation detection, a host of cognitive biases lead us to exaggerate the cross-situational consistency of behavior.

Perhaps because Western culture emphasizes traits so much, we start off with strong expectations that behavior will be consistent. Having inferred from your behavior yesterday that you are friendly, I will expect you to be friendly today as well. Through the lenses of this expectation, your behavior today may seem especially friendly. My expectancies may therefore lead me to see you as more consistent than you really are. There is ample evidence that our expectancies can color our interpretations of behavior (see chapter 2; for a review, see Olson et al. 1996). For example, depending on one's expectancy, the same ambiguously aggressive act may appear highly or moderately aggressive, and the same test performance may be seen as reflecting strong or mediocre ability (Darley and Gross 1983; Sagar and Schofield 1980). By viewing behavior as overly consistent with our expectations, we may impose consistency on an inconsistent world.

Even if we originally see a person's behavior for what it is, we may, on a later date, remember it as more consistent with our current impressions of the person than it really had been. Now that I consider you to be a friendly person, I may remember your behavior toward me when we first met as more friendly than it had actually seemed to me at the time (see chapter 5; for a review, see Ross 1989). By reconstructing our memories in this manner, we may end up viewing others' behaviors as more consistent over time than is warranted even by our own ongoing assessments of these behaviors.

We may also fail to realize that although the many situations in which we observe our acquaintances are quite diverse, they all share an important element—our presence (see Swann 1984). We may not realize that people may behave quite differently when we are not around. In part, this may be because we may not realize the extent to which we compel people to fulfill our expectations of them. A considerable amount of evidence suggests that our expectations of others can be self-fulfilling (for a review, see Jussim 1986; see chapter 8). A teacher's expectation that a child will do well at school can improve that child's performance (e.g., Madon,

Jussim, and Eccles 1997; Rosenthal and Jacobson 1968). Our expectations may also shape they way others treat us. If I expect you to compete with me, I will engage in competitive behaviors that will force you to respond in kind. Indeed, people who believe that everyone else is competitive tend to bring out competitive rather than cooperative behavior in others (Kelley and Stahelski 1970). Thus, we may cause others to behave in a relatively consistent manner toward us, and may not realize that their behavior in our presence is considerably more consistent than is their full range of behaviors in situations that do not include us.

In sum, we may exaggerate the cross-situational consistency of behavior because we see and remember behavior as more consistent than it really is. We may also fail to recognize that even when we encounter a relatively consistent pool of behaviors in an individual, these behaviors may not be representative of the individual's entire repertoire of behavior; the individual may behave quite differently when we are not around. Thus, we may be privy to overly consistent slices of other people's behavior, and then further exaggerate the observed and recalled consistency of what we see.

Redefining Traits
Our notion of traits as broad and stable dispositions that manifest themselves to the same extent in a variety of situations cannot hold water. However, this does not mean that there are no enduring and systematic differences among individuals. My intuitions that I am a very different person from my brother or that my children have predictably different patterns of behavior need not be wrong. Such intuitions may be based on meaningful and stable differences among individuals but not the kind of differences implied by the traditional understanding of traits. Consider the two individuals depicted in figure 9.5. Carol is extremely extraverted in one-on-one situations, is only moderately extraverted when in small groups, and is not at all extraverted in large groups. She will appear very comfortable and outgoing if you meet with her alone, but will clam up and appear very shy and awkward if you encounter her in a

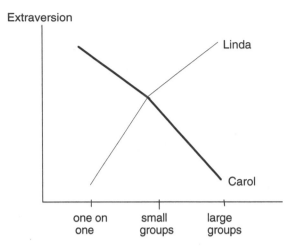

Figure 9.5 Behavior-situation profiles of the degree of extraversion of two hypothetical individuals in different situations. Higher values indicate greater extraversion.

large group setting. Linda has a very different profile. She is extremely extraverted in large groups but not at all extraverted in one-on-one situations. She may appear composed and comfortable when lecturing to a large audience but withdrawn and aloof if you approach her when she is alone.

Both Linda and Carol are quite inconsistent in their extraversion across these three situations. Moreover, if you average their behavior across these situations, you will find them to be equally extraverted. However, by averaging across situations in this manner, as a traditional trait theorist would, you may lose very important information that defines the uniqueness of each of these individuals. Although the behavior of each of these women across these situations is inconsistent, their unique profiles of behavior in these situations may be quite consistent; Carol may always be more outgoing in small than in large groups, and Linda may always be more comfortable in large groups than in one-on-one situations. You may recall that the temporal stability of behavior in each situation is quite high. It follows that profiles depicting behavior in each of several situations should also be high. Walter Mischel and Yuichi Shoda (1995) have argued that these stable patterns of variability in behavior from one situation to another may represent the enduring differences in personality that underlie our intuitions that people are predictably different from one another.

Do people really have stable profiles of behavior across situations? To answer this question, Shoda and his colleagues studied the behavior of 53 troubled children attending a 6–week summer camp (Shoda, Mischel, and Wright 1994). They identified five psychologically meaningful situations: "peer teased, provoked, or threatened," "adult warned the child," "adult gave the child time out," "peer initiated positive social contact," and "adult praised the child verbally." Within each hour of camp activity, observers coded whether each child encountered each of these situations and, if so, coded the child's response along several dimensions of behavior—did the child show verbal or physical aggression, whine, comply, react in a prosocial manner? From these extensive observations, it was possible to create, for each child, a profile depicting the extent to which the child performed each of these behaviors in each situation. The investigators randomly divided each child's behaviors into two sets, and created a behavior-situation profile for each set. Figure 9.6 shows the profiles of verbal aggression obtained for two different children.

The two children have quite different profiles. Child #28 is most verbally aggressive when approached positively by a peer, child #9 is least aggressive in that situation but becomes aggressive when warned by an adult. And each child's profile is quite stable. The investigators calculated the stability of each child's profile of behavior for each dimension (i.e., the correlation between the two profiles obtained from the two set of observations for each child) and averaged the coefficients obtained for each dimension. The obtained average stability coefficients were all significant, ranging from .19 for prosocial talk to .47 for verbal aggression. On average, then, the children were moderately to substantially stable in their behavior-situation profiles. Although the consistency of one's behavior from one situation to another is quite low, one's pattern of variability across different situations can be quite consistent.

Not everyone shows a consistent profile. Whereas some children in this study had extremely stable profiles, others showed very

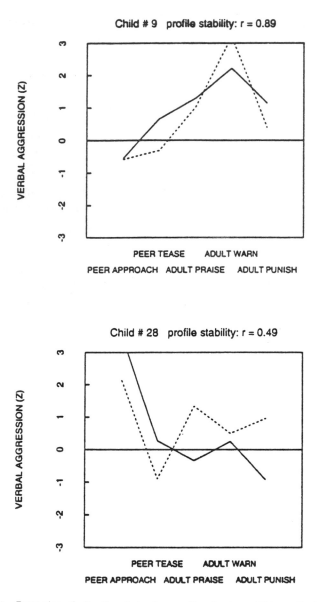

Figure 9.6 Examples of situation-behavior profiles for two children. Each figure portrays verbal aggression in five different situations in two separate sets of occasions in which the child encountered each type of situation as shown in time 1 (solid) and time 2 (broken). Data are shown in standardized scores (Z) relative to the average level of aggression in each kind of situation. From Shoda et al. 1994 (fig. 1, p. 678). Copyright © (1994) by the American Psychological Association. Reprinted with permission.

Table 9.3 The cross-situational consistency and the stability of person-situation profiles in the conscientiousness-related behaviors of students who viewed themselves as high or low in consistency on this dimension

PARTICIPANTS' PERCEIVED CONSISTENCY	CROSS-SITUATIONAL CONSISTENCY	STABILITY OF PROFILE
Low self-perceived consistency	.10	.02
High self perceived consistency	.09	.45

Source: Based on Mischel and Shoda (1995, fig. 3, p. 251). Copyright © (1995) by the American Psychological Association. Adapted with permission.

little stability from one set of observations to another. It occurred to Mischel and Shoda that these variations in profile stability may serve as the basis for people's varying intuitions about the stability of their own behavior. Some people consider themselves to be quite consistent in their behavior on traits such as friendliness or neatness, whereas others consider themselves quite inconsistent. Bem and Allen (1974) argued that the people who considered themselves more consistent would in fact show greater cross-situational consistency, but subsequent research suggested otherwise. An extensive study, described earlier, which examined the conscientiousness of college students in a variety of situations also examined whether those who viewed themselves as consistent on this dimension were in fact more consistent than others (Mischel and Peake 1982). They were not. The cross-situational consistency for students who viewed themselves as highly consistent was just as low as that obtained for students who viewed themselves as inconsistent, as you may see in table 9.3.

However, when Mischel and Shoda (1995) calculated the stability of these students' behavior-situation profiles, they found that students who viewed themselves as consistent did indeed have more consistent profiles than did those who viewed themselves as inconsistent. Clearly, then, our intuitions of consistency are not illusory.

They appear to be based on the extent to which our behavior varies predictably from one situation to another. Individuals who have more stable patterns of variation across situations see themselves as more stable.

Why do different people have enduringly different behavior-situation profiles? Mischel and Shoda's account for this is based on the view of individuals as actively constructing meaning from situations based on their unique patterns of knowledge and experience (for a review, see Cantor and Kihlstrom 1987; see chapter 10). The same situation may have different meanings for different individuals. Each person focuses on different features of the situation, and different people may have different associations and emotional reactions to the same features (see chapter 2). For one child, an invitation to play with another child brings to mind memories of fun activities and good times. This child will see the invitation as a friendly act, will activate the goal of making friends, will feel happy, and will respond positively. For another child, the same invitation brings to mind memories of being teased and bullied. This child will see the invitation as a nasty pretense, will activate the goal of protecting the self, will feel angry and anxious, and will respond aggressively. A different social situation, coming across another child engaged in self-absorbed play, may trigger completely different reactions in each of these children. The first will feel ignored, have memories of being left out, feel angry and offended, and may launch an attack. In contrast, the second child may see this as a nonthreatening situation and initiate prosocial behavior.

In short, we may each have a stable network of interrelated goals, beliefs, and feelings. Different situations will trigger different configurations of these, and so will elicit different behaviors. If each situation usually brings to mind the same thoughts and feelings, we will have a stable profile of behavior across the various situations of our lives. This reconceptualization of traits in terms of behavior-situation profiles helps explain both why our behavior varies from one trait-related situation to another and why we nevertheless view ourselves and other people as quite consistent.

In conclusion, it appears that we are truly quite consistent in our behavior within each situation, and it is quite appropriate to expect such consistency in others. But we run into trouble when we expect this consistency to extend to other situations as well. Even slight variations in the features of a situation can lead to dramatic shifts in people's behavior. Our failure to recognize this can cause us to harbor mistaken beliefs and expectancies about other people. When we jump to conclusions about how a person encountered in one situation will behave in another, we may make costly mistakes in our professional as well as our personal lives.

Summary

Our estimates of the prevalence of various attitudes, beliefs, or choices in the population are often colored by our own standing on these issues. When we favor a particular choice, we may estimate it to be more common than do people making the opposite choice. As a result of this *false consensus effect*, we often exaggerate the extent to which others share our opinions and habits.

On the other hand, sometimes most people fail to realize that others share their own private reactions. Such *pluralistic ignorance* arises when our (and everyone else's) public behavior does not reflect our private attitudes, and we all think that other people's behavior is driven by different causes than our own identical behavior; even though we know that we expressed support for a practice that we in fact oppose only because of our fear of ostracism, we may assume that other people expressed similar support for it because they actually endorse it. This may lead to the perpetuation of norms and behaviors that are in reality quite unpopular.

Despite these biases, we are not blind to social reality. Indeed, we can be remarkably accurate about the distributions of various attitudes, traits, and behaviors within large social groups. We will be especially accurate if we are familiar with the social group in question.

We can, however, be quite mistaken when predicting or explaining an individual's behavior. We often fail to realize that even though people's behavior is typically quite consistent over time within a given situation, they may behave quite differently in other situations. We also do not appreciate the implications of this low cross-situational consistency of trait-related behavior for our ability to predict others' behavior: Even though we can do a pretty good job of predicting how a person will behave, on average, over many situations if we know this person's past average behavior in a comparable range of situations, we cannot predict behavior in one situation from behavior in one other situation with any confidence.

Not recognizing this, we tend to overestimate the predictability afforded by single behaviors and to exaggerate the cross-situational consistency of traits. We make *the fundamental attribution error*, overattributing behavior to dispositions and underattributing it to situations, we consider single behaviors and brief encounters to afford far greater predictability than they actually do, and we spontaneously jump to conclusions about traits from trait-related behavior even when we have no intention of doing so. We often fail to take situations into account because we do not appreciate their power to shape behavior. Even when we do understand situational constraints, we may still make the fundamental attribution error if we lack the mental resources needed to take these constraints into account.

Many factors contribute to our failure to appreciate the low cross-situational consistency of behavior. Accurate detection of co-variation among social behaviors is especially difficult because it is difficult to unitize and score these behaviors. In the absence accurate covariation detection, a host of cognitive biases lead us to exaggerate the cross-situational consistency of behavior: Our expectancies can make us see behavior as more consistent with earlier behavior than it really is. Biases in memory reconstruction can lead us to recall our initial impressions of a person's past behavior as more consistent with that person's current behavior than they really had been. We may also not realize that our own presence may consistently constrain individuals to behave in a certain manner, and that they may behave quite differently in our absence. In short, we are exposed to overly consistent slices of other people's behavior, and then further exaggerate the observed and recalled consistency of what we see.

When we use the term *self*, we have many meanings in mind. My self is the person I am now, the child I once was, the elderly person I expect to become. My self is the person who is my parents' child, my children's parent, my spouse's partner, my co-workers' colleague. My self is the center of my thoughts, feelings, desires, and actions. My self is that part of me which attempts to control my own thoughts, feelings, behaviors, and circumstances and also tries to manage other people's impressions of me. It is clear that the self is so broad a term that it could encompass most of the topics discussed in this book: It is the agent forming impressions and making decisions, recalling the past and simulating the future, using stereotypes and suppressing prejudice, driven by motivation, and subject to emotion (for a review, see Baumeister 1998). In this chapter I will focus more narrowly on research and theory that involves the self explicitly in that it examines actual and desired self-knowledge and its implications for thoughts, feelings, and behavior or examines attempts at self-regulation.

Much of the chapter concerns the ways in which the contents and structure of the self can influence social judgment and behavior. It examines how the nature and the organization of our beliefs about our traits, our sense of our overall self-worth, and our goals relate to the ways we think and feel about ourselves and others and influence our choice of interpersonal strategies and social situations. The chapter also discusses the executive, controlling aspect of the self and examines some general consequences of exercising self-regulation.

Dimensions of Self-knowledge

Self-schemas

Each of us has many self-concepts. One may think of oneself as friendly, smart, lazy, independent, responsible, overweight, and many other things. Hazel Markus (1977) noted that some of these attributes may be more important than others to one's self-definition. My intelligence may be more important than my independence to my sense of who I am as a person. Moreover, people may differ in which attributes they consider central and self-defining. Some people may define themselves predominantly in terms of their friendliness. Others, who also see themselves as friendly, may not consider their friendliness to be as central to their sense of self, and may define themselves, instead, predominantly in terms of their intelligence. So far this line of reasoning is similar to the thinking of Bem and Allen (1974) who also argued that the same trait may be more central and important to some people than to others (see chapter 9). However, Bem and Allen were interested only in the implications for the consistency of people's trait-related behaviors. Markus took these ideas a step further by focusing on their implications for the representation and processing of social information.

Markus (1977) proposed that people who considered a trait such as *friendly* especially important would also have an especially rich set of beliefs and memories about their own friendliness, that is, a *self-schema* for friendliness. A *self-schema* is an integrated set of memories, beliefs, and generalizations about one's behavior in a given domain. A *friendly* self-schemas, for example, may include memories of specific events ("I struck up a conversation with a stranger at the dentist's," "I invited my new neighbors over for dinner") as well as more general beliefs about one's typical reactions in various circumstances ("I am especially happy when I am around my friends," "at parties, I try to make sure everyone is having a good time") and broad self-categorizations ("I am friendly," "I am a warm person"). Based on research about other knowledge structures or schemas, self-schemas can be expected to influence the processing of information about the self and others (for a review of research on other schemas, see Rumelhart, 1984; see chapter 2).

Processing Information about the Self Individuals who have a rich, well-articulated, and salient self-schema as an independent person should process information about their own independence in a different manner than do other individuals who may also describe themselves as independent but who do not have similarly elaborate self-knowledge in this domain. Those who have self-schemas as independent should be able to process information about their independence more efficiently than those who lack self-schemas on this dimension, should be able to back up their claims of independence with a greater number of specific examples, and should be more reluctant to accept as true evidence that challenges their independence.

To examine these ideas, Markus (1977) first identified three kinds of individuals: Individuals with independent self-schemas, individuals with dependent self-schemas, and aschematics, that is, individuals without a self-schema in this domain. Individuals were considered *schematic* if they had rated themselves as extremely independent or as extremely dependent and also rated this dimension as highly important to their self-description. Individuals were considered *aschematic* if they had rated themselves less extremely on this dimension and rated it as relatively unimportant to their self-descriptions. These independent, dependent, and aschematic individuals were invited to the lab and given a variety of tasks designed to assess their processing of self-relevant information.

The first task examined whether the three types of individuals differed in the kinds of adjectives they judged to be self-descriptive and in the speed with which they made such judgments. Trait adjectives were projected on a screen, one at a time. As they saw each, participants were asked to indicate whether or not it described them by pressing a *me* button or a *not me* button. The list of adjectives included 15 that were related to independence (e.g., independent, individualistic, unconventional), 15 that were related to dependence (e.g., dependent, conforming, tactful), and 30 unrelated words. The top panel of figure 10.1 shows the average numbers of dependent and independent adjectives that each group of participants responded *me* to. The three groups clearly differed in their responses: Dependents said *me* to more dependent traits than did independents, whereas independents said *me* to more independent traits than did dependents.

The *me* responses, however, do not tell the whole story. Notice that dependent participants, as might be expected, said *me* to more dependent than independent traits. Independent participants, however, said *me* to as many dependent as independent traits. Does this mean that these independent participants considered dependence to be just as self-defining as independence? Not necessarily. One might say *me* to a dependent adjective such as *tactful* for a variety of reasons. One may do so because one really thinks about oneself habitually as tactful. Alternatively, one may say *me* to tactful because one would like to see oneself as tactful or because, upon reflection, one concludes that one is tactful. These different reasons for saying *me* should result in different reaction times. People who habitually think of themselves as tactful should be able to make the *me* decision relatively fast because their relevant self-knowledge should be extensive and highly accessible. In contrast, people who do not frequently think about themselves in these terms and who therefore need to go through the process of deciding whether their self-knowledge permits a *me* response should be relatively slow to make this response.

It may be seen on the bottom panel of figure 10.1 that although independents said *me* to equal numbers of dependent and independent traits, they responded much faster to the independent traits than to the dependent ones. Most likely, this was because these independent participants had more elaborate and accessible knowledge pointing to their independence than to their dependence. Dependent participants showed a comparable pattern: They were faster to say *me* to dependent than to independent traits. Thus, both independent schematics and dependent schematics were faster to say *me* to adjectives that were congruent with their

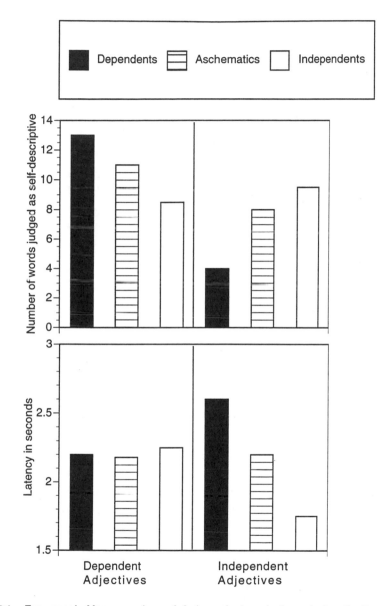

Figure 10.1 *Top panel*: Mean number of independent and dependent adjectives to which dependents, independents, and aschematics responded *me*. *Bottom panel*: Mean latency with which the three groups of participants responded *me* to independent adjectives and to dependent adjective. From Markus (1977, fig. 1, p. 68). Copyright © by the American Psychological Association. Reprinted with permission.

schemas than to incongruent adjectives. Only the aschematics responded with equal speed to the two kinds of adjectives.

It seems likely that schematics were able to process schema-congruent information more efficiently because they had more elaborate self-knowledge in the domain of their schema. This notion gained support from participants' performance on a second task. Participants were given a list of dependent and independent adjectives and were asked to circle those that they considered self-descriptive. Immediately after circling an adjective, they were asked to explain why they considered it self-descriptive by providing specific evidence from their own past behavior. Participants had little trouble coming up with such evidence. For example, to explain why they considered the adjective *conforming* to be self-descriptive, they described incidents such as "I didn't go to any rallies about the teaching-fellow strike because my friends didn't," or "I watched a television show I couldn't stand last night just to save a hassle with my roommates," or "I pierced my ears because all my friends did."

Interestingly, even when they had circled the same dependent words, dependent schematics were able to come up with more such examples of their relevant behavior than were independent schematics. The opposite was true for independent words that both kinds of participants had circled; for these, independents listed more examples of their past behavior than did dependents. In both cases, the aschematics listed an intermediate number of examples. For schematics, then, schema-congruent attributes are associated with an especially rich repertoire of knowledge about their own relevant behaviors. Perhaps because of this rich self-knowledge, schematics were reluctant to accept test results that challenged their self-views. For example, when informed that a test had found them to be highly susceptible to social influence, independents viewed this feedback as less accurate than did aschematics (Markus 1977).

In sum, people who are schematic on a dimension such as dependence or independence can make judgments about their standing on this dimension very efficiently, can back up these judgments with extensive personal examples, and have little faith in evidence that questions their self-views. Self-schemas on other dimensions, such as masculinity and femininity, have been shown to have similar consequences for how people process information about the self (e.g., Markus et al. 1982). All these findings suggest that a self-schema in a given dimension entails an elaborate knowledge structure about this dimension. Such an elaborate knowledge structure should also have implications for how one processes information about others, as discussed next.

Processing Information about Others   Individuals who have a self-schema on the dimension of masculinity may have rich and detailed knowledge not only about their own masculine reactions but also about the very nature of masculinity which kinds of behaviors, clothes, and speech patterns imply masculinity, which kinds of situations and people afford the expression of masculinity, which other traits are associated with masculinity, and so on. In other words, individuals with masculine self-schemas can be considered experts on masculinity. If so, this expertise should influence the way they process information about others.

Experts in other domains such as chess or physics process information in their domain of expertise quite differently from novices (e.g., Chase and Simon 1973). For example, when looking at a snapshot of a chess board taken in the middle of a game, an expert will see meaningful configurations of interrelated pieces, whereas a novice will see only a conglomeration of unrelated pieces. Moreover, a chess expert will be able to shift smoothly between levels of analysis, focusing either on large chunks of pieces or on smaller subsets, as required by the task. Novices, in contrast, will be restricted to a single level of analysis. Markus and her colleagues reasoned that self-schemas may confer similar advantages. If masculine self-schemas entail expertise in masculinity, then individuals who are schematic on this dimension should be especially likely to see meaning and structure in the relevant behaviors of another person.

To examine these ideas, Markus, Smith, and Moreland (1985) first identified two groups of men. One group included men who were schematic on the domain of masculinity, that is, rated themselves very highly on masculine attributes such as *masculine* and *dominant* and rated these as very important to their self-evaluation. The second group included men who were aschematic on masculinity, that is, rated themselves moderately on these attributes and viewed them as relatively unimportant. These schematic and aschematic men were later recruited to participate in a seemingly unrelated study, where they were shown a film of a male student in a dorm room. In the first part of the film, the student performed a series of schema-irrelevant behaviors such as playing a record and eating an apple. In the second part, he performed several stereotypically masculine behaviors such as lifting weights and watching a baseball game. As they watched this film, participants were asked to press a button whenever they saw what was to them a meaningful unit of behavior. The instructions explained that the same behavior could be unitized in different ways, all equally correct. For example, if a person takes ten steps across a room and gets a drink of water, this could be viewed as one meaningful action (going to get a drink), as two meaningful actions (crossing the room and getting a drink), or as 12 meaningful actions (taking ten steps, lifting the glass, and drinking). Would schematics and aschematics differ in how they unitized a film depicting masculine behaviors?

If masculine schematics see more coherent meaning in masculine behaviors than do aschematics, then the schematics should break the flow of masculine behaviors into larger units. This was indeed the case. Schematics' tendency to see larger units when observing the masculine behaviors must have been due to their specialized understanding of these behaviors; when they observed behaviors that were irrelevant to masculinity, for which they had no special expertise, the sizes of their units did not differ from those of aschematics. Perhaps because they were better able to see the relevance of the target's masculine behavior to masculinity, schematics also viewed him as more masculine than did the aschematics (though because there was only one target, it remains possible that schematics would also see more masculinity in individuals who behave neutrally). A follow-up study revealed that schematics also had the flexibility observed for experts in other domains: They were better able than aschematics to shift from large to small units when asked to do so (Markus et al. 1985). Together these data suggest that individuals who have a self-schema for a particular dimension can be considered experts on that dimension; much like experts in any other domain, they are able to chunk domain-relevant information into especially large units, and can also shift readily from one level of analysis to another.

Taken together, research on self-schemas suggests that when we see ourselves as extreme on a particular trait and consider it central to our self-definition we are likely to have an elaborate and accessible self-schema that contains detailed knowledge about our trait-related behavior and that influences the way we process information about ourselves. In addition we possess more general expertise about this trait which we draw upon to make sense of others' behavior (for a review, see Kihlstrom et al. 1988). It is unclear, however, whether our expertise in the domain of our self-schema stems from the self-knowledge or precedes it: Is it the case that people first develop an elaborate self-schema in a given domain and then, as a by-product of their personal interest in this domain, also develop more general knowledge about it? Or is it the case that people first develop expertise in a domain, perhaps because it is emphasized by their parents and teachers, and then, once they are expert, apply this expertise to themselves?

To date, there are no data that can address this question, and the causal relations between self-schemas and domain expertise remain unclear. Moreover, it is possible that people may have elaborate and accessible expertise even in domains where they lack self-schemas. Indeed, one study identified people with chronically accessible knowledge about personality traits such as kindness and shyness not by assessing their self-schemas but by examining the frequency with which these traits appeared in their descriptions of other people (Bargh et al. 1986). Such chronically accessible traits were shown to influence impressions of a target person much like would be expected for self-schemas: Participants for whom shyness was chronically accessible viewed an ambiguously shy person as especially shy, and those for whom kindness was chronically accessible viewed an ambiguously kind person as especially kind. It remains unclear whether people for whom shyness or kindness were chronically accessible also had elaborate self-schemas on these dimensions because self-schemas were not assessed in this study. But it is clear that when a trait is chronically accessible, either because it pertains to one's self-schema or for any other reason, it will figure heavily in one's impressions of others.

The Working Self-concept

The notion of self-schema implies a stable, unchanging self. Individuals identified as schematic or aschematic in one setting behave in predictably different ways when observed weeks later in other settings. People appear to carry their self-knowledge with them as they move from one situation to another, and their enduring self-schemas influence their processing of self-relevant information as well as their impressions of others in a wide variety of situations. However, this view of the self as comprising stable and enduring knowledge structures is put into question by several findings indicating that the self can vary from one situation to another. For example, it is easy to shift people's sense of how shy or outgoing they are: People may come to see themselves as more outgoing if they are asked to furnish examples of their past outgoing behaviors, if they are asked to answer the one-sided question "Are you extraverted?" or if they are led to believe that outgoing individuals are especially likely to succeed (Fazio et al. 1981; see chapter 3; Kunda et al. 1993; see chapter 4; Sanitioso et al. 1990; see chapter 6). Clearly we see ourselves as more outgoing on some occasions than on others.

We vary from one occasion to another not only in how extremely we view ourselves on traits such as extraversion, assertiveness, or masculinity but also in the extent to which any such trait is likely to figure in our self-descriptions in the first place. When considering who we are, we may be especially likely to focus on those dimensions that distinguish us from other people in our current environment. The lone woman in an all male workplace may be especially likely to think of herself as a woman, and token African Americans may be especially likely to define themselves in terms of their ethnicity. Indeed, when school children were asked to "Tell us about yourself," they were especially likely to mention characteristics such as age, gender, or ethnicity if they differed on these from the majority of their classmates (McGuire et al. 1978; McGuire and Padawer-Singer 1976). Different attributes may figure in our self-conceptions on different occasions, depending on the attributes of the people who surround us.

How may one reconcile the malleability implied by such shifts in the extremity and salience of self-conceptions with the stability implied by the enduring impact of self-schemas on information processing? One answer is that we may be malleable only on our nonschematic dimensions, elaborate self schemas may remain consistent over time, whereas other, aschematic aspects of the self may shift with circumstances. This explanation is supported by some evidence suggesting that the self-reports of schematics are indeed more consistent over time than those of aschematics (Markus 1977). Nevertheless, this explanation does not completely solve the puzzle because shifts in self-concepts have been demonstrated even for people who had started off with extreme self-views and who could therefore be considered schematic (Sanitioso et al. 1990; see chapter 6).

Such shifts may be accounted for if one considers the richness and complexity of self-knowledge. The self is not a unitary structure. Rather, it encompasses within its scope many diverse, often conflicting memories and beliefs about one's behavior and attributes (see Greenwald and Pratkanis 1984). One may remember oneself behaving in a friendly and outgoing manner on a variety of occasions and also recall being shy and feeling awkward on other occasions. The self at any given moment—*the working self-concept*—is only a subset of these diverse self-conceptions (Markus and Kunda 1986). The contents of the working self-concept may vary from one occasion to another as various features of the situation highlight different aspects of the self. The stability of the self, then, reflects one's enduring self-knowledge whereas the malleability of the self arises from the fact that different elements of this self-knowledge are activated on different occasions.

This analysis suggests that the malleability of the working self-concept depends on the diversity of one's enduring self-knowledge. To be able to alternate between extraverted and shy self-conceptions, one must be able to recruit memories of one's extraversion as well as memories of one's shyness. If one has only extraverted memories, one will be unable to view oneself as shy regardless of the demands of the situation. There is some evidence that this is so. You may recall that people shift their self-conceptions in response to one-sided questions: People asked "Are you extraverted?" subsequently rate themselves as more extraverted than do people asked "Are you introverted?" (Kunda et al. 1993; see chapter 4). It turns out that such shifts were not obtained for people who had described themselves as relatively invariable in how extraverted or introverted they were; these invariable individuals rated themselves as equally extraverted regardless of the direction of the question they were asked. We may entertain conflicting self-conceptions on different occasions only if our self-knowledge is variable enough to support either one.

Even when self-conceptions do shift, the contents and salience of one's enduring self-knowledge may constrain the magnitude of the shift. An extremely extraverted individual may come to view the self as somewhat more extraverted on some occasions and as somewhat less extraverted on other occasions but is unlikely to ever espouse an extremely introverted self. For such an individual, the small number of available shy self-conceptions may become more or less salient on different occasions, but these will always constitute only a small proportion of the contents of the working self-concept. Indeed, when extreme extraverts were motivated to view themselves as introverted, their self-conceptions did shift in the desired direction. Yet they also remained faithful to their true colors; they still viewed themselves as highly extraverted, and as considerably more extraverted than did extreme introverts who were motivated to see themselves as extraverted (Sanitioso et al. 1990; see chapter 6, figure 6.1).

In sum, our working self-concepts are drawn from our enduring self-knowledge. The variability, extremity, and salience of our lasting self-conceptions will therefore determine and constrain the variability of our temporary, working self-concepts. Note that this analysis is very similar to the analysis of why our trait-related behavior may vary from one occasion to another (Mischel and Shoda 1995; see chapter 9). Both accounts share the assumption that people have an enduring network of knowledge and associations and that they selectively bring to mind different subsets of this knowledge base on different occasions. Different configurations of self-conceptions, beliefs, and affective reactions may be activated in different situations, resulting in different, often inconsistent self-conceptions and behavior.

Self-esteem

Our self-schemas contain knowledge about what we are like in particular domains such as independence, extraversion, or masculinity. In addition to these specific areas of self-knowledge, we also have a more global sense of our overall worthiness or goodness. The term *self-esteem* is commonly used to refer to the positivity of this global self-evaluation. Individuals with high self-esteem regard themselves highly, feel they have much to be proud of, and are generally satisfied with their attributes and performance. They tend to endorse as self-descriptive statements such as "I feel that I'm a person of worth, at least on an equal basis with others," "I feel that I have a number of good qualities," and "On the whole, I am satisfied with myself" (Rosenberg 1965). In contrast, individuals with low self-esteem regard themselves as failures, often feel useless, have little self-respect, and are generally dissatisfied with themselves. They tend to endorse as self-descriptive statements such as "All in all, I am inclined to think I am a failure," "I wish I could have more respect for myself," and "At times I think I am no good at all" (Rosenberg 1965). In popular Western culture, self-esteem is viewed as essential to effective functioning, and most parents and teachers strive to protect and enhance their children's self-esteem.

Psychologists too have a long-standing interest in self-esteem and have conducted thousands of studies to explore its consequences (for reviews, see Baumeister 1998; Blaine and Crocker 1993; for cross-cultural differences in the importance assigned to self-esteem, see chapter 11).

From the perspective of social cognition, self-esteem is viewed as a stable construct that has broad implications for the representation of self-knowledge, for the cognitive strategies that people engage in when processing self-relevant information, and for their reactions to such information.

Self-esteem and the Representation of Self-knowledge People with high self-esteem tend to have a clearer sense of who and what they are (for reviews, see Baumeister 1998; Campbell and Lavallee 1993). In one study demonstrating this, Jennifer Campbell identified individuals with high and low self-esteem and asked them to rate themselves on dimensions such as quite/outspoken and competitive/cooperative and also to indicate how confident they felt about each self-rating (Campbell 1990). Although the two groups did not differ in their mean self-ratings, individuals with low self-esteem rated themselves less extremely and were less confident about their self-ratings than were individuals with high self-esteem. A different set of studies by Ann Baumgardner (1990) also found that individuals with low self-esteem have less clear self-concepts than those with high self-esteem: Low self-esteem individuals reported less confidence about ratings of their personality and were substantially slower to make such self-ratings than were high self-esteem individuals. However, this lack of clarity was restricted to the self; when asked to rate a friend, individuals with low self-esteem were every bit as confident and fast as those with high self-esteem. Thus it is not the case that low self-esteem individuals tend to be wishy-washy and generally reluctant to report extreme and confident opinions. They are only reluctant to do so when reporting on their own attributes, which suggests that their self-knowledge is especially lacking in clarity.

Other studies revealed that the self-knowledge of individuals with low self-esteem is also less internally coherent and less stable over time than that of individuals with high self-esteem (Campbell 1990). Note that these characteristics of the self-knowledge of low self-esteem individuals—low certainty, stability, accessibility, and coherence—are precisely those that have been found to characterize individuals who lack clear, well-articulated self-schemas (Markus 1977). Low self-esteem individuals, then, may be viewed as relatively aschematic in their self-knowledge. Whereas people with high self-esteem tend to have clear, confident, and stable self-knowledge, those with low self-esteem tend to be uncertain and confused about their identities. Perhaps as a result of this identity confusion, low self-esteem individuals appear to be more at the mercy of external events—they show greater fluctuations in moods and behavior than do high self-esteem individuals in reaction to the positive and negative events they experience as they go through life (for a review, see Baumeister, 1998).

Self-esteem and Self-serving Strategies   Although the literature on how individuals with high and low self-esteem differ in their processing of social information is very large and somewhat mixed, there appear to be some systematic differences between the two kinds of individuals. For the most part, people with high self-esteem are more likely than those with low self-esteem to put a positive, self-enhancing spin on social information: High self-esteem individuals are especially likely to claim more responsibility for their successes than for their failures and to preferentially recall information that makes them look superior (for a review, see Blaine and Crocker 1993). Generally, although both high and low self-esteem individuals strive to see themselves in the best possible light, they tend to rely on different strategies for doing so: High self-esteem individuals try to maximize self-enhancing opportunities that will make them look good, whereas low self-esteem individuals try to avoid potentially dangerous situations that will make them look bad (for a review, see Baumeister, 1998. For a more detailed discussion of these two kinds of strategies, see later section on self-guides, and see Higgins, 1998). High self-esteem individuals are also especially likely to engage in self-enhancement strategies that directly boost their personal worth, whereas low-self esteem individuals favor more indirect routes to self-enhancement, whereby the self is boosted through enhancement of one's social group, possibly because they fear they will be unable to defend overly positive characterizations of their personal accomplishments (Brown, Collins, and Schmidt, 1988).

Failure brings the different cognitive strategies used by high and low self-esteem individuals into high relief. Any failure poses a threat to one's general self-worth, but one may be able to diffuse such threats by reminding oneself of one's many positive attributes. High self-esteem individuals respond to failure by focusing on their personal strengths, which become especially accessible in their minds following an experience of failure. Low self-esteem individuals show no such tendency (Dodgson and Wood 1998). This may be why failure can have opposite effects on the self-views of high and low self-esteem individuals. High self-esteem individuals view their interpersonal abilities more positively after failing an achievement test than they do after succeeding at it, whereas the reverse is true for low self-esteem individuals (Brown and Smart 1991). Perhaps because they are unable to boost and restore their self-worth following failure, low self-esteem individuals are more devastated by failure than are high self-esteem individuals. Both groups feel equally positively following success, but low self-esteem individuals feel greater shame and humiliation following failure than do high self-esteem individuals (Brown and Dutton 1995).

Perhaps because of these different orientations toward maintaining their self-worth, high self-esteem individuals are more willing than low self-esteem individuals to take risks in order to obtain self-enhancing information. For example, after discovering that they had performed more poorly than another person on one test, high self-esteem individuals showed an increased desire to seek further comparisons with that individual, most probably with the hope of coming out on top the next time round. In contrast, low self-esteem individuals showed no such increased interest in taking on potentially self-enhancing but highly risky comparisons to the person who had just outperformed them (Wood et al. 1994).

Romantic relationships provide an especially interesting, and saddening, arena for exploring the differing cognitive strategies used by individuals with high and low self-esteem. When you are feeling threatened and vulnerable, perhaps because you have suffered a setback at work or because you realize that you have disappointed the person you love, how will this make you feel about your love relationship? Will you fall back on this relationship as a source of comfort and reassurance, boosting yourself by boosting your partner and embellishing your partner's positive regard for you? Or will you assume that your partner will now lose interest in you, and so try to protect yourself from the pain of this rejection by diminishing your partner and relationship? Which of these strategies you choose may depend on your self-esteem.

In a series of studies, Sandra Murray and her colleagues recruited individuals involved in long-term dating relationships and confronted them with various kinds of threats to their self-worth (Murray et al. 1998). In some of the studies, participants were confronted with a direct threat to their relationship: They were asked to contemplate a time when they had disappointed their romantic partner, or to indicate how often they engaged in inconsiderate behaviors towards their partner. Another study confronted participants with a threat that did not concern their relationship—they were led to believe that they had performed poorly on an intelligence test. After receiving one of these threats, participants responded to a series of questions about their romantic partner and relationship. Control participants responded to these same questions without first receiving any threat.

In all these studies, individuals with high and low self-esteem reacted very differently to these threats. Those with high self-esteem responded to challenges to their self-worth by enhancing their belief in their partner's high regard for them. When confronted with their interpersonal or intellectual failings, these high self-esteem individuals attempted to bolster their threatened self-worth by enhancing the positivity of their romantic relationship; they seemed to use this relationship as a resource for self-affirmation in the face of challenge. In contrast, those with low self-esteem responded to the threats by reducing their belief in their partner's positive regard for them and decreasing the positivity of their own regard for their partner. Sadly, rather than using their partner and relationship as a helpful resource that could mitigate and deflect threats to the self, these low self-esteem individuals seemed to view their relationship as a potential source of yet another threat, rejection, and proceeded to protect themselves against this imminent threat by devaluing their partner and relationship. Oddly, low self-esteem individuals also devalued their relationship after receiving a boost to their self-worth, perhaps because the boost reminded them that their partner's affection was contingent on their continued positive performance and thereby heightened their concern about the possibility of rejection.

In sum, it appears that high self-esteem individuals seek, hope for, and expect the best, and engage in cognitive strategies aimed at maximizing self-enhancement. In contrast, low self-esteem individuals fear and expect the worst, and engage in cognitive strategies aimed at minimizing disappointment and self-deflation. A particularly ironic aspect of the predicament of low self-esteem individuals is that their attempts to prevent loss may in fact bring about the very losses they are trying to forestall. By distancing themselves from their romantic relationships and devaluating their partners, as they do when their confidence in their relationship is shaken, low self-esteem individuals may very well bring about the dissolution of the relationship that they so fear losing.

The research discussed so far has focused on exploring how the contents of self-knowledge on particular dimensions may influence the processing of social information. I turn next to a discussion of how the organization and integration of self-knowledge along a variety of dimensions may influence one's thoughts and feelings.

Organization of Self-knowledge

Self-complexity

Shelly and Karen, both college students, organize their self-knowledge in quite different ways. Shelly's sense of self is based predominantly on being a student; all other aspects of her life—her relationship with her parents, her romantic partner, her recreation activities—are closely tied in with her sense of herself as a student; she values relationships and activities to the extent that they support her academic goals. Karen, too, values being a student. But her self-definition is also based on several additional independent and highly valued components—her sense of self as a daughter, a lover, a music enthusiast. Each of these roles allows her to express and fulfill different aspects of her self and all contribute to her sense of who and what she is. Now imagine that Shelly and Karen both find out that they have failed an important exam. Who do you suppose will be more upset?

Intuitively, it seems that Shelly, whose entire identity rests on her academic self, should be more devastated by an academic setback than Karen, who can still maintain her sense of worthiness by focusing on how good a daughter, a lover, and a musician she is. This intuition gains support from a series of studies by Patricia Linville (1985, 1987). Linville noted that people vary in their *self-complexity*. Some, like Karen, have highly complex self-representations; their self-concepts include many distinct aspects. Others, like Shelly, have less complex self-representations; their self-concepts include a small number of highly interrelated aspects. When people experience a negative event that challenges one aspect of their self, their self-complexity may determine the extent to which their negative feelings will spill over into other aspects of the self. If self-complexity is low and all aspects of the self are highly interrelated, a failure in one area can make one feel incompetent in all other areas as well; a poor grade may mean not only that one is a poor student but also that one is a lousy daughter and an incompetent lover. In contrast, if self-complexity is high and the different aspects of the self are quite distinct from one another, the negative fallout from failure in one area of the self will remain restricted to that area; one may feel like a poor student but still think of oneself as a fine daughter and lover.

Linville (1987) assessed students' self-complexity by asking them to sort a set of diverse personality traits into groups so that each group would describe a meaningful aspect of themselves. The students were instructed that they could form as many groups as they liked and could place any of the traits in as many groups as they wished. From these groupings, it was possible to calculate a measure of self-complexity for each participant, using a formula that took into account the number of self-aspects as well as the degree of overlap between them. Self-complexity was considered higher to the extent that the number of self-aspects was high and the overlap between them low (i.e., each aspect involved different traits).

Can high self-complexity buffer the negative consequences of stressful events? When they encounter stressful events, will individuals with high self-complexity experience fewer psychological difficulties and physiological symptoms than individuals with low self-complexity? To answer these questions, participants were asked to indicate which of a lengthy list of life stresses they had experienced in the previous two weeks. The list included a wide variety of minor and major stressful events common for college students, relating to their social and academic life and to issues such as finances, drugs, legal problems, and accidents. The number of such negative events that students said they had experienced in the previous two weeks ranged from 0 to 17, with an average of about 5. To determine the consequences of these events to well-being, students also completed a measure of depression and indicated which of a variety of physical symptoms (e.g., colds, coughs, stomach pains, headaches) they had experienced over the previous two weeks. Two weeks later, the students returned to the lab and completed all these measures again. This design made it possible to ask whether the stressful events reported at the time of the first measurement exerted a negative impact on students' mental and physical health two weeks later, and whether self-complexity (as measured on the first occasion) buffered this negative impact.

Self-complexity did buffer the negative impact of stressful events. Among students who had experienced many stressful events, those with higher self-complexity faired better: They experienced fewer health problems and less depression. This does not mean that people with high self-complexity will generally feel healthier and happier; among individuals who had experienced few stressful events, those with high self-complexity had no advantage over those with low self-complexity. But when people do experience stress, individuals with high self-complexity may be less vulnerable to its adverse consequences because for such individuals, who have many distinct self-aspects, the negative thoughts and feelings provoked by a negative event that challenges one area of the self are likely to remain confined to that restricted area. These complex individuals may still draw on the unaffected areas of the self to boost their sense of worthiness and, thereby, their mental and physical well-being.

Whereas individuals with low self-complexity are especially vulnerable to stressful events, they may have an advantage when stress is low and when they experience positive events. In such circumstances, their positive affect will spill over into all areas of the self, resulting in stronger positive reactions. For complex individuals, in contrast, following a triumph in one area of the self, other, unaffected self-aspects may still remain relatively mediocre. As a result people low in self-complexity may be subject to greater mood swings than those high in self-complexity, experiencing darker moods in the face of setbacks but greater joy in reaction to successes (Linville 1985; Niedenthal, Setterlund, and Wherry 1992).

Another important aspect of the organization of self-knowledge concerns the positivity and negativity of various aspects of the self. There are different ways in which positive and negative self-knowledge may be organized. Positive and negative beliefs about the self may be separated into distinct compartments, some all positive, others all negative. Alternatively, self-knowledge may be organized such that each aspect contains positive as well as negative beliefs. The extent to which positive and negative components of self-knowledge are compartmentalized can affect well-being (Showers 1992; Showers and Kling 1996). When positive and negative aspects of self-knowledge are delegated to separate compartments, one may be able to focus on the positive without thinking about the negative. Therefore, people experiencing positive events may feel happier if their positive and negative self-conceptions are relatively distinct from each other. In contrast, people experiencing negative events may feel happier if their positive and negative self-conceptions are highly integrated, with each aspect of the self containing positive as well as negative information. This is because when they receive a blow to a particular self-aspect, the positive contents of that self-aspect will buffer negative thoughts. In sum, a highly compartmentalized self may allow one to revel in one's successes but leave one especially vulnerable to failures.

So far discussion has focused on the contents and organization of one's actual, current self. I turn next to the relation between this actual self, on the one hand, and one's hopes, fears, and expectations for oneself, on the other hand, and consider the implications for feelings and thought.

Self-guides

As I try to evaluate my attributes, actions, and accomplishments, that is, my *actual self*, I may measure myself against two different standards: One is my *ideal self*, that is, the kind of person I wish and aspire to be, my hopes, goals, and desires for myself. The other is my *ought self*, that is, the kind of person I feel I should and ought to be, my sense of my duties, obligations, and responsibilities. The two may go hand in hand: I may wish to be a good mother and also feel it is my duty to be one. But the two may sometimes clash: I may aspire to a brilliant career, yet feel obligated to stay home and care for my children. I may also measure myself against standards set for me by other important people in my life: My father's hopes and aspirations for me, my mother's beliefs about my duties and obligations. When my actual self falls short of these ideal and ought selves (my own or those held for me by important others), I will feel badly. An extensive program of research by Tory Higgins and his colleagues has shown that the magnitude and nature of these negative feelings can depend on which standard—ideal or ought—one measures oneself against, on how discrepant one's actual self is from this standard, and on how accessible and salient this discrepancy is. The magnitude and accessibility of these discrepancies may also influence one's processing of information about others (for reviews, see Higgins 1987, 1989, 1998).

Self-discrepancies and Emotional Vulnerability At times I may be driven by the desire to achieve positive outcomes—a happy marriage, professional success, good health. In these cases I may be said to have *promotion goals*; that is, I am driven to promote my well-being, approach positive states, and achieve desired rewards. At other times I may be driven by the desire to avoid negative outcomes—divorce, professional failure, illness. In these cases I may be said to have *prevention goals*; that is, I am driven to avoid negative states, escape punishment, and prevent feared outcomes. When these two different kinds of goals are thwarted, I will experience different negative emotions: Failing to accomplish promotion goals entails loss of positive outcomes—I do not have the good things I desire. Such loss leads to sadness and dejection. Failing to accomplish prevention goals, on the other hand, entails experiencing negative outcomes—I am suffering the negative consequences I had feared. Such punishment leads to anxiety and agitation.

Focusing on one's ideal self entails a focus on promotion goals—the desire to achieve one's hopes and aspirations. Therefore, when one becomes aware of a large discrepancy between one's actual and ideal selves, one focuses on the absence of desired outcomes and feels disappointment, sadness, and dejection. For example, if I aspire to become a doctor, and realize that my grades are not high enough to gain admission to medical school, I may feel sad and disappointed. Focusing on one's ought self, on the other hand, entails a focus on prevention goals—the notion of obligation carries with it the notion that one will be punished for failure to meet this obligation. Therefore, when one becomes aware of a large discrepancy between one's actual and ought selves, one anticipates punishment and feels anxiety, agitation, and guilt. For example, if I believe that I ought to work hard at school but have not been doing so, I may feel guilty and anxious. Based on this analysis, Higgins and his colleagues predicted that salient discrepancies between actual and ideal selves would lead to dejection-related emotions, whereas salient discrepancies between actual and ought selves would lead to anxiety-related emotions (Higgins 1987, 1989, 1998).

People differ in the extent to which their actual selves fall short of their ideal and ought selves. Do the magnitudes of these discrepancies determine people's emotional reactions to negative events? Will people feel sadder the more they fall short of their ideal selves and feel more agitated the more they fall short of their ought selves? To address these questions, Higgins and his colleagues first identified two different groups of individuals, one with large discrepancies between their actual and ideal selves and the other with large discrepancies between their actual and ought selves (Higgins et al. 1986). This was accomplished by asking participants to list the attributes associated with their actual self, the attributes associated with their ideal self, and the attributes associated with their ought self. For each participant, the investigators compared the attributes listed for the actual self to those listed for each self-guide (ideal and ought), and counted the number of matches (i.e., attributes that appeared on the actual self as well as on the self-guide) and the number of mismatches (i.e., cases where an attribute on the self-guide was the opposite of an attribute on the actual self). The discrepancy between the actual self and each self-guide was calculated by subtracting the number of matches between the two from the number of mismatches between the two. Two distinct groups of participants were identified, one with a predominant actual/ideal discrepancy and one with a predominant actual/ought discrepancy (each group was relatively high on its predominant discrepancy and relatively low on the other discrepancy).

The emotional reactions of these participants to negative and positive events were assessed several weeks later. Participants were asked to imagine a negative event such as receiving a poor grade or being rejected by a lover or to imagine a positive event such as receiving a high grade or spending an evening with an admired person. Both before and after this imagination task participants completed a questionnaire that assessed their dejection-related feelings (sad, unhappy, dissatisfied, etc.) and their agitation-related feelings (anxious, frightened, nervous, etc.). The moods that par-

Table 10.1 Dejection and agitation experienced by participants with predominant actual/ideal self-discrepancies or predominant actual/ought self-discrepancies after focusing on a negative event or on a positive event

	NEGATIVE EVENT		POSITIVE EVENT	
PREDOMINANT SELF-DISCREPANCY	DEJECTION	AGITATION	DEJECTION	AGITATION
Actual/ideal	.24	.00	.03	.03
Actual/ought	.04	.11	.06	.09

Source: From Higgins et al. (1986, table 1, p. 9). Copyright © (1986) by the American Psychological Association. Reprinted with permission.
Note: Scores are adjusted for premanipulation mood.

ticipants reported after completing the imagination task are presented in table 10.1. As expected, participants with different kinds of self-discrepancies experienced different emotions when thinking about a negative event: Those with a predominant actual/ideal discrepancy became more dejected whereas those with a predominant actual/ought discrepancy tended to become more agitated instead. This different pattern of emotional reactions was found only for participants who had focused on a negative event; the two kinds of participants did not differ much in their emotional reactions to an imagined positive event. This suggests that individuals experience the kind of negative emotion associated with their predominant discrepancy only when they are contemplating a negative event.

People differ not only in the magnitude of their self-discrepancies but also in the extent to which these discrepancies are accessible to them. Jim and Ron may both believe that they are not doing as well at school as they would like to; both experience a comparable discrepancy between their actual and ideal selves. But they differ in the extent to which they are preoccupied with this discrepancy. Jim's failure to meet his hoped-for academic goals is constantly on his mind, whereas Ron thinks about this failure only occasionally, when he receives a bad grade. As a result the two should also differ in the frequency with which they experience the negative emotion entailed by such an actual/ideal discrepancy, namely dejection. Although the magnitude of this discrepancy is the same for Jim and for Ron, Jim should be more prone to sadness and dejection because this discrepancy is more on his mind. More generally, the magnitude of one's self-discrepancies should exert greater impact on one's emotions when these discrepancies are more accessible.

A series of correlational studies by Higgins and his colleagues lends support to this prediction (Higgins, Shah, and Friedman 1997). These investigators assessed, for each participant, the magnitudes of the actual/ideal discrepancy and the actual/ought discrepancy as well as the accessibility of each of these discrepancies. Participants were asked to generate three to five attributes reflecting their ideal self (i.e., the type of person they hoped, wished or aspired to be) and to generate three to five different attributes reflecting their ought self (i.e., the type of person they believed it was their duty, obligation, or responsibility to be). After generating each attribute, they rated the extent to which they actually had that attribute as well as the extent to which they wanted to have it (for ideal attributes) or the extent to which they ought to have it (for ought attributes). The magnitude of the actual/ideal discrepancy was determined by the difference between participants' ratings of the extent to which they wanted to have the ideal attributes and the extent to which they actually had them, and the accessibility of this discrepancy was determined by the speed with which they made these ratings. The magnitude and accessibility of the actual/ought discrepancies were assessed in a similar manner.

Participants also reported how often they felt dejected and how often they felt agitated. The prediction was that the larger one's actual/ideal discrepancy, the more often one should feel dejected, sad, and disappointed, but only if this discrepancy is highly accessible. Similarly, the larger one's actual/ought discrepancy, the more often one should feel agitated, tense, and on edge, but again, only if this discrepancy is highly accessible. Put differently, the magnitude

Table 10.2 Correlation between the magnitude of actual/ideal discrepancies and dejection and between the magnitude of actual/ought discrepancies and agitation for participants for whom each of these discrepancies is high or low in accessibility

	CORRELATION BETWEEN MAGNITUDE OF ACTUAL/IDEAL DISCREPANCY AND DEJECTION		CORRELATION BETWEEN MAGNITUDE OF ACTUAL/OUGHT DISCREPANCY AND AGITATION	
	HIGH ACCESSIBILITY	LOW ACCESSIBILITY	HIGH ACCESSIBILITY	LOW ACCESSIBILITY
Study 1	.41	−.10	.47	−.32
Study 2	.28	−.15	.27	−.16
Study 3	.20	−.13	.44	−.07

Source: Data from Higgins et al. (1997, studies 1–3).
Note: In each case the alternative type of discrepancy and the alternative negative emotion are controlled for statistically.

of each self-discrepancy should predict the frequency with which one experiences the negative emotion that follows from it if that discrepancy is highly accessible but not otherwise. These predictions were borne out.

Participants were divided by median split into those high and those low in the accessibility of their actual/ideal discrepancies. Within each of these groups, the investigators calculated the correlation between the magnitude of participants' actual/ideal discrepancy and their dejection. Similarly, they calculated the correlation between the magnitude of actual/ought discrepancies and agitation separately for those high and those low in the accessibility of that discrepancy. As may be seen in table 10.2, in all three studies the magnitude of each self-discrepancy was positively correlated with the appropriate negative emotion only among participants for whom that discrepancy was highly accessible (smaller and non-significant negative correlations were obtained for participants low in the accessibility of self-discrepancies). These findings suggest that the extent to which we fall short of the standards we set for ourselves predicts our ongoing negative feelings only if these standards are constantly on our minds. The larger the gap between who we are and who we wish to be, the more dejected we will feel, and the larger the gap between who we are and who we believe we ought to be, the more agitated we will feel, but this will only be true if these gaps are highly accessible to us.

Self-discrepancies that are not chronically accessible may still provoke negative feelings whenever one is reminded of these discrepancies. In a different study, participants who fell short of both their ideal and their ought selves became more dejected when reminded of their ideal selves and became more agitated when reminded of their ought selves (Higgins et al. 1986, study 2). No such mood changes were obtained for participants with low self-discrepancies. Once again, each self-discrepancy gave rise to its particular negative emotion only when it was made accessible.

In sum, discrepancies between our actual selves and our standards for ourselves can result in negative emotions. Different discrepancies will result in different emotions—we will experience dejection if we fall short of our ideal selves and agitation if we fall short of our ought selves. However, each kind of discrepancy will provoke its appropriate negative emotion only if that discrepancy is chronically or temporarily accessible. Self-discrepancies that are not on our mind at any given time are unlikely to influence our feelings at that time.

The work on the emotional consequences of self-discrepancies has focused on the negative emotions that follow from a discrepancy between one's current actual self and the self one wishes to be or believes one ought to be right now. Such discrepancies can be demoralizing. However, discrepancies between one's current self and the selves one hopes or fears one will become in the future can sometimes be motivating and inspiring, if these future selves are deemed possible. Research on the impact of possible future selves that differ from one's current self has not been nearly as extensive as the research on discrepancies among current selves. Still, there is suggestive evidence that people's well-being may be enhanced if they entertain positive possible future selves that offer hope for improvement or if they entertain negative possible future selves that may spur them into preventive action (Markus and Nurius 1986; Oyserman and Markus 1990).

Self-discrepancies and Interpersonal Thought and Tactics A focus on one's ideal self amounts to a focus on positive outcomes—the achievements and accomplishments one hopes and aspires to attain. And, indeed, people who are keenly aware that they fall short of their ideal selves experience the emotions typically associated with the absence of positive outcomes, namely sadness and dejection. A salient concern with one's ideal self may also be associated with a more generalized tendency to focus on the presence and absence of positive outcomes when trying to make sense of other people's life and when planning one's own interpersonal tactics. Such a concern may make people especially likely to notice and remember whether other people have achieved or failed to achieve their desired outcomes, and it may lead people to choose those interpersonal strategies intended to maximize positive outcomes rather than choosing strategies intended to minimize negative outcomes. In contrast, a focus on one's ought self amounts to a focus on negative outcomes—the punishment and guilt one fears and wishes to avoid. And, indeed, people who are keenly aware that they fall short of their ought selves experience the emotions typically associated with the presence of negative outcomes, namely agitation and anxiety. Here too a salient concern with one's ought self may be associated with a more generalized tendency to focus on the presence and absence of negative outcomes. Such a concern may make people especially likely to notice and remember whether others have experienced or avoided misfortunes, and it may lead people to choose those interpersonal strategies intended to minimize negative outcomes rather than choosing strategies intended to maximize positive outcomes.

In one study designed to test these ideas, participants previously identified as having a predominant actual/ideal discrepancy or a predominant actual/ought discrepancy read an essay describing 20 events in the life of a student (Higgins and Tykocinski 1992). Eight of these events focused on the presence or absence of positive outcomes. These included events such as finding a $20 bill (present positive outcome) or discovering that a movie one wanted to see was no longer showing (absence of positive outcome). Eight other events focused on the presence or absence of negative outcomes. These included events such as getting stuck in the subway (present negative outcome) or skipping a particularly unpleasant day at school (absence of negative outcome). The remaining events were neutral fillers. After reading this essay, participants worked on an unrelated task for ten minutes and were then asked, unexpectedly, to recall the essay word for word.

Would participants who were focused on their ideal self, and therefore on the presence and absence of positive outcomes in their own life, be especially likely to remember events in which another person had experienced or had failed to experience a positive outcome? And would participants who were focused on their ought self, and therefore on the presence and absence of negative outcomes in their own life, be especially likely to remember events in which another person had suffered or had escaped negative outcomes? As may be seen in table 10.3, the answer to these ques-

Table 10.3 Number of events involving the presence and absence of positive outcomes and events involving the presence and absence of negative outcomes recalled by participants with a predominant actual/ideal self-discrepancy and by participants with a predominant actual/ought self-discrepancy

PREDOMINANT SELF-DISCREPANCY	POSITIVE OUTCOMES	NEGATIVE OUTCOMES
Actual/ideal	6.2	4.5
Actual/ought	5.1	5.0

Source: Data from Higgins and Tykocinski (1992).

tions was yes. Participants with a predominant actual/ideal self-discrepancy recalled more events involving positive outcomes and fewer events involving negative outcomes than did participants with a predominant actual/ought self-discrepancy. People are especially likely to notice events in other people's lives that match the concerns dictated by their own predominant self-discrepancy—a concern with achieving the positive for those preoccupied with actual/ideal self-discrepancies and a concern with avoiding the negative for those preoccupied with actual/ought self-discrepancies.

Temporarily activated concerns with self-discrepancies can have the same consequences for memory as do chronically activated ones. In another study, participants were first led to focus either on their ideal selves or on their ought selves. Then, in a seemingly unrelated study, they read an essay describing episodes in which another person had attempted to seek positive outcomes on some occasions and to avoid negative outcomes on other occasions (Higgins et al. 1994). As expected, participants who had been led to focus on their ideal selves, and who were therefore presumably contemplating the presence and absence of desired outcomes in their own lives, were especially likely to recall episodes in which the other person had sought positive outcomes. In contrast, participants who had been led to focus on their ought selves, and who were therefore presumably contemplating the presence and absence of unwanted outcomes in their own lives, were especially likely to recall episodes in which the other person had attempted to avoid negative outcomes. When one is focused on positive or on negative outcomes in one's own life, either because one has an ongoing preoccupation with that kind of outcome or because something in the situation has caused one to contemplate such outcomes, one becomes especially sensitive to that kind of outcome in other people's lives as well.

Salient self-discrepancies may also help determine which strategies one uses to achieve important interpersonal goals such as making friends. When you are trying to be a good friend, you may use a variety of strategies. These may be divided into those that focus on seeking positive outcomes such as closeness and trust and those that focus on avoiding negative outcomes such as estrangement and discord. Which of these you prefer may be influenced by the particular self-discrepancy that is predominant in your mind: An ongoing concern with discrepancies from your ideal self, which tends to be associated with an increased sensitivity to positive outcomes, may also be associated with a preference for those interpersonal strategies aimed at attaining positive outcomes. Similarly, an ongoing concern with discrepancies from your ought self, which tends to be associated with an increased sensitivity to negative outcomes, may also be associated with a preference for those interpersonal strategies aimed at preventing negative outcomes.

To test these ideas, Higgins and his colleagues (1994, study 3) selected two groups of participants, one with a predominant actual/ideal self-discrepancy and one with a predominant actual/ought self-discrepancy. These participants were given a list of strategies for friendship that included three that focused on seeking positive outcomes (being generous, supportive, and loving) and three that focused on avoiding negative outcomes (not losing contact with friends, not neglecting them, and not gossiping about them). Participants were asked which three of these strategies for friendship they would choose to use. As expected, participants with a predominant actual/ideal self-discrepancy chose more of the positive-focused strategies (and fewer of the negative focused ones) than did participants with a predominant actual/ought self-discrepancy. Put differently, each group of participants showed a preference for those strategies that were focused on the kind of outcomes highlighted by their predominant self-discrepancy.

In sum, a concern with one's ideal self, be it temporary or ongoing, amounts to a focus on the positive outcomes spelled out in one's hopes and aspirations. Such a focus makes people especially sensitive to the presence and absence of positive outcomes in the lives of others and orients them toward attempting to seek and approach the positive in their social lives. A salient discrepancy between one's actual and ideal selves also leaves people vulnerable to those negative emotions associated with the absence of positive outcomes, namely sadness and dejection. In contrast, a salient concern with one's ought self amounts to a focus on the negative outcomes expected to follow from a failure to meet one's duties and responsibilities. Such a focus makes people especially sensitive to the presence or absence of negative outcomes in the lives of others and orients them toward attempting to avoid and prevent negative outcomes in their social lives. It also leaves them vulnerable to those negative emotions associated with the presence of negative outcomes, namely agitation and anxiety.

Concerns with one's ideal or ought selves may be part of a broader orientation toward focusing on approaching the positive or on avoiding the negative. Some people may be predisposed toward seeking and promoting the good things in life, whereas others may be predisposed toward avoiding and preventing the bad. Situational factors may also cause one to focus temporarily on seeking the positive or on avoiding the negative. People's tendency to focus on their ideal or on their ought selves may be dictated by these broader orientations toward promotion or prevention. Indeed, it is possible to induce people directly to focus on positive or on negative outcomes, without going through their ideal or ought selves, simply by framing their goals in terms of positive outcomes (you will be rewarded for success) or in terms of negative outcomes (you will be penalized for failure). Such direct manipulations of positive or negative focus provoke similar emotional reactions to those provoked by more indirect manipulations that highlight ideal or ought selves (e.g., Higgins et al. 1994; for a review, see Higgins 1998).

Which Self-knowledge Do We Seek?

The eminent British philosopher Isaiah Berlin, who had received numerous honors and kudos for his outstanding achievements, noted modestly: "I have been overestimated all my life. I will not pretend that this has been a source of grave distress. As someone once said to me, it is much nicer to receive more than one's due than one's due, and I cannot deny it. All the same, I cannot deceive myself." (*Globe and Mail*, 11.7.1997). Given the choice, would you too prefer that others see you more positively than you see your-self? Alternatively, would you prefer, instead, that others share your own opinions of yourself, negative as they may be? Or would you want others to see you as accurately as possible, regardless of the kind of person you think you are or wish to be? Put differently, do people seek and prefer information that enhances their self-views, information that verifies their self-views, or information that portrays them accurately? People seem to pursue all these different kinds of information on different occasions. There has been some research pointing to our interest in information that provides us with an accurate appraisal of our abilities, regardless of what we think we are or would like to be (for a review, see Trope 1986). However, most of the research in this area has concentrated on self-enhancement and self-verification needs. I therefore focus on these two needs and on what happens when they come into conflict.

Self-enhancement

There is little doubt that most people in Western societies wish to see themselves in a positive light, strive to enhance their self-views, and actively attempt to maintain and affirm their sense of themselves as worthy individuals (for East-West cultural differ-ences in this regard, see chapter 11). The arsenal of strategies we rely on to maintain and enhance our self-views includes strategies such as changing our attitudes to avoid feeling foolish when our behaviors contradict them, shifting our self-conceptions toward attributes that seem to be associated with success, trivializing the importance of abilities that we do not excel at, and derogating others so as to make ourselves look good by comparison. For the most part, these efforts are successful: We tend to see ourselves in highly positive terms and think that we are better than average at just about everything (for reviews, see Kunda 1990; Taylor and Brown 1988; for more detailed descriptions of relevant studies, see chapter 6).

In view of all these findings, there is little question that the motivation to maintain and enhance one's self-views can play an important role in guiding the way people seek and make sense of information about themselves and others. But do people seek self-enhancement at any cost? In particular, do people prefer self-enhancing information over information that confirms their existing self-views? This question has received a considerable amount of research attention, as discussed next.

Self-verification

Donna has always thought of herself as someone who has trouble interacting with others in large groups; she knows that she becomes shy, awkward, and hesitant in such settings and believes that her interpersonal skills leave much to be desired. What do you suppose she would want others to think of her interpersonal skills? When meeting new people, would she want them to assume that she is highly skilled, or would she rather they saw the weaknesses she sees in herself? What would she want her close friends to think of her interpersonal skills? How about her husband? What would she think of someone who praised her interpersonal skills to the sky? How would she feel upon receiving such praise?

Although we may sometimes enjoy unwarranted praise, we may often prefer others to see our weaknesses, for several reasons. If others have unrealistic expectations of our abilities, they may draw us into situations where we are bound to experience failure, but if they recognize our weaknesses, they may help us through situations that we find difficult. A person lacking interpersonal skills would probably feel very uncomfortable at a party where she knows few people. If her friends are aware of her limitations, they may go out of their way to ensure that she is not left to flounder alone at such a party, but if they are unaware of her interpersonal difficulties, they may leave her to her own inadequate devices. Another reason why we may want others to see us as we see ourselves, warts and all, is that our self-conceptions organize our understanding of ourselves and our social worlds. Any challenge to our self-views therefore constitutes a more general threat to our entire world view. To maintain a stable and consistent sense of ourselves and our social world, we may wish to confirm and verify our self-conceptions even when these are negative.

An extensive program of research by William Swann and his colleagues suggests that people are, indeed, often motivated to verify their self-conceptions. To this end, they may seek self-verifying information from others and may behave in a manner intended to ensure that others will see them as they see themselves. They may also be especially likely to recall self-verifying feedback (for reviews, see Swann 1987, 1990). To demonstrate that people engage in self-verification, it is especially important to show that people seek evidence that confirms their weaknesses. This is because the pursuit of evidence that confirms one's strengths need not be driven by a desire to verify one's self-views; it may be driven, instead, by a desire to enhance one's self-views. In the case of personal strengths, both self-enhancement and self-verification goals dictate the same strategies: To satisfy both these goals, one should seek positive information. In contrast, examination of the kind of information that people seek about their weaknesses may disentangle these two goals because, in the case of personal weaknesses, the two goals dictate opposite strategies: To self-enhance, one should seek positive information about one's areas of weakness, but to verify one's existing, negative self-views, one should seek negative information.

To determine whether people prefer self-verification to self-enhancement, Swann and Read (1981) therefore divided their participants into two groups, those who considered themselves likable and those who considered themselves disagreeable, based on a median split of their responses to a questionnaire assessing this dimension. In the experiment, all participants responded to a series of questions about their beliefs on a variety of controversial topics. They were then informed that their responses had been shown to another participant, their partner in an upcoming get-acquainted conversation, and were led to suspect that their partner viewed them either as likable or as disagreeable (to this end, they were shown a form with the appropriate rating circled and were told that it may have been completed by their partner). They were then

Table 10.4 Amount of time that participants who regarded themselves as likable or as disagreeable spent reading the statements made about them by a partner suspected of having a favorable or an unfavorable impression of them

	PARTNER'S EXPECTED IMPRESSION	
SELF-PERCEIVED LIKABLITY	FAVORABLE	UNFAVORABLE
Likable	16.73	12.93
Disagreeable	12.00	16.27

Source: From Swann and Read (1981, table 1, p. 359). Copyright © (1981) by Academic Press. Reprinted with permission.

given an opportunity to scrutinize a series of statements reflecting their partner's feelings about them. The experimenter recorded how much time they spent reading these statements.

If people seek self-verification, they should be especially interested in their partner's opinion of them when they suspect that their partner shares their self-views. If so, participants who expect their partner's reactions to confirm their self-views should spend more time reading these reactions than participants who expect their partner's reactions to contradict their self-views. This was indeed the case, as may be seen in table 10.4. Not surprisingly, participants who viewed themselves as likable spent more time reading their partner's reactions when they expected a favorable reaction than when they expected an unfavorable reaction. More important, participants who viewed themselves as disagreeable spent more time reading reactions expected to be unfavorable than they spent reading reactions expected to be favorable. These participants, who held a negative view of themselves, were more interested in information that had the potential of confirming this negative self-view than in information that had the potential of boosting their self-view. Apparently they preferred self-verification to self-enhancement.

It should be noted that people who view themselves as disagreeable may spend extra time scrutinizing negative impressions of them not only because they wish to verify their sense of themselves as disagreeable but also because they wish to better understand why they come across so negatively so as to improve themselves. Therefore the findings just described need not imply that such people seek self-verification. However, a follow-up study suggested that individuals who view themselves as disagreeable will also go out of their way to ensure that others share their negative opinions of themselves, which implies that they really do wish to verify these self-views (Swann and Read 1981, experiment 2). Once again, participants were divided into two groups, those who considered themselves likable and those who considered themselves disagreeable. This time participants were given an opportunity to spend about ten minutes chatting with another participant, their partner. Before this interaction they were led to suspect that their partner had formed either a favorable or an unfavorable impression of them, or were given no information about their partner's impression of them.

What do people do when they suspect that their interaction partner harbors the wrong impression of them? Do they go out of their way to correct this mistaken impression? If they do, then people who see themselves as likable but suspect that their partner views them as disagreeable should be extra nice during the interaction to ensure that the partner will come to regard them as positively as they regard themselves. More strikingly, people who see themselves as disagreeable but suspect that their partner views them as likable should be especially unpleasant during the interaction to ensure that their partner sees them for what they are. The impressions formed by the partners to these interactions suggest that participants must have been engaging in such strategies. As may be seen in table 10.5, the partners of participants who regarded themselves as likable came to view these participants as most likable when the participants suspected that these partners viewed them negatively. In contrast, the partners of participants who regarded themselves as disagreeable came to view these partici-

Table 10.5 Impressions that the partners of participants who regarded themselves as likable or as disagreeable formed of these participants when the participants suspected that their partner had a favorable or an unfavorable impression of them or were given no expectation

| | PARTNER'S EXPECTED IMPRESSION | | |
SELF-PERCEIVED LIKABLITY	FAVORABLE	UNFAVORABLE	CONTROL
Likable	43.90	49.40	44.48
Disagreeable	39.90	42.40	43.00

Source. From Swann and Read (1981, table 2, p. 360). Copyright © (1981) by Academic Press. Reprinted with permission.
Note: Higher numbers reflect more favorable impressions.

pants as least likable when the participants suspected that these partners viewed them positively. In short, when they suspected that their partners' impressions of them clashed with their own self-views, both groups of participants somehow managed, during their interaction, to bring their partners' impressions into closer agreement with their own self-views.

Do these findings mean that we are constantly trying to verify our weaknesses? Not necessarily. Most of us have strengths as well as weaknesses. Whenever we can, we may choose to focus on our strengths, and so ensure that we boost and enhance our self-views. But when we do consider our weaknesses, we may seek self-verifying rather than self-enhancing information. Support for these ideas comes from another series of studies by Swann and his colleagues (Swann, Pelham, and Krull 1989). Participants first rated themselves on five attributes: intellectual abilities, skill at sports, physical attractiveness, competency at art and music, and social skills. Using these self-ratings, the investigators identified each participant's best and worst attributes. Participants also completed a series of personality measures and entered their responses onto a computer billed as capable of analyzing personalities. They were then allowed to solicit feedback from this computer. To determine whether participants were more interested in feedback on their strengths or on their weaknesses, they were asked to rank the five attributes based on how much they wanted to get feedback on each. And to determine whether participants were interested in positive or in negative feedback on each attribute, they were shown a set of six questions about each dimension, three probing for favorable feedback (e.g., "What is this person's greatest asset at sports and games?"), and three probing for negative feedback (e.g., "In the area of sports, what is this person's largest problem?"). From each set, they were asked to choose the two questions to which they most wanted to receive answers.

Participants were far more interested in getting feedback on their strongest than on their weakest attribute. For example, a person who thought she excelled intellectually but was poor at music was much more interested in the computer's assessment of her intellectual ability than in its assessment of her musical ability. This suggests that people are especially interested in appraisals that seem likely to enhance their self-views. Yet, when asked to choose between positive and negative feedback on each attribute, the kind of feedback that participants chose for each attribute depended on whether they viewed that attribute as a strength or a weakness. Participants who had one very strong attribute as well as one very weak one sought more positive than negative feedback on their strong attribute, but sought more negative than positive feedback on their weak one. This suggests, for example, that a person who thinks she is very poor at music has little interest in feedback that suggests otherwise.

A follow-up study in which participants were given the opportunity to solicit feedback from a person rather than from a computer obtained similar results (Swann et al. 1989, experiment 2). Once again, participants were more interested in feedback on their strengths than on their weaknesses. But, when seeking feedback on their weaknesses, they preferred negative, self-verifying feedback over positive, self-enhancing feedback. It is important to note, though, that this interest in negative self-verifying feedback may be confined to relatively unimportant and unambiguous domains. This is because a vast majority of participants in these studies identified either arts or sports as their worst attribute, and most identified either intelligence or sociability as their best attribute. It remains possible that people who see themselves as weak in intellectual or social skills will be far less eager than people who see themselves as weak at arts or sports to verify these weaknesses.

Even if we seek feedback that confirms our weaknesses, this does not mean that we will enjoy receiving such feedback; it may be much pleasanter to receive overly positive feedback, even if we doubt its accuracy. In a study that examined this possibility, two groups of participants were recruited, one with extremely positive self-concepts and one with extremely negative ones (Swann et al. 1987). Each participant was asked to deliver a brief speech and was then given feedback on this performance, allegedly written by another participant. For half the participants, this feedback was quite favorable ("... this person seems socially self-confident.... I'd say he [she] probably feels comfortable and at ease around other people he [she] doesn't know very well...."). For the other half, the feedback was quite unfavorable ("... this person doesn't seem real socially self-confident.... I'd say he [she] probably feels somewhat uncomfortable and anxious around other people he [she] doesn't know too well...."). Participants were asked to rate the accuracy of the feedback and also to report their feelings.

As can be seen in table 10.6, both groups of participants viewed the feedback that verified their prior self-conceptions as more accurate than the feedback that contradicted these self-conceptions: Those with positive self-concepts viewed the favorable feedback as more accurate than the unfavorable feedback, whereas those with negative self-concepts viewed the unfavorable feedback as more accurate than the unfavorable feedback. Yet, although the two groups differed in their assessments of the relative accuracy of positive and negative feedback, both groups showed similar affective reactions to the two types of feedback: Both felt worse after

Table 10.6 Affective reactions and judgments of feedback accuracy given by participants with positive or negative self-concepts who had received favorable or unfavorable feedback

	POSITIVE SELF-CONCEPT		NEGATIVE SELF-CONCEPT	
	FAVORABLE FEEDBACK	UNFAVORABLE FEEDBACK	FAVORABLE FEEDBACK	UNFAVORABLE FEEDBACK
Accuracy	32.45	10.5	20.62	29.22
Affect	67.09	55.05	59.85	51.97

Source: Data from Swann et al. (1987, tables 1 and 2, pp. 884 and 885). Copyright © (1987) by the American Psychological Association. Reprinted with permission.
Note: Higher numbers indicate greater perceived accuracy and more positive affect.

receiving negative feedback than after receiving positive feedback. These findings show an interesting pattern for participants with negative self-concepts. Even though these participants viewed the favorable feedback as inaccurate, they enjoyed receiving it far more than they enjoyed receiving the more self-verifying negative feedback (see Jussim, Yen, & Aiello, 1995, for similar results). Like Isaiah Berlin, we may find it much nicer to be overestimated than to be viewed for what we are, even if the praise doesn't ring true.

Intriguing evidence that it feels good to be overestimated comes from research on people's satisfaction with their romantic relationships (Murray, Holmes, and Griffin 1996; see also discussion in chapter 6). Partners in married and dating couples each rated themselves and their partner on a range of positive and negative attributes (e.g., intelligent, kind and affectionate, patient, lazy, thoughtless, complaining). They also rated their satisfaction with their romantic relationship. Which partners would people be happier with, those who see them as they see themselves or those who idealize them? Results pointed to the benefits of idealization: People were happier with their relationship to the extent that their partners viewed them more positively than they viewed themselves. Put differently, the more people were idealized by their romantic partner, the more satisfied they were with their romantic relationship. We may be especially happy with intimate partners who see us through positive lenses, noting the best in us and turning a blind eye on the worst.

A similar study by Swann and his colleagues obtained comparable findings for members of dating couples; these reported greater intimacy with their partner to the extent that their partner viewed them more positively than they viewed themselves (Swann, De La Ronde, and Hixon 1994). However, Swann and his colleagues obtained the opposite pattern for married people; these felt greater intimacy with spouses who saw them as they saw themselves than with spouses who saw them more positively than they saw themselves. One possible reason for the discrepancy between these results and those obtained by Murray and her colleagues may lie in the different measures used by the two groups. Three of the five dimensions assessed by Swann and his colleagues were relatively objective and easy to assess (athletic abilities, skills at arts and music, physical attractiveness). In contrast, the dimensions used by Murray and her colleagues were, for the most part, more subjective and difficult to assess (e.g., kind, thoughtless, patient). It may be that we want our spouses to recognize our obvious weaknesses but to give us a positive spin wherever possible. For example, if I know myself to be tone deaf, I would consider anyone who praised my musical abilities to be either a liar or a fool. Yet, if I believe myself to be unkind, I may be pleased and relieved to know that my partner sees me otherwise, and may find this partner's company especially enjoyable.

In sum, when we can, we will seek feedback on our best attributes. Such feedback has the double advantage of satisfying our desire for self-enhancement while, at the same time, satisfying our desire for self-verification. When pressed to focus on our weaknesses, we may often prefer feedback that verifies these weaknesses over more self-enhancing feedback that contradicts our negative self-views. This may be especially true for clear-cut, unambiguous, and relatively unimportant shortcomings such as poor musical or athletic skills. Although we may seek feedback that verifies our weaknesses, we don't enjoy receiving it. We are happier when we get unwarranted praise than when we receive well-deserved criticism. That may be why we find our romantic relationships more satisfying the more our partner idealizes us.

The Self in Relation to Others

We may find it difficult to contemplate and evaluate the performance and achievements of others without also considering our own. When trying to assess others' traits and accomplishments, we may use our own performance as a yardstick against which we measure theirs. And when confronted with an extraordinary performance by another, we may find ourselves considering the implications for our own self-view.

Using the Self to Judge Others

Chris, a college student, spends about 20 hours a week studying. How studious would you say Chris is? How did you go about answering this question? Many students report that they answer such questions by comparing Chris's behavior to their own (Dunning and Hayes 1996). A very hard working student might reason: "I spend about 30 hours a week studying; Chris, who spends much less time studying than I do, cannot be very studious." A less hard working student using the same strategy might see Chris quite differently: "I spend only 10 hours a week studying; Chris, who spends twice as much time studying as I do, must be pretty studious." If people call upon their own behavior in this manner to make sense of other people's behavior, their own levels of behavior should color their assessments of others: The more time one spends studying, the less one should think of Chris's study habits.

David Dunning and his colleagues found that people rely on such egocentric comparisons when they evaluate others (Dunning and Cohen 1992; Dunning and Hayes 1996). For example, when told about a student who spent about 4 hours a week playing basketball, students who reported spending a considerable amount of time on athletic activities viewed this student as less athletic than did those who reported engaging in virtually no athletic activity. Similar results were obtained when participants were asked to determine how studious, punctual, or mathematically skilled another person was: For all these attributes there were negative correlations between participants' own reported levels of behavior or skill and their evaluations of those of another person. Put differently, the higher their own level of performance, the lower their evaluation of the other person's.

These findings are consistent with the idea that people use knowledge about the self to judge others. But these findings may also be due to other causes. It may be, for example, that people who exercise regularly have a different general understanding of athleticism than do those who never exercise. An athletic person, they may think, is one who exercises for at least 7 hours a week. When evaluating another, they may be relying on this broad trait knowledge rather than comparing the other directly to the self; their own self-knowledge may not come to mind at all. If it could be shown that self-knowledge does comes to mind when one evaluates others, this would provide much stronger evidence that the self is used to judge others. This was the aim of another series of studies by Dunning and Hayes (1996).

In one study Cornell students were shown brief descriptions of another person (e.g., "Alice, a student here at Cornell, tends to be late to class about two times each week"). For each such description, half the participants were asked to judge the described person on the relevant attribute (in this case, punctuality). The other half were asked, instead, to assess the grammar of the sentence, a task not expected to activate self-knowledge. Participants were then asked about their own attribute-related behavior. If people bring their own behavior to mind so as to judge another person, then their self-knowledge on a given trait should be activated if they have just judged another person on this trait. If so, participants who had assessed the trait of the person described in the sentence

Table 10.7 The speed with which participants who had or had not judged another person on a trait reported their own behavior or the behavior of an acquaintance

	JUDGED TARGET ON TRAIT	
REPORTED BEHAVIOR OF	YES	NO
Self	5,173	6,761
Acquaintance	6,503	6,749

Source: Data from Dunning and Hayes (1996, table 4, p. 225). Copyright © (1996) by the American Psychological Association. Reprinted with permission.
Note: Data are presented in milliseconds.

should be faster to report on their own trait-related behavior than participants who had merely assessed the grammaticality of the sentence. As may be seen in the top row of table 10.7, this was indeed the case.

This finding suggests that participants had activated their own behavior so as to judge that of the other. However, evaluating another may have speeded up responses about the self for a different reason: It may be that having to judge the other's trait simply primed and activated the entire trait dimension, making it easier to answer any questions about this dimension; the speed-up of responses about the self may have been due only to that priming. If so, responses about any other person should be speeded up as well. To rule out this possibility, another group of participants went through the identical procedure, but instead of reporting on their own trait-related behavior, they reported on the behavior of an acquaintance. As may be seen in the bottom row of table 10.7, unlike responses about the self, responses about an acquaintance were not speeded up by earlier judgments about another person. This rules out the possibility that the speed-up obtained for judgments about the self was due to priming; if it had been, it should have also occurred for judgments about an acquaintance. Rather, it appears that making social judgments speeds up judgments about the self because people spontaneously think about themselves and their own behaviors when they judge the behavior of others.

We may be especially likely to measure others against ourselves when this can make us feel better about our own performance. If my combined Scholastic Aptitude Test (SAT) score was 1,200, I may wish to view someone who had achieved a higher score, 1,300, as highly intelligent; this allows me to consider myself intelligent as well. In contrast, if my own score was a still more impressive 1,400, I may wish to downgrade the intelligence of the person with the 1,300 score so as to make me look all the more outstanding by comparison. If the tendency to measure others against the self in such a manner is driven by such self-enhancement motives, it should be exaggerated when the motivation to enhance one's self-view is increased, as it is after failure (for a discussion of motivated reasoning, see chapter 6). Indeed, a series of studies testing these ideas revealed that people are more likely to base their judgments of others on their own performance after experiencing failure than they are after experiencing success (Beauregard and Dunning 1998). One reason the self plays an important role in judgments about others is that such judgments can be used to bolster the self.

This line of work suggests that we often use ourselves as a benchmark against which we evaluate others. Other research suggests that we also use others to evaluate ourselves, as discussed next.

Using Others to Judge the Self

In 1995 a group of physicists got together to discuss the string theory of matter. Edward Witten, widely considered the most brilliant theoretical physicist of his generation, gave the first talk of the day. The next speaker, Natty Seiberg, himself a major figure in the field, was so impressed by Witten's talk that he began his own talk with the words "Perhaps I should become a truck driver." Still, the talk he went on to deliver was impressive enough to prompt the speaker that followed him, John Schwarz, one of the founders of string theory, to begin his talk with "I'll get a tricycle" (*Scientific American*, January 1996).

An outstanding performance by another can sometimes make you feel incompetent by comparison. When your brother outperforms you at school, when your best friend turns out to be much better than you at basketball, when your coworker secures a coveted promotion, you may question your own ability and worthiness and feel demoralized and deflated. And yet, on other occasions, an outstanding performance by another can make you feel good about yourself. You may take great pride in your brother's extraordinary musical talent, you may rejoice when your best friend makes an Olympic team, and you may be inspired to match the achievements of the top performer at your workplace. When will a superior performance by another make you feel good about yourself, and when will it make you feel bad? I turn next to research that has addressed this question.

The Self-evaluation Maintenance Model Abraham Tesser and his colleagues developed their *self-evaluation maintenance model* (SEM) to account for people's reactions to superior performances by others (for reviews, see Tesser and Campbell 1983; Tesser 1986, 1991). The model makes several assumptions. First, to have any impact at all on the self, the superior other must seem psychologically close. *Closeness* increases with similarity, family ties, shared place of origin, and anything else that leads one to see a bond between the self and the other or to see the two as belonging to the same psychological unit. For example, a sibling or a friend seem closer than a stranger, a sibling who is close in age to you seems closer than a one who is much older or much younger, a person whose attitudes and personality resemble yours seems closer than one who is very different from you. The closer the superior other seems, the greater the potential impact of this person on the self.

But what determines the direction of this impact? When will it be positive and when negative? The SEM model assumes that a superior performance by a close other can make you feel good about yourself if you don't really care about the domain of performance because it is irrelevant to your own self-definition. In such cases you do not feel personally threatened by the other's superior performance and can relax and bask in the reflected glory of the other's achievements (see Cialdini et al. 1976). For example, if you define yourself in terms of academic excellence and have little interest in music, you may take great pride in your sister's stellar musical achievements without feeling threatened by them. In contrast, if the domain in which you have been outperformed by a close other is relevant to your self-definition—you, too, plan a career in music—you will feel threatened by the close other's superior performance and may question your own self-worth. You feel compelled to compare yourself to such a relevant close other, and find yourself lacking by comparison. In sum, the impact of a close superior other on the self depends on the *self-relevance* of the domain of performance: The superior other exerts a positive impact when the domain is irrelevant (because one basks in the reflected glory) but exerts a negative impact when the domain is relevant (due to an invidious comparison of the self to the other).

The SEM model assumes that people are motivated to maintain a positive view of the self. Therefore, when they are threatened by a superior performance by a close and relevant other, they actively attempt to dispel the threat. To this end, they may reduce their psychological closeness to the other (if the other is not close, I need not compare myself to him or her), they may reduce the self-relevance of the dimension (if this dimension isn't important to me, I need not feel bad about being outperformed on it), or they may minimize the other's performance (if the performance isn't that great, I don't look so bad by comparison). In short, people may engage in motivated reasoning so as to make the other's superior achievements seem less threatening by minimizing their relevance, magnitude, or importance (see chapter 6 for a discussion of motivated reasoning). People may also take action to minimize the threat posed by a close other's superior performance. They may, for example, attempt to undermine this person's future performance.

In one study designed to test these ideas, two pairs of male friends were recruited for each experimental session (Tesser and Cornell 1991). On arrival, the four were seated in separate booths where they completed a verbal skills task. To manipulate the self-relevance of this task, half were told that performance on it was strongly related to intelligence; these were expected to view it as highly self-relevant. The other half were told that the task was merely a game, and that no one knew what it measured; these were expected to view it as low in self-relevance. After they completed the task, participants were shown the scores of all four participants in their session. Each participant was led to believe that he had ranked third, and had been outperformed by his friend and by one of the strangers. Participants were then told that each would perform another such task, but this time with clues provided by their fellow participants. Each participant then had an opportunity to choose clues for each of the others. Importantly, the clues varied in how helpful they were. The key question was, of the two people who had outperformed him, who would the participant want to help more, his friend or the stranger?

The answer depended on how self-relevant the task was. When it was not self-relevant, participants gave more helpful clues to their friend than to the stranger; apparently, when they did not feel threatened by their friend's superior performance, participants expected to take pleasure in his success and so were especially motivated to help him. In contrast, when the task was highly self-relevant, participants gave less helpful clues to their friend than to the stranger. Being outperformed by a close friend on a task that one cares deeply about can be more threatening than being outperformed by a stranger; this may be why participants were especially reluctant to help their friend maintain his superior performance. People's eagerness to help a friend excel at an irrelevant task and their reluctance to help a friend excel at a relevant task may have both stemmed from a desire to boost and maintain their own self-worth. Indeed, both tendencies were eliminated when participants were given an opportunity to boost their self-worth through an alternative route. This suggests that when the need for self-affirmation is satisfied, people feel less pressure to seek opportunities to bask in their friend's reflected glory or to avoid invidious comparisons to their friend.

Similar studies provided support for other aspects of the SEM model (for reviews, see Tesser and Campbell 1983; Tesser 1986, 1991). Taken together, this research suggests that close superior others may boost one's self-views when they outperform one on dimensions that one cares little about, but may threaten one's self-views when they outperform one on dimensions that one also wishes to excel at. More recent research has suggested that people are not always demoralized and deflated by encounters with others who outperform them on highly self-relevant dimensions; sometimes they may be inspired by such individuals, as discussed next.

The Impact of Role Models on the Self The year I was finishing up my dissertation and looking for an academic job as a social psychologist, my own department was conducting a search for an assistant professor in social psychology. Curriculum vitae of top applicants were circulated among us graduate students, and I still recall the awe and horror we all experienced at the sight of one of these vitae. This applicant, who was about to graduate from a top program, had already accumulated a list of publications that put us all to shame. Whereas the best of us had managed to produce two or three publications, the list of this person's publications went on for two pages! For weeks after seeing this extraordinary record of achievement, we all felt miserably incompetent. And yet, I later realized, as students at an outstanding program, we were surrounded by professors of far greater achievement; we had daily conversations with some of the giants in the field. But these superb academics did not make us feel unworthy; if anything, they inspired and motivated us. Why did we find this young applicant so much more threatening than our far more accomplished professors?

The job candidate may have seemed more threatening because this person was at the same career stage as we were. We must have realized that it was already too late for us to achieve in graduate school what this star had managed to accomplish. In contrast, our professors were older than us and more advanced in their careers. We could therefore look up to them with the hope that some time in the future we would be able to emulate their success. This analysis suggests that the impact of a highly self-relevant outstanding other on the self may depend on the *attainability* of the other's achievements: A model of unattainable success may make our own lesser achievements seem paltry by comparison and leave us feeling inferior and discouraged. In contrast, a model of attainable success may illustrate the accomplishments that we too may achieve if we work hard enough, inspire and motivate us to strive for these achievements, and leave us feeling all the more capable of doing so.

To examine these ideas, Penelope Lockwood and I presented participants with a star graduating student whose achievements seemed attainable or unattainable by virtue of each participant's own year at school (Lockwood and Kunda 1997). The star was described, in a bogus newspaper article, as a fourth-year accounting student with a spectacular record of achievement; in addition to winning an important award for academic excellence, this graduating student was active in sports and community service, and was said to be considering job offers from several prominent companies. The participants were students in either their first or their fourth year in a highly selective accounting program. We reasoned that the accomplishments of the graduating star would seem attainable to first-year accounting students whose academic careers still lay ahead of them and for whom superb accomplishments still seemed within reach, given their history of academic excellence. In contrast, we expected that these same accomplishments would seem unattainable to fourth-year students for whom it was already too late to match the star's superior achievements. We therefore expected that first-year students would be inspired and self-enhanced by the star, whereas fourth-year student would be deflated and discouraged by the same star.

After reading about the star, participants rated themselves on a series of adjectives related to career success (e.g., bright, skillful). Control participants completed the same self-ratings without first reading about the star. As may be seen in figure 10.2, first-year students, for whom the star's achievements seemed attainable, were clearly self-enhanced by the star: First-year students exposed to the star rated themselves more highly than did first-year controls

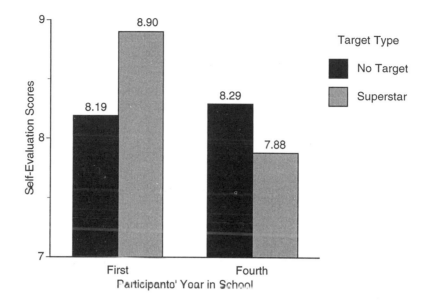

Figure 10.2 Mean self-evaluations made by first- and fourth-year students who were and who were not exposed to an outstanding graduating student. Higher numbers indicate more positive self-evaluations. Based on data reported by Lockwood and Kunda (1989, table 2, p. 97). Copyright © (1989) by the American Psychological Association. Adapted with permission.

who had not been exposed to the star. Fourth-year students, for whom the star's achievements were unattainable, were, if anything, deflated by the star: Fourth-year students exposed to the star rated themselves somewhat less positively than did fourth-year controls, though this difference was not statistically significant.

First- and fourth-year students also differed markedly in the explanations they provided to account for their reactions to the star. A large majority of first-year students (82 percent) reported being inspired by the star (e.g., "... I almost now want to work super-hard so that I can get the award that J. had ..." "... After seeing what J. has accomplished I know what I must strive for." Lockwood and Kunda 1997, p. 98). In contrast, practically none of the fourth-year students (only 6 percent) reported inspiration. Instead, fourth-year students focused their efforts on explaining why the star was irrelevant to them for the purpose of comparison (e.g.,

"... You can't compare 'success' between any two people on the planet because we are all different and successful in our own right." "I'm usually more influenced by how I view myself than by how well I'm compared to my classmates." Lockwood and Kunda 1997, p. 98). Whereas 50 percent of fourth-year students denigrated the comparison process in this manner, practically none of the first-year students (6 percent) did so. Moreover, even though fourth-year students were closer in age and career stage to the star than were first-year students, fourth-year students rated the star as less relevant to them for the purpose of comparison. These findings suggest that only first-year students were inspired by star. Fourth-year students found the star more threatening than inspiring, and attempted to dispel the threat by minimizing the star's relevance to them and by denigrating the value of any social comparison. A relevant star can be inspiring if one believes that one can attain comparable success, but can be demoralizing otherwise.

Other studies by Lockwood and Kunda (1997) also found that a star who had excelled at a highly self-relevant domain can be self-enhancing and inspiring to people who view the star's achievements as attainable. These findings contradict Tesser's SEM model (Tesser 1986, 1991) which assumed that a close other who had outperformed one on a self-relevant domain is bound to have negative consequences for the self. Tesser and his colleagues may have overlooked the possibility that a relevant superior other can provoke inspiration rather than discouragement because in their experiments the achievements of the superior other were generally unattainable: Typically, participants were confronted with another who had outperformed them on a test that neither expected to take again, so participants could entertain little hope of improving their relative standing in the future (for a review, see Major, Testa, and Bylsma 1991). Lockwood and Kunda, too, found that such models of unattainable success can be threatening. However, they also found that models of attainable success can be self-enhancing and inspiring.

There appear to be two different routes through which a superior other can make us feel good about ourselves. A superior other can boost our self-views through a process of *reflection*, which allows us to bask in this person's reflected glory (Cialdini et al. 1976; Tesser and Campbell 1983). A superior other can also boost our self-views by provoking *inspiration*, which leads us to expect and strive for equally stellar achievements (Lockwood and Kunda 1997). To illustrate the differences between these two processes, consider the reactions of different U.S. viewers as they watch an American athlete receive a gold medal at the Olympics. Some budding athletes may be envisioning themselves standing on that same podium four years down the road, and resolve to redouble their efforts toward achieving this goal. These people are inspired. Others, who harbor no athletic aspirations, may simply feel proud to be American. These people are basking in the reflected glory of a fellow American.

The pleasure one takes in the achievements of others and the pleasure one derives from the hope of securing comparable achievements for oneself may engage different aspects of the self: I enjoy another person's triumphs when I think of myself as part of a broader social group, be it my family or my nation; I feel good because my fellow group member made my group look good. In contrast, I enjoy the prospect of my future triumphs when I think of myself as a unique and distinct individual; I feel good because I expect that I personally will look good. In short, reflection boosts one's social, collective self whereas inspiration boosts one's personal, individualistic self (see Brewer and Gardner 1996). The distinction between the personal, individualistic self and the social, collective self has been central to discussions of cultural differences between the East and West (Markus and Kitayama 1991), and will be discussed at length in chapter 11. For now, I focus on the implications for comparisons to superior others.

To fully enjoy another's achievements through reflection, one must hold one's personal self at bay, focusing instead on one's social self. Indeed, people bask in the reflected glory of a close superior other only when that other excels at a domain that they do not themselves aspire to excel at, when they have little need to dwell upon their own self-worth because they are confident in it, and when their social bond with the other is made salient (Brewer and Weber 1994; Pelham and Wachsmuth 1995; Tesser 1988). When they focus on their personal self instead, people may gain personal inspiration from a superior other if they believe that they can eventually attain comparable success (Lockwood and Kunda 1997). However, when one's personal self is salient and the other's superior achievements seem unattainable, the superior other will be threatening and demoralizing.

This discussion has focused on people's reactions to superior others. Of course, inferior others may also influence peoples' thoughts and feelings about themselves. A person who has done much worse than me can make me look good by comparison, boosting my sense of my own self-worth. However, such an inferior person may also highlight the pitfalls that await me. Such a threat may motivate me to shape up and get my act together if I feel capable of warding off similar disaster, but may leave me demoralized and deflated if I feel incapable of avoiding a similar fate (see Major et al. 1991). There is evidence that inferior others can sometimes provoke self-enhancement, and sometimes self-deflation. However, the ideas about when each of these processes will take place remain speculative (for a review, see Major et al. 1991).

More generally, research reviewed in this section suggests that the self is intricately tied in with perceptions of others. We spontaneously use our self-knowledge to make sense of others' behavior. Our own self-views, in turn, are influenced by what we learn about others. Knowledge about others' triumphs and failures may lead us to contemplate our own prospects, to reevaluate our abilities, and to revise our goals.

So far I have focused on the self as a repository of beliefs, feelings, and goals, and I have discussed how the contents, affective tone, and organization of the self can affect one's processing of self-related information and one's interpersonal judgments and behavior, and how one's self-related beliefs and aspirations may in turn be influenced by one's social surroundings. I turn now to another important aspect of the self, namely its executive function. In the following section I discuss the self not as a conglomerate of knowledge but as a controlling agent.

Self-regulation

As should be clear by now, the self is not a passive knowledge structure. Rather, the self actively attempts to control and modify its own thoughts, feelings, and behavior and also to influence and change the environment. The term *self-regulation* refers to this executive, controlling aspect of the self. Many of the topics covered in this chapter, indeed, in this entire book, may be viewed as instances of self-regulation. We engage in self-regulation when we decide which goals to pursue (promotion or prevention, self-enhancement or self-verification), when we determine how to go about pursuing our goals (modify perceptions of self or others, seek or avoid certain kinds of information and situations), when we try to control our mood and its expression, when we attempt to be unprejudiced, when we try to suppress unpleasant thoughts, when we try to stick to a healthy diet and exercise regiment, and the list could go on and on. In view of the enormous scope of relevant research, I will focus in this section only on some general aspects of self-regulation that appear to transcend specific regulatory tasks (for a review, see Baumeister 1998).

Self-regulation Is Adaptive

Much of the early research on self-regulation focused on children's ability to delay gratification. Numerous studies on this topic have used the following paradigm. A child is left alone in a room, and confronted with a choice: The child may wait until the experimenter comes back, and then receive an attractive reward (e.g., two marshmallows) or the child may call the experiment back sooner, and then receive a less attractive reward (only one marshmallow). In this situation, children who are able to withstand the temptation of going for the immediate, albeit small, treat, will be rewarded with a more attractive treat later. Therefore, the longer the child waits before calling the experimenter back the better the child's ability to delay gratification (for reviews, see Mischel 1974, 1996).

It turns out that the ability to delay gratification in this manner reflects highly adaptive skills. In one study, the parents of teenagers who had participated in such delay-of-gratification experiments about ten years earlier, as preschoolers, were asked to rate their now adolescent children on a variety of dimensions. Remarkably, the children's ability to delay gratification in preschool predicted their social and intellectual performance in high school: Those who were able to wait longer for a tempting reward at the age of 4 or 5 were rated by their parents as more academically and socially skilled ten years later! (Mischel, Shoda, and Peake 1988). The ability to delay gratification in early childhood may reflect a broad, enduring, and highly adaptive competence at self-regulation. Success in academic as well as interpersonal domains requires an ability to regulate and control one's thoughts, feelings, and behavior. Children who are capable of such self-regulation when they are young seem to have what it takes to succeed as they mature.

Self-regulation Is Effortful

Self-regulation is not always easy. Several lines of research suggest that controlling one's thoughts and feelings takes effort. Most notably, attempts to suppress unwanted thoughts break down when one in incapable of devoting sufficient effort to the suppression because one's cognitive resources are strained (for a review, see Wegner 1994; see chapter 8 for a detailed discussion). Similarly, attempts to regulate one's facial expressions or to ignore distracters seem to require so much effort that they interfere with other effortful tasks (for a review, see Gilbert, 1989). Moreover, self-regulation can be so exhausting that after attempting one self-regulation task, people are less able to perform another, unrelated task.

In one experiment aimed at demonstrating this, hungry students were recruited for a study on taste perception (they were asked to skip a meal before the experiment). On arrival, participants were taken to a room infused with the delicious aroma of freshly baked cookies and were seated in front of two food displays, one consisting of a stack of appetizing cookies and candy, the other of a heap of radishes (Baumeister et al. 1998). In one condition, participants were left alone in the room for about five minutes with the instruction that they should eat several radishes but not touch the cookie and candy display. In other words, they were asked to exercise self-control and resist the temptation to dig into the cookies. In another condition, participants were instructed, instead, to sample the cookies and candy but leave the radishes untouched. In other words, they were allowed to give in to temptation rather than resist it. There was also a control condition in which participants were not exposed to any food. All participants were subsequently asked to solve a couple of puzzles that were in fact insoluble. The question of interest was how long they would persist at this frustrating task.

If resisting temptation consumes energy, it should leave people with less energy for subsequent tasks. Indeed, participants asked to resist the cookies seemed exhausted by this act of self-control. Whereas cookie-eating and control participants spent about 20 minutes trying to solve the insoluble puzzles, those who had been asked to resist the cookies spent only about 8 minutes at that task before giving up. Follow-up studies revealed that other forms of self-regulation such as stifling one's emotions while watching an emotional movie result in similar depletion of resources and impairment of performance on subsequent tasks (Baumeister et al. 1998; Muraven, Tice, and Baumeister 1998).

In sum, self-regulation can require considerable effort. Successful self-regulation saps the resources available for other concurrent tasks, and depletes the resources and energy remaining for subsequent tasks. People who are adept at such effortful exercises at self-control and willpower seem especially well equipped for dealing with the demands of modern life.

One might argue that many of the processes studied by researchers interested in the goals, organization, and contents of the self also involve self-regulation. Indeed, one exercises self-regulation whenever one seeks certain kinds of knowledge and rejects others, aims for self-verification or self-enhancement, seeks certain interpersonal situations and avoids others, or chooses certain cognitive and interpersonal strategies over others. Some research, such as the recent work on how one's salient self-discrepancies orient one toward particular interpersonal strategies, explicitly links the regulatory aspect of the self to its representation and organization (Higgins 1998). In other research the connections among these different aspects of the self remain implicit. Moreover, despite the pervasiveness of self-regulation, the field still lacks a broad theoretical framework that can tie together the many ways in which we regulate ourselves (see Baumeister 1998).

The search for insights into the nature of the self has long preoccupied thinkers of many stripes, be they poets, philosophers, or psychologists. Social cognition research, for its part, has already contributed considerably to this enterprise, shedding new light on the many ways in which the self colors and is colored by one's understanding on one's social world. Much has been accomplished, and much remains to be done.

Summary

The contents and structure of the self can influence the way we make sense of ourselves and others. People differ in which attributes they consider central and self-defining. For each of our most central attributes, we may develop an elaborate *self-schema*, that is, an integrated set of memories and beliefs about our relevant behaviors. People who are schematic on a trait such as independence can make judgments about their standing on that trait very rapidly, can back these up with extensive personal examples, and are reluctant to accept evidence that questions these self-views. They also possess more general expertise about this trait which they draw upon to make sense of others' behavior. Although we have many stable and enduring memories and beliefs about the self, our *working self-concept,* that is, our sense of self at a given moment, varies from one occasion to another, as different subsets of our self-knowledge become activated.

People also differ in the positivity of their global self-evaluation, or *self-esteem*. People with high self-esteem, who consider themselves worthy and successful, tend to have clear, confident, and stable self-knowledge. In contrast, those with low self-esteem, who consider themselves losers and failures, tend to be uncertain and confused about their identities. The two groups also differ in the strategies they rely on to protect and enhance their self-views. Whereas those with high self-esteem try to maximize self-enhancement, those with low self-esteem try to minimize self-deflation.

The organization of self-knowledge may also influence reactions to self-relevant information. People with high *self-complexity*, whose self-representations include many distinct aspects, are less vulnerable to stressful events than are those with less complex selves, because the negative consequences of a blow to one area of the self remain confined to that area in highly complex individuals but spill into all other areas of the self in less complex individuals.

In addition to our actual selves, we also have notions of the selves we ought to have and the selves we would ideally like to have. People with salient discrepancies between their actual and ideal selves may be preoccupied with the positive outcomes they hope for. This can sensitize them to the presence and absence of positive outcomes in the lives of others and can lead them to seek the positive in their social lives. Such discrepancies can also give rise to sadness and dejection. In contrast, people with salient discrepancies between their actual and ought selves may be preoccupied with the negative outcomes expected to follow from their failure to meet their obligations. This can sensitize them to the presence or absence of negative outcomes in the lives of others and can lead them to avoid negative outcomes in their social lives. Such discrepancies can also give rise to agitation and anxiety.

Beliefs about the self can also influence the kinds of feedback we seek. When we can, we seek feedback on our best attributes, which can be expected to satisfy both our desire for self-enhancement and our desire for self-verification. However, when required to focus on our weaknesses, we may often prefer feedback that verifies these weaknesses over more self-enhancing feedback that contradicts our negative self-views. Yet, although we may seek feedback that verifies our weaknesses, we do not enjoy receiving it. We are happier when we get unwarranted praise than when we receive well-deserved criticism.

Our self-knowledge comes into play when we judge others. We often evaluate other people by comparing their performance to ours. As a result our evaluations of others may depend on our own abilities. We also evaluate ourselves through comparisons to others. Others who outperform us can lead us to experience either inspiration and self-enhancement or discouragement and self-deflation, depending on how threatened we are by their achievements.

The self also has an executive, controlling function. Self-regulation is effortful, and depletes the resources and energy remaining for other tasks. Therefore, after exercising self-restraint in one domain, we may find it difficult to regulate and control other kinds of thoughts and behaviors. The ability to exercise such effortful self-control can be highly adaptive.

III A Cross-cultural Perspective

Anyone reading this book up to this point, or reading the many original articles reviewed in it, may be forgiven for assuming that social cognition research has uncovered universal principles of how people make sense of themselves and of their social worlds. But just how universal are these principles? The vast majority of social cognition research has been conducted in North America, and much of the rest has been conducted in Western Europe. Could it be that some or even most of the findings apply only to North Americans or, more broadly, to Westerners? Just how culture bound is social cognition?

Anthropologists have long noted remarkable differences in how people raised in Western cultures and those raised in Eastern cultures understand themselves and their social worlds (e.g., Shweder and LeVine 1984). To capture the flavor of these differences, consider the following anecdotes: In the United States, "the squeaky wheel gets the grease." But in Japan, "the nail that stands out gets pounded down." American parents trying to get their reluctant children to eat may urge them to think about how much more fortunate they are than all the starving children in Africa. Japanese parents faced with the same dilemma may, instead, urge their children to consider how bad the farmer who had worked so hard to produce their food would feel if they refused to eat it. An American company intent on increasing productivity asked its employees to look in the mirror before coming to work each day and tell themselves "I am beautiful" 100 times. A Japanese company with a similar intent instructed its employees to begin each day by telling a fellow employee that he or she is beautiful (these anecdotes were reported by Markus and Kitayama 1991). American children put together sports teams by appointing two captains who take turns selecting team members. Japanese children reject this method because the last picked child might feel upset. Instead, they form teams by classroom or by the Japanese equivalent of alphabetical order. American mothers want their children to grow up to be happy and successful individuals. Japanese mothers asked what they want for their children may say something like "I just want my kid to grow up so as not to be a nuisance to other people" (N. D. Kristoff, *NYT* 4.12.1998).

Such anecdotes reveal strikingly different understandings of the self and its relation to others. The American examples point to a sense of the self as distinct from others, and highlight the value of being different and special. In contrast, the Japanese examples point to a sense of the self as closely interrelated with and dependent on others, and highlight the value of harmoniously fitting in with one's group. Such differing construals of the self and society may lead to substantial differences in how people think and feel about themselves and others and in how they relate to each other.

Until relatively recently, such cultural differences were explored predominantly by anthropologists whose conclusions rested, for the most part, on observational and ethnographic data. Over the last decade or so, an increasing number of social psychologists have begun investigating the impact of culture on cognition, motivation, and emotion. Their work has resulted in the emergence of a new field, which may be termed *experimental anthropology*; it relies on the rigorous experimental methods developed by social and cognitive psychologists to explore cultural differences. The revealed cultural differences in social cognition are interesting in their own right. In many cases, they may also shed light on topics that have long been central to social psychology such as the fundamental attribution error, dissonance reduction, and the need for self-enhancement.

For example, the fundamental attribution error, that is, people's tendency to exaggerate the extent to which behavior is driven by underlying dispositions and to underestimate the extent to which it is driven by situational forces, has often been explained as resulting from basic perceptual processes. The perceiver, the argument goes, is bound to see the actor as a salient figure against a much less salient ground, the situation. Because of the relative salience of the actor, causal explanations focus on this actor's disposition. Such basic perceptual processes should be universal. Therefore, if it turns out that people in non-Western cultures are less prone than Westerners to the fundamental attribution error, this would challenge the perceptual account of this phenomenon and suggest, instead, that it is rooted in people's culture-bound beliefs and theories about what drives social behavior.

Much of the social psychological research on cultural differences has focused on East-West differences, and therefore most of this chapter will be concerned with these differences. The starting point of research on East-West differences has been the notion that the self is construed quite differently in these two cultures: North Americans and other Westerners typically view the self as independent whereas East Asians typically view the self as interdependent with others (for detailed reviews, see Markus and Kitayama 1991; Triandis 1989). After briefly outlining the basic differences between these two construals of the self, I will describe research that has investigated the implications of these differences for self-representation, attribution, and motivation.

East-West differences are presumed to be so fundamental that they affect one's very sense of selfhood and have wide-ranging implications for the way one perceives and thinks about the self and others and the way one reacts to a wide variety of social situations. Not all cultural differences are so comprehensive, though. Two cultures may differ in their understanding of a particular class of behaviors, even though they view most other aspects of social interaction similarly. Such relatively narrow cultural differences have been found to exist within the United States between Northerners and Southerners. I will describe research pointing to differences in how threats to one's honor are construed in the Northern and Southern regions of the United States, and will discuss the implications of these differences for interpersonal judgment and behavior.

East-West Differences

Independent and Interdependent Construals of the Self

The Independent Self In many Western cultures people are socialized to become unique individuals, to express their thoughts and desires, to strive to accomplish their personal goals, to self-actualize, to realize their potential. The self is viewed as an independent, autonomous, separate being defined by a unique repertoire of attributes, abilities, thoughts, and feelings (I am smart, kind, and responsible, I'm good at math, I am not very musical, I love to travel, I want to outperform my peers). One attempts to express these aspects of the self publicly and to confirm them privately through comparisons with others. It is this repertoire of internal attributes that organizes and gives meaning to one's sense of oneself. One also has knowledge about oneself in a variety of social relations (I'm competitive with my brother, witty with my best friend, shy with members of the opposite sex), but this knowledge is not viewed as central to one's core identity and is not quite as self-defining as one's more global inner attributes. Such independent construals of the self are far more common in Western than in Eastern cultures, although there are considerable variations within each culture.

The Interdependent Self I once heard a Japanese scholar remind his American audience of their sanctified rights and utmost goals, "Life, liberty, and the pursuit of happiness." Suggesting that their forefathers might have overlooked something of great importance, he asked "What about harmony?" In many non-Western societies (e.g., Japan, China, India), people are socialized to strive for harmonious relations with others, to focus on the connectedness of individuals to one another, to adjust themselves to the demands of social situations, and to try to fit in with their social group. The self is viewed as interdependent with others and is experienced as part of a social web. One's behavior, thoughts, and feelings are seen as dependent on those of others in the relationship (I respect my parents, I am sensitive to my spouse's needs, my family sees me as friendly, my coworkers think I travel too much, I want my company to outperform its rivals). One's sense of self is grounded in one's social relationships, and the most meaningful aspects of oneself are those that emerge in relation to others. As a result the self may be experienced as fluid, taking on different colorations in different social settings.

An interdependent self embraces its assigned role, focuses on social duties and obligations, and tries to figure out what others are thinking and feeling so as to best meet their expectations. One acts in accordance with these anticipated expectations of others rather than in accordance with one's own wishes and desires; indeed, acting on one's own wishes is viewed as infantile. Relationships, rather than being a means of realizing one's own goals, become an end in themselves, so much so that others' goals may be experienced as one's own. Note, though, that the interdependent self need not be generally more benevolent and concerned about others' welfare than is the independent self. The interdependent self is not attuned to the needs of all others, only to those of the in-group, and the in-group may be very narrowly defined.

To illustrate how the interactions among individuals with interdependent selves might differ from those among individuals with independent selves, Markus and Kitayama (1991) describe how events might unfold if a person has a friend over for lunch. An American might ask the friend "Hey, Tom, what would you like on your sandwich? I have turkey, salami, and cheese." And Tom would express his preference. The assumption underlying this interaction is that Tom has an inherent right to make a choice that reflects his preferences and desires. Although this assumption is taken for granted by individuals with independent selves, it is not shared by those with interdependent selves. If a Japanese visitor were asked "What do you want on your sandwich?" there would probably be a moment of baffled silence followed by a non-committal "I don't know." To a Japanese, it is the host's responsibility to "read the friend's mind," figure out what the friend would like, and offer it. The friend, in turn, should accept whatever is offered with grace, and be ready to return the favor in the future. In Japan, therefore, the host might say something like "Hey, Tomio, I made you a turkey sandwich because I remember that last week you said you liked turkey more than beef." And Tomio would graciously thank the host (Markus and Kitayama 1991, p. 229).

The experience of seeing the self as crucially connected to others, knowing and trying to do what is best for them, and allowing their goals to take precedence over one's own, is not foreign to Westerners. It is not unusual, for example, for American parents to put their children's needs above their own. Still, the sense of the self as interdependent is more common and pervasive in non-Western than in Western societies. Indeed, several studies have revealed systematic differences among Americans and East Asians in the contents and richness of self-knowledge, as discussed next.

The Structure and Contents of Self-Knowledge

Relative Richness of Self-representation Think of a friend you know very well. How similar are you to this friend in shyness? How similar is your friend to you in shyness? Remarkably, Americans give somewhat different answers to these seemingly identical questions (Holyoak and Gordon 1983). When people are asked to make comparisons between a highly familiar object and a less familiar one, their responses reveal a systematic asymmetry: The unfamiliar object is judged as more similar to the familiar one than vice versa. For example, people who know more about the USA than about Mexico judge Mexico to be more similar to the USA than the USA is to Mexico. Such asymmetries are well-explained by Tversky's contrast model of similarity judgments (Tversky 1977). According to this model, when one is asked a question such as "how similar is the USA to Mexico?" perceived similarity decreases with the number of attributes that are unique to each country. However, similarity is decreased more by the unique attributes of the subject of the comparison (in this case, USA) than by the unique aspects of the referent (in this case, Mexico). Because we are highly familiar with the USA, we are aware that it has many unique attributes (i.e., attributes not shared with Mexico), and so we judge similarity to be relatively low. In contrast, when Mexico is the subject of the comparison (as in "How similar is Mexico to the USA), it is Mexico's unique attributes that one focuses on. Because we know little about Mexico, we can come up with only a small number of attributes unique to it, and so we judge similarity to be relatively high.

The asymmetry obtained for Americans' judgments about their similarity to a close friend therefore reveal something about the relative richness of their representations of self and other. Much like they might judge Mexico to be more similar to the USA than the USA is to Mexico, North Americans judge a friend to be more similar to the self than the self is to the friend (Holyoak and Gordon 1983). For example, I would say that you are more similar to me than I am to you (though you might think otherwise ...). This suggests that the self is more richly represented than the other; because I know much more about my unique attributes than about yours, I judge our similarity to be lower when I am the subject of the comparison (and my unique attributes are salient) than when you are the subject of the comparison (and your unique attributes are salient).

This relatively greater richness and elaboration of self-knowledge as compared to knowledge about close others may be a by-product of a culture that promotes preoccupation with the independent self and its attributes. An interdependent culture may, instead, predispose its members toward developing an elaborate understanding of each other. Individuals whose key social tasks include fitting in with others and reading their minds to anticipate their expectations may accumulate detailed knowledge about close others. Their knowledge of others may be as rich or richer than their self-knowledge. If so, they should not show the same pattern of asymmetry in judgments about the similarity between the self and another person that North Americans tend to show.

A study reported by Markus and Kitayama (1991) supported these predictions. American students and students from India were asked to judge the similarity of the self to another person or the similarity of another person to the self. As in previous studies, the

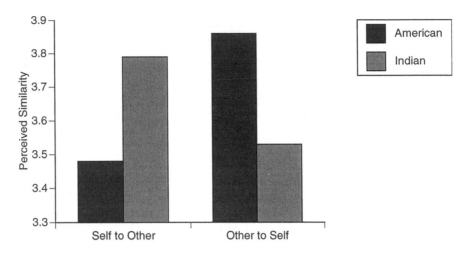

Figure 11.1 Mean perceived similarity of self to other and of other to self by students from American and Indian backgrounds. Data from Markus and Kitayama (1991, fig. 2, p. 231). Copyright © (1991) by the American Psychological Association. Reprinted with permission.

American students believed that the other was more similar to the self than the self was to the other. In contrast, as shown in figure 11.1, this pattern was reversed for the Indian students (though the reversal was not significant). This suggests that for the Indian students, the other was represented at least as richly as the self.

In sum, individuals with independent selves appear to have more rich and elaborate representations of the self than of other individuals. This relative advantage of self-representations over representations of others is eliminated and, possibly, even reversed for individuals with interdependent selves. Individuals with independent and interdependent selves differ not only in the relative richness of their self-knowledge but also in its contents, as discussed next.

Global versus Contextualized Self-descriptions   Imagine you were asked to generate 20 different answers to the question "Who am I?" What would you say? The kinds of responses you provide and the ease with which you can generate them may depend heavily on your cultural background. To an American, this question seems

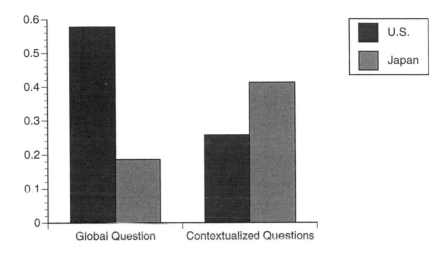

Figure 11.2 Proportion of the self-descriptions made by American students and by Japanese students that were global, unqualified attributes in response to the generalized "Who am I?" question and in response to the contextualized questions. Data from Cousins (1989, table 2, p. 127). Copyright © (1989) by the American Psychological Association. Adapted with permission.

natural and obvious; it permits one to express one's stable, independent inner self. The American will likely respond with a list of global traits, abilities, and preferences. In contrast, a Japanese person confronted with the same question may find that it presupposes an unnatural separation between one's identity and one's social context. To answer the "Who am I?" question, the Japanese may feel compelled to supplement each response with an appropriate social context.

These ideas gained support from a study in which American and Japanese college students were asked to generate self-descriptions (Cousins 1989). The students first provided 20 responses to the global "Who am I?" question. Examination of the five attributes chosen by each student as most self-defining revealed that the Americans were considerably more likely than their Japanese counterparts to respond with global, unqualified traits ("I am honest," "I am easygoing"), as may be seen in figure 11.2. The Japanese students, who were relatively reluctant to describe themselves in terms of global traits, were, instead, especially likely to ground themselves in social affiliations ("a Keio student") and activities ("one who plays Mah-Jongg on Friday nights"). The Japanese students were also considerably more likely than the Americans to fall back on universal abstractions ("a living form," "a person of the twentieth century"). In short, whereas the American students responded to the "Who am I?" question mostly with global traits, the Japanese students responded mostly with social roles, activities, preferences, and abstractions.

A very different pattern emerged when the same students were given a contextualized version of the "Who am I?" questionnaire, one that asked them to describe themselves at home, at school, and with close friends. For Americans, trait terms may lose their global, cross-situational meaning when they are restricted to a particular context, because Americans conceptualize traits as transcending situations. In contrast, for Japanese individuals, the contextualized questions ground the self in its natural social situations, and provide an opportunity for reflecting on the traits one displays in each situation. Indeed, as shown in figure 11.2, Japanese students were considerably more likely than their American counterparts to answer the contextualized questions with unqualified traits (studious, quiet, boastful). Americans, in contrast, were especially likely to provide qualified responses to these contextualized questions (e.g., "I am silly with close friends"). Cousins theorized that such qualifications to an already contextualized question were intended to convey that the self in that context need not reflect one's true, context-free self.

In sum, the Americans were more likely than the Japanese to describe themselves in terms of unqualified, global traits when asked for global context-free self-descriptions, but were less likely than the Japanese to use such traits when asked to describe themselves in particular social contexts. Put differently, the American students were more likely to use traits to describe their global than their contextualized selves, whereas the Japanese students were more likely to use traits to describe their contextualized than their global selves. These findings suggest that the American self is conceptualized as independent of its social milieu, as comprising global, context-free attributes. In contrast, the Japanese self is conceptualized as dependent upon social situations, as comprising context-specific attributes.

Americans' view of the self as characterized by global attributes that transcend situations may be at the root of their tendency to attribute other people's behavior to stable, global attributes. East Asians, who are more likely to see the self as dependent upon one's social roles and situations, are also more likely than Americans to attribute other peoples' behaviors to their roles and situations rather than to their underlying dispositions, as discussed next.

Dispositional versus Situational Attributions

Take a moment to think of something an acquaintance of yours has done recently that you consider wrong. How do you explain your acquaintance's inappropriate behavior? The kind of explanation you come up with may depend on your cultural background. There is considerable evidence that Westerners tend to explain other people's behavior in terms of stable underlying dispositions (see chapter 9; for a review, see Ross and Nisbett 1991). A Westerner will likely attribute an acquaintance's wrongdoing to some ingrained personality flaw: She lied because she is dishonest, he hit because he is aggressive, she insulted because she is insensitive. Such views of social behavior as driven by stable underlying dispositions may be fostered by a culture that encourages its members to view individuals as autonomous, independent agents who are separate from their social context. In contrast, a culture that encourages its members to view people as interdependent with each other and with their social environment, as many non-Western cultures do, may give rise to very different explanations for social behavior. Non-Westerners may see other people's behavior as determined by their social roles and interpersonal situations rather than by their personalities. An East Asian may attribute an acquaintance's wrongdoing to some constraint imposed by the person's role or situation; she lied because she had to defend her

Table 11.1 Proportion of references to general dispositions and to context among American and Hindu adults asked to explain deviant and prosocial behaviors

	DEVIANT BEHAVIORS		PROSOCIAL BEHAVIORS	
REFERENCES TO	UNITED STATES	INDIA	UNITED STATES	INDIA
Dispositions	.45	.15	.35	.22
Context	.14	.32	.22	.49

Source: Data from Miller (1984, table 2, p. 967). Copyright © (1984) by the American Psychological Association. Reprinted with permission.

client's interests, he hit because he was provoked, she insulted because she was stressed out.

Such East-West cultural differences in the way people explain everyday behaviors were demonstrated in an elegant set of studies by Joan Miller (1984). Miller recruited participants from a Western background (Americans in Chicago) and participants from an Eastern background (Hindus in Mysore, a city in South India). Each was asked to recount and explain two examples of a deviant behavior by an acquaintance and two examples of a prosocial behavior (using questions similar to the one at the start of this section). Their explanations were coded as to whether they referred to *dispositions* (e.g., proud, dishonest) or to *context*, which included interpersonal relations (e.g., "She is his aunt," "He has many enemies") as well as location in time and space (e.g., "it was early in the morning," "He lives far away from school").

There were striking differences in how Americans and Hindus explained social behavior. As may be seen in table 11.1, Americans were considerably more likely than Hindus to explain behavior as due to general dispositions whereas Hindus were considerably more likely than Americans to explain behavior as due to aspects of the context. This pattern was especially pronounced for the deviant behaviors. For these, Americans were more than three times as likely to provide dispositional than contextual explanations, whereas Hindus were more than twice as likely to provide contextual than dispositional explanations.

Interestingly, a sample of children from both cultures revealed no differences in how they explained social behavior. Cultural differences in attribution appear to emerge only in mature individuals who have been well-socialized into their culture's view of the person.

Miller reported a couple of examples that illustrate the different kinds of explanations provided by adult Americans and Hindus. One American described the following transgression:

This involved one of the teachers I work with at school. It was a process of scheduling—something to do with scheduling. I came up with an innovative idea of organizing the scheduling, of what we should do. I talked to some of the other faculty members about it, and this first teacher picked it up and quickly went to the principal and presented it as if it were his own idea. (p. 967)

The American's explanation for this behavior was unmistakably dispositional: "He was just a very self-absorbed person. He was interested only in himself."

A rather similar transgression, also involving taking credit for someone else's ideas, was described by one Hindu participant:

This involved a scholar in some other department, and she has got her PhD now. She wanted to publish four or five papers from her thesis. She produced some papers, but the thing is, her advisor, he put his name as first author and this young scholar as the second author. She was very hurt because that means usually the credit goes to the first author. (p. 968)

Rather than attributing this behavior to the advisor's poor character, as the American had for a similar act, this Hindu participant attributed it to social role relations: "She was his student. She would not have the power to do it (publish it) by herself."

Although these findings point to strong cultural differences in attribution, the following objection may be raised: The Americans and the Hindus may have differed not in how they explained behavior but in the kinds of behavior that they had generated; perhaps the Americans were especially likely to narrate acts that are well explained by dispositions, and the Hindus acts that are well explained by situational constraints. Maybe, if given the opportunity, even the Americans would explain the behaviors reported by the Hindus as driven mostly by situational constraints. Miller cleverly anticipated this objection and provided additional data that effectively ruled it out. In the second phase of her research, a new group of Americans listened to an experimenter read a sample of behaviors that had been generated by Hindu participants. Each of these behaviors had been explained by the Hindu participant who had originally described it as due to contextual factors rather than to dispositions (though these original explanations were not shown to the American participants). After hearing about each behavior, the Americans were asked to explain it.

Even when trying to account for behaviors attributed by the Hindus who had generated them to contextual factors, the Americans were considerably more likely to rely on dispositional explanations than on contextual ones; on average, 36 percent of their explanations were dispositional, whereas only 17 percent were based on context. It appears that Americans are predisposed to attribute social behavior to underlying dispositions, whereas Indians are predisposed to attribute behavior to situational constraints. These differences seem to arise from deep cultural differences in the way the person is conceptualized and in how the relations between individuals and their social networks are understood.

The different theories about human nature held by Americans and East Asians color not only their understanding of relatively minor transgressions of the sort reported for acquaintances in Miller's study but also their explanations of far more deviant acts performed by strangers. Michael Morris and Kaiping Peng (1994) examined how American and Chinese individuals explain the actions of a notorious murderer. In the autumn of 1991 there were two similar, highly publicized cases of murder in the United States. In one, a Chinese graduate student at a midwestern university, who had unsuccessfully appealed his loss of an award competition and had subsequently failed to get an academic job, shot and killed his advisor, several other people, and, finally, himself. In the other case, an Irish-American postal worker in Detroit, who had lost his job, had unsuccessfully appealed the decision, and had failed to find an alternative job, shot and killed his supervisor, several other people, and, finally, himself.

Morris and Peng compared the explanations offered for these murders in an English-language newspaper (*The New York Times*) and a Chinese-language newspaper published in the United States (*World News*). All articles published in these newspapers about these two crimes were coded for the presence of dispositional and situational attributions. For the most part, the English articles were more likely than the Chinese ones to focus on both murderers' traits (e.g., "he had a short fuse"), attitudes (e.g., "personal belief that guns were an important means to redress grievances"), and psychological problems (e.g., "darkly disturbed man who drove himself to success and distruction"). In contrast, the Chinese articles were more likely than the English ones to focus on the murderer's interpersonal relationships (e.g., "did not get along with his advisor"), on circumstances (e.g., "had been recently fired"), on problems with Chinese society (e.g., "tragedy reflects lack of religion in Chinese culture"), and on aspects of American society (e.g., "murder can be traced to the availability of guns"). In short, Westerners favored dispositional accounts whereas Easterners favored situational ones.

The same pattern emerged in a subsequent study, in which Chinese and American-born graduate students at the University of Michigan read accounts of these two murders and rated the extent to which each shooting had been caused by a series of dispositional and situational factors which had been gleaned from the various newspaper articles (Morris and Peng 1994). The American students, on average, viewed dispositional explanations focusing on the murderer's pathological character as more causally important than did the Chinese students. In contrast, the Chinese students viewed situational explanations focusing on American culture and circumstances (America's individualistic values and violent movies, the recession) as more causally important than did the Americans.

These studies suggest that Westerners and Easterners subscribe to strikingly different theories about human nature, and differ markedly in their understanding of the causal underpinnings of social behavior. However, studies that involve comparisons among individuals who live in different countries, who use different languages, and who are governed by different social norms are open to a far less interesting, trivializing interpretation. Perhaps the individuals in the two cultures did not differ in their theories about human nature but, instead, differed in their understanding of the meaning and intent of the questions used by the researchers to tap their theories. Easterners, then, may hold the same theories about the causes of behavior as Westerners, but the questions they have been asked, once translated into their language and imported into their cultural context, have not adequately tapped their theories. It would be difficult to sustain this trivializing interpretation of cultural differences in attribution if it could be shown that members of the two cultures do *not* differ in their responses when asked about events for which they hold similar theories. Although Chinese and Americans differ markedly in their theories of social events, they should not differ in their theories about physical events. Therefore, if the two groups understand the attribution questions in the same way, they should provide comparable explanations for physical events even as they differ in their explanations of social events.

Following this logic, Morris and Peng (1994) created two sets of animated cartoons, one depicting social events, the other depicting physical events. The social cartoons all portrayed various interactions among a group of fish. Each showed a blue fish moving in different ways in relation to a group of other fish. In one cartoon, for example, the blue fish moved toward the group and then continued to swim along with it. In another, the group moved toward the blue fish, and the two parties then continued to swim separately. The physical cartoons all portrayed a ball-like object moving across a soccer field. In one cartoon, for example, the moving object stopped, started, and stopped again. In another, it gradually slowed down as if by friction.

The two sets of cartoons were shown to high school students in China and in the United States who were asked to rate the extent to which the movements of the blue fish (in the social scenarios) or of the round object (in the physical scenarios) were influenced by internal factors (e.g., hunger, for the fish, and internal pressure, for the ball) and the extent to which they were influenced by external factors (e.g., the other fish, for the social scenarios, and a person kicking the ball, for the physical ones). This methodology permitted cross-cultural comparisons of attributions about social and physical events. It also had the additional advantage of ensuring that, for both types of events, members of the two cultures were explaining identical scenarios.

Responses to the social events replicated the by now familiar pattern of cultural differences: On average, the Chinese respondents viewed internal factors as less influential than did the Americans and viewed the external factors as more influential than did the Americans. In contrast, the Americans and the Chinese shared the same understanding of the causes of physical events: On average, the two groups did not differ in the extent to which they viewed the internal factors or the external factors as influential.

The Chinese and American students, then, did not differ in their understanding of the questions posed to them by the investigators, nor did they differ in their views of the very nature of causality. Where they held similar theories, as they did for the physical events, they favored the same explanations. The differences in their preferred explanations of social events, therefore, can be assumed to reveal differences in their underlying theories about the nature of social events.

All these studies point to the same conclusion. Westerners tend to view social behavior as driven by internal, stable dispositions such as traits and attitudes. In contrast, Easterners tend to view social behavior as determined by the individual's interpersonal relations, roles, circumstances, and cultural milieu. This conclusion has important implications for the understanding of the fundamental attribution error, namely people's tendency to overestimate the role of dispositions in causing behavior and to underestimate the role of situations. The fundamental attribution error may be fundamental only in Western cultures, where the person is viewed as autonomous, independent, and separate from the surrounding environment. Members of Eastern cultures, where the person is viewed as intricately linked to a web of social relations and as interdependent with others, may show no similar tendency to underestimate the power of the situation.

The hypothesis that East Asians will be less prone than Americans to making the fundamental attribution error was tested in several studies (for a review, see Fiske et al. 1998). In the classic fundamental-attribution-error paradigm, participants observe a person read an essay that either supports or opposes a particular position, say a pro-Castro or an anti-Castro essay. Americans typically assume that the essay reflects the attitudes of the person who read it, even when it is clear that the person had been required to read that particular essay; for example, they believe a person who had been required to read a pro-Castro essay feels more positively about Castro than does a person who had been required to read an anti-Castro essay (for a review, see Jones 1990; see chapter 9). In other words, they fail to appreciate the extent to which the person's actions were influenced by the situation, namely the requirement to read that particular essay. It now appears that Japanese and Korean students also make this error in the original, unmodified paradigm. However, when the paradigm is modified so that the situational constraints are highlighted, Americans continue to make the error, whereas East Asians do not (Choi and Nisbett 1998). These studies suggest that East Asians do sometimes explain behavior in terms of dispositions, much like Westerners do. However, East Asians are more likely than North Americans to pick up on cues pointing to the importance of situational constraints. When the situation is highlighted, they set aside any dispositional explanations that they may have been entertaining in favor of more appropriate situational ones.

It appears, then, that cultural differences between Western and Eastern societies result in marked difference in how people represent, understand, and think about other people and themselves. The fundamental differences in how these two cultures view human nature also appear to influence the kinds of motives that their members strive to fulfill and the social structures through which the cultures sustain these motives, as discussed next.

Choice and Dissonance

Numerous studies on dissonance reduction, conducted mostly in North America, have found that North Americans can be quite distressed by the knowledge that they may have behaved in a puzzling manner or made a poor choice. To reduce this distress, they shift their attitudes toward the position implied by their behavior, thereby making their behavior appear more justifiable. For example, students induced to express public support for raising tuition, something they actually oppose, become more favorable toward tuition raises. And people induced to choose between two equally attractive options come to like the chosen option more and the rejected one less. In both cases the attitude changes serve to make sense of an otherwise inexplicable behavior that might make one appear foolish. Moreover, it is the desire to avoid this appearance of foolishness that drives such attitude change (Festinger 1957; for reviews, see Cooper and Fazio 1984; Greenwald and Ronis 1978; Kunda 1990; see also chapter 6). Steven Heine and Darrin Lehman (1997) reasoned that the desire to avoid the appearance of having behaved foolishly in these types of situations may be unique to Westerners.

If one believes that one's behavior reveals one's global underlying dispositions and, furthermore, bases one's identity on these dispositions, as Westerners do, then foolish behaviors and choices pose a challenge to one's self-worth; if I've made a foolish choice, I must be a fool. If, however, one believes that one's actions are determined by one's social circumstances and, furthermore, one's identity is not based on the attributes that may be implied by these actions, as is the case for Easterners, then behaving in a seemingly "foolish" manner need not provoke distress or challenge one's self-worth; actions and choices that do not reflect one's inner self should not challenge it. If so, Easterners subjected to the dissonance-arousing situations known to provoke attitude change in the West should show no such attitude change. Not experiencing any unpleasant dissonance in such situations, they should have little need to attempt to reduce dissonance by changing their attitudes.

To test these predictions, Heine and Lehman (1997) recruited two groups of participants, English-speaking Canadians and Japanese visitors to Canada, for a study on music preferences. All participants first rated the desirability of 10 different compact discs (CDs) and were then offered a choice between their fifth- and sixth-ranked CDs in return for their participation. Such a choice between two almost equally attractive options can give rise to distressing doubts—"What if I chose the wrong one?" To reduce such concerns and justify one's choice, one may exaggerate the attractiveness of the chosen option and disparage the rejected one. If so, the spread between one's ratings of the chosen and the rejected alternatives should increase following the choice. Indeed, this is the pattern obtained in past studies that offered North Americans such choices (e.g., Brehm 1956). Further, if this increase in the spread of alternatives is driven by the desire to boost one's self-worth by justifying one's choice, it should be especially pronounced following a threat to one's self-worth, when the need to reestablish one's worthiness is exaggerated, and should be reduced following a boost to one's self-worth, when the need to self-enhance is already satisfied (Steele, Spencer, and Lynch, 1993; for a related discussion, see chapter 6). To examine the impact of threats or boosts to self-worth on the extent to which participants would attempt to rationalize their decisions, participants were also given negative or positive feedback about their performance on a personality test, or were given no such feedback. To ensure that this feedback would be relevant to the Japanese participants, it concerned mostly interdependent qualities known to be important to the Japanese such as

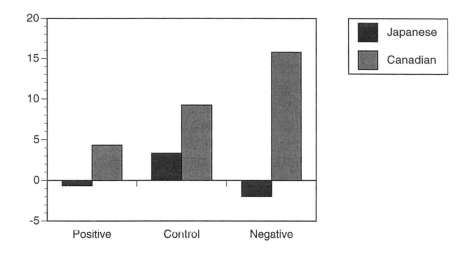

Figure 11.3 Spread of alternatives (i.e., increase in desirability of chosen alternative and decrease in desirability of rejected one) among Japanese and Canadian participants who had received positive, negative, or no feedback on their personality. From Heine and Lehman (1997, fig. 1, p. 396). Copyright © (1997) by Sage Publications, Inc. Reprinted with permission.

loyal, considerate, and cooperative. After making their choice and receiving their personality feedback, participants rated all ten CDs again.

The investigators calculated the distance between participants' ratings of the chosen and rejected CDs at each time point (i.e., before and after the choice) and then computed the difference between these two measures. If participants rationalize their choice by increasing their liking for the CD they have chosen and decreasing their liking for the one they have rejected, the spread between their ratings of the two should be greater after than before the choice. As may be seen in figure 11.3, such an increase in the spread of alternatives was obtained for the Canadian participants but not for the Japanese. The Canadians, then, attempted to rationalize their choices, whereas the Japanese did not. Moreover, for Canadians, the spread of alternatives was also influenced by the personality feedback they had received; their tendency to rationalize their choice by increasing the spread between their chosen and rejected CDs was especially pronounced after they had received negative feedback and was reduced after they had received positive feedback. Apparently, an unrelated threat to their self-worth made the Canadians all the more determined to rationalize their choices, most likely as a means of reestablishing their sense of themselves as rational, worthy individuals who make wise decisions. In contrast, Japanese participants' ratings of the two CDs were not affected by the kind of personality feedback they had received; they showed little inclination to rationalize their choices regardless of how they were made to feel by the personality feedback.

The finding that the Japanese, unlike the Canadians, made little attempt to rationalize their choices suggests that Japanese individuals are less threatened than are North Americans by the possibility that they may have made a poor choice. Moreover, when their self-worth is challenged by negative feedback on their personalities, the Japanese are less inclined to reaffirm their self-worth by painting their choices as especially prudent. These differences may be rooted in the different construals of the self favored in the two cultures—independent in North America, interdependent in Japan. Unlike persons with independent selves, persons with interdependent selves may not view their choices as implicating core aspects of their identities. Therefore, for interdependent individuals, the possibility that one has made a poor choice may not threaten one's integrity, and the knowledge that one has made a fine choice may do little to enhance one's self-worth. As a result they may feel little compulsion to rationalize their choices.

It is also possible that the very concern with protecting, maintaining, and enhancing one's self-worth is more pronounced in the West than in the East, as discussed next.

Self-enhancement versus Self-criticism

Japanese individuals, on average, report lower levels of self-esteem than do North Americans. For example, Japanese students living in Japan as well as those visiting the United States or Canada score lower on measures of self-esteem than do their American and

Canadian counterparts (e.g., Campbell et al. 1996; Diener and Diener 1995; Kitayama et al. 1997). Yet these deflated levels of self-esteem do not seem to make Japanese individuals as unhappy as they might make a North American. In Japan, the correlation between self-esteem and general life satisfaction is substantially lower than it is in the United States or Canada (Diener and Diener 1995). Put differently, in North America, the lower your self-esteem, the less satisfied you are with life, but this is far less true in Japan.

This difference in the extent to which self-esteem is associated with life satisfaction may arise from the by now familiar cultural differences in the construal of the self: North American culture is a highly individualistic one that promotes a focus on the self, whereas Japanese culture is a highly collectivist one that pays less attention to the self, highlighting, instead, one's interdependence with others. The importance of these cultural differences to understanding the value that individuals place on self-esteem was highlighted by a large-scale study that assessed, among other things, the self-esteem and the life satisfaction of students in 31 different countries around the world (Diener and Diener 1995). Each of these countries had been rated by an expert on the extent to which its culture was individualistic versus collectivist. These ratings of each country's culture were strongly associated with the magnitude of the association between its citizens' self-esteem and their satisfaction with life: The more individualistic the country, the stronger the association between self-esteem and life satisfaction in that country.

These findings imply that maintaining and enhancing one's self-esteem may be more important to members of Western cultures, where the self is construed as independent, than to members of Eastern cultures, where the self is construed as interdependent with others. There is considerable evidence that North Americans seek to maintain and enhance the self, and are willing to go to great lengths to ensure that they are seen in the best possible light. Moreover, Westerners' psychological well being and mental health may depend on their ability to see themselves positively (see chapters 6 and 10; for a review, see Taylor and Brown 1988). Although the need for self-enhancement is often discussed as though it were a basic and universal aspect of human nature, it may in fact be a product of Western culture. In a culture that advocates independent, autonomous selves, a positive view of the self—one's traits, abilities, and prospects—may be essential to one's ability to view oneself as a self-sufficient, worthy individual. Because, in such a culture, the self is made meaningful by virtue of its own distinct attributes, one's self-worth depends on the positivity of these attributes, and the motivation to maintain and enhance their positivity is strong.

In contrast, in a culture that advocates a self that is highly inter-dependent with others, as many Eastern cultures do, a positive view of the self does little to promote the key social goals of belonging and fitting in with others. Because, in such cultures, the self is made meaningful by virtue of its social relationships rather than by virtue of its own distinct attributes, one's self-worth need not depend on the positivity of these attributes, and one may have little motivation to maintain and enhance their positivity.

If this analysis is correct, self-enhancement biases, which are so pervasive in the West, may be far less pervasive in the East. Heine and Lehman (1995, 1997) examined this prediction by focusing on one of the most robust and well-documented self-enhancing biases found in the West, namely the belief that one is better off than one's peers. Dozens of studies have shown that North Americans, on average, believe they are better than average: They believe that they are more likely than their peers to have positive attributes and to enjoy desirable outcomes, and that they are less likely than their peers to have negative attributes and to suffer undesirable out-comes (see chapters 6 and 10; for a review, see Taylor and Brown 1988). Are Japanese individuals as likely as North Americans to see themselves as superior to their peers?

To address this question, Heine and Lehman (1997) obtained three samples of students: Japanese students in Japan, Canadian students of Asian heritage, and Canadian students of European heritage. Participants were asked to estimate the percentage of people the same age and gender as themselves who were better than they were on each of 10 traits. The list of traits included 5 that seemed especially likely to be valued by people who construe the self as independent (attractive, interesting, independent, confident, and intelligent) and 5 that seemed especially likely to be valued by people who construe the self as interdependent (cooperative, loyal, considerate, hard-working, and dependable).

People who consider themselves to be about average on a given attribute should estimate that about 50 percent of the population are better than them on that attribute. Estimates should be lower than 50 percent for people who consider themselves better than average, and higher for those who consider themselves worse than average. Of course, Lake Wobegon aside, we can't all be better than average. Therefore, if the mean estimate made by a group is substantially lower than 50 percent, we may reasonably conclude that this group is demonstrating a self-enhancing bias; a substantial proportion of its members must be placing themselves higher than they really are in the distribution. The lower the mean estimate of the proportion of the population that are better than one, the greater the self-enhancing bias. How biased were the three groups of participants?

As may be seen in the top two rows of table 11.2, the European Canadians demonstrated a more pronounced self-enhancement bias than did the Japanese, with the Asian Canadians falling in between the two groups. For independent traits, the Japanese showed practically no bias, believing, on average, that about half of the population was better than them. In contrast, the European Canadians felt, on average, that only about a quarter of the population was better than them on these traits. Remarkably, essentially the same pattern was obtained even for the interdependent traits that the Japanese were expected to value especially highly; even on traits such as loyal and cooperative, which seem to exemplify the culturally promoted goals of the Japanese, the Japanese showed little inclination to place themselves at the top of the distribution, whereas the European Canadians, once again, placed themselves in the top quartile, on average. In short, the Japanese were far less

Table 11.2 Mean estimates of the percentage of the population who are better than the self or a close family member on independent traits and on interdependent traits

RATED TARGET AND TRAIT	JAPANESE	ASIAN CANADIANS	EUROPEAN CANADIANS
Self			
Independent traits	47.3%	36.3%	27.5%
Interdependent traits	43.9%	27.4%	23.7%
Family member			
Independent traits	38.6%	28.0%	23.5%
Interdependent traits	30.6%	20.4%	18.5%

Source: From Heine and Lehman (1997, table 1, p. 1272). Copyright © (1997) by the American Psychological Association. Reprinted with permission.
Note: Estimates were made by Japanese, Asian Canadian, and European Canadian students. Lower numbers represent greater enhancement of the target relative to the population.

prone to self-enhancement than their European Canadian counterparts. Interestingly, Canadians of Asian heritage, who may be assumed to absorb Asian culture at home while being exposed to North American culture everywhere else, fell between the two other groups, showing some but not total adoption of Western cultural patterns.

Is it that the Japanese simply have no desire for self-enhancement? Or could it be, instead, that they are just as motivated to view themselves positively as North Americans are but that they derive their self-worth not from their own attributes but, rather, from a sense of group pride? If so, rather than attempting to aggrandize their selves, as North Americans do, they should attempt to aggrandize their family and other important groups that they belong to. To address this possibility, Heine and Lehman (1997) asked the same three groups of participants to answer the same questions with regards to a close family member.

As may be seen in the bottom two rows of table 11.2, the Japanese students, who had shown little evidence of self-serving bias when asked about themselves, did show some bias when asked about a family member; this time, their estimates were significantly lower than the 50 percent benchmark. Still, they showed considerably less bias than their European Canadian counterparts. It is also apparent that all three groups showed greater bias for the family member than for themselves. We can only speculate on why this was so. It may be that people derive greater pleasure from enhancing a relative than from enhancing the self, it may be that they are less constrained by false modesty when evaluating a relative, or it may be that the participants had simply chosen an especially valued and respected relative to evaluate. In any case, it is clear that the Japanese students in this and similar studies showed less self-enhancement and less family-member-enhancement than did the European Canadians.

It may be argued that questions about a family member cannot really tap one's tendency to enhance one's group because, after all, they focus on an individual rather than on the group. Perhaps, then, the Japanese, who are assumed to derive their self-worth from their association with their social group, will show a greater positive bias than North Americans when asked to evaluate an important group that they belong to. However, another study by Heine and Lehman (1997) found that this was not the case. When asked to rate their own and a rival university, Japanese students, once again, showed less self-enhancing biases than did European Canadians. Whereas the European Canadians tended to boost the relative standing of their own university, the Japanese, if anything, did the opposite; they were more inclined to make self-effacing than self-enhancing ratings of their University. Asian Canadians, once again, showed an intermediate pattern.

These studies suggest that the Japanese are less motivated to enhance themselves, their family members, and their social groups than are North Americans. Although this pattern of responses may stem from basic differences in how people construe and wish to see the self in relation to others, it may also be due to a much less fundamental difference. The obtained differences in how people rank themselves and their associates relative to others may reflect different norms of acceptable discourse rather than true differences in underlying psychology. Perhaps the Japanese are just as inclined as North Americans to view themselves as superior to others but are less inclined to openly express these views. In a culture that urges its members to avoid standing out and distinguishing themselves from their peers, it may be far less socially acceptable than it is in North America to candidly claim superiority of any kind. Although these studies remain vulnerable to this interpretation, other research suggests that the differences among the two cultures do run deeper. Western and Eastern cultures may differ not only in the characteristic motives that they encourage their members to promote but also in the opportunities for satisfying different motives that they provide (Kitayama et al. 1997).

One of the cornerstones of social cognition theory and research is that different individuals may understand the same situation quite differently, if they view it through the lenses of different knowledge structures, goals, and feelings (see chapter 2). Kitayama and his colleagues (1997) reasoned that different cultures may give rise to different collective, culturally shared ways of constructing, defining, and extracting meaning from situations. Similar situations may therefore carry different meanings in different cultures. Moreover, individuals in each culture should drift toward those situations that are best suited to meeting their particular needs. As individuals follow the dictates of their respective cultures, fulfilling the culturally dictated patterns of thought, feeling, and behavior, they ultimately reinforce the very culture that had given rise to these patterns in the first place. As you think and act in accordance with your culture, you support and reproduce it.

Kitayama and his colleagues began with the assumption that Japanese and American individuals differ in their dominant goals. Both ethnographic research and experimental studies such as those described above point to the same cultural differences in how people are motivated to view themselves: Whereas North American culture, as we have seen, promotes self-enhancement, Japanese culture promotes *self-criticism* instead (Kitayama et al. 1997). In an interdependent culture, where one's worthiness depends on one's ability to fit in with one's group, it is important to determine where one falls short of the group's standards so that one can improve oneself and better fit in with the group. Kitayama and his colleagues reasoned that these two culturally dictated motives, self-enhancement in the West and self-criticism in the East, should influence the meaning that individuals in the two cultures attach to relevant situations as well as the nature of situations Easterners and Westerners tend to find themselves in.

To examine these ideas, Kitayama and his colleagues first put together a large list of Japanese and American situations viewed in their country of origin as either self-enhancing or self-deflating, and then examined how Japanese and American students viewed each of these situations. Their first step was to ask a large number of Japanese and American college students to describe situations in which their own self-esteem had increased and situations in which their self-esteem had decreased. The investigators randomly selected 100 success and 100 failure situations that were "made in Japan," and the same numbers of success and failure situations that were "made in America."

Some of the Japanese success situations were: "When I remember a difficult job in the past that I managed to carry through," "When I am told by someone I like, 'I'm glad you were here,'" and "When I feel that nobody is watching me." Some of the Japanese failure situations were: "When I was jilted by someone I was thinking of marrying," "When I was blamed and scolded for something that someone else did," and "When I was the only one ignored in the presence of many people." By comparison, some of the American success situations were: "When I get A+ on my paper or final," "When people tell me I cheer them up whenever I'm around," and "When I make myself a great breakfast just for me." And some of the American failure situations were: "When you are with some friends and they tell you to get lost because they don't want you around," "When you realize many of the people you considered to be friends don't give a damn about what happens to you," and

"When I accidentally ran into someone with my car which may have caused severe injuries" (Kitayama et al. 1997, p. 1267). On the face of it, the Japanese examples may not seem all that different from the American ones when considered one at a time, and most seem meaningful in both cultural contexts. Nevertheless, when taken as a whole, the two sets of situations were quite different, as will soon be apparent.

To examine how these American and Japanese situations would be viewed by members of each culture, the investigators obtained three new groups of participants: Japanese students in Japan, Japanese students temporarily studying in the United States, and White American students. These participants were asked to imagine themselves in each of the 400 situations, to indicate whether their self-esteem would be affected in each and, if so, to indicate in what direction (positive or negative) and to what extent. Do Japanese and American students expect to experience different reactions to the same situations? Do situations made in America elicit different reactions than situations made in Japan? The answer to both these questions was yes.

First, the same situations were viewed differently by Japanese and by American students. American students considered a greater proportion of the success situations (86 percent) than of the failure situations (79 percent) to be self-relevant. Moreover, this was just as true for situations made in Japan as it was for situations made in America. In contrast, Japanese students in Japan considered a greater proportion of the failure situations (82 percent) than of the success situations (74 percent) to be self-relevant. Once again, this was true regardless of where the situations had originated from. Japanese students in the United States showed a pattern that was similar to but a little weaker than that obtained in Japan. Thus, when confronted with the identical set of situations, the Americans were especially likely to find self-relevance in those situations that provide opportunities for increasing self-esteem whereas the Japanese were especially likely to find self-relevance in those situations that give rise to self-criticism and deflation.

The same tendencies were apparent in participants' ratings of the extent to which they expected their self-esteem to increase or decrease in the situations that they deemed self-relevant. Americans thought their self-esteem would increase more in the success situations than it would decrease in the failure situations. In contrast, Japanese students in Japan thought their self-esteem would decrease more in the failure situations than it would increase in the success situations. Once again, Japanese students in the United States showed a pattern that was similar to but weaker than that obtained in Japan. Americans, then, make the most of self-enhancement opportunities and play down the consequences of failure. Japanese, in contrast, seem to do the opposite.

Even more important than these differences between American and Japanese individuals were the differences between American and Japanese situations. Among situations made in America, success situations were judged (by participants in both countries) to have greater impact than failure situations on self-esteem. The very opposite was true for situations made in Japan; for these, failure situations were judged to have greater impact on self-esteem than success situations. Put differently, the positive American situations are more pleasing than the negative ones are distressing, whereas the reverse is true for Japanese situations. Individuals who inhabit a world of American situations will therefore, on balance, be subject to experiences that boost their self-esteem. In contrast, individuals who inhabit a world of Japanese situations will, on balance, be subject to experiences that deflate their self-esteem and provoke self-criticism.

Both the difference between Japanese and American respondents and the difference between Japanese and American situations are portrayed in figure 11.4. The figure depicts a measure of relative self-esteem change obtained by calculating, for each participant, the difference between the average increase in self-esteem expected in success situations and the average decline in self-esteem expected in failure situations. A positive value on this measure indicates that the individual expects self-enhancement in positive situations to be greater than self-deflation in negative situations. Such an individual may be viewed as prone to self-enhancement. In contrast, a negative value on this measure indicates that the

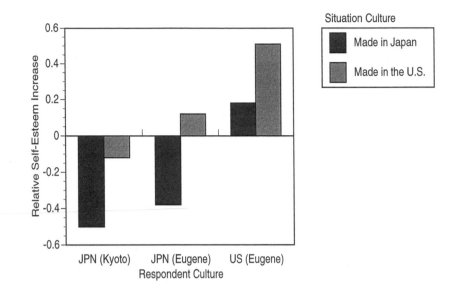

Figure 11.4 Relative self-esteem change (i.e., average increase in self-esteem expected in success situations minus average decrease expected in failure situations) as a function of the culture of origin of respondents and of situations. Based on Kitayama et al. (1997, fig. 1, p. 1253). Copyright © (1997) by the American Psychological Association. Reprinted with permission.

individual expects self-deflation in negative situations to be greater than self-enhancement in positive situations. Such an individual may be viewed as prone to self-criticism. Two scores of relative self-esteem change were calculated for each participant, one for situations made in America, the other for situations made in Japan.

The first thing to note in figure 11.4 is that American and Japanese students showed opposite patterns of relative self-esteem change: The Americans were prone to self-enhancement but the Japanese to self-criticism. The pattern for Japanese students in the United States, as for the previously discussed measures, was similar to that obtained in Japan but somewhat attenuated toward the American pattern. It is important to note that the differences between American students and Japanese students in Japan held regardless of the situations' country of origin: The Americans were more prone to self-enhancement than the Japanese in both American-made and Japanese-made situations. Even when American and Japanese individuals find themselves in the same situations, then, the Americans will be especially likely to extract self-enhancing information from these situations, whereas the Japanese will be especially likely to extract information that highlights their shortcomings.

The second important finding to note in figure 11.4 is that the American-made situations were more conducive to self-enhancement (and less to self-criticism) than the Japanese-made situations. The American students' self-enhancement tendency was especially strong for situations made in America, and the Japanese students' self-criticism tendency was especially strong for situations made in Japan. Put differently, both groups expected, on balance, to experience more positive reactions (or less negative ones) in American-made than in Japanese-made situations. American and Japanese individuals, then, do not inhabit comparable worlds. The positive and negative situations encountered by American students are, on balance, slanted toward providing maximal opportunities for self-enhancement, whereas those encountered by Japanese students are slanted, instead, toward maximizing opportunities for self-criticism. These biases in the nature of Japanese and American situations mirror the biases obtained for Japanese and American individuals—an inclination toward self-criticism in the Japanese and toward self-enhancement in the Americans.

It is important to note, though, that the evidence pointing to the different nature of American and Japanese situations is not conclusive. To draw such conclusions, it is necessary to obtain a random sample of American and Japanese situations. This was not done here. Instead, the situations used were filtered through the eyes of the Japanese and American students who had provided them in the first place, as examples of situations where their self-esteem had increased or decreased. It may be that the American bias toward self-enhancement and the Japanese bias toward self-criticism influenced the kinds of situations both groups of students were willing to report. It remains possible therefore that Americans and Japanese individuals inhabit comparable worlds of situations but choose to describe different subsets of these, with the Americans describing the most positive of their enhancing experiences and the least negative of their deflating experiences, and the Japanese describing the most humiliating of their deflating experiences and the least enhancing of their positive ones. Overall, then, these studies provide strong evidence of bias at the level of individual psychologies in the United States and Japan and weaker evidence of bias at the level of the structure of situations available in the two countries.

The different pattern of responses obtained for American and Japanese students in this study points to differences in their underlying conceptions of social situations and of the self. However, it may also reflect a more superficial difference: Both groups may simply be trying to present themselves in the best possible way, according to the dictates of their respective cultures. If American and Japanese students differed in their ratings of the situations because of such self-presentational tactics, these differences should be eliminated when students are asked to make judgments about someone else, say the typical student, rather than about the self; the motivation to present the typical student positively should not be nearly as strong as the motivation to present the self in the best possible light. A follow-up study addressed this possibility. This time, American and Japanese students assessed the relevance of the same set of 400 situations to the self-esteem of the typical student rather than to their own self-esteem (Kitayama et al. 1997).

Judgments about the typical student followed essentially the same pattern as judgments about the self. Here, too, the Americans expected the typical student to be prone to self-enhancement whereas the Japanese expected the typical student to be prone to self-criticism. And, once again, the American-made situations were judged as more conducive to self-enhancement and less to self-criticism than were the Japanese-made situations. The fact that judgments about the typical student followed the same pattern as judgments about the self suggests that the different self-relevance judgments made by American and Japanese students reflect differences in their underlying theories about the nature of the self and in their definitions of situations rather than attempts to make the self look good.

These studies imply that the American inclination toward self-enhancement and the Japanese inclination toward self-criticism are supported by the opportunities provided within the two cultures as well as by the psychological makeup of the individuals who inhabit them. Americans live in a culture that provides more boosts than blows to self-esteem. This cultural bias towards self-enhancement is further exaggerated by a bias at the level of the individual—Americans seem to make the most of the self-enhancement opportunities that come their way while playing down the relevance and importance of potentially humbling experiences. In stark contrast, the Japanese live in a culture that provides more challenges than boosts to self-esteem. And here, too, the cultural bias towards self-criticism is exaggerated through the psychological makeup of its individual members—the Japanese seem especially likely to find self-relevance and meaning in situations that promote self-criticism, while passing over opportunities for self-enhancement. In this manner the respective cultures and the individuals who reside within them support, reinforce, and maintain each other's proclivities.

The scope of differences between North Americans and East Asians is vast. It is not that surprising that people who differ on key dimensions such as nationality, language, religion, political institutions, and literary and artistic traditions also differ in their psychological makeup. However, culturally determined psychological differences need not be built on such a comprehensive edifice of contrasts. I turn next to a discussion of cultural differences among individuals who live in different regions of the same country—Northerners and Southerners in the United States.

North-South Differences in the United States

Culture of Honor

Do you suppose a man has a right to kill another person so as to protect his family? Is it appropriate for a man to punch a drunk who has insulted his wife? Would you think he wasn't much of a man if he failed to do so? Would most fathers expect their sons to stand up for themselves and fight a child who was bullying them, or would they expect their sons to try to stay away from the bully and avoid fighting him? Your answers to such questions are likely to be influenced by the way insults, violence, honor, and manhood are construed in your culture.

Anthropologists have long noted that some societies have what might be termed a *culture of honor*. Members of such cultures, especially the men, are extremely concerned with maintaining their reputation and protecting their honor. They wish to be seen as "the sort who won't take any shit" rather than "the sort who can be pushed around." To convince others that they are the kind of guy one better not mess with, they feel compelled to respond violently even to seemingly minor threats to themselves, their family, or their honor. Failure to do so brings about ridicule, entails shame, and undercuts one's manhood (for more detailed discussions, see Cohen and Nisbett 1994; Nisbett and Cohen 1996). Such a culture of honor exits in many traditional Catholic, Moslem, and Hindu societies around the Mediterranean basin, the Middle East, Latin America, and elsewhere (Fiske et al. 1998). Richard Nisbett, Dov Cohen, and their colleagues have argued that it also exists in the White Protestant society of the U.S. South.

The American South has long been regarded as more violent than the North. Homicide rates in the two regions support this impression: The rates of homicides by White non-Hispanic males are considerably higher in the South than in the North. This is especially true for smaller cities, where homicide rates for White males are about three times as high in the South than in New England, the least Southern region of the United States. Importantly, Southerners are no more likely than Northerners to commit homicide in the context of another felony such as robbery or burglary. Their elevated homicide rate applies only to those homicides that are related to argument or conflict, such as those stemming from lovers' triangles or barroom quarrels, that is, to circumstances where the killer's honor may have been at stake (for detailed discussion and statistics, see Nisbett 1993). This pattern is consistent with the view that there is a greater concern with honor and the need to protect it through violence in the South than in the North.

Nisbett, Cohen, and their colleagues argued that the South may be home to a culture of honor because historically much of its economy had been based on herding. Herding cultures may be especially likely to promote a culture of honor because, when law enforcement is insufficient, herdsmen stand to lose their property overnight if they are unwilling to defend it. In such a climate it may be especially important to maintain a reputation as someone who should not be messed with (Nisbett 1993; Cohen and Nisbett 1994). Defending one's honor becomes as important as defending one's self because a ruined reputation can entail damage to one's person and property. Therefore it becomes crucial to respond violently even to seemingly minor insults so as to maintain a credible image as someone who should not be trifled with.

Many anecdotal and historical observations support the view that the Southern U.S. regions sustain a culture of honor. These include accounts of juries refusing to convict men accused of murder in response to challenges to their honor, descriptions of child-rearing practices that encourage young boys to lash out violently against anyone who challenges them, and examples of Southern proverbs proclaiming, for instance, that "every man should be sheriff on his own hearth" (Nisbett 1993). In a series of studies Nisbett, Cohen, and their colleagues provided more systematic evidence that Southerners differ from Northerners in their attitudes toward those kinds of violence that are endorsed by a culture of honor as well as in the way they construe and react to personal insults.

In one set of studies, Cohen and Nisbett (1994) compared the responses of Southern and Northern White males to various survey questions that tapped their attitudes toward different kinds of violence. For the most part, Southerners were no more likely than Northerners to endorse statements about violence in general such as "Many people only learn through violence," or "'An eye for an eye and a tooth for a tooth' is a good rule for living." However, Southerners were more likely than Northerners to approve of violence carried out in the service of self-defense or the defense of one's family or home. For example, the percentage of respondents saying that they "agree a great deal" that "A man has a right to kill a person to defend his family" was 80 percent for Southerners but only 67 percent for Northerners, and the percentage who agreed a great deal that "A man has the right to kill another man in the case of self-defense" was 70 percent for Southerners but only 57 percent for Northerners (Cohen and Nisbett 1994, p. 555).

In similar vein, Southerners were more likely than Northerners to approve of punching a stranger who "was drunk and bumped into a man and his wife on the street" (approval rates were 15 percent in the South, 8 percent in the North). Southerners also showed greater approval of violence than Northerners when asked how they thought most fathers would expect a ten-year-old son to react to a bully who had given him a black eye and a bloody nose in front of a crowd of other children. Southerners were considerably more likely than Northerners to think that most fathers would expect the boy to "take a stand and fight the other boy" (this option was chosen by 38 percent of Southerners but only by 24 percent of Northerners).

Southerners were also more likely than Northerners to question the masculinity of a man who did not respond with violence to affronts to his own or his family's honor. When asked to consider cases in which a man fights an acquaintance who had flirted with his girlfriend, had insulted his wife, or had told others that the man is a liar, and cases where a man shoots another who had stolen his wife or had sexually assaulted his daughter, Southerners were, on average, twice as likely than Northerners to say that the man who did not respond with such violence would be "not much of a man" (the average percentages saying this were 12.2 percent of Southerners and 6.1 percent of Northerners). These and similar results reported by Cohen and Nisbett (1994) suggest that Southern culture is more accepting of violence carried out in reaction to threats to oneself, one's family, and one's honor than is the culture that prevails in the Northern regions of the United States.

If it is true that Southerners subscribe to a culture of honor and Northerners do not, then individuals raised in these different cultures should react in predictably different ways when confronted with an identical insult. The different cultural assumptions held by Southerners and by Northerners should lead them to construe and react to the same insult differently: Southerners should be more upset than Northerners by a seemingly minor insult, should be more concerned about the damage it might cause to their reputations, and should be more prepared to respond in kind. A series of inventive experiments by Cohen and his colleagues tested these predictions (Cohen et al. 1996).

Cohen and his colleagues took advantage of the fact that the University of Michigan attracts many students from other states, some Northern and some Southern. In their studies, Northern and Southern White male students were invited to participate, one at a time, in a study on human judgment. In an incident seemingly unrelated to the purported study, each was subjected to the same insult: The participant was instructed to place a questionnaire on a table at the end of a long, narrow hallway. On his way he encountered a male confederate working at a file cabinet in this hall who had to push in an open file drawer so as to make room for the participant to get by. When the participant returned, moments later, the confederate, who had by then reopened the drawer, slammed it shut, bumped into the participant with his shoulder, and called him an "asshole." Control participants went through the same procedures, but without being bumped and insulted. Would Southern and Northern men react differently to such an insult? Several studies employing this procedure suggested that they would.

One of the studies examined participants' physiological reactions to the insult by measuring their levels of two hormones: cortisol, which is associated with high levels of stress, anxiety, and arousal, and testosterone, which is associated with aggression and may play a role in preparing individuals for competitions and dominance contests (Cohen et al. 1996). If Southerners are more upset than Northerners by the insult and are more likely to respond to it by preparing themselves for future aggression, they should show greater increases in the levels of both these hormones, following the insult. This was indeed the case. Northerners showed little change in the levels of both these hormones following the insult, which suggests that they were relatively unaffected by it. In contrast, insulted Southerners showed a marked increase in both cortisol and testosterone levels, suggesting that the insult had upset them and had primed them to prepare for aggression.

Another study provided participants with an opportunity to behave aggressively following the insult (Cohen et al. 1996). This time, after the participant had been bumped and called an asshole, and was continuing his walk down the narrow hallway, another, huge male confederate appeared around the corner and began walking toward him on a collision course. The hallway was so narrow that it was clear that someone would have to give way, and the confederate showed no sign of doing so (except at the last second, to avoid another bumping). Control participants found themselves in the same situation without first being insulted. This set up amounted to a game of "chicken," and the question of interest was at what point would the participant "chicken out" and give way to the hefty confederate. Would Southerners, found in the previous study to begin preparing for aggression following an insult, actually behave more aggressively in this situation?

Once again, only Southerners responded to the insult with increased aggression. As may be seen in figure 11.5, Northerners gave way to the confederate at about the same distance, regardless of whether or not they had been insulted. In contrast, the behavior of Southerners was markedly influenced by the insult. Insulted Southerners went much farther toward the confederate before "chickening out" than did those who had not been insulted. Interestingly, Southerners who had not been insulted were, if anything, more deferential and polite to the confederate than were their Northern counterparts, moving out of his way sooner. However, once insulted, the Southerners became more aggressive than the Northerners.

This experiment also examined what participants expected a witness to their insult to think of them. For some of the insulted participants, the insult took place in the presence of an observer,

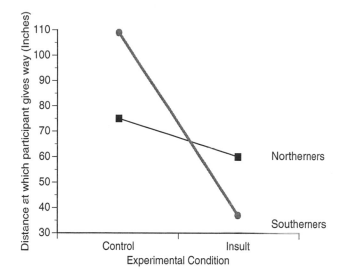

Figure 11.6 Distance at which the participant gave way to the confederate in the "chicken" game, for insulted and noninsulted Southerners and Northerners. From Cohen et al. (1996, fig. 3, p. 954). Copyright © (1996) by the American Psychological Association. Reprinted with permission.

whom they later met very briefly. For other insulted participants, the insult took place privately, with no witnesses. These privately insulted participants and the control, noninsulted ones also met this individual, but for these groups he had not been a witness to their insult. To determine what participants thought this individual would think of them, each was asked to guess how this individual would evaluate him on several masculinity-related dimensions such as manly–not manly, courageous–cowardly, and tough–wimpy. If only Southerners subscribe to a culture of honor, only they should expect their image to be tarnished in the eyes of someone who had seen them being insulted. This was indeed the case.

Northerners expected their evaluator to view them as equally masculine regardless of whether or not he had witnessed them being insulted. In contrast, Southerners who knew that the evaluator had witnessed their insult expected him to think less of their masculinity than did Southerners who believed that the evaluator was unaware that they had suffered any insult because they had been insulted privately or not at all. In short, insulted Southerners expected their reputation to be damaged in the eyes of a witness to their insult, whereas insulted Northerners expected no such damage to their reputation.

In sum, Southerners reacted quite differently than Northerners to the same insult. Southerners were more upset by it, more physiologically primed to respond aggressively, and more likely to believe that the insult had damaged their reputation in front of others. Perhaps for all these reasons, when given an opportunity to show aggression, insulted Southerners behaved more aggressively in a game of "chicken" than did insulted Northerners. Why should Southern and Northern men react so differently to the same insult? There are two possible explanations for this. First, the insult itself may have been perceived as more serious by Southerners, who are accustomed to greater politeness than are Northerners. Second, Southerners and Northerners may have differed in their beliefs about the appropriate reactions to the same insult, with Southerners assuming that a more violent response was in order. In other words, Southerners and Northerners may have differed in their construal of the insult or in their norms for how one should react to it. Cohen and his colleagues (1996) speculated that both these processes contributed to the differing reactions of Southerners and Northerners to the same insult. In either case, it is clear that deep-rooted cultural differences in the meaning attached to insults and aggression among those raised in the Northern and Southern regions of the United States lead Northern and Southern men to react quite differently when they find themselves in a seemingly identical situation.

Implications for Social Cognition

Where do cultural differences in social cognition leave us? In one respect, they reinforce the central tenet of this book, namely that individuals construct their understanding of their social worlds. The meaning that people attach to social events and their resulting thoughts, feelings, and behavior are influenced considerably by each person's unique pattern of associations and feelings. Earlier chapters have reviewed research demonstrating that individuals who enter a situation with different self-schemas, goals, stereotypes, inferential rules, attitudes, beliefs, or feelings will understand and react to it quite differently. Although each individual carries a unique configuration of knowledge structures and associations, the research reviewed in this chapter suggests that individuals inhabiting the same culture may also have many shared ways of understanding themselves and others. Moreover, whereas individuals raised in the same culture will have much in common with one another, they may differ substantially from individuals raised in different cultures. Each culture may bestow its members with distinctive ways of making sense of people.

In this chapter I focused on cultural differences among Western and Eastern societies and on differences among Northern and Southern regions of the United States. Distinctive patterns of making sense of people may also emerge between men and women, between Jews and gentiles, between African Americans and White Americans, between urban and rural individuals, and between professional and working-class individuals. The many ideological and cultural assumptions shared by members of such groups may result in distinctive shared patterns of experiencing their social worlds. Cultures may differ from one another in their basic assumptions about human nature, leading to fundamental differences in how individuals experience themselves and others in the full range of social situations. The East-West differences reviewed in this chapter appear to be of this all encompassing nature. Differences among cultures may also be more narrowly restricted to particular domains of social interaction. The North-South differences reviewed in this chapter appear to be of this more restricted nature. These differences pertain narrowly to honor-related insults and violence. They do not extend to other kinds of violence and are not expected to influence beliefs and interactions that do not involve this aspect of honor.

Although the demonstrated cultural differences are consistent with the constructive view of social cognition that dominates research and theory in this field, such differences also challenge some of the most basic assumptions long held by social psychologists. This is especially true for the differences among Western and Eastern cultures, which appear to result in fundamentally different ways of experiencing the self and the world. Many of the phenomena that North American theorists have considered universal may in fact result from the particular configuration of beliefs and goals that is common in North Americans and other Westerners but is not found in Japanese, Indians, and other East Asians. Individuals who, unlike most Westerners, do not view behavior as caused predominantly by dispositions, may be unlikely to fall prone to that cornerstone of attribution theory, the fundamental attribution error. Individuals who, unlike most Westerners, do not base their identities on their distinct attributes, may be unlikely to show the bias that seems so crucial to the mental health of North·Americans, namely self-enhancement. And individuals who do not assume that their behavior and choices need to reflect their inner attributes may not feel compelled to engage in dissonance reduction so as to justify their behaviors and choices when these seem puzzling. These classic, well-documented, seemingly basic social psychological processes may be basic only in the West.

This is not to say that the many phenomena and processes uncovered by Western social psychologists are not valid. They are, but they must be understood with reference to the culture in which they have been obtained. Research on the impact of culture on social cognition has the potential of shedding new light on the causal underpinnings of many social cognition findings, and it may ultimately lead to an understanding of the many ways in which individuals are shaped by their culture and the ways in which they, in turn, shape it.

Summary

North Americans and other Westerners typically view the self as an independent, autonomous separate being comprising a unique set of global, context-free attributes. In contrast, East Asians typically view the self as interdependent with others, as grounded in a network of social relationships, and as comprising context-specific attributes that vary from one social situation to another. These independent and interdependent construals of the self are associated with different ways of representing and thinking about the self and others.

Individuals with independent selves appear to have more rich and elaborate representations of the self than of other individuals. In contrast, for individuals with interdependent selves, self-representations have no such advantage over representations of others.

Westerners and Easterners also hold very different theories about the causes of social behavior. Westerners, who view individuals as autonomous agents, tend to see other people's behavior as arising from stable underlying dispositions. In contrast, non-Westerners, who view individuals as entwined in a web of social relations, tend to see other people's behavior as determined by their social roles and interpersonal situations rather than by their personalities. Westerners are also more likely than Easterners to base their self-worth on the quality of their actions and choices and may therefore be more threatened by the possibility that they may have behaved foolishly, and may try harder to reduce any dissonance arousing from their actions.

Self-enhancement may be more important to Westerners than to Easterners. Westerners, such as North Americans, are more likely than East Asians, such as the Japanese, to engage in self-enhancement and to view themselves as better than their peers. Moreover, North Americans seem especially likely to find self-relevance in self-enhancement opportunities and to play down the relevance of deflating experiences whereas the Japanese seem especially likely to find self-relevance in opportunities for self-criticism and to play down the relevance of self-enhancing experiences. The respective cultures in North America and Japan appear biased toward providing the kinds of experiences favored by their members—opportunities for self-enhancement in North America and for self-criticism in Japan.

There are also important cultural differences within North America. In the United States, Southern regions are more likely than Northern regions to sustain a *culture of honor*, that is, a culture whose members are extremely concerned with maintaining their reputations and protecting their honor, and are especially likely to respond with violence when their honor is threatened and to sanction violent reactions by others whose honor has been challenged. Perhaps for these reasons, Southern and Northern American men construe and react to the same insults differently. Southerners are more upset than Northerners by a seemingly minor insult, are more concerned that it might damage their reputations, and are more likely to respond in kind.

References

Ajzen, I. (1977). Intuitive theories of events and the effects of base-rate information on prediction. *Journal of Pesonality and Social Psychology, 35*, 303–314.

Allport, F. H. (1933). *Institutional behavior.* Chapel Hill: University of North Carolina Press.

Allport, G. W. (1954). *The nature of prejudice.* Reading, MA: Addison-Wesley.

Allport, G. W., and Odbert, H. S. (1936). Trait-names: A psycho-lexical study. *Psychological Mongraphs, 47,* (No. 211).

Ambady, N., and Rosenthal, R. (1992). Thin slices of expressive behavior as predictors of interpersonal consequences: A meta-analysis. *Psychological Bulletin, 111*, 256–274.

Ambady, N., and Rosenthal, R. (1993). Half a minute: Prediciting teacher evaluations from thin slices of nonverbal behavior and physical attractiveness. *Journal of Personality and Social Psychology, 64*, 431–441.

Andersen, S. A., and Klatzky, R. L. (1987). Traits and social stereotypes: Levels of categorization in person perception. *Journal of Personality and Social Psychology, 53*, 235–246.

Anderson, C. A., and Sechler, E. S. (1986). Effects of explanation and counterexplanation on the development and use of statistical theories. *Journal of Personality and Social Psychology, 50*, 24–34.

Anderson, J. R. (1983). *The architecture of cognition.* Cambridge, MA: Harvard University Press.

Anderson, M. C., and Spellman, B. A. (1995). On the status of inhibitory mechanisms in cognition: Memory retrieval as a model case. *Psychological Review, 102*, 68–100.

Armor, D. A., and Taylor, S. E. (1998). Situated optimism: Specific outcome expectancies and self-regulation. In M. P. Zanna (Ed.), *Advances in Experimental Social Psychology* (Vol. 30, pp. 309–379). San Diego: Academic Press.

Aronson, E. (1968). Dissonance theory: Progress and problems. In R. P. Abelson, E. Aronson, W. J. McGuire, T. M. Newcomb, M. J. Rosenberg, and P. H. Tannenbaum (Eds.), *Theories of cognitive consistency: A sourcebook* (pp. 5–27). Chicago: Rand McNally.

Aronson, E., and Mills, J. (1959). The effect of severity of initiation on liking for a group. *Journal of Abnormal and Social Psychology, 59*, 177–181.

Asch, S. E., and Zukier, H. (1984). Thinking about persons. *Journal of Personality and Social Psychology, 46*, 1230–1240.

Bar-Hillel, M., and Neter, E. (1996). Why are people reluctant to exchange lottery tickets? *Journal of Personality and Social Psychology, 70*, 17–27.

Bar-Hillel, M., and Fischhoff, B. (1981). When do base-rates affect predictions? *Journal of Personality and Social Psychology, 41*, 671–680.

Bargh, J. A. (1989). Conditional automaticity: Varieties of automatic influence in social perception and cognition. In J. A. Bargh and J. S. Uleman (Eds.), *Unintended thought* (pp. 3–51). New York: Guilford Press.

Bargh, J. A. (1994). The four horsemen of automaticity: Awareness, intention, efficiency, and control in social cognition. In J. R. S. Wyer and T. K. Srull (Eds.), *Handbook of social cognition* Hillsdale, NJ: Erlbaum.

Bargh, J. A. (1996). Automaticity in social psychology. In E. T. Higgins and A. W. Kruglanski (Eds.), *Social psychology: Handbook of basic principles* (pp. 169–183). New York: Guilford Press.

Bargh, J. A. (1997). The automaticity of everyday life. In J. R. S. Wyer (Ed.), *Advances in social cognition* (Vol. 10, pp. 1–61). Mahwah, NJ: Erlbaum.

Bargh, J. A., Bond, R. N., Lombardi, W. J., and Tota, M. E. (1986). The additive nature of chronic and temporary sources of construct accessibility. *Journal of Personality and Social Psychology*, *50*, 869–878.

Bargh, J. A., Chaiken, S., Govender, R., and Pratto, F. (1992). The generality of the automatic attitude activation effect. *Journal of Personality and Social Psychology*, *62*, 893–912.

Bargh, J. A., Chaiken, S., Raymond, P., and Hymes, C. (1996a). The automatic evaluation effect: Unconditional automatic attitude activation with a pronunciation task. *Journal of Experimental Social Psychology*, *32*, 104–128.

Bargh, J. A., Chen, M., and Burrows, L. (1996b). Automaticity of social behavior: Direct effects of trait construct and stereotype activation on action. *Journal of Personality and Social Psychology*, *71*, 230–244.

Bargh, J. A., and Pietromonaco, P. (1982). Automatic information processing and social perception: The influence of trait information presented outside of conscious awareness on impression formation. *Journal of Personality and Social Psychology*, *43*, 437–449.

Bargh, J. A., Raymond, P., Pryor, J. B., and Strack, F. (1995). Attractiveness of the underling: An automatic power-sex association and its consequences for sexual harassment and aggression. *Journal of Personality and Social Psychology*, *68*, 768–781.

Bargh, J. A., and Tota, M. E. (1988). Context-dependent automatic processing in depression: Accessibility of negative constructs with regard to self but not others. *Journal of Personality and Social Psychology*, *54*, 925–939.

Barsalou, L. (1985). Ideals, central tendency, and frequency of instantiation as determinants of graded structure categories. *Journal of Experimental Psychology: Learning, Memory, and Cognition*, *11*, 629–654.

Barsalou, L. W. (1983). Ad hoc categories. *Memory and Cognition*, *11*, 211–227.

Baumeister, R. F. (1998). The self. In D. T. Gilbert, S. T. Fiske, and G. Lindzey (Eds.), *Handbook of social psychology* (Vol. 1, 4th ed., pp. 680–740). New York: McGraw-Hill.

Baumeister, R. F., Bratslavsky, E., Muraven, M., and Tice, D. M. (1998). Ego depletion: Is the active self a limited resource? *Journal of Personality and Social Psychology*, *74*, 1252–1265.

Baumgardner, A. H. (1990). To know oneself is to like oneself: Self-certainty and self-affect. *Journal of Personality and Social Psychology*, *58*, 1062–1072.

Beauregard, K. S., and Dunning, D. (1998). Turning up the contrast: Self-enhancement motives prompt egocentric contrast effects in social judgments. *Journal of Personality and Social Psychology*, *74*, 606–621.

Bechera, A., Damasio, H., Tranel, D., and Damasio, A. R. (1997). Deciding advantageously before knowing the advantageous strategy. *Science*, *275*, 1293–1295.

Bellezza, F. S., and Bower, G. H. (1981). Person stereotypes and memory for people. *Journal of Personality and Social Psychology*, *41*, 856–865.

Bem, D. J. (1972). Self-perception theory. In L. Berkowitz (Ed.), *Advances in experimental social psychology* (Vol. 6, pp. 1–62). New York: Academic Press.

Bem, D. J., and Allen, A. (1974). On predicting some of the people some of the time: The search for cross-situational consistencies in behavior. *Psychological Review, 81*, 506–520.

Berscheid, E., Graziano, W., Monson, T., and Dermer, M. (1976). Outcome dependency: Attention, attribution, and attraction. *Journal of Personality and Social Psychology, 34*, 978–989.

Biernat, M., and Manis, M. (1994). Shifting standards and stereotype-based judgments. *Journal of Personality and Social Psychology, 66*, 5–20.

Biernat, M., and Vescio, T. K. (1993). Categorization and stereotyping: Effects of group context on memory and social judgment. *Journal of Experimental Social Psychology, 29*, 166–202.

Blaine, B., and Crocker, J. (1993). Self-esteem and self-serving biases in reactions to positive and negative events: An integrative review. In R. Baumeister (Ed.), *Self-esteem: The puzzle of low self-regard* (pp. 55–85). New York: Plenum.

Blair, I. V., and Banaji, M. R. (1996). Automatic and controlled processes in stereotype priming. *Journal of Personality and Social Psychology, 70*, 1142–1163.

Blaney, P. H. (1986). Affect and memory: A review. *Psychological Bulletin, 99*, 229–246.

Bless, H., Mackie, D. M., and Schwarz, N. (1992). Mood effects on attitude judgments: Independent effects of mood before and after message elaboration. *Journal of Personality and Social Psychology, 63*, 585–595.

Bodenhausen, G. V. (1990). Stereotypes as judgmental heuristics: Evidence of circadian variations in discrimination. *Psychological Science, 1*, 319–322.

Bodenhausen, G. V. (1993). Emotion, arousal, and stereotypic judgments: A heuristic model of affect and stereotyping. In D. M. Mackie and D. L. Hamilton (Eds.), *Affect, cognition, and stereotyping: Interactive processes in group perception* (pp. 13–37). San Diego, CA: Academic Press.

Bodenhausen, G. V., Kramer, G. P., and Süsser, K. (1994a). Happiness and stereotypic thinking in social judgment. *Journal of Personality and Social Psychology, 66*, 621–632.

Bodenhausen, G. V., Sheppard, L. A., and Kramer, G. P. (1994b). Negative affect and social judgment: The differential impact of anger and sadness. *European Journal of Social Psychology, 24*, 45–62.

Bornstein, R. F. (1989). Exposure and affect: Overview and meta-analysis of research. *Psychological Bulletin, 106*, 265–289.

Bornstein, R. F., and D'Agostino, P. R. (1992). Stimulus recognition and the mere exposure effect. *Journal of Personality and Social Psychology, 63*, 545–552.

Bower, G. H. (1981). Mood and memory. *American Psychologist, 36*, 129–148.

Bower, G. H. (1991). Mood congruity of social judgments. In J. P. Forgas (Ed.), *Emotion and social judgments* (pp. 31–54). Oxford: Pergamon.

Bower, G. H., and Mayer, J. D. (1989). In search of mood-dependent retrieval. *Journal of Social Behavior and Personality, 4*, 121–156.

Bowers, K. S., and Farvolden, P. (1996). Revising a century-old Freudian slip—from suggestion disavowed to truth repressed. *Psychological Bulletin, 119*, 355–380.

Brandon, S., Boakes, J., Glaser, D., and Green, R. (1998). Recovered memories of childhood sexual abuse. Implications for clinical practice. *British Journal of Psychiatry, 172*, 296–307.

Brehm, J. (1956). Post-deciosn changes in the desirability of alternatives. *Journal of Abnormal and Social Psychology, 52*, 384–389.

Brewer, M. B. (1988). A dual process model of impression formation. In T. K. Srull and R. S. Wyer (Eds.), *Advances in social cognition* (Vol. 1, pp. 1–36). Hillsdale, NJ: Erlbaum.

Brewer, M. B., Dull, V., and Lui, L. (1981). Perceptions of the elderly: Stereotypes as prototypes. *Journal of Personality and Social Psychology, 41,* 656–670.

Brewer, M. B., and Gardner, W. (1996). Who is this "we"? Levels of collective identity and self representations. *Journal of Personality and Social Psychology, 71,* 83–93.

Brewer, M. B., and Weber, J. G. (1994). Self-evaluation effects on interpersonal versus intergroup social comparison. *Journal of Personality and Social Psychology, 66,* 268–275.

Brewer, W. F. (1992). The theoretical and empirical status of the flashbulb memory hypothesis. In E. Winograd and U. Neisser (Eds.), *Affect and accuracy in recall: Studies of "flashbulb" memories* (pp. 274–305). New York: Cambridge University Press.

Brown, A. S., and Murphy, D. R. (1989). Cryptomnesia: Delineating inadvertent plagiarism. *Journal of Experimental Psychology: Learning, Memory, and Cognition, 15,* 432–442.

Brown, J. D., Collins, R. L., and Schmidt, G. W. (1988). Self-esteem and direct versus indirect forms of self-enhancement. *Journal of Personality and Social Psychology, 55,* 445–453.

Brown, J. D., and Dutton, K. A. (1995). The thrill of victory, the complexity of defeat: Self-esteem and people's emotional reactions to success and failure. *Journal of Personality and Social Psychology, 68,* 712–722.

Brown, J. D., and Smart, S. A. (1991). The self and social conduct: Linking self-representations to prosocial behavior. *Journal of Personality and Social Psychology, 60,* 368–375.

Brown, R., and Kulik, J. (1977). Flashbulb memories. *Cognition, 5,* 73–99.

Bruner, J. S. (1957). Going beyond the information given. In H. Gulber et al. (Eds.), *Contemporary approaches to cognition.* Cambridge, MA: Harvard University Press.

Buss, D. M., and Craik, K. H. (1983). The act frequency approach to personality. *Psychological Review, 90,* 105–126.

Cahill, L., Prins, B., Weber, M., and McGaugh, J. L. (1994). Beta-Adrenergic activation and memory for emotional events. *Nature, 371,* 702–704.

Campbell, J. D. (1990). Self-esteem and clarity of self-concept. *Journal of Personality and Social Psychology, 59,* 538–549.

Campbell, J. D., and Lavallee, L. F. (1993). Who am I? The role of self-concept confusion in understanding the behavior of people with low self-esteem. In R. Baumeister (Ed.), *Self-esteem: The puzzle of low self-regard* (pp. 3–20). New York: Plenum.

Campbell, J. D., Trapnell, P. D., Heine, S. J., Katz, I. M., Lavallee, L. F., and Lehman, D. R. (1996). Self-concept clarity: Measurement, perslonality correlates, and cultural boounndaries. *Journal of Personality and Social Psychology, 70,* 141–156.

Cantor, N., and Kihlstrom, J. F. (1987). *Personality and social intelligence.* Englewood Cliffs, NJ: Prentice-Hall.

Cantor, N., and Mischel, W. (1979). Prototypes in person perception. In L. Berkowitz (Ed.), *Advances in experimental social psychology* (Vol. 12, pp. 3–53). New York: Academic Press.

Carey, S. (1985). *Conceptual change in childhood.* Cambridge, MA: MIT Press.

Carlston, D. E., and Skowronski, J. J. (1994). Savings in the relearning of trait information as evidence for spontaneous inference generation. *Journal of Personality and Social Psychology, 66,* 840–856.

Carlston, D. E., Skowronski, J. J., and Sparks, C. (1995). Saving in relearning: II. On the formation of behavior-based trait associations and inferences. *Journal of Personality and Social Psychology, 69,* 420–436.

Carlston, D. E., and Smith, E. R. (1996). Principles of mental representation. In E. T. Higgins and A. W. Kruglanski (Eds.), *Social psychology: Handbook of basic principles* (pp. 184–210). New York: Guilford Press.

Carrol, J. S. (1978). The effects of imagining an event on expectations for the event: An interpretation in terms of the availability heuristic. *Journal of Experimental Social Psychology*, *14*, 88–96.

Caspi, A., and Bem, D. J. (1990). Personality continuity and change across the life course. In L. A. Pervin (Ed.), *Handbook of personality: Theory and research* (pp. 549–575). New York: Guilford Press.

Chaiken, S., Liberman, A., and Eagly, A. H. (1989). Heuristic and systematic information processing within and beyond the persuasion context. In J. S. Uleman and J. A. Bargh (Eds.), *Unintended thought: Limits of awareness, intention, and control.* (pp. 212–252). New York: Guilford.

Chaiken, S., and Trope, Y. (1999). *Dual-process theories in social psychology*. New York: Guilford.

Chapman, L. J., and Chapman, J. P. (1967). Genesis of popular but erroneous diagnostic observations. *Journal of Abnormal Psychology, 72* 193–204.

Chapman, L. J., and Chapman, J. P. (1969). Illusory correlation as an obstacle to the use of valid psycho-diagnostic signs. *Journal of Abnormal Psychology, 74*, 272–280.

Chase, W. G., and Simon, H. A. (1973). Perception and chess. *Cognitive Psychology, 4*, 55–81.

Chen, M., and Bargh, J. (1997). Nonconscious behavioral confirmation processes: The self-fulfilling consequences of automatic stereotype activation. *Journal of Experimental Social Psychology, 33*, 541–560.

Chi, M., Feltovich, P., and Glaser, R. (1981). Categorization and representation of physics problems by experts and novices. *Cognitive Science, 5*, 121–152.

Choi, I., and Nisbett, R. E. (1998). Situational salience and cultural differences in the correspondence bias and actor-observer bias. *Personality and Social Psychology Bulletin, 24*, 949–960.

Christianson, S. A. (1989). Flashbulb memories: Special, but not so special. *Memory and Cognition, 17*, 435–443.

Cialdini, R. B., Borden, R. J., Thorne, A., Walker, M. R., Freeman, S., and Sloan, L. R. (1976). Basking in reflected glory: Three (football) field studies. *Journal of Personality and Social Psychology, 34*, 366–375.

Cohen, C. (1981). Person categories and social perception: Testing some boundaries of the processing effects of prior knowledge. *Journal of Personality and Social Psychology, 40*, 441–452.

Cohen, D., and Nisbett, R. E. (1994). Self-protection and the culture of honor: Explaining Southern violence. *Personality and Social Psychology Bulletin, 20*, 551–567.

Cohen, D., Nisbett, R. E., Bowdle, B. F., and Schwarz, N. (1996). Insult, aggression, and the southern culture of honor: An "experimental ethnography." *Journal of Personality and Social Psychology, 70*, 945–960.

Collins, A. M., and Loftus, E. F. (1975). A spreading-activation theory of semantic processing. *Psychological Review, 82*, 407–428.

Conway, M., and Ross, M. (1984). Getting what you want by revising what you had. *Journal of Personality and Social Psychology, 47*, 738–748.

Conway, M. A., Anderson, S., J., Larsen, S., F., Donnelly, C. M., McDaniel, M. A., McClelland, A. G. R., Rawles, R. E., and Logie, R. H. (1994). The formation of flashbulb memories. *Memory and Cognition, 22*, 326–343.

Cooper, J., and Fazio, R. H. (1984). A new look at dissonance theory. In L. Berkowitz (Ed.), *Advances in experimental social psychology* (Vol. 17, pp. 229–266). New York: Academic Press.

Cooper, J., Zanna, M. P., and Taves, P. A. (1978). Arousal as a necessary condition for attitude change following induced compliance. *Journal of Personality and Social Psychology, 36*, 1101–1106.

Cose, E. (1993). *The rage of a privileged class.* New York: Harper Collins.

Cousins, S. D. (1989). Culture and self-perception in Japan and the United States. *Journal of Personality and Social Psychology, 56*, 124–131.

Crocker, J. (1981). Judgment of covariation by social perceivers. *Psychological Bulletin, 90*, 272–292.

Crocker, J., and Major, B. (1989). Social stigma and self-esteem: The self-protective properties of stigma. *Psychological Review, 96*, 608–630.

Crocker, J., Voelkl, K., Testa, M., and Major, B. (1991). Social stigma: The affective consequences of attributional ambiguity. *Journal of Personality and Social Psychology, 60*, 218–228.

Damasio, A. R. (1994). *Descartes' error: Emotion, reason, and the human brain.* New York: Putnam.

Darley, J. M., and Berscheid, E. (1967). Increased liking as a result of anticipation of personal contact. *Human Relations, 20*, 29–40.

Darley, J. M., and Gross, P. H. (1983). A hypothesis-confirming bias in labeling effects. *Journal of Personality and Social Psychology, 44*, 20–33.

Davis, C. G., Lehman, D. R., Wortman, C. B., Silver, R. C., and Thompson, S. C. (1995). The undoing of dramatic life events. *Personality and Social Psychology Bulletin, 21*, 109–124.

Dawes, R. M. (1976). Shallow Psychology. In J. Carroll and J. Payne (Eds.), *Cognition and social behavior.* Hillsdale, NJ: Erlbaum.

Dawes, R. M. (1989). Statistical criteria for establishing a truly false consensus effect. *Journal of Experimental Social Psychology, 25*, 1–19.

Deaux, K., and Emswiller, T. (1974). Explanations of successful performance on sex-linked tasks: What is skill for the male is luck for the female. *Journal of Personality and Social Psychology, 29*, 80–85.

Debner, J. A., and Jacoby, L. L. (1994). Unconscious perception: Attention, awareness, and control. *Journal of Experimental Psychology: Learning, Memory, and Cognitions, 20*, 304–317.

Devine, P. G. (1989). Stereotypes and prejudice: Their automatic and controlled components. *Journal of Personality and Social Psychology, 56*, 5–18.

Devine, P. G., and Baker, S. M. (1991). Measurement of racial stereotype subtyping. *Personality and Social Psychology Bulletin, 17*, 44–50.

Devine, P. G., Hirt, E. R., and Gehrke, E. M. (1990). Diagnostic and confirmation strategies in trait hypothesis testing. *Journal of Personality and Social Psychology, 58*, 952–963.

Devine, P. G., Monteith, M. J., Zuwerink, J. R., and Elliot, A. J. (1991). Prejudice with and without compunction. *Journal of Personality and Social Psychology, 60*, 817–830.

Devine, P. G., Sedikides, C., and Fuhrman, R. W. (1989). Goals in social information processing: The case of anticipated interaction. *Journal of Personality and Social Psychology, 56*, 680–690.

Diener, E., and Diener, M. (1995). Cross-cultural correlates of life satisfaction and self-esteem. *Journal of Personality and Social Psychology, 68*, 653–663.

Ditto, P. H., and Lopez, D. F. (1992). Motivated skepticism: Use of differential decision criteria for preferred and nonpreferred conclusions. *Journal of Personality and Social Psychology, 63,* 568–584.

Dodgson, P. G., and Wood, J. V. (1998). Self-esteem and the cognitive accessibility of strengths and weaknesses after failure. *Journal of Personality and Social Psychology, 75,* 178–197.

Doosje, B., Spears, R., and Koomen, W. (1995). When bad isn't all bad: Strategic use of sample information in generalization and stereotyping. *Journal of Personality and Social Psychology, 69,* 642–655.

Dovidio, J. F., Evans, N., and Tyler, R. B. (1986). Racial stereotypes: The contents of their cognitive representations. *Journal of Experimental Social Psychology, 22,* 22–37.

Duncan, B. L. (1976). Differential social perception and attribution of intergroup violence: Testing the lower limits of stereotyping of blacks. *Journal of Personality and Social Psychology, 34,* 590–598.

Dunning, D. (in press). A newer look: Motivated social cognition and the schematic representation of social concepts. *Psychological Inquiry.*

Dunning, D., and Cohen, G. L. (1992). Egocentric definitions of traits and abilities in social judgment. *Journal of Personality and Social Psychology, 63,* 341–355.

Dunning, D., and Hayes, A. F. (1996). Evidence for egocentric comparison in social judgment. *Journal of Personality and Social Psychology, 71,* 213–229.

Dunning, D., Leuenberger, A., and Sherman, D. A. (1995). A new look at motivated inference: Are self-serving theories of success a product of motivational forces? *Journal of Personality and Social Psychology, 69,* 58–68.

Dunning, D., Meyerowitz, J. A., and Holzberg, A. (1989). Ambiguity and self-evaluation: The role of idiosyncratic trait definitions in self-serving assessments of ability. *Journal of Personality and Social Psychology, 57,* 1082–1090.

Dunning, D., Perie, M., and Story, A. L. (1991). Self-serving prototypes of social categories. *Journal of Personality and Social Psychology, 61,* 957–968.

Dunning, D., and Sherman, D. A. (1997). Stereotypes and tacit inference. *Journal of Personality and Social Psychology, 73,* 459–471.

Eagly, A. H., and Chaiken, S. (1993). *The psychology of attitudes.* Fort Worth, TX: Harcourt Brace Jovanovich, Inc.

Eddy, D. (1982). Probabilistic reasoning in clinical medicine: Problems and opportunities. In D. Kahneman, P. Slovic, and A. Tversky (Eds.), *Judgment under uncertainty: Heuristics and biases* (pp. 249–267). Cambridge: Cambridge University Press.

Edwards, K. (1990). The interplay of affect and cognition in attitude formation and change. *Journal of Personality and Social Psychology, 59,* 202–216.

Edwards, K., and Smith, E. E. (1996). A disconfirmation bias in the evaluation of arguments. *Journal of Personality and Social Psychology, 71,* 5–24.

Ehrlichman, H., and Halpern, J. N. (1988). Affect and memory: Effects of pleasant and unpleasant odors on retrieval of happy and unhappy memories. *Journal of Personality and Social Psychology, 55,* 769–779.

Eich, E. (1995). Searching for mood dependent memory. *Psychological Science, 6,* 67–75.

Eich, E., Macaulay, D., and Ryan, L. (1994). Mood dependent memory for events of the personal past. *Journal of Experimental Psychology: General, 123,* 201–215.

Epstein, S. (1979). The stability of behavior: I. On predicting most of the people much of the time. *Journal of Personality and Social Psychology, 37,* 1097–1126.

Epstein, S. (1983). The stability of confusion: A reply to Mischel and Peake. *Psychological Review, 90,* 179–184.

Erber, R. (1991). Affective and semantic priming: Effects of mood on category accessibility and inference. *Journal of Experimental Social Psychology, 27*, 480–498.

Ericsson, K. A., and Simon, H. A. (1980). Verbal reports as data. *Psychological Review, 87*, 215–251.

Esses, V., Haddock, G., and Zanna, M. P. (1993). Values, stereotypes, and emotions as determinants of intergroup attitudes. In D. M. Mackie and D. L. Hamilton (Eds.), *Affect, cognition, and stereotyping: Interactive processes in group perception* (pp. 137–166). San Diego: Academic Press.

Esses, V. M., and Zanna, M. P. (1995). Mood and the expression of ethnic stereotypes. *Journal of Personality and Social Psychology, 69*, 1052–1068.

Farah, M. J. (1988). Is visual imagery really visual? Overlooked evidence from neuropsychology. *Psychological Review, 95*, 385–316.

Fazio, R. H. (1993). Variability in the likelihood of automatic attitude activation: Data reanalysis and commentary on Bargh, Chaiken, Govender, and Pratto (1992). *Journal of Personality and Social Psychology, 64*, 753–758.

Fazio, R. H., Effrein, E. A., and Falender, V. J. (1981). Self-Perception following social interaction. *Journal of Personality and Social Psychology, 41*, 232–242.

Fazio, R. H., Jackson, J. R., Dunton, B. C., and Williams, C. J. (1995). Variability in automatic activation as an unobtrusive measure of racial attitudes: A bona fide pipeline? *Journal of Personality and Social Psychology, 69*, 1013–1027.

Fazio, R. H., Sanbonmatsu, D. M., Powell, M. C., and Kardes, F. R. (1986). On the automatic activation of attitudes. *Journal of Personality and Social Psychology, 50*, 229–238.

Fehr, B. (1988). Prototype analyses of the concepts of love and commitment. *Journal of Personality and Social Psychology, 55*, 557–579.

Fein, S., and Spencer, S. J. (1997). Prejudice as self-image maintenance: Affirming the self through derogating others. *Journal of Personality and Social Psychology, 73*, 31–44.

Festinger, L. (1957). *A theory of cognitive dissonance.* Stanford, CA: Stanford University Press.

Fischhoff, B. (1975). Hindsight $=\backslash=$ Foresight: The effects of outcome knowledge on judgment under uncertainty. *Journal of Experimental Psychology: Human Perception and Performance, 1*, 288–299.

Fischhoff, B. (1977). Perceived informativeness of facts. *Journal of Experimental Psychology: Human Perception and Performance, 3*, 349–358.

Fischhoff, B., and Beyth, R. (1975). "I knew it would happen"—remembered probabilities of once-future things. *Organizational Behavior and Human Performance, 13*, 1–16.

Fiske, A. P., Kitayama, S., Markus, H. R., and Nisbett, R. E. (1998). The cultural matrix of social psychology. In D. T. Gilbert, S. T. Fiske, and G. Lindzey (Eds.), *Handbook of social psychology* (Vol. 2, 4th ed., pp. 915–981). New York: McGraw-Hill.

Fiske, S. T., and Neuberg, S. L. (1990). A continuum of impression formation, from category-based to individuating processes: Influences of information and motivation on attention and interpretation. In M. Zanna (Ed.), *Advances in Experimental Social Psychology* (Vol. 23, pp. 1–74). San Diego, CA: Academic Press.

Fiske, S. T., and Taylor, S. E. (1991). *Social cognition.* New York: Random House.

Fong, G. T., Krantz, D. H., and Nisbett, R. E. (1986). The effects of statistical training on thinking about everyday problems. *Cognitive Psychology, 18*, 253–292.

Forgas, J. P. (1994). Sad and Guilty? Affective influences on the explanation of conflict in close relationships. *Journal of Personality and Social Psychology, 66*, 56–68.

Forgas, J. P. (1995). Mood and judgment: The affect infusion model (AIM). *Psychological Bulletin, 117*, 39–66.

Freund, T., Kruglanski, A. W., and Shpitzajzen, A. (1985). The freezing and unfreezing of impressional primacy: Effects of the need for structure and the fear of invalidity. *Personality and Social Psychology Bulletin, 11*, 479–487.

Freyd, P. (1998). False Memory Syndrome Foundation, World Wide Web Page: http://advicom.net/~fitz/fmsf/.

Garcia-Marques, L., and Hamilton, D. L. (1996). Resolving the apparent discrepancy between the incongruency effect and the expectancy-based illusory correlation effect: The TRAP model. *Journal of Personality and Social Psychology, 71*, 845–860.

Gavanski, I., and Wells, G. L. (1989). Counterfactual processing of normal and exceptional events. *Journal of Experimental Social Psychology, 25*, 314–325.

Gelman, S. A., and Markman, E. M. (1986). Categories and induction in young children. *Cognition, 23*, 183–209.

Gigerenzer, G. (1991). How to make cognitive illusions disappear: Beyond "heuristics and biases." In W. Stroebe and M. Hewstone (Eds.), *European Review of Social Psychology* (pp. 83–115). New York: Wiley.

Gigerenzer, G. (1996). On narrow norms and vauge heuristics: A reply to Kahneman and Tversky (1996). *Psychological Review, 103*, 592–596.

Gigerenzer, G., Hell, W., and Blank, H. (1988). Presentation and content: The use of base rates as a continuous variable. *Journal of Experimental Psychology: Human Perception and Performance, 14*, 513–525.

Gigerenzer, G., Hoffrage, U., and Kleinbolting, H. (1991). Probabilistic mental models: A Brunswikian theory of confidence. *Psychological Review, 90*, 506–528.

Gilbert, D. T. (1989). Thinking lightly about others: Automatic components of the social inference process. In J. A. Bargh and J. S. Uleman (Eds.), *Unintended thought* (pp. 189–211). New York: Guilford.

Gilbert, D. T., Giesler, R. B., and Morris, K. A. (1995). When comparisons arise. *Journal of Personality and Social Psychology, 69*, 227–236.

Gilbert, D. T., and Hixon, J. G. (1991). The trouble of thinking: Activation and application of stereotypic beliefs. *Journal of Personality and Social Psychology, 60*, 509–517.

Gilbert, D. T., Krull, D. S., and Malone, P. S. (1990). Unbelieving the unbelievable: Some problems in the rejection of false information. *Journal of Personality and Social Psychology, 59*, 601–613.

Gilbert, D. T., and Malone, P. S. (1995). The correspondence bias. *Psychological Bulletin, 117*, 21–38.

Gilbert, D. T., Pelham, B. W., and Krull, D. S. (1988). On cognitive busyness: When person perceivers meet persons perceived. *Journal of Personality and Social Psychology, 54*, 733–740.

Gilbert, G. M. (1951). Stereotype persistence and change among college students. *Journal of Abnormal and Social Psychology, 46*, 245–254.

Gillig, P. M., and Greenwald, A. G. (1974). Is it time to lay the sleeper effect to rest? *Journal of Personality and Social Psychology, 29*, 132–139.

Gilovich, T. (1981). Seeing the past in the present: The effect of associations to familiar events on judgments and decisions. *Journal of Personality and Social Psychology, 40*, 797–808.

Gilovich, T. (1983). Biased evaluation and persistence in gambling. *Journal of Personality and Social Psychology, 44*, 1110–1126.

Gilovich, T. (1990). Differential construal and the false consensus effect. *Journal of Personality and Social Psychology, 59*, 623–634.

Gilovich, T. (1991). *How we know what isn't so: The fallibility of human reason in everyday life*. New York: The Free Press.

Gilovich, T., Jennings, D. L., and Jennings, S. (1983). Causal focus and estimates of consensus: An examination of the false-consensus effect. *Journal of Personality and Social Psychology, 45*, 550–559.

Gilovich, T., Kerr, M., and Medvec, V. H. (1993). Effect of temporal perspective on subjective confidence. *Journal of Personality and Social Psychology, 64*, 552–560.

Gilovich, T., and Medvec, V. H. (1994). The temporal pattern to the experience of regret. *Journal of Personality and Social Psychology, 67*, 357–365.

Gilovich, T., and Medvec, V. H. (1995). The experience of regret: What, when, and why. *Psychological Review, 102*, 379–395.

Gilovich, T., Vallone, R., and Tversky, A. (1985). The hot hand in basketball: On the misperception of random sequences. *Cognitive Psychology, 17*, 295–314.

Ginossar, Z., and Trope, Y. (1987). Problem solving in judgment under uncertainty. *Journal of Personality and Social Psychology, 52*, 464–474.

Gleicher, F., Boninger, D. S., Strathman, A., Armor, D., Hetts, J., and Ahn, M. (1995). With an eye toward the future: The impact of counterfactual thinking on affect, attitudes, and behavior. In N. J. Roese and J. M. Olsen (Eds.), *What might have been: The psychology of counterfactual thinking* (pp. 283–304). Mahwah, NJ: Erlbaum.

Gleicher, F., Kost, K. A., Baker, S. M., Strathman, A. J., Richman, S. A., and Sherman, S. J. (1990). The role counterfactual thinking in judgments of affect. *Personality and Social Psychology Bulletin, 16*, 284–295.

Goethals, G. R., and Reckman, R. F. (1973). The perception of consistency in attitudes. *Journal of Experimental and Social Psychology, 9*, 491–501.

Gollwitzer, P. M., and Kinney, R. F. (1989). Effects of deliberative and implemental Mindsets on illusion of control. *Journal of Personality and Social Psychology, 56*, 531–542.

Gollwitzer, P. M., and Moskowitz, G. B. (1996). Goal effects on action and cognition. In E. T. Higgins and A. W. Kruglanski (Eds.), *Social psychology: Handbook of basic principles* (pp. 361–399). New York: Guilford Press.

Greenwald, A. G. (1992). New look 3: Unconscious cognition reclaimed. *American Psychologist, 47*, 766–779.

Greenwald, A. G., and Banaji, M. R. (1995). Implicit social cognition: Attitudes, self-esteem, and stereotypes. *Psychological Review, 102*, 4–27.

Greenwald, A. G., and Gillmore, G. M. (1997). Grading leniency is a removable contaminant of student ratings. *American Psychologist, 52*, 1209–1217.

Greenwald, A. G., and Pratkanis, A. R. (1984). The self. In R. S. Wyer and T. K. Srull (Eds.), *Handbook of social cognition* (Vol. 3, pp. 129–178). Hillsdale, NJ: Erlbaum.

Greenwald, A. G., and Ronis, D. L. (1978). Twenty years of cognitive dissonance: Case study of the evolution of a theory. *Psychological Review, 85*, 53–57.

Gregory, W. L., Cialdini, R. B., and Carpenter, K. M. (1982). Self-relevant scenarios as mediators of liklihood estimates and compliance: Does imagining make it so? *Journal of Personality and Social Psychology, 43*, 89–99.

Grice, H. P. (1975). Logic and conversation. In P. Cole and J. L. Morgan (Eds.), *Syntax and semantics: Vol. 3: Speech acts* (pp. 41–58). New York: Academic Press.

Gruder, C. L., Cook, T. D., Hennigan, K. M., Flay, B. R., Alessis, C., and Halamaji, J. (1978). Empirical tests of the absolute sleeper effect predicted from the discounting cue hypothesis. *Journal of Personality and Social Psychology, 36*, 1061–1074.

Hacking, I. (1975). *The emergence of probability*. New York: Cambridge University Press.

Hamilton, D. L., Dugan, P., and Trolier, T. K. (1985). The formation of stereotypic beliefs: Further evidence for distinctiveness-based illusory correlations. *Journal of Personality and Social Psychology, 48*, 5–17.

Hamilton, D. L., and Gifford, R. K. (1976). Illusory correlation in interpersonal perception: A cognitive basis of stereotypic judgments. *Journal of Experimental Social Psychology, 12*, 392–407.

Hamilton, D. L., Katz, L. B., and Leirer, V. O. (1980). Organizational processes in impression formation. In R. Hastie, T. M. Ostrom, E. B. Ebbeson, R. S. Wyer, D. L. Hamilton, and D. E. Carlston (Eds.), *Person memory: The cognitive basis of social perception* (pp. 155–177). Hillsdale, NJ: Erlbaum.

Hamilton, D. L., and Sherman, J. W. (1994). Stereotypes. In J. R. S. Wyer and T. K. Srull (Eds.), *Handbook of Social Cognition* (2nd ed., pp. 1–68). Hillsdale, NJ: Erlbaum.

Hampson, S. E., John, O. P., and Goldberg, L. R. (1986). Category breadth and hierarchical structure in personality: Studies of asymmetries in judgments of trait implication. *Journal of Personality and Social Psychology, 51*, 37–54.

Hartshorne, H., and May, M. A. (1928). *Studies in deceit.* New York: Macmillan.

Hastie, R. (1980). Memory for information which confirms or contradicts a general impression. In R. Hastie, T. M. Ostrom, E. G. Ebbesen, R. S. Wyer, D. L. Hamilton, and D. E. Carlston (Eds.), *Person memory: The cognitive basis of social perception* (pp. 155–177). Hillsdale, NJ: Erlbaum.

Hastie, R. (1984). Causes and effects of causal attribution. *Journal of Personality and Social Psychology, 47*, 44–56.

Hastie, R., and Kumar, A. P. (1979). Person memory: Personality traits as organizing principles in memory for behaviors. *Journal of Personality and Social Psychology, 37*, 25–38.

Hastie, R., Schroeder, C., and Weber, R. (1990). Creating complex social conjunction categories from simple categories. *Bulletin of the Psychonomic Society, 28*, 242–247.

Hawkins, S. A., and Hastie, R. (1990). Hindsight: Biased judgments of past events after the outcomes are known. *Psychological Bulletin, 107*, 311–327.

Heine, S. J., and Lehman, D. R. (1995). Cultural variation in unrealistic optimism: Does the West feel more invulnerable than the East? *Journal of Personality and Social Psychology, 68*, 595–607.

Heine, S. J., and Lehman, D. R. (1997a). The cultural construction of self-enhancement: An examination of group-serving biases. *Journal of Personality and Social Psychology, 72*, 1268–1283.

Heine, S. J., and Lehman, D. R. (1997b). Culture, dissonance, and self-affirmation. *Personality and Social Psychology Bulletin, 23*, 389–400.

Higgins, E. T. (1987). Self-discrepancy: A theory relating self and affect. *Psychological Review, 94*, 319–340.

Higgins, E. T. (1989). Self-discrepancy theory: What patterns of self-beliefs cause people to suffer? In L. Berkowitz (Ed.), *Advances in experimental social psychology* (Vol. 22, pp. 93–136). New York: Academic Press.

Higgins, E. T. (1996). Knowledge activation: Accessibility, applicability, and salience. In E. T. Higgins and A. W. Kruglanski (Eds.), *Social psychology: Handbook of basic principles* (pp. 133–168). New York: Guilford Press.

Higgins, E. T. (1998). Promotion and prevention: Regulatory focus as a motivational principle. In M. P. Zanna (Ed.), *Advances in experimental social psychology* (Vol. 30, pp. 1–46). New York: Academic Press.

Higgins, E. T., and Bargh, J. A. (1987). Social cognition and social perception. *Annual Review of Psychology, 38*, 369–425.

Higgins, E. T., Bond, R. N., Klein, R., and Strauman, T. (1986). Self-discrepancies and emotional vulnerability: How magnitude, accessibility, and type of discrepancy influence affect. *Journal of Personality and Social Psychology, 51*, 5–15.

Higgins, E. T., and King, G. A. (1981). Accessibility of social constructs: Information-processing consequences of individual and contextual variability. In N. Cantor and J. F. Kihlstrom (Eds.), *Personality, cognition, and social interaction* (pp. 69–121). Hillsdale, NJ: Erlbaum.

Higgins, E. T., King., G. A., and Mavin, G. H. (1982). Individual construct accessiblity and subjective impressions and recall. *Journal of Personality and Social Psychology, 43,* 35–47.

Higgins, E. T., Rholes, W. S., and Jones, C. R. (1976). Category accessibility and impression formation. *Journal of Experimental Social Psychology, 13,* 141–154.

Higgins, E. T., Roney, C. J. R., Crowe, E., and Hymes, C. (1994). Ideal versus ought predilections for approach and avoidance: Distinct self-regulatory systems. *Journal of Personality and Social Psychology, 66,* 276–286.

Higgins, E. T., Shah, J., and Friedman, R. (1997). Emotional responses to goal attainment: Strenth of regulatory focus as moderator. *Journal of Personality and Social Psychology, 72,* 515–525.

Higgins, E. T., and Tykocinski, O. (1992). Self-discrepancies and biographical memory: Personality and cognition at the level of psychological situation. *Personality and Social Psychology Bulletin, 18,* 527–535.

Hilton, J. L., and Fein, S. (1989). The role of typical diagnosticity in stereotype-based judgments. *Journal of Personality and Social Psychology, 57,* 201–211.

Hirt, E. R., Erickson, G. A., and McDonald, H. E. (1993). Role of expectancy timing and outcome consistency in expectancy-guided retrieval. *Journal of Personality and Social Psychology, 65,* 640–656.

Holyoak, K. J., and Gordon, P. C. (1983). Social reference points. *Journal of Personality and Social Psychology, 44,* 881–887.

Hovland, C. I., Janis, I. L., and Kelley, H. H. (1953). *Communication and persuasion.* New Haven, CT: Yale University Press.

Hunter, J. E., and Hunter, R. F. (1984). Validity and utility of alternative predictors of job performance. *Psychological Bulletin, 96,* 72–98.

Hyman, I. E., Husband, T. H., and Billings, F. J. (1995). False memories of childhood experiences. *Applied Cognitive Psychology, 9,* 181–197.

Isen, A. M. (1987). Positive affect, cognitive processes, and social behavior. In L. Berkowitz (Ed.), *Advances in experimental social psychology* (Vol. 20, pp. 203–253). New York: Academic Press.

Isen, A. M., Shalker, T. E., Clark, M., and Karp, L. (1978). Resources required in the construction and reconstruction of conversation. *Journal of Personality and Social Psychology, 36,* 1–12.

Jackson, L. A., Sullivan, L. A., and Hodge, C. N. (1993). Stereotype effects of attributions, predictions, and evaluations: No two social judgments are quite alike. *Journal of Personality and Social Psychology, 65,* 69–84.

Jacoby, L. L., and Dallas, M. (1981). On the relationship between autobiographical memory and perceptual learning. *Journal of Experimental Psychology: General, 110,* 306–340.

Jacoby, L. L., Kelley, C., Brown, J., and Jasechko, J. (1989). Becoming famous overnight: Limits on the ability to avoid unconscious influences of the past. *Journal of Personality and Social Psychology, 56,* 326–338.

Jacoby, L. L., Lindsay, D. S., and Toth, J. P. (1992). Unconscious influences revealed: Attention, awareness, and control. *American Psychologist, 47,* 802–809.

Jamieson, D. W., and Zanna, M. P. (1989). Need for structure in attitude formation and expression. In A. R. Pratkanis, S. J. Breckler, and A. G. Greenwald (Eds.), *Attitude structure and function* (pp. 383–406). Hillsdale, NJ: Erlbaum.

Jenkins, H. M., and Ward, W. C. (1965). Judgments of contingency between responses and outcomes. *Psychological Monographs, 79,* (1, whole issue).

Jennings, D., Amabile, T. M., and Ross, L. (1982). Informal covariation assessment: Data-based vs. theory-based judgments. In A. Tversky, D. Kahneman, and P. Slovic (Eds.), *Judgment under uncertainty: Heuristics and biases* (pp. 211–230). New York: Cambridge University Press.

Jepson, D., Krantz, D. H., and Nisbett, R. E. (1983). Inductive reasoning: Competence or skill? *Behavioral and Brain Sciences, 6,* 494–501.

John, O. P., Hampson, S. E., Goldberg, L. R. (1991). The basic level in personality-trait hierarchies: Studies of trait use and accessibility in different contexts. *Journal of Personality and Social Psychology, 60,* 348–362.

Johnson, E. J., and Tversky, A. (1983). Affect, genaralization, and the perception of risk. *Journal of Personality and Social Psychology, 45,* 20–31.

Johnson, M. K., Hashtroudi, S., and Lindsay, D. S. (1993). Source monitoring. *Psychological Bulletin, 114,* 3–28.

Johnson, M. K., Raye, C. L., Wang, A. Y., and Taylor, T. H. (1979). Fact and fantasy: The roles of accuracy and variability in confusing imaginations with real experiences. *Journal of Experimental Psychology: Human Learning and Memory, 5,* 229–240.

Johnston, L., and Hewstone, M. (1992). Cognitive models of stereotype change: 3. Subtyping and the perceived typicality of disconfirming group members. *Journal of Experimental Social Psychology, 28,* 360–386.

Jones, E. E. (1990). *Interpersonal perception.* New York: W. H. Freeman and Company.

Jones, E. E., and Davis, K. E. (1965). From acts to dispositions: The attribution process in person perception. In L. Berkowitz (Ed.), *Advances in experimental social psychology* (Vol. 2, pp. 219–266). New York: Academic Press.

Jones, E. E., and Harris, V. A. (1967). The attribution of attitudes. *Journal of Experimental Social Psychology, 3,* 1–24.

Jones, E. E., and Nisbett, R. E. (1972). The actor and the observer: Divergent perceptions of the causes of behavior. In E. E. Jones, D. E. Kanouse, H. H. Kelley, R. E. Nisbett, S. Valins, and B. Weiner (Eds.), *Attribution: Perceiving the cause of behavior* (pp. 79–94). Morristown, NJ: General Learning Press.

Judd, C. M., Ryan, C. S., and Park, B. (1991). Accuracy in the judgment of in-group and out-group variability. *Journal of Personality and Social Psychology, 61,* 366–379.

Jussim, L. (1986). Self-fulfilling prophecies: A theoretical and integrative review. *Psychological Review, 93,* 429–445.

Jussim, L., Yen, H., and Aiello, J. R. (1995). Self-consistency, self-enhancement, and accuracy in reactions to feedback. *Journal of Experimental Social Psychology, 31,* 322–356.

Kahneman, D., and Miller, D. T. (1986). Norm theory: Comparing reality to its alternatives. *Psychological Review, 93,* 136–153.

Kahneman, D., and Tversky, A. (1972). Subjective probability: A judgment of representativeness. *Cognitive Psychology, 3,* 430–454.

Kahneman, D., and Tversky, A. (1973). On the psychology of prediction. *Psychological Review, 80,* 237–251.

Kahneman, D., and Tversky, A. (1982). The simulation heuristic. In D. Kahneman, P. Slovic, and A. Tversky (Eds.), *Judgment under uncertainty: Heuristics and biases* (pp. 201–208). New York: Cambridge University Press.

Kahneman, D., and Tversky, A. (1996). On the reality of cognitive illusions. *Psychological Review, 103,* 582–591.

Kaiser, M., Proffitt, D. R., and McClosky, M. (1986). The development of beliefs about falling objects. *Perception and Psychophysics.*

Karlins, M., Coffman, T. L., and Walters, G. (1969). On the fading of social stereotypes: Studies in three generations of college students. *Journal of Personality and Social Psychology, 13,* 1–16.

Katz, D., and Braly, K. (1933). Racial stereotypes in one hundred college students. *Journal of Abnormal and Social Psychology, 13,* 1–16.

Keil, F. C. (1989). *Concepts, kinds, and cognitive development.* Cambridge, MA: MIT Press.

Kelley, H. H. (1950). The warm-cold variable in first impressions of persons. *Journal of Personality, 18,* 431–439.

Kelley, H. H. (1967). Attribution theory in social psychology. *Nebraska symposium on motivation, 14,* 192–241.

Kelley, H. H., and Stahelski, A. J. (1970). Social interaction basis of cooperators' and competitors' beliefs about others. *Journal of Personality and Social Psychology, 16,* 66–91.

Kihlstrom, J. F. (1987). The cognitive unconscious. *Science, 237,* 1445–1452.

Kihlstrom, J. F., Cantor, N., Albright, J. S., Chew, B. R., Klein, S. B., and Neidenthal, P. M. (1988). Information processing and the study of the self. In L. Berkowitz (Ed.), *Advances in experimental social psychology* (Vol. 21, pp. 159–187). San Diego, CA: Academic Press.

Kitayama, S., Markus, H. R., Matsumoto, H., and Norasakkunkit, V. (1997). Individual and collective processes in the construction of the self: Self-enhancement in the United States and self-criticism in Japan. *Journal of Personality and Social Psychology, 72,* 1245–1267.

Klayman, J., and Ha, Y. (1987). Confirmation, disconfirmation, and information in hypothesis testing. *Psychological Review, 94,* 211–228.

Klein, W. M., and Kunda, Z. (1992). Motivated person perception: Constructing justifications for desired beliefs. *Journal of Experimental Social Psychology, 28,* 145–168.

Koehler, D. J. (1991). Explanation, imagination, and confidence in judgment. *Psychological Bulletin, 110,* 499–519.

Krosnick, J. A., Li, F., and Lehman, D. R. (1990). Conversational conventions, order of information acquisition, and the effects of base rates and individuating information on social judgments. *Journal of Personality and Social Psychology, 59,* 1140–1152.

Krueger, J. (1998). On the perception of social consensus. In M. P. Zanna (Ed.), *Advances in experimental social psychology* (Vol. 30, pp. 163–240). San Diego: Academic Press.

Krueger, J., and Rothbart, M. (1988). Use of categorical and individuating information in making inferences about personality. *Journal of Personality and Social Psychology, 55,* 187–195.

Kruglanski, A. W. (1980). Lay epistemology process and contents. *Psychological Review, 87,* 70–87.

Kruglanski, A. W. (1996). Motivated social cognition: Principles of the interface. In E. T. Higgins and A. W. Kruglanski (Eds.), *Social psychology: Handbook of basic principles* (pp. 493–520). New York: Guilford Press.

Kruglanski, A. W., and Freund, T. (1983). The freezing and unfreezing of lay-inferences: Effects on impressional primacy, ethnic stereotyping, and numerical anchoring. *Journal of experimental Social Psychology 19,* 448–468.

Kruglanski, A. W., and Webster, D. M. (1996). Motivated closing of the mind: "Seizing" and "freezing." *Psychological Review, 103,* 263–283.

Kunda, Z. (1987). Motivated inference: Self-serving generation and evaluation of causal theories. *Journal of Personality and Social Psychology, 53*, 636–647.

Kunda, Z. (1990). The case for motivated reasoning. *Psychological Bulletin, 108*, 480–498.

Kunda, Z., Miller, D. T., and Claire, T. (1990). Combining social concepts: The role of causal reasoning. *Cognitive Science, 14*, 551–577.

Kunda, Z., and Nisbett, R. E. (1986). The psychometrics of everyday life. *Cognitive Psychology, 18* 199–224.

Kunda, Z., and Oleson, K. C. (1995). Maintaining stereotypes in the face of disconfirmation: Constructing grounds for subtyping deviants. *Journal of Personality and Social Psychology, 68*, 565–579.

Kunda, Z., and Oleson, K. (1997). When exceptions prove the rule: How extremity of deviance determines deviants' impact on stereotypes. *Journal of Personality and Social Psychology, 72*, 965–979.

Kunda, Z., and Sherman-Williams, B. (1993). Stereotypes and the construal of individuating information. *Personality and Social Psychology Bulletin, 19*, 90–99.

Kunda, Z., and Sinclair, L. (in press). Motivated reasoning with stereotypes: Activation, application, and inhibition. *Psychological Inquiry*.

Kunda, Z., Sinclair, L., and Griffin, D. (1997). Equal ratings but separate meanings: Stereotypes and the construal of traits. *Journal of Personality and Social Psychology, 72*, 720–734.

Kunda, Z., Fong, G. T., Sanitioso, R., and Reber, E. (1993). Directional questions direct self-perceptions *Journal of Experimental Social Psychology, 29* 63–86

Kunda, Z., and Thagard, P. (1996). Forming impressions from stereotypes, traits, and behaviors: A parallel-constraint-satisfaction theory. *Psychological Review, 103*, 284–308.

Kunst-Wilson, W. R., and Zajonc, R. B. (1980). Affective discrimination of stimuli that cannot be recognized. *Science, 207*, 557–558.

Laird, J. D., Wagener, J. J., Halal, M., and Szegda, M. (1982). Remembering what you feel: Effects of emotion on memory. *Journal of Personality and Social Psychology, 42*, 646–657.

Lambert, A. J., Khan, S. R., Lickel, B. A., and Fricke, K. (1997). Mood and the correction of positive versus negative stereotypes. *Journal of Personality and Social Psychology, 72*, 1002–1016.

Landman, J. (1987). Regret and elation following action and inaction. *Personality and Social Psychology Bulletin, 32*, 311–328.

Latane, B., and Darley, J. M. (1970). *The unresponsive bystander: Why doesn't he help?* New York: Appleton-Century Crofts.

Leddo, J., Abelson, R. P., and Gross, P. H. (1984). Conjunctive explanations: When two reasons are better than one. *Journal of Personality and Social Psychology, 47*, 933–943.

LeDoux, J. (1996). *The emotional brain: The mysterious underpinnings of emotional life.* New York: Simon and Schuster.

Lehman, D., and Nisbett, R. E. (1990). A longitudinal study of the effects of undergraduate education on reasoning. *Developmental Psychology, 26*, 952–960.

Lepore, L., and Brown, R. (1997). Category and stereotype activation: Is prejudice inevitable? *Journal of Personality and Social Psychology, 72*, 275–287.

Lerner, M. J., and Miller, D. T. (1978). Just world research and attribution process: Looking back and ahead. *Psychological Bulletin, 85*, 1030–1051.

Lewinsohn, P. M., and Rosenbaum, M. (1987). Recall of parental behavior by acute depressives, remitted depressvies, and nondepressives. *Journal of Personality and Social Psychology, 52*, 611–619.

Linville, P. W. (1985). Self-complexity and affective extremity: Don't put all your eggs in one cognitive basket. *Social Cognition, 3*, 94–120.

Linville, P. W. (1987). Self-complexity as a cognitive buffer against stress-related illness and depression. *Journal of Personality and Social Psychology, 52*, 663–676.

Lippmann, W. (1922). *Public opinion*. New York: Harcourt, Brace.

Locksley, A., Borgida, E., Brekke, N., and Hepburn, C. (1980). Sex stereotypes and social judgment. *Journal of Personality and Social Psychology, 39*, 821–831.

Locksley, A., Hepburn, C., and Ortiz, V. (1982). Social stereotypes and judgments of individuals. *Journal of Experimental Social Psychology, 18*, 23–42.

Lockwood, P., and Kunda, Z. (1997). Superstars and me: Predicting the impact of role models on the self. *Journal of Personality and Social Psychology, 73*, 91–103.

Loftus, E. F., and Coan, J. (in press). The construction of childhood memories. In D. Peters (Ed.), *The child witness in context: Cognitive, social, and legal perspectives* New York: Kluwer.

Loftus, E. F., Feldman, J., and Dashiell, R. (1995). The reality of illusory memories. In D. L. Schacter (Ed.), *Memory distortion: How minds, brains, and societies reconstruct the past* (pp. 47–68). Cambridge, MA: Harvard University Press.

Loftus, E. F., and Palmer, J. C. (1974). Reconstruction of automobile deconstruction: An examination of the interaction between language and memory. *Journal of Verbal Learning and Verbal Behavior, 13*, 585–589.

Lord, C. G., Lepper, M. R., and Preston, E. (1984). Considering the opposite: A corrective strategy for social judgment. *Journal of Personality and Social Psychology, 47*, 1231–1243.

Lord, C. G., Ross, L., and Lepper, M. R. (1979). Biased assimilation and attitude polarization: The effects of prior theories on subsequently considered evidence. *Journal of Personality and Social Psychology, 37*, 2098–2109.

Mackie, D. M., and Worth, L. T. (1989). Processing deficits and the mediation of positive affect in persuasion. *Journal of Personality and Social Psychology, 57*, 27–40.

Mackie, D. M., and Worth, L. T. (1991). "Feeling good but not thinking straight": Positive mood and persuasion. In J. P. Forgas (Ed.), *Emotion and social judgments* (pp. 201–220). Oxford: Pergamon.

Macrae, C. N., Bodenhausen, G. V., and Milne, A. B. (1995). The dissection of selection in person perception: Inhibitory processes in social stereotyping. *Journal of Personality and Social Psychology, 69*, 397–407.

Macrae, C. N., Bodenhausen, G. V., and Milne, A. B. (1998). Saying no to unwanted thoughts: Self-focus and the regulation of mental life. *Journal of Personality and Social Psychology, 74*, 578–589.

Macrae, C. N., Bodenhausen, G. V., Milne, A. B., and Jetten, J. (1994a). Out of mind but back in sight: Stereotypes on the rebound. *Journal of Personality and Social Psychology, 67*, 808–817.

Macrae, C. N., Milne, A. B., and Bodenhausen, G. V. (1994b). Stereotypes as energy-saving devices: A peek inside the cognitive toolbox. *Journal of Personality and Social Psychology, 66*, 37–47.

Madon, S., Jussim, L., and Eccles, J. (1997). In search of the powerful self-fulfilling prophecy. *Journal of Personality and Social Psychology, 72*, 791–809.

Major, B. (1980). Information acquisition and attribution processes. *Journal of Personality and Social Psychology, 39*, 1010–1024.

Major, B., Testa, M., and Bylsma, W. H. (1991). Responses to upward and downward comparisons: The impact of esteem-relevance and perceived control. In J. Suls and T. A. Wills (Eds.), *Social comparison: Contemporary theory and research* (pp. 237–260). Hillsdale, NJ: Erlbaum.

Markman, K. D., Gavanski, I., Sherman, S. J., and McMullen, M. N. (1995). The impact of perceived control on the imagination of better and worse possible worlds. *Personality and Social Psychology Bulletin, 21,* 588–595.

Marks, G., and Miller, N. (1987). Ten years of research on the false-consensus effect: An empirical and theoretical review. *Psychological Bulletin, 102,* 72–90.

Markus, G. B. (1986). Stability and change in political attitudes: Observed, recalled and explained. *Political Behavior, 8,* 21–44.

Markus, H. (1977). Self-schemata and processing information about the self. *Journal of Personality and Social Psychology, 35,* 63–78.

Markus, H., Crane, M., Bernstein, S., and Siladi, M. (1982). Self-schema and gender. *Journal of Personality and Social Psychology, 42,* 38–50.

Markus, H., and Kitayama, S. (1991). Culture and the self: Implications for cognition, emotion, and motivation. *Psychological Review, 98,* 224–252.

Markus, H., and Kunda, Z. (1986). Stability and malleability of the self-concept. *Journal of Personality and Social Psychology, 51,* 858–866.

Markus, H., and Nurius, P. (1986). Possible selves. *American Psychologist, 41,* 954–969.

Markus, H., Smith, J., and Moreland, R. L. (1985). Role of the self-concept in the perception of others. *Journal of Personality and Social Psychology, 49,* 1494–1512.

Markus, H., and Zajonc, R. B. (1985). The cognitive perspective on social psychology. In G. Lindzey and E. Aronson (Eds.), *Handbook of Social Psychology* (pp. 137–230). New York: Random House.

Matza, D. (1964). *Delinquency and drift.* New York: Wiley.

McArthur, L. Z. (1972). The how and what of why: Some determinants and consequences of causal attribution. *Journal of Personality and Social Psychology, 22,* 171–193.

McConahay, J. B. (1986). Modern racism, ambivalence, and the modern racism scale. In J. F. Dovidio and S. L. Gaertner (Eds.), *Prejudice, discrimination, and racism* (pp. 91–125). Orlando, FL: Academic Press.

McDonald, H. E., and Hirt, E. R. (1997). When expectancy meets desire: Motivational effects in reconstructivce memory. *Journal of Personality and Social Psychology, 72,* 5–23.

McFarland, C., and Ross, M. (1987). The relation between current impressions and memories of self and dating partners. *Personality and Social Psychology Bulletin, 13,* 228–238.

McGuire, W. J., McGuire, C. V., Child, P., and Fujioka, T. (1978). Salience of ethnicity in the spontaneous self-concept as a function of one's ethnic distinctiveness in the social enviorenment. *Journal of Personality and Social Psychology, 36,* 511–520.

McGuire, W. J., and Padawer-Singer, A. (1976). Trait salience in the spontaneous self-concept. *Journal of Personality and Social Psychology, 33,* 743–754.

McKean, K. (1985). Decisions. *Discover* (June), 22–31.

Medin, D. L. (1989). Concepts and conceptual structure. *American Psychologist, 44,* 1469–1481.

Medin, D. L., Goldstone, R. L., and Gentner, D. (1993). Respects for similarity. *Psychological Review, 100,* 254–278.

Medin, D. L., Lynch, E. B., and Coley, J. (1997). Categorization and reasoning among tree experts: Do all roads lead to Rome? *Cognitive Psychology, 32,* 49–96.

Medvec, V. H., Madey, S. F., and Gilovich, T. (1995). When less is more: Counterfactual thinking and satisfaction among Olympic medalists. *Journal of Personality and Social Psychology, 69,* 603–610.

Medvec, V. H., and Savitsky, K. (1997). When doing better means feeling worse: The effects of categorical cutoff points on counterfactual thinking and satisfaction. *Journal of Personality and Social Psychology, 72,* 1284–1296.

Meehl, P. E. (1954). *Clinical versus statistical prediction: A theoretical analysis and review of the literature*. Minneapolis: University of Minnesota Press.

Merikle, P. M. (1992). Perception without awareness: Critical issues. *American Psychologist*, *47*, 792–795.

Merikle, P. M., Joordens, S., and Stolz, J. A. (1995). Measuring the relative magnitude of unconscious influences. *Consciousness and Cognition*, *4*, 422–439.

Miller, D. T., and McFarland, C. (1986). Counterfactual thinking and victim compensation: A test of norm theory. *Personality and Social Psychology Bulletin*, *12*, 513–519.

Miller, D. T., and McFarland, C. (1987). Pluralistic ignorance: When similarity is interpreted as dissimilarity. *Journal of Personality and Social Psychology*, *53*, 298–305.

Miller, D. T., and McFarland, C. (1991). When social comparison goes awry: The case of pluralistic ignorance. In J. Suls and T. Wills (Eds.), *Social comparison: Contemporary theory and research* (pp. 287–313). Hillsdale, NJ: Erlbaum.

Miller, D. T., and Prentice, D. A. (1994). Collective errors and errors about the collective. *Personality and Social Psychology Bulletin*, *20*, 541–550.

Miller, D. T., and Ross, M. (1975). Self-serving biases in attribution of causality: Fact or fiction? *Psychological Bulletin*, *82*, 213–225.

Miller, D. T., Taylor, B., and Buck, M. L. (1991). Gender gaps: Who needs to be explained? *Journal of Personality and Social Psychology*, *61*, 5–12.

Miller, D. T., and Taylor, B. R. (1995). Counterfactual thought, regret, and superstition: How to avoid kicking yourself. In N. J. Roese and J. M. Olsen (Eds.), *What might have been: The psychology of counterfactual thinking* (pp. 305–332). Mahwah, NJ: Erlbaum.

Miller, D. T., Turnbull, W., and McFarland, C. (1989). When a coincidence is suspicious: The role of mental simulation. *Journal of Personality and Social Psychology*, *57*, 581–589.

Miller, D. T., Turnbull, W., and McFarland, C. (1990). Counterfactual thinking and social perception: Thinking about what might have been. In M. Zanna (Ed.), *Advances in Experimental Social Psychology* (Vol. 23, pp. 305–331). New York: Academic Press.

Miller, J. G. (1984). Culture and the development of everyday social explanation. *Journal of Personality and Social Psychology*, *46*, 961–978.

Mischel, W. (1968). *Personality and assessment*. New York: Wiley.

Mischel, W. (1974). Processes in delay of gratification. In L. Berkowitz (Ed.), *Advances in experimental social psychology* (Vol. 7, pp. 249–292). San Diego, CA: Academic Press.

Mischel, W., and Peake, P. K. (1982). Beyond deja vu in the search for cross-situational consistency. *Psychological Review*, *89*, 730–755.

Mischel, W., and Shoda, Y. (1995). A cognitive-affective system theory of personality: Reconceptualizing situations, dispositions, dynamics, and the invariance in personality structure. *Psychological Review*, *102*, 246–268.

Mischel, W., Shoda, Y., and Peake, P. K. (1988). The nature of adolescent competencies predicted by preschool delay of gratification. *Journal of Personality and Social Psychology*, *54*, 687–696.

Monteith, M. J. (1993). Self-regulation of prejudiced responses: Implications for progress in prejudice-reduction efforts. *Journal of Personality and Social Psychology*, *65*, 469–485.

Monteith, M. J., Devine, P. G., and Zuwerink, J. R. (1993). Self-directed versus other-directed affect as a consequence of prejudice-related discrepancies. *Journal of Personality and Social Psychology*, *64* 198–210.

Monteith, M. J., Sherman, J. W., and Devine, P. G. (1998). Suppression as a stereotype control strategy. *Personality and Social Psychology Review, 2*, 63–82.

Morris, M. W., and Peng, K. (1994). Culture and cause: American and Chinese attributions for social and physical events. *Journal of Personality and Social Psychology, 67*, 949–971.

Mullen, B., Atkins, J. L., Champion, D. S., Edwards, C., Hardy, D., Story, J. E., and Vanderklok, M. (1985). The false consensus effect: A meta-analysis of 115 hypothesis tests. *Journal of Experimental Social Psychology, 21*, 262–283.

Muraven, M., Tice, D. M., and Baumeister, R. F. (1998). Self-control as limited resource: Regulatory depletion patterns. *Journal of Personality and Social Psychology, 74*, 774–789.

Murphy, G. L., and Medin, D. L. (1985). The role of theories in conceptual coherence. *Psychological Review, 92*, 289–316.

Murray, S. L., Holmes, J. G., and Griffin, D. W. (1996). The benefits of positive illusions: Idealization and the construction of satisfaction in close relationships. *Journal of Personality and Social Psychology, 70*, 79–98.

Murray, S. L., Holmes, J. G., MacDonald, G., and Ellsworth, P. C. (1998). Love me? Love me not? When self-doubts turn into relationship insecurities. *Journal of Personality and Social Psychology, 75*, 1459–1480.

Neely, J. H. (1977). Semantic priming and retrieval from lexical memory: Roles of inhibitionless spreading activation and limited-capacity attention. *Journal of Experimental Psychology: General, 106*, 226–2254.

Neisser, U., and Harsch, N. (1992). Phantom flashbulbs: False recollections of hearing the news about Challenger. In E. Winograd and U. Neisser (Eds.), *Affect and accuracy in recall: Studies of "flashbulb memories"* (pp. 9–31). Cambridge: Cambridge University Press.

Neuberg, S. L., and Fiske, S. T. (1987). Motivational influences on impression formation: Dependency, accuracy-driven attention, and individuating information. *Journal of Personality and Social Psychology, 53*, 431–444.

Newcomb, T. M. (1929). *The consistency of certain extrovert-introvert behavior patterns in 51 problem boys.* New York: Columbia University, Teachers College, Bureau of Publications.

Niedenthal, P. M., Setterlund, M. B., and Wherry, M. B. (1992). Possible self-complexity and affective reactions to goal-relevant evaluation. *Journal of Personality and Social Psychology, 63*, 5–16.

Nisbett, R. E. (1993). Violence and U.S. regional culture. *American Psychologist, 48*, 441–449.

Nisbett, R. E., and Borgida, E. (1975). Attribution and the psychology of prediction. *Journal of Personality and Social Psychology, 32*, 932–943.

Nisbett, R. E., and Cohen, D. (1996). *Culture of honor: The psychology of violence in the South.* Boulder, CO: Westview Press.

Nisbett, R. E., Krantz, D. H., Jepson, C., and Kunda, Z. (1983). The use of statistical heuristics in everyday inductive reasoning. *Psychological Review, 90*, 339–363.

Nisbett, R. E., and Kunda, Z. (1985). Perception of social distributions. *Journal of Personality and Social Psychology, 48*, 297–311.

Nisbett, R. E., and Ross, L. (1980). *Human inference: Strategies and shortcomings of social judgment.* Englewood Cliffs, NJ: Prentice Hall.

Nisbett, R. E., and Wilson, D. (1977). Telling more than we can know: Verbal reports on mental processes. *Psychological Review, 84*, 231–253.

Nisbett, R. E., Zukier, H., and Lemley, R. E. (1981). The dilution effect: Nondiagnostic information weakens the implications of diagnostic information. *Cognitive Psychology*, *13*, 248–277.

Northcraft, G. B., and Neale, M. A. (1987). Experts, amateurs, and real estate: An anchoring-and-adjustment perspective on property pricing decisions. *Organizational Behavior and Human Decision Processes*, *39*, 84–97.

Nunnally, J. C. (1978). *Psychometric theory* (2nd ed.). New York: McGraw Hill.

Olson, J. M., Roese, N. J., and Zanna, M. P. (1996). Expectancies. In E. T. Higgins and A. W. Kruglanski (Eds.), *Social psychology: Handbook of basic principles* (pp. 211–238). New York: Guilford Press.

Oyserman, D., and Markus, H. R. (1990). Possible selves and delinquency. *Journal of Personality and Social Psychology*, *59*, 112–125.

Park, B. (1986). A method for studying the development of impressions of real people. *Journal of Personality and Social Psychology*, *51*, 907–917.

Park, B., DeKay, M. L., and Kraus, S. (1994). Aggregating social behavior into person models: Perceiver-induced consistency. *Journal of Personality and Social Psychology*, *66*, 437–459.

Park, B., and Hastie, R. (1987). Perception of variability in category development: Instance- versus abstraction-based stereotypes. *Journal of Personality and Social Psychology*, *53*, 621–636.

Park, B., Judd, C. M., and Ryan, C. S. (1991). Social categorization and the representation of variablity information. In W. Stroebe and M. Hewstone (Eds.), *European review of social psychology* (pp. 211–245). Chichester, England: Wiley.

Park, B., and Rothbart, M. (1982). Perception of out-group homogeneity and levels of social categorization: Memory for the subordinate attributes of in-group and out-group members. *Journal of Personality and Social Psychology*, *42*, 1051–1068.

Piaget, J. (1962). *Plays, dreams and imitation in childhood*. New York: Norton.

Parrot, G. W., and Sabini, J. (1990). Mood and memory under natural conditions: Evidence for mood incongruent recall. *Journal of Personality and Social Psychology*, *59*, 321–336.

Pelham, B. W., and Neter, E. (1995). The effect of motivation on judgment depends of the difficulty of the judgment. *Journal of Personality and Social Psychology*, *68*, 581–594.

Pelham, B. W., and Wachsmuth, J. O. (1995). The waxing and waning of the social self: Assimilation and contrast in social comparison. *Journal of Personality and Social Psychology*, *69*, 825–838.

Pennington, N., and Hastie, R. (1986). Evidence evaluation in complex decision making. *Journal of Personality and Social Psychology*, *51*, 242–254.

Pennington, N., and Hastie, R. (1988). Explanation-based decision making: effects of memory structure on judgment. *Journal of Experimental Psychology: Learning, Memory, and Cognition*, *14*, 521–533.

Pennington, N., and Hastie, R. (1992). Explaining the evidence: Tests of the story model for juror decision making. *Journal of Personality and Social Psychology*, *62*, 189–206.

Peterson, D. R. (1968). *The clinical study of social behavior*. New York: Appleton.

Pettigrew, T. F. (1979). The ultimate attribution error: Extending Allport's cognitive analysis to prejudice. *Personality and Social Psychology Bulletin*, *5*, 461–476.

Petty, R. E., and Cacioppo, J. T. (1986). The elaboration likelihood model of persuasion. In L. Berkowitz (Ed.), *Advances in experimental social psychology* (Vol. 29, pp. 123–205). New York: Academic Press.

Petty, R. E., Harkins, S. G., and Williams, K. D. (1980). The effects of group diffusion of cognitive effort on attitudes: An information processing view. *Journal of Personality and Social Psychology, 38*, 81–92.

Phillips, L. D., and Edwards, W. (1966). Conservatism in a simple probability inference task. *Journal of Experimental Psychology, 72*, 346–354.

Plous, S. (1989). Thinking the unthinkable: The effects of anchoring on likelihood estimates of nuclear war. *Journal of Applied Social Psychology, 19*, 67–91.

Pratkanis, A. R., Greenwald, A. G., Leippe, M. R., and Baumgardner, M. H. (1988). In search of reliable persuasion effects: III. The sleeper effect is dead. Long live the sleeper effect. *Journal of Personality and Social Psychology, 54*, 203–218.

Prentice, D. A., and Miller, D. T. (1993). Pluralistic ignorance and alcohol use on campus: Some consequences of misperceiving the social norm. *Journal of Personality and Social Psychology, 64*, 243–256.

Prentice, D. A., and Miller, D. T. (1996). Pluralistic ignorance and the perpetuation of social norms by unwitting actors. In M. P. Zanna (Ed.), *Advances in experimental social psychology* (Vol. 28, pp. 161–209). San Diego, CA: Academic Press.

Purdue, C. W., and Gurtman, M. B. (1990). Evidence for the automaticity of ageism. *Journal of Experimental Social Psychology, 26*, 199–216.

Pyszczynski, T., and Greenberg, J. (1987). Toward an integration of cognitive and motivational perspectives on social inference: A biased hypothesis-testing model. In L. Berkowitz (Ed.), *Advances in experimental social psychology* (Vol. 20, pp. 297–340). New York: Academic Press.

Pyszczynski, T., La Prelle, J., and Greenberg, J. (1987). Encoding and retrieval effects of general person characterizations on memory for incongruent and congruent information. *Personality and Social Psychology Bulletin, 13*, 556–567.

Quattrone, G. A. (1982). Overattribution and unit formation: When behavior engulfs the person. *Journal of Personality and Social Psychology, 42*, 593–607.

Quattrone, G. A., and Jones, E. E. (1980). The perception of variability within ingroups and outgroups: Implications for the law of small numbers. *Journal of Personality and Social Psychology, 38*, 141–152.

Ratcliff, R., and McKoon, G. (1988). A retrieval theory of priming in memory. *Psychological Review, 95*, 385–408.

Read, S. J., and Marcus-Newhall, A. (1993). Explanatory coherence in social explanations: A parallel distributed processing account. *Journal of Personality and Social Psychology, 65*, 429–447.

Read, S. J., and Miller, L. C. (1993). Rapist or "regular guy": Explanatory coherence in the construction of mental models of others. *Personality and Social Psychology Bulletin, 19*, 526–541.

Redelmeier, D. A., and Tversky, A. (1996). On the belief that arthritis pain is related to the weather. *Procedures of the National Academy of Science, 93*, 2895–2896.

Roese, N. J. (1994). The functional basis of counterfactual thinking. *Journal of Personality and Social Psychology, 66*, 805–818.

Roese, N. J. (1997). Counterfactual thinking. *Psychological Bulletin, 121*, 133–148.

Roese, N. J., and Olson, J. M. (1995). Functions of counterfactual thinking. In N. J. Roese and J. M. Olson (Eds.), *What might have been: The psychology of counterfactual thinking* (pp. 169–198). Mahwah, NJ: Erlbaum.

Roese, N. J., and Olson, J. M. (1997). Counterfactual thinking: The intersection of affect and function. In M. P. Zanna (Ed.), *Advances in experimental social psychology* (Vol. 29, pp. 1–59). San Diego, CA: Academic Press.

Rosch, E. (1978). Principles of categorization. In E. Rosch and B. B. Lloyd (Eds.), *Cognition and categorization* (pp. 27–48). Hillsdale, NJ: Erlbaum.

Rosch, E., and Mervis, C. (1975). Family resemblances: Studies in the internal structure of categories. *Cognitive Psychology, 7,* 573–605.

Rosch, E., Mervis, C. G., Gray, W. D., Johnson, D. M., and Bayes Braem, P. (1976a). Basic objects in natural categories. *Cognitive Psychology, 8,* 382–439.

Rosch, E., Simpson, C., and Miller, R. S. (1976b). Structural bases of typicality effects. *Journal of Experimental Psychology: Human Perception and Performance, 2,* 491–502.

Rosenberg, M. (1965). *Society and the adolescent self-image.* Princeton: Princeton University Press.

Rosenthal, R., and Jacobson, L. (1968). *Pygmalion in the classroom: Teacher expectations and student intellectual development.* New York: Holt, Rinehart, and Winston.

Ross, L. (1977). The intuitive psychologist and his shortcomings. In L. Berkowitz (Ed.), *Advances in experimental social psychology* (Vol. 10, pp. 173–220). San Diego, CA: Academic Press.

Ross, L., Amabile, T. M., and Steinmetz, J. L. (1977a). Social roles, social control, and biases in social-perception processes. *Journal of Personality and Social Psychology, 35,* 485–494.

Ross, L., Greene, D., and House, P. (1977b). The "false consensus effect": An egocentric bias in social perception and attribution processes. *Journal of Experimental Social Psychology, 13,* 279–301.

Ross, L., Lepper, M. R., and Hubbard, M. (1975). Perseverance in self-perception and social perception: Biased attribution processes in the debriefing paradigm. *Journal of Personality and Social Psychology, 32,* 880–892.

Ross, L., and Nisbett, R. E. (1991). *The person and the situation: Perspectives of social psychology.* New York: McGraw-Hill.

Ross, M. (1997). Validating memories. In N. L. Stein, P. A. Ornstein, B. Tversky, and C. Brainerd (Eds.), *Memory for everyday and emotional events* (pp. 49–81). Mahwah, NJ: Erlbaum.

Ross, M. (1989). Relation of implicit theories to the construction of personal histories. *Psychological Review, 96,* 341–357.

Ross, M., Buehler, R., and Karr, J. W. (1998). Assessing the accuracy of conflicting autobiographical memories. *Memory and Cognition, 26,* 1233–1244.

Ross, M., and Ellard, J. H. (1986). On winnowing: The impact of scarcity on allocators' evaluations of candidates for a resource. *Journal of Experimental Social Psychology, 22,* 374–388.

Ross, M., McFarland, C., and Fletcher, G. J. O. (1981). The effect of attitude on recall of past histories. *Journal of Personality and Social Psychology, 10,* 627–634.

Ross, M., and Sicoly, F. (1979). Egocentric biases in availability and attribution. *Journal of Personality and Social Psychology, 37,* 322–337.

Rothbart, M., and John, O. P. (1985). Social categorization and behavioral episodes: A cognitive analysis of the effects of intergroup contact. *Journal of Social Issues, 41,* 81–104.

Rothbart, M., and Lewis, S. (1988). Inferring category attributes from exemplar attributes: Geometric shapes and social categories. *Journal of Personality and Social Psychology, 55,* 861–872.

Rumelhart, D. E. (1984). Schemata and the cognitive system. In R. S. Wyer and T. K. Srull (Eds.), *Handbook of Social Cognition* Hillsdale (Vol. 1, pp. 161–188). NJ: Erlbaum.

Rumelhart, D. E., and McClelland, J. L. (Eds.). (1986). *Parallel distributed processing: Explorations in the microstructure of cognition.* Cambridge, MA: MIT Press.

Sagar, H. A., and Schofield, J. W. (1980). Racial and behavioral cues in black and white children's perceptions of ambiguously aggressive acts. *Journal of Personality and Social Psychology*, *39*, 590–598.

Salovey, P., and Birnbaum, D. (1989). Influence of mood on health-relevant cognitions. *Journal of Personality and Social Psychology*, *57*, 539–551.

Sanitioso, R., Kunda, Z., and Fong, G. T. (1990). Motivated recruitment of autobiographical memories. *Journal of Personality and Social Psychology*, *59*, 229–241.

Schachter, S., and Singer, J. E. (1962). Cognitive, social, and physiological determinants of emotional state. *Psychological Review*, *69*, 379–399.

Schacter, D. L. (1987). Implicit memory: History and current status. *Journal of Experimental Psychology: Learning, Memory, and Cognition*, *13*, 501–518.

Schacter, D. L. (1996). *Searching for memory: The brain, the mind, and the past*. New York: Basic Books.

Schaller, M. (1992). In-group favoritism and statistical reasoning in social inference: Implications for formation and maintenance of group stereotypes. *Journal of Personality and Social Psychology*, *63*, 61–74.

Schanck, R. L. (1932). A study of community and its group institutions conceived of as behavior of individuals. *Psychological Monographs*, *43*, 1–133.

Schul, Y. (1983). Integration and abstraction in impression formation. *Journal of Personality and Social Psychology*, *44*, 45–54.

Schwarz, N. (1990). Feelings as information: Informational and motivational functions of affective states. In E. T. Higgins and R. Sorrentino (Eds.), *Handbook of motivation and cognition: Foundations of social behavior* (Vol. 2, pp. 527–561). New York: Guilford Press.

Schwarz, N. (1994). Judgement in social context: Biases, shortcomings, and the logic of conversation. In M. P. Zanna (Ed.), *Advances in Experimental Social Psychology* (Vol. 26, pp. 123–162). San Diego: Academic Press.

Schwarz, N., and Bless, H. (1992). Scandals and the public's trust in politicians: Assimilation and contrast effects. *Personality and Social Psychology Bulletin*, *18*, 574–579.

Schwarz, N., Bless, H., Strack, F., Klumpp, G., Rittenauer-Schatka, H., and Simons, A. (1991). Ease of retrieval of information: Another look at the availability heuristic. *Journal of Personality and Social Psychology*, *61* 195–202.

Schwarz, N., and Clore, G. L. (1983). Mood, misattribution, and judgements of well-being: Informative and directive functions of affective states. *Journal of Personality and Social Psychology*, *45*, 513–523.

Schwarz, N., and Clore, G. L. (1996). Feelings and phenomenal experience. In E. T. Higgins and A. W. Kruglanski (Eds.), *Social psychology: Handbook of basic principles* (pp. 433–465). New York: Guilford Press.

Schwarz, N., Strack, F., Hilton, D. J., and Naderer, G. (1991). Base rates, representativeness, and the logic of conversation: The contextual relevance of "irrelevant" information. *Social Cognition*, *9*, 67–84.

Shafir, E. (1993). Choosing versus rejecting: Why some options are both better and worse than others. *Memory and Cognition*, *21*, 546–556.

Sherif, M., Harvey, O. J., White, J., Hood, W., and Sherif, C. (1961). *Intergroup conflict and cooperation: The Robber's Cave experiment*. Norman: University of Oklahoma Institute of Intergroup Relations.

Sherman, J. W., and Klein, S. B. (1994). Development and representation of personality impressions. *Journal of Personality and Social Psychology*, *67*, 972–983.

Sherman, S. J., and McConnell, A. R. (1995). Dysfunctional implications of counterfactual thinking: When alternatives to reality fail us. In N. J. Roese and J. M. Olsen (Eds.),

What might have been: The psychology of counterfactual thinking (pp. 199–232). Mahwah, NJ: Erlbaum.

Sherman, S. J., Presson, C. C., and Chassin, L. (1984). Mechanisms underlying the false consensus effect: The special role of threats to the self. *Personality and Social Psychology Bulletin, 10*, 127–138.

Sherman, S. J., Presson, C. C., Chassin, L., Corty, E., and Olshavsky, P. (1983). The false consensus effect in estimates of smoking prevalence: Underlying mechanisms. *Personality and Social Psychology Bulletin, 9*, 197–207.

Sherman, S. J., Skov, R. B., Hervitz, E. F., and Stock, C. B. (1981). The effects of explaining hypothetical future events: From possibility to actuality and beyond. *Journal of Experimental Social Psychology, 17*, 142–158.

Shiffrin, R. M., and Schneider, W. (1977). Controlled and automatic human information processing: II. Perceptual learning, automatic attending, and general theory. *Psychological Review, 84*, 127–190.

Shilts, R. (1987). *And the band played on: Politics, people, and the AIDS epidemic*. New York: St. Martin's Press.

Shoda, Y., Mischel, W., and Wright, J. C. (1994). Intraindividual stability in the organization and patterning of behavior: Incorporating psychological situations into the idiographic analysis of personality. *Journal of Personality and Social Psychology, 67*, 674–687.

Showers, C. (1992). Compartmentalization of positive and negative self-knowledge: Keeping bad apples out of the bunch. *Journal of Personality and Social Psychology, 62*, 1036–1049.

Showers, C. J., and Kling, K. C. (1996). Organization of self-knowledge: Implications for recovery from sad mood. *Journal of Personality and Social Psychology, 70*, 578–590.

Shultz, T. R., and Lepper, M. R. (1996). Cognitive dissonance reduction as constraint satisfaction. *Psychological Review, 103*, 219–240.

Shweder, R. A., and LeVine, R. A. (1984). *Culture theory: Essays on mind, self, and emotion*. New York: Cambridge University Press.

Simon, H. (1957). *Models of man: Social and rational*. New York: Wiley.

Sinclair, L. (1998). *Justifying desired impressions of evaluators: Motivated activation, application, and inhibition of stereotypes*. Unpublished doctoral dissertation, University of Waterloo.

Singer, J. A., and Salovey, P. (1988). Mood and memory: Evaluating the network theory of affect. *Clinical Psychological Review, 8*, 211–251.

Skinner, B. F. (1963). Operant behavior. *American Psychologist, 18*, 503–515.

Skov, R. B., and Sherman, S. J. (1986). Information gathering processes: Diagnosticity, hypothesis-confirmatory strategies, and perceived hypothesis confirmation. *Journal of Experimental Social Psychology, 22*, 93–121.

Slovic, P., Fischhoff, B., and Lichtenstein, S. (1982). Facts versus fears: Understanding perceived risk. In D. Kahneman, P. Slovic, and A. Tversky (Eds.), *Judgment under uncertainty: Heuristics and biases* (pp. 436–489). New York: Cambridge University Press.

Slusher, M. P., and Anderson, C. A. (1987). When reality monitoring fails: The role of imagination in stereotype maintenance. *Journal of Personality and Social Psychology, 52*, 653–662.

Smelsund, J. (1963). The concept of correlation in adults. *Scandinavian Journal of Psychology, 4*, 165–173.

Smith, E. E. (1990). Categorization. In D. N. Osherson and E. E. Smith (Eds.), *Thinking: An invitation to cognitive science* (pp. 33–53). Cambridge, MA: MIT Press.

Smith, E. E., and Medin, D. L. (1981). *Categories and concepts*. Cambridge, MA: Harvard University Press.

Smith, E. R. (1996). What do connectionism and social psychology offer each other? *Journal of Personality and Social Psychology*, *70*, 893–912.

Smith, E. R. (1998). Mental representations and memory. In D. Gilbert, S. T. Fiske, and G. Lindzey (Eds.), *Handbook of Social Psychology* (Vol. 1, 4th ed. pp. 391–345). New York: McGraw-Hill.

Smith, E. R., Fazio, R. H., and Cejka, M. A. (1996). Accessible attitudes influence categorization of multiply categorizable objects. *Journal of Personality and Social Psychology*, *71*, 888–898.

Smith, E. R., and Miller, F. D. (1978). Limits on perception of cognitive processes: A reply to Nisbett and Wilson. *Psychological Review*, *85*, 355–362.

Smith, E. R., and Zarate, M. A. (1992). Exemplar-based model of social judgment. *Psychological Review*, *99*, 3–21.

Snyder, M. (1984). When belief creates reality. In L. Berkowitz (Ed.), *Advances in experimental social psychology* (Vol. 18, pp. 248–306). New York: Academic Press.

Snyder, M., and Cantor, N. (1979). Testing hypotheses about other people: The use of historical knowledge. *Journal of Experimental Social Psychology*, *15*, 330–342.

Snyder, M., and Swann, W. B. (1978). Hypothesis testing in social interaction. *Journal of Personality and Social Psychology*, *36*, 1202–1212.

Sorrentino, R. M., and Higgins, E. T. (1986). Motivation and cognition: Warming up to synergism. In R. M. Sorrentino and E. T. Higgins (Eds.), *Handbook of motivation and cognition*. (pp. 3–19). New York: Guilford Press.

Sowell, T. (1981). *Ethnic America*. New York: Basic Books.

Spellman, B. A., and Holyoak, K. J. (1992). If Saddam is Hitler then who is George Bush? Analogical mapping between systems of social roles. *Journal of Personality and Social Psychology*, *62*, 913–933.

Spencer, S. J., Fein, S., Wolfe, C., Hodgson, H. L., and Dunn, M. A. (1998). Stereotype activation under cognitive load: The moderating role of self-image threat. *Personality and Social Psychology Bulletin*, *24*, 1139–1152.

Spencer, S. J., Steele, C. M., and Quinn, D. M. (1999). Stereotype threat and women's math performance. *Journal of Experimental Social Psychology*, *35*, 4–28.

Srull, T. K. (1981). Person memory: Some tests of associative storage and retrieval models. *Journal of Experimental Psychology: Human Learning and Memory*, *7*, 440–463.

Srull, T. K., Lichtenstein, M., and Rothbart, M. (1985). Associative storage and retrieval processes in person memory. *Journal of Experimental Psychology: Learning, Memory, and Cognition*, *11*, 316–345.

Srull, T. K., and Wyer, R. S. J. (1979). The role of category accessibility in the interpretation of information about persons: Some determinants and implications. *Journal of Personality and Social Psychology*, *37*, 1660–1672.

Stangor, C., and Lange, J. (1994). Mental representations of social groups: Advances in understanding stereotypes and stereotyping. In M. P. Zanna (Ed.), *Advances in Experimental Social Psychology* (Vol. 26, pp. 357–416). San Diego: Academic Press.

Stangor, C., Lynch, L., Duan, C., and Glass, B. (1992). Categorization of individuals on the basis of mulitple social features. *Journal of Personality and Social Psychology*, *62*, 207–218.

Stangor, C., and McMillan, D. (1992). Memory for expectancy-congruent and expectancy-incongruent information: A review of the social and social developmental literatures. *Psychological Bulletin*, *111*, 42–61.

Steele, C., M., and Liu, T. J. (1983). Dissonance processes as self-affirmation. *Journal of Personality and Social Psychology, 45*, 5–19.

Steele, C. M. (1988). The psychology of self-affirmation: Sustaining the integrity of the self. In L. Berkowitz (Ed.), *Advances in experimental social psychology* (Vol. 21, pp. 261–302). New York: Academic Press.

Steele, C. M. (1997). A threat in the air: How stereotypes shape intellectual identity and performance. *American Psychologist, 52*, 613–629.

Steele, C. M., and Aronson, J. (1995). Stereotype threat and the intellectual test performance of African Americans. *Journal of Personality and Social Psychology, 69*, 797–811.

Steele, C. M., Spencer, S. J., and Lynch, M. (1993). Self-image resilience and dissonance: The role of affirmational resources. *Journal of Personality and Social Psychology, 64*, 885–896.

Stein, M. I. (1966). *Volunteers for peace.* New York: Wiley.

Stephan, W. G. (1985). Intergroup relations. In G. Lindzey and E. Aronson (Eds.), *Handbook of social psychology* (pp. 599–658). New York: Random House.

Strack, F., and Mussweiler, T. (1997). Explaining the enigmatic anchoring effect: Mechanisms of selective accessibility. *Journal of Personality and Social Psychology, 73*, 437–446.

Stroessner, S. J., Hamilton, D. L., and Mackie, D. M. (1992). Affect and stereotyping: The effect of induced mood on distinctiveness-based illusory correlations. *Journal of Personality and Social Psychology, 62*, 564–576.

Swann, W. B. (1984). Quest for accuracy in person perception: A matter of pragmatics. *Psychological Review, 91*, 457–477.

Swann, W. B. (1987). Identity negotiation: Where two roads meet. *Journal of Personality and Social Psychology, 53*, 1038–1051.

Swann, W. B. (1990). To be adored or to be known?: The interplay of self-enhancement and self-verification. In E. T. Higgins and R. Sorrentino (Eds.), *Handbook of motivation and cognition: Foundations of social behavior* (Vol. 2, pp. 527–561). New York: Guilford Press.

Swann, W. B., De La Ronde, C., and Hixon, J. G. (1994). Authenticity and positivity strivings in marriage and courtship. *Journal of Personality and Social Psychology, 66*, 857–869.

Swann, W. B., Griffin, J. J., Predmore, S. C., and Gaines, B. (1987). The cognitive-affective crossfire: When self-consistency confronts self-enhancement. *Journal of Personality and Social Psychology, 52*, 881–889.

Swann, W. B., Pelham, B. W., and Krull, D. S. (1989). Agreeable fancy or disagreeable truth? Reconciling self-enhancement and self-verification. *Journal of Personality and Social Psychology, 57*, 782–791.

Swann, W. B. J., and Read, S. J. (1981). Self-verification processes: How we sustain our self-conceptions. *Journal of Experimental Social Psychology, 17*, 351–370.

Tanaka, J. W., and Taylor, M. (1991). Object categories and expertise: Is the basic level in the eye of the beholder? *Cognitive Psychology, 23*, 457–482.

Taylor, D. M., and Jaggi, V. (1974). Ethnocentrism and causal attribution in a South Indian context. *Journal of Cross-Cultural Psychology, 5*, 162–171.

Taylor, S. E. (1991). Asymmetrical effects of positive and negative events: The mobilization-minimization hypothesis. *Psychological Bulletin, 110*, 67–85.

Taylor, S. E., and Brown, J. D. (1988). Illusion and well-being: A social psychological perspective on mental health. *Psychological Bulletin, 103*, 193–210.

Taylor, S. E., and Fiske, S. T. (1975). Point of view and perceptions of causality. *Journal of Personality and Social Psychology, 32*, 439–445.

Taylor, S. E., and Fiske, S. T. (1978). Salience, attention, and attribution: Top of the head phenomena. In L. Berkowitz (Ed.), *Advances in exprimental social psychology* (Vol. 11, pp. 249–288). New York: Academic Press.

Taylor, S. E., Fiske, S. T., Etcoff, N. L., and Ruderman, A. J. (1978). Categorical and contextual bases of person memory and stereotyping. *Journal of Personality and Social Psychology, 36,* 778–793.

Taylor, S. E., and Golllwitzer, P. M. (1995). Effects of mindset on positive illusions. *Journal of Personality and Social Psychology, 69,* 213–226.

Taylor, S. E., and Crocker, J. (1981). Schematic basis of social information processing. In E. T. Higgins, C. P. Herman, and M. P. Zanna (Eds.), *Social cognition: The Ontario symposium* (Vol. 1, pp. 89–134). Hillsdale, NJ: Erlbaum.

Tesser, A. (1986). Some effects of self-evaluation maintenance on cognition and action. In R. M. Sorrentino and E. T. Higgins (Eds.), *The handbook of motivation and cognition: Foundations of Social Behavior* (pp. 435–464). New York: Guilford Press.

Tesser, A. (1988). Toward a self-evaluation maintenance model of social behavior. In L. Berkowitz (Eds.), *Advances in experimental social psychology* (Vol. 21, pp. 181–227). New York: Academic Press.

Tesser, A. (1991). Emotion in social comparison and reflection processes. In J. Suls and T. A. Wills (Eds.), *Social comparison: Contemporary theory and research* (pp. 115–145). Hillsdale, NJ: Erlbaum.

Tesser, A., and Campbell, J. (1983). Self-definition and self-evaluation maintenance. In J. Suls and A. Greenwald (Eds.), *Social psychological perspectives on the self* (pp. 1–31). Hillsdale, NJ: Erlbaum.

Tesser, A., and Cornell, D. P. (1991). On the confluence of self processes. *Journal of Experimental Social Psychology, 27,* 501–526.

Tetlock, P. E., and Boettger, R. (1989). Accountability: A social magnifier of the dilution effect. *Journal of Personality and Social Psychology, 57,* 388–398.

Tetlock, P. E., and Kim, J. I. (1987). Accountability and judgment processes in a personality prediction task. *Journal of Personality and Social Psychology, 52,* 700–709.

Tetlock, P. E., and Levi, A. (1982). Attribution bias: On the inconclusiveness of the cognition-motivation debate. *Journal of Experimental Social Psychology, 18,* 68–88.

Thagard, P. (1989). Explanatory coherence. *Behavioral and Brain Sciences, 12,* 435–467.

Thagard, P. (1992). *Conceptual revolutions.* Princeton: Princeton University Press.

Thagard, P., and Kunda, Z. (1998). Making sense of people: Coherence mechanisms. In S. J. Read and L. C. Miller (Eds.), *Connectionist models of social reasoning and social behavior* (pp. 3–26). Mahwah, NJ: Erlbaum.

Triandis, H. C. (1989). The self and social behavior in differing cultural contexts. *Psychological Review, 96,* 506–520.

Trope, Y. (1986a). Identification and inferential processes in dispositional attribution. *Psychological Review, 93,* 239–257.

Trope, Y. (1986b). Self-enhancement and self-assessment in achievement behavior. In R. M. Sorrentino and E. T. Higgins (Eds.), *Handbook of motivation and cognition* (pp. 350–378). New York: Guilford Press.

Trope, Y., and Alfieri, T. (1997). Effortfulness and flexibility of dispositional judgment processes. *Journal of Personality and Social Psychology, 73,* 662–674.

Trope, Y., and Bassok, M. (1982). Confirmatory and diagnostic strategies in social information gathering. *Journal of Personality and Social Psychology, 43,* 22–34.

Trope, Y., and Bassok, M. (1983). Information-gathering strategies in hypothesis-testing. *Journal of Experimental Social Psychology* 19, 560–576.

Tulving, E., Schacter, D. L., and Stark, H. (1982). Priming effects in word-fragment completion are independent of recognition memory. *Journal of Experimental Psychology: Learning, Memory, and Cognition, 8,* 336–342.

Tulving, E., and Thomson, D. M. (1973). Encoding specificity and retrieval processes in episodic memory. *Psychological Review, 80,* 352–373.

Turnbull, W. (1981). Naive conceptions of free will and the deterministic paradox. *Canadian Journal of Behavioral Science, 13,* 1–13.

Tversky, A. (1977). Features of similarity. *Psychological Review, 84,* 327–352.

Tversky, A., and Kahneman, D. (1971). Belief in the law of small numbers. *Psychological Bulletin, 76,* 105–110.

Tversky, A., and Kahneman, D. (1973). Availability: A heuristic for judging frequency and probability. *Cognitive Psychology, 5,* 207–232.

Tversky, A., and Kahneman, D. (1974). Judgment under uncertainty: Heuristics and biases. *Science, 185,* 1124–1131.

Tversky, A., and Kahneman, D. (1983). Extensional versus intuitive reasoning: The conjunction fallacy in probability judgment. *Psychological Review, 90,* 293–315.

Uleman, J. S., and Bargh, J. A. (Eds.). (1989). *Unintended thought.* New York: Guilford Press.

Uleman, J. S., Newman, L. S., and Moskowitz, G. B. (1996). People as flexible interpreters: Evidence and issues from spontaneous trait inference. In M. P. Zanna (Ed.), *Advances in Experimental Social Psychology* (Vol. 28, pp. 211–279). San Diego: Academic Press.

Vaillant, G. E. (1977). *Adaption to life.* Boston: Little, Brown.

Vallone, R. P., Griffin, D. W., Lin, S., and Ross, L. (1990). Overconfident prediction of future actions and outcomes by self and others. *Journal of Personality and Social Psychology, 58,* 582–592.

von Hippel, W., Jonides, J., Hilton, J. L., and Narayan, S. (1993). Inhibitory effect of schematic processing on perceptual encoding. *Journal of Personality and Social Psychology, 64,* 921–935.

Wanke, M., Bless, H., and Biller, B. (1996). Subjective experience versus content of information in the construction of attitude judgments. *Personality and Social Psychology Bulletin, 22,* 1105–1113.

Weber, R., and Crocker, J. (1983). Cognitive processes in the revision of stereotypic beliefs. *Journal of Personality and Social Psychology, 45,* 961–977.

Webster, D. M. (1993). Motivated augmentation and reduction of the overattribution bias. *Journal of Personality and Social Psychology, 65,* 261–271.

Wegener, D. T., Petty, R. E., and Smith, S. M. (1995). Positive mood can increase or decrease message scrutiny: The hedonic contingency view of mood and message processing. *Journal of Personality and Social Psychology, 69,* 5–15.

Wegner, D. M. (1994). Ironic processes of mental control. *Psychological Review, 101,* 34–52.

Wegner, D. M., and Bargh, J. A. (1998). Control and automaticity in social life. In D. T. Gilbert, S. T. Fiske, and G. Lindzey (Eds.), *The Handbook of Social Psychology* (Vol. 1, 4th. ed., pp. 446–496). New York: McGraw-Hill.

Wegner, D. M., and Erber, R. (1992). The hyperaccessibility of suppressed thoughts. *Journal of Personality and Social Psychology, 63,* 903–912.

Wells, G. L., and Gavanski, I. (1989). Mental simulation of causality. *Journal of Personality and Social Psychology, 56,* 161–169.

Wilder, D. A., Simon, A. F., and Faith, M. (1996). Enhancing the impact of counter-stereotypic information: Dispositional attributions for deviance. *Journal of Personality and Social Psychology, 71,* 276–287.

Wilson, T. D., and Brekke, N. (1994). Mental contamination and mental correction: Unwanted influences on judgments and evaluations. *Psychological Bulletin, 116,* 117–142.

Wilson, T. D., and LaFleur, S. J. (1995). Knowing what you'll do: Effects of analyzing reasons on self-prediction. *Journal of Personality and Social Psychology, 68,* 21–35.

Wilson, T. D., and Schooler, J. W. (1991). Thinking too much can reduce the quality of preferences and decisions. *Journal of Personality and Social Psychology, 60,* 181–192.

Winter, L., and Uleman, J. S. (1984). When are social judgments made? Evidence for the spontaneousness of trait inferences. *Journal of Personality and Social Psychology, 47,* 237–252.

Winter, L., Uleman, J. S., and Cunniff, C. (1985). How automatic are social judgments? *Journal of Personality and Social Psychology, 49,* 904–917.

Wittenbrink, B., Gist, P. L., and Hilton, J. L. (1997a). Structural properties of stereotypic knowledge and their influences on the construal of social situations. *Journal of Personality and Social Psychology, 72,* 526–543.

Wittenbrink, B., Judd, C. M., and Park, B. (1997b). Evidence for racial prejudice at the implicit level and its relationship with questionnaire measures. *Journal of Personality and Social Psychology, 72,* 262–274.

Wittgenstein, L. (1953). *Philosophical investigations.* New York: Macmillan.

Wong, P., and Weiner, B. (1981). When people ask "why" questions, and the heuristics of attributional search. *Journal of Personality and Social Psychology, 40,* 650–663.

Wood, J. V., Giordano-Beech, M., Taylor, K. L., Michela, J. L., and Gaus, V. (1994). Strategies of social comparison among people with low self-esteem: Self-protection and self-enhancement. *Journal of Personality and Social Psychology, 67,* 713–731.

Word, C. O., Zanna, M. P., and Cooper, J. (1974). The nonverbal mediation of self-fulfilling prophecies in interracial interaction. *Journal of Experimental Social Psychology, 10,* 109–120.

Wyer, R. S., and Gordon, S. (1982). The recall of information about persons and groups. *Journal of Experimental Social Psychology, 18,* 128–164.

Wyer, R. S., and Srull, T. K. (1986). Human cognition in its social context. *Psychological Review, 93,* 322–359.

Yarkin, K. L., Town, J. P., and Wallston, B. S. (1982). Blacks and women must try harder: Stimulus persons' race and sex attributions of causality. *Personality and Social Psychology Bulletin, 8,* 21–24.

Yee, D., and Eccles, J. S. (1988). Parent perceptions and attributions for chidren's math achievement. *Sex Roles, 19,* 317–333.

Zajonc, R. B. (1968). Attitudinal effects of mere exposure. *Journal of Personality and Social Psychology Monographs, 9,* 1–27.

Zajonc, R. B. (1980). Feeling and thinking: Preferences need no inferences. *American Psychologist, 35,* 151–175.

Zanna, M. P., and Cooper, J. (1974). Dissonance and the pill: An attributional approach to studying the arousal properties of dissonance. *Journal of Personality and Social Psychology, 29,* 703–709.

Zbrodoff, N. J., and Logan, G. D. (1986). On the autonomy of mental processes: A case study of mental arithmetic. *Journal of Experimental Psychology: General, 115,* 118–130.

Zuckerman, M., Knee, C. R., Hodgins, H. S., and Kunitate, M. (1995). Hypothesis confirmation: The joint effect of positive test strategy and acquiescence response set. *Journal of Personality and Social Psychology, 68,* 52–60.

Author Index